SOLDIERS OF THE SULTAN

For Louise

who came to love Oman

and dedicated to those who served in the Armoured Car Squadron together with men from the Recce Platoons of Desert, Northern Frontier, Jebel and Muscat Regiments attached to the Squadron

and to friends who survived and those we lost.

SOLDIERS OF THE SULTAN

*Diaries of a Secret War
Dhofar Insurgency 1971-73*

PAUL HODGSON

First published in Great Britain in 2024 Copyright © Paul Hodgson

The moral right of the author has been asserted. All rights reserved.

No part of this publication may be reproduced, stored in a retrieval system, or transmitted, in any form or by any means, without the prior permission in writing of the publisher, nor be otherwise circulated in any form of binding or cover other than that in which it is published and without a similar condition including this condition being imposed on the subsequent purchaser.

Editing, Design, typesetting and publishing by UK Book Publishing
www.ukbookpublishing.com

Cover design - Toby Hodgson
Cover photograph - Alan Howard

ISBN: 978-1-916572-85-0

Contents

Prologue		ix
Introduction: That Question		xi
The Dhofar Chest – An Awakening		xiv
Diaries of a Secret War		xvii
1	Britain's Secret War	1
2	Dawn of the Armoured Car Squadron	23
3	Arrival in Oman	30
4	National Day & Effects of Active Service	58
5	Dhofar	69
6	Incident at Wadi Jardum	85
7	Convoys & Saving a Desert Dragon	96
8	Costello gets his AK47, Phillips receives a Rolex	107
9	'... if you meet a Dhofari'	130
10	Geoff and the Cat	148
11	Saladins at last and Geoff's gun examined	166
12	Akoot Battle Camp	186
13	Wood Convoys, R&R & Ambush	213
14	Christmas 1971	239
15	African Adventure	262

16	Threat to Saladins	298
17	They say never volunteer	332
18	Op Simba	351
19	Battle for Vimy Ridge	378
20	Akoot rearguard	404
21	Habarut attacked	415
22	Last out of Akoot	428
23	Fight to save Janook Airhead	438
24	Grenades, Habarut retaken & Mirbat	464
25	Armoured Bedfords revisited?	489
26	Mike, 'Uncle'	500
27	Tim departs	518
28	The raid into Yemen	530
29	Habarut convoys, a Firqat ambush, The Empty Quarter and Jibjat Road	548
30	Medevac and The Sultan's Palace	578
31	The Last of the Bedu?	602
32	Handover and Farewells	624
33	Valete	639
	Appendices: The Saladin Armoured Car	647
	Glossary	651
	Acknowledgements	656
	Index	657
	Regiments	676
	Addendum	677

"Only those who have been to Dhofar can fully appreciate the severity of the conditions in which the polyglot force fought and flew: at times extreme heat: at others cold, wet, with permanent cloud: and rugged terrain, the equal of which it would be hard to find anywhere . . . Those who fought there, including those who were wounded or died, did not fight in vain"

Field Marshal Lord Carver, Chief of the General Staff 1971-73, commenting on conditions faced soldiering in Dhofar, Southern Oman.

As any child growing up in Africa, we hoped one day to become a soldier warrior, wearing a lion mane headdress.

Prologue

In his classic book, 'Arabian Sands', Wilfred Thesiger exemplifies the hardships and privations men endured in mid 20th century Arabia, writing that when clouds gather and rain falls, men and animals live; when clouds disperse without rain, they die. In the deserts of Southern Arabia the rhythm of seasons fade, marked only by changes in temperature. It is a cruel, unforgiving land and yet over millennia men and animals have lived here, not merely subsisted. Knowing no other way, it was a life the bedu had long accepted, leaving little trace bar the disturbance by footprints and fire-blackened stones as evidence of their existence. Dropped into this then priceless, ageless world suddenly threatened by expansionist Marxist ideology, Britain sent young volunteers to fight a secret guerrilla war against Chinese and competing Soviet trained, armed and led guerrilla forces.

Introduction
THAT QUESTION

It was 1974 and political tensions between Western and OPEC countries had created a crippling oil crisis. World economies crumbled, stock markets crashed, inflation and unemployment soared. The UK's economy and society were in decline. The London Stock Exchange had lost 73% of its value, the index sinking to 146, a market nadir that seems inconceivable today. Weakened by strikes and scandals, the Conservative government fell. Britain was on the ropes.

I'd married and left the Armed Forces to discover what army life doesn't teach: exit strategy on leaving. Joining straight from school, after almost ten years of team membership when possibly one may have been lucky enough to have made some contribution, you're likely to be quite unprepared for the crushing reality of civilian life. I'd seen a promised job disappear, endured confidence-eroding interviews, been diagnosed with kidney damage and undergone invasive surgery at Millbank Military Hospital. Now minus a kidney, rib and piece of lung, within a month I'd secured a position with Chartered Loss Adjusters in Edinburgh as a trainee. The Chairman, an ex-Royal Marine, said he was prepared to 'give me a shot'. Starting again, I'd grasped the bottom rung of a corporate ladder. Breakthrough at last. I was just 26, ready to go again.

Within weeks of joining the firm, I was attending the Glasgow Insurance Institute's annual dinner as a guest of our Scottish regional director. Taking our seats as grace ended, I glanced around at the assembled tables with the realisation that civvy life, corporate speak and codes were still alien. We've all experienced it sometime, the rookie parachuted in amongst strangers. Opposite me sat Ross Logie, a colleague from our Glasgow office. As we had filed into dinner, we'd been introduced briefly and now he leant forward engaging with the leading question:

'So then, I hear you were in the army? . . . Were you an officer?' to which I affirmed 'Yup, correct', wondering where the conversation might be going . . . a pause, then 'Might I ask,' he continued, his Glaswegian inflection demanding attention, 'have you . . . umm . . . ever *killed* anybody?'

I looked back at Ross. What was it he'd just said?

Caught off balance, it hits you. In an instant there's shouting, crashing explosions, screaming in-coming rocket fire, crack-crack, crack-crack as bullets whip past, some striking bodies, that sickening thud of impact with soft tissue. Screaming, groans, the acrid smell of propellant and everlasting stench of burning, torn cloth and flesh, guts and snot, shit and piss, always piss, the pervading stink of war that infects the mind.

How often it takes you by surprise; mostly unwanted and unwished for, yet always at its own bidding. The trigger – a sight, sound, smell or remark to evoke immediate 20/20 vision and bang, recall is complete. A flash and it's there, then gone, buried again. Unresponsive, I stared back at my questioner.

'You *alright*, Army?' he enquired, the sobriquet unnecessary. A voice beside me growled, 'Ross, you arsehole, what a bloody stupid question!' Clearing the air, Doug Simpson, another new acquaintance who'd one day rise to become the firm's Scotland Director and with whom I have remained good friends since.

I wondered if Ross's question might become the ritual opener at introductions between colleagues, an adjunct to the ubiquitous 'and what did you do before?'. In the early 1970s, Brits leading a foreign army in a secret foreign war was unheard of. It shouldn't have been a big deal for we were soldiers; yet to those who'd served, it was.

HE NEVER SPEAKS OF IT

How often we hear that remark about father, uncle or combatant '. . . he never speaks, (or spoke), of his experiences . . .'

Then the inevitable question 'what was it like?' – an open and simple inquiry, but for those questioned, any answer is almost certain to fail, the subject too deep for casual conversation. And generally out of context. Who's to judge? Unless experienced, I'd question whether it is possible to depict in conversation an answer sufficient to conjure the degree of intensity necessary to recreate the mental and physical extremes live action in warfare generates. It's no brutal game of rugby, mad downhill ski chase or Cresta toboggan run. There are no rules. It's life/death/kill/be killed and how you faced it, or didn't. How can the listener be

THAT QUESTION

expected to reasonably relate to what he or she might hear? It was always thus, this disconnection between public conception and soldiers' experience. Wounds may heal, but they leave a scar.

Vivid though the memory may be, actual events will generally exceed the cognitive power demanded to describe in words adequately to those who would seek to imagine or understand. They cannot feel nor really apprehend, and why should they? Film and television are capable of the visual, sometimes leading to revulsion, but they fail in the 'what was it like?' category.

This inability to elucidate experiences too intense for adequate description blocks further discussion. For those questioned it's safer to keep one's counsel and the subject closed. And for some, memories evoked by the question may be too painful to relate. Unintentionally the well-meaning questioner is left feeling excluded, cut off and rebuffed by an inadequate response – through no fault of theirs.

THE DHOFAR CHEST – AN AWAKENING

Concealed in the depths of a 17th century brick and slate roofed barn that over the years had been used as a pigsty then cowshed and now converted to garages, lay a brown stained timber box. To the casual observer a pretty innocuous looking wooden box. Familiarly, it was always referred to as The Dhofar Chest. Piled high with tins of old paint and accumulated junk, the collection coated with dust, swallow guano and old cobwebs – the last evoking memories of stretched camouflage netting – the coffin-sized box had long lain undisturbed, jealous custodian to its secrets.

I'd gone into the garage searching for a particular nut and bolt I hoped might fit my lawnmower, when rummaging through a rusty tin, I came across a key. Rubbing away a film of dirt and rust I caught my breath, as suddenly the thought occurred: was this the lost key to the chest? Would it fit? God, how long had it remained locked? I'd have to work that one out.

Removing the piled junk from the box, I caught myself smiling at finding the bullet-holed and shrapnel-splintered chest still carried diamond-shaped labels printed with EXPLOSIVO, warning of its original contents, four 80mm air-to-ground SURA rockets. Rockets that had been developed and manufactured by Hispano-Suiza, the famous Spanish automotive–engineering company, and fired in action from a jet fighter. Across the chest's hinged lid stencilled in white was my rank, name and unit: Captain PEB Hodgson ACS, the calligraphic work of an Arab soldier, a friend from a life long passed. The neat stencilling had been partially painted over with crude brushstrokes which had raised my rank to major and ACS (Armoured Car Squadron) replaced with "Ah Mud Cars", Arab soldier-speak for 'Armoured Cars', the work of Sgt Lou Costello, stout-hearted and reliable ally, lacking only in the ancient skills of calligraphy. Adapted as a chest, the box held memories intentionally repressed, and at a guess I reckoned probably unopened

THE DHOFAR CHEST - AN AWAKENING

for 38 years. Wondering whether I now dare open this once familiar box, I inserted the rusty key; it fitted and turned, opening the heavy cast metal padlock.

Inside, lay a bundle of faded foxed-marked papers, in the neat Remington script of a battered manual typewriter once used as our only means of writing dispatches. There were also a number of pencilled sheets torn from army message pads, all tucked into a dog-eared buff folder titled "Anti-Guerrilla Operations – Dhofar – Secret". Across the top in Major Tim Cornwell's neat handwriting was written 'Captain Hodgson ACS'.

There too, were several well-used maps, pencil marked and variously annotated, some cut down and covered with Fablon. A black-painted brass prismatic compass, chipped and dented, in its worn brown leather case beside a well-used pair of padded, leather framed army issue desert goggles, the laminate in the glass now bubbled, obscuring vision. Hidden by maps nestled four impact-compressed tail fins, still ingrained with white Omani limestone, the crushed residue of explosive forces. Three were Russian rocket fins, the last a British 3-inch mortar, souvenirs of incomers that'd landed too close for comfort. Beside these were a handful of jagged shrapnel shards, still sharp edged and now rusted. Grouped together were a handful of Russian 12.7mm Shpagin armour piercing rounds, copper jackets scraped or torn on impact to reveal tungsten carbide cores. A dozen or so similarly dented and chipped 7.62mm Kalashnikov spent rounds lay neatly as eggs in a nest, buried amongst more papers. The top sections of three battered Saladin periscopes, alloy frames still containing bullet crazed glass and then below, two 76mm HE shell cases cut down as ashtrays, cold to the touch and heavy to hold, just visible towards the bottom of the chest.

Moving these aside, I found four matching boxes of deteriorating 35mm slides sitting on three diaries wrapped in a faded red, green and white pennant. My diaries! Dogeared, scuffed, worn and oil stained, the diary covers were marked "Dhofar June 1971 / March 1973 – PEBH". Once so familiar as to be my next of kin. The pennant was the Omani national flag I'd proudly flown from a radio aerial. It was punctured with holes. And there, right at the bottom, lay some medals, gifts from an Arabian Sultan, medals from a secret war. A war the British had fought and helped to win.

Dipping into my diaries, I read a few pages and *bang*, with an absolute clarity, it was as if it had all happened yesterday. That came as a shock, causing a shudder through me I'd not expected, sending hairs tingling along arms and back of neck. 'That's enough' I thought, starting to carefully repack the contents. 'That's quite enough of that', and replacing the sacred fragments belonging to another era, I closed the lid, refastening the heavy padlock, once again a prisoner to memories. Then I undid the lock and reopened the box, and started to read.

***

Many books have been written on the Dhofar War and some are very good, and some may stretch it a bit. Generally, they are written from different perspectives. Here in this box I had rediscovered my journals, maps and photographs representing an eyewitness account of two punishing years fighting a desert war, which at the time was considered unwinnable. And yet the war was won, and a little bit of history made. Would revisiting and writing about it, I wondered, be as cathartic as I hoped?

DIARIES OF A SECRET WAR

Over two years loaned to a foreign army fighting a secret war in Southern Arabia, I had kept notes which extended into three diaries, recording each day's events and happenings as witnessed at the time, and in the main as objectively and dispassionately as possible. Not allowed to send detailed reports back to family or friends, I half imagined my jottings might help me relate to what we had experienced, once restrictions on censorship had been lifted.

For the historian writing a book, he or she must undertake exhaustive research of manuscripts, authoritative reports, maps, personal papers, hearsay and interviews, which they then transcribe based upon their own interpretation. A film director does the same.

Those who partake and who attempt to record what they saw and did rely on memories – theirs and others – also jotted notes, old maps, surviving letters and if available, journals. Such is my case. Photographs, reports and the rest tell half the story, but there's an absolute about a diary: they don't lie. The journals represent a two-year timeline of private thoughts documented whilst still being hot branded into memory, events recorded for oneself, reflected first hand. There is no point for untruths or hyperbole in a diary.

They cover a brief period of my life when luck played its part. It does not look back with any particular fondness, nor is it meant to rely on the benefit of hindsight. I have sought to write devoid of dramatic licence and without contrivances. Neither is it written with the disillusion of a civilian life after a hugely fulfilling short career as a soldier.

To simplify rather than offend or confuse, I have used as few Arabic sentences as possible, adopting English to avoid transliteration that might be open to disagreement. Also, certain place names, especially Midway and Shisur, I have used as they were at the time; today known respectively as Thumrait, and Ubar.

Quotations taken from FCO Archives, at the time Secret, or Top Secret, have now recently been declassified. Also as was common at the time, there is a mix of imperial and metric measurements. Ranges, as in distances to targets, and weapon dimensions were metric. Whereas generally distances travelled were in miles, I have endeavoured to use kilometres for clarification. Altitudes I show are measured in feet.

There may be bias for which I apologise, but this only reflects my reliance on personal notes kept at the time. It is a story that relates to experiences gained during a war fought in Arabia's harsh unforgiving deserts, wilderness and mountains. A time spent with some of the unfailingly brave and a few not so. Shared food, water and laughs, excessive heat and on occasions night frosts, gut-wrenching fear juxtaposed with highs of elation. There were periods of mental and physical strain, wounds and death – yet always, there existed a mutual determination to support each other, live through and survive.

THE ARMOURED CAR SQUADRON (ACS)

On loan to the Sultan's Armed Forces I was one of three officers serving with the Armoured Car Squadron (ACS). We operated with two troops of three Saladin Armoured Cars and a troop of six Ferret Scout Cars.

Saladins deployed with three-man crews comprising commander, gunner and driver, whilst Ferrets had two men, commander/gunner and driver. Stripped of doors and windscreens, we also had six Land Rover gunships, fitted with either .30 or .50 calibre Browning machine guns. In support were five Bedford trucks, two being converted as recovery vehicles capable of towing an armoured vehicle along flat ground. Attached to the squadron at any one time were two infantry recce platoons with four Land Rovers. This was the limit of our regular forces, i.e. trained soldiers.

Bringing numbers up to 200 or so were some 25 local militias, villagers armed with .303 rifles, and an additional fifty to sixty ex-enemy irregulars in two separate units, called Firqats. Clannish and at times contemptuous towards outsiders, they lived and operated by their own harsh codes. These were Bedouin tribesmen of the Bayt Kathir and Mahri tribes with a history of inter-tribal skirmishes, blood feuds, rights to use of wells and camel raids. Disillusionment through enforced anti-Islamic ideologies dictated by Marxist leaders and a barbaric cruelty towards nonconforming families, had driven these proud men to defect. Fiercely independent and often indifferent to outside authority, they were the better to have on side for they were brutal fighters.

Remote and isolated from the infantry battalions for much of the time, the Armoured Car Squadron lived as desert Arabs, based at locations bordering the vast desolate loneliness of Arabia's Empty Quarter, and in the rocky mountains and dry wadis of a region called Dhofar, the then war zone in South West Oman.

1
BRITAIN'S SECRET WAR

Active Service with The Sultan's Armed Forces (SAF)

Who we were and why Britain was involved in a secret proxy war fought in the Middle East, a potential flash point when the UK fought Russian and Chinese led and supported troops.

In the early 1970s Oman was a country uniquely untouched by the pervading effects of western influence. There was certainly no tourism. The country was at war and the armed forces were led by a handful of British officers either on loan from Britain's armed forces or on contract as mercenaries. These last included volunteers from the Antipodes and African states of Rhodesia, Kenya and Zambia, French Foreign Legion and also a few ex-Hong Kong Policemen; all were ex-servicemen.

In general the level of issued equipment was woeful. The lack of vital spares was overcome by improvising. Rations were supplemented with locally purchased souk (market) foods. Often we relied on suspect drinking water drawn from desert wells, or jebel streams and rock pools without the reassurance of purification tablets. Water was shared with Bedouin and Jebali (desert and mountain peoples), goats and camels.

As close as brothers, never doubting or questioning but remaining utterly life dependent upon the other, we'd learned to respond without hesitation or request, unconsciously as a body moves a limb. We'd operated in temperatures of unimaginable heat, at other times endured bitter cold; faulty equipment and clothing became a permanent fixture, a handicap that led to unnecessary casualties. Many the occasion we faced instant death or life changing wounds. Close friends died. But we survived, through luck and that special camaraderie born out of danger shared, when heightened senses saw us through intense chaos, unbearable noise and horrendous mess. Fleeting moments would remain stored deeply in the subconscious, hidden and buried out of the necessity to forget and move on.

THE DHOFAR WAR

SECRET   *FCO document September 1971*

From all points of view, the defeat or containment of the Dhofar rebellion is important. Active communism must be halted militarily as far away as possible from Northern Oman. Protection of our current and likely oil sources depends upon a continued presence in Dhofar by SAF. It is clear . . . the Sultanate cannot afford to lose.

The Dhofar War remains a largely unknown story when a small number of mainly young British officers, aged 23 and upwards and being fluent in colloquial Arabic, led a force of Omani and Dhofari Arabs, a force which included other Gulf State Arabs and mercenaries from Baluchestan, Iraq and Iran.

Rebutting America's concern against a diminution of the UK's role in the Arabian Peninsula, the British Government effected the withdrawal of Britain's forces from East of Suez, to be completed by the mid-1970s. With pressure on sterling, this policy was accelerated to 1971. Already an injudicious policy, it now fuelled the growing insurrection in Oman. From minor rebellion in 1962, Dhofar became an East/West proxy war ending in 1975.

Attached on loan to the Sultan's Armed Forces were the UK's elite SAS in squadron strength. Spending four months at a time on active duty before roulement (rotation), they maintained a vital presence in Dhofar. In an effort to disguise their presence in the country, the Foreign Office decreed the SAS be known as the British Army Training Team (BATT). A role never limited to training duties.

In the final stages of the war an Iranian battlegroup together with elements of Jordanian Special Forces arrived to support the young Sultan achieve victory. Without their valuable assistance the war would have festered for many more years, causing chaos in one of the world's most vital regions. We need only look to Yemen today.

Approximately half of the Sultan's officers were seconded on two-year engagements. Essentially this meant they'd been loaned under contract by the MOD to His Majesty Sultan Qaboos bin Said, Sultan of Oman. The remaining 50% of officers and NCOs comprised a mix of three-year contract soldiers. This eclectic group of officers and SAS led their Muslim troops in a hard-fought counterinsurgency, a war which was won, safeguarding the world's Gulf oil supplies and determining the geopolitical composition of today's Arabian Gulf.

British involvement in this desert war was protected with a 'D-Notice' issued by Her Majesty's government, in effect restricting media reporting in the interests of national security. Despite the blanket of secrecy, anti-Vietnam protests in London sought to include Britain's involvement in Dhofar, as an adjunct to America's secret war in Laos. Fortunately for Downing Street, media focus deflected towards domestic troubles in Northern Ireland whilst the continuing conflict in Vietnam attracted growing hysteria around the Cold War's international rivalry at the time.

In the mid-20th century the Western world faced an expanding global threat, Marxist Communism supported by Russia and China. The 19th Century's 'Great Game' had never really ended.

BACKGROUND TO BRITISH TIES WITH OMAN: A SPECIAL RELATIONSHIP

Britain and Oman have been trading partners since the mid-17th century, a time when the East India Company accounted for almost half the world's trade. Increasingly dependent upon British support, Oman became a British Protectorate on 20 March 1891. Never a colony, the treaty suited both countries who benefited from this special relationship.

Arabia's territorial borders, existing only on indistinct maps drawn up by Europeans, became a point of contention in the 20th century with the discovery of oil. Abruptly the question of oil concessions began to focus FCO concerns as hazy borders between Oman and Saudi Arabia gained a sudden and imperative importance.

In the early 1950s the country was still referred to as Muscat and Oman, indicating two autonomous factions – a reflection of historic tribal disputes over land and, more recently, oil. Severely restricted, the Sultan's influence was limited to the coastal areas by an Imam ruling the interior's Omani tribes bordering Al Rub al Khali, Arabia's Empty Quarter.

Enjoying support from Saudi Arabia and Egypt, whose leaders were dedicated to the eradication of British influence in Arabia, the Imam tried to establish his region as an independent state. He issued passports and applied for membership of the Arab League. Unrest that had brewed for decades began to boil over, threatening the Sultanate.

America, already active in Saudi Arabia, sought to exploit their influence in the region when the question became whether the interior of Oman, with its claimed rich oil fields, might feasibly be brought into that county's orbit.

Sultan Said bin Taimur had meanwhile granted a concession to a British company which naturally the British Government steadfastly supported. Britain's decision was met with strongly opposing views held collectively by the Imam, Saudi Arabia, Egypt and American oil companies. The British Government acted, suddenly awake to the realisation that the future of Eastern Arabia's oil fields might to an extent dictate the destinies of GB.

The key to exploring Oman and Abu Dhabi oil fields lay with a collection of nine villages at Al Buraimi Oasis leading to what became called the Buraimi Crisis, a muddle of political and strategic imperatives. Saudi and Egyptian pressure escalated with covert support for their puppet the Imam, causing Britain increasing disquiet. Fanned by Egyptian and Communist propaganda, Saudi black gold and America's self-interest, Saudi troops acted, occupying Buraimi's nine villages, three otherwise controlled by Abu Dhabi, six by Muscat.

Linked to Britain by treaty, Muscat and Abu Dhabi were now pitted against American-supported Saudi Arabia, a country where Britain too sought influence and trade. Of equal concern was the need to avoid upsetting GB/US relations. Finally, in 1955, in a lightning attack, British officers leading Arab soldiers expelled the occupying Saudi garrison. With that, the Imam's power was crushed, the oilfields secured and Muscat & Oman became 'Oman'.

RELIGION IN OMAN – IBADI ISLAM

The leading Muslim faith in Oman is Ibadi Islam. Followers of Abd Allah ibn Ibad, Oman is the only country where they form a majority. Sultan Qaboos was a member of the Ibadi community and within Oman, Ibadis, Sunni and Shiite coexist in harmony. Communist forces attacking from Yemen, intolerant of the Muslim faith, sought to eradicate all religious beliefs, tribal systems and loyalties in favour of a strict Marxist ideology.

BRITAIN'S SECRET WAR

GEOPOLITICAL ASPECTS – OMAN 1971

In the early 1970s this unique land remained a geographical enigma, a mystical country at the South East corner of the Arabian Peninsula.

Map showing the northern tip of Oman, The Musandam, jutting towards Iran creating the choke point at the Straits of Hormuz. The war zone, Dhofar, lies to the southwest bordering communist-controlled Yemen. Intriguingly, a CIA map.

Oman's coastline measures just under 3200km. To the north, Oman shares a 625km boundary with Saudi Arabia and to the northeast, 400km with United Arab Emirates. Jutting out into the Straits of Hormuz is The Musandam, an isolated part of Oman, a peninsula of rocky mountains which fall dramatically into the waters of the Persian Gulf.

And finally in the southwest, marching with Yemen along a 300km boundary, is a region called Dhofar.

Until the arrival of Iranian and Jordanian forces in late 1972, SAF basically comprised four infantry battalions, an artillery regiment, one squadron of armoured cars and Z Company, a Land Rover borne unit. There was a small and experienced air force (SOAF) flying jets, fixed wing STOL aircraft (short take-off and landing) and Huey helicopters, the army's lifeline. In addition, there were two gendarmerie battalions, a number of irregular infantry forces (Firqat) and supporting arms including engineers and headquarters staff.

It is perhaps extraordinary today to imagine the synergy of such a force where Christians leading Muslim soldiers fought against an overtly non-believing Marxist army, advised, trained and led by specialists from the two major communist powers seeking influence at the time, USSR and China.

In a world where the West is widely despised by a significant number from the Middle East, it is perhaps hard to appreciate the degree of trust, comradeship and devotion that existed within the Sultan's forces. A bond shared between the proud Omani soldiers and their white officers, a bond that found an unexpected fulfilment for each in the service of the Sultan.

Comradeship was built through living and eating together, the sharing of drinking water from army issue charguls (canvas water bottles), shared rations of local food, dates, meat and rice. Communal water used for washing, shared sangars and shared cigarettes. Living out of caves or under canvas sheeting stretched between rocks for shelter against a fierce unrelenting sun. We ate food cooked over fires of sticks bleached white and preserved, dried by the merciless sun and radiated heat from limestone rocks, gravel and sand. Such desiccated wood was smokeless.

Also, comradeship developed under shared intensity experienced in battle, or indeed those interminable days in anticipation of battle. A trust that emerges between people of any race, colour or creed facing extremes. That is when such bonds are forged, leading often to spontaneous acts of great bravery, selfless actions, so often unrecorded but recognised in any field of battle. Moments which freeze-frame in the mind.

There is no question such acts were displayed on both sides in equal measure, for the enemy (adoo) lived and fought under the same harsh conditions. Where they lacked the mobility enjoyed by SAF's vehicles and helicopters, the adoo made up for in their astute knowledge of terrain, escape routes, secure hiding places and the vital intelligence of clean water wells.

These experienced fighters must have been astonished at their opponents' lumbering fieldcraft. SAF was an army of young soldiers, many straight out of basic training, some doubtlessly never having lived rough or out in the open before posting to the war zone. In contrast, the adoo, natural fighters, were operating over tribal lands roamed from birth, lands the British-led forces trod as aliens.

Despite the advantages of helicopters, artillery, armoured cars, Land Rovers, trucks and ancient jet fighters, we were nonetheless often found wanting in our cumbersome fieldcraft against a fleet of foot, fast reacting enemy. And likewise with our personal weapons, FN rifles were no match in close quarter fighting to the battle proven SKS and AK-47 Kalashnikov used with such devastation by the Sultan's opponents.

THE COMMUNIST THREAT IN THE MIDDLE EAST

The early 1970s saw the UK supporting an independent Arab state combating communism in the Arabian Gulf, whilst the Americans were heavily committed in their fight against communism in South Vietnam. An MOD report states:

> "While the Americans were fighting what was then becoming a lost cause in Vietnam, a struggle of even greater strategic significance was taking place in the Middle East: the Sultanate of Oman guards the entrance to the Arabian Gulf, at the Straits of Hormuz, a narrow, strategically important shipping lane which at its narrowest is 54 kilometres wide. It is the only sea passage to the open ocean for large areas of the petroleum-exporting Persian Gulf, and is one of the world's most strategically important choke points. Around 20% of the world's oil passes through this strait. It is shared with Persia with whom the movement of oil from that region is potentially controlled. In the 1960s and early 1970s, the Communists tried to seize this artery. Had they succeeded, the consequences for the West and for the Middle East would have been disastrous – and yet, few people have ever heard of this geo-political drama that unfurled at the height of the Cold War."

At the time half the world was under communist rule, influence or threat. The Cold War threatened nuclear oblivion no government dared sanction and the spread of Marxist ideology was spreading relentlessly through civil aid programmes, reaching some countries recently independent of European colonial rule.

Both the Chinese and Russian communist blocks began positioning themselves for greater influence in the Middle East, a part of the world that had witnessed the UK withdraw from bases in Aden and the Arabian Gulf States following retrenchment; a direct result of Government budgetary cutbacks and the reigning back on a fading Imperial Foreign Policy. As the wolves gathered, the back door had been left open.

SECRET   *FOC Briefing*

SOVIET NAVAL PRESENCE (SECRET). AT 1215 ON 23 AUGUST, KOTLIN CLASS DESTROYER NO 407 AND OSKOL CLASS AR - PM 24 WERE SIGHTED AT ANCHOR ABOUT 30 NMS NORTH OF QATAR, OSKOL WEIGHED ANCHOR AFTERWARDS, AND WAS SEEN AGAIN THAT EVENING, APPARENTLY LEAVING GULF. KOTLIN 407 REMAINED AT ANCHOR (EXCEPT FOR ONE 10 NM SHIFT OF POSITION) UNTIL 27 AUGUST, BEING JOINED BY THE OILER VISHERA ON 25 AUGUST. KOTLIN 407 THEN MOVED NORTH AND IS NOW ANCHORED IN POSITION 29 DEGREES 35N 49 DEGREES 46E, AO VISHERA REMAINS AT ANCHOR.

The Americans made clear to the British Government their alarm at the obvious vacuum Britain's withdrawal from the Middle East now posed. They considered this was a void likely either of their two major rivals, Russia or China, would seek to fill. The region that had grown to be one of significant influence was seemingly in danger of being gifted to communist ideology by the withdrawing British.

As the Cold War continued to threaten world peace, NATO forces trained relentlessly to withstand a numerically superior Warsaw Pact onslaught across Europe. The US and their allies fighting in Vietnam were up against an exacting foe in a war that was crippling the perception of American dominance as one of the world's two main military superpowers. America was not used to losing on the scale of losses being sustained, especially given their superior forces, weaponry, military communications and technical expertise. Yet the unthinkable was happening and it was evident that battlefield superiority in technical terms counted for little when faced by determined and often suicidal forces willing to die fighting for their cause – freedom from capitalist imperialism.

With the British Government increasingly preoccupied by the horrors developing at home in Northern Ireland, deepening concern grew at the very real threat of Marxist communism spreading from Britain's recently vacated territories in Yemen and out into the Gulf of Arabia, allowing Soviet Russia to achieve their goal of securing both a warm water port and control of the Straits of Hormuz.

> *FCO Report*
>
> The rest of the Government and the general population of Northern Oman do not fully comprehend the communist threat or the dangers in Oman, The Dhofar rebellion could become as unpopular in Oman as Vietnam is in the U.S.A. All the conditions in Dhofar tend at present to impose a putative stalemate, where SAF is not strong enough to clear out the communists from the Jebel, and the rebels do not have the strength to capture and hold the Salalah plain and coastal villages.
>
> From all points of view, the defeat or containment of the Dhofar rebellion is important. Active communism must be halted militarily as far away as possible from Northern Oman. Protection of our current and likely oil sources depends upon a continued presence in Dhofar by SAF. It is clear . . . the Sultanate cannot afford to lose the (Salalah) plain.

WHEN HARD LEARNED MILITARY TACTICS CHANGED

Vietnam saw the USA swamp their zone with highly equipped, well-trained troops. Vast military bases were established, huge quantities of munitions used. Widely condemned, napalm and Agent Orange cleared jungles of life. Indirectly, whole communities, civilians, women, children and farm animals were consumed in a catastrophic laying waste to regions. Vivid reporting by war journalists with horrifying photographs emerged to illustrate the brutality and senselessness of the American campaign. The predictable ending came with ignominious defeat and withdrawal of the last remnants of America's huge army, soldiers holding out against overwhelming odds as the US Saigon embassy was evacuated on 30 April 1975. A guerrilla army had prevailed against superior forces.

On the Arabian Peninsula the Russians seeking to influence the region backed the People's Democratic Republic of Yemen (PDRY). Emboldened by their success against the British in Yemen, PDRY now pushed eastwards into Oman intent on eventually overthrowing the Gulf's newly independent conservative and wealthy monarchies, with the aim of installing Marxist regimes. Rapidly they set up political cells, commencing recruitment and military training in support of guerrilla fighters already controlling much of Oman's southwest, a region called Dhofar.

These guerrillas had taken up arms against Oman's monocracy. Their aim, to gain recognition and freedom from an outdated feudal regime that left its peoples subjugated and controlled from northern Oman where for centuries the country's rulers had governed. The north/south divide had become intolerable to the disaffected Dhofari tribesmen.

Oman's forces facing the advancing communists comprised a small army of ill-equipped northern Omani soldiers, led by British officers in the service of the elderly Sultan Said bin Taimur. This small force fighting to close off the relentless advance of communism into the Gulf of Arabia was failing. The threat of defeat in Arabia suddenly looked to imitate what was occurring in Saigon.

COUP D'ÉTAT AND A NEW WINDS BLOWS

In 1970 the British-schooled and Sandhurst-educated Qaboos bin Said, son of the Sultan of Oman, was under house arrest. Born and raised in Dhofar, he spent six years between 1958 and 1964 in Britain, attending boarding school before gaining entry to the Royal Military Academy, Sandhurst before being commissioned into the Cameroon Highlanders. Following military service, Qaboos studied a range of subjects including economics, law, politics and administration at university in London before returning to Oman in 1964.

With the rapid advances realised through immeasurable wealth that oil now bestowed on certain Gulf States, Oman began to be left behind in the race to modernise. Jealousies arising from Saudi wealth and advancement fuelled tensions throughout the Middle East, upsetting the status quo as the shift of power and influence moved from established dynasties to the new wealthy.

Oil had yet to be discovered in any significant quantities in Oman. Added to which, in his heart the Sultan held a natural distrust of the modern world's vulgar excesses. He saw only the result of these excesses across his borders where ancient ways were being uprooted, traditions and customs diluted, the very essence of the desert warrior who'd evolved and held sway over centuries lost forever.

Considered by his father a modernist and reformer on his return to Oman, Qaboos was being held as a prisoner at his home in Dhofar.

Presented with perfect timing, the communist regime across Oman's western borders in the People's Democratic Republic of Yemen made their move. Filling the vacuum created by Britain's departure, arrived an aspiringly confident Marxist ideology, fuelling insurgency built on frustration at the lack of political progress in this ancient and noble kingdom. The country appeared doomed to succumb to communist imperialism.

On 18 June 1970 a general election held in the United Kingdom resulted in a surprise victory for the Conservatives. Edward Heath won with a majority of 31 seats. This general election was the first in which people could vote from the age of eighteen, and the first chance to vote for many already serving in the military, as was the case with many of my generation. After four years in the army came my first chance to choose in the enduring hope our votes mattered.

And the greatest threat facing the free world, communism, was on the march in the Middle East. Communist-phobia pitched high on agendas of Western Governments. In a move to halt Marxist expansionism from Yemen eastwards into Oman and onwards to the Gulf States, the West through the agency of Britain went to war.

Foreign Office plans prepared under the Labour Government were suddenly given the green light. On 23 July 1970, just 46 days into the new administration, a small force of Desert Regiment soldiers led by British contract officers, led a coup d'état deposing Sultan Said bin Taimur in a tightly executed military operation allowing his 28-year-old son to ascend the throne. Casualties were light, other than the dead loyal bodyguards caught on the wrong side. Uncertain of the outcome and whether Omanis loyal to the existing ruler would support the obvious interference by Britain, plans were prepared to pull out British personnel in the event of mission failure. Had this occurred, the loss to British influence in the region would have been profound, erasing a relationship built over millennia, extinguishing Britain's already fading light in the Middle East.

This was the gamble Britain's newly elected Conservative Government backed that July. The coup was a success. Forces considered fiercely loyal to the old regime were contained in their camps, until the message had been delivered safely that the new Sultan was now their legitimate ruler.

Unlike other politically waged wars in the area, before and since, there was to be no sledgehammer approach relying solely on military might, but the opposite: the loan of British seconded personnel to join and lead the Sultan's forces in the fight against an increasingly powerful and successful communist insurgency.

Thus it was that serving British military personnel, each having individually sworn oaths of allegiance to Queen and Country, went out to serve with equal resolve and devotion directed towards their country's ally, Sultan Qaboos bin Said al Said, Sultan of Oman. A country with an absolute monarchy where the Sultan ruled and governed as Prime Minister, was Supreme Commander of Armed Forces, Chief Minister of Defence, Foreign Affairs and Finance, and Head of Police.

The concept of creating a military force led by loaned and contract officers from a range of countries to fight alongside their Omani and Middle Eastern and Asiatic comrades in arms, involved the vital winning of 'hearts and minds' of the local population. Understandably, people were initially suspicious and occasionally openly hostile to those whom not unnaturally they regarded as foreign mercenaries and imperialists.

The coup spawned a hive of activity with the building of schools, hospitals and water supplies to villages. Militarily, an additional infantry regiment was formed, Jebel Regiment, the procurement of arms and weaponry hugely extended, and the decision made to create a light armoured car squadron operating two troops of Saladins supported by Ferret Scout Cars. That same July, I was selected for secondment to The Sultan's Armoured Car Squadron and placed on notice to attend an Arabic course.

Of paramount importance at the time, and the stated objective of Western governments, was the need to halt the relentless spread of communism from Yemen. That historic fear, Russian or Chinese influence becoming established across the Gulf states and taking control of a large part of the free world's oil supplies, threatened the world order.

In April 1959 Persia had altered their legal status to the Straits of Hormuz expanding its territorial sea to 12 nautical miles from its southern coastline, declaring it would recognize only innocent passage (non-military) through the newly claimed area. In July 1972, matching Persia's earlier move, Oman also expanded its territorial sea northwards into the straits. Thus, by mid-1972, these 24 miles of water became a bottleneck controlled by the aligned monarchies of Persia and Oman.

To this day the Straits of Hormuz, one of the world's most strategically important choke points, remains a critical flashpoint. In the early 1970s this was one of the most significant conflicts in the world.

The situation continued to deteriorate such that in 1971, a full year after the coup d'état placed Sultan Qaboos on the throne, SAF were losing the Dhofar war. There was every likelihood the province of western Oman would fall to communists already controlling 90% of the region. There was anxiety that Muscat in the north might also fall and Oman, allied to Britain by Treaty, would succumb to communism.

Classified   *FCO Briefing*

ALSO DISCUSSED (Dhofar)... NOT ENTIRELY HAPPY ABOUT THE WAY THINGS ARE GOING... CONSIDER THAT SAF REALLY NEEDS TWO FURTHER BATTALIONS – CLEARLY UNATTAINABLE – TO WIN THE WAR QUICKLY.

THE ADVERSARIES

Friendly Forces

A British Outpost – The RAF stationed at Salalah

Allied to the Sultan's forces was the RAF base at Salalah with its sand runway dating from 1942 when it had been used as a staging post for the RAF and USAAF during WW2. As the US departed, Britain remained, committed by reciprocal treaty whereby Oman ceded use of Masirah, a remote island, conditional to Britain defending Salalah's airfield. Of strategic importance, the Masirah airfield gave a vital link to Britain's Far East interests.

As a consequence RAF Salalah became a British responsibility. By summer 1971 the military situation had deteriorated with almost daily small arms and, increasingly, 75mm RCL (Recoilless Rocket Launcher) and 82mm mortar attacks. Roads around the base were mined. The jebel and surrounding plains beyond a 10-mile radius were under enemy control. The Foreign and Commonwealth Office was becoming concerned.

---

9 Sept 1971 FCO:

Arabian Dept: It was agreed . . . the question of phasing out our dependence on Masirah should also be raised. Masirah has been such a sacred cow with the Ministry of Defence that this suggestion may come as something of a shock to some quarters of the MOD.

17 Sept 1971 FCO:

The situation in Dhofar clearly has implications for the continued RAF presence at Salalah.

SAF – The Sultan's Armed Forces

Infantry Battalions:

- Muscat Regiment (MR) (Firqat As-SaHraa)
- Desert Regiment (DR) (Firqat Masqat)
- Northern Frontier Regiment (NFR) (Firqat Al Hudood Ash-Shimaaliyya)
- Jebel Regiment (JR) (Firqat Al-Gebaal)

Each battalion (Bn) comprised three rifle companies (Coy) of four platoons (Pl) – full strength approximately 30 men each Pl. Bn HQ Coy combined ops/admin/motor mechanics and a medical unit under command of an Indian Army doctor, additionally Mortar, Signal and Reconnaissance platoons. Troop carriers were soft-skinned Bedford three-ton trucks, and Land Rovers. A battalion pioneer platoon cleared mines, built airstrips, ordnance store sangars and latrines – rotten work but of vital importance.

Infantry battalions spent nine months on active service tours in Dhofar, with one battalion alternatively based in the Western Approaches (Akoot), positioned deep in the western jebel patrolling, ambushing and holding the position against repeated attacks. The second was based at Umm al Ghawarif (UAG) camp, home to HQ Dhofar Area, later Brigade (Bde) tasked with covering the Central area, Salalah Plains and Eastern Jebel.

The two other battalions were based in northern Oman, again on nine-month tours. Here they spent their time recruiting, building up casualty-depleted forces and training before roulement and return to the war zone to take over from their counterpart Dhofar battalions.

Oman Artillery: (OA) (Midfaeeyat Umaan)

- RAF Salalah support – Two 25 pounders (pdrs) committed to support RAF Salalah base.
- Central Battalion support –

  — Two 25 pdrs – range 10,800 metres
  — One 5.5 inch (in) Howitzer – range 15,000 metres

- Air portable elements One 25 pdr – air-portable by Skyvan
- Two 75mm pack howitzer – heli-portable – range 8,800 metres
- One 75mm RCL – heli-portable – range 7,000 metres
- Western Approach Battalion support – Three 25 pdrs plus one 5.5in Howitzer

The Armoured Car Squadron: (ACS) (Al-MusaffaHaat)

- Support Troop – Western Approach Battalion at Akoot – three Saladins
- 76mm gun – range 2,000 metres direct, 7,000 metres indirect
- Plains Troop – Central Battalion support – three Saladins & Recce Troop, four Ferret Scout Cars.
- .30 Browning – Saladin – range 2,000 metres: Ferret – range 800 metres

- Four Land Rovers, three Bedford trucks and a fourth converted for vehicle recovery, carrying vehicle spares.

Z Company: (As-Sareeya)

- Company strength based at UAG: a Baluchi unit with Urdu the dominant tongue. Modified Land Rovers known as Gunships, mounted with .50 Brownings – range 3,000 metres.

Dhofar Gendarmerie: (DG) (Gundaarmat Dhofar)

- Battalion strength – two combat coys and HQ Coy comprising 130 Dhofari, 200 Baluchi and 75 Pakistani gendarmes based at Arzat Camp east of Salalah, with a mortar platoon. DG were based also at Taqah, Mirbat and Sudh forts, in fishing villages east from Salalah. Adding to the eclectic mix, the Dhofaris were Khadims, African slaves of the Sultan until freed in the July 1970 coup. The Dhofar battalion was supplemented by two troops of Oman Gendarmerie (OG) on secondment from northern Oman. Located at Taqah were Firqat Jaboob, irregulars from the Eastern Jebel north of Taqah.
- OG (Gundaarmat Oman) were otherwise based at a number of locations in northern Oman tasked with Royal Guard duties, policing and maintaining border security over a considerable area.

Sultan of Oman's Air Force (SOAF) (Al Quwwat Al Jawiya)

- Under command of HQ Dhofar Bde was a Strike Squadron with six jet provost Strikemaster Jets used for ground support.
- A Helicopter Squadron with two Agusta Bell 206s used for observation, recce, liaison and casevac.
- Six Agusta Bell 205s capable of lifting approximately one ton payload or 12 troops (troop, ordnance, water and resupply freight lifts, and casevac duties)
- Two Caribou max load 3.5 tons dependent on airstrip lengths – Short Take-off and Landing (STOL) aircraft
- Three Skyvans capable of carrying 1.75 tons – STOL aircraft.

Sultan of Oman's Navy (SON) (Al Quwwat Al Bahria)

- The Royal Yacht – As Said – armed with 40mm Bofors, range 7,000 metres.
- Occasional commandeered Arab dhows.

Firqats: (Arab irregulars)

- 11 firqats varying from platoon to company strength, consisting of Dhofari desert and hill tribesmen, many of whom had come over from the enemy as surrendered personnel (SEP) to support the Sultan.

Command and Control:

Seconded British lieutenant colonels commanded each of the four SAF infantry battalions and a seconded Wing Commander the air force. Artillery and Armoured Cars were under the command of seconded majors.

Commanders at both HQs, Combined Armed Forces (Oman) and Area/Brigade (Dhofar) were seconded, with acronyms (CASF) and (CDA/B) respectively.

Officers and NCOs were either contracted or seconded. Seconded personnel were volunteers recruited from amongst serving members of Britain's Royal Navy, Army and Royal Air Force. Contracted officers and NCOs were mostly ex-British military. These men were recruited through various channels, including word of mouth and occasionally advertisements placed in broadsheets such as The Daily Telegraph. From this unlikely and eclectic mix of seconded and contract servicemen whose ages ranged from under 24 to late 50s, having all been supposedly pronounced physically fit before recruitment, a cohesive force was established.

Of note, despite the fact overall command at Dhofar HQ was held by a British serving officer, command for operational tasks was selected on the basis of meritocracy – be they contract or seconded commanders. Thus, it was not unusual for seconded British serving personnel to serve under the command of contract officers in the field.

The recruitment of contract personnel, arranging of interviews, appointments and visas was undertaken by Charles Kendall and Partners, of 7 Albert Court, SW7. Those recruited would have their occupation listed as "Government Official". These procurement consultants also issued joining instructions to personnel joining SAF, listing obligatory items of clothing (tropical suits?) and recommended kit, in addition to arranging passport visas. Complying with instructions to travel in tropical suits, we did so, but only once. The suits were never used again.

Charles Kendall also organised visa arrangements for the SAS journeying to Oman. To this day they still operate out of their SW7 offices as a global organisation.

By the mid-1970s the advertised tax-free annual salary for an officer serving a three-year contract would more than have paid for a small London flat in Notting

Sultanate of Oman
CONTRACT APPOINTMENTS

There are currently vacancies available for Officers to be employed on a contract basis for three-year periods with the Armed Forces of the Sultanate of Oman as COMPANY OFFICERS in Infantry Regiments, and as ARMY LIAISON OFFICERS in remote parts of the country.

Applicants must possess the following qualifications:—

(a) Have **recently** served in the British Armed Forces or be due for release within the next three months.

(b) Have appropriate experience as a commissioned officer in the British Army (preferably Infantry), Royal Marines or R.A.F. Regiment, and be able to demonstrate military and administrative competence.

(c) Be physically fit to meet the demands of a varied life in harsh conditions and often in mountainous terrain.

(d) Be between the ages of 25 and 30 (although slightly older men of obvious competence and fitness will be considered).

(e) Be prepared to learn colloquial Arabic (instruction will be given locally).

(f) Be prepared to serve unaccompanied (though there may be opportunities for short family visits).

Successful applicants will be commissioned in the rank of Captain in the Sultan's Armed Forces, which carries emoluments equivalent to approximately £7,700 at current exchange rates. (Emoluments are free of Sultanute tax). Other benefits include free accommodation and services, a generous end-of-contract gratuity, and 60 days home leave per year usually taken in two periods of 30 days) with free air passages.

For further details, write enclosing a brief résumé of your Service qualifications and experience, to:—

S.C.17730, Daily Telegraph, E.C.4.

Advert placed in The Daily Telegraph early 1975, by which time salaries had risen exponentially, more than doubling 1971 rates of pay, when a contract captain earned £3,000.

Hill, W11; £7,700 would have bought a flat in Edinburgh. Seconded personnel remained liable to UK rates of income tax. It was thus a moot point for those who viewed the distinction with a certain degree of irony, given we were equally employed in the service of a foreign country's armed forces – facing the same risks. The big difference of course lay in the fact the contract commissioned and non-commissioned officers held limited term contracts (normally three years) after which they might well be out of a job. Whereas the seconded officer would return to his regiment where he might (he hoped) be appreciated for his hard-earned experience, sufficient perhaps to enhance a military career. As to the tax and emolument advantages, most chose to remain silent on the issue. Argument would have been pointless anyway.

I found I fell between the two camps, seconded and contracted. Ten months earlier in BAOR (British Army of the Rhine) whilst serving with my regiment I'd signed on extending my original three-year Short Service Commission by another three. There was no certainty of gaining a regular commission at the end of my extended service as my regiment was fully subscribed with officers of my age. I thus faced the prospect of having to leave the Army two months following the end of my secondment. The paradox was not lost on me. Financially I'd have been far better off as a contract officer. That, however, had not been a route open to me when I'd volunteered for SAF. Encouragingly though, as regards a regular commission, I had the generous support of our regimental colonel, Lt. Col John Cordy-Simpson CBE MC. *'We'll get you in . . .'* he'd written, adding *'. . . so long as you bloody return from the desert!'*. Something I fully intended to do. I had no regrets.

Enemy Forces

The Adoo

FCO Briefing   *Restricted*

The indoctrinated and trained communist hard-core are believed to number between 700 and 1000. They are supported by an equally imprecise number of inhabitants who bear arms either voluntarily or by coercion. They are ruthless.

Leadership and weapon handling are markedly better than a year ago. Their knowledge of the jebel element is first class and tactical field-craft superior to SAF. Intelligence clearly indicates considerable numbers are receiving leadership and heavy weapon training – China, Korea, Iraq and Syria.

In 1971 communist forces outnumbered SAF stationed in Dhofar and it was common knowledge their fieldcraft was superior.

The Popular Front for the Liberation of Oman and Arabian Gulf (PFLOAG) were known as the *adoo*. Backed by the leading communist states, the adoo were controlled and administered by China, North Korea and Russia. China considered the war in Dhofar next in importance to Vietnam, equally capable of guaranteeing them victory in the region.

The adoo were issued with SKS-45 and AK-47 rifles as personal weapons. Adoo armaments included:

- 75mm RCLs with a range of 7,000 metres.
- 81mm or 82mm mortars with ranges up to 6,400 metres.
- 60mm mortars up to 3,400 metres.
- An unknown number of Shpagin 12.7mm heavy machine guns (HMG), firing range 7,500 metres.
- Light machine guns (LMG), maximum range of 3,600 metres.
- Also within their arsenal were issue Russian TM46 anti-tank and Russian PMN-1 anti-personnel mines, together with Chinese equivalents.

Similar to our irregular troops, the enemy were also formed into firqats, generally 50-man units, split as follows:

Western Approaches

- The Western Military Unit – estimated strength, 150 to 300 combatants in three firqats. These operated across the Yemeni border through which the arterial supply routes passed, feeding their forces with rations, ammunition and ordnance. This area held a hardcore of trained personnel guarding munitions dumps and training camps.

Central Area

- Comprising two firqats, the Lenin and Che Guevara Units numbering 100 to 150 in strength. Positioned to hold the Midway to Salalah road, a distance of approximately 100km, a vital North/South arterial route lost to the adoo after SAF were forced off the jebel in 1970.

Eastern Area

- Three firqats totalling between 100 to 200, operating out of scattered bases on the jebel overlooking Taqah, Mirbat and Sudh, coastal towns east of the Salalah plain.

Ho Chi Minh Unit

- A single firqat of between 100 to 200 were tasked with escorting camel convoys and troop movements north of Adonib through to the Central and the Eastern areas.

RUSSIA AND CHINA EXERT THEIR INFLUENCE

Russia had sought initially to restrain the People's Democratic Republic of Yemen (PDRY) from involvement in a guerrilla war. Not to be circumvented, China stepped in to provide an alternative source of aid, on the ground and militarily with personnel and hardware. Large numbers of guerrillas were taken to training camps in China and later, Yemen. Chinese advisors fought alongside their communist colleagues they'd professionally trained. Seeking to uphold their presence in the area, Russian advisors joined their fellow communists in the conflict. The communist Dhofar Liberation Front (DLF), now supported by Russia and China, were later joined by soldiers from North Korea and subsequently Cuba and East Germany.

The Soviet Union began to transfer ever more sophisticated weaponry to the DLF. Armed and supported by Chinese and Soviet military advisors, Cuban pilots and East German specialist forces, the DLF now threatened to overwhelm the Sultan's forces, reinvigorating a Jebali population's aspirations of victory.

Assisted by a sympathetic civilian population, the guerrillas were kept informed of the government forces' every move, while the Sultan's forces operated blindly in an intelligence vacuum. Adding urgency to an already tense region, in 1970 the DLF cemented ties with their Marxist comrades from Yemen. The Front's name was changed to PFLOAG (Popular Front for the Liberation of the Occupied Arabian Gulf). With forces swelled they began to act in unison.

Suffering significant casualties, SAF lost the battle to keep the Midway/Salalah road open. With that, the adoo won control of this important supply route over the jebel, leaving Salalah heavily reliant on resupply by air, there being no working harbour at the coastal town.

Pushed from their last jebel outposts, SAF was forced back to their base at Salalah. With increasing confidence, the well-trained guerrillas increased their ambushes and raids, wresting the initiative from government forces. The intensity of the war increased from one or two attacks a week, to two or three a day by 1970. It was widely held by SAF and visiting SAS commanders that Salalah was at serious risk, such it was acknowledged 'lose the airfield and you lose the war'.

Arriving in 1970 as the new Forces Commander, CSAF, Brigadier John Graham was aghast at the situation in Dhofar. SAF morale was shot; Marxist guerrillas had forced the Sultan's forces off the surrounding 3,000ft mountains and now encircled Salalah, capital of Dhofar and residence of the Sultan. From their vantage point the Marxists rained mortar and rocket and small arms fire onto government positions protecting the capital and airport. SAF were held at gunpoint with their backs to the sea.

A summary on the situation by the FCO held:

> The causes of SAF's demoralisation are threefold. First, with only two battalions serving at any one time in the south, they do not have numerical superiority essential to achieve victory in Dhofar. Secondly, the terrain favours the rebels. Thirdly, SAF's heart is no longer in the war.
>
> Other factors affecting SAF's morale include the recent direct hits on Salalah by rebel artillery; the length of tours of duty by SAF in Dhofar, which now stand at ten months* and are unlikely to decrease. HMG should realise that the rank-and-file SAF are a very tired force.

and in conclusion:

> ... that it was for HMG to assess the consequences for British interests in Oman as a whole (following) British military withdrawal from the Trucial States. If a resumed autumn campaign failed to achieve any significant success ... and the rebels might be armed for the first time with 105 mm guns, thus continuing an escalation of weaponry ... would tell against fixed bases and demoralised regular troops ... the position is desperately serious.

> *Author correction, nine months

The scene was set for a repeat of a historic communist victory when the French were defeated at Dien Bien Phu on 7 May 1954, leading to the fall of French Indochina. Concerned about regional instability, America went to war in Vietnam only to follow France when they too pulled out, 20 years later.

1970 and 16 years on from that French defeat, with Vietnam concentrating minds in the American administration, the CIA began questioning whether SAF were capable of defending Salalah let alone defeating a Marxist onslaught into Oman. Failure to do so would hand Russian and Chinese backed communists control of that strategically vital region.

With the MOD now conscious of Oman becoming another Vietnam, the period between mid-1970 into 1972 became the nadir in the conflict, the outcome held in balance by an overstretched, outnumbered Sultan's Armed Forces.

D-NOTICE BREACHED

Given today's constant deluge of live 'breaking-news' reporting, there is little doubt that in the 21st century the war in Dhofar could have remained a 'secret war'.

Early in 1972 the 'D-notice' was breached. The media sensed the whiff of a story. Why, given the Labour Government's pledge that British troops had withdrawn from all points East of Suez by December 1971, were British soldiers still being killed in Arabia? Britain's three major broadsheets carried editorials questioning whether, like the Americans in Laos, the UK was fighting a clandestine war in Dhofar? Young Liberals demanded of their constituency MP:

FCO Briefing

... wish to draw your attention to what, at first sight appears to be, not only a dubious role of Her Majesty's Forces in the Middle East, but also to a suspicious silence on the part of the daily press. We refer to the Sultanate of Oman and Dhofar.

Pressure brought to bear closed these stories. Unlike today, when social media and television ensure the public are continuously bombarded with reports on the world's latest developments, the story died.

2

DAWN OF THE ARMOURED CAR SQUADRON

The call for volunteers from amongst serving British and suitable ex-servicemen. Selection and Arabic language course. We learn of an early British casualty killed in action (KIA)

"The Armoured Car Squadron of the Sultan's Armed Forces is quite unique, and it would be pointless to try and equate its organisation and tasks to that of a squadron in the British Army"

Major AJ Cornwell RTR: RAC Centre
Bulletin 1972 – classified 'restricted'.

The distinctive title, 'The Armoured Car Squadron', dates from WW1 with a certain Flight Commander Thomas Hetherington, ex-18th Hussars. A riding accident leaving him no longer able to ride, Hetherington gained his flying certificate and transferred to the Royal Naval Air Service (RNAS). In November 1914 the RNAS built 15 Wolseley armoured cars. These were split into troops of five cars, to form The Armoured Car Squadron whose primary task was rescuing British airmen forced to land behind enemy lines. Operating with spectacular success, they lasted until the advent of trench warfare curtailed operations. Prominent amongst the first section commanders were Hetherington and the Duke of Westminster.

THE CALL FOR VOLUNTEERS

Suddenly things began to move swiftly. Following the coup on 23 July 1970 an immediate order was circulated calling for volunteers to join the Sultan of Oman's Armed Forces on secondment. I applied, gaining selection that same month, coincidentally together with a friend from the adjacent barracks, Mike Campbell, Coldstream Guards. Our regiments, part of 4 Guards Brigade, BAOR, were based at the university city of Münster in north-west Germany. Mike's posting to Oman would precede mine as he was to join an existing infantry regiment, whereas I'd be joining the Armoured Car Squadron being formed early the following year.

In August 1970, my regiment departed for annual firing, a period of gunnery training with live ammunition on the NATO ranges at Bergen-Hohne Training Area on Lüneburg Heath. The month was rain-free; it hadn't rained properly for weeks, leaving the ranges tinder dry.

As troop leader of the regiment's light reconnaissance troop, I had had two days firing .30 Brownings and two days extinguishing fires caused by our tracer rounds. Instructed to spend the remainder of the week practising radio voice procedures, things had become a trifle dull when as occasionally happens and surely some blame must fall to young men's testosterone, matters took an unexpected turn sufficient to threaten my posting to Oman.

On a particularly hot evening following dinner in the ex-Wehrmacht Officers' Mess, a group of unmentionable individuals decided to ambush those of us still seated following dinner, enjoying a quiet drink and conversation with invited guests idly minding our business. Suddenly from nowhere and without warning,

Possibly slightly worse for wear, author and Carter on picquet, ready to take on all comers. The episode in an otherwise unpromising career to date, earned me a string of extra duties which had to be worked off prior to my Oman secondment. My accomplice Carter was excused as a guest led astray.

whoosh then *woosh* again flew curtains of water thrown from fire buckets through an open door. Instantly all seated were drenched. There followed whoops of joy, and shouts of '*on target!*' echoing down the corridor. Bedlam.

With no time to waste and grabbing an antiquated water syphon pump and bucket I was joined by my dinner guest, an equally soaked Anthony Carter, a fellow subaltern with the Blues and Royals, and together we returned fire, dousing our would-be assailants. A lot of water was used that night and a not inconsiderable level of noise made with each attack successfully repulsed. In hot pursuit following our attackers upstairs, we rounded a corner to find an individual standing in our path clad in his pyjamas. Immediately we opened up with a full jet of water. Unfortunately for those of my redoubtable section, we'd just soaked a sleep deprived Lt. Colonel John Howard, my commanding officer. There followed a short lecture on etiquette and the awarding of an inverse number of extra orderly officer duties. It was even hinted that any idea of my Oman posting being realised was now in serious jeopardy. Thankfully that turned out to be no more than a threat expressed in the heat of the moment. Many years later at a regimental funeral Col. John approached to inquire whether I hadn't served during his time as Colonel? I assured him indeed I had, relieved he'd obviously filed both Hodgson and that Hohne evening under 'Forgotten'. Or had he?

That winter, and allocated the duty (duty?) of training and captaining the regimental langlauf and downhill ski teams, I eventually traded the snows of Bavaria and St Moritz for an Arabic language course beginning in March 1971, the same month the first Saladins were being landed ashore from a rickety ferry at Oman's Muscat harbour. The cars remained at SAF headquarters in northern Oman until commissioned for service at the end of April. I arrived two months later.

Just outside the medals, my team managed 4th place out of 17, however, probably not ideal training for war in Oman's deserts. A close friend, Alan Howard, a Royal Marine, followed his selection to SAF by promptly opting for a demolitions course, which was to prove far more useful a year down the line.

Meanwhile, Major AJ (Tim) Cornwell, the Armoured Car Squadron Leader, and his 2ic Mike Offord had arrived in Oman earlier that year. Their task: to set about recruiting and training soldiers in preparation for the imminent arrival in the country of eight new Saladins and four Ferret Scout Cars, with urgent deployment to the war zone in Dhofar.

When eventually the Squadron deployed to Dhofar it would link up with four ancient Ferrets already there, stored in 'light preservation'. Two of the new Saladins and Ferrets would remain at SAF HQ, colloquially known as Bayt al Falaj (BAF), under joint command of 'Q', S/Sgt Pete Minvalla and S/Sgt Geoff Beadle, running the squadron quartermaster stores and recruit training respectively.

By June 1971, the Squadron Officer and NCO strength would be as follows:

- Squadron Leader: Major Tim Cornwell 2 RTR*
- Second in Command: Capt Mike Offord ex-1 RTR
- Plains Troop Leader: Capt Paul Hodgson 13/18th Royal Hussars
- SSM: Stan Piórkowski ex-11th Hussars
- SQMS: S/Sgt Pete Minvalla ex-5th Inniskilling Dragoon Guards, SAS
- D&M: Training S/Sgt Geoff Beadle ex-9/12th Royal Lancers
- Saladin Commanders: S/Sgt Geoff Begley ex-1 RTR
- Sgt Alan Oliver 4 RTR
- Sgt Gerry Fyfe 2 RTR
- Sgt Tony Wright 17/21st Lancers
- Plains Troop Sgt: Sgt Lou Costello Queen's Royal Irish Hussars

— Severely injured in a Land Rover accident, we lost Sgt Wright early. A good man, but following casevac to the UK he never returned.

*RTR – Royal Tank Regiment

ARABIC COURSE
INTER SERVICES SCHOOL OF LANGUAGES, BEACONSFIELD. APRIL 1971

Reporting to Wilton Park, the Army School of Languages at Beaconsfield, I joined seven others, six of us destined for SAF and two for The Trucial Oman Scouts (TOS). We were here to learn Arabic in ten weeks.

Now owned by the MOD, Wilton Park was once home to the Du Pe family. As Governor of Madras in the 18th century, Du Pre had amassed a considerable personal fortune. The original Palladian building with Robert Adam interiors was used to interrogate WW2 Nazi prisoners including Rudolf Hess. Demolished after the war it was replaced with an ugly range of buildings, becoming the MOD's Inter Services School of Languages.

None of us had met before and as at any first meeting between strangers, there was the momentary sizing up of those present as we introduced ourselves. That none had previously met was unusual given the many opportunities to have crossed paths at officer training, or any of the many courses and field exercises held across the UK or BAOR. But we were all new to each other, arriving from different parts of the armed forces, Armour, Infantry, Gunners and the Royal Navy. And from the armoured corps two were from the Royal Tank Regiment, I was the sole Cavalryman. The six of us destined for SAF would be posted to the following regiments:

- Captain Rick Williams (Royal Marines) – Desert Regiment (DR)
- Captain Tom Bremridge (3 Royal Horse Artillery) – Desert Regiment (DR)
- Lt Sandy Blackett (Argyll and Sutherland Highlanders) – Muscat Regiment (MR)
- Lt Paul Hodgson, Sgts Alan Oliver & Gerry Fyfe – Armoured Car Squadron (ACS)

The two sergeants had recently been promoted. In Oman, Sandy and I would hold the rank of captain. Advised I could now wear a third pip, I was delighted to be elevated so rapidly having only recently gained a second to become substantive lieutenant. Regrettably, the army thought best to restrict my service pay until I arrived in Oman. Fortunately, extra 'messing', the levy towards fine dining enjoyed in certain regiments, was not imposed at Beaconsfield, where on recollection the food wasn't worth complaining about. Senior amongst us was the quiet and respected Lt. Colonel John Williams, a Glorious Gloster, veteran of the Battle of Imjin River where a single battalion had famously faced and fought an entire Chinese Division. One evening he told what to expect when under accurate enemy fire, and how afterwards you'd never be the same again. His words hung heavily to receptive ears.

Weekly reports on the war in Dhofar were posted with brief insights on various contacts (actions) and troop movements. Though censored, these were read avidly as the only intelligence available on what was happening in Oman. Towards the end of our course in June, we learned of Stuart Rae's death in action. A fellow Royal Marine, it hit Rick hard. And at lunch that day, gone was the cheeky banter we'd become accustomed to with the pretty Mess waitresses; instead, tears. It was touching and yet shouldn't have been unexpected, for they knew where we were being posted and had been privy to the same weekly war reports posted on the Mess notice board. Stuart had been on the Arabic course immediately prior to ours.

SECRET *FCO Briefing*

ON 12 JUN NORTHERN FRONTIER REGT AND FIRQAT TARIQ BIN ZAID ENCOUNTERED A REBEL GROUP WHILE PATROLLING AREA YU5360 PD   ONE ROYAL MARINE SECONDED OFFICER WAS KILLED (CPT SJ RAE) AND ONE SAF SOLDIER WOUNDED PD

Stuart had joined Northern Frontier Regiment (NFR) at Akoot Camp, a battalion held position established a few months earlier. On 12 June, barely six weeks into his two-year secondment and patrolling south of Akoot, NFR were caught in the open. Pinned down and sensing fire was being concentrated towards another section of his company, Stuart gradually raised his head to locate the enemy. He'd been watched. Waiting for his move, a carefully aimed shot rang out from his flank, wounding Stuart mortally in the throat. He died on the jebel, an already respected soldier taken out long before he'd a chance to fulfil his true potential.

Three years later, quite by chance, I met people who'd known Stuart well. They still felt his loss deeply, a frequent visitor to their rambling house my parents were to purchase as I was leaving the Army in 1974. A large comfortable home with mature gardens, it became an ideal place for the few weeks I would need to convalesce following surgery.

At the end of my Arabic course I had time for one last diversion, a weekend spent at Henley Royal Regatta. A couple of days of escapism juxtaposed with a scramble of last-minute shopping, packing and a final haircut with Mr Bird at Trumpers, 9 Curzon Street, W1.

Seconded from the British Army as 23 to 26-year-olds, promoted captain and completing our Arabic course, we were on our way to join a foreign army. An army we would find comprised many soldiers deemed illiterate, men who despite being able to read and recite the Quran in Islamic text, had no recognised education. For these, signing for pay, identity cards and driving licences was achieved with an inked thumbprint. Signallers messaging in English and taught the Morse Code dot-dash alphabet and numbers without learning English, made for some interesting signals.

Omani soldiers with regional tribal dialects added further complication. Always a surprise was a soldier's unexpected use of English, indicating someone who'd travelled for work or studied in one of the neighbouring Gulf states. Indians and a few Pakistanis spoke excellent English; Zanzibaris, an Arabic/Swahili mix and English, and the Baluchis, Urdu. By definition we made a polyglot force.

Amusingly, a later FCO document relates:

Zanzibaris 5. Aug 1973

The Principal Immigration Officer has (ordered) no more passports should be issued to Zanzibaris claiming Omani nationality. The measure stems apparently from objections by real Omanis to the way East African Omanis are picking up all the best jobs, where English and other skills are in demand. With so many Zanzibaris well placed in the Administration it is probable that the order will not be strictly observed.

3

ARRIVAL IN OMAN

Initial experiences on arrival, introduction to Arab soldiers, language difficulties and training for combat. Issued woefully inadequate equipment we rely on shemaghs for helmets. The Sultan's Royal Stables. Troop training nears completion. Swimming with snakes. The Squadron's first contact. Another early British casualty.

We boarded a BOAC flight out of Heathrow Airport on a gloriously warm summer's day, the 5th of July.

Earlier in the day, feigning a relaxed composure, whilst in truth endeavouring to remain outwardly calm, determined to suppress the excitement and apprehension that had begun to knit in my stomach, I bade farewell to my twin, William and his sweet young wife Catherine, who'd been married less than a year – I'd been best man at their wedding. Seeing me off at a West End bus stop, Catherine gave me two lined notebooks: 'You'll need these to record your experiences, otherwise you'll forget and regret it one day.' We parted, they happily on their familiar way to work, whilst in perfect paradox, I as a great many others before, was off to war.

At the time under strict orders to maintain secret our mission in Oman, none had spoken of it to parents or siblings, in my case, twin and two younger sisters, Ann a student nurse and the youngest, Odeyne, still at school. The secrecy element had made parting all the easier. To all intents and purposes we were being seconded to help modernise, train and run the still fledgling armed forces of Oman.

That was it – no more farewells. No turning back and indeed there never had been any chance of doing so following selection for secondment. Under official army terminology I was now classified 'Officer at ERE' (Extra Regimental

Employment). I was off the regimental pay list. Even then, despite BAOR facing the perceived threat from Soviet Russia, Britain's armed forces were operating on a shoestring. So, a small saving to my regiment was still a saving, a time when annual mileage for tanks and armoured vehicles was strictly limited, and many aspects of military ordnance restricted. I would now be paid from a special reserve fund out of Whitehall, in addition to a loan service package graciously paid by the Sultan during secondment.

At midday I met up with the others, Tom, Rick and Sandy at Heathrow. All four of us were wearing tropical lightweight suits in accordance with SAF joining instructions. Suits we'd had tailored by the doyens of bespoke tropical tailoring, Airey and Wheeler, 11 St George Street, Mayfair, for prices charged that would probably have paid for two Savile Row suits. However, the same suit later washed in a tin bucket by a slightly over-enthusiastic Arab orderly, lasted far longer than many purchased in later years and professionally dry cleaned.

Looking as overdressed as the arriviste, we stuck out as sore thumbs. As we casually looked around, attempting to appear nonchalant, up strode a lightly tanned and sensibly attired Martin Robb, wearing jeans and loose shirt. With a broad grin, he remarked 'You lot must be on your way to Oman', adding 'no one, but no one dresses for travel quite like SAF's new intake'!

Martin Robb, a contract officer serving with Muscat Regiment, had noticed us as soon as we'd entered the departure lounge. Laughingly he joked that everybody subsequently regretted wearing suits on what was then a two-day journey to Oman. He remarked dryly: 'It'll probably be the last time you'll wear suits in Oman and you'll definitely never wear them flying again!' He was right on both counts.

Martin, an ex-Gurkha, was a contract captain returning from a month's leave in the UK to rejoin MR currently stationed at Salalah, Dhofar where Sandy would soon join him as a brother officer.

I was the only one of us 'new boys' to have visited Arabia before. Admittedly that had been as a child, sailing by ship out of Mombasa in 1953, when we docked at Aden for three days to refuel and take on supplies. As a family we had ventured ashore and all I recalled was that it had been unbelievably hot. The onwards voyage followed the Red Sea northwards to the entrance of the Suez Canal, 120 miles of narrow waterway cut through Egyptian desert and out into the blue waters of the Mediterranean, on to the estuarine discoloured English Channel, eventually to make landfall at Southampton docks. Despite having to attend daily school lessons given freely by two of my parents' fellow travellers, for a pair of six-year-old twin boys it had been an enormous adventure.

My family was returning to the UK, my father having accumulated six months' leave as a District Commissioner in East Africa. His province extended from the shores of Lake Victoria eastwards across the Serengeti plains, recently awarded National Park status. We later moved to Moshi in the foothills of Kilimanjaro and later still back to Tanganyika's capital, the city where my brother and I had been born, Dar-es-Salaam, on the coast. It would be difficult to imagine a more perfect upbringing.

With the undaunted confidence of a 23-year-old, I'd optimistically proposed the four of us endeavour to arrange our first leave dates to coincide, when we'd fly to East Africa for adventure. There, with me acting as guide, we'd rent vehicles and equipment and travel freely, visiting game parks and reserves, culminating with a Kilimanjaro climb. The then permanently snow-covered mountain on the Equator still conjured enchantment as a rare and evocative place unspoilt by tourism. As one, all eagerly agreed to the plan with little appreciation as to the practicalities. Two of us did, however, make that journey.

As we casually took our seats on the aircraft, giving the impression of seasoned travellers, an air stewardess approached, waving a small brown envelope, enquiring which one was Captain Paul Hodgson? Cover blown, she held a telegram my mother had kindly sent as a parting gesture: "Wishing you all the very best – much love". The resulting ribbing was altogether predictable. 'Bet you said you're off to win a war?' enquired an incredulous Rick. 'Nope,' I replied truthfully, to a barrage of ribald laughter from my three companions . . . at least the tension was broken.

We were off to Oman, and I recorded the first of my diary entries.

> *6 July – Flight out comfortable. Hiccup at Bahrain Airport – passport query as to why I was a British citizen but born in East Africa. Required to pay transit visa, £2.00 – as had no local currency. Is someone on the make? Taxi out to local hotel. Air-con not working. Very hot. No chance of sleep. Interesting landing at Bayt al Falaj. If Bahrain was hot, Oman's a furnace. Briefing – all cat-napped. 1800 fitted out with uniforms. Unbelievably hot. Suitcase has not arrived Oman. HQ will investigate.*

We flew BOAC (British Overseas Airways Corporation) by the iconic Boeing 747 first brought into service in 1969. In Bahrain there was a delay and we were accommodated in a local one-star hotel with non-functioning air-conditioning. Unaccustomed to the heat, sleep evaded even the Royal Marine who'd boasted he could sleep anywhere. It was a tired group next morning that climbed aboard a Gulf Air flight to Oman. Gone was our spacious Jumbo, swapped for a 28-seater turboprop Fokker F27 Friendship, which appealed to immature minds. Tom took the window seat and promptly slept, his head all but obscuring views to the deserts below. I noticed our fellow passengers comprised Arabs, others from Asia and some chickens – no doubt destined for someone's celebratory meal. Stuck on the bulkhead in front of us, three holes had been taped over with pink sticking plaster, 'Probably holding the aircraft together' commented a rueful Rick. An uneventful flight was made memorable for the close proximity between wingtips to mountains as we flew in a sweeping arc following a dry limestone walled wadi to land with a thump at Bayt al Falaj, Oman's joint military and civilian main airport.

Peering out, blue skies faded to a blistering heat shimmer. Mirages distorted everything between airfield and mountains beyond. Oven-hot air radiated off rocks and barren ground surrounding the apron on the edge of the small airfield. Alien in its ferocity, the heat catches you off guard. It was midday, hottest part of the day. Desert virgins taking an involuntary gulp of air emerging into the glare and heat, discovered too late an atmosphere filled with spent aviation fuel fumes burned parched throats.

Eyes unaccustomed to fierce brightness were instinctively squeezed, the light blinding, such we probably resembled more our enemy's commissars from the Orient than a newly arrived contingent for the Sultan's forces. Descending the gangway leaving the air-conditioned aircraft, clothing stuck, sodden with sweat. A corrugated tin shed passed for customs control where there seemed to be a bit of flap going on. It transpired there'd been a rumour our plane had been hijacked. False alarm.

Our initial visas were still stamped Muscat and Oman, as the country was known until the coup in 1970. By our second year the visa stamp had become Sultanate Of Oman.

Patiently waiting for passports to be checked, we were amazed at the seemingly cool, controlled composure of the middle-aged local customs officer sitting in what could only be described as a hellhole of heat. An oven would have been cooler. Carefully reading our passports, deliberate in action turning each page to study previously stamped entries, he eventually stamped each in turn, bidding us individually 'Welcome, sahb' with a slight and dignified nod of his head after first making direct eye contact. I was impressed.

Then arrived a gangly staff officer, in full khaki uniform, looking as if he'd just stepped off a parade ground. Flushed and sweating almost as much as the new arrivals in crumpled suits, Captain Victor Seely (11th Hussars), tasked with meeting and escorting new arrivals to SAF HQ at Bayt al Falaj camp, welcomed us to Oman.

Bundled into the back of a dusty Land Rover together with what bags we had, we rumbled along a dirt track to the camp gates, passing some desiccated small bushes where I noticed a handful of scruffy looking sparrows had taken refuge – 'Sparrows? Out here?' I thought, amazed they might exist in this seemingly utterly inhospitable environment. I read later that except for Antarctica, sparrows (Passer domesticus) are found on every continent.

Arriving at the ancient colonial style Officers' Mess, a concrete building once painted white, Seely climbed out of the Land Rover with a cheery 'Right you are, sign in, dump your kit in your rooms, see you in the bar for a drink and lunch. After lunch a briefing on what's happening'.

FIRST BRIEFING IN DEPTH – CURRENT STATE OF THE WAR IN DHOFAR

FCO: Re DHOFAR. 1971

BRIGADIER SEMPLE OF THE SAS PASSED THROUGH BAHRAIN ON 10 JUNE AND DISCUSSED WITH ME, AS I BELIEVE HE DID WITH YOU, THE SITUATION IN DHOFAR. WHILE ACCEPTING THAT ANY REALISTIC ASSESSMENT OF THE FUTURE COURSE OF THE WAR IN DHOFAR MUST WAIT UNTIL AFTER THE MONSOON ENDS IN SEPTEMBER, SEMPLE NEVERTHELESS PAINTED A GLOOMY PICTURE OF POLITICAL DISILLUSIONMENT AMONG EVEN THE MOST LOYAL DHOFARIS WITH THE SULTANATE AUTHORITIES AND ARGUED THAT MILITARY OPERATIONS ALONE WOULD BE INSUFFICIENT TO WIN DHOFARI SUPPORT FOR THE SULTAN.

Diligently prepared maps and handouts were distributed as another staff officer, Andrew Rosencrantz (Royal Engineers), outlined the present state of Oman's secret war. Except for geography, it bore all the trademarks of a BAOR seminar, the exception being there was now no mention of nuclear, biological or chemical weapons for which we'd trained endlessly in Western Germany.

Dog-tired after the flight, as yet unaccustomed to the oppressive energy-sapping heat, a cold beer at lunchtime and we were paying for it now. The whirr of a failing air-conditioner's engine vibrating in its housing, added to the sonorous voice of the speaker, only quickened gravity's effect on eyelids. Bliss. I am sure I was not alone, but with my luck it was me who heard a distant voice enquiring 'Ah yes, Hodgson, isn't it? . . . Might I ask whether we are quite comfortable enough?'!

Regardless the seriousness of topic, lack of sleep, seated motionless in an overheated, airless room following a light lunch, I defy anyone to remain fully conscious. The effect is well known to any who've experienced afternoon lectures. Even chewing on a lip had no effect. Biting your tongue didn't work either.

Nudged awake by Tom, I caught the gist of the intended message. In plainest 'military speak' we were being told the aim was to win a decisive and lasting victory against a Russian and Chinese communist backed enemy, who having succeeded in pushing the Sultan's Forces from the jebel, were now holding most of Dhofar, the southwestern region of Oman.

Soldier morale was low. Not without reason. Casualties were mounting and patrols were constantly ambushed. Adoo attacks were effective, seemingly sprung by a superior enemy capable of striking at will before melting into the jebel's wilderness. Soldier recruitment was sluggish and front-line soldiers were disappearing AWOL when granted leave. Weapons were being lost, correctly presumed stolen.

A British contract officer, Eddie Vutirakis, ex-Royal Sussex, ex-SAS (DR), had been shot and killed by one of his soldiers as he slept. The Americans had a term for it, 'fragging', except more usually associated with grenades. The Arab murderer escaped to join the other side.

We learned the enemy had not only swallowed the Marxist ideology but had totally ingested it, to a degree which excluded formerly deeply held religious beliefs. The result was the conversion of Muslim to non-believer, the creation of ideological zealots, setting brother against brother, tribe against tribe.

The briefing continued to describe loosely the various tribal regions in Dhofar, political infighting and long-held distrust between tribes, their faith and their outlook on life. There were mountain tribes, tribesmen from desert and from coastal towns, and east of Salalah was an area given over to a significant group made up of ex-slaves, until recently fiercely loyal to the deposed Sultan Said bin

Taimur. An eclectic mix of different dialects and loyalties promised to make our lives interesting.

We would learn fighting alongside the young, devout soldiers of the Sultan's Forces, many of whom regularly displayed extraordinary acts of bravery, that on occasions we would meet our match in the adoo, whose ideologies so contradicted ours.

As occurs with any close band of fighters, the enemy would be engaged and fought with a matched degree of ferocity for no other reason except the imperative of not letting down those around you, ordinary men trained as soldiers. In the two years I spent in Dhofar, rarely did I meet a politicised soldier, for whilst they would fight the enemy without hesitation, there seemed to be a lack of any hate. Neither was there any particular wish to discuss the loss of faith and conversion to communism. The adoo were simply an enemy who killed or maimed those on our side. And so perpetuating the timeworn traditions of existence and survival in the desert, the bottom line was: they kill ours, we kill theirs. There was little or no emotion involved. Atonement achieved, an eye for an eye.

We'd find that at the death of a soldier emotions were controlled, respect was paramount, the dead buried that day with the short prayer, ending in 'Allah Kareem' – God is Generous. At first intrigued by their philosophy, we grew to understand and value it as part of the desert code essential to their existence. One that had enabled desert peoples to evolve as nomads, mountain men, oasis and village dwellers eking out a living on the edge of unforgiving environments.

In truth it was not difficult but to accept their ways and codes established over millennia. We who were guests in their country grew to admire the straightforward ancient creeds, principles and fortitude, their outstanding loyalty to each other that was graciously extended to us, their British officers.

DRIVING TEST

7 July – Still in suit trousers. Morning spent meeting HQ old sweats. Toured numerous staff offices. Bank. Driving Test – 7 minutes and pass! Swam after lunch – bliss to be back in the Indian Ocean again, or correctly, Arabian Sea.

In common with all newly arrived, none of us had any Omani currency and on day two of our continued initiation to SAF, between introductions to countless HQ personnel, we were driven to a Muscat bank to withdraw cash. On our return each took turns driving the Land Rover, which constituted a driving test. Being as it was one of the easiest vehicles to drive, all passed with ease. That evening we

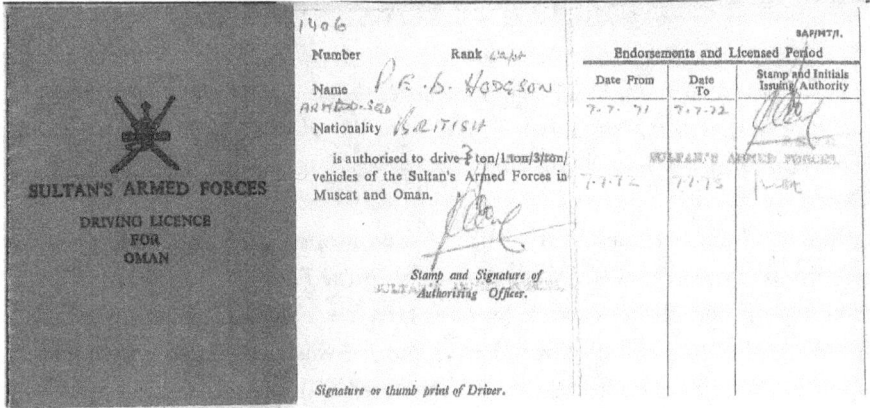

A sample of Oman's 1970s currency, 100 Baiza, One Rial and 5 Rials notes.

were presented with our SAF driving licences. A record any country's licensing authority might only aspire to. Licences were renewed annually.

'You'll get used to the heat – and the country,' remarked the staff officer testing our driving skills. 'Expect to bloody hate the first six months after which you'll gradually get used to it all, the way of life, the soldiering and of course the bloody flies . . .' before adding casually 'that's except those going to Dhofar – you'll find the climate's different, flies are worse, they bite and some chaps never get used to the three months monsoon. Ground level cloud and drizzle blankets Salalah plain and surrounding jebel, bloody treacherous for SAF, great for adoo!'

We glanced at each other but none chose to reply. Unnecessary rancour from an officer constrained by tedium and frustrations of an office-bound existence.

THE SULTAN'S ROYAL STABLES

8 July – afternoon. Still no sign suitcase. Borrowed kit. Rode Arab stallion, a grey – Al Muharib Saeid "The Happy Warrior". Lightly brown spotted. With Francois, French diplomat.

At lunch Victor Seely asked if I'd like a ride on one of the Sultan's horses that afternoon. Answering yes, I was asked to be at the Royal Stables at 4pm. Victor later told me he'd 'checked me out' as one of the few fellow cavalry officers serving in SAF at the time and discovered as he put it I was 'all right'. Inherent elitism prevalent within the British Army and hoped left behind in BAOR was obviously thriving at HQ.

Relishing the offer as probably one never to be repeated, I'd readily accepted. Victor kindly lent me a pair of twill trousers and I duly reported to the Royal Stables, which I found were no more than a single-storey row of cement breeze-block loose boxes with corrugated iron roofing. Stifling hot inside but with walls constructed to leave a half metre gap between blockwork and sheets of iron roofing, they were at least ventilated. That said, the average July daytime temperature was pushing 45C in the shade.

I was introduced to my riding companion, Francois, a French diplomat who'd likewise turned out in khaki slacks and loose shirt. His English, perfect, my French not so, he exuded the enviable air of a professional horseman which turned out to be correct.

Exchanging pleasantries, I walked over to my mount, a magnificent grey, standing between 15 to 16 hands. He looked as fine as any Lipizzaner. Ears forward on a head held high, long white eyelashes framing eager eyes flashing whites around dark pupils. Was this fear or were the horse's eyes naturally partially pigmented? Horse eyes are probably the largest in scale of any land mammal, lenses magnifying what humans see by an additional 50%, giving them an acute advantage over predators. Shadowed pink nostrils flared. Completing the picture, a loose flowing mane and impatient whisking tail held high. A foot stamped on the baked earth. In the sun's glare I imagined him to be white Arab, but drawing closer saw he was speckled as an Appaloosa with faint mottled hide of light brown spots. Naturally I assumed he was a gelding.

I'd experienced nervous horses before so made a conscious effort to remain calm, realising he'd see straight through any attempt to conceal apprehension.

Beautifully turned out with shining tack, brasses gleamed on a saddle sitting securely on a royal red blanket. 'That's smart,' I thought. Then I noticed the important bits – 'Oh shiiiit . . . stallion' flashed my subconscious. Still held by his stable lad, my mount dared me approach, defiant in his stare. Taught to murmur a steady 'hello old chap', I realised perhaps that should have been in Arabic. I reached to rub his muzzle. He glared back at me. I patted his neck. No point in hesitating, taking the proffered reins, putting left foot into the stirrup iron I swung myself into the saddle.

The response, immediate and not anticipated. Rearing up, my mount began bucking furiously in an attempt to throw me forwards over his head between his now flattened ears. Lashing out he was determined to kick anything and anyone foolishly within range of his flailing hooves.

Pride, that first of deadliest sins, probably saved me. A group of His Majesty's undoubtedly curious stable staff, each of whom would easily have ridden the animal bareback, had gathered to witness the white officer 'mount up'. Was it pride that determined what happened in the next few moments or perhaps the stones and hard sun-baked ground that ruled out any thought of an undignified dismount? With no headgear a fall was out of the question. Self-preservation won; I hung on.

For an instant I was transported to a scene 16 years earlier at boarding school in Kenya. A preparatory school located at high altitude on Kenya's plateau that runs to the edge of the Great Rift Valley. My parents then lived on the shores of Lake Victoria in Tanganyika, three days' drive and an antiquated lake ferry crossing away.

Improbable today, but as a school we rode out four days a week before classes. My twin brother and I had first attended boarding school aged five and a half and, now seven, were addicted to riding. I'd ridden my mount, Hell-for-Leather, on a number of occasions before. This morning I'd volunteered to ride bareback.

Halfway through the ride, we'd passed an African village and trotted out onto the open savannah beyond. At the bidding of our teacher, came the anticipated shout – a sign we were to take off at a gallop – "Leopard attack!" (Whilst a serious lesson for school rides in 1950s Kenya, it was always the highlight of the morning's excursion.) Unluckily for me, as we kicked into gallop, a pack of village dogs rushed out, barking wildly, two becoming entangled with my pony's front legs and together we took a head-first fall. My mount landed partially on top of my left side. I regained consciousness as an African boy dragged me clear of pony and barking dogs, all animals remarkably unhurt.

My left arm was shattered at the elbow with a compound fracture. Someone wrapped a handkerchief around my wound and, feeling fairly miserable, I was lifted onto the teacher's saddle before he climbed up behind me to ride back to the stables, 35 minutes away. A brief visit to the sanatorium and a vehicle was quickly prepared to take me to hospital. The make-shift ambulance, an open pick-up truck, transferred me two hours to the only local hospital in the region, along a dusty corrugated earth road. It was extremely uncomfortable but the best mode for transporting a prone casualty. Matron kindly sat with me as escort in the back of the truck and together we were delivered to the hospital, arriving covered in a layer of Kenya's finest red dust. Two weeks of repeat operations with lots of gas followed, when the bones were successfully sewn together. Within six months I was back in the saddle riding out and playing school rugby again. Young bones heal quickly. To this day I remain in awe and indebted to the laudable skills of a talented orthopaedic surgeon, a consultant who just happened to be visiting Eldoret Hospital as I was admitted.

That was 16 years ago. Now with one foot in a stirrup iron and gripping as tight as I could with my knees, leg muscles screeching in protest, I held on and somehow remained in my seat. He put his head down again and bucked to throw me forward once more. With his head remaining low, I managed gently to turn him, keeping his head down, gradually gaining control, bringing him onto the bit. 'F... me,' I thought to myself, 'that was a surprise!'

In what had seemed an age but in reality was only moments, I'd won control and my mount settled down, still trembling, shaking and snorting, ready for a repeat performance. 'Mabrook yaa seedee, mabrook!' which translates roughly as 'good on you, mate' exclaimed the onlookers, having all sensibly backed away during my hapless display of horsemanship.

With heart pounding I heard Seely shout, '... just wanted to see if the 13th/18th could handle a proper horse!' I don't recall my precise reply but I doubt it was cordial. With a grin towards Francois, we set off at a controlled, if bouncy canter away from the stables. 'I enjoyed the spectacle,' remarked my suave French companion, before adding, 'truly magnificent beasts, n'est pas?'

Francois was right, these were amazing animals. Of course, Francois chain-smoked Gauloises. We cantered lightly towards the nearby coastline, arriving shortly at a small fishing village. Slowing our mounts to a walk we rode past white painted flat roofed houses, raising an unwelcome dust trail as we made our way out to the sun and salt encrusted sandy beach. Small children gazed in wonder, adults in curiosity, as two Europeans rode by on the Sultan's prized mounts in the late afternoon sunshine. We would have presented a rare sight owing to the scarcity of such fine horses in Oman at the time.

Looking out over the expanse of an almost white beach, we stopped briefly to take in the spectacle of the blue sea and small breakers lapping the shoreline. A glance and a nod were all it required before we released the pent up power in our magnificent creatures. Acceleration was immediate and astonishing. We galloped; two riders on noble white stallions pounded through the shallows at the water's edge. Uninterrupted bleached sand stretched to the distance, the faintest hint of colours gaining intensity in the late afternoon sunshine. The tide was ebbing, the sand firm. The beach, deserted but for us, had a backdrop of brown, sun-scorched rock, burnt through millennia by blistering sunshine now shimmering in the last radiated heat of the day. Too soon the sun would be setting into the sea and it was time to return our mounts to the grooms at the Sultan's stables.

We arrived back with the sun sinking as an orange ball into the horizon, exhilarated and tired, arms and legs aching from controlling our mounts, the insides of my knees rubbed raw where stirrup leathers had chafed and pinched through seawater-splashed khaki trousers.

The exquisite horses, lathered up and still on their toes, were ready for more but we'd been instructed to be back before dark and for me that meant a return to the real world of soldiering and responsibility. The late afternoon's intensity and exhilaration was gone too quickly. There would be no repeat. It had been an utterly intoxicating experience; one I recall still to this day. By such brief moments you escape reality, they are rare and far removed from what I had volunteered for.

BID BID CAMP

9 July – Long drive to Bid Bid accompanied by Babu Chacko, DR's doctor. Couldn't keep awake, dozed fitfully much to Babu's astonishment anyone able to do so on rough corrugated tracks. Bid Bid camp overlooks Wadi Fanja – a dreamlike setting – proper oasis. Green date palms and clear water running over the whitest of stone and boulders you ever saw

Tom, Rick and I arrived at Bid Bid camp in Northern Oman from SAF HQ, by canvas topped Land Rover. Still white skinned, we were thankful for the sun cover. The road, a simple graded earth track, was heavily corrugated through continuous pounding from army trucks and Land Rovers plying between HQ and outlying posts.

Far away we glimpsed the Hajar Mountain range and Jebel Akhdar, The Green Mountain. The highest peak, Jebel Ash Shams, Mountain of the Sun, so called as being Oman's first landmark at over 9,750ft to be touched by daybreak's rising sun. Through the heat haze distant mountains shimmered blue. In the 10th century the Persian army had invaded Oman and stormed these mountains, fighting their way to the summit of the Hajar. Despite great losses, many were so taken with the place they elected to remain and settle. Descendants of these Persians live there to this day.

On arrival we were again hot, sweaty, covered in dust and thirsty. It was Jumea, Friday, the Islamic weekend. Here I met up with my Squadron Leader, Tim Cornwell, and Mike Offord his 2ic. Showing me to my temporary accommodation, Tim suggested once I'd showered and changed, I meet him in his bayt (room) where he'd brief me. 'See you in 15 minutes. Oh, and keep the windows closed, bloody flies . . .' and he was gone. My room with a shower off, had a steel framed bed, mattress with two clean sheets and single pillow which stank of someone else's sweat, one small bedside cupboard and a solitary 1950s ceiling fan. It was stiflingly hot. The fan was broken.

Over a beer, Tim outlined his plans, I would lead 'Light Troop', eight men in four Ferret Scout Cars. I had three months to fully train my troop before the squadron deployed to Dhofar and the war zone. Ample time then, to get to know my soldiers, perfect my Arabic, acclimatise to the heat and train a troop of Omani soldiers just out of basic infantry training into a battle-worthy light armoured reconnaissance (recce) troop.

Within three days the timescale had changed. Given a fortnight to do all of the above, my troop was ordered to Dhofar, the move precipitated by a disastrous contact involving two lightly armoured vehicles on a recce out of Salalah.

LIGHT TROOP – ACS

Originally designated Light Troop, I'd been allocated Sgt Lou Costello, a man aged between 40 and 45, staunchly loyal, smoked like a chimney and with more than a little liking for an occasional beer. (Oman was a dry country then, except for SAF Officers and Sergeants' Messes.) Unlike his comic Hollywood acting persona, Lou was not past telling the most appallingly crude jokes, often as not, in the most inappropriate circumstances.

Costello had no Arabic and spoke with the unmistakable clipped lilt of the Northern Irish. To my 23-year-old mind he looked old and worn out, but being already proven in battle I could not have hoped for a better man. Someone you would not choose to cross for his quick Celtic temper, yet Lou would also be your first choice to have beside you in a fight. His, that rare ability to read and interpret a critical situation instantly, then pull off the most audacious act, always with a grim smile, which would break into a largely toothless grin spreading slowly from ear to ear once the shooting was over. And his language was truly abominable. The soldiers were very fond of the old man. My troop included two Dhofari khadim, ex-slaves released from the Sultan's household following the 1970 coup. Of African origin and raised under the regime of the previous Sultan, Sultan Said bin Taimur, they'd gained their freedom when he was overthrown almost a year earlier. Sultan Said had decreed his slaves and servants be educated, thus the two khadim were literate. Both had previously served with Dhofar Gendarmerie (DG) based at Arzat camp east of Salalah, where they had excelled at basic training and been promoted.

On hearing that the ACS were recruiting, they'd asked to transfer and a reluctant DG had let them go. Able to read and write, they had risen quickly through the ranks to become non-commissioned officers, LCpls – Abdul Raja Faraz and Abdul Wathik. Faraz also had a smattering of English, which proved very useful in the early days of familiarisation. They were reputed to be good soldiers.

Finally, and certainly not least, I had four Omani Arab drivers, Abdullah Ali, Ali Hamdan, Hilal Ali, and Nasir Hamed, each of whom would individually prove to be pillars of support through the next two years fighting in Dhofar.

THE DAIMLER-BUILT FERRET SCOUT CAR

The Ferret Scout Car (FSC) was still in use with BAOR and a vehicle I knew well from a year commanding Recce Troop with my regiment in Münster, Germany. The four-wheeled Ferret was used for light reconnaissance, capable of moving relatively fast along tracks and roads, but across country the vehicle registered every ditch hit or rutted track crossed with a thump for the crew inside. Whilst comfortable on tarmac, you hung on bloody tight as soon as any cross-country motoring was involved.

British designed and light armoured, these vehicles were produced between 1952 and 1971 by Daimler, at the time part of Jaguar Cars, Coventry, UK. They were currently being phased out from the British Army.

Armament was a M1919 Browning .30 calibre machine gun and six forward facing smoke grenade launchers. Brownings fitted to Ferrets were said to have a range limit of 800m. We discovered they were useful up to 1,000m. Weighing nearly four tonnes and capable of reaching 60mph (90kph) on roads, the four-wheel drive cars, powered by 4.62 litre Rolls-Royce engines, were said to be good for 300km. Across sandy terrain and gravel wadis, it was more likely to be half that. The tyres, like those of the Saladin, were run-flats, essentially puncture proof, enabling crews to continue motoring having sustained small arms fire or HE splinter shrapnel.

Apart from Costello, none of us had yet been tested in battle. Still to learn were skills required to drive and maintain the vehicles, and vitally, tactical

Ferret Scout Car leaving Arzat Camp, Dhofar on a Salalah plains patrol.

cross-country deployment. Without these skills these new recruits were doomed to early graves, the cars, the ignominy of being reduced to hard targets on a remote range somewhere.

TROOP TRAINING FOR COMBAT

> Go easy for the first few weeks. A bad start is difficult to atone for, and the Arabs form their judgments on externals that we ignore.
>
> TE Lawrence

What struck me on meeting my soldiers for the first time were their young ages. The oldest turned out to be a couple of years older than me, but the majority were younger, still mid-teens. Without birth certificates, for there were none at that time, a soldier's age was more or less an objective guess. Lawrence's quotation was as true as it had been when first conceived.

But the quality of their issued clothing surprised me most. Combat kit consisted of thin cotton shirts and khaki trousers, covered with splotches of hand-applied green and/or brown dyes as a concession to camouflage. Footwear, brown canvas topped, rubber soled gym shoes, the like of which BAOR soldiers were issued for PT, little more than slip-ons. Later that day I remarked at the apparent inadequacy of clothing and footwear to which Tim had replied casually, 'you'll find most of them prefer to go barefoot, or wear Nizwa sandals (handmade camel leather sandals). They will only wear their issue shoes on parade'. This I would discover was quite true. The lack of adequate clothing, particularly footwear, would prove to be a significant concern during the winter months patrolling the wadis and foothills bordering the Empty Quarter or living at varying altitudes up to 3,000ft in the mountains of Dhofar. That said, it was rare to hear a complaint about kit – far more likely it'd be one concerning pay or rations.

> *10 July – Training not going too badly seeing there is such a language problem. Think may be best to use in pairs. Costello and I each leading a second car . . . my nose, badly burnt, has started to peel . . . Arabic pretty appalling, thank God for Swahili.*

One immediate problem I faced with training was the need to give orders first in English to Lou, followed immediately by orders in Arabic to the two NCOs before we could get underway. Orders to turn right or left were relatively simple to explain over the air by radio. But the tactical crossing of a defile, wadi or open space required a little more ingenuity.

I took it upon myself to teach Lou selected commands in Arabic, but until such time he grasped the basics, each time I communicated between my cars I continued to repeat orders in both English and Arabic over the radio. We learned quickly to cope with the handicap, but it was more than a little frustrating in those early days when I needed to get to know my men and win their confidence.

L/R- Drivers: Abdullah Ali, Hilal Ali, Ali Hamdan, LCpl Abdul Wathik and Nasir Hamed pose in front of a mined DG Bedford, part of a convoy we were escorting and had recovered back to Arzat Camp.

Sunburn too had begun to matter. We had no sunscreen, or alternatives. Daily exposure to sun and wind driving across country, through wadis and villages, left Lou and I increasingly sunburned. Warned to wear shemaghs over faces, we didn't need reminding. 'You'll get used to sunburn' was the general message. It became a common sight in the squadron for some of the fairer skinned Brits to suffer lengthy periods when noses sported blood red, sunburn blister scabs.

11 July – We ate fresh harvested dates!

Stopping for a brew was always popular – sometimes with the added attraction of local dates picked fresh from palms.

That day after practising patrolling and changing formations, I called a halt. It was time for debrief. And at such moments as these the bond between Arab and Brit began to cement.

Abdullah Ali parked our Ferret neatly in the shade of an ancient date palm. The other three cars fanned out and parked in a circle, turrets facing outwards – 'pretty good' I thought to myself, cheered we'd not all bunched together like lambs suddenly come to a halt after charging around in a field. Turning to me with a wide grin, Abdullah gestured towards the grove of date palms running along the wadi 50m away to our left. Climbing out of the car, he asked if he might call at one of the flat-topped mud and stone built houses visible in the palm grove, saying this was his village. Returning his smile, I told him to make it quick and be back in time to share the brew and debrief on the morning's training.

Abdullah returned before the water boiled, his shemagh filled with fresh dates. A gift to share from his family, he declared. The dates were "first harvest" young, sticky and pale – a treat for desiccated mouths, sweet and delicious. Abdullah claimed they were Al Khalas dates, the most prized in Oman, one of over 250 varieties grown in the country.

12 July – Sandy joins MR today.

Sandy flew down to Dhofar to join MR.

That evening sitting relaxing with Tom and Rick on the terrace outside the Mess, Alex read out the latest bundle of applications submitted by aspiring individuals wishing to join Desert Regiment on contract. Seated around us were those who'd soldiered in Oman, Africa and Vietnam. I sat, witness to an acerbic lesson in the art of character assassination as each would-be mercenary's application underwent the caustic scrutiny of the battle hardened. A time to listen and learn.

ARRIVAL IN OMAN

Much amusement as Alex Lamond read aloud letters received from potentials seeking contracts with Desert Regiment. Some looking to 'fight a mercenary war', others to live as latter-day Lawrences! One in particular – read and instantly discarded – had used a circle to dot each letter i throughout his application. Glad the poor fellow couldn't hear the roar of derision this was met with.

Three days into training a signal arrived from SAF HQ with the cryptic message that Dhofar HQ demanded 'immediate armour presence' on Salalah Plain following a spate of adoo attacks and the loss of an armoured personnel carrier. One British officer killed, another wounded and four Omanis wounded. It had been a shambles.

13 July ... they shot Mike Campbell yesterday afternoon. One of the very few people I knew out here. A contract officer and 4 soldiers wounded, armoured car lost – all same skirmish. What a boost for the adoo – what waste for us. They were in an armoured troop carrier amongst trees, hit by anti-tank rockets. Apparently the novice driver stalled 3 times as the officer ordered him forward ... they escaped from side of vehicle ... without weapons ... what a fucking shambles. Mike's body dragged from the vehicle, searched and I expect photographed. God, I hope he was dead. I cannot get the fact that they hope to use my scout cars, with half inch armour and a .30 mg as TANKS ... More tears at Beaconsfield?

Little news as we had, that night the discussion centred around this latest contact. Victory to the adoo. The question on everyone's minds: 'Who ordered such an idiotic op sending cars into the treeline?' Listening to the 'battle weary' talking, it began to sound as if the episode might have been a joy ride. Remaining quiet, I thought it best to keep my own counsel until I found out the truth.

'What the fuck are we doing out here?' a voice asked rhetorically, for each was a volunteer. And we followed orders. All had undergone periods of extensive training for their individual roles. Some, through parental choice or circumstance, were privately educated, some grammar schooled, but now we were equals having completed the rigours of intensive training to gain commissions. With Mike Campbell and the many like him before the products of a boarding school system, instilled into receptive young minds were the simplistic notions of duty. This too had been hammered into us as officer cadets. So, to a man, each knew there was no going back. Conversely, the man who raised the question, an archetypal would-be mercenary officer, failed to return from his next leave.

Years later I discovered the incident had been recorded in Whitehall, as follows:

SECRET   FCO SITREP

DHOFAR PD 12 JUL AT MOUTH OF WADI JARDUM ZU 1686 RECCE PLATOON A COY MR CMM PATROLLING IN CADILLAC COMMANDO APCS CMM WAS AMBUSHED BY THREE REBEL GROUPS PD LEADING APC WAS HIT BY SEVERAL RPG 2 AND WAS WRITE OFF PD CASUALTIES ONE SECONDED OFFICER KILLED CMM ONE CONTRACT OFFICER AND THREE BALUCHI ORS WOUNDED PD ENEMY CASUALTIES UNKNOWN PD

481742 CAPTAIN MRA CAMPBELL COLDSTREAM GUARDS CMM SECONDED TO MUSCAT REGT SAF CMM KILLED IN ACTION PD IF QUESTIONED BY PRESS INTEND TAKING SAME LINE AS RÉF OMITTING LAST SENTENCE PD

My diary entry ended,

"... what is death? Happens one day anyway. Wonder deep down if it's not death we fear, but more, perhaps fear itself?"

Mike's death affected us all. Those who knew him the more so. In a pensive mood that night I recalled Stuart Rae's death exactly a month earlier and diarised perhaps there'd be more tears at Beaconsfield's Officers' Mess. What had actually happened, I'd discover later.

There it was, a screw-up when a friend died, hastening my troop's move to Salalah, three months ahead of the Squadron. Operating on Salalah Plains, Light Troop would henceforth be called Plains Troop.

COMMANDO CARRIERS AND THE SQUADRON

A month before I arrived, Tim Cornwell and Mike Offord, S/Sgt Pete Minvalla, Sgts Geoff Begley and Lou Costello with eight Omani troopers were flown south to Salalah on a familiarisation visit. The aim, to get an idea of the terrain and conditions the squadron might expect moving to Dhofar in November.

Lt Col Fergus Mackain-Bremner, officer commanding Muscat Regiment, offered them a sortie in two of four US-built Cadillac Gage Commando Carriers based at UAG camp. There was a suggestion the Squadron take on the vehicles. Tim agreed to test them out.

Setting off with skeleton crews driving the cars for the first time, Tim and Mike each commanded a Commando Carrier, whilst Lou Costello and Geoff Begley, a pair of old Ferret Scout Cars. Used occasionally by MR, the Commandos were in reasonable condition; however, the Ferrets hadn't been driven for some time. All seemed to be progressing well when, approaching the jebel towards Raysut, west of Salalah, the cars were ambushed. Ambushes are always sudden. Stopping to rescue a sick child and parents from a Bedu camp close to the foot of the jebel, they'd stayed too long.

This was the squadron's first action and accurate enemy fire was directed towards the armoured cars with total disregard for the civilians grouped around them. With everyone pinned down attempting initially to take cover as best they could, Mike raced to his Commando Carrier followed by a hail of bullets as he scrambled through the open side of the vehicle to immediate but temporary safety. Inside he climbed in behind the .50 Browning machine gun and began to return fire. This gave the others a breathing space, a moment to scramble their passengers and themselves into the comparative protection of the two Commando Carriers and crews into the supporting Ferret Scouts Cars.

Lou Costello, who'd reached his Ferret, pulled forward around Mike's Commando Carrier where he could see Geoff Begley was now feeding ammo into the heavy machine gun (HMG) Mike was firing.

Not fully trusting their loaned vehicles, drivers had remained in their cabs with engines running should they fail to restart. With commanders in cars, Tim began an organised withdrawal out of the ambush.

In his Ferret, Lou opened up at the advancing adoo with his Browning. Leaping forwards from rock to rock sensing a victory, the adoo were firing and yelling their high-pitched calls of delight running at the scene of confusion before them as soldiers and civilians scrambled madly into cars. Mike continued to fire, killing a man firing onto their exposed position. Under accurate covering fire from Mike and Lou's cars, the second Ferret was ordered back, the driver stoically still waiting for his commander, Geoff Begley, to return from assisting Mike.

The rate of fire from the two Commando Carriers and Lou's Ferret halted the advancing adoo who melted away. Good guerrilla tactics, attack, fall back. The firing ceased. Silence. Tim was taking no chances. All were acutely aware a rocket launcher would turn tables in a second and Tim pulled Mike and Lou back some 50m beyond his car and the second Ferret, still without a commander.

The action seemed over almost as soon as it happened. It had in fact lasted 45 minutes. Disengaging, Tim withdrew, allowing Begley to scramble back into his Ferret from Mike's car.

With passengers safe, the four cars made it back to UAG without further incident and the sick were taken to the army medical centre. It was only after parking up they discovered the Commando Carriers were peppered with dents where struck by light machine gun (LMG) rounds, a number of armour piercing rounds still sticking into the vehicle hulls. It had been a narrow escape.

A lack of spare parts and cumbersome off-road capability decided Tim against the Carriers. So it was they remained attached to the Salalah Plains battalion – to be used so disastrously three months later. Mike's steadfastness under fire, accurately returning fire ensuring the safe withdrawal of the cars, crews and rescued passengers without loss, won him The Sultan's Commendation Medal awarded for bravery, a gilt medal hung on a blue medal ribbon with a gold palm leaf. A medal that would be added to his Dhofar campaign medal, awarded to those who had served sufficient time in the war zone.

The Commendation Medal (left), first instituted by Sultan Said bin Taimur in 1960. Awarded for acts of brave conduct.

The Dhofar Campaign Medal (right) awarded to those completing fourteen continuous days on active service, or wounded within that period.

THE TROOP BONDS AS A UNIT

I'd now seventeen days to complete training before we departed for Dhofar. Mike Campbell's death reinforced awareness we had started from scratch, literally strangers to each other. Bonding as a group, basic military tactics, weaponry, radio procedures, simple mechanics and rudimentary driving skills must be mastered quickly. On top of this I still felt very new, very white, and my Arabic, well, monosyllabic at best.

Strangely and possibly a result of my African upbringing, I found no awkwardness, no hesitation, no embarrassment even at my poor Arabic in front of my men. They were a great bunch, enthusiastic as African kids my brother and I used to play soccer with on our annual school holidays in Dar-es-Salaam, ten years earlier. When stuck for the appropriate word, I'd use my Swahili – a language many understood, a result of long-established historical ties gained over years of trading

ARRIVAL IN OMAN

spices, frankincense, myrrh, gold, silver and silks between Oman and East Africa. Many Swahili words derived from Arabic, a lasting legacy of the years Oman ruled a region along the East African coast, reflecting centuries of the Middle East's slave trade.

We were an eclectic group from different tribes, cliques were forming and we needed bonding into a single unit. One that was dependent on the other, able to react impulsively yet in an anticipated, recognised way to whatever dangers or circumstances we would shortly face in Dhofar.

Gradually the searing heat became more bearable with each day that passed, sun induced headaches becoming fewer, but still faces, necks, hands and forearms burned. In learning to cope and accept the still alien heat, constant dust and bleak terrain, we became used to seeing contours of dried sweat appear on shirts and trousers whilst motoring, only to rewet as soon as we stopped for a debrief, breakdown or vehicle recovery. We'd drink as frequently as was practicable from our canvas water bottles, called charguls.

Hydration was essential, more so for newly arrived Brits, and we were never without our charguls, canvas water containers holding on average between 2 to 3

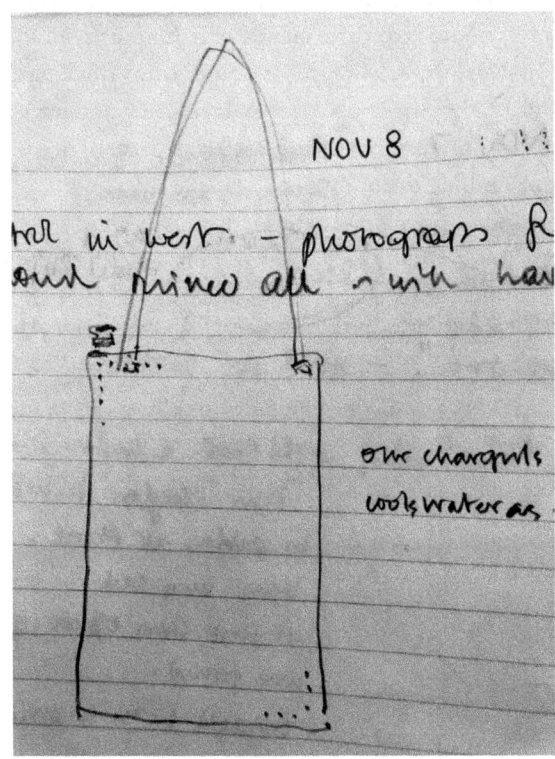

Sketch of a chargul, canvas water bottle.

pints of water. The chargul was designed to allow water to sweat constantly through its semi permeable material, cooling the liquid held inside. Genius.

We were becoming used to each other, Lou was proving to be a quick learner and was soon responding to commands in Arabic; life was becoming a lot easier.

SWEAT – ECCRINE AND APOCRINE GLANDS

Sweat, probably too often mentioned in this record, was a fact of life – as might be expected seemingly affecting Europeans more than our soldiers but thankfully even soldiers sweated. A natural phenomenon – the body's cooling mechanism. There are two categories of sweat produced by the body's eccrine and apocrine glands which react instantly. Dependent upon the extremes of heat or fear, you may soon be drenched.

Sweat associated with heat: The salty fluid is a product of a body's response to rising ambient temperatures making you hot, or the result of burning calories during exercise. (SAF regulations included the issue of salt tablets following an uphill assault. I never saw a salt tablet in two years' service.) When the 'thermostat' in a human brain signals the body's getting too hot, it sends a message to the four million sweat (eccrine) glands to release moisture, glands which are spread all over our largest organ, the skin. This protective layer is about 2mm thick and weighs approximately six pounds (2.7kg) made up of seven layers of ectodermal tissue guarding underlying muscles, bones, ligaments and internal organs. About 90% water, heat sweat evaporates, cooling the body.

Then there's sweat associated with fear: again, a natural response. Stress sweat comes from a spike in the body's response to fear. Scared suddenly, the body releases stress hormones (adrenaline and cortisol, the fight or flight defence). These hormones set the heart pounding, a signal for apocrine glands located in armpits and crotch to react.

Fear sweat is 80% water and 20% fat and protein, the smelly part; that's probably more than enough of that.

MAKING PROGRESS

15 July – Abdul Rajaz is a good shot with the Browning, on par with Costello

We built a makeshift firing range. Using disused, empty 45-gallon (205 litres) oil drums (burmails) half concealed behind rocks and mounds as snap targets, we introduced the troop to .30 Browning live firing. There were no official ranges. Additionally, we instructed the crews in Sub Machine Gun (SMG) drills, at first with hearts in mouths, for not without reason was the 9mm Sterling known for its notorious record of being fired accidentally with catastrophic consequences for those caught in front of the muzzle.

Thankfully, never once did any of my soldiers fire a single burst or round by accident. This was not always the case with others, when soldiers accidentally fired off FM rifles, light machine guns (LMGs), and occasionally AK47s, resulting in a number of fatalities, both on operation, training and on bases.

In addition to getting the drivers used to off-road driving, I was struggling to explain best and thus least dangerous ways to move cars through areas of ambush or attack. Sketches on paper and in sand failed to get the message across. Then I realised all but two were illiterate, none could comprehend a map. Was this the stumbling block? Obvious with hindsight, I cursed myself.

Also needing putting into perspective, despite our half-inch 'fools' gold' armour plating, Ferret Scout Cars remained vulnerable to enfiladed attack, or attack from the rear, and noisy engines equalled total lack of stealth.

Meaning we were:

- vulnerable to RCL or Rocket Propelled Grenade (RPG) – HE or Heat rounds
- vulnerable to both HMG or LMG armour piercing rounds
- vulnerable to anti-tank mines
- and finally, an armoured car presented a prime target – both psychologically and strategically – a prize, a potential war trophy the adoo would probably deem worth dying for.

CRACKED IT!

17 July – Think the message has got through – Don't bloody bunch!!

We'd left camp at 0545 to gain as much of the morning before the worst of Oman's July heat arrived, when hot became 'searingly hot' at 0800. Halting the troop and disembarking, I gathered the soldiers around me. Sheltered in the shade of a thorn tree, each seated cross legged Arab fashion on the bare earth, I sought to put into practice a thought I'd had during a night when heat and sweat stole sleep.

My plan – improvise. Selecting a few small stones as we walked across to the shade, I used these as model scout cars, demonstrating some basic armour tactics. Remembering days spent as a child waging wars against a friend's lead soldiers and cast metal tanks, I now built sand-formed defiles, wadis, hilltops and obstacles through which I drove my stone cars.

The troop looked on in fascination as I re-explained the necessity against bunching, drills if caught in ambush, emergency deployments when attacked and troop car movement across threatening terrain. Also, I explained the basics of escort duty with convoys, arcs of fire and concealment plus anti-tank and anti-personnel mine awareness driving, the need for following directly the tyre marks of the lead vehicle when mines were suspected.

Getting them each to use the stones themselves, they took turns in showing the rest how they would best deal with obstacles which I had the other troop members construct using sand, loose rock and stones. The game caught on and each took a particular pride in demonstrating no matter what obstacle the others put before them, they had an answer to avoid falling into a trap.

It was highly unlikely any had played war games or used stones as toy armoured cars before, yet looking back at eager faces, I realised they'd understood. The improvisation had worked. When we moved off, almost immediately the troop put into practice the moves they'd learned. I could scarcely believe how quickly they'd got the message.

SWIMMING WITH SNAKES

The following day after a morning's training, we stopped off at a wadi just waded. A shallow ford flowing with crystal clear water, sparkling in the bright sunlight. We were each hot and sweat-stained, shirts and trousers clinging rags that stuck to bodies as if we'd been out in the rain. Additionally, we were dust coated from shemagh-covered heads to sweaty desert boots and the men's plimsolls. The water, invitingly clear and cool to the touch, was beyond resistance.

Walking across to a shaded section of stream, where it flowed against a wadi wall worn away to form a cave, was a perfect pool.

Leaving one man on guard, we removed shoes and fell luxuriously into the cooling freshwater stream, ducking beneath the flowing diamond-clear water. The pool was approximately 10m in length, 8m wide. Swimming partially clothed in the chest deep wadi, I looked up into the blue sun-bleached sky, the glare fading colours at its midday hottest and relaxed. The training was going well and the troop bonding into the friendly unit I wished to achieve. A group who in times of danger would I hoped be able to rely on the other without hesitation.

Bursting through contented thoughts came a shout of alarm. We'd disturbed a long snake which swam swiftly across the stream, scything between us, scattering all to the wadi's edge, dry ground and safety. Before I could stop what followed, the metre long snake was chased, caught and summarily dispatched by the boys throwing rocks at it with enviable accuracy. I could not make out whether it was one of Oman's seven or so venomous snakes, but it was now very dead, with pulverised head and body. There are 22 species of snakes in Oman and most are not considered dangerous.

That said, the snake is not a creature exuding apathy among humans. This was a black snake, possibly a Walterinnesia aegyptia. Known commonly as a desert black snake, native throughout the Middle East, and highly venomous. So much for nature conservation, but who was I to preach? The soldiers had grown up dealing with snakes as something done any day of the week. Scorpions, camel spiders and spiny backed lizards were dispatched out of hand, casually and without sentiment. As a youngster growing up in Africa, I too had shared similar views, everything was there to be hunted. Allowed to roam with a .22 rifle, we'd spend nights out under canvas, hunting and shooting guinea fowl for supper. Using a friend's .22 rifle, the result was sometimes messy. Gradually there came a change and from the age of ten or eleven a steady appreciation dawned, leading to an awareness to recognise every creature had its place – so long as it wasn't going to eat you. At twelve my twin and I were catching reptiles and fish for the city museum's live specimen display tanks, on show in the country's capital, Dar-es-Salaam.

And in Dhofar, on the rare occasion I did manage to save the odd creature, I accepted for the most my soldiers' attitude was not one born out of cruelty, but a reflection of the harsh realities through which Arabia's desert peoples had evolved. I learned to let it pass.

We drove back to camp, wet clothing drying rapidly as we motored under a burning sun and average in-the-shade 45C midday heat of an Omani July.

BOULDERING WITH MAKESHIFT ROPES

There remained one aspect I felt still needed putting across. It was our last day of cross-country manoeuvres, and we'd stopped for a brew, sheltering under the shade of a wadi wall. In going through a general debrief, I felt it time to test reactions to avoiding getting into danger without an escape route out.

A thought had occurred to me, and it was a long shot, for I suspected the concept of rock climbing as an exercise might possibly be foreign to them. I hoped if perhaps I used the basics of scrambling or 'bouldering', I might be able to get the message across.

Above us rose a moderate 9m limestone cliff of wadi wall. It was good rock, not too steep and looked free of loose material. Stored in my Ferret were three 'spent' .30 Browning canvas machine gun belts. Measuring 18ft (550cm) by 1 inch (2.5cm), these white woven canvas belts would, I reckoned, be as strong as rope. I asked for a volunteer and Abdullah Ali stepped forward without hesitation. A calibre above the rest, he was an exceptional soldier and one I would come to rely on for his uninhibited response to challenges. Tying the three belts together, I fastened one end around Abdullah's waist and looped the other end through my canvas regimental stable belt. I told him to follow my moves exactly, once I called for him to ascend.

At the back of every climber's mind is one inescapable fact: the pull of gravity. Downward acceleration is about 10 metres per second per second. (actual speed 9.81 metres). A human does not fall at a constant speed but accelerates until hitting the ground or reaching terminal velocity at 53 metres per second, approximately 190 kph, the maximum speed where Earth's gravitational pull is balanced by atmospheric resistance. By altering body profile to reduce atmospheric resistance, skydivers can accelerate their descent beyond this speed.

I rechecked his knotted rope and climbed to the top of our cliff. Fastening a belay, I looked down and gave the go ahead for Abdullah to start climbing. He was good. A natural, he made it straight to the top to join me without faltering. Grinning widely, he confessed he'd been climbing date palms since an early age and had no fear of heights! Well, I should have thought that one through.

Two more made it safely to the top without much effort. This was not going quite to plan, but then it became Abdul Wathik's turn. Secured to the makeshift rope by Lou, gingerly he started upwards. Clearly nervous but encouraged with a tight rope, he moved slowly. Wathik had not climbed before. Halfway and he froze, 'gripped'. I did not want him to lose face in front of the others and giving Abdullah the top rope, I scrambled down to my LCpl. Perched on a ledge beside him I quietly showed Wathik how we would reverse his climb. He wouldn't move. I climbed below him and tapping his foot indicated where he could find a safe foothold. Now he moved. One step at first then another and another as we slowly descended back to ground level.

Now I had the full attention of the troop as I climbed up again to where Abdul Wathik had frozen and then reversed my climb back down as he had done under my direction. It was a crude demonstration of my point of not getting into a position one could not reverse. I then took a different route and this time as Wathik followed, he succeeded to both his and my great relief. Honour was restored.

The boys fell into much discussion on the various alternative routes they might have attempted, each indicating where they considered the best routes to be and

ARRIVAL IN OMAN

those they'd avoid. The palm tree climbers were clearly in a class of their own. I was impressed. Despite the general consensus they'd rather be climbing for dates and coconuts, an important lesson was learned. Rock climbing as a sport had still to be recognised in Oman, without perhaps relying on used .30 Browning ammo belts.

In this way I demonstrated lessons and tactical moves both Lou and I had practised endlessly and perfected on Lüneburg Heath as part of our BAOR existence.

I began to think perhaps we might be ready for Dhofar.

4

NATIONAL DAY & EFFECTS OF ACTIVE SERVICE

Oman's first National Day celebrations. We assist with a cholera epidemic. En route to lead the National Parade through Muscat, we meet a leper. Later Tom and I gain an insight to the mental turmoil of active service.

NATIONAL DAY – FRIDAY 23 JULY 1971

23 July – First Anniversary of The Sultan's Accession

After the usual lengthy greetings, we shook hands with upwards of 50 people, men and boys, before being shown into a barusti for tea, cakes and warm blackcurrant juice. It was about 7.30am. Offered chairs but declined in preference for the floor with our hosts.

A group of young boys were then marched around in the dust before us, a couple of shots in the air followed. We moved to stand within Fanja castle where more shouting and rifle shots punctuated proceedings before a bearded man stood up and read a copy of the Sultan's Ascension Day speech. As the speech ended 10 men appeared brandishing long ceremonial swords dancing and singing before the Wali and guests. Afterwards escorted upstairs into Wali's imposing house. By now 8.15am and we were treated to Halwa, fresh dates and biscuits from large oval dish, mindful to use right hands only. More warm Ribena, then coffee.

NATIONAL DAY & EFFECTS OF ACTIVE SERVICE

One year on from the date Sultan Qaboos deposed his father in the British led coup, the 23rd / 24th July 1971 were declared public holidays commemorating the Sultan's first year of reign.

In response to Radio Aden's daily broadcasted propaganda, Sultan Qaboos gave a personal address to the nation on Oman Radio outlining plans for building schools, hospitals and infrastructure. Great emphasis was put on the fact Islam would remain the foundation of Omani culture, counter to the anti-Muslim communist ideology being fought against in Dhofar. The broadcast was well received.

Tim had asked me to join him with Paul Mangin, Second-in-Command DR and long-term contract officer. Paul, a natural linguist, was fluent in many dialects of both Omani and Dhofari tribesmen. He was also fluent in Serbo-Croat. Greatly respected, and someone I would get to know well whilst attached to DR in their jebel base at Akoot.

We were to pay our respects to the local dignitary, the Wali, the regional Governor who resided in nearby Fanja, a small town famed for hot springs, forts and watchtowers alongside Wadi Bid Bid.

Arriving at 0645 we were greeted royally, in a way I would come to recognise as representing the true Omani spirit, instantly putting us at ease. Shown to a barusti (palm leaf) roofed verandah and offered chairs, we declined, choosing to sit as those already gathered. After sweet tea, followed by a blackcurrant drink and cake, we were feted with a display of the traditional Omani Sword Dance, the Al Razfa Ardah. This involved two lines of men facing each other a few metres apart, dancing whilst brandishing long swords as they sang traditional Bedouin songs. Originally performed as a communal celebration of victory, the performance that day was in honour of the Sultan and his first year of reign. It was spectacular.

Oman's populated regions are divided into 59 districts known as Wilayats, each presided over by a Wali, a provincial governor responsible for settling local disputes, collecting taxes, and maintaining peace, supported by the Sultan's army when necessary. Most Wilayats are relatively small, the exception being the Wilayat of Dhofar, the largest and also the war zone. Whilst each Wali had sworn loyalty to the new regime, the Wali of Dhofar had long been a resolute supporter of the young Sultan.

With the ending of the sword dance, we were taken to the Wali's house and on entering, shown into a dark room. Except for a single small window and open door behind us, there was just sufficient light to allow making out shadowy occupants already seated. The pupils of eyes constrict in bright light to protect the retina, and on leaving the harsh Arabian sunlight, it took minutes before gradually we became accustomed to the darkness of an all but windowless room.

Leaving footwear outside and once again offered chairs, we declined as we took our places on a magnificent Persian rug spreading expansively from wall to wall. Against these walls were displayed a collection of fine Persian cushions, far more comfortable than the carpeted concrete we now sat on, but it was not to be. One of the household entered carrying a dish of water and proceeded to wash our hands before small towels were produced. Formalities over, we were offered black coffee, poured with a single exaggerated action, with a long stream of coffee pouring from the curved spout of a silver Omani coffee pot, into a porcelain finjan (small handleless cup). Filled almost to the top, it's by miracle not a drop is spilled.

Etiquette demands the finjan is held between thumb and two forefingers of your right hand. You drink no more than three cups, offering the emptied finjan for refill until the third is drunk, when with a slight rocking motion of the cup, you indicate politely you've had sufficient, declining more with 'shukraan' (thank you).

In addition we were offered Halwa, fresh dates and sweet biscuits followed by a sweet cordial, served warm through lack of electricity, refrigeration being then limited to military camps. Halwa, orange brown, sticky gelatinous cubes made from sugar, clarified butter (ghee) and flour, each cube portion the size of a generous marshmallow. A Middle Eastern delicacy dating from around 2000 BC, when then the preserve of Egyptian gods and royalty. The halwa and dates were a welcome counter to the coffee's black bitterness. None gave a second thought to sugar count.

Despite the July heat, the house was noticeably cooler inside. The two-storey rectangular building, set amongst shading date palms, its thick walls and flat roof offering respite from the heat outside. Discussion drifted between Dhofar's war to local matters where change was not happening fast enough. Recently, political, tribal and historical tensions had flared, resulting in armed clashes leading to SAF clearing villages. Arms and ammunition caches had been discovered, but the situation was otherwise under a watchful control.

It was not long before the hard floor began to remind what was still an unnatural way to sit, cross legged with either leg tucked beneath the other, bum and ankles pressed hard against an unforgiving surface. You sat so as to avoid showing the soles of your feet, as to do so was impolite. Even with bare feet you may have trodden in something better not revealed that might now be stuck to the bottom of a foot.

Unlike human and dog faeces, dried camel and goat droppings rarely stick to feet or boots. Largely due to diet, but also the fierce sun, these animal droppings soon desiccate in the searing desert heat. Later, lying-up in ambushes, I learned human faeces take longer.

With time seemingly an irrelevance to our host, we sat cross legged on the carpeted floor for quite a while, none moving or stretching a limb to ease circulation, the three of us refusing to admit or display any discomfort that might reveal the truth: our silently protesting Western bodies were more accustomed to soft sofas than solid floors. I wondered whether the old man, the Wali, was secretly testing us.

I followed little of the conversation that day, the local dialect strong and almost incomprehensible to my newly trained, inexperienced ear. The language bore little comparison to the classical Egyptian Arabic taught at the Army School of Languages. I probably managed one word in five.

With Paul disarmingly fluent and Tim, four months ahead of me in colloquial Arabic and conversing unhesitatingly, I realised how imperative the need was I quickly step up to absorb the language with its varied nuances if I was to be of any use to my men, and the squadron.

CHOLERA RESCUE

Leaving Fanja and the Wali, we drove back along the dusty, corrugated earth and stone track that afternoon. The sun, still hot, glared sufficient to dazzle as we came upon a small group standing beside the track, waving us to stop. We discovered an elderly, very ill man accompanied by his equally elderly wife, two men and another female. Shaking and foaming at the mouth it was all too apparent the sick man was probably a cholera casualty, now in need of urgent medical attention. We cleared an area in the back of our Land Rover between our two-soldier escort, laying the patient down gently on a panel of canvas canopy as a makeshift mattress. We could take one other passenger. A heated discussion ensued, the wife desperate to be allowed to accompany her husband, but no, patriarchal authority asserted a man accompany the patient. Leaving the grief-stricken woman and companions at the roadside, we drove back to camp where immediate medical help was administered by DR's doctor, Captain Babu Chacko (IAMC) on secondment from the Indian Army, our friendly Dr Babu.

It was a sharp lesson in Middle Eastern propriety. Despite our sympathies for the woman who doubtlessly feared she'd never see her husband alive again, it was not for us to brush aside recognised customs of this ancient country. The man recovered fully and was returned to his village and wife a week later. Hearing the news from Babu, it helped to reflect perhaps we had shared in making a small contribution. Babu rose to become a close associate of the Sultan, as chief medical officer to the Royal Oman Police.

CHOLERA EPIDEMIC

Injections: cholera, lines of Omani locals – men, women and children. Babu warns of dangers of rectal prolapse!

Oman was suffering a cholera epidemic. Towards the end of our Arabic course, we'd each received double dose vaccinations. The Sultanate ordered a military led vaccination programme and Tim and I volunteered to assist the hard-pressed Babu. Following a remarkably brief instruction, we joined Babu at the head of rows of patiently assembled locals. In essence it entailed giving a small injection, the first of two, two weeks apart. My first patient was a man with matchstick thin arms. 'Shit,' I thought 'nowhere to stick a needle...' Meeting an unconvinced expression I went for the top of his arm at shoulder height where it seemed there was most muscle tissue. I'd made my first jab. Thankfully the man remained stock-still. Looking from needle back to me he grinned widely, 'Thank you, sir, thank you very much', and it was on to the next in line.

After my first attempt, it became easier. A good two hours later, all had been treated. A repeat performance followed, thankfully after I'd departed for Dhofar.

Cholera vaccines were developed in 1885 by Spanish physician Jaime Ferrán, studying under Louis Pasteur. Offering a degree of protection for up to two years after a single shot, three to four years with an annual booster, the risk of death is reduced by 50% in the first year after vaccination. I don't recall any of us succumbing to the disease.

That evening relaxing outside on the Officers' Mess terrace, Babu was recounting various ailments he'd treated and the sort we might expect in Dhofar. Mentioning the obvious such as overheating, sunstroke, dehydration, amoebic dysentery and food poisoning, he casually dropped into the list having recently treated a Brit for rectal prolapse. That caught our attention. 'Lack of liquids leads to constipation,' he warned, 'and overstraining can force the last part of the rectum to protrude from the anus.' In the stunned silence that followed, it was difficult to avoid an involuntary tightening of the gluteus maximus. You could have heard a pin drop on sand as hands reached forward for another drink. Mentally notes were made, keep f...... hydrated. The remedy required surgery with the unfortunate man medevaced to the UK, another not to return.

NATIONAL DAY & EFFECTS OF ACTIVE SERVICE

THE LEPER

24 July – We lead National Day parade through Muscat – 4 Ferrets flying Sultanate pennants, Brownings, ammo. Best kit.

Stopped to assist elderly couple by track to Muscat sheltering beneath flattened out cardboard box pushed into thorn bush for shade. Leprosy. Left hand worst, fingers and thumb eaten to knuckles. Gave them water, my chargul and mug, and some money, all I had. Just like street beggars in Dar-es-Salaam. Outcasts. It's very sad. The boys needed reassurance, don't think they fully believed me. Can't catch leprosy. See Q for another mug and chargul.

Driving to Muscat to join the National Day Parade we'd stopped by the side of the earth road for a pee and drink of water when I noticed an elderly couple crouched beneath salvaged cardboard sheeting wedged into a camel-thornbush. The cramped shelter was no higher than 1m from the ground. Walking over to pass the time of day, I noticed the man's hands. He had leprosy. As I'd approached his wife pulled up her headscarf shielding her face, except for her eyes. She looked startled. Offering the standard greeting, 'Asalaam alaikum' the man replied hesitatingly, 'Wa alaikum assalam' as I squatted to his level. The woman moved round behind the man, looking over his shoulder staring at me above her shayla (half niqab). In an effort to conceal his disfigurement, he'd pulled his hands into the loose clothing around his waist.

I had seen many cases of this disease in Africa, and as kids we'd been taught to give beggars a few cents from our pocket money. I understood these two might appreciate a gesture from a stranger.

Offering water, the man nodded silently. Back at my car, I filled my army issue mug, aluminium and already dented, from my chargul as my astonished driver, Nasir Hamid, looked on. Taking mug and chargul back to the couple I placed the mug on the ground. Looking at the woman, I said 'hadha lak' (this is for you).

At this, she reached behind her husband and produced a battered, recycled tin can clutched tightly in thin fingers. She offered it towards me revealing a bare emaciated arm, gesturing I should fill it from my mug. 'La, hadha lak'. 'No', I replied, 'this is for you', adding 'mae Salaamti' (with Salaams). I insisted she take it – the recycled tin had seen better days. I added my chargul, placing it close to the man. Reaching into my pocket I found three folded red coloured notes, just three riyals, adding them to the chargul by my mug as I wished them well. Undoubted riches for them, loose change in my pocket for me, but it was all I had. He looked up as I rose to go, 'Thank you, Sahb' adding as we exchanged the traditional farewell 'Fee amaam Illah' / 'Fee amaam al kareem' (Go with God).

Once seen, we had to offer something, respecting their predicament as outcasts from society. There was no hospital in Oman to treat him then, added to which the cholera epidemic was already testing the fledgling regime. I knew his wife would remain by his side until the end. Desert life is hard, for a leper and his wife, unimaginably so.

'You never fucking touched him did you, sir?' asked an open-mouthed Costello. 'No.' I smiled in reply as we climbed into our cars and moved off. I'd learned in Africa, you don't catch Hansen's disease, leprosy, by casual touch. In the USA, there are accounts of Armadillos with the disease, the only other mammal known to be naturally infected by this bacteria, Mycobacterium leprae.

* * *

That same month, Steve Bidmead, a Royal Marine serving with MR, was wounded in the stomach by his own men. Two officers with a MR half company were returning to their 'Hedgehog', one of five fortified outposts defending Salalah airfield, when mistaken for approaching adoo, they were immediately engaged by a nervous night picquet.

Accompanying Steve was an ex-RGJ (Royal Green Jacket) captain serving with DR on Dhofar familiarisation prior to roulement in October. He wore his beret after the French, cap badge above left temple, claiming he'd served with French forces in Vietnam, generating a few amusing comments from fellow officers. Seeing the MR officer drop, he crawled over and, viewing Steve's wounds, asked nervously, 'Have you any words you'd like me to give your mother?' Steve groaned 'For fuck's sake, just get me a medic' before complimenting his soldiers' efforts, 'well at least they hit me . . .'

Steve thankfully made a full recovery. The incident, occurring within sight of the RAF Salalah base and the SAS Field Surgical Team (FST), where a team of British Army doctors highly qualified as trauma surgeons, saved him. One very lucky man. And the Vietnam veteran? He failed to return from his next UK leave.

WE LEAD A PARADE THROUGH MUSCAT

Day two of the Sultan's National Day celebrations saw my troop back at HQ to lead a column of soldiers and police through the streets of Muscat. As we assembled, an elderly Brit contract medic approached Lou and I, introducing himself as the one who'd had to 'tidy up' Mike Campbell's body before repatriation to the UK. Keen to impress and without stopping for breath, he began elaborating on detail – to be jointly told to fuck off; our precise words. What an idiot. If meant to disturb, regrettably it worked.

Setting off with pennants flying from aerials, our Ferrets led the column of soldiers in a collection of vehicles around a predetermined route through the town. Whether the obnoxious medic had heightened awareness, Lou and I couldn't help but notice not everyone appeared that happy to see us. There were still those yet to be convinced about Britain's involvement in the change of regime twelve months earlier. Arms caches had been discovered, people arrested and later, an attempted mutiny against the sovereign.

Perhaps it was rookie paranoia, for nothing came of it and as the parade ended we found ourselves chatting with a group of policemen I discovered were all Zanzibar-born. They had paraded behind us in Land Rovers. Much to their amusement, I practised my broken Swahili with them. Then an expat British lady came over to greet us, sweetly commenting on how smart we all looked in our armoured cars. She was perfumed and looked a picture in white shirt and jeans and large straw sunhat. Somewhat taken aback and doubtlessly blushing, I turned to my troop and translated the compliment to them. I could hear Lou chuckling. Given his lack of Arabic he'd absolutely no idea what I was telling the boys, but relished the fact I was flustered by the lady's direct approach. 'Telling 'em you caught the sun today . . . eh, sir?'

Chatting easily for a while, it became evident she'd not seen a Ferret Scout Car at close quarters before. Endeavouring to answer her direct questions, I hoped to God it might be interesting for she was the first pretty lady I'd seen since arriving in Oman, and I was not about to make a hash of the chance meeting.

I don't exactly recall the precise moment, maybe when explaining the finer attributes of the .30 Browning perhaps, when quite to my surprise she interrupted to invite me to join her and her oil engineer husband at lunch the following Friday (Jumea, the Arabian weekend) at the PDO Camp.

'Gosh she's pretty,' I thought, carefully reminding myself 'Hodgson, she's married!' as retaining my composure I replied I was very sorry but had to decline for we were off to Dhofar in two days, only to receive a shocked 'No, but you're too young for Dhofar . . .?' Subsequently told this had caused an additional flush of embarrassment to already sun-tanned cheeks, a grinning Costello was quick to relate to all who'd listen '. . . should have seen his fucking face!'

Too soon it seemed, we received orders to return to camp 50km away at Bid Bid. As we moved off, against my better judgement I glanced back to meet her gaze from amongst the crowd, she raised a hand and I waved. There's much truth in Seifert's poem:

> "goodbye, goodbye pretty girls
> we met today
> and will never meet again"

Probably a very good thing.

INSIGHT TO THE EFFECTS OF ACTIVE SERVICE

After dinner that evening, we sat as usual on the terrace, the warm still night, arched with crystal stars shining minute spotlights through an unpolluted atmosphere.

Seated next to me, Tom and Mike Ryan, a contract major, ex-Paras and 3 Coy commander, DR. Quiet, measured, a veteran of many years in SAF, he abruptly announced he was giving up soldiering. He'd not take another Dhofar tour and went on to explain his reasons for turning his back on soldiering. The final straw had been a patrol during his last tour. Returning late one afternoon, they'd walked into an ambush. The firefight lasted until dark. Nothing too special in that except the feeling of inadequacy this particular contact had left in Mike. Almost as soon as the shooting started, Mike realised he'd be unable to do anything to save a man. This had impacted deeply into his subconscious.

In the initial burst of fire, soldiers fell, one mortally wounded. As men scattered for cover, Mike dragged another wounded man to the comparative safety of a rock. Attacked from above and with bullets striking around them, they now couldn't move. Then came the cry for help beyond the rock Mike sheltered behind.

Pinned down, it was impossible to reach the soldier without being cut in half by the nearest AK47 firing about 75m away. Too late in the day to call for jets, sniping continued until dusk as his patrol were held to the ground, the adoo retaining the initiative. Mike told how the wounded soldier's body was repeatedly used for target practice. There'd been one scream, then silence. But for Mike, the nightmare continued with each subsequent crack/thud as single bullets struck the now lifeless body. With darkness the patrol extricated themselves, withdrawing to safety, carrying their dead and wounded. The day had left an indelible mark on this professional soldier, he was redeeming his SAF contract and returning to Britain, in search of easier employment.

Listening, I couldn't help but think what a waste of a good officer. I didn't know at the time, but Mike had been decorated for bravery in action, winning the Sultan's second highest award for gallantry under fire, The Sultan's Bravery Medal, the WB. Naively, I put it to him returning to Dhofar might sort out his demons – only to be met with a silent look and slow shake of the head. It was a conversation I would recall in moments of reflection, when I'd learned to understand the realities of this business. As Mike rose, he replied with a haunting maxim; whether his or not, it remained with me. 'War's always been someone else's decision where, when and sometimes how your friends die, or if it's your turn.'

Returning to the UK, Mike tried his luck as a civilian only to find the life he'd excelled at held a greater draw than any desk alternative. He rejoined the Paras. Word reached us he'd not been allowed to wear his medals as they'd been awarded to him as a mercenary.

'WHAT THOUGHTS DID YOU GIVE TO BEING TAKEN PRISONER?' – FIONA WARTON

Seven years earlier a SAS eight-man patrol operating in Arabia's Radfan became trapped. Lying-up during daylight concealed in caves, they'd been discovered when a goatherd stumbled upon them. Turning to shout an alarm, he was shot. Immediately, the position was compromised. Alerted, the enemy moved in, securing the high ground surrounding the caves. The SAS patrol held out all day, supported by Hawker Hunter jet fighters flown out of RAF Aden. Having walked in, the patrol was out of helicopter reinforcement or rescue range. With the enemy closing, remaining calm and professional, the men fired only at visible targets; the need to conserve limited ammo each carried, paramount.

With darkness, the jets had to withdraw. The patrol began their escape. Under constant fire, pulling back through scrub and steep walled limestone wadis, two were killed and left. Next morning the enemy displayed their victims' heads in the Yemeni town of Taiz. Photographs of the disaster became headline news. Britain had to admit to SAS presence in Radfan.

Notwithstanding the action was recent history, it was still heeded by Brits in Oman. Fleeting thoughts might steal into the subconscious, for we were fighting the same ideology, intensity and callousness. There were men consumed with a hatred for the Westerner. No quarter could be expected, no compassion towards those taken, wounded or prisoner. And bodies would be mutilated.

We were all versed in Geneva Convention rules – rules that apply in "armed conflict setting standards intended to protect people no longer taking part in hostilities; to include the sick and wounded of armed forces on the field of battle". Laudable philosophy, but such codes of chivalry were unknown in Dhofar. It was laughable to expect the adoo to know, let alone abide by such humanitarian principles.

When asked of any SAF officer what thoughts he might have in the event of capture, I doubt there'd have been one admit to being unafraid at the prospect, before replying 'Don't get taken alive – they don't fucking take prisoners'.

Three weeks into training, my orders arrived for deployment to Dhofar.

5

DHOFAR

A camel spider and our departure for Dhofar. The sorry state of the Sultan's airforce in July 1971. Salalah, capital of Dhofar. Arrival in the war zone under fire. I meet Geoff Mawle, and first introductions to landmines and mine protection. Dhofar's monsoon, al Khareef. A Beau Geste fort. Meet Harry Wooley and camp commandant Chris Phillips. Issued armoured cars without radios, we resort to communication by semaphore.

WE LEAVE FOR DHOFAR AND ARZAT CAMP

I was to take over four Ferret Scout Cars recently released from the Palace compound where previously they'd been used for ceremonial duties. Assured the cars were 'fit for role' (battle ready), we were in for a surprise. The remainder of the Squadron and our impressive new Saladins would join us in three months' time. Going into landmine, rocket and armour piercing ammo territory, I'd have preferred a Saladin, but such is the lot of a junior officer.

We'd be attached to Muscat Regiment, the Salalah Plains Battalion nearing the end of their nine-month tour of duty. They were based at Dhofar HQ, a camp called Umm Al Ghawarif (UAG) at Salalah, whilst we would be based at Arzat Camp with the Dhofar Gendarmerie, a battalion largely comprising freed slaves (khadim), previously the personal property of the former Sultan. In command, a major with two captains, all ex-British forces.

1st August and my last night at Bid Bid. Following dinner, we sat on the now familiar terrace adjacent to the Officers' Mess. Some smoked as we each held whiskies or iced cold beers streaming condensation. The mood was quiet and reflective. Endlessly black, the sky seemed to rain stars onto surrounding mountains in silhouette around us.

As we were departing early next day, I'd decided to turn in. Tom and Rick had wished me good luck as we three walked towards our rooms when in the shadow-filled light cast by the still lit Officer's Mess, a slight movement alerted us from treading on a hand-sized insect. 'Ughh, God they're revolting!' exclaimed Rick. One of nature's more hideous incarnations with notoriety to match, the 'mind-your-own-business' Camel Spider. (Order Solifugae: so neither true scorpion, Scorpione, nor true spider, Arachnid. Specimens grow to six inches including legs.) Spectacularly rumoured to eat earlobes of sleeping humans, whilst actually they are rated of negligible danger.

Anecdotal stories and evil reputation aside, it was the beast's size that repelled. Just dragging its body past you causes an involuntary shudder. We watched spellbound as the creature scurried away, leaving its trademark furrow in the sand. I shuddered, was it revulsion or tension building before tomorrow's flight to Dhofar? Tom and I had made a pact promising each would write to the other's parents should either be the first to fall.

Up at 0400 the next day, I supped a mug of warm sweet tea prepared by an already awake Mess Staff, grabbed a prepared sandwich (fish paste – only at Bid Bid!) and joined my troop loading kit onto our transport, a canvas-topped Bedford 3-tonner. Leaving at 0430 we arrived at Bayt al Falaj airport after an uneventful, dusty drive. On the concrete apron, we met the aircrew and immediately boarded an awaiting Caribou military transport bound for Salalah. The aircraft was capacity loaded with ordnance.

We were aboard one of two SOAF Caribous, twin-engined planes built by de Havilland in Canada since 1958. A short take-off and landing (STOL) cargo aircraft, used extensively by the USAF and Royal Australian Air Force in Vietnam. Requiring landing strips of only 365 metres favoured Dhofar's airstrips, many no more than a level piece of ground cleared of tree stumps, rocks and boulders.

The de Havilland Canada DHC-4C aircraft was crewed by two pilots and an air loadmaster. Having a payload limit of 8,000 lb (3630kg) they could carry 32 troops or 14 casualty stretchers. Two × Pratt and Whitney engines gave a maximum speed of 220 mph (360 kph). Flying up to 24,800ft, they had a range of 400km with a full payload.

SOAF IN JULY 1971

Our destination was Salalah, SOAF's airbase in Dhofar, shared with the RAF. That July, SOAF morale was low after a jet had crashed on 18th July, killing Flt Lt Del Moore attempting a low-level manoeuvre near Mudhai, in Dhofar's northern jebel and three aircraft damaged on the ground by 75mm RCL rounds. Whilst jets and transport continued to perform well, SOAF helicopters were all but grounded. Operational pilot numbers had halved to four through resignations and sickness. Airworks, the contracted specialist engineers, were down to just two after resignations. SOAF was down to one Jet-ranger 206 and a single Huey 205, this last with just under 20 hours' flying time before major servicing.

From this nadir, matters improved dramatically in August with the arrival of new pilots and engineers. Jets, transport and helicopters were vital to Salalah and SAF operations. It'd been a close call.

Added to SOAF's predicament, the daily attacks on Salalah and the recent armoured car loss on 12 July, CSAF had ordered an immediate armoured presence in Dhofar. We were four car commanders, two still learning and four rookie drivers in four ancient scout cars. We might as well have had L plates. Hardly the cavalry.

SALALAH – CAPITAL OF DHOFAR

The ancient coastal town of Salalah faces the Arabian Sea. Flat plains behind and to both sides rise from sea level to approximately 60m in height. A fertile coastline, some 65km wide by approximately 10km deep towards the foothills, is crisscrossed by dry wadis (riverbeds) which run with water during the khareef (monsoon), a time when mountain wadis are fed into a system of aflaj (singular falaj), small irrigation channels dug in the earth to carry water. Over generations, these aflaj have enabled farmers to create a lush patchwork of tiny yet productive fields. Towards the eastern reaches of the plain, a narrow, elegant stone-built aqueduct carried water from the jebel to the plains. An obvious adoo target, it'd been destroyed leaving a bare, useless skeleton, a poor cousin to France's Pont du Gard. Yet despite the odds, the Sultanate still held an ace, Salalah's fresh water was supplied by aquifer, refilled annually by rainfall in the mountains. The Dhofar capital and SAF had drinking water.

The plains sit below the high mountain range of Jebel Al Qara. Simultaneously beautiful and majestic, in 1971 they were filled with menace and foreboding. Covered in verdant green for three months of the khareef/monsoon, the mountain vegetation dries a desiccated buff-brown for the rest of the year. During the khareef or even when dry, the adoo enjoyed perfect cover for guerilla operations. Holding this high ground encircling Salalah having captured the arterial road over the jebel, they held the plains in an ominous embrace. Without road access or port, Salalah was totally reliant on aircraft and local fishing dhows for supplies. Dhows would anchor off the coastline whilst small boats plied back and forth, unloading provisions for the beleaguered town. However, as highlighted by the FCO:

> The monsoon (khareef) also brings with it the heavy seas which force a halt in the sea supply of our forces in Dhofar.

On arrival and taking stock of the situation, CSAF was heard to mutter 'this (situation) . . . is truly wretched'.

* * *

I looked at my troop sitting quietly, the aircraft's engines drowning out normal conversation. Of my seven, five were no older than 20. Only Lou at 44 had seen active service. The embodiment of calm, a veteran combatant who'd been here before. He looked cool as mustard whilst others quietly contemplated what might lie ahead.

The twin-engined plane vibrated alarmingly and the air we breathed smelled strongly of kerosene used to refuel the aircraft that morning. Seated on aluminium-framed canvas seats bolted to the deck, surrounding us were resupplies for the beleaguered Salalah garrison, steel and wooden boxes containing mortar bombs, metal belted .72mm and the canvas belted .30 Browning machine gun ammo. A load shift and the result was finality, as had happened at Akoot six weeks earlier. I glanced towards the smartly dressed Baluchi sergeant loadmaster; he smiled back. Of course! With aircraft known to be hit by machine gun fire, flying into a war zone in a thin-skinned aircraft, seated amongst high explosive, why worry about load shift? Grinning at Lou, I shouted to my Irish sergeant, 'You might offer a small prayer for a safe landing please, Lou'.

Our canvas seating had seen better days. Aching backs and limbs numbed where pressed against tubular frames were stretched to ease cramped muscles. It'd been a bumpy ride flying south along the coast to cooler cloud-hidden Dhofar. Nearing our destination and beckoned forward to the flight deck, I was shown Dhofar's mountain summits floating above low cloud. Shouted above the engines' roar 'welcome to your home for the next two years' before cryptically 'rather you than either of us two, mate!' We began our descent towards the rust browns, bleached whites and buff colours of Salalah plain and earth airstrip, hidden below in the mist.

Seated under the aircraft's wings we watched the landing gear shudder then thump, locking into position ready for landing. The ground came into view revealing the desert plain, crisscrossed with what turned out to be camel tracks. There were coconut palms, date palms and thorn bushes. On our final approach emerged clusters of the white hewn coral stone and mud-built townhouses: Salalah. With thoughts turning to offloading on landing, a sudden expletive came from the cockpit as engines screamed, sending the aircraft into a steep climb. We were pushed back into flimsy seats as the aircraft climbed, shuddering sufficient to shake apart until reaching and breaking through the low cloud base. 'Airstrip's under attack,' the senior pilot yelled, 'rockets and small arms, we remain up here until ordered otherwise.'

'Right,' I mused ... fleetingly reflecting on the chances of our flight being ordered to return north, wishful thoughts of constant sunshine and Desert Regiment's convivial existence at Bid Bid sounding eminently preferable to Dhofar. Lazy beach weekends swimming ... that invitation to lunch? More time to acclimatise, complete training and perfect my Arabic. Hell yes! Might even work up a tan to match the 'bronzed' with their months or indeed years of Omani sunshine ahead of me.

That was never going to happen. Thirty minutes after the aborted landing, the all-clear was given, freeing us to land. Dropping rapidly through the monsoon cloud base, a sudden bump then another announced we were down, racing along the sand airfield, the shortest landing I'd experienced. Engines straining in reverse thrust, the pilots brought us to an abrupt stop, before taxiing to a single storey block which passed for Salalah's arrivals and departures terminal.

With engines left running, we scrambled out to be met by a contingent of walking wounded, non-serious medevacs. At the front, a British contract major admirably still carrying his rifle and in place of shemagh, a spotless white gauze head bandage through which a neat patch of red had begun to ooze. If intended to impress, annoyingly it worked.

'Hello, you look new,' he quipped looking me up and down before exclaiming 'Fucking hell! They're now sending us bloody schoolboys!' Aboard the aircraft, so gaining height advantage, he turned. 'Been told yet you're too bloody white? Yellow hair? You might last a week, mate! Welcome to fucking Dhofar!' Disappearing into the Caribou he took the seat I'd vacated moments before. The friendly loadmaster waved, busy directing operations as wounded took their seats, hurrying, ready for a rapid escape back to Muscat and safety.

'Yer man's shyte – might've ferking said 'How do' eh, sir?' muttered a rueful Costello.

'Sergeant Costello, regrettably we're not all as well-mannered as the Queen's Royal Irish Hussars,' I replied, thinking of the bandaged hero, as I muttered 'What a pretentious prick!' . . . Great welcome though, hadn't expected that. Revived first day memories at English boarding schools. Lou was right. Yet given the man had recently been under enemy fire and obviously suffered a head wound, perhaps understandable. Mind you, it was difficult dismissing the thought it'd all been to impress. Our paths never crossed again. I learned later he'd struck his head seeking cover. Easily done, as I would discover myself.

Making our way towards the range of sandbagged buildings, I noticed striding towards us a tall rangy officer with a broad smile of greeting, 'Hello, see you've met the lucky sods escaping back to Oman for the cushy life? Reckon you must be Paul Hodgson, I'm Geoff Mawle – I'm to take you to Arzat where you're with us at DG – it's about 30 minutes' drive away. Let's grab your kit'.

Appreciating his uncomplicated, easy-going manner, I introduced Geoff to Sgt Costello and each of my troop. Formalities over we set off, I and one other in Geoff's open Land Rover, Lou and the remainder boarding an open-topped Bedford. These 4.9 litre, four-wheel drive vehicles were the backbone of motor transport in BAOR and armies around the world. Manufactured by Bedford (General Motors) between the mid-1950s until early 1970s, here they served as

A convoy of Bedford trucks at rest, parked alongside my Land Rover flying the Sultan's pennant. To the right of the photograph, the Fitter's pick-up. We were returning from resupplying a SAF position on the Yemeni border.

personnel carriers, but also for transporting ordnance, munitions, water, rations and firewood. Some were fitted out for vehicle recovery. Simple in design and hence in repair, they were versatile, dependable vehicles.

As we left the airfield Geoff pointed towards the jebel at some obviously manmade constructions, 'Hedgehogs, manned by MR to protect the airfield'. Looking like vast molehills, they were built utilising empty 200-litre fuel drums, placed three or four deep and three high, filled with sand and stone. The rust-coloured fortifications supported corrugated iron roofs layered with more earth and stone, the whole sufficiently strong to withstand mortar, rocket and machine gun attack. Unlike the enduring Czech hedgehogs, static star shaped anti-tank obstacles constructed from angle iron against advancing tanks, Salalah's hedgehogs were built as defensive positions against infantry and artillery attacks. Originally five in number and identified phonetically Alpha to Echo, these incongruous-looking bastions formed a defensive semicircle around the vital airfield and RAF base. They absorbed many adoo incomers, reducing attacks on the airfield behind. Foxtrot, a sixth Hedgehog, was added that August following increasing rocket attacks, built I later learned by Sandy and his men from MR.

Geoff's Land Rover was stripped of doors, windscreen, canvas roof and overhead rails, anything that might hurt in an explosion. The sandbagged floor forced knees to chest level – neither dignified nor comfortable for travelling. 'Mine protection . . . about as good as it gets' Geoff's answer to my enquiring look. 'You'll get used to it, we all do . . .' and with that we roared off in clouds of powder fine dust, across the flat countryside around Salalah's northern barbed wire perimeter. Half a mile on we came to the first mined vehicle, a Bedford truck, with what remained of the cab pitched forward into the ground. The front offside wheel, front wing and bonnet gone, blown away in the explosion. 'Landmine,' shouted Geoff cheerily, 'yesterday morning, poor sods, unprotected, five casualties, driver killed, others bloody lucky, minor injuries – nasty business, mines,' he added as an afterthought.

Efforts to mine-proof vehicles were fairly ad hoc, if not Heath Robinson. In addition to sandbagged floors, quarter inch steel plates were welded beneath vehicle cabs and front wheel arches to deflect a mine's explosive forces. Plating extending just beyond the petrol tank beneath the commander's seat provided little consolation.

Unfortunately, brake, clutch and accelerator pedals were unprotected. As a result, on detonation pedals flew into the driver's cab, generally with fatal consequences.

A glance confirmed soft skinned vehicles stood no hope against mines. 'The procedure,' Geoff shouted, 'follow the lead vehicle's tracks, never deviate.'

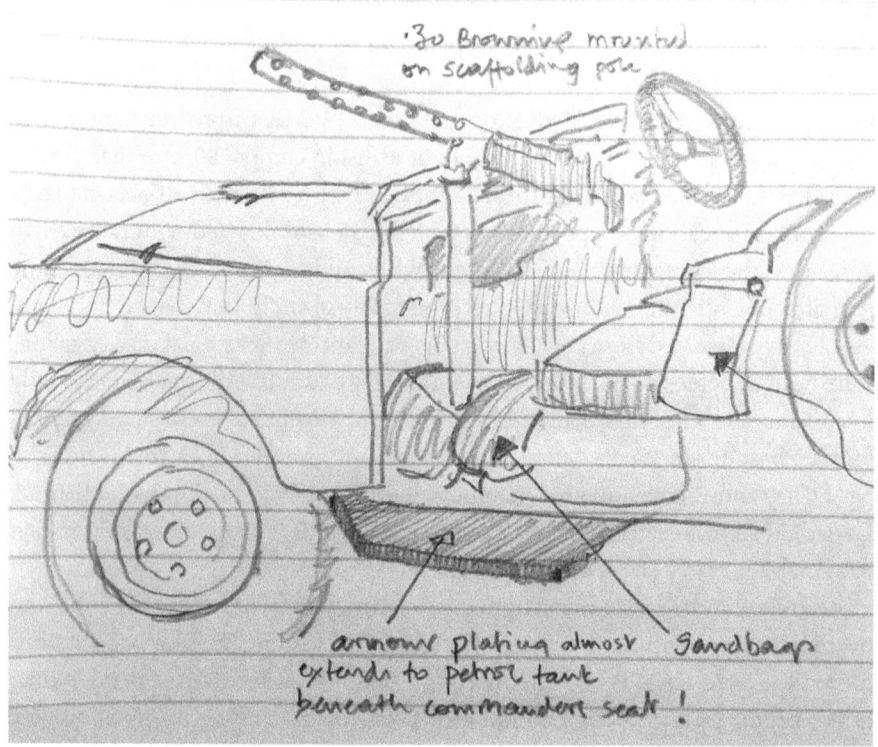

Sketch of mine protection on my Land Rover adapted to carry a .30 Browning. Never intended as a long-term measure, the Browning was slotted into a section of scaffolding pole welded to the vehicle.

Laughing, he shouted, 'Bedfords have wider axles than Land Rovers!' Before adding reassuringly, 'Mine sweeping patrols clear these tracks each morning, but even so SAF regularly hit mines . . . drivers not concentrating!' Turning with a broad grin he added, '*I* am concentrating – what a bloody way to make a living?'

Unconsciously I'd pulled my legs into my body, such that I was now in danger of toppling out. 'Better hang on!' yelled Geoff. 'Everyone sits like gnomes at first, but sitting like that gives away you're new!' Mortified, I immediately stretched out my legs.

Our two vehicles left dust clouds billowing in the still air as we crossed sand and gravel plains motoring eastwards leaving Salalah behind. Looking left and up towards the jebel I reckoned we were visible from miles away as Geoff shouted, 'We're watched from there the whole time – like the poor French buggers in Vietnam!'

'And that didn't end too well,' I thought, remembering a visit to the French Foreign Legion where an officer had recounted one of many stories to emerge from Vietnam, the siege at Dien Bien Phu, when a French garrison fell and 10,300 soldiers were taken prisoner. In the Legionnaire's Mess, he'd shown me a row of portraits honouring Legionnaires who'd died in the final stages. The hauntingly simple pencil drawings stared impassively out at the observer devoid of emotion, and I realised the artist must have drawn from their ID cards. The siege lasted one month, three weeks and three days. The well-equipped French had held out against overwhelming odds until gradually one position after another was overrun. Towards the end, the garrison's senior artillery officer committed suicide. He'd used a hand grenade, some feat having earlier lost an arm in battle. Out of ammunition and with enemy closing rapidly, the last remaining survivors of a Legionnaire company fixed bayonets and charged from their trenches roaring 'À Camarón!', choosing glory over surrender. Famously their battle cry since 1861. It was a story to resonate with any young soldier; would you be that brave?

In December 1967, Soviet Union backed Yemeni Marxists had taken on a well-equipped modern army, forcing the British to withdraw from their long-established base at Aden. Declaring the situation untenable, Britain's 'permanent garrison East of Suez' was abandoned, leaving behind large quantities of valuable ordnance, weapons and live ammunition now being used against us in SAF. And here we were, three years on, likewise contained by a Soviet Union and Chinese trained guerrilla army in control of the surrounding high ground. Would history repeat? A beleaguered garrison, encircled by mines and bombed with impunity by an enemy sensing victory, the fall of Salalah had become the talk of Officers' Messes across the country. Unbeknown to us, Whitehall too were concerned. Was this really another Dien Bien Phu, I wondered?

SECRET

In the longer term, if things go badly this autumn, we cannot rule out the possibility of the Sultan eventually being forced to abandon Dhofar. In that event it is difficult to predict what the reaction would be in the rest of Oman, with implications for the continued use of (RAF) Masirah as a staging post.

AA Acland, Arabian Dept. FCO

Shortly afterwards we arrived at Wadi Sahalnawt. Rising in enemy held mountains, storm waters had created gorges cut into the limestone in places 60m deep, yet here at Khawr ad Dahariz the steep sided wadi was reduced to a shallow ford.

The 45m wide khawr (lagoon) emptied unpolluted waters into the Arabian Sea. Approximately 30cm deep, fresh water flowed south across a limestone pebbled riverbed. Fist sized, hard and once razor-sharp stones worn smooth by nature's caress, and now increasingly by the urgency of army trucks' wheels.

'This spot's frequently mined' Geoff remarked as we crossed the wadi, 'cleared it coming to meet you'. A task we would undertake daily, as we took turns attending Brigade HQ briefings at SAF's base, UAG, just east of Salalah.

Suddenly through the mist loomed the silhouette of a tower, at first sight an archetypal Beau Geste fort. Closer, the building was far smaller yet still impressive. No doubt a forbidding sight to passing nomads at a time before vehicles. Now the camp's entrance gate and guardroom, the two-storeyed and mud-brown construction with whitewashed castellations gave the appearance of a giant coffee cake, topped with cream. Above flew the Sultan's national flag.

Arzat Fort - gatehouse to the camp.

Chairman Mao Zedong's Little Red Book

In a little over three months at Arzat, three adoo surrendered at the gatehouse. Arriving undetected, each carried a loaded Kalashnikov, spare magazines and an Arabic version of Mao's 'little red book'. Reputedly translated into over 50 languages, and which every Chinese citizen was required to own, read and carry during the Cultural Revolution.

ARZAT CAMP

'Welcome to your new home,' remarked Geoff. Flimsy lengths of barbed wire carried on wooden poles enclosed the camp. Behind the fortress, an 81mm mortar sat behind a sandbagged pit for protection. Beyond, a range of stone-coloured buildings.

Geoff pointed to my left, 'That's your vehicle park, and men's quarters, Sergeants' Mess just beyond. We're over there –' he gestured towards another white painted bungalow, beneath ubiquitous corrugated steel roofing. 'Not bad, no fly-screens on windows, no air con, shared toilet and shower block – only the OC, Chris, has his own facilities?' he added with questioning intonation. Later I'd come to appreciate the nuance.

'Lucky him,' I replied, adding, 'think I'll have a quick look at the men's quarters and Sgt Costello's, join you afterwards. Can you dump my kit at the Mess please?' I added: 'Owe you a drink for collecting us.' 'It'll be a beer.' Geoff grinned, driving towards the Officers' Mess.

The soldiers' accommodation was Spartan, devoid of beds or storage cupboards, standard issue in the British Army. Expected to sleep on blue 120cm x 180cm SAF cotton prayer mats, kit stored in canvas kit bags, SMGs by their sides. 'I'll get beds,' I told them, receiving the stoical reply 'Allah Kareem sahb', (God is generous), which I took to mean 'thanks, sahb, you can try'. Turning to Lou, I muttered 'We must be able to improve on concrete floors . . .'

Lou's room was much the same. (Chris refused to allow Lou to use the Officers' Mess, so he lived with the Pakistani and Dhofari Sergeants.) At least he had a bed, rusty but with a mattress and slow revolving ceiling fan. 'You'll be very comfortable, Lou,' I remarked. 'Sure, I'll be fine, thank you, sir – bet it's no worse than yours. Can't wait till squadron arrives and we get our own accommodation.' Never a truer word. 'One day,' I replied, unsure when that would happen, 'meanwhile, we're guests of DG, I'll sort beds for the boys. We'll have a look at the Ferrets after lunch.'

In the Mess, I met ex-Gurkha Harry Wooley MBE, who'd fought through WW2 as a commander of a Vickers machine gun carrier. Mentioned in dispatches during the Italian campaign, on leaving the Gurkhas, he'd served with various foreign armies. As DG Quartermaster he'd become a confidant and supplier of extra kit others denied us.

Harry showed me my room. 'One of our best, almost ensuite,' he chuckled, 'washroom in that block, quite clean. The drains smell, you'll get used to it – lunch at one' and he was off. I would pick my time to discuss beds for the boys. After the men's accommodation, mine was five-star, foot polished concrete floors, interiors much in need of a coat of whitewash. Bare steel rafters carried minutely holed corrugated sheeting creating daylight stars. Already baking hot, and this the 'cool' monsoon season. The bed, steel-framed, with an old mattress again reeking of others' sweat was damp to the touch. My new home.

Seldom seen without his pipe, a keen gardener collecting rocks for the Officers' Mess gardens at Arzat.

The two glassless window openings were fitted with diamond design wire security grills, replicas of those found in East African schools and homes. Looking up past tiny shafts of sunlight, I thought I made out movement. Camel Spider. Ugly dark brown mandibles and grotesque body just visible. Quiet, still and beyond reach, the creature watched, taking in this new occupant to an already claimed space. 'Following me?' I asked out loud, adding 'You'll have to stay,' thinking to myself I'd ask Harry if stores might supply a mosquito net. Whilst a net would be a precaution against any accidental meeting between spider and human, mosquito nets were not always issued as at the time Oman was declared free of the malaria-carrying Anopheles mosquito.

A quick wash then lunch where I met Chris Phillips, Officer Commanding DG. Ex-3rd Carabiniers (Prince of Wales Dragoon Guards). Twice my age, balding, ruddy-faced with fine girth and a liking for gin and tonic, Chris epitomised the archetypal retired major. Unfulfilled military career and past disappointments now eclipsed by the gift of command.

That first evening with conversation light and cordial, Chris suddenly announced 'Understand, Paul, although you're outside my operational command, on base, you and your men are (under my command). You'll take your turn at orderly officer duties, and your men will perform guard and other duties around camp. I expect you to make that very clear to your Arabs.' 'Naturally, Chris,' I replied slightly taken aback, and catching Geoff's eye, he grinned. 'Saw that coming,' he said afterwards. Probably more bluster than blood, but a man to treat warily. Battle lines were drawn.

Chris had highlighted a distinction: four of my troop were Arabs from northern Oman and two were khadim from Dhofar, the tribe who formed the largest tribe at Arzat camp. The distinction would come back to trouble me later.

Harry became known as 'Uncle', a nickname that made him smile. (Much later, the squadron's Mike Offord, though younger than Harry, was also Uncle.) Harry's laconic smile was generally hidden behind a habitual briar pipe, billowing smoke or empty, held tight between tobacco-stained teeth. Smoking an abominable variety of tobacco he claimed killed every variety of fly – I never noticed any decrease in their numbers.

One night, enquiring why he was still soldiering, he'd replied '. . . a long story, but I can tell you this, just make sure you have children whilst you're young . . .' A worthy life lesson. A year later he became QM to the newly formed regiment of irregulars, the Firqat Forces, made up largely of ex-adoo fighters. Already a recipient of a Commendation Medal for bravery, he was later awarded the WKhM, the Sultan's Distinguished Service Medal.

Ahead of me in Dhofar by a couple of months, Geoff, ex-Duke of Edinburgh's Royal Regiment (DERR) was DG Operations Officer. He'd been recruited into SAF by Ray Kane, whom I'd known at Bid Bid camp and was destined to serve alongside later. Ray, the singularly offbeat, ferociously brave Red Coy Commander was also ex-DERR.

NO RADIOS!

2 Aug – Unbelievable – NO RADIOS!? They're promised. Ferrets at first glance are a disappointment from those at Bid Bid. However, think we'll manage.

We had been issued armoured cars without radios but I was promised they'd soon be delivered. Confident we could make the cars roadworthy by the addition of a few spares – it was unbelievable we'd been issued cars with no means of communication. We'd have been better off on horseback.

3 Aug – Much cooler than Bayt al Falaj, more like Dar. Saw the jebel today quite clearly, green and beautiful, grass and trees. Life very different here, never without loaded weapon, and never out of camp without escort. Cleaning weapons a daily task because of damp. Both mornings so far, wet drizzle. Gardens pretty, bougainvillea, jasmine, shrubs and annuals. Air-conditioning not needed here. Room comfortable. Surf pounding on beach clearly audible from camp. Must take a look. 3 letters and pc from home – quite a surprise.

DHOFAR'S KHAREEF – WELCOME INTERLUDE IN A DESERT'S YEAR

Dhofar's monsoon season, called the khareef, arrives each June, heralding fine mists and light rain. The damp atmosphere is filled with scents as jasmine blooms whilst droplets of moisture coat clothing, exposed face and arms, shemagh, vehicle and weapons constantly. Drizzle-covered surfaces would glisten if there was sunshine. Remaining exposed for any period soaks all who venture out in open vehicles. The monsoon lasts until September; by then Salalah's plains and jebels have been transformed from dust bowls and dry wadis, to verdant carpets of grasses, trees and shrubs all brought back to life. Temperatures reminded me of the rainy season in Dar-es-Salaam, when the East African countryside would burst into green following 'the rains'. Here, lasting little more than ten to twelve weeks, the heat and dryness return quickly to desiccate tender grasses and plant life. Yet the annual gift of the khareef is not wasted, the many varieties of grasses and wildflowers having flowered and set seed in readiness for a repeat of this Arabian miracle the following June. And wadis run with water.

> *... drove into Umm al Ghawarif this morning to be informed radios still at Bayt al Falaj! Am assured they'll be sent down soon and in the meantime we're not expected to be operational until after they arrive.*

Leaving Lou with the troop overhauling the Ferrets, accompanied by LCpl Abdul Raja Faraz and my driver Nasir Hamid as escorts, I drove to Brigade HQ to enquire about radios. The route had already been cleared for mines that morning as Geoff attended the daily O group at HQ. To my surprise, I discovered no one had clocked our lack of radios. My first introduction to problems Tim faced daily building the Squadron against an infantry bias at SAF and Dhofar HQs. Inevitable really: we were new, the infantry well established.

Hearing we'd no radios, Tim messaged us warning I should be awake to recognising the ascendancy infantry claimed over newcomer, armour. We'd have to fight our corner. That day, having won assurances on delivery of radios, my orders were clear: get the cars roadworthy but remain non-operational.

I had a shopping list for Ferret spare parts and called next at HQ workshops where I introduced myself to Bert Kenyon, Warrant Officer First Class running the Sultan's Forces Electrical and Mechanical Engineers (FEME). A welcoming smile, firm handshake and positive outlook, Mr Kenyon was instantly likeable, fortunately for us with our numerous calls on his expertise. 'Bert' as he was known, became one of the Squadron's most staunch supporters at HQ. Discussing immediate issues, he arranged to send an engineer to resolve the few snagging problems we'd discovered. A worthwhile visit in many ways.

Later that afternoon at Arzat, I called at the QM stores where I found Harry seated behind a desk of papers and a variety of kit being sorted with his QMS, Baluchi staff sergeant Noor Mohamed. In a tiny hot office sat Harry partially hidden by his pipe's smokescreen. I hoped his QMS was more than just a passive smoker. Despite only recently met, I'd found a receptive ear. This old warrior, listening to my concerns about men's lack of beds, promised to find some.

'One other thing, I wonder could you possibly assist with some small flags?' I enquired. Explaining our perilous lack of radios I wondered if he might have some flags we could use for signalling between the cars. 'Hmmm,' came the reply, before asking 'would green and red do?' 'Harry, that'd be excellent,' I replied, 'of course, port and starboard!'

'I've some in store for rifle ranges' and with that, we were gifted four sets of flags, one for each car. Next, I taught the troop the significance of the colours – green, right; red, left.

Little did I realise how soon we'd need our improvised means of communication. That same afternoon came the order to escort a three-vehicle convoy carrying soldiers east into Taqah, a fishing village along the coast. We were to liaise with the Bedfords as they arrived at Arzat from UAG. Bert had sent a vehicle mechanic to travel with the convoy as backup. Our Brownings, stripped, cleaned and reassembled had already been tested. The guns worked. So it was, we set off on our first active convoy escort, four cars without radios, suspect engines and gearboxes, leaking hydraulics and one car, a fragile starter motor which needed a hammer blow to persuade the thing to work.

Hilarious but for being so serious, the small matter of inter-car communication. Relying on the ancient craft of semaphore for communicating between the armoured cars, a system first invented by Frenchman Claude Chappe in 1792, we set off escorting the trucks. Using hand signals, we communicated between Ferrets and the Bedfords. Costello's views on senior officers would have earned him a court-martial in BAOR.

The convoy passed without incident. On return to camp I discovered, true to his word, Harry had delivered beds to my soldiers' block. From those early meetings with Harry and Geoff, life under an occasionally difficult atmosphere became tolerable through a shared companionship that did much to counter the often irascible moods of the camp commandant.

Our orders to remain non-operational had lasted three hours.

6

INCIDENT AT WADI JARDUM

I meet Bob Tomlinson and learn details of Mike's death 21 days earlier. Warning – do not be taken alive. Spike Powell and a soldier's yarn.

INTERVIEWING THE COMMANDO CARRIER CREW

"....in the sombre wars of modern democracy there is little place for chivalry"
Winston Churchill

3rd Aug – Commando Carrier, two crewmen and Bob Tomlinson!

I return to the Muscat Regiment contact three weeks earlier when Mike Campbell was killed. On arrival in Dhofar, no one seemed to be able to give me a clear explanation of events. It was not until I'd met up with Sandy and a friend from BAOR, that matters became clearer.

MR was commanded by Lt. Col Fergus Mackain-Bremner, Royal Anglian Regiment, ex-King's African Rifles stationed in Dar-es-Salaam, Tanganyika. Although never making the connection during my secondment, a young Captain Fergus had been best man at the wedding of Alison, the daughter of our neighbours, Sir Richard and Beatrice Turnbull, Britain's last Governor of Tanganyika, when my sister Ann was a bridesmaid. Attached to MR between that August and October, I worked closely with Fergus as his armoured reconnaissance troop.

That day we'd called at HQ workshops to repair a vehicle. Adjacent were parked two M706 Cadillac Gage Commando Carriers, the type used by the Americans in Vietnam as armoured personnel carriers. Four-wheel drive and battle ready, they weigh approximately 9.8 tonnes, and can carry nine soldiers in addition to four crew, commander, gunner, radio operator and driver. Classified as Armoured Personnel Carriers (APC) as opposed to our heavier Saladins armed with 76mm guns which were categorised as Armoured Fighting Vehicles (AFV).

Access was through two side doors and turret cupola. Closed down, all round vision was provided by armoured glass and periscopes. Within the revolving turret, either side of the gunner were a pair of machine guns, .50 and .30 calibre Brownings. With the imminent arrival of Saladins, the squadron had declined the Commandos, leaving them with MR for use as personnel carriers. Designed for amphibious operations during the Vietnam War, they were also used as armed escort by Military Police.

Tim had warned me that whilst they looked impressive, not to be tempted for they were actually useless as armoured cars.

I walked over to the parked cars and was surprised by an involuntary shudder as my hackles raised, imagining being captured alive, wounded and dragged out of the car, when a touch on the shoulder made me turn quickly. 'Made you jump,

My rough sketch of an American M706 Cadillac Gage Commando Carrier.

INCIDENT AT WADI JARDUM

Hodgson! You donkey waller' (time-honoured RTR welcome to cavalry). Grinning broadly, there stood a finely whiskered officer wearing a red Muscat Regiment beret. 'Robert Tomlinson!' I exclaimed, rescued instantly from nightmare.

I had no idea he was in Dhofar. Exchanging greetings, we recalled last meeting nine months earlier on a wet Lüneburg Heath in Germany. Bob, aka 'Poppo', had been in Dhofar for six months, seconded from 2 RTR and serving with MR. Promoted later to Company Commander, he completed his secondment in 1972, before returning on contract with DR, serving with distinction, winning the Sultan's Commendation Medal for bravery.

'Same car as Mike was killed in, huge roaring V8 turbocharged engine, guaranteed to stir perceptions of invincibility in the mind of the gung-ho, never a bloody substitute for clearheaded thought and common sense! Terrible business, should never have happened,' Bob remarked, nodding at the cars as two Baluchi soldiers approached extending greetings 'Salaam Alaikum', 'Wa Alaikum as-Salaam' we replied. They too were MR, and wanted to talk. They'd been with Mike in the captured Commando Carrier.

As a lead-in to what emerged that 12th July, I quote from a singularly frank and personal recollection of a partial witness, Sandy. Remaining at Bayt al Falaj for a flight south, Sandy eventually flew to Dhofar, joining MR on the 12th July.

Sandy writes:

"I can, however, now report details of the operation leading to Mike Campbell's death. It was my first day in MR. As I was to join A Company MR, of which Mike was 2ic, he met me from the aircraft from Muscat, took me to my room, then to the QM's Stores to draw items of MR uniform, issue for living in the field kit etc, to the Company Stores to draw my rifle and ammunition, to the Mess for lunch and then to the Operations Room for a briefing by Martin Robb, the Operations Officer. Willie Harris, OC HQ Company, came into the Operations Room. He invited me to join him on patrol that afternoon. I did not know how to reply: on one hand, I knew I was unprepared, unbriefed, rifle not zeroed etc, and on the other hand I did not want to be considered a funk. Martin Robb saved the day and almost certainly my life by informing Willie that as I was due to meet the CO, Fergus Mackain-Bremner, later that afternoon I could not join the patrol.

The patrol comprised two (of three based on the Dhofar Plain) American Commando Carriers, four-wheeled armoured cars crewed by Willie, Mike, plus Patrick Freke-Evans, A Coy Commander, the drivers and about six to eight soldiers.

Patrick was commanding the second vehicle. Mike, a passenger in the first commanded by Willie Harris. The patrol had an objective: Patrick wished to plan an ambush in the area of the entrance to the Wadi Jardum, and the patrol was to recce the ground. As Mike was then 2ic A Company, it made sense that he, too, was on the patrol.

Willie led, entering the scrub leading towards Ayn Jardum. You may remember there were small mounds of earth/hillocks there. Willie followed the track through them: crazy without dismounted infantry support and, being constrained by the hillocks, the route was predictable. And he was ex RTR! Knowing Willie, as I came to do later, I think he wanted a contact just to be able to report a story to friends; as OC HQ Company he may have been frustrated, wanting action; in writing that, I may be being unfair, but that is what I think.

As the patrol moved into the scrub, Patrick became concerned at Willie's seeming recklessness and suggested to Willie over the radio that they were too near, or in, the thicker scrub etc and should return to the open plain. Ignoring that advice, Willie led on.

Patrick heard a bang and saw smoke which probably was the first RPG shot which missed Willie's vehicle. Willie ordered his driver to turn the vehicle around and he and the gunner returned fire. Having turned the vehicle around and heading back the way they had approached, Willie's vehicle stalled.

A second RPG round hit the back door of the vehicle penetrating the armour wounding Mike, Willie and at least two others. At close range, the adoo engaged the vehicle with machine guns, rifles and RPG. I do not know how many adoo were present.

Willie and (his) soldiers debussed and ran back. A few, including Willie, were wounded. Mike managed to debus, but was too badly wounded to move fast. The adoo caught and killed him near his vehicle. The remainder of the story is unchanged."

'Should never have happened,' Bob had said.

The two MR soldiers had been with Mike and Harris, crewing the lead Commando Carrier. As my troopers exchanged greetings, I asked the men to describe what occurred on 12th July. We listened as they related their version of events, corroborating Sandy's account.

Reaching the treeline, Harris continued into the scrub. Sparse at first it becomes increasingly dense towards the steeply sloped jebel. Thornbush and large anthills slowed progress. The second car held back.

As the inexperienced driver attempted to manoeuvre around an anthill, they came face to face with between thirty to forty adoo, standing in the open, waiting. The driver stalled. The nightmare had begun.

The Commandos' powerful eight-cylinder engines would have been heard passing the airbase, or conceivably seen even earlier creating dust clouds leaving Salalah's perimeter fence.

The adoo opened up with a fusillade of AK47 Kalashnikov and SKS, the semi-automatic Simonov designed assault rifle. Not all carried Kalashnikovs. Following the initial burst, silence. The adoo disappeared. Looking through the armoured glass to his front, Harris ordered the driver to restart the engine. It kicked into life, and Harris shouted again 'Yala! Yala!!' (Go on! Go on!) At this, Mike shouted, 'No, get back!' only to hear 'I want a body!'.

And at this, adding emphasis to his account, the soldier made a repeated grabbing action towards us with his hand, miming Harris' reply to Mike. Harris now opened up with the .50 Browning, but the adoo had melted into the trees and the many 1.5m tall earth anthills. At this point, the best move would have been to break off. Ambushed from such close cover, the two cars were at a considerable disadvantage. Fatally, Harris pushed forward after the disappearing adoo.

Advancing, the young driver then braked suddenly, shouting he could see men encircling their flanks. An explosion erupted in front as a rocket landed short. Harris, thrown forward by the braking vehicle, yelled to the driver 'warra! warra! warra!' (back! back! back!) who without hesitation swung the vehicle round, to stall again. That was it. Khalaas (Finished).

The next rocket hit the rear of the vehicle, a HEAT round (High Explosive Anti-Tank) designed on exploding to scatter molten metal inside the target vehicle. Mike shouted he'd been hit. Momentarily concussed, peering through smoke, dust and explosive gases, Harris took in the damage. Mike, wounded badly, two soldiers with him, flesh wounds, driver and another OK.

A fire started as electric cabling ignited.

The second Commando carrier had moved forward to about 200 metres behind the stricken car, the attack witnessed by an unbelieving crew, astonished at the unravelling events. This was meant to be a lightly armed recce, not an operational patrol! Inside the smoke-filled car, expecting a second rocket to strike at any moment and realising Mike was not going to make it, Harris yelled 'Dismount!', shoving open the side door away from the incoming automatic rifle fire. Leaping out he fell, breaking an arm. On his feet again, Harris urged the soldiers run to the other Commando. Pausing to look back at Mike's collapsed body, he turned to run after his men, crouching low, cradling a broken arm. What was going through the man's mind must have been unimaginable. Behind him, alone at the gates of Hades, he'd left a badly wounded man.

With the second car now putting down covering fire, the crewmen made it to safety. Apart from Harris's arm, the soldiers had escaped with minor flesh wounds. Climbing through the Commando's opened hatch to safety, Harris shouted Mike was dead.

Escaping leaving personal weapons, rifles, pistols and webbing, the Baluchi soldiers had run barefoot, discarding army issue plimsoles to run across flesh-cutting limestone gravel and sunbaked earth, as only those raised in desert or mountain are capable of. A Westerner's bare feet would have been cut to shreds after two paces.

I looked at the two young soldiers standing in front of us having related their story first hand. They expressed a wish to transfer from MR to join the ACS, but I had to decline. Two ordinary blokes, with no apparent axe to grind, who'd eloquently and seemingly without exaggeration told of the events experienced that 12 July. Not for the last time, I marvelled at these people's acceptance of death, "Allah Kareem" they'd say "God is Generous".

Bob filled in on the rest; the surviving Commando had returned directly to HQ. Alerted to the contact, Strikemaster jets had scrambled and flown over the area but without seeing movement. An enemy too expert at fieldcraft to be caught in the open had disappeared, taking weapons discarded by the fleeing soldiers and personal possessions from Mike's body.

Mike had been taken alive. Using a linen handkerchief, he'd applied a tourniquet above his leg wound to staunch the bleeding. His blood trail showed he'd dragged himself into the commander's seat in an effort to engage the enemy with the turret-mounted Brownings. But to no avail: the side of the car was open and the adoo would have swarmed over the stricken vehicle with their shrill whoops and cries of victory unique to the mountain Arab.

The gleeful shouting would have been terrifying. No matter how brave, a soldier's sweat-awakening nightmare is being taken alive by those who hate you. With sickening recognition, the complete sense of hopelessness would have hit hard being taken alive. Pulled roughly out of the vehicle he was dragged to be propped into a sitting position beneath a thorn tree. Ransacking the Commando, the adoo stripped what they could carry. Shortly afterwards they murdered Mike. Executed without mercy, the intention to humiliate and demoralise those who would eventually return to rescue him. The adoo knew the army would go to great lengths to retrieve their wounded. And they'd find out what happened to captured British soldiers. A coup for the enemy.

As intended, the barbarism appalled. And if not fully appreciated before, now it was clear there'd be no nod towards the Geneva Convention out here. Simple message: 'don't get taken alive' and all that that implied. We'd been warned.

Following a hasty briefing, Col Fergus assembled a rescue mission. Given Patrick's immediate involvement with the contact, his A Coy MR would lead, accompanied by Z (Zulu) Company, the Baluchi manned unit based at Dhofar HQ, used for mine clearance duties, convoy escorts, but in particular as an emergency back-up known as Strike Force, to which my troop would soon become attached.

Dismounting from their Bedford trucks, they advanced, securing the area before Z Company moved through led by their commander, Spike Powell, an accomplished veteran. Under covering fire, Spike ran forward with a section, found Mike's body and retrieved it without taking casualties. The adoo had sensibly disappeared. Brave to the point of recklessness, Spike was without equal in Dhofar.

Two weeks earlier, on learning of Mike's death I'd written:

> "They shot Mike Campbell last night. One of the very few people I knew out here. One contract officer wounded and four soldiers too? All same skirmish. They were in an armoured troop carrier, hit by an anti-tank rocket... we hear great deal of speculation on Mike's death, hard what to believe... but the main line is it was a 'swan'... Big .50 was jammed, adoo couldn't get it out of its fixing. Mike's body recovered. Zulu Coy."

Various aspects troubled us at DR – why had Harris abandoned Mike alive? We'd heard of British soldiers taken alive in Aden less than four years earlier and that hadn't been pretty. Returning from firing practice and in compliance with British army regulations, they'd "made safe" their rifles and emptied magazines before leaving the ranges. Dragged out of their ambushed Bedford truck by a murderous Aden mob, the soldiers' empty rifles were of little use in the butchery that followed.

But Harris was trained in tank warfare. Why then, on reaching the second car hadn't they pulled back 500 to 750 metres if necessary whilst putting down covering fire using the, not insignificant, Commando's weaponry? Might possibly have kept the adoo at bay, away from Mike's car, until reinforcements arrived? Acknowledged, the adoo had RPG – but that's a gun requiring manual re-sighting each time to lay on to target, and Harris had four wheels allowing constant switching of positions. And Jets to give top cover.

Yet here we were, safe and at ease 600 miles (1,000km) north of Salalah, discussing what we'd imagined might have happened, when each privately knew conjecture's the poverty of truth. They may have been low on ammunition? Like Harris, they may also have had inexperienced crews? And anyway, who were we to judge? We were no better than the despised armchair warriors who debate actions they were never at. Except for those present that afternoon, not one of us was there to do things otherwise. We could only hope that when and if caught in similar circumstances, we'd act differently. And of course, Mike was presumed left for dead.

That night at Bid Bid, scant on detail, talk had revolved on being abandoned, left alive. Many had made pacts with those they trusted – if when seriously wounded and incapable of rescue, double dose the morphine syrettes carried around our necks. At the back of our minds we knew too – no syrette, no time, gun. Don't leave people alive for the vultures, human or avian. Towards the end of the evening, when conversation had all but dried, leaving each to their thoughts, a silence was broken by the gravelly voice of Graham Sherwell offering quietly, "Funny, isn't it? In English when desert is used as a noun, how different it is from the verb."

I add Sandy's concluding thoughts, as one of the luckiest men alive.

> "I did not see Mike's body, but following its recovery he was laid in the room in the Mess that had been allocated to me and the air-conditioning was switched on. I think that his body was evacuated to the UK very soon, perhaps the following day. I heard that he had multiple wounds. I spent my first night in MR in Willy Harris' room; *his bed sheets*! I remember that his "library" comprised training pamphlets, particularly US Army ones. I thought and continued to think he was an immature "cowboy".
>
> If I had joined the patrol, I would have probably been in Mike's vehicle. If he sat in the rear, as I understand he did, I would have sat either adjacent to or opposite him. It is near certain that I also would have been wounded. I like to think that I would have tried to assist Mike; if so, we would have been captured and killed together. If I had not assisted Mike, I would have been ashamed of myself for the remainder of my life.
>
> Harris was casevaced to the UK. He returned after about six months to command B Company. He was removed from post by the CO after the first three weeks of the next Dhofar tour; I replaced him. Willie was moved to HQ SAF or somewhere like that . . ."

For those who know him, there is no one who would doubt Sandy would have acted other than exactly as he writes. In the very best traditions of the 91st/93rd of Foot, when shit happens he'd be one to have beside you.

That night in my room, before I switched off the bare bulb hanging beyond the broken ceiling fan, mulling over what we'd heard earlier that day, I wrote in my diary,

> *"You tie a tourniquet when you can still fight, when there's still hope, it's hope, the last thing to die. Mike was alive."*

At a reunion recently, someone commented that Mike had had a death wish. When questioned, he admitted to not having been in Oman at the time. How utterly crass.

RECOVERING MIKE'S BODY

'Spike' (Neville) Powell had run forward unhesitatingly to recover Mike's body. Carrying him back through MR's lines to the vehicles, all withdrew successfully. SOAF Jet cover had kept the adoo at bay. No further casualties were taken. The Commando Carrier was left where it had stalled, stripped of equipment, except for the .50 Browning stuck in its housing, jammed pointing uselessly to the ground, ammunition gone, impotent and empty.

The adoo had successfully hit back against a superior force. They had prevailed over one of the Sultan's armoured vehicles, using rocket propelled grenades and armour piercing rounds. An assortment of weapons had been captured. But significantly, they had captured and killed a British officer. All this, without sustaining casualties on their side. The news spread rapidly throughout the jebel, the army could be beaten, again. More importantly, the Sultan's armoured vehicles were no match for rocket launched missiles nor indeed armour-piercing tungsten carbide rounds which pierced their armoured skins.

SAF retreated to the safety of UAG some 1,000 metres back, to take on board lessons learned that day, lessons that would not be forgotten.

It later transpired Mike had been carrying sensitive documents when killed. Involved recently in mapping defensive minefields north of the Hedgehog positions, Mike had his marked map with him. It was never recovered. Required for the patrol, it was presumed to have been with him when captured. Of the spoils taken that day, the weapons, ammo and radios, together with Mike's personal effects, none measured in worth to the location of these mines, relatively easily lifted, ready to lay again.

SPIKE POWELL MBE, WB, WKHM (G) – ZULU COMPANY'S LEGENDARY COMMANDER

Spike was awarded the WB, the Sultan's Bravery Medal, equivalent to the DSO for Gallantry and second only to the Sultan's Gallantry Medal, equivalent to the British VC.

Equipped with .50 Brownings mounted on Land Rovers, Z Company patrolled Salalah Plains. 'Spike's gunships' were part of Strike Force, the rapid response unit on permanent standby located at UAG and Arzat. Comprising a half rifle company, Z Coy and my troop of Ferret Scout Cars covered responses to attacks on the Hedgehogs and SAF ops, but also incidents within Salalah, as would occur on 20th September with an attempted assassination of the Sultan's uncle.

Spike had become a professional soldier after service with the King's African Rifles fighting the Mau Mau in Kenya, where he won a military MBE. Raised in East Africa, he'd served with the Rhodesian Light Infantry and also as part of Col Mike Hoare's forces fighting Maoist-inspired 'Simba' terrorists in the Congo wars between 1961-65.

Born in India in 1919, Mike Hoare, known as "Mad Mike", was raised in Ireland and though educated in England, retained his Irish nationality. A chartered accountant, he joined the London Irish Regiment, serving in the Far East on Earl Mountbatten's staff during WW2. Later Hoare became the ideal mercenary leader. Well groomed, charming, quietly spoken and confident, the archetypal officer and gentleman. In the early 1960s the Congolese Prime Minister, Moïse Tshombe, hired Hoare to fight communist terrorists. In sixteen months, he'd raised and trained a small army. While paid to fight, the mercenaries were as motivated by anti-communism as a lust for adventure. Although outnumbered, the force began to push back their Congolese adversaries.

Liberating Stanleyville, they freed hundreds of European hostages, including a Christian convent's nuns, many of whom had been raped, beaten and tortured. Hoare's men finally restored law and order to the Congo in November 1965. Unpopular throughout the Communist Bloc, he was known as "the mad bloodhound Hoare". Surviving to reach his 100th year in February 2020, he outlived many of those who'd served with him. Sadly, one of those was Spike.

The Sultan's Bravery Medal (WB) was instituted by Sultan Said bin Taimur in January 1968 for brave and distinguished conduct in the face of the enemy. British forces seconded to the Sultan of Oman's Armed Forces who were decorated with this award were granted unrestricted permission by Her Majesty the Queen to wear the medal.

The circular medal, measuring 37mm in diameter, is manufactured in gilt cupro-nickel. The obverse bears in the centre the Omani coat of arms, a crowned pair of crossed Omani swords in scabbards, a sheathed Khunjar (Omani curved dagger) with belt attachments, the emblem having engraved inscriptions in Arabic above and below. The reverse bears a central Arabic inscription, "gallantry", surrounded by a palm laurel wreath. The medal is suspended from a straight bar suspender. The multi-coloured ribbon has five vertical stripes of dark blue, red, green, yellow and light blue.

The Sultan's Bravery Medal – "Wisam Al Jura'at"

A SOLDIER'S YARN

After several months in Dhofar and on 24hr R&R from Akoot Camp in the Western jebel, I was sharing a few beers with Spike at the UAG Mess. It was late as Spike and I sat reminiscing on a shared heritage of childhoods in East Africa.

Others had retired for the night when I'd asked him about his exploits in the war against the loathsome Simba during the Congo's communist wars. He smiled, replying that a lot of what people had written and spoken was 'ng'ombe kinyesi' (Kiswahili for bullshit). And with a grin he leaned forward. 'But there's one story, man, that'll make you laugh . . .' the undisguised inflection revealing his East African/Rhodesian heritage. I'd already heard the story, but I hoped to hear his version first hand. I was not to be disappointed.

His platoon had come up against UN peacekeepers who'd attacked his position. It'd been a stand-off contact with each side firing small arms, but to little effect. Spike's platoon of Katangese Gendarmes (more police than soldiers) were armed with .303 rifles but also a .50 Browning machine gun. Dug in, they were defending an upper slope looking down onto a railway line below which a double tracked road passed through a short tunnel.

The attacking UN force consisted of Southern Irish infantrymen in battalion strength. As the Irish attempted to rush the tunnel, Spike's men opened fire and sensibly the Irish hit the deck and withdrew. 'Good,' thought Spike, 'now bugger off!' only to see his opponents re-group and attempt a second, followed by a third assault through the tunnel. On each occasion, Spike's 30 men drove the Irish back with a steady rate of rifle fire and the Browning HMG. Platoon against battalion and winning.

After the third attempt and exasperated at the 'singular stupidity' of the Irish, Spike yelled down to them in his clipped Kenyan English 'Oh . . . for fuck's sake man! Bugger off, you fucking idiots!!' before pausing and shouting 'I've the whole fucking area covered' adding the lie 'We're dug in, battalion strength and we'll slaughter the next fucking idiot who attempts to enter the fucking tunnel'!

To Spike's astonishment the UN's Irish decided perhaps discretion might be the better part of valour and retreated. The battle was over. Under cover of darkness Spike withdrew his outnumbered Gendarmes. Victors against a UN battalion, unharmed and bursting with pride, each with stories to relate into old age. Sipping his beer, Spike growled 'To win, man – just believe you're the bloody best!'

Such were the tales by which Spike had earned his deserved reputation.

7

CONVOYS & SAVING A DESERT DRAGON

First official operational convoy. Mine shudder and the art of lifting mines. Meeting CSAF, Commander Sultan's Armed Forces, and saving a desert dragon.

FIRST OFFICIAL TAQAH RESUPPLY CONVOY, 4TH AUGUST

At the easternmost reaches of Salalah plain, the Qara mountains drop towards a turquoise sea lapping white sands along the coastline at Taqah, a small fishing village with a fortress on a rocky headland.

Comprising little more than a hundred mud and stone buildings, the village's sand-filled streets are strewn with desiccated droppings of camel and goat, the absence of litter explained by these creatures' insatiable appetites. Survivors, desert herbivores will eat almost anything.

Rising above the village stands a stone fort occupied by the Wali, the Regional Governor. The majority of the population was Al-Ma'sheni, the tribe of the Sultan's mother. Hence the frequency of attacks against the town.

Dhofar Gendarmerie maintained a platoon at the fort under the command of a Dhofari Khadim Sergeant. Armed with FN rifles and a light machine gun, these men bolstered the Wali's own militia called askars, armed with bolt-action Lee–Enfield .303 rifles. Preferring to live separate from the fort, a well-armed BATT section occupied a village building. In addition to their machine guns, the team would use a French artillery piece, a WW2 Giat 90mm anti-tank gun. I return to this weapon later.

The BATT were employed recruiting men to join the fight against the adoo and importantly administer medical aid to the locals as a means of winning hearts and minds. Taking resupply convoys into Taqah at regular intervals we'd meet up with the team who were a great bunch. On occasions as a troop we would spend the night at the fort with the Arzat based DG gendarmes.

Many years later, the Sultan's mother, Sultanah Mazoon bint Ahmad Ali Al-Ma'sheni, was buried at Taqah, her tribal home. Within her inner circle of the Royal Household, the highly respected Sultanah was known affectionately as Bibi.

On the 4th August, my four Ferrets and Geoff's gendarmes in two Bedfords joined the resupply convoy of five Bedfords arriving from UAG. I was leading with Abdul Raja Faraz as my second car commander, and Costello brought up the rear with Abdul Wathik, in a dust cloud visible for miles. Reaching the high ground west of the small fishing village, we'd taken hull-down firing positions facing the adoo-held jebel when DG got into a muddle. Scampering to picquet the high ground, men dashed off in all directions, bunching and huddling together seemingly unsure what they were meant to be achieving. At this point, Geoff lost his rag, running amongst his men, rifle in hand, gesticulating madly and shouting at them to move to higher ground, spread out and not bunch together. All the while this tall lanky officer, a good foot taller than his men, presented the simplest of shots to any watching sniper.

I wrote in my diary

> "... whilst everything seemed to go wrong for him, Geoff I thought got unreasonably mad at his men."

He was very angry. Doubtlessly realising the danger he and his men had placed themselves in, but more the fact we as a group were meant to be the official convoy escort. I waved the convoy through as we sat hull down, engines purring, powerful Brownings loaded and cocked, facing the jebel. Eyes straining through binoculars, we waited, searching for any movement. Warned to expect mortars or machine guns, I hoped we were ready. As it dawned, our first proper op had actually gone quite well. All credit to the troop, together now just four weeks. The sweat, frustrations, and moments of doubt were behind us. Proud of the way my troop had performed, I couldn't believe how well they'd adapted to flag waved instructions; it might be primitive but it worked. On the other hand, being operational without radios was sheer lunacy.

I felt for Geoff as he struggled to organise his men. His was the far greater challenge, that of transforming gendarmes more used to ceremonial duties into a fighting force. He still had some way to go. We returned to Arzat without incident. In contrast to how pleased I was with my troop's performance, Geoff was still sore with his men. Dismissing them with an abrupt dressing down, he stalked off to the Mess in a foul mood. After we'd cleaned weapons and made an attempt to wipe down the accumulated fine dust lodged inside our cars, I caught up with my frustrated friend slumped in a chair on the Mess verandah. Offering him a beer, I enquired 'You OK?' to receive a grunt in reply.

I then made the mistake of asking how he reckoned things had gone. At this, Geoff rounded on me, having a go at how 'fucking easy' it was for the 'bloody cavalry!' . . . 'You've seven men against the hundreds I have to train – so don't bloody ask me how things went – you were there, dammit . . . what a bloody shambles!'

Thankfully, any tension between us lasted no longer than that one evening. Geoff apologised for his outburst. As the only two combatant officers at Arzat, it was important we got along and this was generally the case. I volunteered to give him a hand in training his men. Together we worked out a programme combining our troops, the two of us teaching the rudimentary principles of fire and movement, and basic tactical moves. They learned quickly.

NERVOUS DRIVERS

6 Aug – This paper is damp, khareef affects everything. Yesterday four car patrol with Sgt Costello, LCpls Wathik and Faraz, working road Salalah to Raysut. At wadi Adonib, decided we'd pushed far enough towards tree line and ordered Hilal Ali "About" (turn around). He promptly stalled. Both front wheels stuck in a gully, he proceeded to flood engine trying to restart. Tapping him on shoulder I called "Quf!" (Stop!). He was sweating profusely – bad place to stall. Told him to wait before trying again. Signalled Costello to move forward to cover open right flank. Other two cars in depth.

In BAOR, when a tank stalls, it stalls, so what? Here it might mean sudden death. Minutes dragged as we waited. "Alaan!" (Now!) I commanded – it worked, engine kicked into life and we reversed out of the gully, out of trouble and away. We'd had a fright. Easy target. Hilal tries hard, but an engine stalls in wrong gear . . . he's got to gun it! Stalling – exactly same scenario when Mike killed.

A constant problem with newly trained drivers, a reluctance to use the engine's power for fear of losing control of the car. Four-wheel drive, with limited slip differential, designed to eliminate wheel spin through loss of traction, Ferret engines needed 'gunning' to power wheels free from obstacles such as holes or ditches. It was a skill learned with confidence and practice.

O GROUP – DHOFAR BRIGADE HQ AND MINE SHUDDER

7th Aug – attended O Group at HQ

It was my turn to attend HQ's morning briefing and waiting with three armed troopers in my vehicle, DG's escort arrived with eight squashed into a second Land Rover. In answer to my query, the Sergeant pointed out two ashen-faced men needing delivery to SAF's hospital. One glance at the men was sufficient, and ordering two DG pioneers onto my uncrowded vehicle, we set off. Pioneers cleared mines.

Avoiding adoo-mined tracks, we drove across country, arriving at Wadi Sahalnawt's 45m wide ford, 'Khawr ad Dahariz', gurgling 30cm deep over rounded limestone gravel and as any clear Alpine stream. Beguilingly innocent, many an army vehicle had been caught approaching this ford, where there was little choice of route. Halting, my escort fanned out, taking up firing positions. Removing my boots and treading gingerly barefoot, I accompanied the two trained in mine clearance, watching closely these experts search meticulously, wary for any visible disturbance, indentation, loose material or upturned stones, signature of man, not nature. There was a lot to learn.

Many will know the involuntary stomach clench. That instant the gut tightens when sixth sense warns danger threatens. It can occur in the moments before ambush or attack. With mines, as quick as the mind translates 'shiit . . . MINE!', it's probably already too late.

Despite a cool khareef morning, sweat began trickling from armpits and between shoulder blades wetting my shirt. Hairs bristled like a Rhodesian Ridgeback along backs of neck and arms. Driving over suspicious seen-too-late hollows has the same effect. You never got used to it. I called it mine-shudder.

No matter how hot a desert's heat, an involuntary shiver induces goosebumps. Charles Darwin held that goosebumps were a vestige of evolution, when our hairy ancestors reacted like animals still do today, alarmed, raising their fur to increase body size in an effort to intimidate the attacker. This is called a vestigial reflex

– caused by fear but also euphoria or sexual arousal (negative in desert warfare). Another surviving vestigial reflex is ear-perking, when sixth sense makes ears twitch. Indiscernible yet felt before becoming aware of a sound, a mechanism triggers information to the brain for analysis. This fraction-of-a-second advantage explains the evolutionary selection for this response.

Working ahead of me, devoid of any blast protection, the mine clearers advanced gingerly, delicately prodding the ground with steel spikes, searching for soft ground, listening intently for any giveaway onomatopoeic 'clunk' against their spikes. Metallic for anti-tank (AT), softer clunk for Bakelite anti-personnel mine (AP).

With an increasing heart rate, I watched nonetheless fascinated as these men edged forward into the shallow water-filled wadi. Following with boots tied together over one shoulder, trousers rolled above the knee, carrying my submachine gun, we eventually walked out to dry land. Turning, they indicated the all-clear. I waved the cars forward. My first experience of mine clearing, something we would become skilled at.

We drove on as I marvelled at these two unprotected men who'd crossed the wadi barefoot, using steel spikes to clear the way. Unlike British Army sappers burdened with the unenviable task of clearing mines, here I'd witnessed mine detection in its most primitive form. It was all we had. Their metal spikes were manufactured by SAF's vehicle mechanics. Later, we'd use hunting knives we'd purchased ourselves as armed with Sterling submachine guns as opposed to rifles, we were never issued with the soldier's last desperate means of defence, a bayonet.

We drove on towards Salalah arriving on time for my first Dhofar HQ Orders Group, (O group – commander's orders to his subordinates). On another occasion arriving late after being held up clearing a mine, I was bollocked and told to get up earlier. It hadn't helped either, when parking hurriedly my driver left the Land Rover in gear as he switched the ignition off, sending the vehicle bang into the Ops Room outer wall. I believe a little dust was disturbed behind the maps inside. We knew how to make an entrance.

MEETING CSAF

7 Aug – Met CSAF. Had I had a contact yet?

My first meeting with Commander Sultan's Armed Forces (CSAF), Brigadier John Graham was that morning outside Dhofar HQ ops room. Down from SAF HQ in northern Oman, he was standing in for Dhofar Commander, Col Mike Harvey, away on UK leave. I saluted (unlike in the field, here on base we saluted senior officers). Our Force Commander was dressed officially, immaculate uniform, red beret and badges of rank. Feeling distinctly shabby, I'd already noticed the smart scarlet berets and pressed khaki uniforms of MR's officers. Setting out for HQ that morning suitably dressed for my first O group, my best kit was no longer clean, dampened by khareef mist and mud-spattered driving across from Arzat. In place of parade beret, I wore a shemagh.

'Ah!' came a rapid-fire greeting, 'Hodgson – Armoured Cars? Welcome to Dhofar, had a contact yet?' returning my salute and adding without pause 'until you've had two contacts' (emphasised by Churchillian V sign) 'you're little use to me!' He extended his right hand which I shook in greeting, CSAF's opening fusillade being matched only by a vice-like grip. An impressive man, looked you straight in the eye, daring you look away. Broad of shoulder and solidly built, John Graham epitomised the archetypal para officer.

It was difficult to avoid feeling 'le nouveau arrivé'. Everyone but the newly arrived had seen some sort of action. That is, they'd been at the receiving end of either direct or indirect enemy fire. I doubted somehow the Brigadier would accept the airfield attack on landing might count as a contact. Subsequently, someone far better qualified than I, described this same welcome on arrival as to feeling he'd just crawled out from under a stone. Pretty good description.

Momentarily caught off balance, I decided against mentioning I'd not yet been here five days. Clearly, he bloody meant it. 'Good morning, Brigadier,' I replied, 'yes, Hodgson, no contact but I'll see what I can do.'

To which CSAF growled: 'Don't give me any of your cavalry flippancy, this ain't BAOR. Here, we need good infantry officers. I've yet to be convinced we need cavalry in armoured cars fighting a guerilla war.' Adding for clarity: 'Meant what I said about two contacts, first you'll shit yourself, second, you might be useful! Now follow me, welcome to your first O group'. Subsequently I learned I'd received CSAF's standard greeting to each new boy, army, navy, air force, seconded or contract, the lot.

John Graham had form; enlisting in August 1941 aged 18 as a private in the Argyll and Sutherland Highlanders, he was commissioned a year later. Wounded in North West Europe and mentioned in dispatches, he later transferred to the airborne division. Promoted brigadier to command SAF he'd arrived to find a Sultan refusing to implement change or accept the Dhofar war was out of control, maintaining it would fizzle out in time. Yet the adoo now held 90% of Dhofar, and Muscat itself was threatened.

There were elements in the MOD and FCO who maintained Oman might fall to communism within the year. John Graham arrived in March 1970 with clear orders from the Vice Chief General Staff (VCGS), to first, support the Sultan, and second, resolve growing criticism within the country but also SAF who knew the war was being lost.

On Thursday 18 June 1970 the Labour Government lost to the Conservatives. With the change of power, one aspect loomed large: the stark realisation that 50% of the UK's oil was supplied through an increasingly threatened Straits of Hormuz. Faced with a looming crisis in Oman, on 23 July a British orchestrated coup successfully replaced Sultan Said bin Taimur with his son, Sultan Qaboos. John Graham had been in the country just four months, hitting the ground at a run; he never stopped.

Highly regarded by his officers, CSAF worked tirelessly; with scant regard to his own health he pushed himself to the limit until eventually collapsing, requiring hospitalisation. Through his drive and determination, foundations were laid, turning the tide of war. An extraordinarily fine leader, the right man at the right time for Oman.

As to his welcoming challenge, what I suspect he meant was 'have you felt fear yet?'. We all feel fear despite how hard we think we are. In training, no matter how

Parked outside HQ Dhofar Ops Room – where my driver later unceremoniously announced our late arrival.

harshly inflicted, subconsciously fear is managed for there's always someone in control. Not so on active service when nothing compares to that initial shock when ambushed. Bullets crack past, ricochets spin, bombs or mines explode, and men are hurt. That's when fear can consume, that's when you grab it first, and throw it back at your attackers. Act, get hot angry, don't lose your cool, and you survive.

8th Aug – DG lose one killed and others wounded to AP mine in Taqah, one lost an eye. Affects morale. MR suffer casualty at Bravo (Hedgehog) and NFR two KIA, one WIA on op. out of Akoot. Taqah roads mined as we continue convoys. We alternate times to keep adoo guessing . . . Still no front bearings for Brownings, told they're on way. Can't believe we're sent out in such dilapidated vehicles, but am told Ferrets boost convoy soldiers' morale.

The Taqah platoon lost a man to a PMN-1 anti-personnel mine, another was badly wounded. The adoo had managed to mine a night piquet's position. Quite when, we never discovered, but it reinforced the need for caution walking along any form of track. How we hated mines.

One of the world's most widely used and commonly discovered mines found during de-mining operations, the Russian PMN-1 (противопехотная мина нажимная – anti-personnel pressure mine). Designed and manufactured in the Soviet Union, the mine dates from the 1950s and is particularly lethal compared to most other anti-personnel landmines, having an unusually large explosive filling. Anti-personnel blast mines generally contain around 50 grams of high explosive, typically destroying a victim's foot. PMN-1 mines contain 249 grams, sufficient to destroy a victim's entire leg in addition to inflicting severe injuries to the adjacent limb. The palm sized mines are cylindrical and filled with TNT. Constructed with a brown or black Bakelite case with a black rubber pressure-plate, they're armed

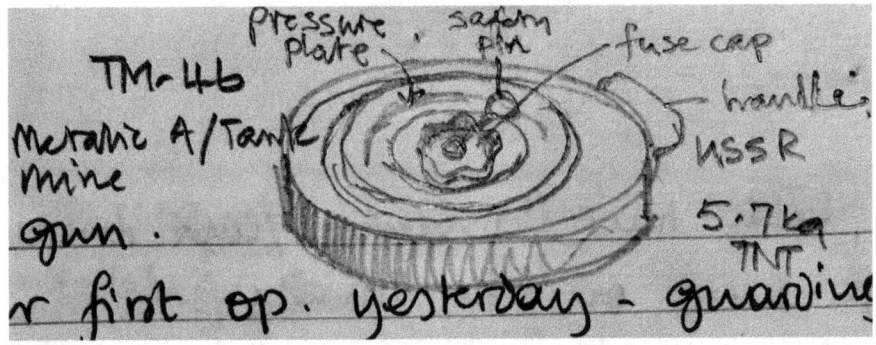

TM46 anti-tank mines held 5.7 kg TNT, against the PMN-1 anti-personnel mine's 249 grams.

by removing a steel ring-pull at the end of the horizontal fuse. The ring-pull holds back a spring-loaded striker from a stab-detonator. An average man's weight is 90 kg; it takes roughly 5.8kg on a pressure plate to detonate the mine. Loathsome.

LIFTING MINES

The going rate for a recovered mine was 50 Riyals, a sizeable sum and obvious incentive. Aware we were becoming adept at lifting mines, the adoo set anti-personnel mines under the larger anti-tank weapons, planned to trigger as the larger mine was lifted. In the end, I think more adoo were killed booby-trapping mines than we lost trying to lift them.

SPIKE POWELL'S UNIQUE ART OF MINE CLEARING

The "... look – the best way, man" lesson in lifting mines was taught to us by Spike Powell. Finding a mine, clear the area of loose earth and stones, expose the top. Next, slowly unscrew the firing pin mechanism on top of the mine, holding the casing firmly without exerting any downward pressure. Once done, mine's essentially defused. Next, tie a length of field telephone wire to its carrying handle, walk away feeding out the line and tie this to your vehicle parked 40m away. With everyone out of blast range tow the mine clear. Any booby-trap devices beneath would hopefully be ineffective, leaving the cleared mine relatively unscathed, and you the new owner, richer by 50 Riyals.

Despite my respect for Spike's undoubted talents, I never put into practice his "utterly failsafe" technique. Preferring instead, once the top was exposed as demonstrated, to leave well alone and from the safety of approximately 50m, blast it with my .303 rifle, hoping my aim was good. Otherwise, the trusty .30 Browning, when a short burst would always do the trick. Very satisfying – but no bounty.

* * *

SIBELIUS – SAVING A DESERT DRAGON

Walking to my room at the end of the day, I passed two DG soldiers carrying a stick of acacia on which clung a mature chameleon, Dhofar's single species

(Chamaeleo Arabicus). Gazing fixedly with independently watchful eyes that display contempt for lesser mankind, it's little wonder they're called dragons, demon tormentors of small invertebrates. A plentiful supply of flies ensures its desert survival.

The widespread thorny acacia (Vachellia tortilis), also found across East Africa, plays a vital role in tolerating drought and a wide range of soil types, including that tainted by salinity. Possibly its greatest attribute is taking nitrogen from the atmosphere (78% nitrogen gas) to fix into the soil, benefiting the majority of plant life incapable of pulling N2 from the air.

The reptile was a noticeably fine specimen about 25 cm long from tail tip to magnificent head. Only Marty Feldman had eyes to match. Now transformed into a shade of lime green to match the foliage, it clung, rocking slowly back and forth, watching, probably wondering what the hell was going to happen next.

Enquiring what they intended to do with the creature, they replied expressing surprise: 'kill it, of course, Shab . . .' Asking why, they insisted the creature had been created by the Devil. Faced with such intransigence and not wishing to appear to be befriending Satan's agent, I still wished no harm to the Dhofari chameleon.

I wondered whether by defending the creature this would only emphasise the differences in cultures, something I was consciously working to avoid. Making a decision I hoped wouldn't backfire, I asked if I might have the animal to help deal with the fly problem in my room. The two looked at me in amazement – then back to the still-swaying chameleon. A moment's hesitation before a shrug of a shoulder and the chameleon was passed to me.

Departing with warnings never to touch its skin, I thanked them, grateful for their advice, silent to the fact I had grown up with chameleons as pets. Suddenly I had the ideal solution to the numerous flies which constantly flew in and out of our open windows. The bedroom window security bars might have kept an honest man out, but never a human intent on entering, and likewise were no deterrent to flies.

I named the chameleon Jean Sibelius and he flourished in his new habitat, earning my respect as Flycatcher First Class. With his wandering eyes you were constantly under observation and you'd wonder if he hadn't a grin on his face – 'what,' I'd ask, 'is it you find so amusing?'!

Geoff was convinced I was mad and admitted to being repulsed by the creatures he said smelt of lizard, steadfastly refusing to have anything to do with Sibelius. Growing up with pet chameleons, I'd remained fascinated by them. Newly hatched they were particularly enchanting. How extraordinary was evolution to produce an animal with independently roving eyes, an ability to change colour, a fierce grip enabling them to hang from just one limb assisted by a tail used as a fifth limb. And finally, equipped with a super accurate extendable tongue, fatal to flies. There was nothing wrong with admiring a chameleon, or sharing a room with one.

Despite the offer as a fly deterrent, Geoff adamantly refused to have Sibelius anywhere near him.

8

COSTELLO GETS HIS AK47, PHILLIPS RECEIVES A ROLEX

Still no radios. Royal Jasmine. Mutiny at Arzat and first indication of racial tensions. Grenades. Squadron moves to Dhofar. Costello gets his Kalashnikov. Looting from the dead. Geoff on patrol. Phillips gets a Rolex. Bagpipes. My sergeant oversleeps.

WE USE FLAGS

7-21 Aug – Still operating without radios. Quite successful using flags to indicate left/right manoeuvres. Red/port – green/starboard. Nautical – but works.

More Taqah convoys as village needs constant resupply. Returning today found suspect mine. No time to stop – marked with red flag. Returned later by Land Rover, four DG and one Ferret, Costello and Ali Hamdan. Discovered site of mine was empty – old, probably lifted and re-laid elsewhere. Visible signs past explosions, craters and pieces of destroyed vehicles. Makes you tread carefully.

3 letters from home – Father in Turkey to coordinate British assistance to Red Crescent post-earthquakes, Mum and Odeyne. For a 13 yr old, O's handwriting now much more mature . . . nice surprise. Once read, realised perhaps should have read on consecutive days.

We continued using flags to indicate manoeuvres when motoring across country, absurd on reflection, but like everyone else we'd had to improvise to get by.

My father was leading a mission to Turkey where the British Red Cross was assisting the Turkish Red Crescent after earthquakes destroyed 90% of Bingol city. As happens in soldiers' families, my sisters were still teenagers, the youngest still at school whilst I was abroad on active service. Neither knew my circumstances, I was simply in Arabia. Before departure for the Middle East, I'd dug out the family's atlas and pointed out Oman, bottom right of the Arabian Peninsula, 4,500 miles (7250km) from Britain, but that was it. They certainly knew nothing of the war. The deception, besides the Official Secrets Act, was common to any soldier seeking to avoid unnecessary concern amongst immediate family.

How reassuring to receive news from home seen through uncomplicated perspectives of school life and nursing college, and their undented perceptions of life amongst sand dunes and date palms, camels, hot sun and blue skies. The references to school discipline made me smile, seemingly at odds with Odeyne's 13-year-old rebellious attitude pitted constantly against a headmistress's controlling qualities. My sympathies lay with Sister Marina, the convent's elegant Mother Superior. Like many of her generation, she'd lost her fiancé in the Somme's mud, leading a platoon of the 60th Rifles. In response, she'd become a nun.

And 55 years later as head of a convent school I suspect there was little she didn't know about hormonal teenage girls, and she had a close rapport with my mother having two daughters at the school and whose father too had served with the KRRC at the Somme. Little did Odeyne realise, the tales of school life frustrations were a perfect juxtaposition between innocence and reality.

The following day Arzat had lost a man killed and a number of others hideously wounded to an anti-personnel mine.

Every letter was re-read.

> *8th Aug – At last! Issued with a Racal TRA 906 Squadcal radio with handset.* ***But only one****! Comms with fitted antenna I've strapped to back of turret as won't fit inside, so unable to close down without cutting cable. One bullet will knock it out, but I have communication. Other three cars still work to my flags. What a way to run a war! Long range s/a contact as we departed Taqah – ineffective. No cas.*

We had our first meaningful contact on 8th August. It was long range small arms as we left Taqah. Moving forward into firing positions we engaged with Brownings, and the engagement ceased after about ten minutes. The thin-skinned convoy of Bedfords sped past safely and we suffered no casualties. Baptised, we'd

View back towards Salalah as we return to Arzat, along a graded road cleared of mines that morning.

had our first contact, now we needed a second to satisfy CSAF we might be 'of any use' to him.

10th Aug – Returning from Taqah, Nasir Hamid stalled at bottom of Wadi Arzat. Engine wouldn't restart. We'd already two convoy Bedfords in tow, when the Dodge truck carrying 81mm mortar and crew broke down requiring a tow as well. Fitter struck starter with hammer, it worked and we were off out of danger. (Solenoid jammed.) Had Costello been there he'd have got Ferret started straight away – claims it's a fairly common problem. Live and learn. His Ferret off-road – choke stuck on . . . .

Practised diamond formation, as best way crossing open country fast. Found out soldier killed at Taqah had been blown in half . . . not very nice.

13 Aug – Jumea, no patrols today! Visited HQ, once roads cleared. Everyone in weekend mood. Hilal Ali had picked a dozen or so scented flowers of jasmine from behind Mess and placed them on Land Rover's empty front parcel shelf. Crushed flowers release heavy perfumed scent.

Dropped Nasir Hamid off with askars at Salalah perimeter wire. Boys back on DG transport later. Met DR's Col. Nigel who's down here to visit Arzat.

Saw Bert Kenyon, still no front mounting bolts. Improvised with steel rods he'd had made. Returning, met Nasir at perimeter encampment. Invited to join his uncle and cousins for coffee. Sat next to his uncle, a local dignitary, courteous, graciously mannered, welcoming. Watched as coffee beans first roasted over small charcoal fire, then mashed in homemade, battered steel mortar using a makeshift steel pestle. Coffee jet black, strong and bitter, and flavoured with cardamom, delicious.

Dismissing my attempts to uphold traditional three finjans, we drank coffees twice over and feasted on chopped pineapple chunks and dates, welcome counter to the black coffee. Eventually after excuses to leave accepted, I rose and bending for my shoes nearly fell over with pins and needles after sitting crossed legged too long. What a novice! Hopefully disguised the fact ... Returning, gave Nasir driving lesson. He'd not driven Land Rovers.

The dates would have been imported from northern Oman, where there is sufficient heat for them to fruit successfully. At the time Dhofar's main crop was coconut, although pawpaw (papaya) was also grown. The diversity of crops and fruit grown on the Salalah plains today is quite extraordinary. An interesting point I was to learn from a one-time guide, Mohammad Salaam of the Mahri tribe, was that whereas coffee had long been the preferred beverage of the Omani and Salalah peoples, traditionally tea was the hot drink of the Dhofar Jebalis living in the mountains. Today both are consumed in equal measures.

"Alyasimayn Almalakiu" (Royal Jasmine) Jasminum Grandiflorum grew freely in the Mess gardens of Salalah, but also the steep sided wooded wadis of the jebel enclosing Salalah plains.

COSTELLO GETS HIS AK47, PHILLIPS RECEIVES A ROLEX

14 Aug – SMG range practice – managed lowest score in troop!! There's a lesson! Painted suitably ugly looking faces on targets made from hardboard donated by Harry – much appreciated by the boys. They're good shots.

Need for vigilance around our range, clearing for mines each time we use it. Today, added more dannert wire – but still needs clearing. Finding some 9mm rounds are duds – misfires – old ammo?

16 Aug – Brilliant news – secured loan x3 radios from Harry. Took Abdullah Ali as driver on Taqah run today – he's easily the best. Hilal Ali still timid, so stalls.

Geoff out on fighting patrol tonight, towards Ayn Arzat. My troop on standby. All RTB, nil contact.

20 Aug – Jumea
Breakfasted with Sandy as guest of MR. They do eat well!
Fruit salad – mangoes, papaya and bananas, followed by porridge, then fishcakes, Full English, toast and coffees! We're poor cousins living at Arzat.

21 Aug – Chris Phillips with hangover changed his mind saying he couldn't think straight this morning! Refused loan of promised radios just as I was signing for them with Harry. UNBELIEVABLE. Man has exaggerated sense of self-worth. Told him to keep his f.... radios and took Troop to HQ. Found John Speakes and David Venn both extremely helpful and loaned 3 more Squadcals – at last all cars have radios – strapped to backs of cars.

Patrolled out to Raysut and back north of Alpha H/Hog.
Drive back not a success – whatever I tell him, Hilal Ali won't keep revs up. Stalled twice. Strapping handset to bulkhead, we swapped seats, told him to watch and learn and we set off again. Ferrets are fun to drive. For all his talk, Hilal lacks confidence.
Made peace with Phillips. Searching for escaped Sibelius discovered Tabakh (cook) growing 3 tomato plants in kitchen's open drain. <u>Two fine tomatoes</u>! Found Sibelius, Mess garden.

Diary entry says it all. Exasperated at Phillips' behaviour, I drove out to UAG where John Speakes, who ran Dhofar HQ's signals troop, and David Venn of JR, between them loaned me three radios ending a frustrating three weeks relying on semaphore signals. All four cars now had radios, albeit strapped to outsides of turrets and vulnerable. I was happy.

Not for the first time Sibelius vanished. Searching behind the Officers' Mess kitchen I found cook had grown three fine tomato plants from fresh tomato seeds, supporting two ripening tomatoes. Beaming with pride, cook forbid me touch the fruits destined for our table. Growing in the greasy fat-stained, fly infested open drain, I did wonder what the fruit might taste like; however, I don't recall any ill effects. I discovered Sibelius eyeing me from a Mess garden acacia tree. Climbing to catch him wasn't a problem; enticing him off his perch was. Eventually I got him onto a twig then onto my shirt back and together we descended safely. Promptly returned to my room and his fly hunting duties – I wondered whether he'd learnt his lesson as he never escaped again.

23 Aug – Sent out by Col Fergus to patrol east of Wadi Adonib again. Thought we had a contact. About to engage four men with rifles running away. Skidded to stop with Faraz to my right. Grabbing binos had a look – could make out three had FN rifles – firqat? Hearing us, two turned waving shemaghs and holding rifles in air. With Costello and Wathik behind, moved with Rajaz towards the men – FAN (Firqat Al Nasr) chasing suspects who turned out to be two women and a boy! Greetings exchanged – Don't think they realised how close a call that'd been. We've orders to seek and take out likely adoo mine layers known to be in the area. Good for adrenaline? Bloody hell!

29 Aug – used Wathik's car – younger model. Turret swings around easier, and Nasr Mohamed, good driver. Might change cars and crews around. Discovered Taylor Woodrow with grader levelling road towards Arzat. OK – makes for temporary smoother road, but leaves ground soft and easier for mine laying. Col Mike (Commander Dhofar) furious when he heard my radio message to Red Zero (MR HQ) – he'd explicitly told TW to cease road works.

Saw group men through mist on plains, advancing to 600 metres, had pulled cocking lever on Browning as we moved into firing positions when one removed his shemagh and threw it in the air. FAN – outside their area again. Moved up to have word, greetings all round. Difficult to make them understand they'd be better remaining in their designated zones.

Learned an interesting point today: The accepted signal indicating friendly intentions is to grab a handful of dust and throw it into the air – except during the khareef when the soil's damp, they use shemaghs instead. Live and learn.

31 Aug – Suddenly realise I'm a day away from birthday. 24 – God, I am getting OLD!
Taqah convoy with DG yesterday – have changed cars and crew. Much happier. Wathik content with the move. Not sure about him.

Today the inevitable – car radio gave up the ghost. Swapped cars with Rajaz who then relied on my hand signals as we moved off. Convoy: building materials – went well.

Geoff lost it with his DG boys, swearing at them in English . . . caught his eye, shouted my boys understood some of his comments, at which he calmed down. He didn't speak to me again. Difficult. He'd had row with Chris that morning for taking two platoons leaving camp 'vulnerable'. All are stressed. It's not BAOR soldiering.

PM. Geoff flew to Sudh – three days – arranging DG withdrawal. Sudh has no khareef, but has foul water.

4 Sept – Costello and I on Raysut road clearance again this morning, followed by a plains patrol. After July Commando Carrier incident, orders we maintain 2,000 metres distance from tree line. In dense mist today, found we were 1,000 metres ahead of Hedgehog Foxtrot position. Too bloody close to jebel. Khareef mist disorientates – like driving in fog, hard to judge distances. Called Sandy, shouted messages as we passed H.H. Foxtrot – don't envy their living conditions. Poor chap's got toothache, off to Bayt al Falaj for treatment. Beats Hedgehog life.

Sandy's men built Foxtrot, the sixth Hedgehog. Raysut was the site of the Squadron's first contact where six months earlier Mike Offord won his Commendation Medal for bravery. On this occasion all was quiet.

MUTINY AT ARZAT

FCO progress report 1971	*Restricted*

Dhofar Gendarmerie . . . the recruitment of an additional 450 Baluch askars will further strengthen the defences of the Salalah plain and enable the SAF Battalion based on Um al Ghawaraf to be redeployed against the main enemy threat on the jebel.

5th Sept – Christopher is having trouble with DG after news new draft of Baluchi soldiers caused trouble in the north. Soldiers outside the Mess shouting . . . 'la Baluch hina, kifaaya!' (no Baluch here, we've enough)

Talk of mutiny? Apocryphal story Baluchi officers were murdered at this very camp, their throats slit. Not best bedtime story! DG soldiers threatening to take matters into their own hands over Baluch question.

Geoff back.

6th Sept – Taqah convoy. Came under s/a and mortar attack, Firqat piquet west of Taqah also attacked. We again drew adoo fire as convoy rushed through without casualties.

Returning from escorting a convoy into and out of Taqah that had involved a long-range small arms and mortar contact without taking casualties, we arrived back to find Arzat in a state of hysteria. Men on foot rushing about, others in trucks tearing around the camp at breakneck speed. Following the morning attack at Taqah, we were still on edge. What the hell was going on at Arzat?

Chris Phillips had left early to brief Dhofar HQ, taking Geoff in two Land Rovers with a Baluch section as escort. Only afterwards I learned our Camp Commandant had felt it necessary to travel in person to warn Brigade HQ of the worsening relations between his Khadim and Baluchi troops, against risking a telegraph message being intercepted, complicating an already deteriorating situation.

Parking up as normal we unloaded our gear and began stripping dust-coated, post contact Brownings from scout cars for cleaning. At that instant, shots were fired from behind an accommodation block as a Bedford emerged with excited DG soldiers firing wildly skywards, shouting and waving FN rifles above their heads. They all seemed to be Khadims. I had no idea what the commotion was about – was it some sort of Eid festival? Realising perhaps the behaviour was a little more irrational than celebratory, I glanced towards Costello for any reaction to see him rapidly reassembling his partly stripped Kalashnikov. Then I noticed my soldiers, two Dhofari Khadim and four Omani Arabs, had edged forwards so now they sat in a circle, facing outwards as they hastily reassembled and loaded machine guns. We waited. Twenty taut minutes passed as bedlam continued. Round and round drove the Bedford trucks, men chanting and firing into the air.

Then as it had begun, abruptly it ended, seemingly without explanation. But there was. Unnoticed by us, Chris and Geoff had returned with their combined armed escorts. An uneasy truce had been called and we'd only learn why later.

I looked at the men around me, encouraged by their response. They'd acted not on command, but out of instinct. I'd thought we had yet to achieve that special bond I hoped to attain – when intuitively a group acts as one to danger. Maybe it was already here?

Taking no chances, I instructed my best three, Costello, Abdul Faraz and Abdullah Ali to keep their weapons loaded, on guard, as I joined the rest cleaning Brownings. Once completed, weapons were immediately re-loaded. SMGs next, ensuring we weren't without loaded weapons. Costello growled. 'DG are ferking crazy, sir . . . what'd you think that was all about?' he asked as he stripped his prized Kalashnikov. 'I've not a bloody clue,' I replied truthfully, 'we'll just keep our wits about us . . . I'll find out from Major Phillips.'

My chance came at lunch that day. Harry had demanded to know what it was all about. He'd too been away in Salalah, arranging delivery of fresh provisions that morning and only learned of the episode on his return from a worried Baluchi SQMS. Chris had left the camp in the charge of his Baluchi officers. Given what was happening elsewhere, perhaps that was ill-advised.

Chris elaborated on an incident within the last few days when an Oman garrison in the north had had to act rapidly to defuse a potentially disastrous flashpoint arising from growing animosity between factions of Arab and Baluchi soldiers. Considered potentially so serious, the imminent arrival of DG bound Balochistan reinforcements had now been cancelled. Despite shortages of manpower, DG would no longer take Baluchi soldiers. The Baluchi reinforcements would instead be stationed separately at Raysut west of Salalah. Honour satisfied, the matter had been settled, rumblings of mutiny diffused.

That evening with routine inspections of camp guards completed, we relaxed on the Mess verandah, the atmosphere light-hearted for a change. Inevitably discussion continued around the Dhofari Khadim v Baluchi tensions within DG. We hoped the crisis had passed, yet menacingly the word 'Mutiny' haunted conversation.

What of Arzat's apocryphal story of mutiny when DG slaughtered their Baluchi officers, three on this very verandah? Harry commented, 'We're sitting on the murder scene', evoking secrets the polished concrete floor still held. The discussion's downward spiral was broken only by Geoff suggesting we get pissed.

With more beers ordered, I reckoned the atmosphere needed lightening up. With no better idea, I went to my room off the verandah and fetched a Mills 36 from my kit. Carrying the grenade I rejoined the others to see Chris, who'd been sinking ever lower into his chair, jolt bolt upright. 'Just what the fucking hell do you think you're doing?' he demanded.

At HQ, firearms were forbidden inside the Mess. The result, the incongruous sight of rifles left propped against a whitewashed wall outside the Mess bar door.

I never heard anyone lose a weapon from this rule, a procedure which undoubtedly helped avoid accidents. There were more than a few heavy drinkers.

'This is not a firearm, Chris,' I reasoned, 'and given the current situation, I feel I should demonstrate an important point.' As I was speaking and without waiting for an answer, I'd unscrewed and removed the grenade's base plug and four second fuse. I now had the most attentive of audiences. Grinning at Geoff, my fellow conspirator, I rolled the grenade in an uneven bouncing arc across the polished floor to bump up against his shoe, 2m away. 'Now that's the noise we need to remember – brrrrr brrrrr *clunk* brrrrr brrrrr *clunk* . . . the safety lever's still there, someone's forgotten to pull the pin out! A continuous brrrr brrrr brrrr brrrr brrrr – and it's '*Ohhh SHIT!*'

Simultaneously, Geoff and Harry burst out laughing at what I judged demonstrated a seriously overlooked lesson in surviving a grenade attack. And I hoped, eased tensions.

Regrettably, the 3rd Carabinier's sense of humour failed, erupting into an attack on my colonial background, upbringing, Kenyan schooling, regiment and lastly Sibelius, 'that fucking chameleon'. In BAOR, thunderflashes and hose pipes had earned me extra duties; here an unarmed grenade equalled monumental bollocking. The incident, duly reported to Tim, my OC in northern Oman, was fortunately overlooked.

GRENADES

The Mills 36 grenade with its ferocious energy comes in the seductive shape of the innocent pineapple. Grooved cast iron casing was designed for easier grip as opposed to shattering along segmented lines. At its core, a spring-loaded striker is held in tension by a safety lever, secured by a safety split pin. Weighing 765g and designed for a defensive role, thrown to wound by fragmentation. The alternative offensive grenades don't fragment but rely on lethal short-range blast to wound or stun, reducing danger to the thrower as grenade fragments travel greater distances than blast material. Whilst a competent thrower might achieve 15m with reasonable accuracy, an exploding Mills 36 grenade flings lethal fragments 90m across hard open ground. Inevitably these defensive grenades were used offensively. A weapon of last resort. I kept a box of 12 which I primed before each patrol, issuing two to each car commander.

Mills 36s came encased in hardened preservative grease needing focused attention when scraping clean using a sharp knife. I taught my men to strip, clean, prime and throw these weapons. They make a loud bang and it's not a time for sweaty hands. Instructing grenade drills must measure as one of a young officer's least favourite duties.

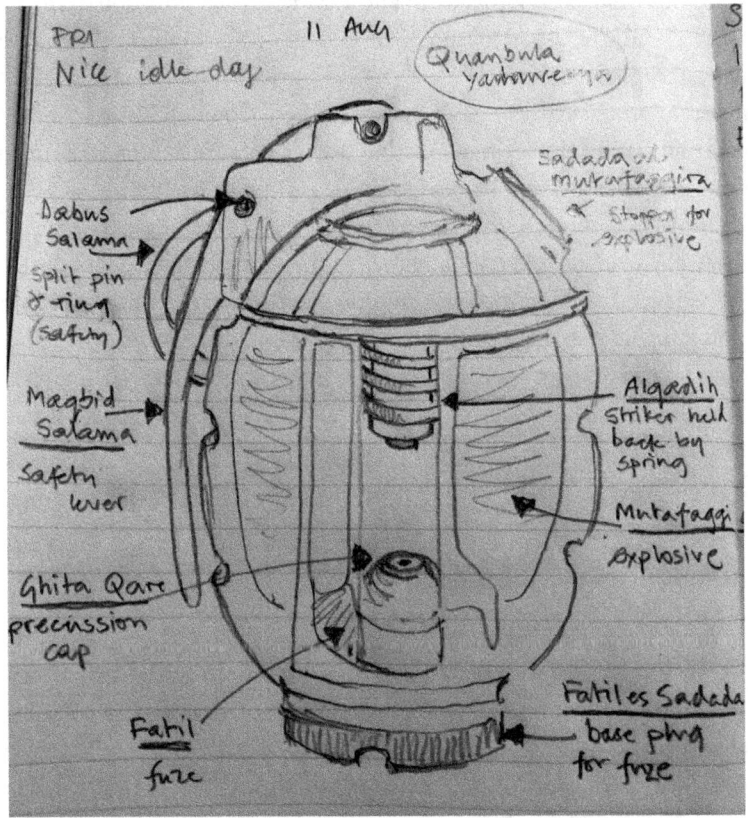

My cutaway sketch copied from an army manual, used to inform my troop the workings of a Mills 36 hand grenade.

7th, 8th Sept – Patrolling Bravo and Charlie sectors. At w. Jardum we were called back to HH Bravo under s.a attack – Thimrin. Saw nothing – firing ceased when we arrived.

THE SQUADRON MOVES TO DHOFAR

On 10th September the Squadron moved to Midway. Men and their kit were flown down from Bayt al Falaj by Caribou to Salalah, and on up to Midway by Skyvan.

Vehicles followed overland on a 900km journey taking three days. Six Saladins carried on monster Kenworth low loaders each capable of carrying up to 35 tons, and two Ferrets on Bedford 3-tonners departed Bid Bid leading the convoy. Passing desert villages of Sumail, Iski and Adam, they circumvented the Wahiba Sands, then south to desert outposts of Hayma, Mugshin and Dawqah before eventually arriving at Midway.

The already considerable convoy was joined along the way by additional Bedford trucks and vehicles transporting urgently needed supplies of ordnance, munitions, rations, fuel and stores required in Dhofar. Eventually more than 50 vehicles lumbered south across desert to Northern Dhofar, at times stretching 40km between lead vehicle and tailender as drivers sought to avoid dust kicked up by vehicles in front. Numerous punctures and trucks getting stuck axle deep in the soft going ensured progress was painfully slow. Three days of dust, heat and breakdowns, every convoy commander's logistical nightmare.

Today, travelling in an air-conditioned vehicle along tarmacadam roads, the same route can be covered in eight hours.

HOW COSTELLO ACQUIRED HIS AK47

Shortly after the Raysut ambush in June, Tim had taken the Commandos and Ferrets patrolling east of Arzat towards Ayn Arzat. Approaching a dry, steep sided wadi, they were ambushed. Staccato small arms fire from up the wadi struck the ground around Costello's car. Lou in his Ferret Scout Car immediately returned fire as the other cars joined in.

There appeared to be just two men firing from behind rocks when one made a dash for better cover. Lou saw him and opened fire again, bursts of .30 Browning following the leaping man heading towards the safety of the ridge. Suddenly on target, the man was flung to one side where he remained, motionless. Costello kept firing at the now lifeless body until it tumbled down the slope coming to rest twenty metres in front of his Ferret. Attached to the body by a sling was an AK47.

As suddenly as the ambush was sprung, the firing ceased. The second adoo had disappeared. Waiting for any signs of movement, everyone held their breath. Perhaps eight to ten minutes passed before over the radio came Lou's voice 'I'm getting myself a Kalashnikov!' Driving forward to the prone body, he was out of his turret in a flash, snatching the weapon before leaping back inside his car. It had taken seconds, executed in one single fluid movement. Bloody idiot. Had there been watching adoo, Lou wouldn't have made it halfway out of the turret.

Tim gave the order to withdraw, and the lead Ferrets swung round to cover the Commandos, which soon followed suit. Withdrawal was achieved without further contact. It was assumed the adoo pair had chosen to try their luck. A suicidal decision taking on armoured cars given the imbalance in fire power. Possibly the casualty had been the senior man and the reason the contact ended so abruptly.

It was a salutary reflection that many ACS soldiers were probably no older than their mid-teens. The adoo were equally young. In a country lacking birth certificates, ages were a matter for conjecture and I doubt much inquiry was made into each new recruit's date of birth. Nationally, there was a push to recruit sufficient to meet the challenges of the casualty rate. Generally speaking, so long as the man was tall enough and eager, he was accepted for training. Apart from the few who had transferred from other fighting units, none serving in the ACS had experienced active service. Recruited from villages and towns, most were naturally adept on the firing range, hitting bullseyes with ease, but like any newly recruited, experiencing an enemy firing directly at you was an entirely different matter.

The Ferret crews the day Costello snatched his AK47 were subsequently promoted to Saladins. None of my Ferret troop had had battle experience except for the Irishman. That August a long-range contact at Taqah had been our baptism, an undramatic standoff machine gun attack making the air whistle and crack. We four Ferrets had moved forward drawing the adoo fire, returning fire with our Brownings, as the convoy sped through the defile at Khawr Sawli. Initiation for Plains Troop was complete – and their officer, six years older than the youngest man at barely 17, was one of them. First titled Light Troop, then Plains Troop, that day MR's Col Fergus decided he'd call us Sabre Troop. Our call signs remained unchanged, Tango 6I, Alpha, Bravo and Charlie.

LOOTING FROM THE DEAD

... to the victor – the spoils

The roots to the English word "loot" stem from the days of the British Raj, where in Hindustani "lut" referred to the spoils of war.

In Dhofar it was common practice for the dead of each side to be robbed of military kit. Every weapon and bandolier of ammunition captured was a loss to the opponent's arsenal and such ordnance could be re-used against the enemy. Weapons have long been taken from dead opponents as trophies, and equally to be used again. There was the additional matter of gained esteem for the owner of looted weaponry, an inescapable fact of war that has existed since man first took up arms against fellow man. Identification discs, books and maps or manuscripts were taken for intelligence. Personal items looted as souvenirs. To the victor the spoils.

Whilst I accepted the capture of weaponry was important to the individual making the capture, I felt less comfortable with the theft of personal items taken from the dead. Few as these items were, given the spartan levels of equipment the adoo carried into battle, there was often intelligence to be gained from gathering the dead's effects. However, an AK47 was a prized trophy, carried by a number of SAF's officers and soldiers, and also BATT. The latest to join that elite group had included one Sgt. Lou Costello.

Early on following Mike Campbell's lonely death, when venturing out on patrols never fully knowing the outcome, I would resolutely remove both my watch and signet ring, 21st birthday gifts I'd no wish ending up adorning some adoo fighter. This lasted a couple of weeks as gradually such negativity was lost, amounting to a recklessness soldiers adopt unerringly through surviving.

When one of my men later presented me with a captured, part-bloodstained bandolier together with a wicked looking knife sheathed in handmade camel

LCpl Rasul Bux cleaning a .30 Browning on return from patrol. An army issue prayer mat is used on which cleaned items are placed keeping them dust free before reassembly.

leather, I took it as a point of honour, accepting the gesture in the manner it was intended. The occasion had followed a contact, one where we had narrowly escaped with our lives. The man who gifted me the items had been a good soldier and friend, LCpl Rasul Bux, a tough, honest and resilient Baluchi from the mountainous Shashan region of Baluchestan. A quiet man from a region with a reputation for toughness, loyalty and tenacity to hold ground; rated by their British East India Company officers as only equalled by Gurkhas. Famous regiments such as the Duke of Connaught's Own Baluchis had won VCs. Rasul Bux came to Oman to earn money regularly sent home to family. It was a good wage relative to people's incomes in Baluchestan. Uniquely popular with Arab and Baluchi alike, it was a sad day when RB was killed in action, June 1972. Such a waste.

The belt and knife were to remain with me until I prepared to depart at the end of my loan service. I gave the trophies to another soldier, LCpl Abdullah Ali Al Shibili, a man who would later rise to be commissioned in the expanding Sultan's Armoured Regiment. The Squadron's best gunner, a remarkable man, utterly faithful and of unswerving courage, who'd served steadfastly alongside me for two years.

10 Sept – First op. with infantry. Spent night at Adonib, 1 Coy JR – Paul (Tiger) Wright, Bob Aplin, Mike Austin. Great bunch, looked after us very well. Slept remarkably badly and relieved when woken 0430 with mug of tea and chapati. Left camp 0500 to RV with Tiger's advance half coy. group, mouth of wadi Jardum. They'd left 0300. Swept westwards from this point to Nahr Sayqah. Engaged adoo OP at mouth of wadi. Saw no enemy but Tiger asked we put down fire on likely escape routes. JR blasted area with mortars. I was interested to note tracer burns out at 1,000m. Stoppage jammed gun. Damp belt? Cleared OK. Rough going all day – all whacked tonight. Tiger praised the Brownings, saying it boosted men's confidence.

Khalfan and Rajab called round to my room to welcome me back saying all troop flat out on beds asleep! God what a boost to be amongst proper soldiers – instead isolated at Arzat – can't wait to leave. Chris Phillips apparently unpopular everywhere – arrogant and tactless. One thing about this op. don't want to see another rock wadi again – we're cut and bruised!!

Our first operation working closely with infantry was with 1 Company JR, who had recently arrived in Dhofar after nine months in the north recruiting and training. They were JR's advance company leading to a full deployment of the regiment on roulement in October.

Leaving before dawn to RV west of Wadi Jardum, it ended up as a Browning 'fire power' demonstration on a known adoo OP (observation post). Afterwards we patrolled back towards Adonib. JR were on foot, so it was slow work. A full day and we returned to Arzat at last light, whacked.

GEOFF ON FERRET PATROL

Next day, Geoff asked to accompany me on patrol and I agreed. Standing Lou down for the afternoon, Geoff took his car.

At Commander Dhofar's O Group, irreverently referred to as morning prayers, I'd received orders to photograph the entire length of the enemy held escarpment enclosing Salalah plain – between the western reaches at Adonib which JR held, east towards Wadi Umran, past the Hedgehogs onto Arzat where we were stationed, and out to Taqah. The distance was some 60km skirting the foothills of Jebel Al Qara, the mountain range enclosing Salalah plain. We began in the east and worked our way slowly westwards, under strict orders to take our time and avoid at all costs a repeat of the 12 July fiasco which killed Mike. Easy targets in our small Ferrets, this was one order I fully intended to comply with.

Not having travelled in a scout car before, Geoff wanted "to see how the cavalry skived footslogging . . ." I'd show him. We left at 1300 with the camp quiet, men stood down before parading again at 1630 and stand-to at last light 90 minutes later. Afternoon patrols were always hot.

We motored in diamond formation, my car on point, Geoff to my left back keeping approximate station, with Abdul Raja Faraz to my right back, and finally Abdul Wathik bringing up the rear. This had become our favoured formation crossing the exposed plain and ensured vehicle commanders remained tactically spread out. Also, each car commander had a clear line of sight to me, and by loosely maintaining formation, we each knew roughly where the other cars were at any one time.

We did not need to present the watching adoo with an easy kill by bunching together – as often occurred with escorted convoys when trucks closed up to the vehicle in front. No matter how many times we tried to spread trucks apart, they'd eventually end up nose to tail, fearful of being ambushed alone. A characteristic throughout the animal kingdom, of which man is part.

We maintained our attacking formation, being unable to move with stealth given the noise of our engines but also the giveaway clouds of powder dust disturbed by our wheels. Nature, blameless casualty of war, suffered unprotestingly as vehicles ploughed their way ruining forever the virgin sunburned desert crust of baked sand and stone. Formed over millennia and able to withstand the trodden foot of man, camel and goat, the surfaces were no match for pneumatic tyres. And in places, what resulted became an increasing series of vehicle tracks, filled with super-fine dust, more akin to an expensive talcum powder, but devoid of sensuous scent.

Desert sands of the Middle East hold an unexpectedly large fungal biodiversity, adapted for survival in the extreme and environmentally challenging conditions. Over thousands of years, photosynthetic microfungi have adapted to the intense light to play a vital role in colonisation of bare sand, developing hard crusts on which, should it rain, mosses will grow. Fungal crusts in Dhofar appear burned black, remaining dormant for long periods until disturbed, when they can unleash toxic spores causing serious illnesses. Seen clearly from aircraft at 30,000ft and lasting beyond human lifespans, deserts scarred by vehicle traffic are probably visible from outer space.

That afternoon we drove out to Wadi Sahalnawt, which drops 3,000ft from Jebel Al Qara north of our camp at Arzat. We'd patrolled here before, searching caves carved out of 9m high wadi walls offering man and beast shelter from the heat of the day, but equally enemy mine layers hiding from SAF ground and air patrols. Cut deep into the limestone mountain, the wadi cuts across Salalah plain towards the sea.

On this occasion we drew a blank. But I had photographs to complete and stopping at intervals below the intimidating tree lined slopes of rising jebel, I photographed the panoramic sweep of escarpment rising above us. Signalling the three cars covering me I was calling it a day, we turned for home. No one had stalled, struck any of the numerous rocks or anthill obstacles, radios had worked and cars all maintained sensible distances. Back at camp it was one happy troop leader who climbed out of his car on parking up.

With a groan and emerging from his cramped commander's seat, Geoff stretched his six-foot-three frame, shaking his head in dismay, exclaiming he'd not be transferring from the infantry. Driving his father's tractors had been noisy enough, 'but your screaming Ferret engines are beyond belief!'. Farmer Geoff had joined the Duke of Edinburgh's Royal Regiment, where by sheer coincidence, he was quick to assure me, the regimental quick march was "The Farmer's Boy". Naturally this became a point he was not allowed to forget. Tragically, within a month Geoff was killed.

13 Sept – 0930 – 1500 Taqah convoy – picqueted Khawr Sawli 3hrs whilst DG with BATT rolled fixed wing airfield west of town. Returned by northern route. NTR.

We were in Taqah giving cover whilst engineers and DG soldiers under BATT supervision using a mechanical road roller flattened the earth airstrip cut up by fixed wing aircraft. It had become a maintenance task repeated on a regular basis.

14 Sept – Eastern sector – Umran, saw nothing. Interesting to note no water now flowing out of Umran. Reported 200 camels and 18 Bedouin tents – grid 013948.

BAGPIPES AND CHANTERS

Following an early patrol that'd gone well, I'd debriefed the troop and planned an hour's small arms practice on our range constructed beyond the camp's perimeter. Whilst first cleaning our Brownings, the cheerful banter was suddenly interrupted by the unmistakable sound of chanters being practised, badly.

'D'yer hear that?' asked an incredulous Lou Costello. Wide eyed he turned, asking, 'You don't mind, sir, me leaving you cleaning weapons? I have to sort this out!' It was said more in statement than question.

'OK,' I replied, adding, 'only don't upset anyone, they're boys – and they're the Sultan's pipers!' wondering what on earth he was hoping to "sort out". The screeching noise stopped abruptly, followed by a moment's silence before softly came the sound of a single chanter, in tune, producing a melody! Lou Costello played the pipes! Was there no limit to the man's talents?

16 Sept – 0600-1100 patrolled western sector – crossed Ayn Jarsis at grid AD 892919. Mike's commando carrier clearly visible at Jardum, ZU 165861?

17 Sept – Jumea – Taqah convoy – back midday. Northern route. No incidents. Sitting having a beer before lunch, you had to be blind not to notice our esteemed Camp Commandant was wearing a rather smart, shiny new steel watch.

BULLSHIT BAFFLES BRAINS – JUST REWARDS FOR THE DESERVING FEW

Jumea, the Arabian weekend (Friday) and ostensibly our day off, we'd taken a small convoy into Taqah early and, arriving back, I joined the others relaxing on the Mess verandah.

Chris was sporting a gleaming new watch. It was no ordinary watch. As yet unscratched, the Rolex's highly polished watch glass and steel bracelet glinted in bright sunlight shining through onto the west-facing verandah. I glanced at Geoff, then Harry. Both had noticed the conspicuous display of new acquisition. Unable to contain himself, Geoff enquired, 'New watch, Chris?' There followed a short pause before with an intake of breath to ensure maximum effect, Chris replied, 'Well yes actually, just arrived – gift from the Sultan'.

Holding out his arm, we looked incredulously from shiny watch to owner's face for explanation. Who gets a watch from the Sultan? Chris revelled in the moment. It was pretty clear the three of us were at a loss to recall any specific action or deed warranting such approval from His Majesty. What on earth had Chris done to garner such praise?

Anyway, who'd heard of anyone gifted watches? In the slightly awkward silence that followed I proffered 'Follow that, Geoff' to receive a wide grin and 'V' sign in return. Savouring the moment, Chris continued: 'The Sultan gave me this watch following DG Boy's Pipe Band's first parade,' adding boastfully, 'no doubt there'll be more rewards as my band progresses!' There was no polite answer to that.

A couple of days later a message was received from Victor Seely at SAF HQ. He who two months earlier had arranged an unforgettable afternoon's ride for me on one of the Sultan's string of horses in northern Oman. Victor's overseeing of building the stable block, training men as grooms and stable lads at the Sultan's Royal Stables had gained him a special award from an appreciative Sultan. For Victor the reward for this noble role, one gold Rolex. Hearing of Christopher's, Victor had immediately signalled, which to his credit Chris showed us:

To Sunray DG

"Congratulations steel Rolex.
For services to His Majesty's nags, received gold Rolex.
Only proves horseshit beats bullshit!"

Staff Capt 'A' Works

AYN UMRAN

18 Sept – Patrol to Ayn Umran
Slept badly. 0500 start. Long day. Drove to w. Umran, set up a cauldron and searched Ayn Umran. No sign adoo activity. Beautiful wadi. Later photograph patrol with Geoff in Land Rovers – W. Arzat to Sahalnawt

to Nahiz – returned 1700 to Bedu camp with medical aid. Strikemaster crashed between Hedgehogs and airfield. Pilot escaped, badly injured.

I'd slept fitfully, uneasy with the mission we'd been allocated. At morning prayers two days earlier at UAG, we'd been tasked with patrolling in Ferrets out to Wadi Umran, northwest of Taqah.

I planned to leave before daybreak. My orders were to approach Wadi Umran, a well-known adoo area (Tony Jeapes in his book SAS Secret War quotes "the Jebel Aram had always been a favourite adoo area and it was easy to see why"). Our mission was to 'search for traces of activity in the area, such as tracks, extinguished fires, discarded cigarette ends, faeces, in fact any signs of recent human occupation.'

With no infantry support, we'd be moving to the tree line, albeit the eastern limits of the plains were probably safer than Salalah's immediate north. But it was a known area the adoo used when shelling Taqah. To my as yet relatively inexperienced thinking, I wondered whether infantry minds at HQ were fully aware the noise 4.26 litre engines made working hard motoring across country. Forget stealth or covert approach to the objective, Ferret engines don't purr, they scream. Even maintaining low engine revs, we'd be audible from miles away, particularly the hills above the plain. And the dust would give us away.

I decided we'd bet on speed. Get in quick, get info and out. It had to be that. Rapid approach and exit. We'd rely on our .30 Brownings and the Daimler's 6 to 16mm armour plating. I was not a happy young man.

0500 hours, ready to leave. Brownings loaded with canvas belted 250 x .30 rounds, engines idling, crews alert for my signal to depart. All ready, except for the absence of one Sgt Costello.

Leaping from my lead car, I strode fuming to the sergeant's mess and Lou's billet. Approaching, I heard snoring before I reached his door. As expected, the door was locked – all slept behind locked doors after a fracking incident when an officer was shot whilst he slept.

I hammered on the door and hissed 'Costello! Wake up!' or something similar... the snoring stopped abruptly. I heard a shuffling noise, the door unlocked, opening to reveal an unshaven, slightly worse for wear Costello. Give him his due, he was fully dressed, booted and armed with Kalashnikov, 'Ferk me! What time issit?' he mumbled inquiringly, to which I replied sharply 'After five!'.

Exasperated, I pushed past him into his room, grabbed a half glass of water, turned and emptied it over his head – adding bluntly 'We leave now – bloody stay awake, you're coming with us'!

I was livid. A bad night with little sleep didn't help. I'd briefed the troop the evening before. Costello knew my concerns about the mission and the need for an early start. His drinking, of which I'd been warned, would have to be sorted out if he was to remain with me. Climbing into my Ferret, I felt a tap on my arm. 'Ferking sorry letting you down, sir, it'll ferking never happen again, that's my promise.' Glaring angrily back at him there was something about his demeanour that struck me, and I replied, 'That's a promise I'll collect'. Giving the order, we moved out. We were ten minutes late. He never once let me down again.

In the event we made good progress out from Arzat, moving across the barren landscape towards Wadi Umran. We approached our objective without hiccup. Keeping the cars well spaced, slowly we edged forwards. Leapfrogging, two cars advanced whilst the other pair covered them forward. Taking up position with Faraz to my left flank, we gazed into the wadi and small oasis that was Ayn Umran. At any other time I'd have longed to explore this Garden of Eden below, but right now I couldn't afford such indulgence, acutely aware we were trespassers in adoo territory.

Costello and Abdul Wathik covered us from 50m to our rear. Nothing moved. It was deathly quiet and still. Scanning the area through Barr and Stroud 30x8 binoculars, I saw no obvious evidence of recent activity around the well. I pulled Costello and Wathik to new positions below and to our front. Once in position, Faraz and I manoeuvred forward, dropping to the wadi floor. It was relatively open, but the dense tree line was less than 200m away. With pounding heart I advanced to the well. Looking about, there was clear evidence of activity leading to and from the well – but this was to be expected, the plains Bedu, their goats and camels frequented the place on a regular basis. I called Costello to say I was dismounting, to receive his response, profane and to do with sex and hades, but he confirmed he had the area covered from his position. I despaired at his mindset – the vocabulary of a sewer; what my Arabs thought I hardly dared think; the antithesis to my Arab soldiers whom I never heard swear, even under extreme duress. And I trusted Costello with my life.

I climbed out of my car conscious I was armed solely with a house clearance weapon, outranged and little less than useless against adoo weapons. We knew FN rifles wouldn't fit into Ferrets, hence we were stuck with Sterlings. To a man we'd all have preferred Kalashnikovs, like Costello's, stolen on the battlefield.

Pulling back, cocking the firing mechanism, safety catch off – the light machine gun was now a spider's thread away from bursting into life should I need to open fire. Equally it'd happen should I accidentally stumble and fall. Keeping Faraz wide, 15m to my left, we moved forward cautiously. I was searching specifically for imprints of issue Chinese canvas and rubber soled boots as worn by the adoo. We found nothing; the footprints were all barefooted.

Satisfied the evidence was none other than the expected passage of human, goat and camel and desiccated faeces of the latter two, I decided it was time to leave. The place, though idyllic, was not somewhere to linger. I climbed into my Ferret with a sense of relief at being back in the ostensibly protective cab of my little armoured car. With Faraz we withdrew through the other two cars covering us, to take up covering positions for their withdrawal.

'Seen enough, no signs of adoo,' I radioed Costello, 'time to go – fan out,' I ordered as we drove away and out from danger. A negative report was still a worthwhile report, I told myself, as I determined to speak my mind with Commander Dhofar. I needed to spell out that without infantry support, armoured cars were not best suited for patrolling into the tree line, the adoo's chosen ground. This had been proven beyond doubt eight weeks earlier. We were back at Arzat Camp before midday.

On a previous op, Muscat Regiment with two troops of SAS leading two firqats, Salahadin and Kalid bin Waalid, had conducted a joint operation to locate the adoo's base plates used firing onto Taqah. They'd run into adoo, suffering casualties and endured a three-day battle before finally withdrawing. As SAF descended the jebel, the adoo confidently stood skylined, firing their classic departing bursts of automatic fire, the telltale "fuck you!". Both sides claimed victory, yet possibly the numerically smaller group of Marxists claimed the greater satisfaction.

That afternoon we patrolled out towards Wadi Arzat to investigate a possible adoo OP following intermittent long range small arms attacks on Arzat. I needed also to continue my photographs of the jebel. Geoff joined us in two Land Rovers. We swept the area from Wadi Arzat west through wadis Sahalnawt on to Nahiz. We drew blank, stopping off at two Bedu camps enquiring after any adoo activity. The Bedu appeared suspicious of the jaysh (army) and that night I wrote in my journal *"they're probably bloody adoo sympathisers anyway"*.

One of our tasks was to check the Bedouin carried no more than .25kg of salt per man, the precious commodity vital to nomadic existence. Invariably this led to tensions. Whilst cordial, meetings were distant with suspicion. Unaccustomed to intrusive searches by soldiers, it was perhaps inevitable we received cold welcomes. Occasionally we'd administer first aid. That day, approached by a man and his son, I cleaned and dried the boy's weeping burns on a small arm before applying a dry white bandage., I was certain the clean bandage's whiteness was probably all the medication required as he proudly displayed his wrapped arm. After another lengthy day in our Ferrets, we arrived back at Arzat in time for stand-to, more than satisfied with ourselves.

Next day we learned a SOAF Strikemaster had crashed the evening before and the pilot badly injured using his ejection seat to escape at 40m, far too low to survive. As the seat separated from beneath him, his parachute opened partially, stalling a rapid descent. Striking the ground hard, he'd broken his back at T7, but lived. Flt Lt Barrie Williams' jet flying days ended then and there. When he was flown home to the UK for treatment, his spinal cord was subsequently discovered to be miraculously still intact. After intensive rehabilitation at Headley Court, Barrie received confirmation he might fly again – no more jets but the equally important SAF lifeline, transport aircraft. One very lucky man, one great pilot, and once fit he returned to Oman.

9

'... IF YOU MEET A DHOFARI'

We dine on barracuda. An attempted assassination. A lesson learned and I lose two NCOs. Racial tensions. The 'Huey Achievement'. SEP incident. Beach convoys and ghost crabs. An absence of body armour.

BARRACUDA LUNCH

After servicing cars all morning, the afternoon was mine to catch up with troop paperwork and letters from home before evening stand-to at 1800hrs. The lunch menu that day was locally caught fish. Taking a mouthful, I asked Harry as Messing Officer, what the fish was. 'Delicious,' came the reply, wide grin wrinkling his eyes, 'Salalah beach market Barracuda, fresh as Billingsgate!'

Instinctively I stopped chewing the lumpy white fish – hadn't Tanganyika's fishermen warned, "samaki sumu" (old barracuda, poison on fishbone). About to mention the African warning, Chris put his fork down, spluttering through a mouthful of fish, 'Barracuda can make you ill'.

Also, I thought, recalling an incident 13 years earlier whilst snorkelling with my twin brother, the fish have an unhealthy interest in humans. Our family were at Leopards Cove, out from Dar-es-Salaam, a remote sandy beach approached through a sisal plantation and coastline scrub, dense enough to dissuade all but the adventurous. A favourite place.

Taking harpoon guns, we'd swum out to investigate fishermen's nets set above coral reefs about two hundred metres out. Stone weights secured finely woven sisal string nets, kept afloat with lumps of rough cork bark. A calm sea made swimming easy. With increasing anticipation at what we might find trapped in the nets, on arrival all we saw were barracuda! The vertical nets held a mass of these writhing silver and black barbed fish. Our approach sent them into a frenzy, razor sharp jaws snapping at us. Thrilling our eleven-year-old imaginations, we watched fascinated as the fish tried to attack, becoming ever more entangled in the nets.

My brother, swimming too close as he dived deep to collect an interesting shell, snagged his snorkel near the bottom of the nets and began struggling to free himself. 'Rip it off!' I shouted into my mouthpiece, only to choke, gulping seawater. As I swam down to him, William's instinct for self-preservation kicked in. Tearing off mask and snorkel, kicking hard with his flippers, he shot upwards to arrive gasping at the surface. I swam towards him. We looked at each other, horrified. Nothing was said. Now it was my turn. Removing my mask and snorkel, I handed them to William treading water. Taking a deep breath I dived down to the entangled net, cutting free the trapped snorkel and mask with my diver's knife, 5 inches (12.7cm) of razor sharp blade with cork float handle. Each carried one strapped around skinny waists. Freeing the snorkel, I swam back to the surface, lungs bursting. Frequently we'd swim holding our breath underwater, managing a minute plus easily, competing to last the longest, as brothers do.

Neptune smiled on us that day, brother William in particular. We swam back to shore. In our absence our parents had started cooking supper, three stones arranged for a stove, tinder dry grasses and driftwood for fuel. Our two younger sisters were playing at the water's edge, Mother was singing "The night they invented champagne . . ." Father, adding more wood to a fierce little fire, looked up as we arrived, 'Ahh . . . there you are, we could do with some more kooni . . .' (Swahili for firewood). We never did own up to the fishing net episode, guilty at having cut the fishermen's nets freeing the snorkel.

And yet our deepest 'dare dive' had been a year earlier, off the side of a luxury yacht our parents would occasionally charter for a weekend. Steel hulled, mahogany decked, Captain's bridge, engine room, a proper funnel, cabins and crew of six, by any standards a very smart boat. As children it impressed us immensely. Moored off Honeymoon Island, an uninhabited wooded islet with pale sandy beach, we were there for the weekend. Now known as Mbudya, it remains uninhabited, one of four small islands part of a marine reserve off Dar-es-Salaam.

Diving off the side we'd swum down to investigate the keel's depth, the ship's draught. After a couple of exploratory attempts wearing goggles, we reckoned if we dived off the boat without goggles we'd have sufficient momentum to swim deep, pass beneath the hull and up the other side. To get around the buoyancy problem full lungs presented, we reckoned you'd need to let your air out as you swam down past the hull. Not for a moment did we consider what appealed to immature adventurous imaginations perhaps lacked a certain degree of cerebral thinking. The idea seemed eminently sensible to our young minds.

As neither could agree who should go first, we decided we'd dive together. A count of three, deep breath and we launched ourselves headfirst over the starboard side of the boat, disappearing beneath the clear turquoise sea. Swimming down past the bulk of the boat's hull, we emptied our lungs, this time not turning back but straight on under the keel. It was then when looking up, the nightmare hit home, the childish nightmare of becoming stuck on the keel of a barnacle encrusted hull. Every pirate story had such a tale, that of being deep underwater, caught by the foot in a giant clam. Urged on by fear, we swam up towards the teasingly out-of-reach luminous surface, small waves seeming to mock effort – 'enough oxygen' they'd enquire?

Bursting through the surface together, spitting out sea water and gasping for air, adrenalin filled and suddenly high on achievement, we yelled excitedly, banging hands against the boat's hull in delight. Unfortunately, this impulsive display of exuberance brought a flabbergasted mother to the boat's port side, understandably concerned having seen us disappear off the starboard side, not to reappear. That evening, on coming up to our mosquito-netted verandah bedroom to wish us goodnight, Father told us he was proud of what we'd achieved, but to perhaps let them know what we might be planning next time. Encouraged by him to take (sensible) risks, looking back I wonder what influence his friendship had had as a fellow Scot with David Stirling whilst a postgraduate at Trinity College Cambridge, and earlier, a particular friend of Jock Lewis when part of the successful Oxford boat race crews of 1936, 37. Mother wasn't that easily won over, and we remained grounded for a while.

On matters barnacle, as any self-respecting cirripedologist (studies barnacles – over 1,000 species) would tell us 'barnacles are related to crabs and lobsters'.

And, 'Ciguatera' food poisoning is a nasty complaint that results from eating reef fish. None at Arzat that day suffered any ill effects at all; Harry was right: the barracuda was delicious.

FCO APRIL 1971   *(SECRET – DELICATE SOURCE)*

SOME WEEKS AGO IT WAS RUMOURED THAT 30 OMANIS HAD BEEN RECRUITED IN KUWAIT FOR TRAINING IN N KOREA, THREE SEPARATE SOURCES NOW REPORT THAT THE GROUP HAS RETURNED TO ADEN, AND HAS RECEIVED SPECIAL TRAINING IN ASSASSINATION TECHNIQUES

ARABIAN DEPT SECRET

'... IF YOU MEET A DHOFARI'

SAVING THE SULTAN'S UNCLE

20 Sept – Summoned urgently from patrol to respond to rubsha (trouble) in Salalah. Made it in 20 minutes beyond H/hogs to town – must be record. Someone shot at the Sultan's Uncle, Sheikh Issa. Splitting troop to block off area, my 3 cars covered separate street junctions, leaving us exposed as MR arrived to search house to house. Of 4 adoo hunted, 2 found, 2 escaped. Guns discovered. Once flurry of excitement over, broke off back to patrol. Lunched on sweet tea and hardtack biscuits beneath acacia bush. Found 2 small yellow scorpions, so we squatted rather than sat! Sgt Costello away testing new drivers around the town missed the action. Wathik becoming a problem, pushing to fly 'sick' relatives to Muscat for treatment. Faraz says it's a try-on. He's a good man.

Soldiers are trained to react to the unexpected. On an otherwise ordinary day, the unexpected happened. Radioed to move directly into Salalah to establish a cordon, I was to liaise with MR already en route there. Told "just move like lightning" with no explanation given. Taking just twenty minutes from jebel to town to be met by a fever of activity, I was ordered to cut off the immediate area around the Palace, blocking entry to the gathering crowds. The cost of doing so isolated my cars from each other, but MR were arriving in numbers.

Running past, a Brit officer shouted there'd been an assassination attempt on Sheikh Issa al Ma'sheni, a brother of the Sultan's mother, whose tribe came from the jebel above Taqah. In a civil war, frequently there is no knowing who the enemy is. Every civilian carried a weapon, all wore similar clothing and many in town were legitimate visitors from the jebali tribes. You scan faces staring at you, some agitated, some sullen, and you wait. A prescient shiver, and at the back of neck, hands and arms, hairs rise and sweat trickles between shoulder blades.

There are few more unnerving moments than looking along the barrel of a primed machine gun at watching crowds whom days before you considered were friendly, now wondering if any had a concealed weapon, ready to claim a scalp.

We maintained station for about an hour. MR were after four men, two were captured and two disappeared. After receiving the all-clear, I decided we'd return to the plains and gradually patrol back towards Arzat. Approaching midday, it was hot and we were all thirsty. Seeking a suitable spot, we halted for a quick brew and debrief. Our lunch, hardtack biscuits and tea. We'd be back in time for the men's main meal, curried or spiced goat on traditional flat dish of rice with chapatis, served each day at 1500.

Author, Hilal Ali, Abdullah Ali, and Abdul Wathik. Photo taken with my camera by Abdul Raja Faraz on watch from his Ferret. We kept one car on point at every break. Here we crouched rather than sat after finding some of the stones concealed small scorpions.

Waiting for the small fire of desiccated smokeless sticks to boil a brew, we discussed the incident. Surprisingly unconcerned by the assassination attempt, their nonchalance only reinforced the difference in cultures, and our media driven appetite for sensationally reported news.

'Brewed and peed', we drove out to the southern approaches of Hedgehog Alpha before turning east, back to Arzat. MR did well capturing two of the attempted assassins, the other two (apparently known to SAF intelligence officers) melted away and escaped.

That evening, showered, changed and relaxing on the verandah before dinner, I was relating the day's events to Harry and Geoff when Chris appeared. With his usual bluster he enquired 'Armoured Cars do anything useful today?' to which Harry replied, 'He's saved the Sultan's Uncle!' as Geoff added 'Probably get a gold watch!'. Despite himself, Chris beamed, 'Bollocks, takes more than that!'

* * *

Abdul Wathik, increasingly diffident, was beginning to wear me down. Incessantly requesting I organise Muscat flights for his family to receive medical treatment he claimed was unavailable in Salalah. Being a Khadim family from Salalah, Muscat to them must have held utopian possibilities, largely the result of their son's exaggerated stories when attending his training in the north with the Squadron. The family members, seen and treated by Salalah doctors, were fine, but Wathik remained insistent Muscat medication was better and demanded I arrange flights. I told him I couldn't, we were fighting a war. We had stalemate.

> *21 Sept – Things hotting up with end of khareef. Patrolling programme has been stepped up. Big push expected next 2 weeks. Adoo very quiet at present. Another long day – Taqah convoy am followed by 4 hour patrol in front H.Hogs Bravo and Alpha. Tasked with recceing Wadis Jarsis and Nahiz. Saw nothing. Said bin Ghia helped clear for mines. Three cars only – 4th VOR. Front wheel collapsed outside camp – required recovery.*

We patrolled daily between 22nd and 25th, stopping to check Bedouin with camels, all fairly routine. A quarter of a mile out from camp a Ferret's wheel collapsed; a mechanic's error, fortunately not an everyday occurrence. But the cars were ancient. The acronym VOR 'Vehicle Off Road' was used to denote a broken-down car or truck.

We were accompanied by Said bin Ghia, of the Bayt Qatan, a tribe inhabiting the jebel directly north of Salalah. He'd defected from the adoo and was now working as an agent for the Sultan's Intelligence services based at UAG, Salalah. Although he was considered untrustworthy and unpopular by many, I got on well with him. Crossing wadis he'd help clearing for mines, seemingly capable of knowing exactly where mines might be laid. He was, after all, an ex-adoo commander.

POST ADONIB AND PLAINS PATROL INCIDENT

Having left camp at daybreak we'd completed our morning mission to patrol towards Raysut, beyond Salalah. With JR established further to our west, the area east of Raysut was deemed secure in daylight. Parking our cars close to the top of the huge cliffs jutting out into the Arabian Sea we sat spending a few moments admiring the dramatic views. It was below these cliffs that Captain Ian Jones (RAMC), a doctor attached to the SAS, had tragically perished.

Raysut offered the chance for a dip in the sea for those stationed at HQ. On 28th May a small group had gone swimming in the bay. Unnoticed, the sea became

Sabre Troop take a break above the beach where Ian Jones died. Left to right - LCpl Abdul Raja Faraz, Tpr Nasir Hamid (without shemagh & shoes), LCpl Abdul Wathik, Tprs Hilal Ali, Abdullah Ali and Ali Hamdan. Lou on watch in his Ferret. My unloaded SMG in the foreground.

increasingly challenging as the tide turned and a rip current swept one of them out of the bay towards the open sea. There was nothing anybody could do to help: there was no boat; there weren't any ropes. Ian Jones yelled he was alright but obvious to all present the situation had become suddenly ominous. If he could only stay afloat and keep his head above the waves, he might be able to swim out to sea and then make it back into the bay, or even round the bluff and into the next towards Khaftawt.

But that didn't happen. Caught in the strong currents he was swept back towards the limestone cliffs. On the beach they could only watch. Running to the clifftop some 175m above, they'd witnessed Jones swept out of the bay then agonisingly back towards where the cliffs plunged into the sea. Here the blue sea becomes white with spume pounding vertical limestone. With each wave his body was thrown angrily against the rocks. It was not a soundless death. An accident. The needless waste of a fine soldier doctor, someone others relied upon when they themselves became ill, suffered infection or were wounded. But none could save him.

We had returned to Jebel Regiment's forward patrol base at Adonib we'd last visited on 10th September, for a joint operation. Commanded by Major Paul Wright (RE, ex-SAS) with Captains Mike Austin (ex-Devonshire and Dorset Regiment) and Bob Aplin (Royal Anglian), I Coy JR were tasked with cutting adoo supply routes eastwards from Yemen, and patrolling the western approaches to Salalah plain. Despite the SAF base at Adonib, the adoo still got through to attack RAF Salalah, SAF and BATT positions beyond, the Hedgehogs, Arzat, Taqah, Mirbat and Tawi Ateer. The tracks leading to these SAF locations were constantly mined, including those around RAF Salalah's airfield.

Early that morning we'd carefully checked for mines along the tracks to Adonib. We found none on this occasion, but regularly mined; this route later claimed a Saladin to a Soviet TM46 mine. The crew escaped injury, but such a mine would have destroyed a Ferret and crew.

Making our way back towards Arzat, weary and satisfied having cleared the route for mines, we halted in a small clearing. A freshwater stream flowed through reed beds. A place known to one of my troop drivers, Naser Hamid, who confirmed the water was sweet.

I felt chuffed. The short weeks of training and patrols had paid off. Without my having to signal, the cars had parked in a circle as we halted, 30m apart, facing outwards. 'It's beginning to come together,' I thought, dismounting and walking to the stream. Although an area designated safe, I still took the precaution of leaving a car on guard. We all carried submachine guns. Abdul Wathik had first shift in his Ferret. Crassly, I'd let deep-rooted defences drop.

IF YOU MEET A DHOFARI . . .

We filled bottles and scooped water by hand to parched mouths, splashing the clear liquid across faces, wiping away the morning's fine layer of dust. Tasting of sand and declared 'tamaam' (good) by my men, the water was also sublimely cool. SMGs by our sides, we remained alert yet relaxed. It was a moment to enjoy, at ease following our early start and now completed patrol.

A light touch on my shoulder triggered a sixth sense awareness as Ali Hamdan whispered slowly, 'adoo, sahb' . . . Whoever you are, your heart stops. I knew instantly something was very wrong. It hits hard, precipitating an involuntary shudder. Hairs rise on arms and nape of neck. I raised my head from sipping water still cupped in my right hand to find I was staring down the wrong end of an AK47 Kalashnikov. I heard a switch go off inside my head.

One theory on fear claims our primal brains, positioned at the back of our heads, are reptilian. Over millennia of evolution mammalian brains were added and gradually over time, primate ones and finally human. When placed under extreme threat we revert to our reptile brains: rock bottom instinct – flight or fight? The intensity is magnified by realisation, heaving instinct above experience, intellect or emotion. I had become reptile.

I raised my eyes from the seductive tip of chrome lined rifle barrel pointing chest level towards me, my heartbeat thumping as a kettledrum in ears fit to burst. Surely he must hear it too, this man who'd materialised from thin air. All had heard the ancient Omani proverb, one much quoted by my Northern Omani soldiers: "On a path, if you meet a snake and a Dhofari – first shoot the Dhofari". Motionless as a cobra, standing less than 5m away, pitch black uncaring eyes watched, absorbing the scene, revealing nothing, exquisitely confident in the victor's skill, the hunter's superiority of surprise.

Dressed as adoo, loose khaki shirt over patterned wizar (traditional wrap-around cloth similar to a sarong, reaching from waist to above ankle), a shemagh worn as a turban in Dhofari fashion and across his chest a cross-belt glinting where sunshine touched a row of 7.62mm rounds. Strapped nonchalantly at his waist, not a khunjar but a simple curved dagger in a goatskin sheath.

I stared back at the dark eyes, expressionless above a wide African nose and full mouth set in an arrogant face, framed in long plaits of wild jet-black hair falling from his temples, typical of Dhofari tribesmen. He held my stare, his as disinterested as a cat's.

Was that a flicker of a smile on an otherwise murderous face? Does a pathological killer remain so still and expressionless?

In the instant it took to take in every detail, no one moved and we were seven

'... IF YOU MEET A DHOFARI'

to one. Additionally, I had a man in an armed Ferret behind me on picquet. Yet all of little consequence, for the Dhofari held an automatic weapon levelled at us, my chest the first hapless target.

Stupidly, and demonstrating a naivety to be expected of a raw recruit, believing we'd safely patrolled the area, I'd made the basic and potentially final error of allowing our guard to drop, placing my men in a critical situation. It was imperative no one did anything rash. The man holding the Kalashnikov continued to stand motionless, eyes fixed with steady stare at mine. A game warden in Tanganyika once remarked "all the cruelty of Africa can be seen in the pitiless yellow stare of a lion". Apart from the lack of yellow eyes, right at that moment an armed Jebali had much the same impact. Momentarily stunned, it was my move.

What'd seemed minutes had been seconds.

Coming to my senses, maintaining steady eye contact with Kalashnikov man, I offered the universal Islamic greeting 'As Salaam Alaikum'. There followed a slight pause, before I received the courteous reply 'Wa Alaikum Assalam'.

Slowly I rose to greet him, letting my SMG drop at my left side. I extended my right hand to shake his as he stepped forward through the shallow stream to join us. Obvious or not – and I prayed not – relief surged through me as I shook his hand.

There followed the customary enquiries as to his health, those of his family and tribe, ending with 'peace be with you', as we exchanged greetings with a growing cordiality. We discovered he was ex-adoo and Bayt Kathir, a warrior tribe and largest on the jebel. After surrendering two months earlier, he'd joined the recently formed firqat, FAN, Firqat al Nasr undergoing training with members of BATT out of UAG.

Fortunately, he spoke Arabic, enabling us to converse easily. We'd discovered some Bayt Kathir chose only to speak Jebali interspersed with Arabic, making dialogue difficult even for my soldiers, impossible at the time for me. I discovered he'd been washing in the stream up from us and thought he'd surprise us by approaching quietly "mithal el adoo ..." (like adoo) adding emphasis by jabbing his finger twice, hard into my chest. At this his lined face broke into a wide toothless grin behind whiskery beard, transforming a fearsome countenance into instantly likeable rogue. We've all met them sometime.

Pleasantries exchanged, I offered him a lift on the back of my scout car to his base at Mamurah where the FAN were currently stationed, a collection of ancient traditional mud and stone, flat roofed buildings. Climbing onto the rear decks, I told him to hang on tight as we moved off. Perched leaning against me, gnarled bare feet wedged against the engine decks for purchase, loaded Kalashnikov somehow pressed hard against my back, we moved off and even the rushing wind failed to mitigate the distinctive aroma of Jebali male as we motored towards Marmurah.

Astonished at the Ferret's perceived cross-country capabilities, he'd thump my shoulder, yelling with glee each time we hit a bump or rut as we managed no more than 20mph over the rough terrain. Neither the powerful .30 Browning loaded with a full box of 250 belted rounds, nor our boxes of Mills 36 and white phosphorus smoke grenades strapped with gaffer tape inside my turret, but the high-pitched roar of the six-cylinder Rolls-Royce engine that impressed most. 'Shadeed, waajid shadeed!' (colloquially – 'bloody marvellous!').

I told him he would have been doubly impressed had he ridden on a six-wheeled Saladin and promised to give him a lift if, heaven forbid, we ever met in similar circumstances again. With a knowing smile, as we dropped him off he declared we were now life-long friends. Departing for Arzat I heard the shout 'Albaqa' fi halat tahab' (stay alert!).

We'd been fortunate that day. A lesson learned without cost, except to my conscience. I had let the men down. I'd not drop my guard again.

I LOSE MY JUNIOR NCOS

Back at camp, I drew Abdul Wathik aside. I challenged him for not seeing the man approach. He claimed he'd needed a pee and looking about, considered it was safe to leave his Ferret. Kneeling behind the vehicle, he'd relieved himself. (Peeing in the open, men knelt to pee, in theory to present less of a target – in practice, less splashing.) He'd not seen a thing until it was over.

Holding back my anger, I knew you didn't bawl out these men, but reasoned with them. So began our game of chess. Asking whether he felt he'd acted in our best interests allowing an armed man to approach unchallenged to within five paces of us, he countered it'd not have happened had we stopped for a pee earlier. Check.

I explained leaving his post had endangered others and did he understand how serious this was? Check. He shrugged. Check. I wasn't going to get any further. Realising the matter was one best dealt with cold, I ordered him to report to me next morning after first parade. Placing him on a charge would lead to court martial, something I wished to avoid. I was still in check. It wasn't going well.

Recently I'd become aware of a growing resentment between the most obvious of tribal groups in the troop, the north/south divide. At first putting it down to LCpls pulling rank, I now wondered if it wasn't something more serious. My first priority was discipline, now it seemed my second was to eliminate the emerging rift between one Dhofari Khadim and my Omani tribesmen. I'd noticed Wathik's propensity to express his superior education when pulling rank, which naturally rankled with my illiterate Omani Arabs. Endeavouring to build a cohesive unit, there could be no room for schisms.

HQ SAF OFFICERS MANUAL – ANTI-GUERRILLA OPERATIONS

Prepared and written as the Sultanate emerged from 38 years of division and autocratic rule, an operational manual recently issued to expatriate Officers and senior NCOs defined 'Tribes of Dhofar' as being almost as intolerant of their neighbours as Scottish clans. Intended to educate the expatriate, it was never intended as a diplomatic document.

> "The tribes of Dhofar . . . tend to treat each other with scorn . . . of African stock, the Khadim originate from East Africa from whence their ancestors were imported into South Arabia as slaves. They form a close knit and prolific community. The Khadim are widely disliked and distrusted by other tribes owing to their position as slaves and to their overbearing way in which they carried out the orders of Sultan bin Taimur."

The previous sultan, Sultan Said bin Taimur, had formed a Khadim regiment, the Dhofar Gendarmerie now based at Arzat. He'd ensured men were taught to read and write, with some learning English, rare in Oman at the time.

The British-led coup in 1970 a year earlier had won the Khadim slaves their freedom. Once fiercely loyal to earlier sultans, all now gave allegiance to the young Sultan Qaboos. We'd hear at first hand examples of gallantry by the Khadim matching in courage their Arab cousins. And in the ACS a Khadim and someone who became a loyal and good friend, Greadh Jummah, after attending training in Jordan was commissioned in January 1972, becoming the squadron's first Arab officer.

Back to Wathik: in the event a solution presented itself when he called at my room early that evening requesting to see me. It was not uncommon for soldiers to call upon their officers unannounced seeking a private audience; most cases concerned money or worries on compassionate grounds. Looking awkward, he shuffled from one foot to the other, before saying it was impossible to work with the troop's Omanis. He requested immediate release back to DG, his previous unit. It didn't need a degree in psychology to realise this was more likely an excuse to avoid facing serious repercussions for his actions that day, but it did ease my decision making somewhat. I said I would consider his request.

That night in the mess I asked Chris whether he had any strong objections to taking back Abdul Wathik, a man he'd known before volunteering for the ACS fifteen weeks earlier. Chris liked Wathik and warmed to the idea, but wanted more. There'd be a price. Taking Abdul Wathik, I'd have to release Abdul Raja Faraz, a man Chris had been sore losing to us.

'Hell,' I thought, 'Faraz's a good man.' We got on well. I liked his no-nonsense can-do attitude, so different from his ex-DG companion. I'd no option. I would have to release both men to lose Wathik. With little choice, I agreed on condition Faraz was amenable. Next day Faraz confided he'd be sorry to go, then surprised me saying he'd been considering requesting to leave anyway – a bad leg hurt each time his Ferret hit a bump!

Holding back a smile to avoid giving offence, I told him I'd had no knowledge of his affliction and congratulated him on concealing the injury for so long. Reluctantly I accepted his departure, so losing both my junior NCOs. Despite the gammy leg story, I knew I'd lost a good soldier.

With Wathik's departure, and the arrival of two more Arab replacements, the troop were buoyed; to a man they claimed Wathik's attitude towards them had irked. I suspected there was also an element of Omani tribesman vs Dhofari Khadim, unschooled vs schooled, each camp considering themselves superior to the other. It was vital I had a close-knit troop which my gut told me I now had. That day the change in atmosphere was palpable. Checkmate.

When Tim heard, he was not too pleased as he considered we'd lost two good men. One, I agreed we had. My decision held. It helped that Tim was 800km away in northern Oman building and training the squadron, but I was in Dhofar, on patrol daily or on convoy escorts.

A year later the two NCOs and I met again. I'd been medevaced to FST Salalah with a fungal pneumonia, an environmental pathogen not then considered contagious person to person. It may well have been MERS-CoV, now recognised as Middle East respiratory syndrome coronavirus, which can develop into pneumonia. Its source is from contact with camel milk, or camel secretions, i.e. water tainted by camels. How often we'd accepted a Bedu's generosity to drink from a dish, mud lined and woven from reeds, to sup eagerly freshly drawn camel milk, or drunk thirstily, water from wells shared with camels?

Hearing I was in hospital, they'd called and been allowed entry by an inattentive medic who believed they were ACS. I should have welcomed visitors, but the meeting was an ordeal. With difficulty breathing and unable to sit up, I received my guests lying prone to hear a lengthy petition (I use the word loosely) for their transfer back to the Squadron, and yes, as officers. Too much water had passed. With the medic's arrival to administer another two penicillin injections, tactfully as possible I refused their requests.

SEPTEMBER 1971: MONTH OF "THE HUEY ACHIEVEMENT" AND SOLDIER MORALE

That September HQ SAF declared the introduction of helicopters had been a huge success, in that they significantly increased men's chances of survival; which on the face of it, didn't need much explanation. Perhaps it would have been better left at that. But the intended morale boosting pronouncement went on to elucidate that since January, as the little over 70 officers and men wounded, none had died, was to be considered a singular achievement. Casualty numbers, until now not widely broadcast, came as a bit of a shock to us in Dhofar, at a stroke achieving the direct opposite to the message intended. Soldiers have a phrase for it.

With the monsoon ending, CSAF ordered the Sultan's Forces take the initiative to the adoo still holding the mountains surrounding Salalah, seemingly with impunity. Yet Dhofar forces were tired, battered and frustrated by their inability to remain on the jebel for any length of time, particularly during the khareef when visibility might be reduced to tens of metres. Added to the logistical problem of keeping supplied sufficient numbers in the mountains to withstand attacks, operationally there was doubt men nearing completion of yet another tour had the stomach for it. Roulement when DR and JR would arrive from the north to take over from the Dhofar battalions, MR and NFR, would happen in October. The thirst for battle was not uppermost in young men's minds.

Until now, soldiers saw only a constant repetition of high casualty, nine-month Dhofar tours when willing them on, most seconded officers served but one and a half tours before they were gone, returned home to their British regiments. And big battles always seemed to come towards the end of yet another tour. Dhofar morale was generally low. Six months later, the bold gamble of Op Simba would change all that.

SEP INCIDENT – ARZAT GATEHOUSE

As Duty Officer I was called to deal with a Kalashnikov armed Dhofari who'd presented himself at the gatehouse. Approaching, I noticed the man's lack of headdress, revealing a cleanly shaven head. Significantly, this indicated acceptance of death. Suicide bombers still an unknown threat at the time, I nevertheless approached the man under the gatehouse archway with growing apprehension. For some reason, he'd not been disarmed, yet three DG soldiers stood to one side, FN rifles levelled at the man's chest. With Kalashnikov balanced casually at rest on his left shoulder, left hand loosely clasping the muzzle end of the barrel, he embodied the relaxed tribesman's pose for carrying arms, be they Bedu, Jebali, our soldiers or adoo.

A camel stick was held in his right hand. These crafted, half-metre long whittled acacia sticks are used habitually to control camels or goats, but also for adding emphasis to conversation by prodding the earth whilst seated cross legged on the ground. Watching me approach, he looked as relaxed as someone at a garden party.

A week or so earlier, another two had surrendered at Arzat to join the local firqat, where they'd been greeted with enthusiasm. More than likely this man wished to do the same. Exchanging greetings politely, I asked him to place his rifle on the ground beside where he stood. Without objecting, he concurred. I explained we needed to search him for other weapons; again he acceded. We found none, to my relief.

On questioning it transpired he'd fully expected to be shot, claiming that was a nobler end to remaining with the Marxists on the jebel. He was surrendering to join the Sultan's forces having become disillusioned with the ideology forced cruelly upon Jebali tribesmen, their women and children by people who'd forsaken their religion. Mothers refusing to allow their children to be taken away for training as soldiers had been killed in front of their children, protesting old men executed barbarically.

After food and water at the guardhouse, he was transferred to Firqat al Nasr (FAN) at Mamurah later that afternoon. SEP (surrendered enemy personnel) was an anomaly as the word 'enemy' was never used as such; they were adoo. However, the acronym remained the recognised classification for surrendered adoo.

BEACH CONVOYS

25 Sept – Two Ferrets VOR – have had to resort escorting convoys to Taqah by Land Rovers with Bedfords. Tide out, decided we'd try the beach run. Joined at Khawr ad Dahariz 3km west of Arzat where beach accessible with ease. Doubling back south of the camp progress good – except for soft sand at wadi creeks. One Bedford stuck but towed out successfully. Noticeably, the beach is covered with white crabs. Alarmed, they scurry sideways back and forth as we approach. Unable to avoid the vehicles, the creatures die in their hundreds to repetitive crunching symphony splat! splat! splat! splat! on and on. Food for seagulls.

Whilst the beach offered rapid access to Taqah, we only rarely used the route to avoid giving the adoo an undue advantage. Overuse would have allowed them a string of choice ambush positions from behind sand dunes and khawrs (small creeks) along the beach edge. We alternated departure times in an effort to avoid setting patterns the adoo might exploit.

Looking back as we sped east towards Taqah, my Bedford truck with convoy stretching out behind, keeping to the water's edge and firmest sand. You had to travel fast to avoid sinking.

GHOST CRABS OF OMAN

The dominant variety of crab along this section of coastline is known as the 'Ghost Crab of Oman'. Ocypodidae Saratan have the crab's atypical shaving-bowl-like armoured body, thick elongated eyestalks and one claw larger than the other. Primarily nocturnal scavengers and predators of smaller creatures, they broke curfew every time we used the beach as a road. Despite evolving to wear suits of armour, it was never a match to mankind's evolutionary progress. They died by the hundreds to the sound of hitting motorway cats' eyes, the appalling clatter of tyre crushing exoskeleton. Luckily for us they didn't scream, at least that is, audibly above engine noise.

BODY ARMOUR

On the subject of body armour my diarised thoughts comment:

> *Body armour here is zilch – no helmets, no leather gloves which would save knuckle rash. Our sole protection – a cotton shemagh, issued dyed green from original red/white Saudi shemaghs, where they're called 'Ghutra'. Once washed and beaten against stone they soften to a comfortable fabric.*

Arabian Gulf States primarily wear the ghutra draped over the head, kept in place by a fine coil of black rope, an 'Iqal'. The ghutra and iqal are not often worn in the southern states of Oman or Yemen, where exclusively the shemagh dominates, traditionally worn as a turban tied securely around the head.

At approximately 4 ft sq (0.37 sq m) and tied in a fashion of folds around the head, dust shielding shemaghs offered the added benefit of protection against inevitable cuts and bruises when striking unforgiving steel inside an armoured car.

Arab soldiers relished regaling others about war and daring deeds, and would embellish stories in the knowledge unsuspecting and trusting teenage recruits were 'all ears'. But with us Brits, their particular delight was in explaining the benefits and intricacies of the multi-purpose army shemagh. Conspiratorially, they'd explain how these uniquely versatile items of kit had four distinct uses over protecting against sun, bangs to the head, bullets and shrapnel. Summarising, they'd emphasise how each corner had an individual purpose. Laying out your shemagh, they would point to each corner in turn with the following solemn explanation:

> First corner – use spit and wash eyes.
> Second – same, clean teeth.
> Third – same, clean and oil rifle.
> Fourth – same, wipe your arse.

Ending, they'd warn, best never forget which was which in the dark! Guaranteed to raise peals of laughter, every time.

George Sommerfield (ex-3rd Carabiniers) joined the Squadron in late 1972. Arriving as we'd all done, burdened with designated essential kit, he possessed an item of which he was particularly proud. A present from his mother, an academic who ran the University Arboretum at Aberdeen. Her token to body armour was a blacksmith crafted, steel cased cigarette case she'd had made. Presenting him with the case were strict instructions it be worn over his heart. Unbeknown to George's dear mother the adoo rarely shot at the heart, perfecting a head shot.

Another officer arrived with a hunting rifle he'd purchased in the UK, in preference to the then issue .303s. And one I served with at Desert Regiment preferred alpine boots with soles reinforced by steel plates he thought might offer protection against mines. More than a little optimistic, as everyone knew anti-personnel mines nearly always removed foot and leg past the knee, on their way to meet torso, neck and face.

Whilst the majority of us simply got on with what we were issued with, possibly my most useful piece of kit was a Wildebeest tail fly-whisk – with which I attempted to control the ever-persistent swarms of flies.

10

GEOFF AND THE CAT

The Sultanah's Royal Guard. Near disaster at Wadi Jardum. Roulement and post monsoon operations, Op Jaguar and Job's tomb. Another routine Taqah convoy, the SAS and the cat. Geoff killed.

ROYAL GUARD DUTIES

26 Sept – Guard duty: Sultan's mother arriving Salalah Palace – Strike Force – Z Coy and us – Guard helipad and HM's safe escort to Palace. We need to practise this. We're meant to look for trouble, not gape at the person we're guarding!

Towards the end of the month, as part of Strike Force we were summoned to take up positions around the Palace, to protect the Sultan's mother arriving by helicopter from her royal residence in northern Oman. In the event it was all over in a moment, the Huey arrived, hovered, landed, and with blades still running, out stepped the royal party to be ushered hurriedly from aircraft into the palace and safely away. My four-car troop, impressively fanned out as we'd mounted guard, crews alert and awake to possible dangers, had the landing area covered and secured. Or so I thought. As the Huey landed, I'd glanced across at the other cars, only to find the crews were all craning their necks, hoping to catch a glimpse of the royal party. Admittedly, it was highly unlikely they'd ever seen the Sultanah before, and a short command barked over the radio broke the royal watchers' trance – and luckily, order resumed.

WADI JARDUM – NEAR DISASTER

Photograph shows the steep ravine carved through the jebel as Wadi Jardum exits onto Salalah plain. One of a series of photographs I was tasked with taking for OC HQ Dhofar, soon after my arrival. The series stretched west to east along the adoo-held Jebel al Qarar, encircling Salalah plain. Forming a panorama, enlarged photographs were displayed around the walls of the HQ Command Ops room, used as points of reference in planning operations.

26 Sept – Haircut, day before yesterday by Said Abdullah – God what a mess! First shearing since old Mr Bird at Trumpers few days before leaving for Oman in July, mind you haircut long overdue.

Near Disaster today – patrolling north of Hedgehogs Bravo and Charlie taking photographs of wadis Jardum out towards aqabat Thifah. At Jardum, whilst reversing, over-eager Nasir Hamid hit the floor (accelerator pedal) at same time pulling wheel hard left, sending us back fiercely when Bang! we were stranded 4 wheels spinning, hull grounded, stuck on a boulder.

Back hurt where I'd slammed against turret as we came to abrupt halt. Instantly I knew what had happened. Called T1A for push off rock – unhesitatingly he motored up behind me – without stopping crashed his Ferret into our rear, thumping us forward off the boulder. Abdullah Ali, his driver, stopped short of beaching his car as they hit us. Freed suddenly, both cars beat hasty retreat together, then moved on to complete patrol and photos. Back mid afternoon. That Costello is owed a drink.

It had been a lucky escape. What had occurred was entirely my fault – it's the vehicle commander's responsibility to direct his reversing driver. For expediency, we'd tap the driver's shoulder to direct left or right when getting out of trouble fast, either reversing or moving off forwards. A tap in the head was straight ahead. Having given Nasir the command to reverse straight back, I bent forward to secure my precious camera and in doing so nudged his left shoulder. Reversing hard to avoid stalling, he'd spun the steering wheel to the left and *bang* we landed on a lump of rock, one designed to catch a scout car. The violent force of grounding smashed each of us into the car's superstructure which hurt more than usual. There was no time to think of bruised bones as I radioed Costello for assistance.

Such was the bond that'd developed, I knew instinctively he'd see what was necessary. This was not the place or time for conventional tow ropes or recovery vehicles. Telling Nasir to engage "tars wahid" (1st gear) I shouted a warning to him as we braced ourselves against the approaching impact. Without stopping, Costello crashed into us, shoving us clear. Thankfully, his accomplished driver Abdullah Ali hit his brakes at the moment of impact, avoiding stranding on the same rock.

With no more than a glance at the front end of his car, I gave Costello a thumbs up and we roared off to join the other cars, hull down giving us cover 150m back. Driving through their position we regrouped in a shallow wadi sufficient to allow Costello and I to leave our cars safely. Shaking hands with my sergeant and Abdullah warmly, I thanked them as we checked the cars. Apart from having to free one front mudguard rubbing against a tyre, we found no other damage.

A promise to Lou of beers on me and we continued westwards to photograph Aqabat Thifah (Thifar pass). I often look back at how lucky we were that day.

ROULEMENT OCTOBER 1971 AND POST MONSOON OPERATIONS

October saw MR and Sandy moving back to northern Oman, replaced by the balance of JR as Plains Battalion based at Salalah. NFR also returned north after handing over to DR in the Western reaches of Dhofar, at Akoot battle camp on the mountain range called Jebel al Qamar where Rick and Tom were now based, and where we'd meet again in a month's time.

Before roulement was completed, there were a couple of joint operations involving Z company and my Ferret troop, more as familiarisation exercises for the incoming battalion but with live ammunition and a possible enemy.

OP MACBETH; A FINAL FLING

27 Sept – 0400-1830 Op Macbeth. MR, A & C Coys, 1 Coy JR, Golf 11, Strikemasters and composite troop six mortars, Z Coy, and 4 Ferrets. Protection mortars. Small s/a contacts – we covered withdrawal across plains.

Op Macbeth was launched on 27th September. A Search and Destroy mission starting at 0400. We returned at last light. At battalion strength, the op included A and C Coys MR, 1 Coy JR, artillery, jets and my four Ferrets with Z Coy carrying six mortars. My job was to protect the mortars and cover the withdrawal. Expecting a contact, we drew blank receiving a few long-range shots that caused us no discomfort. The typical "F... you" gesture from a confident adoo.

Chatting with Spike Powell, he put it to me that if we all survived, I'd come to see Macbeth followed a pattern each departing battalion undertook at roulement. One last operation, one last bash at glory by an outgoing battalion heading for nine months' quiet in Northern Oman. Spike, similarly deployed in Dhofar on a permanent basis, warned 'be watchful, man, at roulement times, the buggers'll want to go out with a bang!' It'd reoccur too, each occasion a senior officer reached the end of his loan service. The need to make a mark. It's a common phenomenon: legacies are not the exclusive province of the military.

POST-MONSOON OPERATIONS: OCTOBER 1971 – JUNE 1972

FCO cabinet office briefing 31 Aug 1971

THE REBELS ARE PLANNING AN ATTACK IN STRENGTH ON TAQA BEFORE THE END OF THE MONSOON

1 Oct – Taqah convoy – took 5.5 into town, Z Coy piquetted Khawr Sawli, Strike Force at Loan Tree. Strikemasters on call. All went smoothly.

2-6 Oct daily plains patrols.

7 Oct – Brought 5.5 out from Taqah. Z Coy Khawr Sawli, DG and Asslt Pioneers cleared for mines. 1 Coy MR deployed at Loan Tree. 5.5 required for Jaguar.

PHASE 1 – OP. JAGUAR

The October roulement coincided with the end of the 1971 khareef, and the launch of Op Jaguar. This was to be the first of three operations we'd been promised by CSAF as the post-khareef offensive to destroy the adoo's dominance across the Qara jebel encircling Salalah. The objective: strangle the adoo supply routes through the western approaches, the Qamar jebel bordering Yemen, using fresh troops of the newly arrived battalions.

Of the many complications for SAF high command to consider was the potentially significant fact that the Holy Month of Ramadan commenced on 21 October. Whilst the war had been declared a Holy War fought against communism, an ideology that actively denounced the Muslim faith, there remained doubt as to how the troops might react to the launch of a big operation during the Holy Month. A decree issued by the Sultan as both religious and secular head of state, had been reinforced by an absolution from the senior religious cleric in Oman authorising troops to disregard fasting during military operations. Notwithstanding both royal decree and absolution, some would still adhere to their fast.

With Ramadan in mind, HQ felt the best chance of success was to push ahead immediately, launching Op Jaguar at the beginning of October. A wait until November post-Ramadan would be too late. Inevitably, by the time the op kicked off on 2 October, rumours were rife with expectation of a major push to take the jebel post-monsoon.

Three distinct operations would dovetail to secure the objective.

Phase 1 – Op Jaguar: Combined Operation: put troops onto the jebel in strength and positions where they would remain. Mounting the op would be elements of HQ MR/JR, I Coy JR, Strike Force with my four Ferret Scout Cars, two squadrons of BATT and the recently formed Dhofari firqats. Further, ensure continued security of the Salalah plains area, together with the coastal strip from Mughsayl in the west, eastwards past Taqah, Mirbat and Sudh coastal villages east of Salalah.

Phase 2 – Op Vulture: The ACS to establish/hold three desert locations at Midway, Mudhai and Habarut; patrol and control movement north of jebel.

Op Leopard (following in November): JR to the west of Salalah, would establish three positions north of Adonib as further attempts to stop adoo arms traffic.

Phase 3 – Op Simba: DR-led operation to establish battalion operational base from which SAF would be able to control and effectively cut off the present unhindered flow of adoo supplies and munitions to their bases within Dhofar.

GEOFF AND THE CAT

9 Oct – Deployed with Spike's Strike Force to Jardum area. Directed 5.5 fire onto adoo positions. Firqat reported seeing two adoo, we advanced and in ensuing chase, my driver Said Sulleman managed to hit a gully where there were none – he'd hit 'Lone Tree' given half a chance. Cut eyebrow against Browning – messy. Said mortified on seeing my cut face. My temporary driver as Abdullah Ali and Nasir Hamid away on leave. Decent lad, he'll make good driver eventually.

Adoo turned out to be ghazal. At two thousand metres with naked eye, I've made same mistake. Jaguar established.

Ali Hamdan surpassed himself last night by responding to a wager he couldn't drink 10 coconuts dry. He managed 13 and is off sick today – wonder if coconut milk toxic? (Thankfully, Ali Hamdan, the young fool, made a full recovery after a long day at the camp's latrines.)

Lone Tree as the name implies, was an emaciated acacia thorn tree, withered and offering no shade. Nevertheless, there it stood, lone sentinel north of Salalah's rusting barbed wire perimeter defences. Remarkably, against all odds the tree survived as the surrounding desert gravel plain gradually succumbed to powder dust-bowl following the endless passage of army vehicles plying SAF bases. To those travelling the plain, this otherwise nondescript ancient tree became a talisman and landmark no driver willingly passed without appreciation.

Rare sightings of ghazal (gazelle) always excited. These were the Arabian species – Gazella Arabica, about a metre high and weighing approximately 25kg. Very similar in size and markings to the Thomson's Gazelle found extensively across the plains of East Africa. We found them more frequently north of the jebel, in the wilderness and scrubland bordering the Empty Quarter.

Local intelligence gleaned from jebali would suggest adoo build up to Arzat's front at Umran and Sahalanawt. Thought to be in retaliation to Op. Jaguar.

Jaguar, the combined operation in which Spike and I played but a bit part, successfully established SAF and BATT with firqat in strength on the eastern jebel. The region chosen for Phase One had been selected as presenting the easiest to win and hold in an attempt to strangle the adoo's lengthy resupply chain from Yemen eastwards into Dhofar.

In an effort to deflect adoo attention, diversionary tactics were implemented intended to confuse. This was our task, and deploying with Strike Force, my four

Ferrets protected a 5.5in Howitzer to fire into Wadi Jardum and various targets north of Salalah.

JOB'S TOMB

East of Jardum lies Wadi Thimrin. Unknown to me, and I suspect many of us Brits at the time, the place is the home to a special site of pilgrimage respected by the Abrahamic faiths of Islam, Christianity and Judaism; the tomb of Job. Today, there stands a small building described as serenely banal, modest and unadorned, yet a place of quiet beauty. I shudder to think how frequently the area was shelled during operations.

Tony Jeapes in his excellently researched book, "SAS Secret War", relates of Jaguar, "by 9th October, the battle was won". My diary entry at the end of a week-plus of frenetic activity on the plains for us with Strike Force, and much greater effort for those on the jebel concluded with the following:

> "BATT losses seem high, but confirmed adoo kills are 25 which is good for 9 days' action. Desert Regt today lost one KIA and five WIA on their first familiarisation op. out of Akoot. Not so good."

I paraphrase what others have written concerning the BATT operations on Jaguar:

> Following prolonged bouts of fighting both SAS Squadrons were exhausted. They'd suffered losses although reportedly the adoo were sustaining the greater casualties. Most contacts became stand-off long range affairs. Squadron commanders agonised at their casualty rate. There seemed to be no progress against a determined foe. Constant patrols night after night, water rationing and poor rations resulted in some men losing over a stone in weight. Many, including their commanding officer Johnnie Watts, were suffering chest infections, reducing effectiveness for covert operations. Then three firqats decided after all they'd observe the Holy Month and refused to participate any further until Ramadan ended in another 10 days. Fed up with the extraordinary change of events and believing the loss of so many of his men had seemingly been for no purpose, one squadron leader refused to send out further patrols. He only agreed to do so following the intervention of his commander and the fight continued. More SAS casualties were taken, but the fierce fighting eventually broke the adoo's hold in the region. "... the battle was won."

It'd be one of many.

On the 10th October and now released from Jaguar, it was a day when fate played her hand.

10 OCTOBER – JUST ANOTHER ROUTINE TAQAH CONVOY

I had taken a convoy into Taqah that morning with a 5.5in Howitzer and gun crew. Firqat and BATT were soon to move out. Geoff had picqueted positions on the outskirts of Taqah, to safeguard our entry and exit. On leaving later, I stopped for a brief word as the convoy rumbled past.

Entering Taqah, I was met by the SAS troop leader who invited me for a mug of tea and catch-up on 'plains' news. The largish team of twelve from G squadron had arrived in Dhofar at the start of a four-month tour mid-August. We'd met on earlier visits to Taqah. During our conversation I became aware a small creature had entered the room. We were sitting on ammo boxes as there were no chairs when a kitten leapt onto my lap. 'Ahh,' remarked my host, 'hoped that might happen', before explaining they'd found the kitten after a mortar shell struck a mud-built house, killing its siblings and mother.

The 5.5 passes my Ferret at Geoff's picquet as we approach Taqah on a mine cleared track.

Following the attack, a search was made, wounded dealt with, helicopters arranged and casualties evacuated. Searching for unexploded ordnance, but also pieces of shrapnel, mortar and rocket fins as aids in identifying adoo weaponry, they'd examine the angle of impact to determine the general direction the shell had been fired from. At one such site they'd found the kitten, its eyes still unopened. Blowing off the worst dust and grit, the protesting kitten was placed in a jacket pocket before the troop continued clearing the area. Their quarters, a mud building loaned by the Wali of Taqah, had an inner courtyard and sand floor leading to a larger flat-roofed structure with small parapet wall, offering measurably cooler accommodation at night but more importantly, views over the town. BATT had declined to use the fort, as being too restrictive. An unexpected bonus of mud buildings was the material's ability to absorb shards of exploding HE shrapnel, in stark contrast to the devastating effects ricocheting shrapnel, stone chips and bullets caused flying off limestone rock, an element of the war we shared equally with the adoo.

Instantly adopted, the kitten was handed over to the patrol medic, also an Arab speaker. In sharp contrast to the archetypal image of hardened SAS trooper, he set about cleaning the tiny creature, whilst another mixed a teaspoonful of British army compo milk powder with some water.

Predictably first attempts to persuade the kitten to drink directly from a mess tin failed – and licking the solution off a finger wasn't accepted either. 'Got it!' exclaimed one, as digging out an eye-drop dispenser borrowed from the patrol's medical supplies, he filled the glass tube with milk and squeezed it into the kitten's mouth. Slowly at first, the patient was soon lapping at the glass dispenser. 'Welcome to BATT life,' remarked an onlooker. The improvisation worked and the kitten never looked back. Responding well to such intensive care, progress from wretchedness to a bouncy kitten was achieved. A week later, I arrived on the scene.

Now purring trustingly in my lap, the creature had a certain gift of helpless charm. What an idiot! I'd fallen for the oldest trick in the book – 'looks like you've been adopted, you'll have a friend for life . . .' 'Oh yes?' I replied, wondering what Chris Phillips would have to say about a kitten in the Officers' Mess? To his credit he didn't object.

I was introduced to the eye-drop dispenser – hand rearing SAS style. The paradox was these herculean individuals, the army's best trained in the limitless arts of killing, could in equal measure be so soft about a kitten. The dispenser worked first time. Simple really. A delighted BATT guardsman assured me the cat was fully house trained (!), easy to feed and would prove excellent at killing rats presumably flourishing at Arzat as naturally they did at Taqah. Funny, I couldn't immediately recall there'd been much evidence of rats at Arzat. It occurred to me too, how'd I keep him away from Sibelius? I needn't have worried; each maintained a courteous deference to the other.

The SAS were moving out. Responsibility for Taqah was being ceded to Geoff's DG platoon, so they couldn't take the cat. Apparently, Geoff had refused ownership, and finding myself outnumbered twelve plus kitten to one, I became the unexpected owner of a small, furry, sharp clawed and toothed war refugee tomcat. Numbers obviously had nothing to do with the decision.

When I introduced the cat to my driver Nasir Hamed, I could tell he'd probably need convincing about an additional crew member. A Ferret Scout Car was not built to carry excess baggage. Tin cases of .30 Browning ammunition, two sterling machine guns, loaded spare magazines, boxes of 9mm ammo, a box of Mills 36 plus smoke grenades and flares, maps and on this occasion a spare radio, there was little space left for additional passengers. The driver sits directly in front of the commander, which meant that at just over 6ft (1.83m) tall, my knees ended up wedged uncomfortably tight either side of the driver's seat backrest. By wedging my knees offered greater stability travelling across rough terrain. However, gaffer-taping canvas wadding to the seat-back, to save knees from chafing against the sides of the car's interior, had reduced space further.

Looking in towards the cab at Nasir Hamed's now incredulous expression, I had to admit there was definitely little room for passengers, even a tiny cat. Undeterred, I gave the order 'start up' and holding the cat in one hand, SMG slung over my shoulder, I climbed aboard. Slipping into the commander's turret, I settled on my seat and with a flash of inspiration tucked the hapless kitten into the Browning's attached canvas bag, known officially as a "spent-case-cartridge-bag". The bag is designed to collect burning hot .30 brass spent-cases when the machine gun is fired to avoid these dropping to litter the turret floor, or fall down inside the driver's shirt. I hoped the cat would stay put – a hope which proved a little optimistic given that escape to a small inquisitive cat was all he desired.

SPENT-CASE-CARTRIDGE-BAG

As frequently mentioned, it's imperative to hang on very tight when travelling over rough ground to avoid being thrown and injured against unforgiving armour plating. The trip soon became one where the cat's recent rescue was seriously called into doubt as I struggled to keep the animal in the canvas bag away from the back of Nasir's head and shoulders, whilst at the same time trying to brace myself from being thrown around the turret.

"Spent-Case-Cartridge-Bag" lived in my hat for a while . . . Feline, (family Felidae), the 37 species include among others – cheetah, puma, jaguar, leopard, lion, lynx, tiger, and domestic cat.

Leading the convoy of trucks, we headed back to Geoff and his platoon of gendarmes piqueting our exit route. Lou Costello brought up the rear and the other two Ferrets midway along the line of trucks, working the flanks. I pulled up at Geoff's sangar, signalling Lou to take the convoy through whilst I caught up with my friend. I'd then cover the rear of the convoy through the defile to where the higher ground broke to Salalah Plains.

Geoff was angry. Bloody angry. Why'd I spent so long in town? His mood worsened when in reply, I answered I'd stopped for tea with his mates at Taqah – only to receive an anguished 'They're *NOT* my fucking mates'!

The SAS operate as close-knit squads, trained to standards well beyond others in the British army. What they achieve is extraordinary soldiering, arguably the best in the world. Operating in small units, each man an expert in at least one specialised skill, gives each group the capabilities of a considerably larger force that when required will be implemented to devastating effect. To pass selection each man would have endured and passed an exhaustive, challenging process. The regiment's underlying advantage over other units was that of being an intimate close-knit force, committed to ensuring absolute reliability to each other.

But by working and getting to know certain individuals broke through any aloofness, the logical consequence born out of being members of the British

Army's best. For whatever reason, Geoff hadn't managed to achieve this, and during his brief posting to Taqah, he'd established his own quarters separate from the BATT lines. When my troop deployed with Geoff and his men, it was to the old Portuguese fort, utilitarian and certainly basic, but no more than might be expected of a 19th century fort in Arabia. High external walls with parapets, having an inner central core, all built of mud and/or hewn coral blocks and stone. The dense wooden doors elaborately carved in an Arabesque style were reminiscent of carved doors found in Zanzibar and other buildings along the East African coast, outposts of the once extensive Omani empire. The fort at Taqah stood alone at the northern edge of town and it was here Geoff had made his base.

Geoff had assumed we'd been taking an inordinate time to unload the trucks. Both of us being hot, dusty and stressed, unnecessary words were said. To my enduring sadness and regret, following a heated exchange between friends, we parted, neither looking back. I never saw him alive again.

Moving off to catch the rear of the convoy, I recognised Geoff had a valid point. Exposed on picquet guarding our safe exit out of Taqah, I'd been enjoying sweet tea and compo ration biscuits with the BATT crowd. Geoff reckoned he'd been left exposed to the increasing danger of attack by a competent enemy. Positioned within range of their weapons used previously in attacking convoys through the defile at Khawr Sawli, the creek west of Taqah, Geoff was sitting on an adoo's registered target area.

GEOFF AND THE GIAT 90MM ANTI-TANK GUN

That night Geoff took it upon himself to use the Taqah field gun, a piece of artillery requisitioned from the previous Sultan's palace in Salalah following the coup a year earlier. One of a pair used previously for ceremonial duties, the gun had stood outside the palace, more a symbol of power than any particular military purpose.

The artillery piece was French, manufactured by the French armament group Giat (Groupement Industriel de l'Armement Terrestre) as a WW2, 90mm anti-tank gun. Following the coup, the two guns had been cleaned of their deep preservation (manufacturer's original protective grease) before being requisitioned by SAF for use in the war effort.

We had delivered one of the guns to Taqah by convoy a short while before, in an effort to bolster defences in response to the adoo's increased shelling of the town when, interestingly, they had begun using VT fuses – variable time fuses.

These had given them the capability to fire air-bursts, shells that explode in the air, a lethal weapon against anyone caught without suitable overhead cover.

Now part of Taqah's ordnance, the French gun had been put into service where it was used infrequently by BATT. Its stock of ancient ammunition comprised high explosive, finned shells. At the time, this was already an ancient weapon and the gun's full history unknown. When attacked BATT had taken to remote-firing the gun, attaching a long lanyard of mine tape from gun, back to their vantage point at the top of the fort. Having previously registered the target area, they'd fire a single round in the direction of the adoo in the hope of success, and in their own words 'not bothering to reload (the suspect weapon) until the contact was over'. So that was the SAS professional view of the gun. Such was the degree of confidence in this particular piece of artillery, it was rarely used.

From his map it is apparent Geoff intended to fire a salvo of shots he'd earlier identified as possible adoo base plates (mortar positions). These were points on the jebel he'd identified on the high ground overlooking the small town from where the adoo had successfully fired into Taqah, causing a number of casualties. Collecting a crew of two of his DG soldiers, Geoff commenced preparations.

One might question whether he should have sought assistance from one of the BATT team and it remains a mystery why he acted alone, relying solely on a couple of inexperienced gendarmes to assist him loading and firing the French gun. Despite his rank as a captain in the Sultan's Armed Forces, as a contract officer Geoff had no authority over the BATT stationed with him at Taqah. The SAS/BATT operated as self-contained units, with their own kit, communications, rations, ordnance and ammo. They reported directly to their autonomous HQ based at UAG, SAF's Brigade HQ compound. Independent and in command of his platoon of gendarmes, Geoff reported to his commander, Chris Phillips at Arzat, and then to Dhofar Bde HQ.

An accomplished soldier, Geoff was mortar trained. I had seen him in action firing mortars from Arzat. One evening he had demonstrated to me the basics of live firing. The 81mm mortar is noisy up close. Good at his job, he would have been quietly confident of his soldiering abilities and more than capable of handling the weaponry now at his disposal.

At the time, it was no doubt considered reasonable that someone of Geoff's ability would be able to operate and fire the gun supported by his Arab soldiers. But this weapon was not standard issue armament. Dating from 1926, the French 90mm anti-tank gun was almost a museum piece. Not long since rescued from Salalah palace, the gun, including my four Ferret cars, had been part of a huge arsenal of weapons and ammunition hoarded by the Sultan's father. That evening the gun was Geoff's weapon of choice.

As we'd discovered with my ancient Ferrets, all had required extensive mechanical overhauling and cleaning of deeply encrusted paint and old grease. The French gun was probably in need of a similar overhaul and commissioning before issue to Taqah. The ammunition was most likely out of date and probably should have been condemned and destroyed a long time ago. With less severe results, we discovered the point proven frequently with blinds, main armament and machine gun ordnance which failed on live firing. Laughable but for the consequences.

There are published accounts that mention Geoff was standing too close behind the gun as the breech recoiled on firing, killing him. This is not what happened.

Inspecting the gun four days later, I interviewed the DG gendarmes under Geoff's command to learn that the gun's breech had jammed as Geoff attempted to fire the first round. Loaded into the chamber was a live HE shell. The breech had failed to close properly. The soldiers told me they saw smoke escaping from around the jammed breech. From his position immediately to the right of the gun, in a flash of recognition the trained mortar officer would have realised what must happen next. Roaring a warning to his two crewmen standing off to his left, it was already too late as Geoff made to spring sideways away to his right when the breech exploded.

Geoff's shout undoubtedly saved the lives of those two gendarmes. It beggars belief no one else was seriously injured. Unbelievable. The right side of the gun had exploded towards Geoff, killing him instantly. The two gun crew standing off to his left had escaped injury, seemingly protected by the gun shield deflecting the blast away. On seeing Geoff's lifeless body, one side unmarked as if asleep, the other grotesquely wounded, Costello remarked simply it looked like he'd been cut in two. What hit home, Geoff had known there was no hope the instant he yelled his warning to his soldiers immediately before the explosion. Geoff, that big strapping farmer's lad, he of chiselled chin and direct stare, had died saving his men.

Geoff's body was recovered by Land Rover in the dark. The only safe route out and back, avoiding ambush or the ever-present land mines and mine-laying parties, was along the wet sand of that night's low tide beach stretching all the way between Salalah and Taqah, the fine sandy beach we used intermittently to resupply the Taqah position. When wet, the pale yellow sand was firm enough to support Land Rovers and Bedford trucks driven at speed below the high tide mark. That night the return journey was back to Arzat camp then on to the BATT doctors at 55 Field Surgical Team, at the SAS base in Salalah.

Later Geoff's body was flown back to Muscat and buried in the SAF graveyard with full military honours. SAF had lost a good man. A thoughtful and considerate soldier. One who in his short time in Dhofar had made a difference.

Earlier in conversation one evening, Geoff and I had discovered we shared a common passion for Joan Baez songs; both in agreement on her relationship with Dylan. Indeed, I'd once known a girl who sang Baez songs almost as well as the star herself. At the time one of the most popular and haunting was 'There but for Fortune' which told it for all young soldiers facing sudden death; the lyrics hold a repeat

> 'And I'll show you a young man
> With so many reasons why
> there but for fortune, go you or I'

Geoff's death was sore, sore for us all at Arzat but particularly so for Ray Kane serving with Desert Regiment and who had recruited him into SAF. Out of the same parent regiment, Ray felt the loss as much as we who'd recently served closely with Geoff at DG. What angered was that the death of this young officer was unnecessary and avoidable but for faulty equipment.

> *10 Oct: Geoff killed today at around 1800 in Taqah when the 90mm he was firing blew up in his face ... he was firing WW2 gun and ammo!! Why are we using vintage weapons and ammo??! Words exchanged returning from taking the 5.5 back into Taqah ... claimed we'd kept him waiting too long on picquet. Unnecessary argument between mates. He died instantly, what a senseless waste. Will miss the easy companionship, much needed at Arzat, a good bloke. We're all shocked. Wrote to Geoff's parents.*

RAY KANE WB

Ray is published on the Dhofar war, sometimes he's provocative yet always eloquent; vivid reporting by one who experienced close and long-distance battles. He was pivotal in some of the more significant actions between 1970 and '72. Recalling his friend, Ray writes simply, "Rest in Peace, Good Friend".

Widely reported and written about, the July 1970 Palace Coup in Salalah saw the overthrow of Sultan Said bin Taimur and immediate replacement with his son, Sultan Qaboos bin Said al Said, held by his father in house arrest at the time.

Given less than a 50/50 likelihood of success, Ray led the assault, an audacious operation to storm the palace defended by loyal armed guards, and successfully capture alive the country's sovereign. The small force of Red Company, DR struck fast and hard. Ray accompanied by his 2ic, David Wood, captured Sultan Said, wounded but alive. Also wounded in the leg by a ricochet, Ray had seen the mission through. For their actions that day Ray and David were each deservedly awarded the Sultan's Bravery Medal, the WB.

Responding to Ray's suggestion that he volunteer, Geoff had joined SAF where, to quote, 'there's some proper soldiering to be had with men loyal and fearless, that is, once you've proven yourself in battle'. Geoff had, and likewise the respect of his soldiers and brother officers.

AFTER GEOFF

With Geoff's easy going manner it'd not been difficult becoming friends. Two months sharing danger, you get to know people well. We'd shared duties guarding Arzat, training soldiers in weaponry, rifle ranges, mine clearance, grenade throwing, field tactics and radio procedures. Shared too, ambushes, patrols and convoys. It had been a full two months.

After Geoff the mood at Arzat changed, the camaraderie never quite returned in the same way. Those who remained, Chris, Harry, Lou and I were the poorer for it. Life moves on, but you don't forget. On learning of his death, Geoff's parents wrote back to us, to say he had sent news home telling how he felt he was at last beginning to make a contribution to the life of his soldiers and their country. The poignancy was not lost on us.

Geoff had had a lot to offer and would have achieved much in the fight to help win the peace which at the time still remained a doubtful prospect. He had wanted to be a part of, and be involved with, the beginnings of a new country, helping in Oman's ascendance from what was basically still a mediaeval feudal state, to what would become a modern 20th century democratic and free country.

I realised my feelings of wretchedness in part reflected the way we'd argued that afternoon on Taqah's westly piquet. Geoff standing beside my car as I sat on the Ferret's rear deck, both ridiculously exposed to any adoo watching. Unnecessarily harsh words were batted between us, hit fast and hard as a squash ball. That's not how friends should part.

Detailed by Chris, I found myself sorting through and packing a fallen soldier's personal belongings to be sent home to his parents. It is a wretched, desolate, lonely business. Nothing comes close nor matches the abject sadness felt packing someone else's kit, stuff you'd seen worn and used on a daily basis, borrowed on occasion, but which now had no further point or usefulness, no longer cherished, as with Geoff's new Minolta camera. Inanimate, cold, defunct.

I think what gets you are the boots. There is something inherently unique about a person's footwear. Of all that is no longer required, boots are always singular to the individual. You notice the worn heel, the difference of wear between the two soles, one boot scuffed more than the other. Of course, they'd never be used again, but still you pack the boots. And you pack with a thoughtfulness and special care, a friend's kit going back to grieving parents and two brothers, Robert and Bill, on a farm 4,500 miles away in England. Taking pains in folding and packing as neatly as you can, sensitive to the knowledge who will unpack at the other end.

Unlike his seconded brothers in arms, as a contract officer Geoff's body was not being repatriated to the UK but buried with full military honours at the Christian cemetery in Northern Oman. The distinction between seconded and contract officers was never more apparent than in death. A painful and to my thinking unnecessarily coldhearted financial measure, whereby seconded dead were repatriated for burial in the UK, contract dead were buried in Oman; "a corner of a foreign field that is forever England".

Out of choice, we'd volunteered. As senior officers repeatedly briefed, the importance of our role was to defeat an ideology intent on spreading Chinese and Russian communism throughout the Middle East. BAOR soldiers faced the same threat but with the absence of live ammunition fired at them. Soldiers in Northern Ireland of course faced those same perils. We receive orders and counter orders and we do our best. The majority in Oman were junior ranked officers, either serving or ex-British Army lieutenants and sergeants aged 23 or 24, officers temporarily promoted Captain. It fell to us to carry out strategies senior officers planned at remote locations, away from bombs, mines and bullets. Geoff was 26.

What was unexpectedly reassuring was my soldiers' attitude to mortality. Whether in battle or accident, theirs was an implicit acceptance, born out of a desert existence. A mindset that had sustained their psyche over millennia. Acknowledging death, they'd respond 'Allah Kareem' (God is generous) and move on. This superiority over loss of life sent a subliminal message to those who observed. There's a Bedu saying, "Be aware the sound of your own feet upon your chosen path". 'Tis well said.

For a while Geoff's wasteful death remained foremost in our minds. We were a small unit. We knew death with all its finality might call any moment, yet when it did, it still upset. In his book, "Looking for Trouble", Peter de la Billière touches on the endemic weakness of small units such as the SAS squadrons, where people living under stresses and dangers of campaigns at close quarters are hit all the harder when losses occur. He is right. The Sultan's officers and NCOs were equally hit hard, owing to the very few serving in Dhofar.

A great many years later I learned that Geoff's parents, with his younger brother Bill, had journeyed to Oman later the same year he was killed, to visit Geoff's grave. It was December 1971 and to many of us it would have been inconceivable that such a visit might occur. Stationed and under constant attack with DR at Akoot by then, I was completely unaware of the Mawles' family visit. I would have liked to have met with them, but we were at war in Dhofar. I am sure none of my contemporaries heard of the family's visit, and Ray Kane would have moved heaven and earth to be able to meet the Mawles. That said, I am told they were looked after with great sympathy and compassion.

11

SALADINS AT LAST AND GEOFF'S GUN EXAMINED

Squadron arrives in Dhofar. My first operation with Saladins. Geoff's gun inspected. Lou and the rat and farewell to Arzat, the cat and Sibelius as Saladins arrive at Salalah. Court Martial duty. Tim KIA. Remembrance Sunday and last days with Sabre Troop Ferrets.

Callsigns: T19 – Tim Cornwell T12 – Paul Hodgson
T19A – Mike Offord T12A – Sgt Gerry Fyffe
T19B – SSM Stan Piórkowski T12B – Sgt Alan Oliver

OP BROADSIDE

11-12 Oct – Left Lou in charge, servicing Ferrets. Summoned to Midway, I joined Squadron for Op. Broadside as T12. Op was a bit of a flop – lead Saladin got lost! But we RV'd OK and moved forward into foothills to fire 76mm – on target. Noticed how clean cars were, asking how many ops/patrols they'd done – apparently just 3. So against us out every day, I don't mind a little dust in our cars. Saladins very comfortable across country.

Flying to Midway I joined the Squadron for Op Broadside commanding Tango 12 (T12), the squadron's Second troop, and with me were Sgts Oliver and Fyffe, colleagues from our Arabic course. First troop was Tim's, T19, which included Mike and SSM Piórkowskii. This was a first for the Squadron, mounting two Saladin troops operationally. It was also my first introduction to these large six-wheeled armoured cars, leaving me very impressed at the smooth ride across country. Despite my diarising the op as a 'flop' when the lead Saladin initially took the wrong route, we reached our objective on time and engaged the suspected enemy positions indicated by our firqat guides, Firqat al Badiyah (FAB). Withdrawing at last light, we made comfortable and rapid progress, initially through scrubland of thorn trees then across the rolling desert gravel plains, reaching Midway in the dark, the waning moon and bright stars producing sufficient light to find our way.

Memories of night training under damp West German skies in 55-ton tanks rumbling across neatly managed countryside on BAOR anti-Warsaw Pact manoeuvres, causing immeasurable damage to crops and ancient field systems, seemed a pointless age away. Yet, communist forces never did march into Western Europe.

Impressed how clean the Saladin turrets were, I was intrigued to learn this was just the Squadron's third op out of Midway, due mainly to maintenance problems. Knowing my cars would need a thorough deep clean before a Tim visit, I was buoyed that our Ferrets had patrolled practically every day since the beginning of August.

GEOFF'S GUN EXAMINED

14 Oct – Took beach convoy into Taqah with Huw Jones (JR) as Geoff's replacement. Also two forensic experts to inspect the 90mm. Saw flamingos en route, Khawr Sawli. White with black wing markings.

SAF EME . . . a major and his ASM didn't trust their Omani driver, so the major drove succeeding in flooding engine with sea water once, getting stuck, twice!

Ex-Royal Welsh Fusiliers (RWF) Huw Jones, JR's Intelligence Officer (IO) was loaned to DG as a temporary replacement for Geoff in Taqah. I was to take him and two Brit EME (Electrical & Mechanical Engineers) to examine Geoff's gun. The tide was right and I'd decided to take the beach run. Briefing drivers as I did each convoy to watch for soft sand, we set off, lightly armed in two Land Rovers with a Bedford truck of DG as escort. We made good time until the first sandy creek, Khawr Qanat, where I watched the EME major charge through the shallows, flooding his Land Rover engine. Stopping and ordering everyone into defensive positions around our small convoy, we waited whilst a red faced EME and passenger hurriedly dried plugs and distributor cap.

The British major, not trusting his Omani driver with the beach conditions, had taken the wheel himself. Setting off once more and fearful of flooding the engine again, our hapless officer succeeded in ploughing axle deep into soft sand at the berm, the top of the foreshore. Not once, but twice. Freeing the Land Rover both times meant we dismounted, securing the area as the Bedford turned around to use its winch attachment. It worked, saving us digging out and precious time, but by this stage Huw and I were hardly speaking to our EME senior officer.

We arrived safely, later than planned but the tide still favoured our return journey, if the inspection could be kept brief. Taking Huw over to the fort to meet his new command, I introduced him to the Wali and gave him a quick tour of the position. We then joined the group inspecting Geoff's gun.

The remains of the Giat 90mm still pointing towards the adoo positions.

Remains of the charge can be seen still in the breech which exploded to the right as Geoff tried to leap clear.

I'd seen enough and bid Huw 'bon chance' as we climbed into our vehicles, shouting encouragement we'd be back. I suggested perhaps Major EME follow my tracks on the return journey, and with that we sped rapidly along the beach, arriving safely back at Arzat in time for a snatched lunch.

The Khawr Sawli flamingos (greater flamingo: Phoenicopterus roseus) were a surprise, not the pink of their African cousins but white. They were young birds, unmistakably flamingo with their hooked beaks and long matchstick legs. Growing to 5ft (150cm) high, these 10-pound (4.5kg) birds can live to 60 years, and whilst ungainly on ground, fly with ease at 35mph (56kph). Diet affects their colouring, the pink shading in adult birds being the result of a carotenoid pigment present in an African-algae-and-crustaceans diet.

> *PM patrolled Nahiz to Umran. Took Sgt Morrison, Irish Guards, with me as third car commander.*
> *He is very good.*

That afternoon, with a patrol schedule to maintain, I offered Sgt Morrison, Irish Guards and on temporary loan to SAF, a short trip across the plain. A weapons expert, he was fully versed with the .30 Browning. He was also an excellent soldier.

> *Found 18 men sitting in a cave where wadi Nahiz meets wadi Sahalnawt. Unmoving, they sat looking at us from the dark shade as I radioed Grey Zero who came back to me – "Noted – do not engage". I couldn't really get out of my car and ask "are you adoo or friend?" Considered it – briefly. 18 against six? Couldn't see any weapons. As instructed moved off. Perhaps should have called Grey Zero for clarification they'd understood my message. We could have held them until support arrived. 'theirs not to make reply / reason why!'*

This incident has often returned to bother me – what were JR duty ops thinking? Was this a case of the newly arrived in Dhofar missing the point? More likely Grey Zero knew more about the men than had been put out, although with a detailed record of my patrols programme they would have been aware of my troop's planned patrols, day by day. With Lou off sick, there was another factor: I had taken Sgt Morrison with me commanding the third Ferret. Officially not in the country, it was paramount nothing happened to him that might get back to cause embarrassment in the UK. He and the affable Captain Peter Le Marchand (Scots Guards) were on four weeks' loan to SAF from the UK garrison at Sharjah. Their task was to instruct DG in mortar skills following Geoff's death. The two of them did a marvellous job, for within four weeks DG had the competency to safely fire their mortars in the right direction. A source of much amusement, Peter, still under 30, was never seen without his walking stick. He insisted it was a regimental tradition.

At about this time, date unrecorded in my diaries, Ray Barker-Scofield arrived at Arzat as second-in-command, DG. Chris had been out to Salalah to collect him from the airport. Meeting outside the Mess as they drove up in a Land Rover, Chris, as ever correct in etiquette, introduced our new arrival, 'Paul, this is Captain Ray Barker-Scofield, my new 2ic, Ray, may I introduce Captain Paul Hodgson, 13th/18th Royal Hussars, serving with the Armoured Car Squadron?'

With his extravagant accent, Ray greeted me, 'Very pleased to meet you, I'm sure'. 'Come on!' I thought, 'Nobody speaks like that off-stage?' Taking the proffered, soft palmed hand, an already well tanned Ray B-S smiled broadly, revealing film star teeth beneath a classic David Niven moustache. Convinced it was a Phillips wind-up, I very nearly put my foot in it, only to discover no, not a wind-up! Ray's was the perfect burlesque accent.

Chris had remained seated in his open Land Rover, sitting like the proverbial Cheshire cat, grinning from ear to ear. Positive it was a put-on, I'd glanced at Chris then back to Barker-Scofield, Chris giving nothing away. Then Harry appeared. He too received the same introduction and only by a whisker I'd avoided making an unnecessary faux pas.

Barker-Schofield, WW2 veteran, paratrooper instructor, veteran of Indian, African, Middle and various Far Eastern armies, claimed to be the archetypal mercenary. Emphatic in his denial he was anything other than a professional soldier following his calling, this man of the suspect inflection would rise to take over DG at Arzat dislodging the once in-favour Christopher and his Rolex. Later interviewed on Thames Television, Ray Barker-Scofield attained immortality.

> *17 Oct – Long day today starting at 0615. Had planned for 0545 move off, but thwarted by Ramadan prayers which I'd overlooked. My fault. Blessing in disguise as I hadn't been able to raise Grey Zero by radio until 0700 – after we'd moved out. No signs any movement, except a herd of approx 50 cattle grazing out towards Umran, one herdsman. Reported Grey Zero –"noted" came the reply. Very quiet – Have SAF operations sealed jebel to the East?*

This was one of our last patrols out of Arzat before joining the Squadron moving down to UAG after two months operating out of their Midway desert base.

That day there were no signs of adoo activity and only a single Bedu to investigate, crossing the plain with his cattle. Still required to stop him, we needed to check he was carrying the permissible quantities of salt and provisions, the allowances recently further reduced in an effort to control the illicit trade in commodities reaching the adoo. This general lack of enemy activity seemed to reinforce the successes of Op Jaguar.

> *18 Oct – Op Rabies 11. Two Ferrets, two Z Coy LRs, Patrick Freke-Evans' half Coy MR, and two 25 pdrs. Grid 0877, Adonib HF* tasks onto jebel. Scout cars – flank protection.*

*HF relates to Harassing Fire, artillery fire missions effected to demoralise the enemy rather than firing at any specific target. It is a form of psychological warfare intended to wear down an opponent.

20th Oct – Deployed with Strike Force, 2 Ferrets, half Coy MR, & JR mortars. Flank protection again, search w. Jardum for 75 base plate – grid sqs 1683 - 82 - 1581 - 82.

We drew a blank on both days. These were the last of JR's familiarisation operations with MR whose nine months of Dhofar soldiering were now ending. After they left for the north, Z Coy and Sabre Troop ACS would now be operating with JR, the new Plains Battalion.

LOU AND THE RAT

19 Oct – Taqah fort for night.

I'd taken the Ferrets into Taqah to deliver a radio to Huw now comfortably residing at the fort. We'd orders to remain overnight, which went against my preferred judgement, for I reckoned we'd be watched entering the town and would be vulnerable to both ambush and newly laid mines on our departure the following day, and with Ferrets we'd not the option of using the beach route. In the event neither occurred. Following an excellent curry and rice supper shared with soldiers, Huw, Lou and I had retired to the fort's flat roof for a quiet beer or two, before turning in. After a while, when we'd discussed the vastness of the night sky, the invisible new moon and stars at their brightest, we'd gradually drifted off into contented sleep. But for an occasional voice rising from the village, all was quiet and peaceful until about 0300 when sleep was shattered by a demoniac scream. Feeling pressure on his chest, Lou awoke to find a large rat sitting on him. His yell 'Ughhhh, God! . . . *Shiiiit!* – it's a ferking RAT!!' drifted out across the town's rooftops.

That sent the fort's defenders scrambling to stand-to positions. Heard through the melee of rifles being cocked, orders shouted and feet pounding came 'D'yer ferking see size o'that?' from my incredulous sergeant. 'It's a rat,' replied a drowsy Huw, as together we burst out laughing, relief easing tension, 'it's only a bloody rat|!' Now wide awake, we delighted in regaling him how rats had been known to eat the toes of sleeping soldiers on the Western Front in 1916. Lou never did live that one down.

The large rodent was probably a well-fed Nile Rat (Arvicanthus Niloticus), found widely across Dhofar's jebel grasslands, and in townships, drawn by man's wasteful habits. The species are related closely to the African Grass Rat. None of us liked rats, period.

23 Oct – About five days ago . . . caught in sandstorm whilst returning from Umm al Ghawarif, which preceded sudden rain deluge! First covered by sand, rain washed my escorts and I clean, leaving us soaked to skin . . . Costello and the boys greatly amused on our arrival back.

Two further ops. with Strike Force but no contacts. There has been no physical contact with adoo for almost a month on Plains, other than mines. They still lob mortars and 75mm shells around. Again little seems to be happening on the plains. Jaguar success?

25 Oct – Wonder how the Regiment is celebrating Balaklava Day?

Despite my absence from Regimental life (with the 13th/18th Royal Hussars), the annual Balaklava Day celebrations in honour of our principal battle honour, remained imprinted in the mind.

LEAVING ARZAT AND PARTING WITH SIBELIUS AND CAT

Living in my room at night and ranging around the Mess during the day, the tiny cat had now become the accepted Officers' Mess Cat-in-Residence. Partial to scraps of food readily accepted from Mohamed the Mess cook, Spent-Case-Cartridge-Bag with his convoluted name now shortened simply to 'Cat', flourished. Whilst not sure about the rat population, Cat kept the more numerous and tropically sized, large shiny brown cockroaches at bay. I have no doubt these are delicious, but not raw and crunchy as he preferred. Cat was growing fast and would one day be the scourge of any creature smaller than himself venturing to make a home in or around the Officers' Mess. When I left, he remained at Arzat answerable only to Harry who spoiled him rotten. It was a wise QM who saw the benefit of an excellent rodent and cockroach hunter. Harry kept me posted on Cat's progress and it turned out he became a firm favourite with the Mess staff too. When Harry moved to join the Firqat as QM, he left a contented and well-fed Cat at Arzat with Ray Barker-Scofield, newly appointed Officer Commanding DG.

On 29th October my troop were eventually moved from Arzat to rejoin the squadron based at UAG. It was early, just after first light as we left. I was to rendezvous with Mike Offord, Squadron 2ic, at UAG having been allocated the job of overseeing unloading Saladins being flown from Midway.

With our kit packed the night before into Land Rovers and a Bedford truck, we rose at 0545. Even Lou, never the best early riser, was at his car with the boys as I walked over carrying SMG, magazine ammo belt, binos, freshly filled chargul and map. Clinging tightly to my shirt across one shoulder was Sibelius, with his chameleon's superior demeanour. Promising my driver Ali Hamdan I would not let Sibelius anywhere near him, I gave the order 'mount up' and we drove slowly in line away from the camp that'd been home for the past three months. I would miss Harry, but I was glad to be leaving.

We made a detour across to Mamurah's ancient and once-splendid gardens. Amongst a collection of majestic coconut trees (Cocos nucifera) there remained a few sad-looking relics of vegetation, plants just recognisable despite the combined effects of neglect, lack of water, grazing goats and camels.

It was hard to visualise what once must have been a magnificent ornamental garden. But a few bougainvillaea survived, an evergreen climber that scrambles over host plants. These bushes added a touch of colour, quite unexpected in an otherwise desolate landscape, thin papery bracts glowed in the sunlight with shades of magenta, purples and reds. Stunted shrubs, all that remained of the deserted Royal Gardens, the property of the Sultan's mother, this collection of 'Bougainvillaea glabra' hung tenaciously to life.

Fifty years on, the gardens remain a botanical jewel on Salalah plain that has become a major coconut-producing region in the Middle East. Halting the convoy briefly, in the still early dawn light, I set Sibelius free. Placing him on a tangle of bougainvillaea, my companion didn't give me a second glance as he made off.

Ever anxious Sibelius

With the purposeful gait of his species, the master of camouflage inched his way into the shrub gradually osmosing leaf colour. Momentarily he stopped to turn his head, one roving eye fixed on me, a forefoot held out before him as if in bewildered benediction, a free chameleon once again.

THE SALADINS ARRIVE AT SALALAH

29 Oct – Support Troop T12 commanded by SSM Stan Piórkowski, with Sgts Alan Oliver and Gerry Fyffe posted to Akoot, joining DR roulement convoy as they relieve NFR at the end of nine month operational tour in Dhofar. Due to deteriorating situation here, Saladins required on Salalah Plains. Three cars plus two Ferrets and support vehicles flown down from Midway. Airlift undertaken by RAF Hercules on special loan to SAF for operation. Mike and I met each aircraft as they landed. Incredible aircraft. Someone took a shot at us as we waited, possibly a Martini-Henry – heard report as it passed overhead, followed by boom from Salalah. Some idiot showing off? Made us duck though!

T12 under Squadron Sergeant Major Piórkowski were joining DR as part of the Akoot defence. In response to increasing attacks on the RAF base, HQ redeployed the three remaining Saladins and two Ferrets to Salalah from Midway. The cars were flown down in two C130 aircraft, on loan to SAF from the UK for the operational move. With Mike we unloaded each of the armoured cars without hitch, more than a little relieved not to have caused any damage to Her Majesty's RAF Hercules, damage which might have been difficult to explain back in the UK.

As the last cars unloaded we heard a bullet '*crack*' overhead. Involuntarily ducking, we looked at each other with a 'what the fuck?' exclamation and in no time the C130's crew were back on board. With engines roaring, billowing great dust clouds over us, the aircraft rumbled away across the airfield to take-off and safety.

With the dust settling, we looked back towards the palm trees bordering Salalah in the distance but couldn't make out any sign of movement, in fact anybody. Still as a desert's midday, nothing moving except the heat haze, that optical illusion caused by the varying temperatures between sun baked ground and cooler air above it. 'Martini Henry, I think,' Mike's comment carried a far greater conviction than I felt. As the bullet had cracked as it passed, I wondered if a Martini Henry's would have done the same. 'At least we'll have a Saladin and Ferret escort back to camp,' he added. There was never any explanation for the

SALADINS AT LAST AND GEOFF'S GUN EXAMINED

Saladins arrive at Salalah flown south from Midway, ferried with gun turrets facing backwards to avoid denting the C130 fuselage.

Mike watches as the last two Ferret Scout Cars offload. The adoo-held Qara jebel in the distance.

shot and reflecting later, I reckoned it was probably a .303 round, possibly fired to remind us there were still other types of weapons in Oman, weapons that would do the job just as satisfactorily as any modern high velocity rifle. Or perhaps it'd been just a case of bloody mindedness? We never found out and arrived back at UAG without further incident.

The Squadron had been reorganised. T12, commanded by Squadron Sergeant Major Piórkowski with three cars were deployed to Akoot with DR in the Western jebel. T13, third troop, was soon deployed to Adonib under Mike, in support of JR's company position.

After almost four months, I had rejoined the squadron as Sabre Troop Leader, now with six Ferret Scout Cars. My role as a Recce Troop was unchanged, patrolling Salalah Plains and escorting convoys whilst remaining part of Strike Force, based at Umm Al Ghawarif, Dhofar HQ. Tim, ostensibly based at Midway, spent his time flying between his scattered squadron, Adonib, Akoot, Midway, where our stores were maintained, and back to Bayt al Falaj in northern Oman, where he continued the battle for urgently needed spares and equipment.

5 Nov – The Squadron now patrolling with the Saladins. Limousines compared to my Ferrets. Escorted Saladins on familiarisation patrols around Hedgehogs, followed by Hearts and Minds patrol through Arzat village.

COURT MARTIAL

Unexpectedly, I'd replaced Mike, officiating at a court martial after he had been taken ill. Acting as principal adjudicator was a senior staff officer, Major RHJ Anderson who had flown down from SAF HQ at Bayt al Falaj, Muscat. Commissioned in 1941, he'd served with the Rajputana Rifles during WW2, before transferring to the Green Howards. On retiring from the British Army, he joined SAF where he continued to serve until a second retirement in 1973. A man who'd acquired a considerable girth and perhaps unfairly been described as choleric, he'd nonetheless attained a reverence throughout SAF as 'The Drum'. Assisting him, a 45-year-old Baluchi lieutenant, also flown down from SAF HQ and then myself, taken off active patrolling to sit on a court martial.

In freshly laundered, carefully ironed shirt and khaki trousers, I reported at 0700 to the makeshift courtroom, a Dhofar HQ staff officer's rapidly rearranged office. On arrival, court procedures were explained with what I felt alarming alacrity. We were sitting as a Field General Court Martial (FGCM), as used in wartime. Just three commissioned officers were needed to be present, and the decision had to be unanimous for the death penalty to be imposed. Death penalty? The Drum went on, there would be no right to appeal.

He then laid out the charges against the defendants, three young Desert Regiment soldiers from Red Coy. They were up for 'desertion in the field'. As a group, they'd refused orders to join a patrol out of Akoot and downed arms. Refusing such an order on active service carried the ultimate penalty, death by firing squad. I glanced across at the third officer sitting the other side of The Drum in the air-conditioned room and despite being immaculately turned out, he'd begun to sweat. Similarly caught off balance, he met my eyes and his look was as mine, stunned at what we'd just learned about this court martial.

I learnt defence would be led by Rick, DR's 2 Company commander also down from Akoot. Knowing Rick so well and added to the fact four months earlier I'd served with Red Coy training in Oman, I realised there might be a conflict of interest, which I voiced. The reply received was the sort one might have expected from an overbearing headmaster on your first day at school, precisely as the one I had attended, run by a ferocious monocle-wearing ex-Indian Army colonel, too handy with a cane. Blunt and to the point, the reply was frankly he'd not time to wait for another officer so I'd better bloody get on with it. A man known for his booming persona, this was not an altercation I was going to win and dutifully I gave way to his 20 plus stone (130 kg) against my humble 11½ (73 kg). HQ officers always did eat better than field.

The three Red Company defendants were Ray Kane's men. Baluchis, young men with whom I'd possibly shared meals and lived amongst, volunteers recruited from Quetta, capital city of Balochistan, some 1500km away. Living in what was then a destitute country, they'd joined SAF for the money. Their interest wasn't with the Sultan's war, but their pay to send home to feed families. Fed up with being led into contacts by career furthering or gung-ho British officers, these soldiers just wanted to earn, survive and return home one day.

Suffice to say Rick put in an Oscar-winning performance, reminding me of the handful of attempts I'd tried to do as well as he, when hours spent carefully researching and writing up Pleas in Mitigation, I'd endeavoured to excuse generally good men who'd 'gone AWOL' in BAOR. Here the seriousness of the charges was altogether different. Evidence heard, and the courtroom cleared, the two of us less distinguished officers listened patiently as The Drum expounded on the importance of making an example of 'men who refused to fight!'. Garrison Commander Bayt al Falaj, Major RGH Anderson WKhM (distinguished service) was unquestionably an extremely experienced Staff Officer, who'd served in SAF for longer than most could remember. But at that particular moment I doubted whether he could recall when he'd last carried a rifle into battle.

The Baluchi officer and I broke off to talk things over. It was soon quite clear we each considered the Drum's seemingly unshakeable stance needed serious tempering. Reaching agreement, we took our seats either side of the great man and argued for sentences that reflected far greater clemency than that he seemed to propose. Touch and go, but eventually we reached a compromise with the adjudicating officer. Sentences were agreed: two years' jail and a return to regimental duties. It would be no ordinary jail, but a darkened dungeon at Jelali Fort in Muscat, a veritable hellhole, the most notorious of Oman's prisons and known for its appalling conditions. Due to recruiting shortages, the men were back serving with their regiment within the year.

Eighteen months later at a separate court martial, a handful of men were tried for plotting mutiny. Facing capital punishment, they were duly sentenced and executed by firing squad. They had plotted to attack Izki Camp in the north and murder DR's British officers, 2 Company's Rick and Alan, so would have expected no mercy. I was greatly relieved not to have been called to sit on that trial.

1 Nov – Patrolled towards Raysut with Strike Force, mobilised out to Khawr Sawli.

2 Nov – Taqah Convoy – nothing to report.

3, 4 Nov – OPs Room HQ – Orderly Officer

5 Nov – Raysut sector again today – when going into danger, it is very reassuring to look back and see a Saladin hull down in a firing position, covering you forward. Tim told me today I may have to go up to Akoot as SSM Piórkowski not being quite as diplomatic as perhaps he might be. Saladins at last?

6 Nov – Visited DG en route Khaw Sawli patrol. Paid exorbitant Mess bill! Be glad to get to Akoot.

SALADINS AT LAST!

Whilst relishing being free from Chris Phillips' constant interference in my operational role out of Arzat, I sorely missed the autonomy enjoyed over the last three months. Gone, the satisfaction of running my own operations out of Arzat, reporting directly to Commander Dhofar, Colonel Mike Harvey or in his absence, CSAF, Brigadier John Graham. Now back with the Squadron and working as Plains

Recce Troop, I was once again, and quite rightly, subordinate to Tim commanding the Squadron. I missed the freedom of planning patrols, or ad hoc, joining Z Company when together we'd carried out sorties across the plains and out towards adoo-held wadis at the foot of the jebel. Hence with the hint of a possible move to take over the Saladin troop in action at Akoot, my spirits rose immediately.

Excited at the prospect of Saladins, my delight was tempered by losing Costello who was to remain in Ferrets for continuity reasons. However, he would be re-joining me one day, I made sure of that. Tim knew how well we worked together and promised to send Costello to join me once Plains Recce Troop had settled in with Piórkowski. In my favour I knew there were few who would put up with his idiosyncrasies, and 'Irish', as he later became known, would follow me to Akoot sooner than later.

And that same month, a FCO briefing announced a new firqat was being formed,

"... of Western Mahra tribesmen to start training at Midway sometime after 7 November for deployment west of Akoot".

Eleven months on, driving Land Rovers and Bedford trucks, these same gentlemen with a troop of my soldiers involved, would form part of a daring clandestine raid into Yemen.

TIM TAYLOR, SULTAN'S COMMENDATION MEDAL

7 Nov – Remembrance Sunday
Tim Taylor killed today. Very, very sad. Remembrance Sunday service here at SAS base. Need smock for Akoot – see Q.

Tim was mortally wounded at Akoot, SAF's forward operating base on the 3,400ft Jebel al Qamar, a rocky, windswept, dusty place some 35km east of Yemen's border.

The attack as always came out of the blue. A sudden whistle building to scream announces an incoming rocket, supported by machine guns firing bullets that crack overhead, seeking targets randomly, direct or by ricochet, as these weapons are designed to do.

The Akoot battalion were effectively contained, encircled on three sides by the communists who controlled the southern approaches from west to east. An enemy with a seemingly endless supply of ordnance attacked with impunity, firing rockets, mortars, heavy and light machine guns, causing a growing number of casualties amongst DR who'd been there a month. The camp was also encircled by mines.

Tim was hit by shrapnel from an exploding rocket fired from a RCL, a recoilless rocket launcher. As the first incomers arrived, he'd run back to the Mess tent for his binoculars. 2 Coy Officers' Mess sat snug in a ravine, across which an army brown canvas marquee had been stretched taut and secured with boulders between the two wadi walls.

Four camp chairs, a trestle table and small coffee table counted for furniture. There was a paraffin refrigerator and the place was lit by a paraffin pressure lamp. The floor had a canvas sheet, swept twice daily. There was a cook and a couple of Mess waiters. Tim's high standards, enjoyed by his 2ic, Rick, and the battalion's Mortar Officer, Tom, ensured the heights of comfort with all mod cons sufficient to maintain morale during a gruelling nine-month tour ahead. It might have been Raffles in Singapore. They certainly had gin.

Tim entered the tent as a 75mm RCL round landed, exploding into a hellfire of burning shrapnel and stone splinters ricocheting against everything within the wadi walls of the open plan tent. He never had a chance. Nothing inside the tent escaped the penetrating shards of exploding rocket. Tim was still standing, bleeding profusely from multiple wounds as Rick, then Tom ran back into the tent. Calmly, and probably unable to hear anything but the high-pitched inner ear scream that follows a close explosion, he asked for morphine. He would have realised how badly he was hit but remained quiet; fixing his two officers with a steady stare, he again asked for morphine.

Momentarily frozen in disbelief, it was a second before automatic responses kicked in and they caught Tim before he fell. Rick tore a syrette from his neck and administered a shot of pain-easing morphine into Tim's arm. Finding a gaping wound to Tim's chest, Tom grabbed a pillow, pressing it against the wound to staunch the blood loss. Tim needed immediate attention and lifting their company commander the two carried him to their Land Rover, driving directly down to the battalion HQ and Babu's marquee hospital. Babu now took over as weakening, yet still the consummate soldier, Tim ordered his two officers away, Rick to take command of the company, Tom the mortars.

A few days later, the battalion doctor to whom we turned unhesitatingly in times of medical need, Babu, recounted to me the unequal struggle to save Tim. The chest wound, though serious, was not the main concern. Unnoticed by his two officers due to his extensive wounds, Tim had been hit in the groin by a shard of shrapnel. Fighting against time, Babu found he was unable to stem the blood flowing from this primary wound, a badly severed femoral artery high in Tim's groin. With little more than field dressings to staunch the blood loss, Babu continued his fight to keep Tim awake, trying to calm his patient as his loss of blood became ever more critical, whilst the attack continued and the agonising wait for a helicopter lengthened.

Babu explained how the ends of a cut artery spring back beneath the skin like a rubber band and he couldn't reach into the wound sufficiently to stem the flow of life-giving blood. Growing agitated, Tim demanded yet more morphine. Babu couldn't risk giving him a further shot, the need to keep his patient conscious overriding the temptation to alleviate pain. It was paramount to keep him calm, the mounting anguish Babu felt matching only the pain of his friend.

The helicopter arrived 40 minutes after scrambling from Salalah. Given that timescale, Tim's chances were nil. He died from his wounds on the flight to the Field Surgical Team Hospital in Salalah. A gifted soldier, greatly admired by his men, he'd always a ready word of encouragement for us younger officers. Cool in temperament and calm under fire. A champion Bisley shot. The Green Jackets had lost one of their best. In addition to those of his command, his brother officers and his devastated family, Tim left a young fiancée. A life which once had held so much promise, now unfulfilled.

As with anyone who has dealt with the severely wounded, there is an inevitability in wondering if it might not have been possible to do more. The two carried these doubts needlessly, until the reality was fully explained by our mutual friend, Dr Babu. One can only imagine the effect on Tim's two younger officers who'd escaped injury to survive as helpless witnesses to the mortal wounding of their company commander and friend. Nothing they could have done would have altered the outcome.

One moment it had been just another attack when each man grabbed rifle and kit before scrambling to predetermined positions. As Rick said later, 'Tim went back for his binos and the next moment, BANG! – the tent was hit. The fucking *Mess tent!*' At Akoot, that'd constitute a joke, except someone was inside.

Positioned in a small ravine, rockets were not meant to penetrate the cocooned safe area, snug behind the robust stone-protected walls of the purposely selected Officers' Mess tent site. Surely beyond doubt a safe area? Yet the presumption that any part of the battalion base was safe from rocket or mortar attack was a ludicrous misconception, as it proved that evening.

This was war and it was imperative the battalion remained focused; Rick was promoted to the rank of major commanding 2 Company, Tom to second-in-command and SAF began recruiting for a 3rd company officer. That December, fresh from his Arabic course at the Army School of Education, Alan Howard, Royal Marines, arrived on a two-year secondment, another young lieutenant promoted captain.

Tim had been one of those instantly likeable characters, welcoming and easy going. I'd held an affinity with the Royal Green Jackets from my time as a potential officer (in the ranks) where I'd served at the Army's Outward Bound School at Morfa Camp, Towyn, North Wales. Additionally, there was a family connection through my maternal grandfather who'd commanded a battalion of the KRRC at the Somme. But for being hijacked to join the 13th/18th RH by the then adjutant Robert ffrench-Blake, I'd have remained a Green Jacket, proud to have once been called a Rifleman with 2 RGJ (Kings Royal Rifle Corps), now one of the highly respected battalions that make up The Rifles.

On his first Dhofar tour nine months earlier, Tim had been awarded the Sultan's Commendation Medal for bravery in the field of battle. As volunteers, we were young, fit and strong, at an age when you feel invincible. You've trained as soldiers to deal with the unexpected. It works bloody well, until circumstances and fate play their hand. Curiously at the time I couldn't get over that it was Tim. People like Tim didn't get killed. Sadly it was fact and should have been expected, but never is when you are young.

Avoidable death hits home hard. Ranulph Fiennes in his intuitive book "Where Soldiers Fear to Tread" makes mention of a badly wounded officer shot in the stomach, whilst on patrol deep in the jebel. Although in radio contact with his battalion, he was beyond immediate rescue and SAF was still a year away from being supplied with helicopters. Too distant to reach him with life-saving medical aid, the casualty would have to be carried off the jebel by men on foot, back to an awaiting vehicle and back to the battalion's doctor. On this occasion, too seriously wounded to move, Battalion HQ could only listen as the young man's voiced radio messages grew weaker. Remaining conscious long enough he finally dictated a message to circling SOAF fighter pilots who promised to relay his words to his mother back in the UK. His last call told of growing cold; the ambient temperature was 55 degrees centigrade. He might have lived had there been helicopters.

Despite the advent of life-saving Hueys to lift wounded off the jebel for surgery at Salalah's Field Surgical Team's hospital, whilst never admitted, skulking at the back of each soldier's mind lurked the real possibility rescue would arrive too late. And at the time, Hueys didn't fly at night.

War stories abound with anecdotes of young soldiers' deaths and one recounted by a British WW2 soldier, has always stuck. He'd written home describing how after a night spent listening, motionless, not daring to move for fear of alerting the enemy surrounding a shallow ditch he'd dropped into during a close contact, he'd found the body of a dead German soldier about his same age. The man was dead and had lain almost within reach on the other side of the hedge which had separated them. The dead soldier's identity papers (Wehrpass) confirmed he was 17. He'd cried for his mother during the night.

Unfailingly, Housman's haunting lines would come back to haunt as one more friend was killed. Following the loss of another many knew, the charming, bright, easy going Huw Jones, who queried as we sat sharing a beer in the fading light of another day, seated in the gardens of UAG, 'what a stupid, stupid fucking way for young men to earn a living'. Huw, like many of us, was still in his early twenties but his destiny would be to die in a mined Bedford truck.

On the evening Tim was killed, I wrote in my diary – a sentiment that'd recur again in my writings, hopelessly mashing the poet's gifted prose,

death is nothing to be afraid of, unless one is young,
and it's the young who die.

Sadly, and as should have been expected but never is when you are young, this note would recur again in my writings.

By cruel coincidence, Tim was killed on Remembrance Sunday, the Sunday closest to November 11th. Free to attend a late afternoon service held before stand-to, I joined British members of Dhofar HQ and BATT at the camp's open air cinema where the SAS Padre conducted the annual Service of Remembrance. The roofless cinema was basic: white painted cement block wall for a screen, dwarf walls to either side and tiered bench seating. The floor was sand. The solemn service was short and spoken. The padre listed names of the most recent casualties, and already included, was Tim's. Throughout the service watching from the sidelines stood a curious, respectful group of Arab and Baluchi soldiers, silent witnesses to a Christian ceremony.

A fortnight later at Akoot Camp, DR's HQ Company commander Graham Sherwell was relaxing whilst reading the Daily Telegraph's weekly overseas edition when he found a short piece confirming that a Major Tim Taylor, Royal Green Jackets, had been killed on active service in Oman. There was no mention of further details, the "D-Notice" effecting press silence through the British Government's enforced censorship. 'That's nicely put,' remarked Graham, putting down the flimsy overseas edition delivered earlier that day from Salalah.

As soldiers felt the loss of close friends in battle, detached within the distant safe corridors of Whitehall, discussions on Dhofar continued to address bright minds.

FCO – restricted

The daunting problems of fighting a conflict in Dhofar, surely one of the remotest corners of the world, primitive, wild and inaccessible, are such as to make the most skilled logistic planner blanch.

Political factors sometimes have to override military logic. Having rather primly said that, one must concede the truly remarkable achieve ments (sic). This fast growing force has never been hungry, without some form of shelter, without arms or ammunition, or unpaid. It administers its multi-racial self and its complex equipment in most trying conditions, with a staff miniscule in comparison to that which a similar sized Western force would expect. God (sic) lessons are learned here by young British officers.

LAST DAYS WITH SABRETROOP

8, 9, 10 Nov – Patrolled western plains – final photographs for Bde HQ. Low cloud spoiled views so had to repeat. Patrolled area to Adonib from Wadi Naar.

Hoping to complete photographing Salalah's surrounding jebel, I returned to the Western plains with four Ferrets. A low cloud base necessitated returning on consecutive days to finish the job. My move to Akoot was on hold until I finished the job first begun two weeks earlier. Why either Tim or Mike, or indeed any of the senior NCOs, weren't deemed fit for the task was never explained.

Returning on consecutive days may have been one reason the adoo became interested in the repeat Ferret patrols. Previously I had been careful to alternate patrols to avoid setting trends. Whatever the reason, the adoo were sighted in the area north of Adonib on 11 November and I was sent out with three Saladins to engage their positions in Wadi Sarit. I was conscious by the time we'd arrived from UAG the adoo would long since have departed. Still, it was an opportunity for some additional 76mm firing practice.

11 Nov – AM – relief Duty Officer Ops room. Ranges pm – Recruits live firing on the ranges. Recced NE of Arzat. MG and main armament. 6 x rounds HESH / HE per gunner. Range to targets 2400 metres. T1B - 24 HESH, 6 HE.

'Stood-to' late pm – 3 Saladins to Adonib – we fired at reported 30 adoo seen in wadi Sarit – 5 x HE and 1 x HESH.

SALADINS AT LAST AND GEOFF'S GUN EXAMINED

12 Nov – SAF Association copy must be finished by end of day. Duty Officer 0700 - 0700

13 Nov – Mike on relief.

Crewing: Akoot

T12	T12A	T12B
Hodgson	Fyffe	Oliver
Gnr: LCpl Nasir Mohamed	Sgt Jan Mohamed	Mubarik Ali
Dvr: Nasir Hamid	Said Mohamed	Hamdan Khalfan
		(Jumea Musalim 25 Nov)

Duty Officer was an inescapable chore of Brigade HQ existence. Despite the occasional drama, generally there was little to do but maintain radio contact with the outlying Ops Officers in Battalion and Company positions. At least my troop personnel were now confirmed, and whilst I knew the Brit NCOs, the Arab and Baluchi soldiers were new to me.

13, 14 Nov – More firing practice – 12 x long range HESH. Called to Arzat en route to UAG, met Lou with Ferrets and Sgt Morrison who's returning to Sharjah. Kit packed, ready to go.

My last day was spent assisting practice firing for new recruits followed by a visit to Arzat to wish them well. Sgt Morrison was returning to the Irish Guards at Sharjah. I'd heard he'd done great things with the DG boys who were now pretty efficient on mortars. With kit packed, I was at last joining Saladins at Akoot.

12

AKOOT BATTLE CAMP

Daily attacks on our mountain held position, sangars and trenches and life under fire. Op Longknives. Ramadan ends & Eid al Fitr. An interrupted dinner and a too close for comfort brush with a Colt .45.

Callsigns
Desert Regiment – Sand
OC – Sand 9
Red Coy – Sand 1
2 Coy – Sand 2
3 Coy – Sand 3
ACS – Tango 12, 12A, 12B
Artillery – Golf 2

FTZ – Firqat were issued with Panasonic handheld radios and used names to identify a caller's ID, having not yet advanced to using SAF voice procedures.

AKOOT BATTLE CAMP

'Akoot: a dreadful place, surrounded by minefields...'

Rowland White

15 Nov – Akoot? At last YES!
Self, LCpl Nasir Mohamed, Hamdan Khalfan, Mubarik Ali : Skyvan flight.
T12, 12B on ridge – no contact.

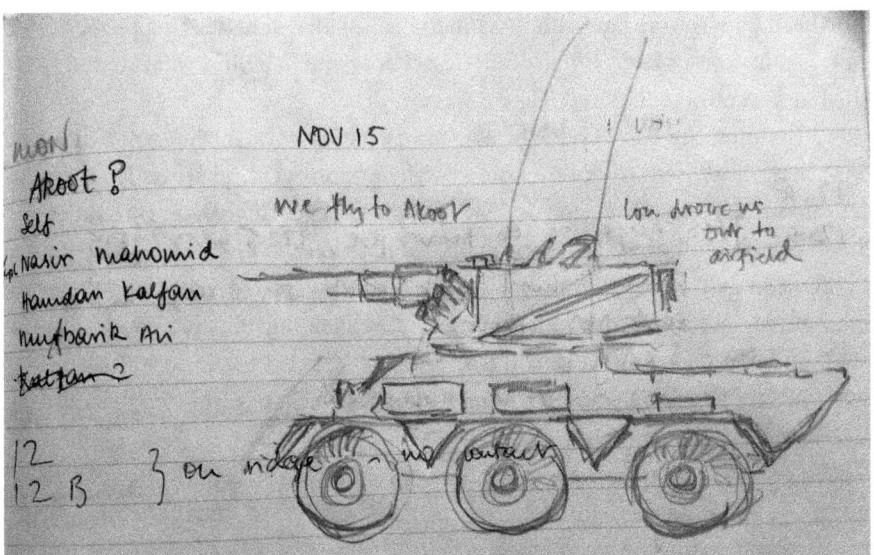

Diarised sketch of a Saladin at Akoot

At last I was on my way, with three crewmen, LCpl Nasir Mohamed, Troopers Hamdan Khalfan and Mubarik Ali. Lou drove us to the airfield at Salalah to catch the only Akoot flight that day. Accompanying him, Abdullah Ali and Ali Hamdan came to see us off. Departing, we shook hands formally and I promised we'd serve together again. They were a great bunch.

Climbing through the Skyvan's gaping loading bay, I saw we weren't the only passengers. We'd be accompanying the battalion's resupply of rations that included six live goats, tethered inside plastic bags with heads free, successfully reducing both mess and goat fragrance. Ordnance, mail, my crews' kit, our personal weapons plus my now increasingly battered blue Globetrotter suitcase and canvas rucksack completed the load. After an uneventful noisy flight, we landed at Akoot. The dusty airfield was set on the only flat ground at the northern edge of camp. Perfect tactically as being farthest away from incomers, but a recurring problem otherwise as each aircraft landing and taking off produced great clouds of dust that drifted over the camp, depositing a film of the desert's best soft powder over everything.

Jebel al Qamar's alpine atmosphere was hot and arid during summer months, in winter when temperatures dropped, rationed water froze in shaving bowls or outside your sangar where spat brushing teeth the night before. With chill winds blowing increasing the levels of discomfort, it was bitter, for none had adequate clothing. Gloves were unheard of, and soldiers accustomed to warmer climes of

Northern Oman were particularly vulnerable, sockless and wearing rubber soled canvas plimsolls or later, thin leather desert boots. In Saladins, we wrapped spare shemaghs around necks and feet for warmth.

Arriving at the base I had the briefest of meetings with the larger-than-life SSM Stan Piórkowski. We'd met only briefly a month earlier when I was up for Op Broadside, as he had been on leave during my initial weeks at Bid Bid camp. Scrambling out of the Skyvan, we caught up on matters. With less than ten minutes to fill me in on the troop's status before the aircraft departed, I gathered this large man might have a problem with SAF hierarchy. 'Fucking officers – sorry, not you, sir!' he assured me whilst confirming the men were in fine fettle but vehicle spares were 'fucking non-existent!'. This point had been one of the causes for his row with Col Nigel. A point I took on board.

An exceptional man, the teenage Stan had escaped the chaotic tumult of Nazi occupation in Poland, making his way to Paris where he'd joined the Resistance,

Stan crouching, and Lou show a fitter how it's done.

fighting alongside the French for the remainder of WW2. At the war's end not only had he mastered passable French, he'd also picked up a smattering of English working with British SOE operatives. Unemployed with the ending of hostilities, a series of chance introductions found him recruited into the British army, joining the 11th Hussars. Reaching retirement, he was now contract soldiering with SAF.

Undeniably a capable soldier, he was also a natural mechanic and as strong as an ox. Oblivious of whom he upset, quick to temper, with no time for 'Fuk'n idiots' and a liking for the occasional dram had earned him the epithet 'Purewhisky'. He also answered to Popski.

As SSM he'd been given command of Saladin troop, Tango 12 (T12). Together with Sgts Alan Oliver and Gerry Fyffe, he'd moved to support DR recently deployed at Akoot. They'd arrived escorting a roulement convoy travelling via Mudhai from Midway. Known for his short fuse, he'd unfortunately managed to cross swords with OC DR, Colonel Nigel Knocker, who'd demanded his immediate replacement. In the right place, at the right time, Stan would go on to prove his worth over and over again. In recognition of his unwavering support to the Squadron, Stan was awarded the WKhM, the Sultan's Distinguished Service Medal in 1974.

ALEX LAMOND WKHM DESERT REGIMENT

Tearing along an uneven track a Land Rover skidded to a halt, showering everyone in stones and dust. Alex Lamond (45 Commando Royal Artillery) never did things by half measures. DR's Ops Officer was to prove one of those rare individuals in life, filled with an inexhaustible supply of hubris and almost childlike infectious energy. Alex had missed his vocation as an entertainer treading the boards; the West End's loss, the army's gain. Reassuringly quick with a grin which spread ear to ear, his welcoming voice boomed, barked from beneath a ridiculously full, reddish brown handlebar moustache. He also had a huge laugh. Endeavouring to take in all he was saying and despite his warning an attack was expected at any time, the abiding image was of a moustache as splendid as Falstaff's.

With his customary bonhomie, he'd driven over to welcome me at the airfield and loading us and kit into his battered Land Rover, we'd driven bouncing over the rocky terrain to my troop's position. A group of sangars shielded four canvas tents lashed to sangar walls. Set aside was a Bedford truck's canopy strapped onto a sangar wall. 'That's yours!' before pointing out the three Saladin sangars, two empty and one holding a stationary armoured car. Unloading our gear from his Land Rover, he shouted, 'Your sergeants will be returning from the ridge, once we've the all-clear! Make yourself comfortable!' With a wave of his hand and a backwards shout 'Colonel's expecting you in fifteen minutes, the boys will show you where HQ is', Alex disappeared in a cloud of dust.

Shortly afterwards the two Saladins returned and I was introduced to my troop. Sgts Alan Oliver and Gerry Fyffe from our language course greeted me with six Omani crew members, a qualified fitter (electrical/mechanical engineer) and my new orderly.

'Welcome, sir,' grinned Sgt Oliver, nodding towards the Bedford canopy, 'better than Buckingham Palace!' It was indeed very smart. 'Ideal,' I replied as we entered the dark interior from the bright sunshine's glare and immediately struck my head against the tubular steel frame. Sgt Oliver quipped, 'Oh yes, you're going to have to watch the height, Popski's shorter than you.'

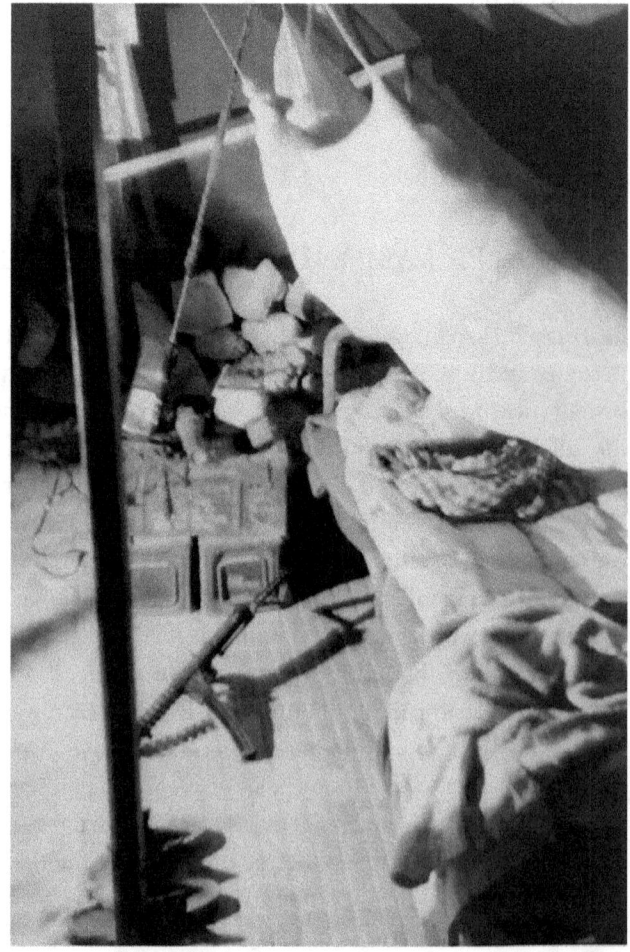

My home for the next four months. Hard sprung bed, off-ground and scorpion free, sleeping bag, shemagh, fly/mosquito net, blankets, no pillow, personal weapon and handset radio.

AKOOT BATTLE CAMP

By my bed, the troop Mills 36 hand grenades and morphine syrettes store. Alarm clock. Woven grass matting on earth floor. There were no mosquitoes, but a net protected against biting flies, ferocious in their search for life-giving moisture, of any and every sort. The alarm clock, gifted by my brother, remained with me until eventually meeting its demise chewed to pieces by an infuriated cocker spaniel puppy, five years later.

Following introductions with each of my men, I left to meet DR's Col Nigel. Battalion HQ was 600 metres away set up under a brown canvas marquee across a small wadi, an enclave deemed safe from enemy direct fire. With a soft canvas roof, it presented a prize kill zone to a lucky adoo mortar or RCL gunner.

The Akoot battle group, comprised DR's three rifle coys of four platoons, plus mortar, pioneer and MT platoons, an artillery light detachment (three 25 pounders and a 5.5in Howitzer), my three Saladins, and a firqat, Jebali irregulars named Firqat Tariq bin Ziyad (FTZ). As with each firqat attached to SAF, their numbers included men who had recently fought as our enemy. With a change of loyalties and for some, the lure of 100 Saudi Riyals apiece – then approximately worth £100 – they'd come over to fight for the Sultan. At the time, the bounty was an attractive sum.

The FTZ were positioned behind me to my near right flank, a point that was to have a particular relevance less than three weeks later when in the early hours of a particularly black moonless night, nervous members of the FTZ woke us, having mistaken a hyena for advancing adoo. Blasting away into the darkness, they were soon firing directly towards our tents. Believing we were under attack when several rounds passed cleanly through our canvases and onwards towards Battalion HQ, we'd scrambled to cars.

Briefly trying to determine where the shots were coming from, for it seemed everywhere was lit by tracer, I gave the order to move to our predetermined emergency defence positions. Ten minutes of frenetic radio activity followed whilst the firqat continued pouring automatic fire into the darkness. During this period, Col Nigel radioed with orders to immediately fall back to Defensive Position 1, adjacent to Battalion HQ. (Position 2 defended the airstrip and ammo dump further to our rear.) I replied I was already there. To my relief this was met with 'Bloody good, await orders'. Sunray (Col Nigel) sounded pleased. Taking the initiative, pre-empting a commanding officer's order is always dicey, it might have been difficult had he wanted me elsewhere. Once the shooting ended we were stood-down and returned to cold beds, cursing those who mistook hyenas for adoo, for it was not an isolated incident.

At my first briefing with my new commanding officer, Col Nigel with Alex gave me a full low down on the latest military situation, enemy positions, the

Sheershitti caves (adoo stronghold), the daily rate of incoming rocket, mortar and machine gun attacks, casualties, mine fields (ours), patrols, ambushes, harassing fire, my stand-to duties, patrols and arcs of fire. Stoically, I made notes and marked up my maps. Finally, Alex pointed out the location of the officer's loo, more of which later.

I returned to my troop's quarters and called them together in front of their accommodation, together with the two sergeants. I then told them I would brief them each morning after attending prayers, the Colonel's daily orders group. After that we would carry out vehicle maintenance as necessary, ready for afternoon duties picquetting Akoot ridge. There would be SMG drills and live firing, which I knew was lacking with the Saladin crews, and I warned we'd be doing some physical training which we all needed to combat the long hours spent on watch sitting in cars. Also, I would send for a volleyball and net which was met with much enthusiasm. Finally, any questions? That, as usual, opened a floodgate of queries about rations, pay, compassionate, sick and annual leave . . . I really should have known better.

At last I got away to unpack. My new accommodation had been well built, thick walls of limestone boulders supporting the cannibalised Bedford truck canopy as a roof. The truck I discovered had recently been blown up on an anti-tank mine travelling to Akoot. Whilst the truck had disintegrated, the canopy frame was otherwise unscathed, complete with its original canvas-clad topping. Holed in places told of its recent history, otherwise it looked the height of post-modern architecture. Already warned to watch my head on the frame, it offered more space than a tent.

The indispensable Bedford 3-ton truck was a bastion of troop, munitions, food and water transport for the Sultan's army. Likewise as important within the British Army, BAOR and all other postings where Her Majesty's Forces were deployed around the globe. Later I would use these dependable trucks on patrols, convoys, troop movements and occasionally for transporting army donkeys, selfless animals of burden used for carrying ammunition on foot patrols in the jebel. We used them also to carry our wounded.

Inside my tent, grass matting covered the earth floor, reducing greatly the amount of persistent dust that seemed to penetrate even the tightest bound bag, rucksack or suitcase. There was a stretched and slightly sagging steel sprung bed (Popski's weight being slightly greater than mine), plus a couple of chairs and small wooden table. It looked very comfortable.

Otherwise, one of the three Saladins was in army jargon VOR, 'vehicle off road'. Not a promising start. LCpl Habeeb Bullah the Baluchi fitter promised to have the car fixed by the next day and that afternoon I took the two roadworthy

An armed Saladin on patrol in Wadi Gharah, North Dhofar. Sgt Lou Costello in T12B moves past my car, south east of Mudhai, in March 1972, when we'd been tasked with finding a suitable route onto the plateau of Jebel al Qamar at the western reaches of Dhofar. The gunner/radio operator sitting beside him, is Mubarik Ali, educated, likeable and English speaking but a rogue who defected to the adoo in early 1973.

cars T12A and 12B up to our positions, hull down along Akoot ridge, facing adoo territory, a task we would undertake daily for the next four months unless on operations out of camp.

Crossing dry wadis, the cars would sometimes sink 45 centimetres into the loose bed of rounded stones. It never ceased to amaze that devoid of life but for the occasional withered thorn tree baking in temperatures approaching 55 Celsius, these wadis of evaporated moisture had once run with water sufficient to erode hard limestone rocks into smooth rounded stones.

Tim and the rest of the squadron were fully occupied on Salalah Plain supporting SAF infantry, but also BATT operations, running convoys to Taqah and patrolling the plain. Once again I was left to my own devices where we were employed on battalion piquet duties, escorts for resupply transport, supporting patrols on ambushes and escorting essential firewood collection missions.

I was happy to be left alone and increasingly surprised at Tim's apparent confidence in my ability not to damage or misuse his beloved Saladins. Noticeably absent, he only once visited us at Akoot where we were under almost daily attack from rocket, mortar, heavy machine gun and small arms fire. His faith was just fine with me.

Sgt Gerry Fyffe had begun to suffer repeated attacks of fevers and high temperatures. Doctor Babu, finding no sign of any obvious infection or reason for Fyffe's condition, decided to send him back to Salalah for tests. In answer to my request, Lou Costello, now tiring of the tedium of Salalah plains patrolling, joined us. Freed from repeated convoy duties east to Taqah and Rauzut to the west of the 30 mile (48km) plain, for a while he was a happy man. Once Gerry was better, he returned and Lou was transferred back to Salalah. But we would serve together again.

Our days at Akoot now fell into a familiar routine, each afternoon picqueting the southern ridge of the camp's basin position, interspersed with 'stand-to' responses every time we were attacked. Be it day or night we'd deploy to whichever of the numerous firing positions best suited to respond to the attack being launched. Each morning I endeavoured to take the boys through a few warm-up exercises, short runs around our sector of the camp, followed with PT, and of course volleyball, exercises which they seemed to enjoy, such that they grumbled if a session were ever missed due to attacks, necessary vehicle maintenance or patrols out of camp!

Also, we built a small arms shooting range to keep the crews gun-safe and proficient in the use of personal weapons. The otherwise excellent, simple to use, and clean but unpredictable and accident-prone SMG 9mm submachine gun was a weapon if dropped on its butt was likely to let loose a burst of automatic fire. I am glad to say that none of my men ever discharged his machine gun accidentally, an occurrence on active service that can be all too common when each man permanently carries and lives with a loaded weapon. I return to this weapon in greater detail later in the book.

Apart from our daily routine, there were patrols when we joined one or other of the three DR companies and occasionally DR's Recce platoon. The reliability of our cars was a constant worry, primarily due to the acute lack of vehicle spares, but also it must be said, through soldier inexperience, inevitable in the circumstances for none had been armoured car crewmen longer than four or five months. As yet, and still a nascent part of the recently expanded army and war effort, stretching the country's finances to the limit, Tim had the unenviable struggle sourcing his front-line troops with sufficient parts to ensure we remained battleworthy.

During those early days following the Squadron's formation, it was due solely to Tim's unstinting and courageous determination that we remained 90% fit for battle whilst constantly on the front line. Sad to relate, HQ SAF would never repay or recognise properly the considerable debt owed to Tim for his inexhaustible qualities and tenacious willpower ensuring the ACS remained a fighting force within SAF.

Apart from time spent on picquet along Akoot ridge, sitting hull-down (turret only exposed) in firing positions, we 'stood to' at dawn and dusk, historically the expected time of attack. The adoo were wise to this unavoidable pattern and registered the ridge which they bombed repeatedly. So much so it became almost a game. For much of the time it was quiet, each side observing the other, waiting for the first to make a false move, or through inaction, become complacent.

There were long periods of inactivity as we sat in our hot Saladins. Eyes grew tired straining for signs of movement through binoculars, new sangars or any evidence of disturbance to the rocky hilltops around us, up to 1,000m away. During these periods it was not difficult to find one's mind drifting from the present to far-off places and people left behind, particularly girlfriends. We were normal young men. The lack of female company was naturally a regular cause for discussion during evenings sat around the stone built open fireplace ingeniously constructed and cut through the Mess marquee's wall. Remarkably, there was never any evidence of scorching to the canvas wall.

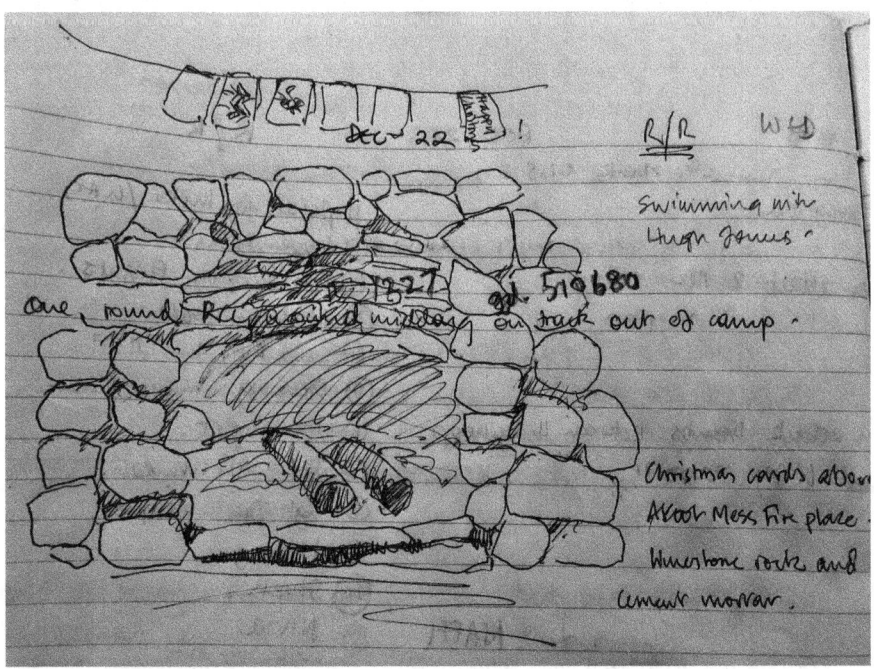

The Mess fireplace, with our displayed Christmas cards.

Girls. God, how we missed girls. Not that any of us were in any way presentable to the fairer sex given four to five weeks living on the jebel between much needed R&R visits to HQ. Showered, shaved, haircut, change of clothes, a meal and drink at the Mess bar, we might attempt presentability for barely 20 hours before catching a helicopter or Skyvan back to Akoot.

Each held remembered loves found or lost or perhaps left in limbo. Forgotten memories that'd creep uninvited into the subconscious, leaving a pang of remorse at how possibly once shared love might have been saved, now irretrievably lost. For most of us, the situation was probably determined by a combination of neglect, distance and life choice. So then, our fault. But that didn't count a jot to those in their early twenties, knowing what fun friends were enjoying back in the UK, or indeed West Germany. Undoubtedly, we'd too much time to think. Yet how much worse for those older men either married or engaged and forced to live 7,250km apart, fighting a war in a foreign land, a war nobody was meant to know about. Sadly, one heard of relationships that failed. It had been bad enough in BAOR, but with the added uncertainties of active service and distance, I was thankful to be unattached.

Inevitably there were times when we reflected on our choice of career. Off-duty and relaxing on R&R at headquarters, UAG, the career choice question might be raised. Measured against the apparent abandonment civilian friends were enjoying in the post flower-power revolution, it seemed hedonism still blossomed across the free world, particularly in Britain, Europe and the USA. To young men suffering enforced celibacy, it didn't help we'd volunteered!

> *16 Nov – adoo mor fire 1725, 1815hrs*
> *nine bombs – most just short 3 Coy in east Akoot – no casualties today.*
> *T12A,12B 2 Coy, T12 with 3 Coy – engaged with HE*

Periods spent musing over such thoughts vanished explosively that afternoon as the first of nine incoming rounds screamed in to smash into the ridge close to our cars. In an instant you revert to the soldier at war. The mortars dropped close to my car and I engaged with HE, 3 Coy's 2ic, Dick Morgan-Evans having located and passed on the suspected adoo position.

We took no casualties that day.

> *17 Nov – 2 Coy + recce + T12A, 12B to Manston – helicopter op.*
> *More a training exercise – use of armour and infantry working together.*
> *T12 off rd – suspected electrical problem – distributor? no spares.*
> *PH duty in Ops tent – 1300/1600 and 0300/0500 tomorrow.*

Olly and Lou escorted 2 Coy north to Manston and returned without incident whilst I was on duty in the Ops tent, my car VOR with distributor problems. With no spares, such a minor problem grounded one of the Sultan's six fighting Saladins, a ludicrous situation but one we had become used to living with. Everyone, be they infantry, guns or armour was short on spares and ordnance; even the air force suffered. However, it was clear as a numerically small but particularly expensive entity, the ACS would suffer disproportionately. We just had to get on with it.

> 18 Nov – 0300/0500 on Ops duty
> T19 – Daily calls – 0800, and if any answer needed, call again 1300 or 1700hrs.
> Op. Longknives 5 – O group – Recce Vimy Ridge
> Aim – ambush adoo routes twds Akoot
> Op Longknives 5 – Vimy
> Execution:
> 1 – Red and 3 Coy into posns night 19th
> 2 – Amd Cars group – 0545 first light 20th – with half recce pl L/rovers + ammo and Tom + 4 mortars + half recce pl + donkeys for mortars + FTZ
> 3 – Cars group – withdraw last light
> 4 – Followed by Red and 3 Coys
> 5 – Red posn 4763 – Alex FOO
> 6 – 2 Coy in reserve – Tom (mortars/donkeys)
> 7 – 3 Coy posn 4963 – Chris Long-Price FOO
>
> Fired 4 rds HE onto sangar Vimy ridge – two adoo @ 2600m.

At 0800 daily I'd check in with Tim (T19) at UAG, giving him a report on vehicles, men and any provisions we required. Contact reports were submitted daily to HQ Dhofar.

On picquet that afternoon Abdullah Ali spotted movement, two men in a sangar on Vimy Ridge, to our south. We engaged with four rounds HE demolishing the stone fortifications. Possible mine layers? No further movement was seen. Op Longknives was a recce towards Vimy Ridge to our south on the 19th, followed by taking the ridge on the 20th, and we needed it to be clear of adoo and mines.

> 19 Nov – Op Longknives 5 – Take & hold Vimy
> T12 – i/c Recce Group in Land Rovers, DR recce and Firqat FTZ. Tom – mortars with donkeys. L/rovers.
> T12A, 12B move with Recce group.
> Move out first light to Vimy Ridge.

0500 reveille
0530 RV – T12 take Recce pl to ramp
0545 – leave camp by forward ramp
0645 – in posn
1700 – Withdraw – T12A, 12B – cover withdrawal.
1745 – T12 and Land Rovers RTB
Casevac – Donkey by night: Chopper by day

Ramadan ends? Naam!! (Yes!)
Mechanic cleaning spark plugs let sand fall into engine. On stand-to following attack, Rasul Bux started up against orders – now car definitely V.O.R.

Undoubtedly an inauspicious day for my troop. My diary entry says it all. Fine sand, the bane of our lives was a constant problem. When responding to attacks we'd race to our cars and move out at top speed to firing positions, inevitably creating an all-enveloping dust cloud. And moving out twice daily to take up picquet positions, the reverse was true when we motored in low gears, in an attempt to reduce the dust problem, but also conceal our exact positions, hull down on the Akoot ridge line. Yet still dust got everywhere. And no matter how often we oiled and cleaned surfaces, it returned to mock our futile efforts.

That day, the inevitable happened: whilst removing spark plugs for cleaning, our fitter, failing to notice he'd caught a scoop of fine powdered sand in the sleeve of his overalls, poured it directly into two of the open spark plug housings. That was it, there was nothing further we could do given the lack of specialised equipment. None too pleased with life, I went off to radio for an urgent EME visit (mechanical engineer) the next day. But the day's problems had hardly begun.

As I'd walked away, Sgt Oliver and the crew closed the engine decks, leaving the car parked in its sangar by my tent. We were attacked ten minutes later by 82mm mortar. Nasir Hamid, my usual driver, was away on compassionate leave, his father having recently died. In his place I'd been sent a newly qualified, ultra keen young Baluchi driver, trooper Rasul Bux (not to be confused with the dependable Corporal Rasul Bux). My replacement driver ran from his tented quarters 30 metres away, leapt into the open driver's compartment of my VOR Saladin and immediately pressed the starter button. A horrible noise was heard as the powerful V8 turned over and Sgt Oliver, running past to respond to the attack, screamed at the hapless rookie 'Fucking stop!'. I'd a rule profanity be used only against ourselves or circumstances, for it caused offence, disproportionately. Olly's outburst was rare and understandable. I heard him apologise later to the young trooper. The army adverb we've taught the world.

The car remained VOR until repaired on 21st Nov after a visit from SAF's mechanical 'God' – Bert Kenyon, WOI in charge of Dhofar Area workshops, whom I'd got to know well when commanding Sabre Troop Ferrets. With no car, I'd volunteered to take command of DR Recce in Land Rovers and together with my two remaining Saladins and FTZ, I would be joining Tom and his mortars for the op. All was set for an early start at daybreak the next day.

News that evening received by morse code from Dhofar HQ, confirmed the crescent moon had been sighted and religious leaders declared Ramadan officially over. There was quiet relief throughout the camp and we learned Eid al-Fitr would be officially celebrated in two days' time.

20 Nov – Op. Longknives 5
Contact 508647 – men seen/engaged

Feeling naked out of my Saladin, I led DR Recce platoon in Land Rovers as T12A and 12B leap-frogged ahead to secure the ridge we knew as Vimy. Red and 3 Coys were already in position the day before, to our left and right flanks, 2 Coy mortars behind in depth.

We moved through Tom's mortars dropping off additional 81mm ammo with his donkey section, not only SAF's archaic carriers but also our best means of evacuating wounded at night. Despite a good start, we were delayed reaching Vimy through Land Rover punctures, the razor-sharp limestone playing hell, slicing soft walled pneumatic tyres.

Adoo were spotted around midday moving through scrub at grids 490610 and 496643 and engaged using mortars. Too far to accurately judge effectiveness, but sighted movement justified engagement. The day wore on quietly otherwise until preparing to withdraw, a man was spotted running towards us and immediately engaged, grid 508647 to our south east. Undoubtedly there'd have been more, but firing ceased and later all returned to base safely.

THE MIND WANDERS – ROCK, 'EAGLE', GENUINE HOSPITALITY AND RANK SOCKS

It's a kindness that the mind can go where it pleases.

Ovid

21 Nov – Fix commanders .30 Browning's ammunition feed
Contact reports 19/20 Nov – done

> *ammo state post op – done*
> *T12 repaired by 1100. Bert is Superman. On picquet from midday. Nothing happening, fondly recalled BAOR adventures. Eye strain.*

Often at a day's end, eyes ached from straining too long through 8x30 binos searching for signs of movement, dust raised, or a dark shape that might indicate man at 1,000, or 2,500m, absorbing, not reflecting light. As the sun slipped to the west, it became all the harder to peer into the horizon against a setting sun's blinding glare.

Sitting in a turret for long periods, minutes became hours, hours became days when thoughts might return to forgotten adventures. In BAOR, 'Adventure training' was a pseudonym for escaping the tedium of tank maintenance to go rock climbing, canoeing or, in the winter, skiing. Recalling one occasion accompanied by my troop corporal, Steve Davies, we'd taken a group of men rock climbing. During a brief lull in tank warfare exercises on Lüneburg Heath, we took off for a weekend in a Bedford packed with my climbing ropes and gear, army rations, cookers and sleeping bags. We'd no helmets, now sensibly considered a prerequisite with rock climbing. And we'd no tents: it was summer.

Equipment was non-existent: I had two climbing ropes and a handful of heavy steel carabiners, relics of my teenage posting at the Army's Outward Bound School in Snowdonia. Commanded by the charismatic Brigadier Charles Storrs Howard, DSO, late Ghurkas, it'd been a spartan life of leaking Nissen huts, cold showers and pre-breakfast daily mile run to plunge into Cardigan Bay's icy waters.

Semi-retired, ruddy faced and standing at over six foot five inches (two metres), Brigadier Howard towered over us all. Seldom without his blackthorn thumbstick, he'd be seen striding purposefully about the camp, a pair of black labradors at his heels, followed by plumes of white smoke wafting from an old briar pipe, clenched between his teeth. Anyone who dared complain, be it the wet or cold or blisters or scrapes would be labelled 'a girl'. Straight out of Kipling, hugely respected by us all, like many of his generation, he'd lived and fought through both world wars and various insurgencies. Completing my February outward bound course, I'd somehow managed to convince the army they should retain me as an assistant climbing instructor. To my astonishment, for the role didn't exist, I was accepted and so remained at Morfa rather than rejoin my infantry regiment. A week into my new post and on hearing I was awaiting entry to Mons Officer Cadet School, the Brigadier graciously insisted I live in the Officers' Mess as a precursor to one day gaining a commission. I'd just turned 18 and was a potential officer (PO) serving in the ranks. To their credit the instructors accepted my temporary elevation, making me very welcome.

Famously, the Commandant's greeting at breakfast was a hearty 'Good morning, Comrades!' – a hangover from his time fighting communists in Malaya. Sadly, after a full and eventful life, he died suddenly in September that year. By sheer coincidence one of the mountaineering course students that month was a Sandhurst Officer Cadet, Sandy Blackett. Small world.

Back to the rock-climbing weekend in Germany. Approaching a rockface we hoped to climb, we'd given a lift to a local who'd introduced himself as 'Adler – in English, that's Eagle'. A climber with rope slung across shoulders, he was on his way for some solo work. Knowing the area well, Adler kindly offered to assist in choice of routes, on one occasion giving me a top rope through a daunting overhang well beyond my comfort zone. We must have looked a sight climbing dressed in our tank overalls and combat jackets. Without helmets, or harnesses and belayed by bowline, we climbed in issue DMS, rubber soled boots, not the most sensitive of climbing footwear when searching for small footholds.

In the afternoon, our newly recruited mountain guide and I taught the boys the classic abseil, the Dülfersitz, a non-mechanical abseiling technique named after its mountaineer inventor Hans Dülfer. Used infrequently today since the introduction of belay devices, I know no better emergency off-the-rocks escape. Passed around the body, rope friction against clothing controls the speed of descent.

Knowing how to Dülfersitz, ropes are spared unnecessary wear often experienced with belay devices. It remains essential ropes don't kink, for that hurts. Sufficient thickness of clothing is needed to avoid friction burns where running ropes slide past shoulder, neck and groin, which will make your eyes water. As the novices learned that afternoon, a controlled descent certainly minimises the unwelcome effects of rope burn to sensitive areas.

Bidding farewell to our German companion, we returned tired and sunburned, with sinews stretched, hands and knuckles rock-grazed and bodies bruised. Back at our truck the mood was upbeat. There was much bravado talk brought on by a sense of achievement and I was proud of these young Yorkshire Hussars, for none had climbed before.

Sitting on my sleeping bag with my back against a tree, sipping a brew, I listened contentedly to the cheerful banter whilst two troopers prepared supper, bully beef mash. We'd had a great day, climbing and abseiling; the sun had shone and the rocks were dry. Thoughts of tank drills, gunnery and radio procedures, engine maintenance, BAOR tactical O groups and map reading temporarily forgotten.

As we cleared our makeshift cookhouse, we were approached by an elderly couple whom I had noticed observing us from their nearby farmhouse. We'd spoken briefly that morning on arrival when I'd introduced my lot, seeking permission to park up for the day. The hulk of a Bedford takes up a lot of room on a farm track and we'd parked respectfully, gaining their consent to stay.

I rose up to greet them as they insisted we use their hay barn as shelter. Expressing my gratitude, we moved camp across to the farm steading to settle in for the night, beneath the welcome cover of the ancient shingle clad, clay tiled barn. We were then further invited, this time into their home for coffee. Oh God, I groaned inwardly, knowing I must accept their additional kindness. This elderly couple, I thought, have obviously never experienced, or long since forgotten, young soldiers who've lived and slept in oil-stained clothes in evil-smelling tanks for over a week.

Entering the large utilitarian farmhouse kitchen with its imposing green tiled heating and cooking kiln oven, belting out heat, we politely removed our boots and sat down around the kitchen table. Mugs of hot coffee and biscuits soon followed.

In that warm atmosphere, it was no time at all before the aroma of dairy farmyard was eclipsed by nine pairs of sweat stained green army issue, 65% acrylic, 20% wool and 15% indestructible nylon socks.

Not a word of complaint was heard. But the stench! As soon as we'd finished our coffees, I caught Steve Davies's 'time to go' expression and thanking our hosts once again, made our excuses, professing the need to be away early the next morning. The memory brought a smile – perhaps farmyard smells imbue the nostril's natural olfactory receptors? I hoped so, they were decent people. Stevie Davies, at no taller than about 5ft 6 inches, later rose to become RSM and then won a Queen's commission. A remarkable soldier.

> *22 Nov – Monday but Jumea routine – Eid al Fitr. feast with the boys.*
> *First adoo attack 1000 – 7 rounds RCL*
> *Second adoo attack –1705 – T12A scores direct hit on adoo sangar. 2 killed.*
> *Third adoo attack – 2000 – 81mm mortars, RCL, heavy machine gun and small arms.*
> *Fourth adoo attack – 2300 – one 81mm mortar*
> *Fifth adoo attack – 0600 23 Nov – one mortar*
> *Dinner with 2 Coy Rick/Tom – post stand-to. They've chosen to retain shrapnel pitted fridge which still works. Bit macabre.*
> *Attack 2000 – mortars, RCL and Shpagin plus small arms. Two RCL over 2 Coy Mess tent, landing metres beyond. Ordered to rejoin Troop – missed dinner. Dick saw Sphaghin rounds striking ground under my Land Rover – presented me with a round as Talisman – nearly ran him over!*
> *Long day responding to nuisance attacks. 2 Coy Mess tent RCLs very near thing.*

EID AL FITR – 22 NOVEMBER

A Caribou departs, taking off to the north out of adoo range, leaving its customary trail of fine dust to drift over the base. Within five months, the adoo had registered the airfield, their rockets effectively denying Akoot resupply by fixed wing aircraft.

The ending of Ramadan brought a sense of relief and celebration, lifting spirits. The boys had been making preparations for their feast since earlier that morning, nonchalantly working around the adoo's first attack.

The colonel's order for 'Jumea routines', meant duties were limited to 'stand-to' and daily weapons cleaning, a necessary constant. Each afternoon a wind blew to whip dust into every conceivable crevice, be it weapon, armoured car, tent, clothing, mouth, nose, eyes and ears. Sun, winds, heat, cold, flies, the realities of desert life.

Predictably the adoo decided to augment Eid celebrations with nuisance attacks over 24 hours. To their credit, my troop still managed to produce a mouth-scorching, heavily spiced celebratory meal. Given our usual restricted rations, what was produced was a feast. With Eid approaching and deserving of a reward, I'd placed a special order with DR's quartermaster. Paying cash, I arranged for a live goat to be flown up from Salalah market and the animal had been delivered by Skyvan the day before.

To fresh goat was added sweated onions, raisins and a lethal variety of chilli peppers. Over an open fire set between three rugby ball sized stones, the meal was carefully cooked by a couple of would-be chefs. Albeit recipients of a continuous stream of unheeded advice from onlookers, they worked studiously and with particular pride. The finished dish, a warm reddish-brown stew was gently and deliberately poured over steaming hot, boiled white rice already overflowing a large oval tin dish, in a familiar display of the desert people's generous hospitality.

The soldiers' main meal of the day was taken at 1500. Invited earlier to join them, we three Brits had foregone lunch. I was catching up on paperwork when Nasir Mohamed entered my tent, grinning widely, to announce the feast was ready. Needing no further persuasion, I called Olly and Gerry to join us. As we approached, the troop rose graciously from their places seated in a circle, shuffling aside indicating where we should take our seats. 'Tafaddal Sahb, tafaddal,' Nasir Mohamed and Nasir Hamid enjoined, bidding me sit between them on the ground as we settled cross-legged in a tight group encircling the sumptuous feast piled too high on an overfilled circular dish.

Tender goat pulled off the bone, served with caramelised onion, chilli peppers, raisins and fresh herbs, pungent flavours that sent taste buds into meltdown. Eager fingers picked out prize pieces of cheek muscle which were lifted carefully around the dish and placed in front of the three of us car commanders, a tradition of honouring guests, which equally, tradition forbade even polite refusal.

We ate with our right hands, dexterously and single-handedly forming a cup out of the malleable soft boiled rice. Steaming hot – this required nimble fingers to escape scalding, always a cause of much merriment when failing to do so. Surviving this test, the trick was then to dip your rice cup into the juicy meat, scoop a portion and in a single movement lift it up into your mouth avoiding at all costs drips, let alone spillages onto clothing or the ground. Between each mouthful there was constant chatter. Sometimes there'd be earnest questions about British dining habits, the whole gamut of cooking and food preparation, life in the UK, had we met the Queen, did she live in a fort or castle? Eating in the local fashion was an art form, but once mastered it seemed the most natural way to feed. My first Eid al Fitr feast was one of those memorable meals that leave a lasting imprint.

Chillies left a protesting, burning mouth that the meal's finishing black coffee and sweets did little to extinguish. On patrols months later, sharing similar dishes after days subjected to desert sun and winds, we found fresh chopped chillies were purgatory to sunburned mouths. Getting food past burned lips was always going to be difficult. Already sore, cracked and sometimes bleeding, it stung like hell, needing wiping quickly with a wetted corner of shemagh. No one laughed then. Laughing split burned lips anyway.

The second attack came at 1705. Already up on the ridge towards end of day stand-to, we were watching and waiting. T12A, seeing two men firing from a sangar at 600m, opened up and claimed a direct hit, later confirmed on Radio Aden making their regular propaganda announcements as to casualties SAF had suffered, whilst also disclosing two of the Front's fighters had been killed at Akoot. There were two further attacks that evening, another at first-light next day.

DINNER WITH TOM AND RICK

22 Nov – Quite a day: Attacked four times, the third as I was having pre-dinner drinks with Tom and Rick. Two 75mm rockets exploded behind Mess tent. Think I hit the floor first, 2nd time – first caught me by surprise! Their reflexes! Tom and Rick, quickest in Akoot?! Also small arms and Shpagin. Reaching Tom's sangar, was quite happy talking with him as he directed mortars – without slightest intention of re-joining my Saladins – both sergeants were there and with only two cars motorable, felt justified staying put. As it was, bullets were ricocheting off wadi walls behind us, so driving along the ridge considered suicidal.

Then Col Nigel ordered me back to my Saladins. I wilcoed as Tom and I exchanged astonished glances and I rushed to my Land Rover. Took off as fast as it would go. Silhouetted by flares, learned later bullets followed my progress, striking ground around and under Land Rover. Lady luck on my side.

Having received an invitation to join 2 Company for dinner that evening after stand-down, in accordance with British Officers' Mess etiquette I'd booked myself out for dinner advising I'd be dining with 2 Coy. So far, so good.

Following evening stand-down, leaving my two serviceable Saladins in their blast sangars, a quick debrief and orders for the night guard, I dismissed the troop before driving out to 2 Coy's position. Carried with me, my loaded Sterling, magazines and Panasonic radio, a soldier's arm extensions.

Driving towards our earlier picquets I followed a route west, skirting below Akoot's southern ridgeline along a dusty, potholed track strewn with incomer blast-holes and occasional lump of limestone. Driving past where we'd spent that afternoon on stand-to, I arrived at the western most point of Akoot camp, 2 Coy's position. Sangars dug in depth and sighted just below the skyline from the adoo's perspective, it presented a strong defensive position. But the adoo had it registered.

Arriving, I found the Mess tent's new brown canvas marquee stretched across a narrow ravine, much as ours further back at HQ. Substantial two-metre-high stone walls built at both front and rear entrances offered blast protection from exploding bombs and ricochets. The sides were vertical wadi walls. As with HQ Coy's Mess, the entrance protection had been constructed with two offset walls allowing passage for one man to pass through diagonally. But it was difficult not to reflect perhaps the protection was flawed, the soft skinned canvas roof offering sun protection only. The case proven 15 days earlier when an exploding rocket had left Tim mortally wounded.

I had been looking forward to a reunion meal with my fellow Arabic course attendees, and heard 2 Coy's Royal Marine and Royal Horse Artillery gunner dined well. Who said beggars can't be choosers? Entering the messing tent, it came as quite a shock to observe everything, the spartan furniture, canvas floor and Mess paraffin refrigerator still bore the scars of rocket shrapnel that had killed Tim. As I took in my surroundings, Rick saw me glancing at the motley assortment of their furnishings. 'Fridge's working, so why change it? Furniture's OK too, don't you think?' quizzed Rick. 'Sure,' I remarked, forcing my gaze away from the horrendously pockmarked fridge. 'Great to see you two again' as I accepted a beer thrust at me, sitting gingerly not quite trusting the badly holed chair.

Tim's death still a vivid memory, I wondered whether it'd been wise to accept their invitation to dinner, but any awkwardness was soon lost as we began reminiscing of our idle time at the army language school. All we needed was Sandy, now back in northern Oman with MR, to complete the circle. The four of us had got along famously and we'd enjoyed a string of noisy evenings in the admittedly utilitarian Beaconsfield Mess bar, but also local pubs and parties. Rick's engagement bash was one in particular. Sandy, with parents in Scotland, had spent the occasional weekend with me at my family home in Sussex.

I'd decided to avoid the subject of Tim's death, but it'd been unavoidable given the evidence all around us. I think it was Rick who broached the subject first and I listened without interruption or question to the grim reality, still first-degree burn raw for my two friends. Hearing them talk, I could only hope it was somehow a cathartic exercise for the two of them. Thirty minutes passed. First beers downed and the conversation eased, lifting to our proposed African expedition in February when we planned to visit East Africa's game parks and climb Kilimanjaro. I could sense anticipation mounting as I outlined my plans.

Screeeam – BANG! Without warning, but then it's always without warning: the banshee screech that heralded incoming rockets. The explosion was just beyond the tent's walled exit. I'd ducked my head, remaining seated. The other two, only too aware of the awful consequences had leapt spring-loaded to flatten themselves under the small table with an alacrity that'd have impressed an olympic scout. 'Fuck . . . whaaat was that?' I heard myself say as the other two raised themselves from flattened positions on the floor. 'Fucking RCL!' replied Rick hoarsely, adding needlessly, 'new noise eh?' A second rocket screamed in. This time I hit the floor first, wishing it'd been softer; even better, very deep.

'Shit! Shit! Shit!' I heard Rick's yell through the whistling now occupying my ears. The second round had landed closer, dust and small stones arriving to bounce, drumming noisily on the stretched flimsy tent covering, shrapnel thudding into the solid rock walls at the entrance. One behind, one in front, we were bracketed. 'OUT!' Rick barked as he and Tom, simultaneously grabbing rifles and radios, made a dash for the front exit, scrambling past the protective wall opening. Hot on their heels and stooping low out of instinct, I ran with them to the first sangar with Tom, as Rick sprinted on to another further up the slope, 2 Coy command sangar.

More rockets landed and adding to the cacophony of noise a Shpagin opened up, tracer rounds lighting Akoot's lengthy ridge as they struck bouncing ricochets overhead. Then Douglas Maclaine's guns roared in response. The artillery doing what they do best. 'Hurts the ears?' enquired Tom, more statement than question. 'Best keep your mouth open, reduces explosive pressure on eardrums.'

Oman Artillery's Captain Douglas Maclaine was a first-class gunner who won a WB. Operating as a Forward Observation Officer with MR, he'd been wounded in a contact and inexplicably left behind when the battalion withdrew. It was a stomach wound and he couldn't move. Only the courage of his Baluchi signaller saved Douglas. Remaining with his officer, the operator bent his radio aerial flat against the ground to avoid detection as the adoo moved forward towards MR's recently vacated position. Not able to speak for fear of giving away their position, the signaller quietly tapped out a message using morse code, alerting TAC HQ to their predicament. A rapid counterattack followed and the couple were successfully rescued. Being left behind is every soldier's nightmare. Douglas made a full recovery and duly returned to active service. Brave man.

Standing beside a grinning Tom in his mortar platoon sangar, he berated my sluggish reactions when the first rocket landed, adding how impressed he'd been with my moves as the second came in! Responding to the banter, I was pointing out I'd noticed the gunner was the faster of us three, when our radios crackled with a staccato call from Sunray DR, 'Tango – WHERE ARE YOU?'

'Tango 12, with Sand 29A,' I replied, adding I was hoping to have dinner with 2 Coy. This clearly failed to register, as abruptly came an unrepeatable rebuke ordering me to return immediately to my position at the far end of the Akoot basin. 'Wilco, out' was all I could reply. Glancing towards an astonished Tom who added simply 'not a happy Sunray', I called up my two Salidins. 'Meet you on the track,' I ordered as I looked up at the mass of Shpagin rounds illuminating the night sky, producing a firework display as bullets bounced manically off the ridge and my route back. In a typically British surreal moment, we shook hands, 'Sorry about dinner,' Tom added. 'Not at all,' I replied, 'perhaps another time?' Not waiting for an answer, I ran to my Land Rover.

'Best of luck!' shouted Rick as I hurtled past his command sangar, Land Rover tyres spinning in the dirt track, out towards the now brightly lit skylined track along Akoot's ridgeline. Someone had fired flares illuminating the area. 'Oh great!' I thought through gritted teeth.

Seeing the orange tracer flying about the sky and bouncing off the ridge, 'Go! Go! Go!' I shouted willing my vehicle greater speed. Clenched tight in my hands the protesting steering wheel jarred furiously at each large stone or pothole struck as I sped through the darkness lit only by tracer and illuminating rounds.

Suddenly the dark bulk of Saladin loomed ahead, strobe-lit by incoming tracer. In that instant I slammed on the brakes skidding to a halt, fighting momentum and gravity on a downward slope, stopping just metres from the lead Saladin, Olly in T12B. 'That was close!' he yelled down at me encouragingly, as crashing gears into reverse, I reversed in a dust cloud, swinging the Land Rover to one side before leaping out to run across to T12A, Sgt Fyffe's car. 'Take it back, we'll see you there,' then to Olly: 'same positions as earlier!' climbing easily past Gerry's diminutive driver, Said Mohamed, up to the commander's hatch, to join my smiling gunner, Nasir Mohamed. Gerry's gunner, Sgt Jan Mohamed, had remained behind, guarding our position. I was back in business.

Yet I wasn't. Despite the insane drive, the adrenaline rush, the danger, once in position on the ridge, we could only watch as the attack continued, unable to fire our main armament due to the lack of 'p' bulbs – tiny light bulbs our gun sights required to enable the gunner to lay accurately onto target on a pitch-black night.

Down but not beaten, seeing the graceful arcs of incoming tracer, we used registered targets to hit back with Douglas' 25prs. In contrast to the Saladin's direct fire, it felt torturously slow directing guns, but we dropped rounds around the targets and the heavy machine guns fell silent. I suspected this had more to do with ammo shortages than a hit on target, but the effect was the same: the adoo ceased firing. Finally stood down, we returned to our night positions adjacent to the firqat sangars.

Giving stand-down, Col Nigel ordered I report next morning with an explanation as to why we'd not engaged with our 76mm main armament. 'Wilco, out' was again all I replied, thinking *'Bloody hell!!'* as we climbed off our cars. 'Tell him, sir, we can't fucking fire at night with blind sights!' shouted Olly from his car.

'Leave him to me, Olly,' I replied, keeping my cool – whilst I seethed, thinking to myself 'shouting at officers over the air – thought that shit had been left behind in Germany!' It wasn't as if I was some newly joined rookie officer. My pride hurt.

Parked up, and the troop back in their sangars with guards set, I walked down to the Mess kitchens hoping to find a bite to eat. Too late, the cooks had long gone, having taken cover as the first rockets landed on 2 Coy. They had then returned later to clear the dining and cookhouse areas against the nightly visits of Akoot's rodent and cockroach populations. Hungry and feeling sorry for myself, I walked back to my position in the darkness. On reaching my tent I decided I'd call in on the lads. Drifting down towards me was the faintest smell of coffee and I could make out the low hum of voices. 'That's what I need,' I thought, 'conversation with good men and a mug of coffee.' Making my way across to their tents and challenged on approach, I was soon welcomed and invited to sit down with them. The still mountain air was filled with the heavy aroma of coffee, charcoal and hot blackened stones used as a stove. The very welcome drink was hot, strong and bitter, the result of crushed beans freshly roasted over glowing charcoal.

On regaling how the incoming rockets had sent me diving beneath a low coffee table already riddled with shrapnel holes, the group collapsed with laughter. I seriously imagined some might die laughing. Once they'd recovered their composure, we chatted on, inconsequentially, the mood easy and relaxed. There was more coffee when Mubarik Ali asked inquiringly what I'd had to eat. I replied wearily the HQ Mess cooks had disappeared by the time we'd got back. Expressing amazement, first Nasr Mohamed, then another reached behind into the folds of their tent and out came chapattis wrapped in shemaghs. 'Eat, sahb, please.' The proffered chapatis, still warm and soft, were undoubtedly being kept for snacking during their stag duties on guard. I declined their kind offers, but that was never going to work. In face of fierce insistence and indeed desert etiquette, I had no alternative but to give way and accept their offer with humble gratitude. I have rarely tasted better chapattis. By such simple acts are friendships forged, memories deep branded.

There followed two further attacks overnight, at 2300 and 0600 the next morning, resulting in us tearing back up to the ridge in our cars, to stare out into the dark waiting for any sign of giveaway movement or accidental light. Predictably there was none, as we'd grown to expect and respect of men accustomed to a life without light during the hours of darkness. As intended, it was a long night for those at the receiving end of adoo incomers.

UP BEFORE THE BATTALION COMMANDER AND 'P' BULBS

Ten minutes before his daily briefing, I reported to Col Nigel to answer for the previous evening. To my surprise Alex was there too. Asked first to explain my absence from HQ Mess the previous night – I explained having signed out for dinner, I was legitimately visiting 2 Coy, not AWOL. Suspecting Alex had reminded the CO before I arrived, my answer was accepted, but for tactical reasons, it was made clear there'd be 'no further dining out' for me.

Then I explained to an incredulous Battalion Commander the consequences of night sights without their illuminating 'p' bulbs, where the lack of these tiny bulbs effectively ruled us out of night firing. Questioned why hadn't I fired directly back at the incoming tracer, I replied why demonstrate our inability for accuracy at night? It'd only have advertised a weakness in our ability to operate after dark – a fact any intelligent adoo or their communist advisers would be soon to capitalise on. So I'd directed artillery fire instead. I ended by saying the troop had been waiting for 'p' bulbs since arriving at Akoot.

In response, the air cleared and to his credit Col Nigel promised more support on vehicle spares. And as if by magic the long-awaited bulbs were delivered on the next resupply aircraft. I have no idea where they'd been sourced – possibly cannibalised from the Plains Troop Saladins south at Salalah? Selfishly, I didn't care – we had night firing capacity.

'OF COURSE IT'S FUCKING LOADED'

At prayers that morning, each company commander was present and reported on the night's attacks. Next to me sat Red Coy OC, Ray Kane. 'Good dinner last night?' he quipped. 'Heard Nigel was happy.' 'Happy as Larry,' I replied. All listening on their handsets would have heard the colonel's radioed messages to me the night before.

Then suddenly, with an involuntary shiver, I sat very still. Was it sixth sense? No. Too bloody obvious. Nestled in Ray's open smock pocket stared the gaping muzzle of a pistol pointing loosely at my left torso, by my reckoning somewhere around the base of my left rib cage. Sitting less than six inches from the business end of a .45 calibre automatic pistol is never recommended at any time. And when pointed at your body, the .45 has an offensively wide muzzle. It is also something that preoccupies, demanding your immediate concentration.

Ray was a hard man, qualified by fearless action in the field, with a reputation for ruthlessness. The archetypal professional soldier on contract serving with SAF.

Ray's pistol, butt down with barrel pointing mockingly up at me from the waist pocket of his WW2 British army camouflage smock, was a Colt M1911. A one-shot-stop category of weapon. The bullet makes a big hole entering and larger one leaving. There is no argument with this particular piece of military hardware. Looted from the previous Sultan's considerable arsenal, it was Ray's favoured personal weapon. Not without his detractors, Ray Kane was intolerant of those he considered not up to the mark, demanding total loyalty and blind obedience from those he led. He'd countenance no valid excuse. A hard man you did not quickly cross. It was Ray's men who'd faced the court martial at Salalah in October.

We couldn't have had more different backgrounds. Possibly for that we got on well despite him openly deriding cavalry officers in general. Never to my knowledge did he malign me. Stood up to, I believe he respected those who did. Of colourful language and strong views, yet modest of his achievements, he was characteristically loyal to his friends, a quality that one day would only quicken his departure from SAF.

That morning, 23 November, Col Nigel was outlining plans for a 3 Coy led operation. It was quite involved; Op 'Devil's Delight' involved my three armoured cars in support. Whilst concentrating hard to catch every detail, scribbling notes on my pad, radio frequencies, codes and marking up my map, it was difficult to dismiss the constancy of my neighbour's .45 pointing up at me. Not wishing to unnecessarily interrupt a now pacified colonel in full flow, I scribbled across a page of my notebook, 'RAY – that thing loaded?'

Back came the hissed dismissive: 'No fucking good empty?'!

Shit! Question or statement? One glance at Ray's wide grin and realisation dawned. He's not fucking joking. Pride alone allowed for only the slightest adjustment of posture. Hoping it wasn't too obvious, very gradually I bent forward, 'praying for a miracle'.

With the O group concluded, we were collecting radios and weapons left inside the tent's door when 3 Coy's 2ic, Dick Morgan-Evans, came across to greet me. 'What a night!' he exclaimed, adding, 'You bloody fucking near ran me over!'

It transpired as he was trying to reach his forward sangars, he'd been forced to take shelter with three men behind a small mound close to the track. They'd watched my approach, followed by a stream of Shpagin tracer striking the earth kicking up lethal combinations of stone splinters and ricochets. Not only was I drawing fire towards their exposed position, I'd only just avoided running them over. Worryingly, I never saw sight of him or his men. Typical of Dick, he'd been fascinated (his words) watching Sphagin tracer pass beneath my skylined Land Rover.

'Here,' he said, reaching into his jacket pocket to pull out a spent 12.7mm round. 'From last night's firework display, went right under your Land Rover as

Tom's Land Rover peppered with the minute shards of steel shrapnel, the type that caused such devastation to a body's soft tissue.

you drove past like a maniac,' adding, 'have a souvenir, or talisman – as if you bloody needed one; wounded at night, no fucking helicopters!'

The Shpagin round remained with me for another 15 months in Dhofar, carried in a trouser pocket. On a number of occasions it was picked up and returned to me by a soldier sharing a sangar or meal after it'd dropped out of my pocket. On one patrol along the northern reaches of Wadi Mitan bordering the Empty Quarter, we'd slept beside Land Rovers and my signaller found it in the sand as we broke camp at first light. Talisman? It may well have been at the time. Twenty-five years later, the bullet, secure in a small camphor-wood chest I'd owned since a young boy in Zanzibar, was stolen along with many other personal effects during a miserable burglary.

I wonder what was made of the Sphagin's armour-piercing round, metallic grey tungsten carbide core showing where the damaged copper casing had been scraped off as the round ricocheted on impact, to reveal the secret to the projectile's unexpected weight, a little over 64 grams.

The loss of this inanimate, 51mm length of metal upset me to a far greater degree I suspect than any benefit that might have accrued to the new owner. Once polished through months of being carried in my pocket, the shine had dulled over time. The memories though, never do.

13

WOOD CONVOYS, R&R & AMBUSH

Convoy escorts, routine ops Fanbelt, Spiders Web, Pandora's Box, Sandbeach. And significantly Op Sandmartin, the recce for SAF's spring offensive, Op Simba. Alan Howard arrives at 2 Coy. SOAF bomb adoo caves complex, ineffectively. R&R and Op Gold Block ambush. Conjunctivitis. A new shemagh and thoughts turn to Christmas.

ROUTINE SETS IN AT AKOOT

23 Nov – O gp. Op Devils Delight
Mission – shell / destroy adoo training camp Grid YU 297 464
3 Coy move out x 4 Hueys to Manston. Secure.
Elements – 3 Coy, half 2 Coy, Mortar pl, SOAF, OA – 75mm and crew, Armd Cars
Execution – move to Manston – join 3 Coy.
2 Coy in reserve – 2 pls and 2 mortar crews, remain standby at Akoot.
Armd cars – escort transport to Manston, protect pick-up point. 3 Coy return Akoot by Bedfords.
Recce pl with Armd cars escort group Akoot/Manston/Akoot
Timings – 0530 start.
Frequency – Channel 4.
Codewords: Snapper = abort op. Tin Can = LZ. Alternative pick-up point = Poppy.
Fanbelts!!

The mission was accomplished without casualties. On return together with Recce platoon we secured an area of scrubland whilst 3 Coy collected urgently required firewood for Akoot's kitchens. The only incident of note was when my car overheated. Climbing out we opened up the engine covers to discover three of the five drive belts had failed, one had fully disintegrated. We carried no spares. Enquiring as to the delay, Col Nigel was singularly unimpressed when in answer to his question, I replied there were none at camp either. Whilst Sunray fumed back at Akoot, I had more pressing issues to resolve. Looking down at the hapless frayed belts, I reckoned if we cut away the ragged pieces to leave as much semblance of belt as possible, and moved the two surviving belts across to balance the drive, it might work. Using my pocket knife, I cut away the shredded reinforced rubber as we rearranged the modified belts and once re-tightened, we were all set. I asked Nasir Hamid to start the engine gently. It worked! Commanding Nasser to keep the revs low, we limped back to camp. At Col Nigel's insistence Tim dispatched replacement engine belts which arrived the following day by Skyvan. Again I have no idea where he'd managed to source them. Without sufficient equipment to function, the Squadron was running on empty, yet still SAF HQ procrastinated over spare parts.

> *24 Nov – 0800 call: 1. Dvr Said Mohamed – mother ill – news?*
> *2. Troop Fitter for T12 – news?*
> *Red Coy may be loaned to Op Jaguar?*
> *Water convoy to Mudhai – half 2 Coy.*
> *5 RCL into 2 Coy posn. T12 bracketed. adoo fire fm B12, 13, 14 areas. Engaged. Also B22 – rht 500.*

This was the first occasion my car had been bracketed, necessitating some deft manoeuvring between firing positions. And each time we'd kick up clouds of dust revealing our new position. But at a range of 2,000m, I reckoned the adoo needed to be very lucky to secure a direct hit with RCL. Shrapnel and blast stones didn't hurt us as it did our infantry friends. Identifying three adoo positions near registered targets, B12,13, 14, we engaged. Again later 500m right of B22 where adoo were seen.

The morning call to Tim was fairly typical, requesting news of a soldier's sick mother, and chasing up a troop mechanic for my troop.

> *25 - 28 Nov – Op Civet – Red Coy away 3 day ambush and patrols – in support Op Jaguar*

WOOD CONVOYS, R&R & AMBUSH

26 - 27 Nov – Op Fanbelt – Armd Cars, Sand 60, Pioneer pl and FTZ – Recce alternative pick-up points for Manston. Ambush Wadi Aydim
HF - 1315 - 5.5 - Sheershitti
1640 - B22
1750 - B21

Naming this operation Op Fanbelt, whilst an obvious dig at my expense, was also Alex's idea of lightening the tension between our commanding officer and his armoured support. Col Nigel, under immense pressure, certainly didn't need the worry of losing a Saladin in the field through lack of spares.

28 Nov – FTZ + 1 pl 3 Coy - Vimy Ridge – search adoo mortar base plate. Tangos 12, 12A in posn. On ridge, by 1st light 0545
Contact – 3 Coy pl ambushed – no cas – 100m N C15 – poss 2 adoo KIA
1210 Western mortar area
1600 B22
1750 B21

HQ gossip was Western Reaches battalion weren't being sufficiently aggressive. Rumour had it DR was holding back in readiness for the spring offensive, Simba. Incorrect. Reflecting on my diary entries, life with DR was one long slog of fighting patrols, ambushes, reconnaissance patrols, mine clearing, road building and repairs, airfield maintenance, water and wood convoys and artillery fire missions. Desert Regiment was busy.

29 Nov – O Group – Rick and recce pm. *Akoot on helicopter diet!*
FEME here today *Towing drills – 3-tonners –*
  Armd cars 1000hrs

Shelldrake HF
1744 - B22 1 x 25
1805 - B21
2330 - Sheershitti
0340 - C40
0500 - Sheershitti

News reached us helicopter missions were to be rationed, to save flight hours but also due to lack of spares. So the ACS weren't the only unit starved of spares. At 1000hrs we practised vehicle recovery drills, Bedfords towing Saladins. Undignified, but it worked.

Douglas's artillery HF harassing fire missions interrupted beauty sleep. Needing kip we hoped it did likewise for the other side.

30 Nov – Letters home for Christmas – done.
M&D to E.A.
O Group 1600
0805 - 25   Suspected sighting 5 adoo on Vimy 0800
1735 - 25
1737 - 5.5
Op. Spider's Web: 1 - 2 Dec
3 pls, 1 sect 60mm mortar, Armd Cars, G2, 3 Coy 81mms.
Ambush with Armd Cars – Tango Group moves out a.m. 2 Dec to LUP*.
<u>*Phase 1: Dec 1st*</u> *– Tom, Rick – 2200 – out fm airfield – LUP – C11 (firm base). Rick by lone tree. Dug in by 0500.*
<u>*Phase 2: Dec 2nd*</u> *– Amd Cars + Alex + 2 pls + Art to LUP – with convoy – in posn 0800. Armd cars Posn 3.*
<u>*Phase 3*</u> *– Posn 1, C11: Posn 2, Mortars 528660: Posn 3, ACS:530645*
On completion – withdraw 1815 to C11. Breakdowns: Inf. fwd.
New DF 525636. Mortars lay on 636634 East. C/S 29,29A,29B,25, 24,21,23, T12,A,B – channel 4.

*LUP – Lie up point, used to observe a target

Spider's Web was a joint op with three platoons from 2 Coy with 3 Coy's mortars, east from Akoot to a wadi complex known to be used by adoo mortar teams. Joining my group, DR's Ops Officer, Alex, enjoying an escape from camp. It was good to have him along as a spare gunner. The op went according to plan. As an exercise we performed well, but failed to draw the adoo who no doubt viewed the whole operation from afar with indifference. In hindsight my briefing notes became ever more cryptic as we settled into set procedures. There was no contact, probably explaining the scant detail recorded.

On the domestic side – I'd managed to send off my Christmas mail to family, girlfriends and the Regiment. My parents were off to East Africa for a family funeral, a cousin of my father's. Collected and delivered by resupply aircraft, our mail was an important morale booster. Adhering to censorship rules, it was an effort to maintain a balance between what we did each day and what we might write home about. Additionally, the onus to avoid needlessly raising concern with family made for some creative writing.

News from home would expound on life's trivialities yet it was the commonplace that gained a disproportionate importance. On occasion two letters would arrive at once. When this occurred I now opened one that day, the second the next. We all envied those receiving a letter, delivered by SOAF in a canvas sack along with official papers.

2,3 Dec – Op Pandora's Box: Red Coy + 2 x BATT + FTZ and Andrew Rosencrantz from BAF.
Ambush 4866
0930 - B22 - 25   Alan Howard RM arrives – 3 Dec
0935 - Sherri - 5.5   joins Rick and Tom at 2 Coy
1750 – 2 Coy mortars adoo's western mortar area
2335 - C40 - 5.5   PM contact – RCL, no cas

Ray Kane and Ben Hodson, accompanied by BATT and the firqat, FTZ departed to lay an ambush south west of Akoot. An area of steep wadis, tributaries of the great Wadi Aydim stretching north into Arabia's Empty Quarter. Running off Aydim at a confluence north of Tudho lies Wadi Madi, the convoy route we later established to supply Habarut, a SAF outpost on the Yemeni border, territory the Squadron would patrol frequently with Firqat al Badiyah (FAB) as part of Op Vulture. Although the ambush drew a blank, the operation continued the important relationship building between SAF, BATT and firqat working together. Nearing the end of his secondment, Andrew Rosencrantz (Royal Engineers), the staff officer who had briefed us as newcomers four months earlier was down from SAF HQ, as an observer.

And significantly, Alan Howard, Royal Marines arrived to join 2 Coy. Later he wrote to remind me of that day:

> "... met Jim Parsons at Salalah when I disembarked from Yimkin Airways on 3rd December 1971 – gave me my ammo and a rifle and pointed me to a Skyvan which was just leaving. Tom met me at Akoot and took me to the 2 Coy position, where I met up with Rick. Two minutes later we had incomers, so he said "follow me" – we dashed to the front in a Land Rover and we jumped into a trench. I was still wearing a bright blue polo shirt and stone levis cords!! I only ever saw Jim in Salalah. He was contract and DR's QM. I think he visited Akoot to help with final planning on Op Simba, but I was away (with you and Tim) on the Mudhai convoy at the time."

Early the following year, Alan and I were destined to share two exposed positions on Op Simba's front line, digging in. 'Yimkin', used here by Alan, translates as 'Maybe'.

5 Dec – HM Sultan's birthday
3 Coy Op Sandbeach – track blasting.
Shelldrake missions
1010 - Sher 5.5
1520 - B22 - 25
1735 – Vimy – mortars – Tom
1740 - b21 - 25
Col Mike Harvey visit
Op Sandmartin: FTZ with Paul – Huey lift to western border region for recce: Dick Morgan-Evans and two plns 3 Coy.
3 Coy for dinner – John and Jonathan Gough-Crispin – haircuts, polo, beards

Commander Dhofar, Col Mike paid us a flying visit to attend the morning briefing. My troop went forward of Akoot with half 3 Coy under command of John Neville (Queen's Lancashire Regiment) and newly arrived Jonathan Gough-Crispin (Royal Irish Rangers). Jonathan was later promoted major taking over from John completing his secondment. We were protecting a workforce of pioneers with picks, shovels and dynamite widening a ramp leading south off Akoot ridge to take Saladins. Fully exposed as any road off a summit would be, it offered the adoo a grandstand view from their many vantage points to our south, with the result working parties were sporadically fired upon, albeit generally from a long distance. The presence of the three Saladins may well have been the sole factor in keeping the adoo at a 1,000m distance. Modifications to the ramp were completed in a day without casualties. The ramp now much improved for our Saladins.

In the finest traditions of trench warfare, Shelldrake (artillery) fired off increasing amounts of high explosive intending to divert the adoo's attention.

OP SANDMARTIN: 6-8 DECEMBER

Paul Mangin, DR's second-in-command, led a covert patrol within sight of the Yemeni border. Their mission: recce suitability of the Mainbrace and Yardarm features pivotal to mounting Op Simba in the New Year, either March or April.

Simba, the open secret operation to secure the border severing adoo supply lines, was freely discussed between young officers at Akoot. None knew exactly when it would happen, just that it would and before DR returned north on roulement next June.

Paul with Dick Morgan-Evans and two platoons from 3 Coy, were to be accompanied by ten members of the FTZ. The small force was airlifted by helicopter on 6th Dec, returning on the 8th. Owing to the significance of the reconnaissance, OC Dhofar Area, Col Mike Harvey was at Akoot for the operational briefing.

Despite the sense of excitement that we were at last taking the initiative against the communists, life within the camp otherwise went on as normal. Wood collection convoys were sent out, 2 Company were planning a move to a new position and blind artillery shells, both ours and adoo incomers were blown up and destroyed.

> 6 Dec – Wood convoy – Firefly on Sheershitti – burmails of benzene – rockets.
> Paul at 0700 at 215496 all OK – but reports men tired!
> 2 Coy will be away in Mugsail for 3 months or so – 10 Dec.
> HF
> 1620 - B22 - 25   Arms – rewards
> 1750 - B21 - 25   automatic/semi auto handguns
> 2200 - C40 - 5.5   40 Riyals – pistols, grenades etc
> 2205 - C40 - 5.5
> 2300 - C40 - 5.5
>   1030 – 2 Coy contact – 5 adoo on 'lip' between B13 & B14

FIREFLY

Firefly – was the code name for SOAF undertaking an incendiary attack. On this occasion first dropping burmails filled with benzene before firing SURA rockets as a means of ignition. This was the only incident I recall when SAF attempted the use of this type of warfare. If there were others, HQ were silent on the matter. The target was the large Sheershitti caves complex, the adoo's primary arsenal in Dhofar. The caves had remained a key SOAF target, following earlier attempts to approach the area had provoked a stronger response than the overstretched infantry could counter. In the event, the attack failed, and the caves remained impregnable, a constant thorn in the side of SAF for a further four years.

Paul radioed to confirm all was well, apart from some men complaining of tiredness. Logical given DR's static existence at Akoot where despite patrols and ambushes, men were ferried part way by helicopter, Bedford or Land Rover. Recognising a potential problem with my Saladin crews seated in cars each day, we'd continued our 30 minutes' strenuous PE every morning, sufficient to raise heart rates and get sweaty. With strict water rationing, the latter did nothing for the retention of best friends.

WOOD CONVOYS

Another firewood convoy for the men's kitchens. Extravagantly this same precious commodity was used in the Officers' Mess where a stone built open fire had been constructed by NFR's pioneer platoon when they'd established the camp. We collected wood every three weeks, sooner if supplies ran low. SAF had occupied the position for almost a year now and we were forced ever further foraging for firewood, pushing deeper into adoo territory, the treeline southeast of Akoot, lending a certain piquancy to an otherwise mundane yet necessary task. Whilst every effort was made to concentrate on seeking dead and dry wood, the pity was that living frankincense, myrrh and young acacia trees often fell to machetes, depleting an already sparse scrubland. Twelve months of a battalion collecting firewood would leave its mark.

And yet what was happening then occurs today across the globe. Populations increase and expand into unspoiled wilderness, be that unique and remote mountain habitats of Southern Arabia, Amazonian forests, or Africa's iconic Serengeti National Park where I grew up: man moves in, cutting down native vegetation for firewood, cultivation or grazing. Here it was war, not agriculture that ravaged.

Ready to return to base, laden with locally sourced wood from wadis east of Akoot.

HARASSING FIRE (HF)

The almost daily incomers fired into Akoot, rocket, mortar, heavy machine gun and small arms were adoo harassing fire, meant to demoralise but also intended to wound or kill. Likewise, SAF responded with the same intent. It is a facet of war and has existed since man first took up arms against fellow man.

Douglas MacLaine's harassing fire had become a feature of Akoot life. HF schedules were given out at morning prayers. Whilst guaranteeing the artillery useful practice, it doubtlessly added to the adoo's impression we'd ordnance to waste measured against their limited supplies carried through mountain passes, hidden in caves and used sparingly as and when the opportunity presented. My troop too would receive HF orders, though less frequently due to 76mm ammo shortages. Given selected registered targets to hit, we remained in practice too. Whether or not effective, we never knew.

I quote from a technical report Tim wrote:

"It is possible to see a very long way in most parts of Arabia, and when the other side can engage you at 7000m with 75mm RCL, you quickly find out that the

L-R, Mohamed Said, Sgt Jan Mohamed, Ali Hamdan, Nasir Hamid and Sgt Gerry Fyffe cleaning weapons and re-loading 76mm HE.

76mm can be used at quite absurd ranges. By running up a small slope we have achieved observed fire at a range of about 9000m. You may question whether or not this can be called effective fire at that sort of range. As far as we were concerned, if it stops them engaging you, makes them redeploy, or prevents them moving and buys you time, then it is effective."

We used the co-axial .30 Browning effectively up to 2,000m, and were directed to put down HF machine gunfire at selected registered targets. As Tim also penned,

"At ranges up to 2000m, we range with the co-ax, stop them with the main armament and finish them off with the co-ax. The two weapons are complementary and are taught as such."

That afternoon, 2 Coy had a contact whilst my troop was out with a party collecting wood, south and west of Akoot. Five adoo were seen at registered targets, B13 and 14, approximately 3,000m due south and engaged with mortars. The adoo were becoming increasingly brazen in their disregard to our artillery and mortar fire; that and brave.

> *7 Dec – Paul to be picked up between 1500 - 1530 – day early*
> *3 Coy mortar trg 1000hrs*
> *OA – 5.5 blind blown 1100hrs*
> *HF*
> *1215 - A22 - 25*
> *1620 - B28 - 25*
> *1800 - B21 - 25*

The Simba recce group were lifted from the Yemeni border region having completed all objectives a day ahead of their planned RTB. Back at Akoot, Dick was upbeat about the recce. He could not believe the Arabian Sea was so close, just over 3,000m south from the escarpment edge that would become Mainbrace's southern border. DR soldiers had performed well; however, the firqat irregulars had questioned the constant toing and froing, leaving them 'exhausted'!

Whilst accepted by soldiers the world over as "... someone must know what they're fucking doing?" the irregulars never quite grasped the benefits of a professional's need for detail.

Ingrained in their psyche almost as if without choice, a firqat did not hesitate making a decision, so reliant were they upon instinct over time spent planning. Often this impulsiveness led to disaster, but equally too, the chance for honour and victory.

On this occasion, deep inside enemy territory the task was to identify the numerous defensive positions DR's battle group required, including a viable airstrip, to be cleared of rock and stone obstacles, with earth surface suitable for fixed wing aircraft. In addition to DR, two companies NFR, a Light Section of Oman Artillery, three pioneer platoons and of course the irregulars FTZ, needed siting. Mapping the extensive area, Paul completed his reconnaissance a day ahead of schedule, a significant achievement.

New rules were introduced for surrendered weapons, with rewards for types of weapon retrieved. Forty riyals was a not insignificant sum. Despite the temptation, Lou hung defiantly to his AK.

R&R

Down from Akoot for a night's R&R, I'd booked into the Mess and been allocated borrowed accommodation from an officer out on patrol. On arrival, I'd met Ray Kane who offered me a lift to Umm al Ghawarif, Dhofar HQ. Passing the RAF's rubbish dump east of the base, without warning Ray suddenly slammed on the brakes, skidding to a dusty halt.

'Fuck! Just look at those!' he hissed, gesturing towards a flock of large birds circling the rubbish heap 75m away. A number sat perched on rusting drums.

'Just watch this!' he whispered. Swinging an AK47 off his lap, he levelled it, took aim and simultaneously loosed off a burst of automatic, blasting an inoffensive roosting bird into a cloud of white feathers. 'Jesus, I just hate shite hawks!' he said with a venom you'd expect more directed towards a despised enemy. Putting away his weapon as the rest of the birds disappeared in alarm, we drove on as I corrected him: 'You might find they were Egyptian Vultures . . . sacred in Egypt.' His reply, something to do with sex and ornithology was lost to a rapidly revving engine. SAF's answer to Paddy Mayne.

Photograph taken from Ray's matchless book, 'Coup D'd'état Oman'. A hard man, frequently seen barefoot.

As a footnote to this episode, we later learned RAF's fortified base had stood-to on hearing the blast of automatic gunfire so close to their outer perimeter fencing. Ray received an almighty bollocking, not for the first time, nor would it be his last. I was found guilty by association. Army justice.

That evening, sitting peacefully in the Officers' Mess gardens, I relaxed in the dark, the sun gone. Tim and Mike had left to shower before dinner. Sitting contentedly at a small table with the remains of my beer I realised the garden was empty, everyone back in their rooms or already at the bar. Light shone through the dining room's uncurtained windows, glowing softly across the small garden. An unexpected moment of serenity in the blackness, the Arabian night's air filled with the warm scent of jasmine's creamy white flowers in full bloom. Bougainvillaea fused with climbing jasmine had spread into the shading trees. Mixed with heavy botanical fragrances, wafted the delicate scent of recently dampened earth, the gardens refreshed by their daily sprinkling of hose-fed water by a 'bustani' (gardener) earlier that afternoon.

Mosquitos neither hummed nor whined as might be expected of a tropical garden at sunset, the Mess staff having sprayed liberal doses of DDT that had surprisingly now dissipated. The only sounds beyond the hum of air-conditioners, unhurried murmuring of kitchen and Mess staff preparing dinner, setting tables and clearing empty beer glasses, detritus of grateful men at ease on R&R. Away from the daily pressures of command and responsibility for those who looked to you for advice, their compassionate concerns, money problems, careers, leadership and of course home leave, the UAG gardens became a too infrequent refuge for silent reflection.

> *10 Dec – 2 Coy move to Mugshail, part of Op Puma. Leaves us bit stretched here. It's December! Regt. ski teams will now be in Bavaria training. Where's the year gone?*
>
> *12 - 15 Dec – 1100hrs 12 rounds RCL into 3 and Red Coys positions; 3 now manned by ACS and recce pl. Fired fm B22 area.*
>
> *3 Coy escorting convoy fm Mudhai. 3 tonner hit AP mine – simply blew tyre off – changed wheel and motored on! Spike Powell here for talk on "Nasties" TM46 No.6 – how to lift, when not to. Fuse instantaneous – orange.*

Briefly thoughts returned to my usual occupation commencing each December, when as captain of the downhill and langlauf ski teams, we'd be in the Bavarian mountains training in preparation for the annual Army Ski Championships beginning in January. It seemed a million miles away from a sangar in Dhofar.

With Rick's 2 Coy move to Mugshail from Akoot, my troop with Desert Regiment's recce pl took over 3 Coy's area, with Red and 3 Coys spreading west to cover 2 Coy's vacant position. The adoo gave us a reception salvo.

SPIKE'S BRIEFING TO DR ON MINES – ANTI TANK/ANTI PERSONNEL

Following a spate of mine casualties, Spike was sent up from HQ to brief us on mines, specifically how and when to lift them, or blow in situ. He concentrated on the adoo's most common blast mines, the metal-cased anti-tank Russian TM-46 and the Bakelite-cased anti-personnel PMN-I.

Summarising an interesting talk, Spike quoted from SAF's issue manual on anti-guerrilla warfare, the following various instructive precautionary measures: (*my added parentheses*)

a) All vehicles must be either mine-plated or sandbagged. (*very few were*)
b) Vehicles to have doors or cab windows removed – to allow occupants to be blown clear – reducing degree of injury.
c) Passengers to sit with knees bent, feet well back – in this position they are more likely to be blown clear without injury. (*with no helmets, and stony ground, there was little chance of landing gently*)
d) Since it is not possible to race a mine blast – 9,000m per second – travel slowly in order to:

   i) Observe track in front for disturbance
   ii) Reduce damage if mine struck – combination of 60 mph plus mine blast will result in more damage than 20 mph plus mine blast. (*unbelievable!*)

Saladins are not to be used to clear mines – they're too expensive. (*affirmative*)
Ferrets will stand up to AP mines, but hitting an anti-tank mine the crew will almost certainly come off worse than the occupants of a Land Rover. (*affirmative*)

And helpfully under the title "Sweeping for mines":

a) Use mine detector
b) Prodding
c) Visual Inspection
d) Drive over them!

(d. *wasn't amusing, other than to a bored staff officer compiling the list.*)

Other instructions that stuck in the mind included:

a) ... mine (lifting) is no task for the enthusiastic amateur.
b) The SAF Mk4A detector is no good for detecting the Russian PMN anti personnel.
c) Use a thin rod – flick dust and stones away, don't prod vigorously.
d) ... Once you have contacted a mine, flick dust clear with shemagh.
e) PMN mines cannot be lifted – blow up on spot.
f) It should be noted the TM46(N) ... has a booby trap in its base, an anti-handling device. Additionally PMN mines can be laid easily beneath TM46 mines ... pull with a cord from a safe distance.
g) Avoid taking obvious cover when blowing mine. That will be mined also.

And finally – If at any time ... dealing with a mine ... booby trap ... no further clearance should be attempted. Report immediately to HQ DHOFAR, copy to OC ZULU Company. (*Spike's men*)

With a smile Spike added wryly the last instruction was of little use to us. 'You poor buggers on the jebel, or away on convoys, you're on your own man; just blow the bugger!' So ended our mine handling tutorial.

AMBUSHES

"in war ... everything is uncertain ... all military action is intertwined with psychological forces and effects."

Count Carl von Clausewitz.

In the subconscious exists a deep-rooted moral quandary that every soldier must face and one that may return to haunt. Ambushes. 'All is fair in love and war' cites John Lyly's proverb. Leaving love aside, in war and given the choice, which frequently will be rare, the best form of attack is from a position of strength. The hunter attacks his prey having first seized, taken or been presented with the advantage, and most importantly that prized element – surprise. No matter what physical attributes a particular soldier may or may not possess, the element of surprise is his best advantage – his position of strength, giving even the outnumbered/outgunned a chance of success.

Probably the most lethal form of surprise is ambush. Caught in a well set ambush the hunted face a murderous rate of gunfire exploding from concealed positions, when advantage is lost with a dreadful immediacy and the hunted become trapped in a fight to the death. Ambushes are set to kill every member venturing into the 'killing zone'. The aim: eliminate the opposition as rapidly as possible, denying them time to react, take cover, fire back, regroup, summon assistance. Since time immemorial armies have used surprise to overcome an opponent. Soldiers are trained to set and respond to ambushes from basic training as raw recruits.

The enemy is the intended target for an ambush. The psychological quagmire arises if or when there's doubt as to who is entering the ambush killing zone. What if suddenly women and children with camels appear amongst the intended target group? What of the single goatherd innocently shepherding his flock, or women out to fetch water from a distant well who wander unwittingly into the trap? And what if one of these unintended targets notices an ill-concealed ambusher, or an accompanying dog scents a hidden man and barks in alarm? And how to tell who or what is walking past when moonlight disappears behind a cloud, or on a moonless pitch-black night when the first indication of people walking into the ambush appear as indistinct dark shapes, manifesting only from the sound of a dislodged stone, or foot scraped across loose gravel?

It's the classic dilemma peculiar to ambushes, omission over commission. Omission and people walk free. But were they carrying mines, ammunition, weapons or much needed provisions? Failure. Commission and hit the target group. Success.

Whilst hitting the wrong group is a disaster, it may also invite disaster. Not only have innocent people been killed, the gunfire may alert others. Those alerted may be in greater numbers than the ambush party. There is no doubting the response. Disturb a hornet's nest and expect a furious counterattack using any and every local advantage to rout the ambusher. And those who escape will carry the psychological trauma of having killed the wrong group.

OP GOLD BLOCK – MARBOOSH 15-18 DEC

Increasingly the adoo had become more daring in their attacks on Akoot and Col Nigel ordered his company commanders to mount ambushes, taking 'the battle to the enemy'. During the previous morning's 'O' group, Alex was outlining Red Coy's mission when interrupted by Col Nigel. Turning to me, he asked casually as I had only two armoured cars roadworthy at the time, would I accompany Ben as his 2ic on a half company ambush patrol? Adding, unnecessarily I thought, that perhaps my two sergeants could look after things in my absence?

The unpredictable nature of operating Saladins in desert and mountain conditions had taken its toll. No matter the effort to overcome the elements, car engines and gun equipment still clogged with dust, fan belts in particular suffered, and lack of spares compounded by inexperienced mechanics and young soldiers meant that rarely had we three cars roadworthy together.

As might be expected, whilst the cars' poor reliability was becoming an irritant for OC DR, it was a constant source of embarrassment to me. I'd no other response but to accept as I mused quietly 'Talk about a bloody ambush . . .'

Typically, a couple of days before an ambush party left, what passed for routine personal hygiene ceased. So, no washing, soap, shaving. Normally fastidious in washing habits, our soldiers frequently applied oils to dry skin and hair after washing. Unfortunately these oils were heavily scented, common practice in the region. The disadvantage was obvious, scents carried on the air could be smelt for miles around, especially by an adoo living in the mountains with little time for the fancy habits of their Northern town cousins and Baluchi mercenaries. I don't recall any Brit using scented shaving soaps or hair oils serving on the jebel. Perhaps a gap in the market for the likes of Messrs Trumpers, Taylors, Truefitt & Hill?

On the 15th we moved out with recce platoon in Land Rovers and packed tight, two platoons plus kit in Bedfords. Driving north then west along the high open plateau behind Akoot, we knew we'd be seen from miles away and hoped the adoo would assume the army were out again collecting firewood. Dropping down into a wadi, we halted and disembarked. Gear unloaded, our transport returned to Akoot escorted by recce platoon in Land Rovers as any wood convoy might, whilst we counted on the subterfuge working, concealing the fact a half company of infantry had been left behind.

Moving off in two columns, spaced apart carrying our equipment, weapons, ammo, trip wires, rations and water for two nights, we trekked through the mountains to our daytime positions. On arrival concealed picquets were set whilst the main body of soldiers hid, sheltering in caves of the wadi complex we'd reached.

Settled in, we sipped our water and ate lightly, conscious of the need to conserve meagre rations. Once again Ben went over the planned ambush drills with his NCOs. Relieved picquets were fed, watered and briefed. We all cleaned weapons and rested, catching up on sleep in the knowledge none would sleep that night.

With darkness Ben lined up each platoon and between us we made each soldier carry out an obligatory standing jump on the spot, repeated a second time, essential to ensure none made a sound with loose kit. Standard procedure before any patrol departed camp, but particularly important prior to leaving on ambush. Impressively, no man rattled. Webbing such as it was, was worn tight, grenades and rifle magazines carried snug and secured. These men, some no older than 15 or 16, had been on active service now for over two months. Those who'd joined as new recruits only six months earlier were now experienced soldiers. We moved out in four sections to set up the night ambush leaving a small group to guard our daylight position holding our water, supplies and rations. They'd radio contact with Ben, and would be maintaining strict radio silence to be broken only in emergency.

We found the planned ambush site with relative ease, having memorised air photographs supplied by SOAF before departure. Quietly and with commendable stealth, the men crept into positions directed as we prepared the ambush. With no moon, darkness cast its shroud, a starlit sky ensuring sufficient night vision to the wadi floor. The ambush was set.

We waited, rifles levelled at the killing zone, eyes peering for movement, ears straining for any sound. Lying rock-still, I recalled the dictum if ambushed: 'hit the ground, take cover, and shout orders so the men know you're still alive and in command'. I wondered what tactics the adoo might employ.

There followed a long night with movement restricted to breathing lightly, stretching soundlessly and remaining acutely alert. Despite the tension, thoughts returned to the 'what ifs . . .'. At the ambush briefing, our orders were clear: anyone moving at night was to be considered adoo. The presumption: non-combatants had no need to move at night. Broadcast widely by leaflet drop, movement on the jebel after dark was forbidden and any breach would be treated as adoo and engaged. Still it was not a situation that rested easily in the subconscious. Not many jebalis could read.

In wars sometimes the innocent are killed. No one wants to be a party to that. Comfortably remote from the action, politicians and world leaders send servicemen to wars, ordering bombing raids killing non-combatants, now termed collateral damage. To an extent, aircrews dropping bombs and artillerymen with indirect bombardments are remote too. It's at the muzzle end of a soldier's rifle that it gets personal and when the results are witnessed first hand. Shot at, gone's the time for indecision, no time to think if he's raising his rifle. About to fire or surrender? When it comes to an ambush killing zone, there's less than an instant to decide let live or kill. Where's the line drawn? I wasn't sure I wanted to find out.

We drew a blank that night. Before daybreak, we moved quietly out on Ben's command and made our way tactically to our daylight positions. Having not peed since setting out the night before, there was now a general need for people to answer the demands of their bladders. At times like these there's no opportunity nor excuse for inhibitions and a soldier just gets on with it.

Despite the lack of contact, the operation had gone smoothly and having congratulated the men, we relaxed with our dry rations and a brew.

Something I'd eaten the early evening before now returned with a vengeance. Grabbing the first opportunity to leave the cave I shared with Ben, I disappeared around the corner and climbed over a small rise, to relieve an aching belly, guts and bladder. Without going into detail, I found I'd joined three other soldiers suffering as I and we just got on with the necessary bodily functions, discreetly facing away from each other. Not a word was said. Relief was instantaneous. Returning to the sanctity of my shared shelter, Ben enquired 'Better?', making his way past me to the 'boul' area (army Arabic for designated fresh-air latrines). Grinning, I replied in the affirmative, 'watch how you go, there's not much room, pretty busy and messy . . .'

Soldiering is no place for inhibitions. A particular apocryphal story had a newly arrived British officer who'd taken himself off to answer a call of nature. Given little immediate cover, he'd wandered some distance from the convoy seeking privacy. When time came for the vehicles to move, the young Land Rover driver couldn't find his officer. As the convoy began to move away, assuming his passenger had joined another officer's vehicle and fearful of being left behind, the driver rapidly set off in pursuit of the fast departing trucks. It was a story regularly referred to around an early evening's dying fire in the desert, when to much merriment soldiers would recall the hapless victim's predicament, with dire warnings not to wander too far for a crap. Luckily the officer had a hand held radio and was soon afterwards picked up.

For hygiene, boul areas were set away from living areas, but this was not always practicable on ambushes. Human waste was left for nature's cleaners: foxes, hyenas, dung beetles or feral dogs. With day temperatures rising above 50C in the shade, sunlight soon dried liquids and desiccated soft matter. Lying up through the day with little else to do, our inactive minds delighted in deciding the definitive sequence for ageing faeces:

  1 day old = raw to rare
  2 days old = medium
  3 days old = well done to burnt

Important to know if caught short after dark, unable to use torch or match.

Both of us were fine afterwards, as were the men. Whether a result of our cooking but more probably the numerous flies which followed us everywhere, British officers in particular regularly suffered from diarrhoea. Severe bouts would last for several days when keeping hydrated was vital. At least constipation

Ben and I share a cave during the day. His bed and radio to the right. Ben, on his way to a MBA, improves his mind reading something cerebrally challenging, whilst I sought distraction in a Wilber Smith. Photograph taken by Ben's radio operator.

was uncommon, occurring generally when drinking water was severely rationed. Despite the remoteness, be it desert or isolated mountain passes, flies found you out. With stubborn inevitability they'd arrive as soon as you occupied a position. Then began the constant battle to keep mouths, ears, noses and eyes, food and tea mugs fly-free. Only darkness brought respite.

Eating tinned sardines and chapattis, brewing tea on our hexamine solid fuel stoves, we rested all day eking out individual water supplies. Weapons were cleaned, ammunition and magazines re-checked and lost sleep caught in naps. Towards sundown, there followed a further briefing on the second night's ambush and under cover of darkness, we took up fire positions overlooking a different section of wadi and suspected adoo track.

Earlier that day Ben and I had debated the general topic of ambush and the psychology relating to such forms of warfare. Deep stuff, but we had the time. The essence of ambush, we reflected, was to engage the enemy without warning, utilising complete surprise. Firing stops only once all in the killing zone have been eliminated. That way success is achieved. I put it to Ben that, isolated from the theatre of war, would he consider the concept of an ambush an act of premeditated murder, killing in cold blood? He'd thought for a while before

Ben chats casually with the boys as we relax before moving back to our night ambush positions.

responding: 'SAF has decreed those moving on the jebel at night are the enemy. What's the difference, say, to a sniper taking out a target at long range? Or when we lay mines? What of the artillery or your Saladins firing HF? Or bringing in a jet strike. And when we advance to contact you want first strike. You take out the adoo before he does you.' It almost scanned.

For a second night we again drew blank. It'd been a long night, the accumulative effect of sleepless nights always are. It was a tired and weary group that made it back to our daylight positions. Radioing ahead for transport, we trekked out avoiding our potentially mined earlier route, successfully meeting up at the RV. Here parched men who'd stretched out meagre supplies to last two days gratefully replenished their almost empty charguls with jerrycan stored water.

There'd been no contact, yet Ben and I were pleased with the way things had gone. It was not uncommon on night operations for someone to accidentally trip, slip on loose stone, fall, drop a weapon or rifle magazine, or in the worst case accidentally squeeze a trigger, shattering any secrecy of silence. Such events occurred, on one occasion the wildly firing weapon leaving six men dead.

Ben was later wounded, twice. The first occasion was with Ray and a gallant signaller holding a position against an advancing adoo when a Kalashnikov round cut neatly through Ben's left forearm cradling his rifle, to smash hard against his binos hanging around his neck, before ricocheting harmlessly away. It was at that moment they realised the rest of the patrol of twenty or so had fled to better cover, leaving the three exposed on a rock outcrop. Returning fire, Ray called for mortar support. Fortunate in their choice of mortar officer, "Bomber" Bremridge (a sobriquet to cause maximum embarrassment), responded by landing bombs bang on target, allowing the three to gallop back to where their men were now returning fire from decent cover. Crouched behind rocks, a medic attended to Ben's arm whilst Ray directed mortars onto a now retreating adoo. It'd been one of those flashpoint contacts, over almost as soon as begun.

Hoping perhaps it was a 'blighty', Ben's spirits rose, only to be dashed when told there'd be no UK return this time. The bullet had missed bone and main blood vessels to leave neat entry and exit holes, expertly stitched to leave two star-shaped scars. Wrist strapped with gleaming white plaster of Paris cast, he was returned to Red Company. The second wounding was far less dramatic, but, he claimed, just as painful. Ben was awarded the Sultan's Commendation Medal in 1971 and in 1972 the Distinguished Service Medal (Gallantry).

18 Dec – Al hilal – very new moon, and Col Nigel departs on Christmas Leave. Returned Op Goldblock with Red Coy. Attack 1730 – RCL

Our trip back to Akoot was uneventful. This was always a considerable relief as all routes were scattered with undetected mines. We'd taken casualties before and a number of trucks and Land Rovers lost – any of which we could ill afford.

Nights spent on ambushes and trekking by foot across desert and mountain terrain brought it home to me why I had opted for the armoured corps. It was with an inner sigh of relief I returned to Akoot to the good news that all three Saladins were now roadworthy and battle fit. And as always the boys seemed relieved to have me back – no more than I was to be with them.

A welcoming party insisted I accompany them to their tented quarters. Wafting from a sangar drifted the beguiling aroma of brewing coffee. On entering, I saw a pot of the freshly made brew beside which glistened a patterned enamelled tin plate, piled with light brown Omani dates. The fresh dates had been brought up from Salalah by Hamdan Khalfan, following his once-a-month's Salalah R&R.

As we shared gossip, without warning Nasir Mohamed turned round to reach behind him to produce a neatly folded shemagh. Understated as ever, he passed it to me. 'Alsalaam wa nurahib ya sayidi' (salaams and welcome back, sir).

Taken aback at this unexpected gesture, I replied 'shukraan Nasir' and reached out for the shemagh held towards me. One look and I realised instantly the

LCpl Nasir Mohamed Mahoon of the Salmi tribe from Nizwa, my utterly dependable gunner with me at Akoot. He later won the Sultan's Commendation Medal for bravery in action. A true and loyal friend.

headgear was not the normal army issue shemagh dyed army camouflage green; this headgear was of a far superior material, soft and silk-like, heavier too than our shemaghs worn daily. On closer inspection I noticed the edges were decorated with an elaborate lacework having three-inch silk tassels attached at intervals. It was a work of art. Caught completely off guard by this gesture I repeated 'this is very handsome, thank you very much'.

I unfastened my filthy headwear I'd worn daily (and regularly washed) since issue five months earlier. Wiping grease and dirt from my forehead, I wrapped the new garment around my head. 'Thank you, it is very generous.'

Needing to recover my composure rapidly, I regaled them with tales of my exploits over the past few days away with Red Company, causing much hilarity at my acute discomfort apropos the effects the rations and/or flies had inflicted, ending with a rush to Red Company's shared toilet facilities!

By now invigorated by strong coffee and sweet dates, I made my excuses and left for my tented sangar. After just three days out, it was sheer bliss to wash, and delight in the exquisite taste of peppermint toothpaste. So aptly put in David Niven's "The Moon's a Balloon", I'd a mouth with furry teeth – 'tasting like the bottom of a parrot's cage'. I now felt human again. And R&R was just a fortnight away.

My finely fashioned new shemagh and a Sultan's Armed Forces cap badge.

Rationed to eight litres of water a day per man, and having three Saladins, a Land Rover and Bedford truck to keep filled, we became very adept at saving water. Finally excused shaving, we'd make four inches of progressively soapy water last a week. None of us smelt that pleasant, some worse than others.

PINK EYE

Shortly after my return we had three cases of conjunctivitis, an infection in the outer membrane of the eyeball, commonly known as 'pink eye'. Seeking Babu's advice, antibiotics were prescribed, and recommending we thoroughly clean cars and weapons, we set to washing down each Saladin's interior to reduce the contagion spreading. We used swabs of cotton-waste dipped in petrol as disinfectant, after I'd banned smoking in cars for a week. This seemed to work as no-one else became infected. A miserable condition. Thankfully all recovered quickly.

THOUGHTS TURN TO CHRISTMAS

With Col Nigel's departure on leave back in the UK, command passed to his 2ic, Paul Mangin, also commanding FTZ, our mercurial firqat irregulars on base. In support, we had the larger than life ex-Northamptonshire Regiment, ex-Zambian Army major, Graham Sherwell, commanding HQ Coy. Responsible for maintaining Akoot's airfield known as 'Karlsberg Airport', Graham had procured a tiny bulldozer to clear potholes and ruts on the packed earth airstrip. Realistically, it proved no more than a toy, but kept Graham amused for hours.

Letters enclosing cards arrived reminding us it was Christmas and someone thought it would be a good idea to decorate the interior of the Mess tent. I'd recently volunteered to take on the role of Messing Officer, a duty not without its risks. As Messing Officer, you were open to complaints about menu repetition, flavours, quantities and food hygiene. Flies in soup were thankfully accepted as extra meat rations, whilst there was no worse censure a Messing Officer might receive than fellow members declaring "Mar Bars on the Messing Officer" when said delicacy would be added to his Mess bar bill. With the absence of chocolate at Akoot this naturally translated to whisky.

The Sherwell demonstrates his bulldozing techniques whilst his driver and Land Rover follow behind, more out of curiosity than any sense of duty.

My Officers' Mess kitchen staff, two cooks in smocks, the others, mess waiters and bottle washers.

Permanent members of the Mess included Col Nigel, Majors Paul Mangin and Graham Sherwell, Captains Alex Lamond, Douglas Maclaine, Babu and we three Saladin commanders, Sgts Fyffe, Oliver and myself. Visitors would include passing HQ visitors and SOAF pilots who rarely ever stayed the night.

I saw as one of my first tasks was to sort out kitchen hygiene. The open sided kitchen sheltered under canvas stretched between two wadi walls. We had a paraffin cooker on bare earth floor. Washing up was done in two cut down drums, burmails, holding an unspeakable grey liquid.

I discovered three milk jugs, rims and spouts congealed with 5mm of yellowed milk powder. Just two of many examples which made me wonder if perhaps I had volunteered too quickly? And then there were cockroaches. These beasts were huge – the largest we found was over three centimetres long. And fat. Few invertebrates attract greater abhorrence, although one Madagascan variety, the Hissing Cockroach, and kept as pets can grow to 7.5 centimetres. An urban legend holds that cockroaches are immortal. They may certainly inherit the Earth one day.

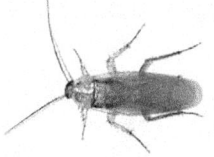

Although unidentified at Akoot, Turkestan cockroaches are a species native to the Middle East and throughout Central Asia. SAF suggested we deal with the invertebrate infestation by spraying DDT, one of man's more toxic pesticides generally suspected of having side effects dangerous to humans, yet remaining in use worldwide. Ironically, we all knew Joni Mitchell's 1970 hit song 'Big Yellow Taxi' in which she pleads "Hey, farmer, farmer, put away your DDT . . ."

In 1972, the USA's Environment Protection Agency finally banned Dichlorodiphenyl-trichloroethane (DDT) for its adverse environmental effects to wildlife but also potential health risks to humans. Reportedly there's a relationship between DDT exposure and reproductive effects in humans. In addition, the pesticide left some animals with liver tumours; today it is classified as a probable human carcinogen.

The Mess had a paraffin powered fridge, which though small could store fresh meat and fish for short periods, longer in winter. So it was organised for Skyvans delivering mail and stores every three to four days to also deliver my selection of fresh provisions. On a recent R&R visit to UAG, I'd arranged through the friendly Mess kitchen staff, for the purchase and supply of fresh rations which SAOF kindly flew up to us on resupply trips.

It fell to me to make arrangements for Christmas. Volunteering as Messing Officer I'd hoped to revive dulled taste buds following endless meals poured from tins. We'd existed largely on imported British army rations, not bad short term but tedious month after month. I introduced occasional fresh meat, goat, slaughtered and prepared by the cooks. Suddenly goat curry and fresh fish were on the menu.

On finding a glass jar in the kitchen that had been used for storing ghee (clarified butter), I had it washed out then I filled it with small onions and added vinegar. Setting the jar on a rock I instructed the cooks to keep an eye on it as the midday sun got to work. Two days later we had pickled onions. But for my pièce de résistance, I made a chilli-sherry. Comprising a heady mix of DR's best sherry, I added red and green chillies plus black peppercorns mixed in a bottle. This fiery concoction was left to brew in the sun for a week. We called it "Chillisherryshitti" in deference to Col Nigel's continued HF shelling of the impregnable Sheershitti caves complex, the adoo arsenal safely sheltered deep underground to our south.

14

CHRISTMAS 1971

First Christmas on active service. More operations. Hurricane warning. Christmas carols. Hand wounds and the horror of 'overs'. Winter's bitter cold. Night attack. Father Christmas. Local officers to lunch. Drilling for water. Saladins' continued mechanical problems.

PREPARATIONS FOR CHRISTMAS

In preparation for Christmas, on his last R&R, Sgt Oliver had been tasked with 'borrowing' a few hymn sheets from Dhofar HQ at Umm Al Ghawarif. To his credit he returned not only clean after his monthly shower but armed with five Church of England hymn books. 'Silly question, Olly, you did ask?' I'd enquired, receiving a wide grin through his red beard; 'Nope' came the reply. It did cross my mind how officialdom might view our ruse, but feelings of guilt were tempered by conviction Higher Authority might have approved.

Then to tent decorations. Requisitioning two post-op maps, illegibly scrawled over in Alex's red crayon and calligraphy, we cut strips making hoops assembled together into chains using a chapati flour and water paste. Alex's artistry only added to the otherwise tans and greys of the original less than accurate 1:250,000 scaled maps. These MOD-issue 'Joint Operations Graphic-Ground' maps came printed with the encouraging footnote – written in minute text:

"NOTE – Users are requested to mark corrections on this graphic and send it to Director of Military Survey. Ministry of Defence, London. Through the normal channels"

Map reading in BAOR had not been without the occasional acerbic bollocking from an exasperated Squadron Leader, and there we'd used 1:25,000 scale maps with contours, but also towns, villages, roads, rivers and landmarks, infinitely clearer than these we were forced to rely upon.

For a Christmas tree I used branches of frankincense, caught on the side of our cars escorting the latest DR wood foraging party. Arranged and displayed against the canvas marquee wall, decorated with a collection of cut-out stars, shepherd shapes and lambs made from tin cans, we could not have asked for a more perfect Christmas tree. All was set – as perfect as it was ever going to be without that single 'want' each listed uppermost in dreams – girls . . . and that wasn't going to happen.

Stand-to and sunrise on Akoot ridge, December 1971.

CHRISTMAS 1971

On Christmas Eve, Alex had one of his many bright ideas. We'd make a recording using a portable cassette machine recently purchased on a R&R visit to Salalah. A particular song that resonated with us at the time was Simon and Garfunkel's "7 O' Clock News/Silent Night". A rendition of Silent Night mixed to juxtapose with a simulated news bulletin.

Alex planned to read out daily sitreps from Dhofar HQ, whilst at various intervals David's 5.5in Howitzer would fire into the night at Sheershitti caves, of course. Whilst this was going on, the esteemed members of the Mess choir would give a sober rendition of Silent Night, now we'd acquired carol sheets.

We had been shelled constantly in the lead up to Christmas, so were more than ready to lighten spirits with our version of the 1966 hit. The event, meticulously coordinated by the two gunners Lamond and Maclaine, would kick off after dinner, when, bolstered by a few beers it was hoped we'd be in good voice, if not perfect pitch as demanded by Alex, self-proclaimed recording producer.

No time for rehearsals, but relying on spontaneity, we'd hoped to record in harmony backed by David's fire mission. Alex started reading his interpretation of Dhofar Brigade's sit-rep reports as Simon and Garfunkel's music began, the ex-choristers amongst us adding admittedly little as the ground shook with the first 100lb shell fired. Briefly, imagining we'd reached the necessary perfect pitch Alex required, the tape broke and sadly all evidence of a classic performance was lost.

Not to be downhearted by our failure to produce an Akoot 1971 Christmas hit, we reached for more beers and all was forgotten once we'd agreed to sack our Manager, Producer and Agent, Alex. It was his tape machine.

HURRICANE WARNING AND FINGERS – WHAT IS IT WITH HANDS?

19 Dec
Venom on Shrerrshitti - 483558 - 1030 . . . postponed, low cloud
B34	*1130*	*25*	*2rds*
C27	*1230*	*25*	*2rds*

1200 – *Hurricane warning for 1800 this pm. We secured tent stays with additional rocks. Found DR driver trapped by fan belt – had to cut hands loose. One finger off, messy. Delivered hosp. RCL attack 1600. Met casualty later in Babu's hospital tent, very cheerful, may lose 3 fingers. . . . Later heard just two fingers lost and 4 finger tips. Lucky.

* Big non event – high winds only.

Venom was the codeword for a SOAF airstrike and a jet strike on Sheershitti caves was cancelled due to low cloud. With Col Nigel's departure on leave, a relaxed air descended on the camp. Being attacked on a daily basis was wearying, but the real threat was one of complacency as yet more RCL rockets crashed into the Akoot basin. Each time we'd respond, infantry to sangars, my troop to cars before roaring to firing positions on the camp's ridgeline.

On this occasion running to my car carrying SMG and hand radio, between explosions I heard screaming coming from a Bedford over to my left. It was stationary. Screaming has a commanding, unavoidable power, urgent, high pitched and pained. Turning towards the truck, I radioed my sergeants to respond to the attack. Approaching, the screaming ceased. Crouched under the off-side wheel arch sat a small man looking up at me. Shocked horror evident across his brown face lined with pain and tears, eyes beseeching help.

Incongruously his arms extended up into the engine compartment and a glance past the freely flowing blood soaking his shirt made my gut wrench. Caught by both hands, his fingers were being slowly but repeatedly chewed into a mash where caught by the stalling engine's fanbelt. Leaping into the cab I switched off the coughing engine. Try as I could though, his hands wouldn't budge, stuck fast by the reinforced black and frayed rubber belt. 'La tataharak!' (don't move!) I said as I got up, noticing my crass remark had generated a painful twitch at the corners of his mouth – poor sod, he wasn't going anywhere. 'Ureed as sikkim' (I need a knife). I ran the 60 metres to my tent, rushing in to find my pocket knife, 'Shit it's small, have to do' and running out I jumped into my Land Rover I'd need ferrying the man to the hospital tent. Racing back, I screeched to a halt, sending dust and stone flying everywhere.

The soldier had fainted and was now slumped in a heap, hanging by hands still caught by the fan belt. Once I'd reached past to free his hands, he recovered consciousness but this time without screaming, just a quiet prayer in Baluchi.

Sawing hard with my pathetic bone handled pocket knife, I cut past loose skin to free his hands, swearing I would buy a proper hunting knife at the first bloody opportunity. Snap! The belt parted and I caught him as he fell back. Half carrying, half walking him to my Land Rover, I eased him into the passenger seat. I looked at his hands he now held in astonishment before him, as if momentarily caught in an act of supplication, the finger ends shredded and pumping blood. With a thumb and uninjured finger he pulled a torn tendon from a pulped finger, then another as I stopped him. 'Laa, kifaaya!' (No, enough!)

Radioing ahead to Babu I had a casualty, I drove the 600 metres across ruts and rough ground to the battalion hospital tent steering with my right hand whilst gripping the man's shirt with my left to stop him falling out of the doorless vehicle.

CHRISTMAS 1971

Dropping the patient off with a waiting Babu, I then drove back across to my Saladin and waiting crew. We joined the other two cars on the ridge, but the adoo had long since disappeared, mission completed, their tit-for-tat rockets in reply to our 25 pounder HF earlier that day.

On my way to dinner that evening, I called at the hospital to visit the casualty and found a man uninhibited in his joy to see me. Tears streaming down his face he held up his two very white bandaged hands, the absorbent gauze red tipped but otherwise clean and hygienic, 'Shukran Sahb, shukran, shukran'. I stood by his bed and we chatted in broken Arabic for a while. The young Baluchi was probably no older than 17. He'd probably served just a year with SAF where he hoped to build a career. He already had a good command of army Arabic. A proud Pashtun, with family north of the town of Quetta, whom I knew he'd be supporting with the greater part of his pay. A brave young man.

And another day had ended at Akoot.

Flown to Salalah on the resupply Skyvan the following morning to receive further treatment, the Baluchi soldier was back at Akoot within two weeks, on light duties but otherwise fully recovered. Meeting me he proudly displayed his hands – they'd healed and despite the original prognosis, the final tally was two fingers lost to the knuckle and distal phalanges (fingertips) from four fingers. His injuries, though nasty, were fortunately light enough to allow him to remain as a frontline soldier with DR.

'Lucky' as I wrote in my diary.

Like the rest of us, we were all witness to some horrendous wounds, bullet, mine blast, shrapnel, accident, yet the memory of chewed fingers haunted – what is it with hands?

20 - 23 Dec – Sgt Oliver on leave. Costello here.
With 3 Coy – Op Sandfly: grid sq 6772.
0600 Manston wood convoy
Found camel tracks gd. 523766. T12A engaged posn. 538653 - 3 HE.
En attacks 1010, 1500, 1600hrs – 6 RCL, track out of camp, & 2 Coy
Bayt al Falaj flooded out! Poor old HQ wallahs!! Heavy rains.
Bloody cold here on jebel
R&R!! 21st – Met up with Huw – swam Salalah beach. He's not convinced Oman best place to spend 'young lives' . . . he's on 3 yr contract.
midday flight out, back midday 22nd. RCL attack pm.
Dec 23 – SOAF Venom attack on Sheershitti – claimed v. accurate 500 lbs bombs.
2 x RCL and LMG attacks 1000 and 1100.

*24 Dec – Built new sangars for boys' tents and relocated to new sangars.
DR local officers in Mess for lunch.
3 Coy lose three tonner returning to Akoot – TM46. A mess.*

Building a replacement sangar with the troop. That stone was equal to Mohamed Salim's body weight, just under 200llbs (90 kg). When challenged, I could barely roll it!

COLD AND THE 'OVERS'

"If it happens, you can bet it was planned that way . . . death doesn't bargain"
F.D. Roosevelt.

Life at Akkot was becoming tougher. It had turned very cold. With insufficient warm clothing and biting winds, keeping warm was an effort. Paul Mangin opened a morning O Group with news there'd been frost overnight, his shaving bowl water had frozen. Weapons and steel hulled Saladins were ice-chill to the touch. Winter in Southern Arabia's mountains can be unforgivingly cold. Life otherwise continued as normal, joint ops with DR out from Akoot, wood and water convoys and daily attacks. RCL rockets were now striking the route out of camp to our rear. The adoo artillery was accurate. Landmines took their toll. Yet many attacks were nuisance value only. Most casualties were sustained when bombs landed amongst sangars or catching men in the open, dropping unheard until the final baleful scream of rocket or whoosh-whoosh of mortar announced incomers.

Then there were the 'overs'. The adoo had taken to firing light machine guns, LMGs and Kalashnikovs from extreme range. The desired effect was to drop bullets flopping out of the blue sky, tumbling arse over tit as their velocity expired. These unwelcome guests fell like steel hail, creating horrible wounds as they hit soft tissue or ricocheted wildly off limestone rock. The casual nature of these 7.62mm rounds dropping randomly out of the sky with a whisper quietness was unnerving, affecting morale even amongst the most fatalistic. The dangerous high velocity had gone, but the tumbling bullet wounds were still serious. Chance inevitably plays its part, as it does in any aspect of life, but none wished we tempted it.

LOCAL OFFICERS' LUNCH

Desert Regiment's Arab officers were invited for lunch in the Mess, a rare event organised by our Arabist 2ic, Paul Mangin. Never reconciled that local officers had their Mess separate from ours, whenever Arab officers were attached to ACS camps, we ate together. The Squadron being recently formed and operating in small units may have been unique in this approach. Change takes time and SAF's long established culture was thankfully evolving, as Arab officers were promoted and segregation fell away.

25 DEC

Christmas Day was celebrated with our artillery, Shelldrake, carrying out no less than 17 fire missions. 25 pdrs commenced at 0001 through to 1900 with a final blast from the 5.5in. So as not to be left out, I'd received orders for 15 fire missions. All in all a busy day which unsurprisingly the adoo treated with their customary disdain, responding proportionately to our somewhat wasteful exercise, a modest two rounds of RCL landed harmlessly in the middle of Akoot camp. I doubt our lengthy fire-power demonstration impressed the adoo or caused any casualties, and equally none were taken.

Naturally the adoo attack had coincided with a Huey delivering Christmas mail, SOAF showing great form delivering Father Christmas! *'He exists!'* I penned in my diary. Good old SOAF.

Father Christmas arrives in person, dispelling any adult myths concerning his existence.

26 - 30 Dec – Thank you letters, Never received so many gifts from home – sponge from Odeyne, pen Ann, notebook William. Sussex churches calendar and books from parents, v. lucky.
Write report on dvr losing fingers 19 Dec.
Tom, Rick and Alan having daily attacks, mortar and SA.
SMG trg - made range - 1030 - 1230hrs

<u>Pay Shortages</u>
Mubarik - 27
Abdullah -22
Jan <u>11</u> - !!
Hamood - 43
Khalifa - 18

Firing SMGs at oil drums placed on my make-shift range was a welcome diversion to days spent in Saladins. Whilst accomplished shots, I dreaded us ever having to pitch these weapons against the exceptional Kalashnikov. On this occasion the empty 45 gallon (205ltr) oil drums never had a chance. In case it's noticed, I'll admit that's my loaded SMG between 2 and 3 on the firing point, contravening every rule in the book on small arms Range Drills. Bad habits gained from Ray Kane's ethos, 'it's no f…..g good empty'.

CHRISTMAS 1971

Live firing on our makeshift SMG range

10 rds automatic	25 yds – standing	Adoo attack – two bombs as yet unidentified
10 rds R	50 yds – kneeling	I've a beer on mortar – close to 2 Coy,
15 rds R	100 yds – prone	very nasty, didn't hear first coming in.
15 rds R	200 yds – prone	and late, 1825.

The SAF Officers handbook had this to say about our issued personal weapons:

> "SMGs . . . of no value. Most engagements are well outside their range . . . they fail to penetrate branches in scrub at close range."

What the handbook said was true, but you'd never fit FN rifles inside a turret, not to mention in a hurried dismount. And a SMG could be fired with one hand to clear the immediate area around a vehicle. The unavailable alternative, the rare AK47, was as easy to stow inside a Saladin as a SMG, and as Lou was quick to add, as easy to dismount with in a hurry.

29th December brought end of month servicing and soldiers' pay day. Flown up monthly from Dhofar HQ, a Pay Sergeant would arrive for pay parade.

Occasionally there'd be shortages leading to inevitable disgruntlement but generally resolved on the spot. However, when on picquet, shortages discovered only after we'd returned to our lines and the Pay Sergeant long gone, I'd end up promising to correct shortfalls, occasionally lending cash to tide a soldier over until the matter had been officially resolved. The shortfalls this month were in baizas, tiny but in principle huge. (With 1,000 baizas to an Omani Rial, at today's rate Jan Mohamed's shortage, although important as a matter of principle, was just 2p.)

End of month servicing undertaken in relays ensured we'd have two cars at battle readiness. At 1055, whilst on piquet four RCL landed close by the cars on piquet, a near miss close to mine (TI2) forcing us to jockey for alternative firing positions. A third sailed overhead by 30m, the fourth was a blind. I wrote afterwards:

> "difficulty blowing the blind and only at third attempt, using a 5.5 shell for a charge did it explode. Thought I'd take a photograph post explosion, but it was raining stones and shrapnel as I attempted to open my cupola, much to Jan's amusement!"

Sgt Jan Mohamed, SAF number 312 was my mature 30-year-old Baluchi troop sergeant. Already an 'old soldier', quick to volunteer and equally so to smile at misfortune, he had been born in Muttrah, northern Oman, the son of a serving SAF Baluchi soldier. I never discovered the reason behind his seemingly senior army number; the next most senior in my troop was the loyal LCpl Nasir Mohamed, 9183, an Omani Arab.

This was not a theatre of war involving heavy bombardment. Each enemy round fired into Akoot had had to be carried by camel train from across the border, some thirty kilometres distant, having been shipped by dhow to the adoo port of Hawf, Yemen. The arms cache at Sheershitti caves had to be constantly resupplied, a logistical headache for any army. The fact the communists did so, so successfully and for so long, remains a tribute to their determination and organisational abilities.

It has been said that Akoot and afterwards Simba were unnecessary drains on the fledgling country's war chest. At Simba, located almost on the border of Yemen, far greater numbers of incomers were experienced. Although never succeeding to cork the flow of munitions into Dhofar, both positions nevertheless absorbed ordnance that would otherwise have been fired into Salalah and the RAF airport. That the adoo failed to bombard Salalah represented a singular victory for SAF forces. The fact that the Sultan's troops remained dug in on the jebel sending out fighting patrols and ambushes to thwart the adoo's previous monopoly of the jebel was a further significant victory in this continuing guerilla war that until recently, as with other current communist insurgencies, had seemed unwinnable.

SECRET

Assistance to the Sultan of Oman: FCO – HM Defence Secretary

Since the present Sultan of Oman came to power in 1970, we have been providing him with covert military support for his campaign against the rebels in Dhofar on a steadily increasing scale, until by September 71 we were providing two SAS squadrons. Force levels have been subject to frequent review and one SAS squadron (will be) withdrawn in March 1972. The Chiefs of Staff have now completed a further review, in conjunction with the FCO and have put forward their proposals for 1972.

Apart from our political and economic interests in Oman, we have a direct defence interest in the stability of the Sultan's regime through our continued requirement for the airfield at Masirah, which provides an important link on the CENTO air route to the Far East and is a valuable deployment airfield in support of CENTO and for maritime reconnaissance purposes. Part of the price we pay for Masirah is the commitment to provide airfield services and support at Salalah in the Dhofar, where the Sultan's forces are carrying out their major campaign against rebels, supported from PDRY.

CENTO, The Central Treaty Organization, was a Cold War military alliance, formed in 1955 between Iran, Iraq, Pakistan, Turkey and the United Kingdom. Modelled after NATO, CENTO committed the nation members to mutual cooperation and protection, as well as non-intervention in each other's affairs. Its goal: to contain the USSR by having a line of strong states along the Soviet Union's southwestern frontier.

1972

1 - 13 Jan – CFTs

	T12	80	1906
	12A	72	2417
	12B	70	2355

Midway convoy out
Sgts Fyffe & Jan Mohamed and Salim Makeera back from leave.

Bloody cold all day. Stand-to until 1845.
SEP in at 0700.

CFT stood for Combat Fitness Test. These applied to both men and vehicles, basically at Akoot I kept my crews fit with morning PT exercises and volleyball (homemade net and a football), the cars being continually maintained fit for battle.

Announcing their arrival with a series of shouts, SEPs would surrender at one of the perimeter sangars at first light. It would have been suicidal to surrender at night when trigger happy soldiers and firqat would blast a minimum 50 rounds of LMG at anything that moved.

Once disarmed and searched, the man would be questioned before being incarcerated pending a flight to Salalah. His cell comprised a Dannert wired square compound, situated uncomfortably close to my tent. 'What's wrong with that?' replied a querulous Alex from behind his walrus moustache to my suggestion perhaps the compound might be relocated, 'they've been disarmed, there're DR guards on duty, safe as bloody Dartmoor!' Whilst there was never a problem, I was quietly relieved after each ex-adoo had been collected and flown to Salalah for interrogation.

Despite regular attacks on Akoot and 2 Coy at Mughsayl, thoughts turned to our East African trip in four weeks with plans to climb Kilimanjaro and visit game reserves. Hoping to gain 'indulgence flights' with the RAF, I'd submitted paperwork, Tom doing likewise from his position at Mughsayl as it was becoming increasingly unlikely either Sandy or Rick could join us.

6 Jan – Breach blocks out/clean. Dhobi to UAG
Caribou 0830, Skyvan 0930. Salim Nakharra AWOL 2 days. New tent – very grand.
Douglas' .55 shell struck 3 metres to my right, bounced off ridge to spin away. One lucky drop-short!

Weapons were cleaned and lightly oiled daily, main armament breach blocks stripped fortnightly or after firing.

On piquet duty that afternoon, the gun detachment fired a .55in at too low a trajectory, the shell ricocheting off the ridge 3m from my car. It happened so quickly, the incident was over before we realised what had occurred. To our

CHRISTMAS 1971

My new home completed, a stone walled tent in which I could stand upright after nearly two months cracking my head on the Bedford canopy SSM Popski had built before he left.

intense relief the next HF round found greater elevation. Some choice words won a suitable apology and a beer from Douglas.

10 Jan – Ali Hamdan requires loan for father's bayt repairs.

I loaned Ali 40 Rials to tide him over to pay-day, he was my driver and utterly trustworthy. The loan to repair his father's house was repaid in two months.

Not too good. Dirty water?

Feeling under the weather, I retired to my bed with a high temperature, handing command to Sgt Fyffe in my absence. By the 14th I'd penned *"Better!"* A four day sweating fever and blistering headache left me weakened but otherwise over the worst. Luckily no vomiting or diarrhoea this time. Babu's paracetamol and my troop's sweet tea seemed to do the trick.

COLONEL RETURNS FROM CHRISTMAS LEAVE

Col Nigel back.
Down to 2 Saladins – 80 towed back to Midway arrived safely 17 Jan.

With continuing engine problems, my car, registration no. 80, was towed back to Midway accompanying the January resupply convoy. Two days later, a smiling Sgt Jan Mohamed arrived back at Akoot with a replacement car.

Attacked on piquet at 2 Coy's thinly manned position, I engaged with 25pdr close to registered targets, B11 and 13. Calling also for mortars, 400m plus of B12, incoming firing ceased. The next day the adoo responded with RCL from the same area – prompting me to diary: *"obviously didn't get them last night!"* adding later, *"however, Radio Aden report 4 adoo KIA"*.

5.5 and 25pdr harassing fire missions continued on a daily basis, typically:

HF 17 Jan	*1140*	*C24 rght 200*	*25pdr x1*
	1210	*C24 add 400*	*25pdr x1*
	1640	*B21*	*25pdr x1*
	1940	*C24 left 400*	*25pdr x1*
18 Jan	*1025*	*B42 add 1500!*	*5.5 x1*
	1155	*B42 add 1500 left 200*	*5.5 x1*
	1520	*C41 rht 1000 drop 500*	*5.5 x2*
19 Jan	*2015*	*C41*	*5.5 x1*
	2210	*C41 rht 200*	*5.5 x2*
	2300	*C40*	*5.5 x1*

As a form of psychological warfare harassing fire is meant to demoralise an enemy by its random nature, intentionally unpredictable and intermittent, and at night to deprive the opponent sleep and rest. None were sure what the adoo felt about Akoot Commander's efforts, but each explosive report of the mighty 5.5in firing into the night certainly kept *us* awake.

When not under fire, Mughsayl-by-the-sea was an idyllic position, a relaxed Tom and Rick outside 2 Coy Mess Tent. The beach, within walking distance, kept them fresh as daisies!

CHRISTMAS 1971

Alan and friend wonder why they never joined the cavalry.

19 Jan – Sangar building for Pioneer Platoon – also decoy sangars – 5 pioneers, 5 MT drivers, and boys building sangars.
1215 SCOs – meeting in Mess with CO. 1500 RCL attack.

Col Nigel's return triggered a flurry of changes at the camp. Stretched thinly over Akoot's extensive area following 2 Coy's move to Mughsayl, the CO now gave orders to build decoy sangars in an effort to disguise Akoot's reduced strength. 3 Coy were spread more thinly facing southwest whilst my troop and DR Recce were joined by their Pioneer platoon and the local firqat, FTZ.

This increased activity didn't escape unnoticed. Mid-afternoon, RCL rounds landed around us, sending men diving into sangars, car commanders and crews into Saladins. The closest round fell 50m short of our cars without inflicting casualties.

Jets called up – but found no target.

Calling an O Group to include SCOs (Sultan's Commissioned Officers), the CO announced revised Immediate Action (IA) drills in the event of an assault on base.

My duties in particular were affected; pulled back from attack to a defensive role, leaving the camp's perimeter defence to instead defending HQ – noted as follows:

IA drills in event adoo breakthrough outer defences

Attack fm N – 2 cars posn 2, 3rd to ammo dump
ditto fm E – (firqat FTZ posn) – All cars posn 2
ditto fm S – (2 x recce pls) – 1 car posn 1 – other 2 – posn 2
ditto fm W – (Red coy) – 1 car posn 1, 2 cars posn 2.

Requested burmails painted white at corners of dannert wired areas.

Shortly afterwards we were attacked in the middle of a moonless black night. As I rolled out of bed onto the ground, scrambling for weapon and radio, I realised I couldn't open my eyes – they hurt, stinging like hell. I crawled, with eyes tight shut to where I knew my canvas water bucket sat on the tent floor. Plunging my face into the conserved soapy water I rubbed my eyes hard against the burning pain. It worked: I could see again. 'Shit!' I thought. 'What's happening to my eyes?' There was no time to dwell on that – 'get dressed, go! *GO!*'

The attack had come from the east. Bullets cracking overhead, I crouched beneath the tent's stone wall, pulling on trousers, jersey and jacket and tying on desert boots, before I grabbed my SMG and radio to scramble running stooped and low to my car. Ali and Abdullah arrived at the same moment. 'Start up, Ali' I whispered as we got to the car. 'Why am I whispering,' I thought, 'with all this racket going on?' I radioed the other two cars – 'load weapons – start up' as immediately both cars kicked into life. We had powered traverse for guns.

Starting a six litre Saladin V8 engine isn't a quiet business, but ticking over the sound deadens, especially under gunfire. Told later our cars were inaudible from 150m away in the ops tent, the order came to move. With engines already running, we deployed immediately to our predetermined IA positions.

A Saladin isn't noiseless at full revs. Engines howled to echo around the Akoot basin, putting a whole new perspective to Turandot's 'Nessun dorma'. Like clockwork, we reached our 1A positions without hiccup, newly painted white burmails clearly marking areas to avoid.

'Bravo! Tango 12' came the laconic response from a wide-awake Alex busy with his maps, marker pens and taking orders from a sleep interrupted Commanding Officer.

CHRISTMAS 1971

Two photographs show the extensive spread of Camp Akoot, looking south towards the ridge we sat each day, hulled down, searching, waiting for the adoo to appear.

Though I am sure our presence surrounding the HQ tents brought a degree of comfort to those sheltering inside, in reality it was illusory. Whilst we now had 'p' bulbs enabling us to fire at night, at close quarters within the confines of the camp, it would have been catastrophic to start firing at shadows in the dark. There'd always have been a friend beyond.

Stretched as we were across the wide Akoot basin, a determined night attack pushed hard would probably have been decisive, as regularly demonstrated by the Long Range Desert Group in WW2, and as the East India Company achieved in the 18th century.

Despite lacking vehicles, an overwhelming assault on Akoot, if successful, might have turned the war. The loss of a British led battalion, artillery and armoured cars group would have presented a severe setback. The repercussions would have had huge impact, both nationally to the country's young leader but also internationally in this, Britain's covert war. The adoo missed a trick there.

I saw Babu later that day and mentioned the eye problem. Quick to reassure it was nothing more than a symptom of harsh sunlight on 'European blue eyes!' he stressed again the importance of wearing sunglasses to protect the 'Caucasian condition'. Glasses presented a difficulty on active service when anything reflective was best covered with material as we did with handset aerials, or smeared with grease to avoid triggering a heliograph message. Binocular use needed particular care to avoid giving away your position.

A bespectacled British officer was shot and killed leading his men. That reflected sunlight may have given him away only added to the already increased risk of pale complexion and above average height ensuring he stood out from his soldiers. The recipient of the Sultan's Bravery Medal, courageously leading from the front, he was shot through a lens of his prescription glasses.

The decoy sangars were a small part of the build-up to Simba. Despite intense secrecy, the anticipated Big Push westwards to sever adoo supply lines and hopefully win the war was no secret. Although half-company ambush patrols were sent out from Akoot and short-term company ops undertaken, the main emphasis was to take as few casualties as possible, train hard and build maximum battle efficiency the battalion would need to accomplish Simba.

Planning for such an audacious operation fell to Col Nigel and his Ops Officer Alex who were wholly absorbed in the minutiae, calculations and checks to ensure Simba's success. It was now past mid-January and DR would be returning to the North in June after their nine-month tour in Dhofar. The date for executing the operation drew ever nearer. Tensions began to manifest in shortened fuses, tempers normally controlled were noticeably quick to flare. With the gift of hindsight, wholly understandable. Adding to the weight resting on Col Nigel's shoulders, an impatient CSAF and in the background, the Royal Palace itself.

20 Jan – Sgt Oliver back? – no – only one plane today.
JR sitrep – contact north Taqah, East w. Darbat. Claimed 12 adoo killed.
Col Nigel ordered stand-to channel will be 19? It's been that for the past week! Radio Aden confirmed 5 KIA, 2 WIA.

21st January – Odeyne's birthday – 14!   HF 0920 C24 rht 200 – 25pdr
JR – I adoo KIA, 1 captured, 1 SEP.   0930 C41   5.5
DR– 2 Coy heavy contact – no cas.   1215 C24 add 400 –25pdr
                                                                         1605 B22   25 pdr

Finished off sangars. Olly back fm leave. Delighted to be back, says he missed us. Yeah.

22 Jan/23 Jan – R&R – submitted indulgence forms at RAF Salalah. Heard SSM Piórkowski was interviewed on BBC whilst on leave. Good old Stan – it's a bloody secret war!!

Life continued much as normal, JR had a large contact north of Taqah. Rick's 2 Coy were under increased attacks whilst incomers still arrived at Akoot. Down for my first R&R in six weeks, it was good to shower and relax. Borrowing a Land Rover out to the RAF base, I submitted my flight indulgence forms, Tom having already done so. The plan, get to Cyprus then hopefully catch RAF transport to Nairobi. In the event wishful thinking on the Nairobi connection. Unfortunately, it was now confirmed neither Rick nor Sandy were free to join us.

CHRISTMAS 1971

During long hours picquetting, with thoughts turning to our African trip, my eye would occasionally catch a passing contrail in the faded blue sky overhead. I'd guess, 30,000ft? Well out of range until Katyusha rockets arrived. Civilian aircraft flying people on holiday, romance and adventure, or just cargo? Either way, guaranteed all would be unaware of the war being fought below. A unique anomaly of a soldier's life.

24 Jan – Practice stand-to against daylight attack on Akoot. NB – all radio coms on practice stand-to to be preceded by 'Exercise'. Otherwise No Duff.
HF – 5.5 on Rakhyut
Tim visit from Bayt
Wood convoy – 0815 one Bedford blown up on TM46. grid 535718. Casevac dvr. Back in camp 1000.

No matter how careful drivers were, it was almost inevitable one of the wood convoy trucks would get blown up. The now heavily rutted routes north from camp were becoming ever more numerous with each sortie to collect wood. Laying landmines in the soft broken earth and camouflaging manmade tracks consequently was neither difficult nor much effort. Given SAF's lack of mine detection equipment, it was a highly profitable exercise for the adoo and they struck bullseye most convoys. It made for jittery men, and soldiers who'd normally shrug off danger with a cheerful 'Allah kareem' became noticeably nervous travellers when sent out to collect the vital necessity, kitchen firewood. Later, on Habarut convoys we used mine protected 'Messtin' Bedfords to lead convoys, the commander and driver carefully scouting the route ahead.

However, even from the open cab of a 'Messtin', when it was meant to be easier to recognise signs of recently disturbed ground, it was imperative the following trucks didn't stray for the lead vehicle's tracks. But inevitably, occasionally they did. That said, we'd no such vehicles at Akoot.

27, 28 Jan - Eid al-Adha - fuddal with troops. Delicious hot spicy lamb.
HF 1120 A24   25pdr - Sheershitti
*   1125 A25   25pdr - Sheershitti   1430 FTZ began firing into the air*
*   1240 B26   25pdr   set whole camp on stand-to!*
*   1520 B22   25pdr*
*   1755 B21   25pdr*
*   1730 B21   81mm mortar - 25rds*

Recovering mined truck, north of Akoot

The annual Eid al Adha (Feast of the Sacrifice) honours Abraham's act of obedience to God's command, his willingness to sacrifice his son. At Akoot we suffered no attacks that day, albeit were stood-to by a few over enthusiastic firqat soldiers firing weapons into the sky. Later that afternoon and before evening stand-to, Sgts Oliver, Fyffe and I were treated to a 'fuddal' (colloquially a meal) of hot spicy goat meat that melted in the mouth served on a dish of white boiled rice. Naturally assiduous in preparation, the meal was cooked to perfection. And to complement the meal, as before, a seating plan had us three Brits embarrassingly designated most favoured seats, on carefully folded army issue prayer mats, crews seated either side of their commanders. The four MT drivers, seemingly happy to be designated the role of waiters, served water and coffees afterwards. Anticipating an explosion of hot spiced food of tender fresh goat meat infused with herbs and chilli peppers, I relaxed as in time honoured fashion the best pieces of meat – cheek muscle – were carefully picked out and placed before me to eat. 'Tafaddal Shab, tafaddal' they beseeched us start so they could likewise begin. Tafaddal is a common imperative, meaning 'be kind', essentially an invitation to partake, it being an act of kindness to accept the invitation. What a meal we had sitting crossed legged on the ground beside the makeshift three stone kitchen fire, the last burning embers of frankincense and acacia branches scenting the air with a hint of hot charcoal, heated rock and burned earth.

Following morning stand-to Sgt Jan takes early morning PE to warm up Saladin crews

30 Jan – CFTs 70 - 2496, 72 - 2497, 80 - 2177
issue Battle rations
adoo attack – 1005 – two rounds RCL onto Red Coy's football ground. Poss. fired from B12 – returned fire 15 mors. (Sand 15).
Later discovered RCL was in fact heat round, worked out fired fm B29. I was wrong, owe Paul M. a beer!

31 Jan – Op Sandcloud. Red Coy – Sandcastle recce – Cancelled – low cloud. 1045 RCL, small arms attacks. C20, B22, SO x2 RCLs. Saw RCL engaged. T12A VOR.
So just 2 Amd Cars to Marboosh – Escort drilling rig convoy back to Akoot. Power cut in wadi defile! Bedford breakdowns forced night at Marboosh – MT dvrs kept up noise all night! Adoo would have heard us miles away. Akoot – 15 incomers, RCL & 80 mors into centre of camp. 1 WIA. Babu's Land Rover hit, attending wounded. One mor 60 yds from our tents – newly arrived orderly, Rashid, says 'afdal bkthyr min alsiynama' (much better than cinema!)

With reliance on monthly convoys to Mudhai's wells, supplemented by aircraft ferried water ever increasing the financial burden of maintaining the position at Akoot, it was decided to drill locally for this most precious desert commodity.

With my second car, T12A again inoperative, I was dispatched to escort the drilling rig into Akoot, with just two cars and DR's recce platoon. Negotiating a narrow defile, my car's engine died. 'Sahb, bataariat musataha!' (flat battery!) my driver shouted: no radio, no intercom. This was ambush country. In disbelief, I climbed into the driver's seat. 'Shit!' I thought, 'ignition?' Reaching behind the steering wheel I found a loose wire. Squeezing into the confined space, I reattached the wire and immediately the ignition light came on. Pressing the starter, six litres of Rolls-Royce best kicked into life.

'How d'you manage that?' queried Gerry. 'Magic,' I replied as we motored on, sweating, relief incalculable. How *had* I managed that?

On our return, two convoy Bedfords broke down just west of Janook. Setting piquets, we waited as MT crews worked on their trucks. Night fell as we kept vigil in adoo territory, to be rewarded with a magnificent firepower display of tracer rounds over Akoot, first adoo then DR in response.

The civilian engineer was German with little spoken English. I recall with embarrassment how little German I could remember. Barely ten months of speaking Arabic had consumed my German vocabulary on which I'd relied running the regimental ski courses and ski chalet. Engineer Henrich never did find water and the project was curtailed shortly afterwards.

Beyond Akoot runway, the rig is offloaded. In the background my Land Rover flies the Sultanate flag.

CHRISTMAS 1971

Not long following his arrival at Akoot, an earnest Rashid appeared with a borrowed, loaded FN rifle in an attempt to persuade me he was man enough to become a soldier. Stretching to full height, he was barely taller than the rifle, 1.1m in length and weighing 5.15 kg. I had to admire his keenness. Telling him what a good job he was doing with the laundry, I said I'd keep him on only if he remained on dhobi duties. He agreed, if I'd agree to promote him one day. He was Bedu, had to have the last word. We'd reached a fair compromise.

Rashid our newest recruit arrived, tasked with laundry, sweeping tent floors and tea making. Too young to join up, boy soldiers were recruited for non-combative roles. He was probably no older than 13 when sent up to Akoot. As with many of my soldiers, few had date of birth records.

When I look back it amazes me that a British-led organisation was party to these youngsters being posted to active service areas, but at the time it didn't appear out of the ordinary. Each Officers' Mess, including DR's at Akoot, employed boy waiters as a route to an army career.

The communists were abducting youngsters from families across the jebel. Beguiled by lies, some parents acquiesced; others, those remaining loyal to the Sultan, had their children forcibly taken. Easily trained in fieldcraft skills and weaponry, the youngsters filled a niche in adoo forces, leading to talk of a 'Boy's Brigade', young teenagers led by adult communists.

3 February had arrived – and I was on leave. I left my troop at Akoot in the hands of Sgts Oliver, Fyffe and Jan Mohamed. My car was VOR again. There was talk the troop would soon be moved back to consolidate with the Squadron at Mudhai.

15

AFRICAN ADVENTURE

After seven months, our first leave and Tom and I escape to East Africa, via Masirah Island, Cyprus, Israel and Ethiopia.

3 Feb – Order Yard-O-Led – Ann will be 21!
81 went up on TM46 this p.m. – centre wheel left side?
Flight – Akoot / Salalah – met up with Tom.
Swam off Salalah beach

Leaving Akoot I caught a returning Skyvan back to Salalah and met up with Tom. After checking we were booked on a RAF C130 Hercules the following day, we took ourselves off to Salalah's beach for a long-anticipated swim. My sister Ann was about to reach 21 – historically the age you were allowed to vote, marry without consent and enter into contracts. I'd promised her a silver propelling pencil so she could change her mind on any of the aforementioned as often as she wished. Three years her older and wiser brother, I'd come to assume this was a young lady's prerogative.

Driving to Adonib, Sgt Begley's Saladin, reg. no. 81, hit a Soviet TM46 anti-tank mine. Exploding beneath the middle of three wheels, the first had missed the powerful weapon's top screwed pressure fuse. Designed to cause maximum damage to vehicles, unlike armoured cars, soft skinned Bedfords and Land Rovers suffered catastrophically, as would have a Ferret Scout Car. Sgt Begley's crew luckily received no lasting injuries apart from the expected temporary hearing loss. The Saladin, however, was rendered VOR for a year through lack of spares.

4 Feb – 11.45 Indulgence flight on Herc. to Masirah Island – "Masirah a hole!" Stayed at RAF Officers' Mess.
Invited to walk to end of runway to view "Arabs living in tented camp, walls built from burmails!" Declined – it's what we've been living in for months . . .

There was very little to commend Masirah's bleak, arid, litter scattered landscape. A result of many years of RAF usage and unconcerned fishermen encamped beyond the airfield's Dannert wire perimeter fencing.

5 Feb - 8 Feb – Indulgence flight to Cyprus. Hope to continue same to Nairobi. Cyprus cold, RAF Mess comfortable.
No luck with Nairobi indulgence flights for a month! Arranged EL AL flight to Jerusalem tomorrow – Israel 4 days then Kenya!
Hired car. Visited Paphos – interesting.
Island quiet and dull – Like Isle of Wight off-season. Pretty orange groves and Mt Troodos has snow! Turkish sector run down and Turks unfriendly. Lunched Nicosia. Visited War Graves. Sombre. Drove north to Kyrenia, pleasant seaside town, worn at edges, unsophisticated.

CYPRUS

Arriving at RAF Akrotiri we booked into the Officers' Mess, before seeking RAF indulgence flights to Nairobi we'd heard were fairly frequent. We were unlucky. Learning there'd be no Kenya flights for another month, we visited a travel agent and booked the first available flight to Tel Aviv and a second, on to Nairobi. This gave us an unscheduled stay of two days on the island. Hiring a car, we became tourists. Following months living in Oman's mountains with little evidence of fresh fruit other than the tinned variety, the groves of ripening oranges were mouthwatering. Eschewing childhood temptations of scrumping, we drove on to Paphos, mythical birthplace of Aphrodite. De-bussed before our arrival, a large group of tourists were in no obvious hurry to move on. Finally, we saw Aphrodite's waterfall, but the oranges made the greater impact.

After Paphos we visited Kyrenia on the north coast, looking sad and rundown, then south through brighter Nicosia to Larnaca, eating at tavernas and cafes. The island was green and beautiful but by the second day I was growing impatient to get on with our planned trip to Kenya and Tanzania. Thankfully at the time little did I realise nine months on I'd be returning to Cyprus on a stretcher.

ISRAEL

8 Feb – Flight out 18.30 – Tel Aviv. Bus very crowded, bags everywhere. Hotel Elat – cheap and cheerful.

9, 10 Feb – Arrived Jerusalem midday – snow on approaches, also burned out military vehicles beside roads and in fields – remnants of '67 war. Are they there as shrines?
Comfortable hotel Casa Nova – once a monastery.

Jerusalem spoiled by cheap commercialism; plagued by would-be guides and souvenir gift sellers. Old City remains as imagined, largely unchanged, stinking, noisy and dirty – perfect!
Met group old Arabs in narrow alley at table smoking hookahs – whom when greeted in Arabic immediately insisted we join them. Made friends through use of Arabic. Promise of taxi tomorrow to take us around sights. Unbelievably generous.

10 Feb – Driver arrived sharp at 0830 – visited Bethlehem, Jericho, Dead Sea, and Lazarus' grave at Bethany, ending with sunset over Jerusalem from Gardens of Gethsemane. Monumental day. Despite protestations he refused payment for chauffeuring services.

Bethlehem disappointed: garish, busy and filled with people jostling for best photographs. Every inanimate object seemed to be either gilded or silver. The crib with too many incense burners, screens, candelabra and pilgrim-worn marbled floors all somehow cheapened by the crush of gawping tourists. On reflection, what we should have expected.

Jericho was a delight: bustling with friendly open market stalls displaying all manner of vegetables, fruits and huge oranges on which we gorged. The Dead Sea looked inviting but for the stretches of stinking mud needed to reach the water's edge.

We returned to an indelible memory. Strolling through Gethsemane's empty gardens, we touched ancient olive trees, a red sun slipped beyond Jerusalem and we watched, reflective, wishing time'd not pass. Our Arab companion waited patiently, refusing payment for our remarkable day.

Boarding our 0230hrs Nairobi flight I realised the Dead Sea visit had taken us almost 1,000ft below sea level. Not the best acclimatisation preparation for climbing Kilimanjaro's almost 20,000ft.

11 Feb – Our El Al flight landed at Addis Ababa on a scheduled stopover at 0810 local time. On take-off the pilots lost control. The VC10 aquaplaned off the runway to a shuddering halt into soft ground. Stuck wheel deep in African mud on Ethiopia's high plateau at 7,700ft. We weren't going anywhere very fast.

A terrific noise awakened drowsy passengers as the aircraft ploughed off the end of the runway. A second's silence before pandemonium as hysterical passengers jumped to their feet, rushing about like headless chickens. Ushered off the aircraft by a suddenly attentive crew, we stood on the airfield gazing at the chaos.

Fishing my Kodak instamatic camera from a pocket, I began taking photographs, unfortunately attracting the immediate attention of two large Israeli cabin staff. Without warning my camera was snatched from me and before I could protest, the back opened, successfully exposing the entire film. 'No photographs!' was shouted into my face as they ran to another hapless photographer hoping for a scoop. Given the heightened security on El Al flights, bordering almost on paranoia following recent terrorist hijackings and bombings, cabin staff/security guards were best obeyed.

Looking at the aircraft, we'd been lucky, for less than two months later a Vickers VC10 crashed on takeoff at Addis. Forty-three passengers died when spilled aviation fuel ignited.

After a tedious day held at the airport and an overnight stay at an Addis hotel, we finally caught an onward flight next day. However, we'd lost 24 hours in our tight schedule.

AFRICA – KENYA

12 Feb – Nairobi AT LAST
Only just found a room as all accommodation taken. The Impala Hotel. By 1400 this hotel full too. Managed to hire car fairly cheaply. 1xKS a mile. VW beetle. Things looking up!
Drive-in cinema – Music Lovers – utterly forgettable.

Exhilarated to be back in East Africa, I was buzzing with remembered excitement. I'd been too long absent. The scents, smells, noises and that ultramarine, high altitude, cloudless sky. A continent brimming with surprises including Nairobi's altitude: 5,889ft above sea level. It felt great to be back.

Kenya's capital appeared surprisingly crammed with people. From an airport payphone I began calling hotels only to find all were fully booked until discovering the 2-star Impala Hotel. It was comfortable even if cockroaches had arrived first. Unbeknown to us, our visit had coincided with the 1st All-African World Trade Fair. Held in Nairobi, 37 member states from the Organisation of African Unity were participating. By 2pm our hotel was also fully booked.

Next I searched a well thumbed telephone directory for a car hire firm. Finding just a single car left, the rest also all pre-booked, I secured a deal on an almost white, slightly dented VW Beetle at one Kenyan shilling a mile. Not bad.

13 Feb – Nairobi National Park
Amazing day. Saw many species. Good rhino. Buffalo. Sleepy hippo. Impala. Eland. Bushbuck. Waterbuck. Zebra. Wildebeest. Cheetah – way too tame? No lion. Cars arriving late p.m. drove us away.

Small in comparison to Africa's main game reserves, Nairobi Park extends across 120 sq km of the Athi plains south and west of the city, on land set aside as a game park in the early 20th century by the revered British conservationist Mervyn Cowie.

Originally settlers had had to put up with roaming wildlife threatening man and property, especially after nightfall. Today, electric fencing protects Nairobi. With easy access, the park with its city skyline can soon become crowded with casual visitors. The disinterested cheetah had probably become immune to gawking tourists. We'd just joined their number.

14 Feb – Visited British High Commission and Col Taylor 14th/20th H – v. helpful letting us have 2 bivouacs and camping gear. Hearing our plans to climb Kilimanjaro and visit game parks, he's forbidden we travel to Tanzania. Serving British military personnel not permitted visit to former colony. So we're restricted to reserves in Kenya? Lunched at Hilton, Tsvao Restaurant – just 15 shillings – excellent meal.

Decided Tanzania was still on. Bought road map. Left Nairobi late at 6pm, arriving Hunters Lodge in the dark. 100 miles. Too late for tents, so booked room. £5 12s 50c B&B – good value. Dined in. Obnoxious tourist guests at another table complaining their rare steaks were raw!? Idiots.

15 Feb – Up at 0545. Tom slept on. Drove to small reserve half mile from Hunters. Saw warthog, giraffe and hornbills. Found still warm elephant spoor on track. Heard branch crack then saw an elephant – lone bull, red brown with local dust, side on, quietly feeding 50m away.

Reckoning I'd photograph, left car and approached. Two photographs and film ended! Instamatic camera. Changed film slowly, b. waterproof wrapper noisy! Noticed elephant had raw wound on hind leg dragging long wire noose. Time to back off. Back at Hunters, reported wounded elephant to hotel staff, but met with indifference. Astonishing. Africa's changed. Tom sorry he'd missed elephant.

Leaving Hunters, drove south through Tsavo seeing 19 elephant, some zebra, five hippo, a python, giraffe, and variety of buck. VW has poor ground clearance limiting cross-country impulses. Stopped Mzima Springs, saw large crocodile.

Camped at exit to Tsavo West Reserve, fixing bivouacs to either side to VW car doors. It worked. Tom cooked excellent meal. Couple of Beers. Comfortable night. Saw Kibo from road. We have to climb.

The camera used was a 35mm single lens Instamatic. The films came in waterproof plastic wrappings impossible to open quietly, but thankfully the elephant took no notice.

Dragging a leg it was clear something was wrong. Then I saw one of its hind legs was raw from the knee down, revealing partially dried flesh. A flap of grey and red dust covered skin hung from its far leg dragging a wire rope, embedded

Taken with an Instamatic camera, 35mm photograph of the wounded elephant, lonely and in pain, left wounded by an uncaring mankind.

around a foot. Raw flesh where there should have been skin was fly encrusted. There was nothing I could do. Sickened, I returned to the hotel a mile away. At reception I raised the matter with a European only to receive a shrug and supercilious 'What the heck you expect us to do eh, man?' 'Shoot it,' I replied, to a contemptuous stare. The level of indifference shocked – ten years earlier a game warden would have been alerted and the matter dealt with. 'Poor bloody animal,' I said in reply, wishing I'd had a rifle. Still angry, we paid our bill and left.

Witnessing the animal's suffering and callous disregard at the hotel, I couldn't help but lament how priorities had changed in the short while since I'd lived in Africa. Left to suffer, the animal faced a prolonged and painful death, unless first killed by lion.

Journeying south we saw Tom's first wild elephant and also some wild game. Reaching the Tanzanian border, we pitched camp for the night beside the track. That afternoon we'd caught our first glimpses of Kilimanjaro, the landscape stretching towards the slopes accentuating a floating snowcap above clouds. During the fleeting moment when equatorial daylight fades to mineral pitch darkness, we were rewarded with Kibo's distinctive dome reflecting the many hues of an African sunset, shades of pink like a cloud of flamingos.

The name of Africa's tallest mountain is an amalgam of two names, Kilima (mountain) and Njaro (whiteness). The giant stratovolcano, Kilima, Africa's Goliath, is a large steep-sided volcano comprising alternating layers of igneous rock, lava, ash and cinders. Njaro, the icecap.

The 19,340ft summit is called Uhuru Peak (Freedom), the youngest of three volcanic cones comprising the massif. To the east, Mawenzi (Friend) at 16,890ft. On the western slopes, the most ancient cone, Shira, once the tallest of the three volcanoes, now eroded over millennia stands at 13,140ft.

TANZANIA

16 Feb – Crossed into Tanzania after a brush & tidy-up, washed, shaved and clean shirts. Luckily no problem at border control. Drove straight to Marangu Hotel and booked climb departing tomorrow! Brilliant timing. To Moshi – haircut and provisions – sultanas and chocolate. Indian barber claims he remembered father as Moshi's DC – 13 years ago? I thanked him for a fine haircut – tipping far too well. Bought an oiled Chinese paper umbrella, just in case! Marangu – erected tents behind hotel beneath gum trees and scented firs, scent evoking memories of Kenya school days. Saw mountain from campsite. Seems a lot of snow. Morale exceptionally high. Excitement indescribable.

MARANGU 6,000FT

I'd known Marangu Hotel from the late 1950s living at Moshi, birthplace of my youngest sister Odeyne, now at school in England. Sixty kilometres from Moshi amongst Kilimanjaro's wooded slopes, the hotel was originally the main residence to a coffee farm. The buildings were still owned by the original settlers who'd arrived in 1907. Buying a small acreage from the local Chagga tribe, the Lenys first farmed coffee before enterprisingly diversifying to run Kilimanjaro expeditions.

Marangu translates as 'full of water'. The natural springs would have seemed heaven sent to the settlers after weeks spent trekking 320km from Kenya's coast across arid savannah plains towards Kilimanjaro's foothills. At an altitude of 6,000ft, Marangu must have captivated then as now, sublimely beautiful, cool and wooded. Idyllic.

Discovering a climb was scheduled to start the next day we'd booked to join immediately. The two indomitable lady organisers, Erika Leny and Peggy Brice-Bennet fitted us out with hired boots and windproof jackets, worn but serviceable. Last but not least we were issued hand crafted wooden staves, four feet in length, skilfully engraved with an anti-slip crosshatched pattern at the handle end, a hand crafted steel spike at the other. Straight and strong, the stave doubled as both walking pole and ice axe, achieving best friend status during arduous days ahead. Available to purchase on return – for those who successfully summited.

Looking up at the mountain, it slightly concerned me how low the snowline appeared, aware it'd be tough going in deep snow, a factor that had occasionally defeated climbers when we lived in Moshi.

> *17 Feb – Left 1115 having hung around too long, delayed by a late arrival. We're now party of 5, two Canadian girls, the late comer, a Brit accountant from Arusha, Tom and me. Light rain at midday – my umbrella causes amusement. Lunched in corrugated tin shed. 4 spongers have attached themselves to our group causing slight tensions. Bismark Hut by mid afternoon. Great to be back. Umbrella works!*

The route up to Bismark Hut, our first accommodation on the trek, followed a dirt track, heavily rutted by rain runoff but otherwise undemanding, passing through banana groves and small farms with mud walled, conical thatched rondavels. Each building seemed to be emitting blue smoke as the women prepared meals over open fires. The Chagga tribe's friendly reputation endured, villagers constantly greeting us along the way. Tiny children rushing up were delighted at my poor

Rain fell off and on, and the recently purchased umbrella became my latest chat-up line.

Swahili, offering freshly picked bananas from parents' plantations for the princely sum of 5 cents, approx 3p.

Raining hard, we'd taken shelter under a timber and corrugated iron lean-to and were snacking on sandwiches when four strangers arrived, squeezing under our temporary cover, announcing they wished to join our climb. I enquired of the guides whether there'd be sufficient room in the bivvy huts and received grudging confirmation. Plainly our guides were unhappy the group had doubled in size with people who'd not paid for their services.

Poorly equipped, it was clear the group, one Brit, two Americans and a German would have to share our accommodation but also rations. A heated discussion ensued at which Tom and I attempted to mediate, finally reaching a compromise. Despite protestations, it was agreed each of the newcomers would make a contribution towards the extra costs against cooking and purchase of additional rations which thankfully the guides were able to procure from local villagers. At the conclusion of this minor hiatus, Tom and I looked at each other grinning – more than used to resolving such issues between SAF soldiers, problems which so often looked intractable until resolved.

AFRICAN ADVENTURE

BISMARK HUT 8,907FT

Subsequently renamed Mandara Hut, after the famous Chagga tribe leader.

On arrival at Bismark Hut, we were relieved to find there were sufficient beds for all. Open plan and austere, the room contained basic wooden bunk beds with typical African rope netting supporting thin, damp canvas-covered, cotton-waste filled mattresses. Fairly ripe toilets were located adjacent to a washroom with basins. Our home for the night was stone built with corrugated iron sheets on a timber framed pitched roof. Ancient whitewashed exterior added to its authentic colonial appeal. The name a hangover from when Tanganyika had been a German colony.

At this altitude breathing was already noticeably laboured and we still had a further 10,000ft to climb.

18 Feb – Started out in brilliant sunshine – no sign rain. Track's mud sticky. Diarrhoea, slowing me down. Tom very supportive by remaining behind. Reached Peter's Hut 1300. Group getting on well including the four spongers. A fifth ! arrived last night at Bismark but couldn't manage the climb today.

On leaving Bismark's clearing, the track disappears beneath a giant heather forest, Erica Arborea (tree heath). The Kilimanjaro variety reaches 6m in height, bearing numerous tiny honey-scented, bell-shaped white flowers and dark green needle leaves. Walking through this forest is one of the climb's early highlights.

Without warning I suffered diarrhoea attacks necessitating mad scrambles into the undergrowth. Fleetingly recalling leopards once roamed this forest, thoughts of being caught with pants down and eaten by leopard failed to diminish the urgency of my gut's demands. The night before, I'd slept badly, twice having to visit the filthy latrines. I'd noticed too, my resting heart rate of around 36 had raced to double that, yet otherwise I felt fine and put it down to the altitude. Gradually the bouts of diarrhoea became less frequent. By midday I'd recovered sufficiently to enjoy a strip wash in a cold but invigorating gently flowing stream, before the last climb to reach Peter's hut which was spacious yet utilitarian, consisting of a rough timber frame, all sheeted in rusting corrugated iron.

Tom had remained with me, patiently observing from a distance my frequent dashes to crouch behind bushes or one of the many rock outcrops. We arrived last at 1300, well behind the others but in time to enjoy a warm cup of tea and later a meal of hot stew prepared by 'mpichi' (cook). During the evening, conversation turned to occupations. Of the four newcomers, the men, English, American and German were 'travelling'. The diminutive Bridget was escaping an abusive father, a Texan rancher.

Our original group comprised two Canadian girls, Joan, a recent divorcee seeking a cathartic escape, accompanied by her pretty younger friend, Beverly. Then there was Richard, a Brit expat accountant working in Arusha 80km west of Moshi, Tom and me. In deflecting interest, we made out we worked for the UK's Department for Overseas Aid, successfully stymieing further enquiry. Enquiring of my spoken Swahili I owned up to having lived in Moshi as a child, adding I'd climbed the mountain with my twin brother as we turned teenagers. As I'd hoped, this brought the group back to the climb and days ahead on the mountain. Turning in, I was relieved to be feeling much better and slept well.

PETERS HUT 12,250FT

Subsequently renamed Horombo hut – 'horombo' is Chagga for 'peace'.

Rumour had it the hut was originally named after a German colonial autocrat, Dr Karl Peters. In the 1890s Peters was the Reichskommissar (Imperial High Commissioner) Kilimanjaro Region, ruling from his headquarters at Moshi. Peters had taken a Chagga mistress. On discovering she had a secret lover, he had them both hanged. This shocking incident, added to an appalling record for mistreating Chagga tribes-peoples, led to an insurrection. Recalled to Germany, Peters was tried and dismissed from service. But that was not the end of it, well connected, he was shortly reinstated by the Kaiser himself, with all previous titles returned, plus a lifetime pension to be paid out of the Kaiser's personal estate. Adding to the injustice, 20 years following his death, Peters was rehabilitated officially on the personal decree of Adolf Hitler. Horombo is a far more fitting name.

> *19 Feb – Kibo hut 1400. Another glorious day. Hidden all morning, Kibo looked magnificent suddenly appearing from behind a ridge as we climbed. Heart's beating like a mad drum, is it the altitude? Tom and I otherwise in good shape. Think all 9 should reach the top. Accommodation cramped. Have to share bunks – girls chose partners. I'm sharing with Beverly. Don't think Tom's happy with his bunk mate. American who'd gone back for extra kit arrived 8pm – fm Bismark to Kibo hut!*

That first sighting of the huge and magnificent dome of snow was sufficient to force stopping to gaze in astonishment at the massive bulk that was Uhuru peak. Looking to one's right, Mawenzi as beautiful, yet whereas Kibo was smoothly rounded and vast, Mawenzi rose jagged, dark rock spiked with ice filled crags, and formidable. We were now climbing through high altitude desert terrain. Once onto the saddle, between Mwenzi and Kibo, we'd reached 14,000ft where we faced a howling gale blowing north to south. The winds were relentless. With the increased altitude and the constant buffeting, the going was slow. It seemed the tiny hut catching sunlight at the foot of Kibo's final ascent remained as distant as a mirage, never getting any closer despite each step taken towards it.

KIBO HUT 15,600FT

This hut seemed more basic than Peters, also constructed of rough hewn timbers clad in weathered corrugated iron, of which two loosened sheets rattled irritatingly in the persistent winds. Utterly utilitarian, a shining shed 15,600ft above sea level on a desolate mountainside was never going to win any architectural prizes, but it served its purpose.

Both Tom and I felt in good shape and the rest of the party looked fit. Remarkably, Will the American, having turned back to collect equipment from Bismark hut, had then trekked past Peters to join us at Kibo hut. An astonishing achievement for a novice mountaineer. But he'd overdone it and unfortunately never made the summit.

The lack of bunk beds left us with no alternative but to share. The girls, asked if they would choose whom they shared with, Beverly immediately claimed that as the youngest, I was the only trustworthy one 'at this altitude'! I never did quite work that one out. Gaps in the structure funnelled wind through tin walls and devoid of artificial heating, temperatures dropped below minus 15C. Trying to sleep there came a plaintive whisper beside me, 'I've *never* been so cold, and another thing, I *don't* believe you two are civil servants!' Our cover was blown. Continuing to grow perishingly cold all were thankful for the additional body warmth of a companion.

Woken at 2300 with a cup of hot tea and some broken Rich Tea biscuits. 'Chai ya Englishi sana' (very English tea) beamed a wide awake Gibson our guide, 'tayari kwenda dakika tano!' (ready to go in five minutes!) We'd all slept fully dressed. Tom and I in our inadequate Omani service gear wore two pairs of khaki drill trousers supplemented with our hired jackets. Outside the hut, we formed into single file for the final ascent.

We set off at a slow measured pace, out of necessity for all were gasping for breath at the unaccustomed altitude. Reaching Hans Meyer's cave at 17,000ft we stopped for more sweet biscuits and water from our carried bottles. The cave, named after the first European to summit Kibo, gave us welcome shelter from the biting winds. After this staging point, the going becomes progressively more laboured due to decreasing levels of oxygen and the calf-deep energy sapping lava scree. For every three steps attempted in ascent, just one is gained. 'Poli, Poli' (slowly, slowly) cajoled Gibson, 'hutaki kufa' – 'What's he saying?' gasped Tom beside me. 'You don't want to die,' I translated.

Hypoxia is a medical condition occurring at any altitude where the concentration of atmospheric oxygen is too low to sustain permanent habitation, generally accepted as above 16,000ft. It can lead to loss of brain function, and ultimately death. For the unacclimatized, it is often known as the Death Zone; we were past this height.

Moving slowly following a zig zag route, progress was governed by the weakest in the group. Patience is a virtue lost at altitude. Each deals differently with the crucible of another's irritating habits; the constant complainer I find the worst. Hans, our German freeloader, began swearing at Gibson to speed up. Unable to let this pass, I turned to remind him the guides were ours and perhaps he should f… off., I stared at him in the darkness, bigger than me; each of us was gasping for oxygen and the thought of a fight at this altitude was beyond nightmare. Then Tom moved to my side. With an oath, the man turned on his heel and made off down the mountain. 'Why give up?' I managed to shout. We never saw him again.

Sunrise beyond Mawenzi

Gradually our numbers reduced as mountain sickness took its toll and people dropped off to return to Kibo's hut. We lost our American, Will, and Canadian Joan. Needing only the slightest encouragement, the game Beverly, with Tom, Richard and I reached Gilman's Point 18,750ft, named after the British geographer who in 1921 climbed and accurately calculated Kilimanjaro's altitude.

Reaching Gilman's, we turned to gaze at the unforgettable golden sunrise silhouetting the rock and snow peaks of Mawenzi. Four out of an original group of 10 had made it to Gilman's. With another 590ft to climb only Tom, accountant Richard and I left to tramp on around the crater's edge. The rock hard ice began to dazzle in the sunlight, and peering down the steep sided, sulphur smelling crater was sufficient to concentrate altitude-addled minds.

UHURU PEAK 19,340FT

"We were in an amiable frame of mind . . . notwithstanding all the toil and trouble my self-appointed task had cost me, I don't think I would that moment have changed places with anybody in the world."

Professor Hans Meyer 1889 on reaching the summit which he named, Kaiser-Wilhelm-Spitze after Wilhelm II, Emperor of Germany, King of Prussia, Imperial ruler of German East Africa until 1918 when the Country became a British Protectorate, as Oman had in 1891.

Progress became progressively tortuous. With bursting headache, eyes streaming and chest hurting like hell, it seemed vital energy had deserted with the increasing sun's glare bouncing off the blue-white ice. I could make out the other two ahead and had to force myself to place one foot forward then the other, all the while fighting an overwhelming desire to lie down and sleep, 'usingizi wa wafu' (sleep of the dead) warned Gibson. They say reason is lost through lack of oxygen, but for Gibson I'd have probably embraced such sleep. Catching up with Tom and Richard, I joined them, tired and exhilarated on the frozen glacial summit of Uhuru Peak, the roof of Africa.

Today much of Kilimanjaro's once revered icecap no longer exists; Africa's snow summit has lost 82% of its ice cap since 1912 and 55% of its glaciers since 1962. With over a century's rising global temperatures the once magnificent white topped peak of Africa, 330km south of the equator, was only ever destined to be transient.

Descending, Gibson allowed me five minutes of restorative kip sheltering beneath a rock overhang. With every step downwards it became easier to breathe,

The glacier is named after Walter Furtwangler who, with a colleague, Siegfried Konig, were the fourth European expedition to reach the summit in 1910.

Some 83 years after the first successful European ascent, an exhausted author in hired hat, jacket, trousers, boots and goggles takes 'five' alongside Gibson, our experienced chief guide.

until soon we were leaping and sliding down the scree to Kibo hut. Gathering our kit, we continued to Peters hut where amongst much rejoicing, we were generously fed and watered before collapsing gratefully into single bunks and deep uninterrupted sleep. We had walked, climbed, crawled and slid that day for over 16 hours, ascended 3,500ft to the summit of Africa and descended some 7,100ft. As Meyer before, we'd beaten the altitude and lack of oxygen, overcoming inner doubts – marvelling that the achievement should be such a triumph. Next morning each summiteer received a presentation of everlasting flowers woven into garlands, as we bade farewell to Gibson and his father Joshua, our guides and the porters.

21 Feb – Long walk back – took it slowly, seeing so much more than had we rushed. Others seemed keen to be off the mountain. Beverly struggling with sore knees. BATH at last!

Back at Marangu we booked ourselves into a room. I'd offered the Canadians a chance to share our bathroom before they caught their taxi and pre-booked accommodation in Arusha. Last to bathe, I turned the taps on full, watching a stream of rust coloured liquid pour out, reminding me of Kenya schooldays when our weekly bathwater had only ever been brown. Letting it run to almost full, I climbed in, sinking until totally submerged when silence is broken only by the sound of heartbeat. Occasionally distant gurgling filters through, water drawn in pipes as other baths are run, secret code of a hotel's plumbing system.

Joshua, Gibson's father, weaves a summiteer's garland

The Kilimanjaro garland made from flowers of the wild everlasting Helichrysum Kilimanjari, growing at 16,000ft.

Celibacy is all very well when taken voluntarily, but few young men necessarily seek it as their first-choice vocation. The girls having departed with tearful farewells, it was a contemplative pair of servicemen who later sat alone in the hotel bar, cold Tusker beers their monastic choice of company. Beverely had guessed we were soldiers, saying it was our optimism and that she'd known all along. I let her have my BFPO address – ensuring our posting remained secure. Letters followed from Canada, delivered by Huey pilots to sangars and various positions in Dhofar, reminding of gentler, softer times. I'd write back whenever possible until eventually the enquiring correspondence faded, as inevitably as flowers on mountain garlands.

THE UNHESITATING GENEROSITY OF FRIENDS

That evening I telephoned the Freemans, longstanding friends of my parents. They still lived in Arusha Chini, 25km south of Moshi, working for the Tanganyika Planting Company Ltd, a sugarcane plantation first established in 1936. We later learned the annual harvest was an impressive 50,000 tonnes a season. Despite the country's name change to Tanzania, the sugar plantation had retained their original Tanganyika designation. Unhesitatingly the Freemans insisted we visit.

Fifteen years earlier, as nine-year-olds, my brother and I had stayed with the Freemans during quarantine following chickenpox. The otherwise simple condition of quarantine was complicated by the fact my father, recently promoted, had had to move 600km away to take up a senior post at Government House, Dar-es-Salaam on the coast. Father's posting, delayed to coincide with the end of school holidays, could not be put off any longer. My mother, left alone with four children, a household to move and unwell at the time, was saved when the Freemans resolutely came to the rescue. The house move went ahead, and my brother and I were transferred to the Freemans where we were spoiled rotten for 10 days before being put on a passenger and goods train to travel the two days to school accompanied by our well travelled school trunks. We had been Kenya boarders since the age of five.

Train services were run by an organisation first established in 1948 under the splendid title: The East African Railways and Harbours Corporation (EAR&H), which operated rail services across Kenya, Uganda and Tanganyika. 'Harbours' reflected various inland shipping services on Lake Victoria and other lakes and waterways in East Africa. The corporation flourished until dissolved in 1977 when broken up to create independent services within the three independent countries.

The trains, part passenger and part freight, were pulled by steam locomotives. Our journey took 40 hours travelling between Moshi in Tanganyika, east around Kilimanjaro then northwest to Nairobi onwards to Eldoret in northern Kenya. Passing through plantations of green sisal stretching between horizons, we travelled through Tsavo Game Reserve meandering gently around the eastern slopes of Kilimanjaro before turning northwest and steaming on to Kenya. The last stop before our destination at Eldoret was Timboroa on the Equator, at just over 9,000ft, the highest railway station in East Africa. By then we'd skirted the Aberdares, mountain refuge of the Mau Mau terrorists. The walking speed of trains at this point necessitated escort by a platoon of the King's African Rifles, carried in two open wagons. It was cold inside our carriages, it must have been bitter in open wagons.

Our 450-mile trip involved two changes: first at Voi, just over the border into Kenya; and then Nairobi before eventually arriving at Eldoret, a small town at an altitude of 6,897ft. Thirty-five kilometres east at 8,250ft was our school at Kaptagat, on the edge of the Rift Valley where today Kenya's long distance athletes train for marathons.

As the furthermost children attending the school, we'd grumble in vain at the repeated loss of a day's travelling either end of our holidays. School friends lived mostly in Kenya and eastern Uganda, within a day's journey to school. Despite the certainty of end-of-holiday misery, journeys home pitched high in our lives. In today's often unpredictable world, it is perhaps astonishing to imagine it was once not uncommon for nine-year-old children to travel to school by train unaccompanied for two days across Africa, and for half that journey as the sole Europeans. On one trip, immediately following our September birthdays, we were at least armed with small alloy cap-guns and boxes of caps.

22 Feb – Freemans for tea – they insist we stay. Funny how well I remember them and their house. They are very generous. Faces now peeling badly.

We arrived in time for afternoon tea, served on the verandah. It was especially good to see the Freemans again after such a length of time, their kindness unforgotten. The house was a typical colonial bungalow, whitewashed throughout with polished concrete floors painted a dull red mostly hidden by any number of scattered Persian rugs and wooden furniture, sofa adorned with a leopard skin. Shading the house, a magnificent avocado tree sagged with fruit. Seeing this Tom had muttered 'A tree like that would be worth a fortune in the UK!' Luckily for us, avocado was on the menu that evening for dinner.

NGURDOTO – CRATER RIM 5984FT

23 Feb – Ngurdoto – Arusha National Park. Saw forest elephant, buff, colobus but no lion for Tom. However, a good park. Stopped off at lookout – picnic lunch – Ellen had prepared delicious hamper. Peered deep into jungle crater. Quite extraordinary, expected to meet Allan Quartermain at any moment!

Our welcoming hosts suggested we stay a second night. Before sunset we visited the home of the Plessings, a Danish family running the sugar plantation, but sadly they were away visiting Denmark. The Plessings were my sister's Godparents and old family friends, with whom we'd spent many enjoyable visits in the past. Their whitewashed house under a huge thatched roof was surrounded by the most exquisite gardens and one of the best uninterrupted views of Kilimanjaro.

Ngurdoto Crater is a steep sided caldera forming a unique reserve within Arusha Game Reserve on the western slopes of Kilimanjaro. Small for an African game park, the caldera's diameter is just 3km at its widest and 500m deep to a flat, marshy base. Surrounded by dense equatorial forest in every colour green, in it we saw cape buffalo and a number of rare colobus monkeys and especially, the elusive small Forest Elephant.

The colobus (Colobus guerezais) a black and white primate has a white framed face, bushy white tip to long tail and flowing afghan hound-like flanks giving the appearance of a mantle. Regrettably they are much hunted for their fine hide worn as celebratory headdresses, and for bushmeat. And with the loss of habitat, this simian is an endangered species.

The wider known African Bush elephant (Loxodonta africana) we'd seen driving south from Nairobi stands 3.95m at the shoulder, whereas the smaller Forest elephant (Loxodonta cyclotis) living deep in Africa's mountain forests, reaches a shoulder height of 2.4m.

As promised by the Freemans, we saw just one other vehicle that day visiting Ngurdoto. The solitude added to the sense of timelessness, alone in a pristine world, as yet undiminished by 20th century demands. Truly a natural successor to the biblical Garden of Eden.

FAREWELL TO WILDNESS

As I write today, a note about the mountain they call Kibo. When I first climbed Kilimanjaro as a 13-year-old, we found snow at 15,000ft sugarcoating Africa's shimmering dome. There were occasions when snow accumulated to depths

Kilimanjaro's peak, Kibo, rises above the forests, as a small herd of Maasai giraffes (Giraffa tippelskirchi) amble gracefully by.

sufficient to thwart many a successful summit attempt. Indeed you hoped not to find deep snow anywhere near that altitude. Global warming has seen an end to the snows, the summit recently bereft of ice. Now plans have been approved to build a cable car onto the Shira Plateau at an altitude of 12,600ft where tourists may disembark to experience views presently restricted to climbers. Plans allow for 15 cars each carrying six passengers with rides lasting about twenty minutes each way. Countries approached to undertake the engineering project include China.

Since 1975 fixed ropes and Chinese installed aluminium ladders assist the ascent of Everest. It's called high altitude tourism. Already mooted as possible, how long before engineers drill an Eiger type tunnel to reach Everest's summit? Progress or regress? Subdue wildness and it's gone forever. Thesiger lamented vehicles in Arabia's Empty Quarter; now we deplore these projects that remove the edge we each need.

THE CHINESE FACTOR

Aware we were servicemen, Ellen took me to one side soon after we'd arrived and confided: 'Please, whatever you do, don't admit to anybody you're British

Army. Recently two RAF officers were arrested and their hosts almost forced to leave the country for having British servicemen to stay on their mountain coffee farm. No one quite knows the full story, but please do take care not to advertise your backgrounds.' That afternoon a neighbour of Ellen's happened to call by who remembered my family well. Moshi had been a close community. Learning we were serving soldiers, she confirmed Chinese military advisors had recently been seen in the area. Employed training Tanzanian troops, they were using the mountain's forests to simulate jungle warfare. One of their tactics, the use of roadblocks in practising ambush drills, involved stopping cars at random and strip searching the occupants.

With passports holding valid Omani visas, our occupations as "Government Officials" and a passably military bearing, short hair as opposed to hippy hair, the accepted norm of westerners, it wouldn't have taken long to establish our true occupations.

Whilst President Julius Nyerere's socialism differed from that promoted by Marxism-Leninism, Tanzania's leader had developed close links with Mao Zedong's Marxist-governed China. We certainly couldn't risk incriminating our hosts. And we didn't relish investigation by the Chinese, seeing as we were currently fighting a covert war in which these people were involved.

I'd originally planned to explore the foothills north of Moshi, an old stamping ground where my father, brother and I had fished for trout, and swum in clear mountain streams. In light of what we'd learned, these plans were abandoned. Additionally, it was suggested we forego my planned Nogorongoro trip and instead visit the more remote Ngurdoto Crater with its fewer tourists and the likelihood of having the place to ourselves. Assured it was full of game and a place not to miss, I was glad we'd followed our hosts' recommendation. Ngurdoto was a paradise.

Unexpectedly, the Chinese question would return within the week.

24 Feb – Left F'mans for Lake Manyara. Violent rain shower turning off Dodoma road. Arrived Manyara 5pm. Erected tents. Noticed elephant droppings 10 paces from tents. Lit good fire. Tom cooked curry supper – he's a formidable cook! Slept well. Have to record – Tom's cooking better than his scary driving! Found porcupine quills close to site. No one else camping. Some smart coffee plantations along the way. Arusha vibrant and busy – Moshi now a poor second. Very sad.

Arusha seemed to be in a different league to rundown Moshi. Once preeminent amongst Colonial Service postings, the township now played second fiddle to successful Arusha. Refreshed after our brief stay with the Freemans, we arrived

Tom, an exceptionally fine cook, prepares dinner alongside our army bivouacs and VW Beetle.

at Manyara Reserve where following negotiations with Park Rangers we were permitted to camp close to the reserve's entrance gates. As I pitched our tents Tom prepared an excellent dinner.

MANYARA RESERVE

Next morning, I showed Tom some 30mm black and white banded porcupine quills I had found. He'd only ever seen quills in museums, cut as pens. Whilst finding porcupine quills wasn't rare, I was surprised to find them close to our tents. When attacked, the animal scurries back impaling their aggressor with sharp quills; barbed, they are difficult to remove, as our family's dogs never failed to learn.

An African brush-tailed porcupine (Atherurus africanus) can weigh up to 70 pounds (32kg) and measure almost a metre in length. Surprisingly given its lethal spines, porcupines are predated by leopard and python.

> *25 Feb – Met bad tempered rhino – forcing hasty retreat. Masses of tembo*. Park estimated to hold 500. Elephants in mud bath, tiny chap charged car! Saw herd 250 buffalo. All animals here are wilder than in Kenya's parks.*

Brewing tea beneath acacia, Land Rover approached. White lady with two rangers – Oria Douglas-Hamilton to whom we offered tea. She cautioned care as lions in area. That night leopard coughed close by as we sat with beers after another delicious Bremridge supper! Built up fire. Monkeys noisy early a.m.

*tembo – swahili for elephant

What a memorable day. A mile out from camp, rounding a bend we almost ran smack into an adult rhino blocking our way. With lowered head, front foot scraping the ground raising dust, his intentions were only too obvious. Driving at 40km/h on the dry rutted track, we'd still skidded to a halt. 'Black rhino!' I'd shouted above the VW's protesting air-cooled engine as I furiously swung the car round, accelerating away through 60cm desiccated grass, desperately avoiding anthills and back onto the dirt track.

'Shiiiiit! *SHIIIIT!*' exclaimed Tom, adding the day's understatement 'He looked unfriendly!' A heavyweight at 1300 kg and standing 1.6 m at the shoulder, a charging black rhino (Diceros bicornis) reaches speeds of 55km/h. Against 800 kg of VW Beetle, no contest. 'They're called Faru in Swahili,' I replied as we sped away, 'I don't care, just keep going!' We weren't chased, but it'd been a close call.

The Northern White Rhino (Ceratotherium simum), standing 1.8 m at the shoulder weighs approximately 2500 kg. These are identified by their wide straight mouth, evolved for eating grasses. The slightly smaller black rhino has a noticeably

A small elephant made a sham charge towards us, stopping short as others watched dismissively whilst luxuriating in a muddy waterhole. The gestation period for an African elephant is 22 months. This chap, probably only months old and already keen to show how brave he was, impressed with his display. We were grateful for his tiny size.

Finally, the matriarch considered perhaps it was time we should leave and beating a retreat, we motored on looking for a suitable shady tree to shelter beneath and possibly have a morning brew.

pointed, prehensile upper lip used for feeding on scrubland bush and herbaceous plants, with a particular liking for thorny acacias. The black rhino has the greater propensity for unpredictability, known for charging blindly at perceived threats. Handsome, but bad tempered beasts.

All in all, it'd been an exciting start to a day when we also saw elephant, buffalo, buck and ostrich. Time for a brew.

The first tree selected looked perfect. Parking in the shade, we got out and it was then we realised our mistake, for suddenly mobbed by biting flies we were forced hurriedly back into the car and another speedy retreat. Each had bites on arms and necks. The flies were Tsetse flies (Glossina species). Their bites hurt, cause a large lump, and if the insect is infected can 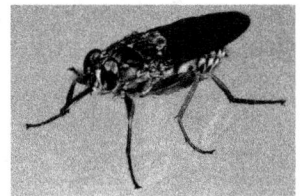 leave you with a serious medical condition called African Trypanosomiasis. Also known as "sleeping sickness", a condition caused by microscopic parasites of the species Trypanosoma brucei transmitted by tsetse fly and found only in sub-Saharan Africa. Luckily neither suffered any ill effects other than itchy wheals on arms and necks. A lump or wheal following a bite is caused by histamine, produced by the body's immune system. Histamine increases blood flow and white blood cell count around the affected area, which causes inflammation or swelling. Fly and mosquito bites itch because histamine also sends a signal to the nerves around the bite. Regrettably we'd no antihistamine; however, we'd been fortunate the flies weren't infected.

At a safe distance away and parked under another tree, we'd no sooner lit our small gas cooker when a Land Rover approached, driven by a European accompanied by two African rangers. Climbing out, an elegant lady looked inquiringly at us as we exchanged courtesies, before my adding an exchange in Swahili with the two rangers. At this, our visitor turned to me to ask where we were from. Explaining we were on holiday and camping at the entrance gate, I mentioned my family had once lived at Musoma on the western approaches of the Serengeti. Straightway the atmosphere thawed. Accepting an invitation to join us necessitated a scramble to produce two mugs and three mess tins in which we managed to serve tea and offered dried tea biscuits.

The lady turned out to be Kenya-raised Oria Douglas-Hamilton, who with her husband Iain had begun a pivotal campaign against the senseless poaching and slaughter of African elephants for ivory.

Conversation turned to the Douglas-Hamiltons' project. She knew my godfather Sir Hugh Elliott and his close involvement with the development of Tanganyika's Game Parks, the creation of the Serengeti National Park in 1951 and the Ngorongoro Conservation Area, my father's provinces when District

Commissioner at Musoma. She brought us up to date on the constant battle against ivory poachers. Incredibly, against all odds, they were achieving remarkable results, with the Manyara elephant count then approaching 500, and buffalo, over 250. A pride of lions was in the area, although we failed to see any that day. The Douglas-Hamilton children, Swahili named Saba (*Seven*) and Dudu (*Bug*) would later become leading lights in the battle to enlighten the world to the perils facing East Africa's elephants. Some say it was in Oria's destiny, for the children's book "Baba the Elephant" was written by her mother's cousin. Arguably, but for the extraordinary efforts of this heroic family, the species Loxodonta Africana would have been decimated in East Africa, if not wiped out.

That night as Tom cooked, I began a poem I'd finish many years later.

TALL AS TREES

Once elephants roamed wherever they pleased,
Africa's battalions, proud and free.
Unhurried, the sun rose over bare backs
As proudly they walked, noble, tall as trees.

Hunted for food . . . by humanity?
. . . before too soon it became just ivory

Farewell Africa's noble giants,
Species: Loxodonta Africana.
Always it seems, destined for history,
Was no fault of yours you grew ivory.

AFRICAN ADVENTURE

NGORONGORO AND ON TO THE SERENGETI

Over the next two days, we drove north past the massive caldera of Ngorongoro, viewing the 16km wide crater from viewpoints and from a modern hotel. One of Africa's wonders, the unique crater is as magnificent as its name evokes, that is but for the hordes of tourists. I'd diarised:

> *Hotel huge, modern, luxurious, full of tourists wearing big-game-hunter hats ringed with fake leopard skin bands, all buying souvenirs – Wildness tamed.*

My disappointment was entirely subjective. Twenty years earlier and growing up on the Serengeti's fringes, there'd been no tourists. In 1959, just 22 tourist permits were issued to travel onto the Serengeti Plains. Now a world-famous Game Reserve, tourists arrive in their thousands, arguably the saviours of East Africa's game parks.

Safaris were always an adventure. My father and Peter Bramwell, the Game Warden based at Banagi, a hamlet on the Serengeti, had led many expeditions in attempts to control the Maasai grazing their Rinderpest infected cattle on the reserves; that and the perennial problem of poaching. Occasionally we'd find poachers' lairs filled with animal hides, strung taut between tree branches to dry, and sadly too, rhino horn, hippo and elephant ivory.

Rinderpest, a viral disease kills even-toed hoofed animals, ungulates. Cattle wandering into game parks spread the disease to buffalo, giraffe, antelope and warthog. The highly communicable virus is transmitted by droplets, infected faeces or contaminated water at drinking holes. With a 100% mortality rate, it was a serious problem for the guardians of East Africa's nascent Game Reserves. The disease was eventually eradicated in 2011.

The word Serengeti means endless plains in Maasai, Siringet: 'the place where land runs forever'. In colloquial Swahili an 'i' is often added to create a noun, for instance a naval destroyer becomes 'Manowari'. At Akoot, a thought had amused me during hours staring through binoculars into enemy territory, willing something to happen, that perhaps an 'i' had been added to Sheershitti, the infamous caves we bombed endlessly? I liked to think so, though I doubt an etymologist would have entirely agreed. Still, it helped pass the time.

> *26 Feb – Reached Seronera at 4pm. Serengeti green. Large numbers Wildebeest, but few Zebra. Hyena, Thomson's and Grant's gazelle, Ostrich, Giraffe, Kongoni, Topi, Reedbuck and Waterbuck. Also Saddlebill. Camped Seronera – surrounded by lions roaring through night – Africa's night sounds.*

Buffalo grazing close to camp, so close, heard their rumbling stomachs. Tom said how much he was enjoying the trip, but again mentioned what awaited our return to Oman and the big push to Yemeni border. Suppose back to Akoot for me?

Increasingly Dhofar reawakened thoughts we'd hoped left behind, Tom would be returning for Op Simba, SAF's big offensive planned for April/June, whereas it was likely a return to Akoot for me? I had no idea.

Akoot's open secret Op Simba would now regularly creep into conversation as we relaxed over beers after a dinner. Tom felt it more than I and both knew the op into the jebel between Oman and Yemen would not directly involve armoured cars. So I'd be out of it. But Tom as DR's mortar officer and 2 Company's 2ic, would be in the thick of it. I tried offering encouragement, but there was no escaping Simba would be the largest military push attempted by the Sultan's forces in the war to date. Given the element of surprise, a battalion-plus airborne assault should knock the adoo sideways. SAF would quickly be dug in ready to withstand any counterattack before the adoo had time to gather their senses. Hopefully.

None knew for certain, we could only guess what the outcome might be, taking and holding a position so close to Yemen's border. No one knew what forces the other side might muster or in what strength given the proximity to Yemen and better supply lines. I knew Tim's death three months earlier had hit hard, a loss still felt acutely at Akoot. It was a reflective Tom who retired to his tent that evening.

SERONERA TO BANAGI

27 Feb – Left camp at sunrise after snatched brew. Drove 12 miles north to Banagi, once home to game warden, Peter Bramwell. Original mud block walls, corrugated iron roofed bungalow, now in need of a little maintenance. Bad tsetse fly frustrated longer stay and we returned towards Seronera. Driving off-road, suddenly spotted two pairs twitching yellow ears. Lion. Five young lions, very sleepy, resting in long grass. Tom's first wild lion. At last.

P.M. followed Nyabogati river – saw pregnant leopard resting in large spreading acacia tree.
Back to Seronera met Tom Moore at Research Centre. Invited to stay overnight. Approaching dusk returned with a sceptical Tom Moore. But leopard hadn't moved. Wasn't long before she stood up, stretched and climbed heavily down the tree. Unexpectedly she leapt last 10ft, landing gracefully on the ground.

What happened next was a first for me, likewise our Seronera scientist. Coiled as a spring at the base of the tree we could now make out the chilling sight of a black snake, spitting cobra which the she Leopard saw off. Unheard-of, never seen the like.

The she leopard descends the Acacia tree to meet the spitting cobra at the tree's base.

Leopard and cobra had eye contact as the snake rose slowly to strike. Spellbound, we watched an extraordinary vignette unfold: leopard meets spitting cobra. Snarling, lips pulled back revealing its killing incisors, the cat turned slowly keeping an eye on its adversary whilst gradually backing her rear end towards the snake. Suddenly, she'd whipped her tail across the snake's face, which in turn feigned a strike as the leopard's tail lashed back again, forcing the snake's retreat. Lasting barely seconds, the encounter ceased, animal and reptile parting company, neither seemingly any worse for the spat. 'Remarkable, absolutely remarkable, never witnessed anything like that before,' exclaimed our astonished scientist. Tom and I had watched spellbound, utterly mesmerised. Top cat!

(Naja nigricollis) moderately sized, these snakes can grow to 2.2m in length and weigh up to six kilos. Their prey is primarily small rodents. In defence these snakes emit a fine sticky spray up to 2m distance, which hitting an eye will cause permanent blindness if untreated. They may also strike and bite. The celebrated herpetologist, Captain Charles Pitman writes in A Guide to The Snakes of Uganda, "the poison, a neurotoxin . . . of these snakes chiefly affects the nervous system and produces paralysis of various muscles . . . followed by respiratory paralysis, convulsions and death by respiratory failure". Best left very well alone.

* * *

At an altitude of 5,000ft you'd expect Seronera's nights to be cool, but it was an ambient 15C, glorious after daily temperatures over 30C. At school we'd learned that given Africa's varied altitudes, for the world's oceans to lap at Lake Victoria's shores, the source of the White Nile, global sea levels would have to rise by 3,745ft. And it is a sombre thought that whilst today's wars are fought over oil and gas, in the future those countries supplied by the Nile basin may go to war over riparian rights and water.

That evening we feasted on Cape Buffalo steak having received assurances the animal had been culled, off-reserve. Late into the evening Tom Moore amused us with life at modern Serengeti and the serious work of the Research Institute established 11 years earlier, in 1961. We learned how lucky we were to have found leopard, for all but a few had been poached along the Nyabogati River, indeed the whole region around the fabled Institute. And I heard again the theory that if caught by leopard, never let it turn you on your back, it'd rip out your intestines with its razor sharp hind claws. We retired glad to be sleeping in a house that night.

28 Feb – Up early to discover VW had puncture – fixed at local garage. Stopped for lunch at Lobo Lodge sitting below a kopje. Wrote thank you letters. Headed on to Maasai Mara reserve intending to stay at Keekorok Lodge – to discover our budget wouldn't stretch to their rates! Motored on to Park's exit where forced to spend remaining Tanzanian shillings, currency forbidden for export to Kenya! Bought rungu. Camped off-road. Lit large fire as lion cubs had been seen playing on dirt road leaving the park. Tom – excellent supper. We gathered useful pile of kooni for a long night's fire. Using thorn branches we constructed mini Maasai corrals around tents. Slept armed with newly purchased rungu. Woken by lion roaring close, just after midnight. Scrambling out of bivouac added more wood to fire as Tom emerged to rush to VW and switch on car's interior light . . . sure it made all the difference?

Five lion cubs on the track, too close to where we camped.

Historically, Maasai raiding parties used long spears and shields; however, feared most by other tribesmen were the Maasai's throwing clubs, orinkas, pronounced rungu, literal translation pumpkin. Made from African hardwood, orinkas are carved to have a slim handle up to 60cm long, with a rounded pumpkin shaped end. These clubs can be accurately thrown to strike a target from up to 70 paces. In Maasai hands these heavy clubs were a lethal weapon.

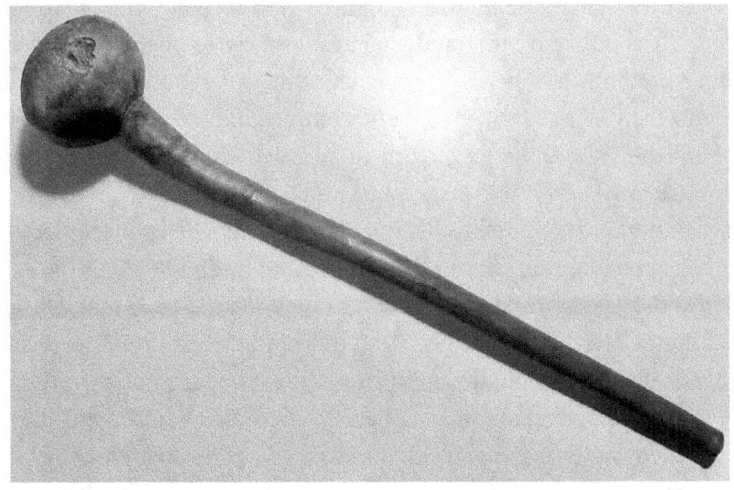

Last line of defence, my Maasai hardwood hunting club.

STILL ALIVE!

29 Feb – Still alive! Lion b. close last night. A few miles on, roadside notice forbidding camping – due to lion danger. Recognised camping a little rash last night. No option as night falling. Back on tarmac into Nairobi. Reported to Col Taylor at Embassy. Received bollocking for visiting Tanzania – otherwise cordial. Sad news, SAF bound Donald Rankin 16/5 killed on exercise in Kenya. Apparently live round fired amongst blanks. Unbelievable.

For those brought up in Africa, many held a primaeval fear of coming face to face with a big cat, pulled to pieces and eaten still not dead, by lion or leopard. That night in our small tents, drifting off to sleep surrounded by Africa's cacophony of night noises, we were acutely aware just a single layer of brown army bivouac canvas was all that stood between us and prowling cats. Just as nasty, we'd heard hyena calling too.

The first roar awakened recurring childhood nightmares of walking alone along a track, high desiccated grass either side, when in front appears the unmistakable outline of lion filling your path. Tawny coated, lions are easily camouflaged except for golden, mascara rimmed eyes surrounding black pupils that gaze mercilessly. Vile stench from open jaws reveal yellow stained incisors framing a strangely hypnotic pink tongue dripping saliva. That's the waking point. Not daring to move, you lie perfectly still, dripping sweat as realisation dawns: any movement is useless, your position's already betrayed.

In hindsight we, or rather I, had been bonkers to have even considered camping so soon after leaving Maasai Mara's boundary. We'd seen lions and photographed their cubs. We should have motored on, but I'd wanted to pitch camp before dark. As soon as the lions had begun roaring close by was the time to have climbed quickly into the VW and remained there, cramped but safe for the night. Despite building up the fire, we were every bit in as much danger as under rocket and mortar attack at Akoot. It was insane, but we'd survived.

Ten years earlier at Seronera, on a warm night a man had gone to sleep leaving his tent flaps open hoping for ventilation. Around midnight a pair of male lions walked into the camp. Hungry, they soon came upon the open tent. Dinner.

Reaching in, one sunk his teeth into the sleeping man's head, the second lion bit deep into the man's shoulder and together they dragged the unfortunate man out of his tent. His screams woke others in the party who on rushing out of their tents saw what was happening. Shouting and throwing what they could at the lions was sufficient to alarm the cats into promptly dropping their meal and running off into the darkness. The victim's wounds were gruesome: he'd lost an eye, his head was a mess and his shoulder had been crushed like matchwood. Incredibly he survived long enough to be flown to Nairobi early next day for surgery, but died on the operating table.

"*Still alive*" I wrote in my diary the next morning as we ate breakfast. We'd been lucky, really bloody lucky.

DONALD RANKIN 16TH/5TH LANCERS

It was shocking to hear the news of Donald Rankin's death. A Rhodesian and fellow cavalryman serving with the Royal Armoured Corps (RAC) Para Squadron. We'd met langlauf skiing when in opposing teams in Germany. He was exceptionally fit. Due to join the Sultan's army shortly, he would be sorely missed by both his parent regiment and SAF. He was a fine soldier killed by accident whilst training.

After returning our loaned army equipment, we'd two days R&R in Nairobi. We had haircuts, I indulged in a new camera, a Bowie hunting knife many wore as standard kit in Dhofar, and we both purchased gifts. Staying at the enduring Norfolk Hotel, utterly relaxed, we swam and dined well. Yet again making its insidious return, came thoughts of our return to bullets, bombs and mines. I diarised:

Neither sure we wish to go back at all . . . such is the soldier's lot.

3 Mar – Sad leaving Kenya. Been great time. 1230 East African Airways VC10 flight – Nairobi to Karachi. Scheduled to put down at Aden to drop off passengers, then on to Karachi. Karachi then Muscat. EAA emphatic no disembarkation at Aden.

Aden! Ordered off plane to transit lounge, smoke filled, standing room only. Passports taken. Thought we were in deep shit. But all OK. Stay limited to 35 mins before all ordered back on plane. Passports returned. 9 Chinese in blue Mao suits and 4 long haired jebalis disembarked. Interesting, could have been disastrous. Aden looking very run down. Photographed Mig fighters: 17s or 19s?

FLYING WITH THE ENEMY – ADEN STOP OVER

'This will be interesting' Tom remarked casually as without warning we were ordered to disembark at Aden. We'd noticed earlier for it was impossible not to, the Yemeni/Dhofari men distinctive in their Jebali dress seated beside their Chinese companions in blue uniforms, seated towards the front of the plane.

Uniformly wild haired, wearing traditional southern Arabian wizars, khaki shirts worn loose, embroidered leather belts and over one shoulder camel wool shawls, these were unmistakably southern Arabian Jebalis. The noble appearance of indomitable nomad, utterly independent, submissive to none.

The Chinese wore plainly cut unisex Maoist uniforms, blue two-piece suits, jackets buttoned to the neck with turned down collars and no ties. Each jacket had five buttons down the front, representing the branches of China's government (executive, legislative, judicial, examination, control). Four breast jacket pockets represented the four virtues of propriety, justice, honesty and shame. The symbols of totalitarianism were oddly menacing, repression in its absolute form, all the more so to non-party members.

Occasionally the group would glance back down the aircraft at their fellow passengers seated behind. We were an eclectic mix, the majority being Asians, there were a few Africans and then us two Brits. 'Whatever you do, just look blank,' whispered Tom. 'Easy for you,' I replied, hoping to ease the growing tension, to receive a grunt from my friend. 'As the more senior officer, and with better prospects, I've probably more to lose!' Touché.

Landing at Aden with the expected bumpy touchdown we'd taxied to a standstill in front of a range of dilapidated post-colonial buildings. None were new. The group of Arabs and Chinese were first to leave their seats and moved towards the exit. Disembarking, some turned again and casually looked back at their fellow travellers. Simple curiosity, or intentional? Avoiding eye contact, we successfully escaped a staring match. It was imperative to remain bloody calm. Beginning to sweat in the sudden blast of Aden's heat rushing through the open exit, we waited patiently for the doors to close.

Then came the order to disembark and my gut gave an involuntary clench. Out on the cracked, oil-stained apron, we walked nonchalantly to catch up with the first passengers queuing outside a utilitarian concrete building roofed in corrugated iron. Unforgotten radiated heat shimmered off the concrete apron. Waiting, sweating in the blistering sun, the queue moved slowly forward. Fading whitewashed walls with neglected windows stained opaque by layers of dust and grime greeted us. Once inside, two lazily revolving ceiling fans presented the face of Marxist ideology to the world arriving at Aden's International Airport transit lounge. All too apparent, any desire to wipe out vestiges of British tutelage was failing in the promotional stakes.

We shuffled from bright sunlight into gloom to be met by a brusque official collecting everyone's passports. There was no alternative but to consent. Things were not looking good. Doing our best to remain calm, both admitted later to pounding hearts. There followed a taut 35 minutes' wait in that stifling room before suddenly ordered out and back across the apron to the aircraft. Seated again, an East African Airways steward approached, handing out passports, efficient and polite. I don't think I've ever been quite so glad to see my battered blue passport.

'How long can someone hold their breath?' I wondered, before abruptly the fuselage door slammed shut and with relief we heard the VC10 engines kick into life. '*Shiiit*,' we each exclaimed, grinning like Cheshire cats, 'that was unnecessarily close . . . why make us disembark?' murmured Tom. 'I've no idea,' I replied, adding 'do you think they took us for oil men?' 'Unlikely, but better than brush salesmen' came the reply, Tom back at his laconic best . . .

For just over half an hour we'd stood stifling, crowded in an airless room, expecting at any moment to be summoned by people almost guaranteed to be hostile. Certainly they'd have been disinclined to believe any answers as to why our passports were stamped with Omani visas. Standing in the sweltering heat it had crossed my mind what might be the repercussions should we be arrested, when inevitably it would have come to light that a Field Marshal's ex ADC and the son of Britain's Director General of the British Red Cross were being held by Marxists in Aden?

Sitting in our aircraft seats now hopefully safe, neither could quite believe what had just occurred. Not only had we shared a flight on an aircraft, there had been exchanged questioning glances, each looking at the other with the knowledge, probable for them, absolute for us, that we were opponents in a guerrilla war and that without a doubt should we meet again each would be trying to be the first to kill the other.

Marxist Aden was Adoo HQ. Reportedly there were 600 Russian 'advisors' stationed in Yemen, not all but a number aiding Syrian, Iraqi and Arab mercenary pilots flying Mig fighters and Russian supplied transport aircraft, Antonov An-24s. Other nationalities including East Europeans were operational with ground troops. Chinese Maoists were there in similar numbers, concentrated mainly with ground forces.

Nightly, Radio Aden broadcasts were made and received throughout Dhofar, reporting on the war with Oman, casualties caused, suffered and victories won. The blunt, unsophisticated propaganda was met with a mixture of stoicism and humour by our soldiers, yet to adoo ears, no doubt it was ideological music.

Shortly after our return to Oman, Radio Aden stepped up its vitriol. Broadcasts now offered bounties for slaying SAF's mercenary commanders, identified by regiment and rank. Over a relatively short period, bounties for named individuals increased significantly.

Taxiing for take-off, I managed a couple of distant photographs of parked Russian Mig fighters.

3rd March continued:

Karachi – chaos: apparently I'd no up to date yellow fever. Tom had, so departed for hotel. I, with a Lebanese bloke, plus two Kenya girls, spent night at isolation hospital. Empty wards, bare beds, no blankets. Whisky though.

Frustratingly my passport hadn't a valid Yellow Fever inoculation stamp, a prerequisite to disembarking at Karachi. Taken to an isolation hospital with three others, a Lebanese businessman and two Kenyan Indian ladies, all whose passports had also failed the test. We talked into the night, we men sharing a half bottle of my new friend's Glenfiddich whisky. A good taste in whisky outweighed his right wing views on Lebanon's future. Beirut was known as "The Paris of the Middle East" owing to its beau monde lifestyle and financial power in the region.

By May 1972, the PDRY had twenty Mig fighter jets, as FCO correspondence reveals.

9. With the build-up of Russian built aircraft in PDRY, including the provision of MIG 21's, there is an increasing potential threat to Salalah

I often wondered what happened to him in the 1975 Civil War which lasted for the next 15 years, tearing the heart out of the country.

4 Mar – 1130 – Bumpy flight out of Karachi. Arrived Muscat 1300. Temp cool. Post holiday blues! Heard good news Sqn had been deployed to Midway – no more Akoot!

We'd made it back to Oman. And the squadron had redeployed, I was no longer based at Akoot. I felt for Tom; he was en route back to the jebel base at Akoot and the big push that would be Op Simba.

16

THREAT TO SALADINS

Return from leave and to reality. Squadron consolidates. Midway and the end for Saladins? Sandstorms and accommodation woes. Phase 2: Op Vulture and patrols to secure a route onto the jebel plateau. Mudhai camp. Geodes, flints and Johnson. Jordanian visitor. Mike not well. Lead up to Phase 3: Op Simba. The Bedu clock, sunburn, another girlfriend marries, a scorpion incident and soldiers' welfare.

BACK IN OMAN

On arrival at Bayt al Falaj in northern Oman and allocated rooms left vacant by Staff Officers on home leave, we met Major David Glazebrook, a personable friendly contact at SAF HQ. Reporting on the Mig fighters at Aden, David immediately asked for my 35mm film, which he'd have developed and returned to me once copied. The slides were with me within a fortnight.

At dinner David passed on the heartening news my troop had been redeployed to Midway, where I would rejoin them. Ten years earlier Midway had been an oil depot, situated some 80km north of coastal Salalah, positioned on an ancient frankincense trade route over the jebel from Salalah. Whilst delighted to be away from Akoot, I'd miss DR's good company following a four-month attachment. Midway, however, was to be no picnic.

FCO report for 1972

So long as the war goes on without successful conclusion, so will weariness grow in SAF and indifference to its outcome among the people of the North.

RETURN TO DUTY

Tom was returning to Akoot and Simba preparations, the ghost that had haunted his leave. Officially secret, we'd worked out the push would come in April. That evening, using a borrowed projector we put on a slideshow from film we'd had developed in Nairobi. It was a small but appreciative audience, expressing envy at our exploits – far removed from UK or BAOR leaves married officers with family responsibilities were restricted to. The Mess bar had closed and it was late when we'd finished. Remarkably for a slideshow, none had dozed. Pretty good for old soldiers.

Memories fade as all are aware and even after the best of times we discover but few attain permanence in an overfilled consciousness. Tom, who would follow a successful military career rising to become a brigadier, wrote recently on reacquaintance disclosing our East African trip as probably the most fulfilling period of his army career. A man known for his sincerity, I was touched by this insight given what must have been an outwardly rewarding life for him as a soldier. For my part, I could not have chosen a more decent travelling companion.

THE SQUADRON CONSOLIDATES

During my leave two of my Saladins had suffered serious mechanical failure. In desperation Tim made the decision to withdraw the cars from Akoot. So it was that my troop was pulled back from the front line, two Saladins suffering the ignominy of having to be towed by Bedford trucks approximately 160km back to Midway.

Added to this move, the two remaining Saladins used for training and based at SAF HQ were brought down from northern Oman to join the Squadron consolidating at Midway. The Saladin strength in Dhofar now increased to seven cars, the eighth still VOR having struck a TM46 Russian anti-tank mine and awaiting spares. Two Ferrets were also based at Midway, the other six remaining as Plains Troop located at Umm Al Ghawarif, Dhofar HQ, Salalah. The ACS were now fully deployed in Dhofar.

5 Mar – Leave ends. Shopped Muscat for essentials, shaving soap, toothpaste and two new wizars. We used to call them kangas in E.Africa.

6 Mar – News from Midway – required asap. Hitching flight on Skyvan tomorrow.

7 Mar – 0705 – Skyvan to Masirah – 1200 to Salalah – 1440 to Midway.
PM Firing .30s from Land Rovers – works quite well.
Great to meet up with the boys. I have new crew – Dvr Ali Hamdan, Gnr (now LCpl) Abdullah Ali.
End of month servicing. Saladins.
Accmd – another Bedford awning over frame as at Akoot. High winds, sand and cold at night. Day temp pleasant. All SOAF transport and jets here till 9th – new runway being built at Salalah. Order kit through Q.

I'd managed hitching a skyvan flight via Masirah, then Salalah, and finally to Midway. A small carrier perfect for short haul, the slow Skyvan is definitely not recommended for longer flights. Arriving at 1530, I grabbed a sandwich from the Mess, dumped my kit, changed from holiday jeans and shirt to join my troop for .30 Browning practice. I was back with the squadron. In my absence, Tim had modified our Land Rovers, mounting .30 Brownings on tripods welded in front of the commander's seat. Soft-skinned, these vehicles never offered protection; the thinking behind Tim's mounted Brownings idea was that it was better than Sterling Machine Guns.

Another two Land Rovers had been fitted with .50 calibre heavy machine guns (HMG), with tripods welded to the rear decking. These weapons made a terrific noise. When fired the vibrations almost shook the Land Rovers apart, but the welds held. Tim was in his designer element, eyes shining with enthusiasm, he told me he'd been working on prototypes for three weeks. 'What'd you think?' he enquired after a session firing at stone filled burmails that rapidly fell apart at 800 metres.

'Pretty good, but I'd rather be in a Saladin than a Heath Robinson alternative.' The raw memory still vivid following four months being on the receiving end of rocket, mortar and machine gunfire, I'd never have chosen these modified Land Rovers. Witness to what tiny pieces of shrapnel, stone and rock splinters did to soft skinned vehicles, let alone the poor sodding occupants, I asked, 'Are you going to tell me what this is all about?'

A FCO paper proposed:

The existing armoured car squadron . . . be expanded to form a regiment. Detailed establishments are presently under consideration. The current equipment, the Saladin, (has suffered from) serious delays in the provision of spare parts and difficulties over recovery and repair. SAF have not yet got the knowledgeable and experienced personnel needed to get the best from such relatively complex equipment. The same remarks must apply to ordnance.

It is unfair to condemn an AFV of such quality when the fault lies in the areas described, but something has to be done before the Saladins are relegated to static gun platforms, a suggestion seriously under consideration some months ago.

The new scheme of things, under current discussion, envisages a regiment of three squadrons based upon some form of unarmoured, load carrying vehicle with a good cross-country performance, capable of modification to carry mounted MGs, a dismountable gun similar to the 75mm RCL or, alternatively, members of an infantry support section . . . armed with support weapons normally held by infantry battalions. It is anticipated that the new equipment will give the regiment the following advantages:

Easier maintenance. Greater mileage. Simpler recovery. A load carrying capacity. A troop carrying (alternative) capability. Less demanding crew skills. A financial saving.

END OF THE SULTAN'S SALADINS?

Tim's reply came as an unwelcome shock. 'No secret, Saladins are costly weapons in this infantry led war' adding, growing angry, 'there've been murmurings about disbanding the cars in favour of LRDG* style operations, Land Rovers and Bedford trucks with. . . .' his voice trailed off. I thought, 'God, all that effort, that hard work to build the Squadron . . .' Disappointment showed in Tim's posture, his shoulders sagged; gone the cheerful outgoing disposition, the unstoppable enthusiasm we admired. Astonished, I waited for more. He looked back at me, before taking a deep breath and shrugging his shoulders; back came his smile, 'Sod them all! Come and meet the SOAF boys,' and turning we walked over to the Mess, a whitewashed concrete block with corrugated iron roof.

Midway Officers' Mess housed a bar, dining area and scattering of utilitarian furniture, basically garden furniture with matching tables. Overflowing sand-filled ashtrays with extinguished cigarette ends, told a story. That day the Mess was filled with friendly, noisy SOAF jet pilots. The sun-baked sand runway, oil sprayed against dust, currently held the Sultan's full complement of Strikemasters and STOL aircraft flown up from Salalah where a tarmacadam runway was being built.

---

*LRDG – The Long Range Desert Group: British reconnaissance and raiding unit in WW2.

SOAF gave us a barbecue and a taste of RAF haute cuisine – roast meats and curries, fresh fruits and ice cream (!), a menu Midway Mess cooks could only dream about. The crews remained with us until flying back two days later on 9th March, their absence all the more noticeable with the return to sobriety, reduced decibels and menu.

Impatient for more detail, I wanted to press Tim further, but he kept his counsel and the matter was set aside. As often happens, new orders arrived eclipsing further debate – we were about to become very busy again.

AN IMPROVEMENT IN ACCOMMODATION

My accommodation returning from leave was spartan. Back to living under a Bedford canopy with walls of burmails and no door, failing miserably on all counts except for providing shade. When the dust and northern sandstorm 'Ash Shimaal' blew, it lasted three to five days with wind speeds reaching up to 70km/h. And sand got everywhere.

Moving into shared accommodation of dilapidated portacabins significantly improved morale, if only in the escape from the ceaseless dust. I was sharing with

A view towards Tim's HQ with a Ferret parked outside during a regular sandstorm. My bedroom, my bayt, is on the right.

THREAT TO SALADINS

Front right, my bayt again with Sgts Oliver, Fyffe, Costello and Beadle's behind left. Weighted down truck canopies were held in place by filled sandbags on sand filled burmails. We moved into portacabins shortly afterwards.

the fastidious 2ic, Mike, whose example I endeavoured to match, as both agreed the new accommodation was a welcome change. Forced to share with the same gender can become onerous, yet despite the differences in age and character, there was never a cross word. Undoubtedly Mike it was who made the greater sacrifices.

As expected, blown sand fills and covers everything. During severe storms, breathing is possible only through face wrapped shemaghs. Exposed skin is stung, eyes especially hurt. Soldiers told of sandstorms scouring skin off faces, and painted surfaces stripped in minutes. Fortunately never experiencing such extreme conditions, on the edge of the Empty Quarter sandstorms were the bane of our existence.

'Q', the master provider of all essentials, had discovered a Hong Kong mail order catalogue, which enabled us to replace shortages and essentials: khaki jeans, shirts, socks and underwear, 35mm film and dark glasses could be ordered for delivery with the weekly mail to your sangar, tent, or Midway base, all posted direct from HK. A great innovation at the time.

PHASE 2 – OP VULTURE

Phase 1 of the SAF offensive commenced post-monsoon October 1971 as Op Jaguar continued with limited successes against an enemy which still controlled large areas of the jebel west and north of Salalah. Under Phase 2, Op Vulture, the Armoured Car Squadron had responsibility for controlling an area known as Al Negd (The Highlands), the area north of the westerly Qamar jebel which extended eastwards to become the Qara jebel north of Salalah. Our role was to prevent the adoo circling around SAF-held positions in the mountains. The northern Oman/Yemen border offered a clear run from the Empty Quarter into Dhofar. It was imperative that Oman's secret oil exploration close to the border be protected, and politically, the continued construction of community centres recently commenced. This huge area extended north to Saudi Arabia and west to Yemen, where constrained by Diplomatic and HQ SAF orders, Saladins were forbidden to venture to within 1000m of these borders. This was despite our remaining the armoured support for SAF's Akoot and Habarut outposts, with

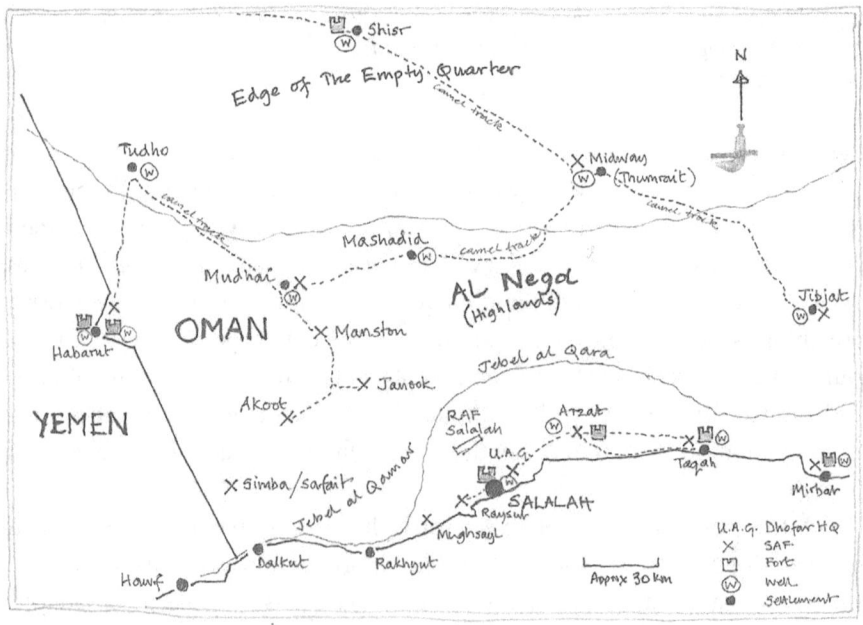

Map shows the area operated by the Armoured Car Squadron, the Al Negd highlands out to the southern reaches of Al Rub Al Khali (The Empty Quarter) and its vague border with Saudi Arabia. Westwards we patrolled out to Oman's equally indistinct border with Yemen. The routes we followed crossed empty deserts and gravel plains, sometimes scrubland and at other times along dried wadi beds, all originally ancient camel tracks between wells.

Akoot in the western mountains and Habarut, a SAF position sited bang on the Oman/Yemen border.

Attached to the Squadron, our numbers were increased by two (occasionally three) infantry recce platoons and two firqat, the Mahri firqat, Firqat al Badiyah (FAB) who would be based largely out of Habarut and the Bayt Kathir Camel Firqat, Firqat al-Hudud al-Gharbiyah (FHG), based at Mudhai.

Tasked under Op Vulture with the control and coordination of all movement within our designated area, we sought intelligence on adoo presence and influence. We patrolled, mounted ambushes, cleared mines from tracks and around wells, and searched the numerous wadi caves for arms caches.

LEAD UP TO PHASE 3 – OP: SIMBA

9 Mar – Mike with half Grey 60 and new .30 fitted Land Rovers left for Mudhai. New camp.
Cars: T12 - 80 - 2809 miles – VOR – new engine fitted – now OK
T12A - 72 - 2915 miles – gearbox oil leak – rectified
T12B - 70 - 2855 miles – VOR – new flywheel – ready 11th?

Mike reported in – Mudhai windy and dusty. Windy here too.

Mike's troop with a Land Rover convoy departed to establish our new base under canvas at Mudhai where my Saladin troop, Tango 12, would join him in a week's time.

The constant demands expected of the cars, one moment axle deep in soft sand, the next navigating boulders the size of kettle drums, dense penetrating dust, all compounded by lack of spares, was taking its toll on our ability to remain at two troop strength. Despite genuine willingness, our fitters came to us more accustomed to dealing with trucks, cars and motorbikes, with the result the lack of armoured car experience was expensive mechanical failure. Lou's car awaited a new flywheel before we could move out.

10 Mar – T12B nearly ready – OK for tomorrow.
Windy, sand everywhere. Letters home, Westfields.

Friday, our day off, was spent working on Lou's car replacing the flywheel by nightfall. I found time to write home, in particular to my grandmother, before a test drive next day and T12B was ready for our first Op Vulture patrol.

11 Mar – Out for the day –
test driving cars.
Maps – fablon
NEW BAYT!

Sitrep: Taqah/Darbat rd open
after 3 yrs. Ammo cache
found RCL + mortar

1630 – Orders Gp: Op Vulture: T12 and Grey 60 – explore alternative route Midway – Mudhai via Ma Shadid. Radio Freqs. Day – 6200 / Night 3500 / Spare 2400

1700 draw rations
News from Mudhai – 6 adoo tracks seen 15 miles SW Mudhai – look out for mines Mudhai/Akoot road.
'Q' kit arrives fm HK

The Jebel Regiment sitrep, effectively breaking news, that the Taqah to Darbat route had been reopened was welcome; heavily mined, it'd been closed for three years. Mike reported mines near Mudhai, we'd been warned.

12 - 14 Mar
Op Vulture patrol
Move out 1000
3 cars, 1x 3 ton - 1 dvr, 2 x Ld/rovers – 11 men Grey 60
Midway to Khadim – 34 miles – good going. No problems in sandy wadis. Wadi Ghadun first real wadi with walls between 100 to 200ft. One man and four camels stopped eight miles from Midway – Hamid bin Rashid – he and family live near waterhole at Khadim. Four Bedu tents, one man says brother in FAB. Checked out. Wadi Ghadun sandy, poss. crossing at Ma Shadid. Old airstrip not suitable fixed wing.
T12A (72) returning to Midway tmw – slight oil leak gearbox – take one Ld/rover. Tim to RV.

Undertaking 'hearts and minds' we administered medical supplies and support to the Bedouin roaming the arid area between mountain, wadi and great sand dunes of the Empty Quarter. With upwards of 250 men we covered an area of a little over 40,000 sq km. As mentioned, given our role of emergency support for Akoot and Habarut outposts, irrationally, armoured vehicles were expressly forbidden to approach within 10km of the Yemeni border. Neither were we allowed to return fire if attacked from across this border. Whilst diplomats in distant offices presumably knew the reasons why, it confounded men on the ground.

That May following attacks on SAF's position at Habarut on Oman's Yemeni border and receiving no countermanding order, on each three-week relief convoy,

THREAT TO SALADINS

I made damn certain each of my Saladins and Ferrets ran with a full load of ammunition and weapons primed. Attack and we'd fight back with all we had, asinine diplomacy lost on soldiers.

We were going well when Sgt Oliver's car developed a gearbox oil leak. Tim agreed for the car to return escorted by a JR recce section. Tim would take two cars to RV with Olly. I would continue, to find a route through to Mudhai with Sgt Costello and the balance of Grey 60, JR recce led by 2/Lt Nasib.

> *13 Mar – Ma Shadid waterhole smells: snakes, scorpions and bats. Accessible with care. Bedouin descend easily to fetch water 60ft down. Wadi not bad going. Recced south to Habkah YV8/3 wadi Ghadun. Going not good at Habkah. Defence laager YV785353. T12B blown fuses and drained batteries. Discovered loose fitting on power supply. Jump start once tightened – ran engine to charge. OK. We desperately need experienced fitters.*
> *T12A back safe. V. cold winds during night. Tim BAF.*

The mine clearing party returns having cleared the route out as we leave the well at Ma Shadid.

Ma Shadid, where 'Ma' translates as 'water', 'Shadid' as 'intense, strong' – so basically 'good water'. Steeply sided, the well is 18m deep, a natural hole in limestone rock holding drinkable water, knee deep and flowing.

Twenty-five years earlier Thesiger had visited here, before journeying into the Empty Quarter. His guides had assured the great man water flowed underground from Ayun, a small lake on the Qara jebel, and then on beneath Wadi Ayun into Wadi Ghadun and on to Ma Shadid. Our maps confirmed this was probably correct. Ranulph Fiennes leading MR recce platoon two years prior to our visit had also explored this isolated well, an experience he describes in some graphic detail and which I'm not sure he particularly enjoyed, telling his soldiers on exiting he'd rather die of thirst than descend another Arab well. Nasib joined me scrambling down into the shaft of the well using hemp ropes. Dark and eerie but rewardingly degrees cooler than surface temperatures. The well smelled of creatures inhabiting the place, possibly Sind Bats common to Oman and Yemen, yet equally the Arabian Pipistrelle found only in Oman. The snakes I refer to in my diary would have been vipers, but we saw none. Although utterly remote, there were legions of black flies near the well's surface and any number of bugs including mosquitoes, the latter easily supporting a single bat's 500 bugs-a-night appetite. Nasib and I saw no snakes or scorpions during our exploration, and both of us were pleased to escape the stench of stale air on exiting the well. The water was perfectly drinkable.

The electrical fault was soon fixed by Costello and we turned our attention to the batteries, in the knowledge we should never let Saladin batteries run low. Using long-boiled water once cooled, we topped up the batteries and after a jump start Costello's T12B was back on the road. It never ceased to amaze how easily these large imposing cars could so easily be brought down; it only took the smallest electrical fault, or broken hydraulic. A fact of life for all who've served in the Royal Armoured Corps.

A Bedford truck carried petrol and water in green battered steel jerrycans, spare ammo, vehicle spares and rations. The shortage of qualified fitters meant we'd no supporting vehicle mechanics. But with Lou and Olly, I was blessed with both mechanical and electrical magicians. T12A met up with Tim safely and returned to Midway. Many an occasion we'd revert to improvising and we never failed to get a car back to base, admittedly often by the skin of our teeth.

Scouting south to a confluence in the wadi system at Habkah the going became difficult and we pulled back before striking west from Ma Shadid, laagering for another cold night. Apart from the fact the two wadis converged, there were no other distinguishing features, nor routes out of the high walled wadi system.

THREAT TO SALADINS

14 Mar – Wadi Thuayt deep sand – Saladins just make it across. Mubarik Salim driving 3 tonner very well. Saw antelope.
Going good except for couple of ramps. Found old, damaged 303 at 683343 Wadi Banut. Broken, rusty – left it. Otherwise nothing of interest in caves. Arrived Mudhai 1440 dusty and tired. Mike's right, Mudhai is windy. First meeting with Johnson.

MUDHAI

Making decent time to Mudhai it was good to see Mike again. The men's tents were ranged alongside our Mess tent, a large, faded turquoise-green marquee. Having radioed ahead our ETA, we arrived in time to share a meal with Mike's men: curried sardines in tomato sauce and hot rice with raisins served with lifesaving sweet tea. Delicious that day, but after a while this simple menu would become a source of discontent.

Looking from a picquet towards our base. In the foreground, date palms, the Civil Aid Centre under construction and beyond, the Sultanate flag flies above our tents, two Saladins in sangars and my Land Rover.

Fed, our gear unloaded, we made ourselves comfortable. Mike had been right: afternoon winds would blow down Wadi Ahboot to blitz Mudhai with stinging sand, before dying away to stillness at sunset. On the boundaries of the Empty Quarter, Mudhai's blown sand occasionally reduced vision to a few metres. And we'd sighted distant antelope in an area of constantly discovered contrasts, desert and wilderness juxtaposed, as yet untamed, beautiful, protected through its desolate wildness.

Ancient date palms provided palm fronds for barusti shelters and animal enclosures. Goats roamed freely, as did camels, the property of the Camel Firqat. Later, with materials convoyed from Midway, the Civil Aid Centre's first buildings took shape, bringing much needed facilities to win over desert tribes.

The walls of the wadi were predominately bleached whites and creams, often studded with rock and stone in the full range of ochres. Amongst the extraordinary spectrum of colours found in Dhofar's mountains and deserts many belong to a family of earth pigments, including golden yellows, reds, purples, sienna and umber. Iron oxide and traces of iron are the major ingredients of all ochres. A reaction to radiative heat affects both umber and sienna hues chemically and here in the arid desert, the sun's strength turns reds into burnt umber and sienna. Colours were best early morning or at sunset, when the sun's glare mellowed.

Bedu children of the Bayt Kathir tribe sit idly admiring the spring-fed dam at Mudhai, recently constructed using local limestone rock.

One of the many geodes I found, nodular stones lined with crystals.

Worked flints which littered wadi caves we searched, or in which we took shelter.

Mudhai's spring water flowed from the base of the wadi's limestone wall, clear, cold and pure, sweet to taste, a miracle in an otherwise cauldron of heat. A small dam was constructed across the wadi collecting flowing water. Legends aside, Mudhai had every claim to revered status, offering life-saving water in an otherwise desiccated landscape. It was also exceptionally clean tasting water.

The spring at Mudhai lies approximately 4km south from the Wadi Ahboot/Gharah confluence. Further north Gharah joins the great Ghadun, running towards the Empty Quarter to disappear buried beneath the huge sand dunes of Ramlat Umm Hayat. Ramlat translates as sand, Umm Hayat as Mother of Life where there's a waterhole, Amilhayt, which translates as saline. Here and at Ramlat Fasad 70km to the west, well water was drinkable but stank of rotten eggs, sulphur (hydrogen sulphide). Fasad translates as rotten, putrid – aptly illustrating the point.

Lying undisturbed amongst the wadi's sandy floored caves could be found amongst dried sheep and camel droppings, any number of half buried geodes. Varying in size from two inches (5cm) to seven inches (18cm) there were a few splendid specimens, scattered as discarded geological litter. Cave roofs too were set with these magical spherical stone globes, some with spikes, others with rounded, bulbous surfaces. Found within sedimentary and volcanic rock, geodes are hollow, most containing tiny clear crystals, some tinged with blues and purples. Collecting a number they adorned a small table in my tent, together with a collection of limestone flints found scattered around ancient cave habitations.

JOHNSON – FAITHFUL COMPANION

With picquets inspected and the camp stood-down, there's often a moment's stillness after sunset. Darkness blankets day, merging shadows into suspicious silhouettes, before moonrise lends definition to shapes remembered in daylight. Mudhai was deemed secure enough to allow small paraffin lamps in tents and as I set to with overdue paperwork, a dog appeared at my tent entrance.

Looking in, he entered and sat down. Motionless but for a penetrating stare, mascara-ringed doe-like eyes found locally only with Bedu women. Dogs were a rare sight. I'd not seen any north of the jebel, or for that matter, out of Salalah. An escapee from a Jebali encampment, or intriguingly had he wandered away from an enemy position? He didn't look in too bad shape – where'd he sprung from?

'Hello,' I greeted as friendly as possible, forgetting he may never have heard spoken English, before adding, 'well, what have we here?' Rising, I approached warily, expecting a growl before he'd bolt. He didn't look ferocious. No foaming mouth, a clue to possible rabies, and approaching I noticed the faintest quiver at the tip of his long tail. 'Good sign,' I thought and reaching out I slowly offered the back of my outstretched hand, touching him briefly on the side of his head. This prompted a drop to the sandy floor and rolling onto his back, he lay wagging his tail. 'Expect you could do with some water?' I enquired. 'We might even muster up something to eat.' The dog just stared back, tail thumping sand.

Mohamed, my orderly, appeared at that moment, and on seeing the animal made to shoo it out of the tent. 'No, Mohamed, he's my guest today, fetch some water please and ask cook for some tinned fish,' our staple diet.

In a good place, safe and secure, Johnson dozes beside my bed, stretched out on an army issue prayer mat. Photograph taken by Brian Jayes with whom I briefly shared a dilapidated portacabin in Midway. Brian also held an affinity with dogs.

A few weeks later this same fish diet manifested as an avoidable headache. Staging an impromptu sit-in at my tent, my soldiers argued for a return to goat meat. Stupidly I'd not noticed the monotony of a sardine diet they now complained so passionately against. Breakfast was fried chapati and sardines, main meal, stone baked chapati and curried sardines. It was patrol food, not base camp food, they argued. My fault, I quite liked sardines. Persuading HQ we required to be fed at least as well if not better than those in Salalah, I was able to arrange the supply of goats and a return to happy soldiers.

Taking my hunting knife, I cut a section from the tent's entrance flap, and lining a scoop in the sand made a temporary water dish for my guest. 'And how long will you stay with us?' I wondered aloud, catching Lou walking past my tent. 'Got yerrself another animal to mind, sir? What're you going to call this one?' recalling the rescued cat and chameleon at Arzat, and lastly 'Twizzel' the cat shared with Graham at Akoot. 'What name – Bedu dog?' I wondered.

Bedu dog became Johnson after LBJ, the US President, who was bombing the hell out of Viet Cong communists. Stoically apolitical, Johnson the dog always responded with a wag to his tail at the mention of his new name also headlining news of an unwinnable war which ultimately the United States would lose.

Rapidly establishing his residency, Johnson became Mess Tent Sentry. Provenance remained doubtful, all we knew was he'd arrived ribcage skinny otherwise in good condition. Greyhound tall, long legged, big feet and curled tail sufficient to confirm dubious breeding. A combination of grin and mascara lined brown eyes fooled everybody. Insanely, his party trick was night ambush. Inspecting sentry posts, you'd hear pounding feet then *wallop!* With adrenaline screaming fight or flight – a dog would land on your back.

Reeling round, you'd have this gambolling clown looking up, tail wagging furiously, pawing in delight at having given you the fright of your life. Worked every time! Yet doing so risked serious injury to dog and others for all carried loaded weapons, in particular Sterlings with their hair-trigger temperament. He was beyond training. 'One day, Johnson, I swear it . . .' And the perilous game went on.

A BACKWARD COUNTRY

15 Mar – 1230 Huey 205 arrived with Jordanian major looking very smart remarking 'I have never visited such a backward country!' Willy Harris as liaison officer. Uneasy, poor chap.
Rebuilt kitchen to accommodate us all. Arab food not too bad – will help lose some weight! Mudhai very sandy and wind blows it everywhere. Starting

> *sometimes at 0845 lasts till 1500, regular as clockwork. Sand gets into everything. Tent needs additional support. Mudhai's water good. Patrol in couple of days – Land Rovers. Nairobi fly-whisk a boon.*
> *Air cleaners / guns.*
> *Contractors Paulings building civil aid centre.*

Surprised by an unannounced Huey visit, we discovered the VIP major was touring Dhofar positions leading to deployment of Jordanian Special Forces. Charming, immaculately turned out and interested in all we were doing, we introduced him to the men, hurriedly assembled by Sgt. Ali, standing stiffly to attention in front of their cars; our Jordanian guest chatted to each in person, Arab, Baluch and Brit. Very professional. Accompanying him was Willie Harris. It was the first time we'd met since Mike Campbell's death the previous July. He knew I'd known Mike in Germany. Clearly uncomfortable in his new role, Harris avoided eye contact with me. It was hard not to feel sorry for the man. Poor sod. As I escorted our VIP, Mike chatted with Harris as a fellow ex-RTR.

Departing with the usual blast of dust, the Huey's massive double blades acting like a giant's hairdryer, I wondered who were we to judge the man. None of us had been present that July afternoon; it'd been only Willie Harris, Mike Campbell and four MR jundees (soldiers). We never met again.

Lou steals a nap after a day patrolling, Old Irish.

THREAT TO SALADINS

Flies, the persistent problem you never got used to but endured, were particularly infuriating when stationary in armoured car, Land Rover or back at base in a stifling tent. Flies having an unquenchable thirst for sweat, are perhaps at their worst as you eat, crawling over face and lips, working the edges of your mouth, eager for first taste of your curried sardines, goat, chapati or mug of sweet tea. And it was inevitable you'd swallow a fly a day. Despite my fly-whisk it was always an unwinnable contest.

16 Mar – SMG inspection – Sgt Ali Abdullah
2 ACS Land Rovers and 4 JR Recce Land Rovers – patrol east from Mudhai, really only route possible, same area patrolled earlier with Saladins patrolling from Midway via Ma Shadid. Wind has dropped.

17 Mar – Back at Ma Shadid. 74km. Pickets out. Pitched camp beside roughly cleared airstrip, wind has got up again. Broken sump on a JR Land Rover – fixed by caulking with rag. Radioed for new sump – arrive tomorrow? Will recce south with half patrol, leave Lou at Ma Shadid to await aircraft supply.

2/Lt Nasib bin Hamad al Ruwehi – Grey 60, at Ma Shadid's well, which we decided to descend by ropes.

My diary entries recording distances covered were a rough navigation gauge. Despite an odometer's inaccuracy across country, when forced to retrace routes around obstacles, steep sided wadis or potential ambush sites, it did assist map reading. Distances diarised in miles reflected journeys in Brit-built Saladins, whereas our Spanish-built Land Rovers had odometers set to kilometres.

18 Mar – 5am start – Recced south from Ma Shadid searching routes out of wadi Ghadun eastwards – no luck. Returned Ma Shadid – met Beaver 1530hrs – new sump delivered safely. Pilot friendly. "Wouldn't bloody swap with you mate!" and left.
Later patrolled north up Wadi Ghadun to YV8739 – then East down Wadi Hayla. Nasib in good form, shot an antelope which we had for supper. V. Good, spiced well. Delicious. Cold night.

Beaver landing at Ma Shadid delivering new Land Rover sump.

19 Mar – Recced north from YU9933 with 2 Land Rovers. Found camel and vehicle tracks? Followed for distance before stopping – we hadn't enough men to picket and move ahead, too obvious as ambush sites. Dismounted, picketed and watched for signs of life. All quiet. Returned to collect others and drove back over jebel to camp above Wadi Ayun. Reported no routes out of wadis.

AGAIN FAREWELL TO SALADINS?
EXPEDIENCY OR VALID ARGUMENT?

20 Mar – After another cold night left early to drive back to Midway, arriving for breakfast. Very tired and dirty. Good to see Tim again.

Startling news. Squadron will be reorganised and Saladins fazed out!! As replacements we're to be equipped with standard Bedfords, upgraded with mine-plating. Each truck armed with mounted 20mm cannon on the rear deck. Also armoured Land Rovers with .50 m/gs. Our role: "long range strike force" patrolling West through the Empty Quarter to Yemen border. No protection, could be interesting. Mike back.

Tim broke the news of a now probable change from armoured cars to Land Rovers fitted with machine guns, Bedford trucks with cannons. It was to be kept secret so as not to affect morale. He was unclear when these plans might be implemented, and until then, we'd carry on as we were, pursuing Op Vulture to the best our stretched resources would allow.

21 Mar – Drew out 303s for the boys. Took a group out beyond perimeter fencing to sand dunes. Set up targets of empty tins to give lessons in rifle shooting. Boys delighted to fire rifles in place of Sterlings – now they've rifles to match mine! Rest of day spent idly around camp. Water here tastes of sulphur against Mudhai's sweet spring water.

Zeroing sights, the men mastered these rifles as I'd expected, almost instantly. It was in their genes, ensuring a familiarity with weapons, firing and hitting a target was second nature to them. Cheered at their weapon handling skills, it was a proud young officer who reported to Tim later that evening how well the ad hoc session had gone. Looking forward to further outings, all realised the 303 was in reality no more than a target weapon, no match for the world-beating design of our enemy's Kalashnikovs.

22 Mar – Welded and fitted .30 Browning to last of Land Rovers. Mike left for Mudhai 0700hrs with petrol convoy, JR recce in escort.

PM shooting with Tim – sore shoulder. Never learn. PDRY threatening at Habarut on Oman/Yemen border. No shooting as yet. We leave tomorrow for Mudhai. T12A finally back on road.

It was a recurring problem: no sooner had one Saladin been fixed, another would blow a gasket, suffer an electrical fault, transmission failure or hydraulic problems. Inevitably the correct spare parts being unavailable at Midway meant ordering from Salalah, or Muscat. Occasionally parts had to be sent from the UK, resulting in frustrating delays.

Little wonder an infantry commanded SAF were concerned, unused to the idiosyncrasies of armoured vehicles designed for European theatres and now operating in desert conditions. Hence the appeal to hurry the Saladin's demise for the less sophisticated armoured trucks and Land Rovers.

ANOTHER PATROL – AND MIKE'S NOT WELL

In temperatures frequently reaching the high 40s Centigrade, we were constantly watchful when refuelling, for spilled petrol onto a hot exhaust and we'd have lost a car. Here we refuel at our Mudhai POL point (petrol, oil, lubricant), comprising 44 gallon (200 litre) burmails, from which we'd pour fuel into five gallon (22 litre) jerrycans then into our Saladins's thirsty fuel tanks – a laborious but necessary task.

23 Mar – Leave after early breakfast – 2 Land Rovers, a Saladin, 2 Bedfords for Mudhai. Northern route. Saladin overheated. Bedfords got stuck in sand. Arrived Mudhai 1700hrs. Fyffe's Saladin 12A no first gear. Dusty journey.

24 Mar – Back along Midway route to Wadi Ghadun: RV with convoy from Midway. Mike ill and stuck somewhere in Wadi Ghadun. Wrong grid ref.

Costello's Land Rover has broken half-shaft. Fyffe got his Saladin stuck again. Recovered using two Bedfords. Not happy. Saladin now has no second gear.

Found Mike – stuck to axles. Got him out only for him to get stuck three more times!? Suggested perhaps he leave driving to his Arab driver. Escorted Mike back to Midway. En route Mike had a puncture – tyres had been deflated to drive out of soft sand and not reflated for gravel plains. And *then Land Rover <u>caught fire</u>. Ali claims back tyre overheated? Oh yeah? – I suspect Ali Abdullah's cigarette!*

Ammo box ignited and ammunition began exploding . . . sand thrown onto fire – extinguished. No one hurt, extraordinary!

Mike had reckoned ammo old so was going to dump it at Midway. Not that old it wouldn't explode? Returned Midway OK, eventually! Midway water really is foul – but food good in Mess. Mike still unwell. Suspected jaundice? Loathe powder dust, gets everywhere, into weapons, ammunition, water, clothes, body, eyes, nose. Hate it! It was quite a day. Showered, fed, good kip.

The original plan was to RV with Mike and Sgt Fyffe with his repaired Saladin, being relocated to Mudhai. I'd take the convoy on to Mudhai and Mike would return to Midway. It turned out to be one of those days when everything that could, would go wrong. Mike repeatedly got his Land Rover stuck in soft sand at Wadi Ghadun. Lou stripped a Land Rover half-shaft trying to assist Mike. Gerry Fyffe's Saladin became firmly stuck too, and only by hitching two Bedfords in line did we extricate his car. Mike's vehicle then punctured after he'd failed to reflate the tyres on being hauled out of the sand. We would deflate tyres to assist crossing extra soft sand, but the secret was to then reflate before carrying on. Finally a canvas holdall containing belted .30 Browning ammo caught fire in the rear of Mike's Land Rover. With ammo exploding, we threw sand over the bag, using shovels still to hand after the many excavations earlier. Amazingly we extinguished the burning bag, smothering it with sand. No one had taken cover, all had rushed to extinguish the blaze. And no one was hurt. Shaken, we looked at the ammo, deciding to leave it covered with sand. Mike was probably correct, the ammo was old, it might have been a very different story otherwise. A tyre overheated they said. It was obvious a cigarette had ignited the fire. Sgt Abdullah Ali looked too innocent, a blank expressionless face with raised eyebrows. I let it pass, there was no way I'd prove anything. A good man, he was Tim's troop sergeant, but I'd mention my doubts to Tim later. It was difficult to ban smoking. We all smoked in Land Rovers and armoured cars, sitting with the constant smell of petrol fumes, surrounded by high explosive. We reckoned smoke kept the flies away.

With Mike looking ill, I decided to escort him back to Midway, sending Lou and Gerry Fyffe in his Saladin on to Mudhai with the convoy. Mike was medevaced to Salalah FST hospital the following day, with suspected jaundice.

Reaching Midway, all my vehicle's crew of five wanted was a shower, supper and an uninterrupted night's sleep in a bed. We'd deserved it, it'd been a long day.

> *25 Mar – Before first-light, left for Mudhai with six Bayt Kathir, Tim and Gordon. Journey slow and hot. Wadi Batina met Jebalis; no reports of adoo. Generously offered camel milk, milked into a mud lined, grass weaved basket. Salty, frothy, delicious.*

The camel milk was offered in a mud lined woven grass basket, watertight to an extent. The trick was to blow the froth and dubious bits aside before taking a sip. Urged to drink more, we did, knowing they'd go hungry but not wishing to insult our hosts. A camel will remain in milk for almost four years and give about one litre twice a day. With a working life of 20 years, they may calve as many as 12 times.

THE BEDU CLOCK

The Bedu measure the time of day without sophistication's need to rely on clock or watch. Patrolling we'd often come across a family or individual with whom we'd stop to exchange greetings and news. Occasionally we'd wish to determine the time of incident or reference, not just which day but time of day. In 1972 it was doubtful many Bedu had seen, let alone owned a watch. They measured time against the sun's position. For mornings, the answer would be before or after 'Ash shams taskhan' when the sun gets hot, around 0800. Sunrise, sunset and midday were easy markers. 'Akl' (food) indicated mid-afternoon, the main meal of the day.

> *26 Mar – Patrolled out to Tudho on Wadi Aydim. Accompanied by the FHG to be shown birthplace of their leader, Said Barakat of the Bayt Kathir. An ancient and obviously hallowed place. Dark shaded deep cave with strong odour of goat. Scattered around cave floor, any number of geodes which I knew would contain quartz crystals, amethyst, agate or jasper – no telling until the stone's broken in half. But these specimens had to stay untouched given the umbilical connection the place had to our firqat leader.*
>
> *1300, 1700 calls – reports and grids.*
> *Enjoyed delicious fuddal in a cave with firqat.*
> *Another broken LR half-shaft. Wadis are heavy going over large stone. One LR reduced to front wheel drive, slow going. Useless in sand – needed towing across wadis.*
>
> *Returned to Mudhai in dark – by moonlight. Long day.*

A brief stop on patrol and Grey 60 soldiers prepare breakfast. Noticeably a few soldiers were now wearing desert boots purchased from Salalah souq, in preference to the inadequate issued plimsolls.

The vain soldier sporting chrome framed sunglasses was only allowed to wear them at halts. The others understood the reason why.

Accompanied by the Camel Firqat (approx 35 irregulars) we'd patrolled out to Tudho. Accompanying me, Tim and Gordon Dawson, a SAF Intelligence Officer based at Midway. Gordon, a respected Arabist, had earlier lived and worked in Yemen's Hadramawt mountains before joining SAF. In his early fifties, short and slightly overweight, he'd a full moustache and ready smile. With faultless Arabic and an inspiring memory for names, he always looked hot, yet never complained.

When on patrol we'd call to check in with Squadron HQ (SHQ) daily at 1300 and 1700. A call to confirm progress and grid reference. This patrol was more PR than active patrol but equally important, cementing relations. It was dark as we returned to Mudhai, but three days short of a full moon ensured ample light for the careful driver without vehicle lights, all illumination disconnected.

27 Mar – Day spent repairing vehicles. Sun hot. Sunburned. Visited pickets checking sangar maintenance – went over fields of fire with firqat sections. Letters to AIWH, MF, Valerie, Sandy and bank. Fuddal with Sgt Said Mubarak OG and his men on loan to us at Mudhai. After too much coffee, slept badly.

Soldiers of Oman Gendarmerie arrived to take over Mudhai base, as the squadron departed on operations. My troop would be returning to Akoot. The remainder to follow under Tim's command to secure an airhead north-east of Akoot as DR launched Simba at a date still unknown to us, but in reality, three weeks' time.

Amongst letters written that day, I'd replied to Valerie, my beautiful cousin for whom I'd held an unrequited love since aged seven and she twice my age. Discovering an anathema to administering hypodermics during nurse training at St Thomas's, Valerie had joined the Foreign Office where, a world away from needles, she'd enjoyed far greater success.

SANDY, THE A&SH AND AN 'AU REVOIR'

MR were busy training pre-return to Dhofar. Meaning to write earlier, I sent Sandy congratulations on the rebirth of his famous regiment, the Argyll and Sutherland Highlanders. The spirited 'Save the Argylls' campaign had secured the regiment's return to full battalion strength eight weeks earlier. I wrote also to my grandmother, for she had followed the campaign with interest. A long-time supporter of the regiment her brother had served with until his death at Ypres. Staying with my grandmother one leave from Germany when my family was abroad, she showed me letters received following my great-uncle's death. One contained the haunting words of a Highlander, who recovering from wounds had written:

> before going into action, everything down to the most minute detail was fully explained, maps studied and questions answered. A final address always finished with an appeal to every man's honour to do what he thought was right. On the eve of the 31st July Captain Kidston, our Coy Commander, had ended, saying 'Men, we go forward together to do what we can.'
>
> LCpl Cleghorn A&SH

They'd walked against machine guns. A special breed of men.

I hoped to see Sandy on his return to Dhofar, but our paths never crossed again until our return to the UK. Nearing the end of his secondment, Sandy trekked with two soldiers using donkeys to carry provisions high on Jebel Akhdar, the Green Mountain in northern Oman. It was quite an expedition. Regrettably I only ever saw the evocative mountain from a distance, hazy blue hue floating through a heat shimmer.

MF (Marie-France) was a pretty Parisian girl I'd met skiing. A hippy friend, part of a Parisian set, all comfortably well off and vociferous anti-Vietnam pacifists.

Catching a train to Paris, there were fun weekends. MF neither understood nor forgave my volunteering for Arabia. Learning I'd chosen Arabic over French "... mais non, non, non! Pourquoi?? Pourquoi soldat dans le désert d'Arabie?" she'd written despondently. Now out of the blue, a letter confirming her engagement to a Frenchman! 'C'est la vie mon ami,' Tim consoled, adding, 'anyway, you'd have made a deplorable Frenchman.' He was probably right, yet still it reinforced the soldier's curse of overseas postings: 'The reason letters fade? Some other b... moves in!'

The letter from my bank was just that, a bank letter.

28 Mar – Patrol by Land Rovers down wadi Gharah South East of Mudhai. Found route out of wadi after clearing a ramp. Possibly too steep for 3-tonners. However, after about 20km, it became too rocky and we had to turn back. Scorching sun. Burnt.

SUNBURN

Sunburn features often in my diaries. Living off vehicles without windscreens or doors we all suffered varying degrees of sunburn. The fairer skinned the worst. Blisters along nose bridges burst, forming protective scabs which flies constantly worried at, causing bleeding. Without suncream, shemaghs were best protection. Wetting a corner and placing it across the sunburned area each night helped relieve the pain, until the following day's motoring increased the discomfort.

Sgts Oliver, Fyffe, Mike and I were each similarly afflicted – all being fair skinned. The worst to suffer was Brian Jayes who joined us mid-1972 from DR. Enviably, Tim, blessed with Mediterranean skin, rarely suffered sunburn. The old Celt, Lou, should have suffered badly but rarely did and if he had, never complained.

29 Mar – Day spent on sangars, vehs, and air recce in Beaver along yesterday's route. Could see no way through. Will have to travel down W. Gharah tmw. and maybe find another ramp. Half-shaft on my car now gone.
Nasib upset about rats.
Mike to be medevaced to England for special treatment.

Rats had become a problem. How, we wondered, had they arrived at the edge of Arabia's Empty Quarter? Recce platoon's 2/Lt Nasib was not enamoured of rats. As we'd found at Taqah's fort eight months earlier, rats were everywhere. We needed a couple of Jack Russells.

Mike was clearly not well. Visiting him in the FST hospital whilst on R&R, I found him in pain. His condition was not improving. For a while he'd suffered in silence until mentioning his concern it might be kidneys. Relying on wells frequented by Bedu, their goats and camels, the water sometimes tasted of camel. Others were infested with bats and it was possible Mike may have picked up an infection. Following a recurrence of his problems in May and again hospitalised, the SAS doctors deemed his condition warranted repatriation to the UK for treatment. Bidding him farewell, we hoped whatever was causing him these fevers and discomfort might finally be resolved. Mike (now referred to as Uncle), returned to us later that July, his health much improved, bringing us back to full strength.

SCORPION INCIDENT AND ANNUAL CONFIDENTIAL REPORT

On an otherwise ordinary afternoon in Mudhai, relaxing under the shade of our canvas marquee, I was marking up maps and notes as Lou cleaned his AK47 before our patrol the next day. Suddenly a small scorpion scuttled across the table between various pieces of stripped-down machine gun, pens and map. Yellowish-green, two inches (5cm) long, possibly a small 'deathstalker' with painful sting? It stopped to stare at us in surprise at the unexpected meeting between species. Without a thought I brought my pencil down quickly, trapping the creature against the table top.

'Kill it, Sahb!' shrieked a worried Said, our Mess orderly just entering the tent. 'Matchbox, Lou!' I called as he unhesitatingly emptied a Swan Vestas box across the table. (It should perhaps be noted that Tim smoked a pipe and was the owner of said matches.) We were used to finding small scorpions around the base of our tents, and occasionally we'd catch one to set free well away from our accommodation. Placing the upturned inner box over the still held arachnid, I slid the outer case over it. One captured scorpion. 'We'll show it to Tim on his return,' I said, triumphant. Unfortunately, circumstances turned out a little differently to that planned.

Arriving back from his rounds checking piquets, Tim sat down, filled his pipe, and reached for the matchbox. Called away to deal with a troop matter, I heard a yell of outrage from 200 metres away. Tim had discovered the scorpion. 'Oh shit!' I thought, or words closely associated.

Suddenly freed from its box, the scorpion scuttled up Tim's shirtless forearm; with a yell that echoed around the valley, he swept the creature off his now upper arm, stamping hard, squashing the hapless creature against the canvas covered floor. Pretty impressive, given he was wearing his favoured open leather sandals at the time.

Tim was not amused. Accepting full responsibility, although typically Lou insisted he share the blame, there followed a decidedly awkward evening before Tim departed early next morning. Having threatened to include the incident in my Confidential Report, he didn't. Possibly later events contributed to that decision.

Even in the remotest places on earth, the British Army's Annual Confidential Reports are written by seniors on their subordinates, recording attributes, successes and failings, the report to be read and signed by each reportee. I can't recall if there ever was any chance of appeal. It was part of the system.

That night, I made a note to myself, next time write SCORPION on lid.

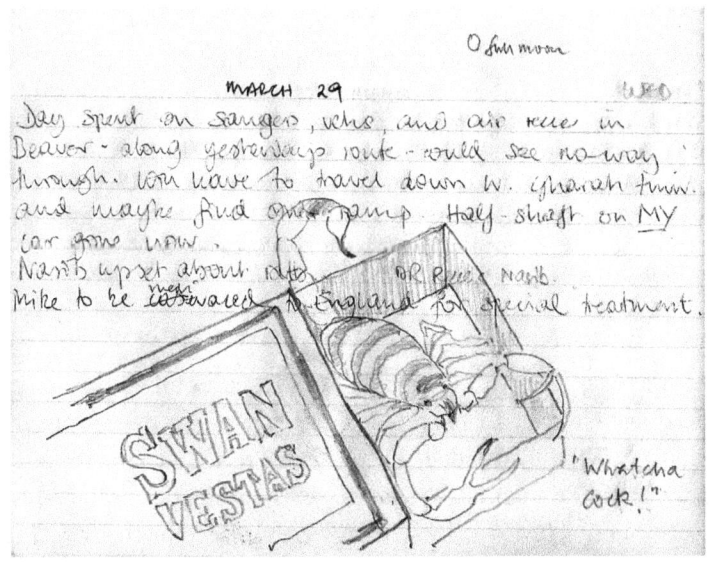

Deathstalker scorpion (Leiurus quinquestriatus) common throughout Oman.

SEARCHES CONTINUE FOR ROUTE ONTO JEBEL

30 Mar – Tim's convoy left for Midway at sparrows, taking Sgt Fyffe, two LRovers and Bedford.
We left to meet up with the Bayt Kathir at first light after Lou had changed LRover's half-shaft. After 3 punctures, torn tyres on three cars, we were down to x2 spares left between 4 Land Rovers.

Met Ahmed bin Salim, Bayt Kathir, drove with him to his cave. Discovered another firqat there, apparently on compassionate leave? Father dead. Shared camel milk. Warm, gritty, dirty.

Bayt Kathir very doubtful we'd find route out of wadi to jebel. 1630, 4th cut tyre puncture. Aborted patrol. Returned safely without further punctures to Mudhai for night. Return tomorrow to recce possible alternative route. Take extra spare tyres!

Tim departed early for Midway, as we drove out on a four-vehicle patrol. Our task remained finding an alternative route onto the jebel plateau and then to Akoot, hoping to avoid reliance on the now heavily mined existing route. The going was tough. After four punctures, we were forced to return for repairs. Most wadi stones were round and smooth, but unseen sharp edges ripped our soft walled tyres.

31 Mar – Op Leopard – 5 adoo KIA and 9 JR wounded by booby trap. 3 x SEP, 2 with SKS.
RCL attack on Taqah.

Flights: fill in leave application for 747 flight – Weds fm Muscat, Thurs fm Bahrain.

Op Leopard had a successful contact. As Vulture, part of the Phase 2 operations commenced last October following Jaguar, this latest op had involved JR with SAS. Against nine JR wounded, five adoo were killed and three captured together with two Russian SKS-45 rifles, semi-automatics designed by Sergei Gavrilovich Simonov in 1945. These rifles were replaced by the AK-47 designed by Mikhail Kalashnikov in 1947. Almost three million SKS and an estimated 100 million AK rifles have been produced, exported widely to communist countries and factions opposing Western governments. Both rifles fire 7.62mm rounds.

Looking ahead to UK leave in July saw me completing necessary paperwork for submission to SAF HQ, who organised air tickets, travel visas and flights. Born outside the UK in Tanganyika, it was deemed necessary for my kind having to apply for transit visas through the Gulf States. The bureaucracy seemed all the more frustrating for someone serving in the UK forces. When the time came, my passport held both Bahraini and Omani visas, clearing my journey home and return four weeks later.

THREAT TO SALADINS

31 Mar – Set off with 4 vehicles – leaving Lou at camp repairing sangars, mending punctures – last two rubber patches left. Requested more. NFR recce join us – Ruqaishi seems solid, think we'll get along well. Met one Bedu but no info.

Still no suitable ramps out of wadis. Green 60 LRover punctured. Ali Hamdan's request – fuloos for father's bayt. Any news?? Met Said bin Salim bin Athar Bayt Sharik with wife and sick camel. No adoo seen, seems genuine. Can't treat camels. Further on, set ambush.

Leaving Lou mending punctures, my patrol set out with four Land Rovers, each with six men, a mix of ACS and newly arrived NFR Recce, led by the redoubtable Green 60, 2/Lt Mohammad bin Said bin Zahran al Ruqaishi WB, holder of the Sultan's Bravery Medal. We were to become firm friends.

After dark, sixteen of us walked a kilometre up the wadi to set our ambush. Old hands, these men knew what to do. Ruqaishi allocated stags. In reserve, guarding Land Rovers, Sgt Abdullah Hamed of NFR recce platoon. Gut wounded by Kalashnikov fire on a previous tour, Abdullah was lucky to be alive. As Ruqaishi, a formidable soldier. He'd guard our backs.

Limbs ache lying prone between rocks, motionless, eyes and ears straining for movement, a stone scrape or rock disturbed by man moving. Taking turns to catnap, we passed a long night. In the absolute quiet of desert, eclipsed by starglow darkness, concealed sound raises body hair. Despite heightened alertness, it still catches you out. No matter how alert, the reaction is genetically hardwired into each of us, an impulse to a cue, until explained.

Humans, birds and on occasions, apes walk bipedally. At night they move with stealth fearing ambush, alternatively stalking prey. Added to this group, many lizards (and cockroaches at speed) run bipedally. We weren't waiting for lizards or cockroaches that night. Once again we drew a blank, and we moved off early the next morning.

SOLDIERS' WELFARE

No matter whether on patrol or at camp, it wasn't rare for a soldier to approach his officer with domestic worries. Unexpected and often at an inappropriate time, most concerns were about money, but sometimes it was on compassionate grounds and it was important to try and resolve matters as best one could there and then. My Saladin driver, the coconut-juice-drinking champion, Ali Hamdan,

My two crew members, LCpl Abdullah Ali brews tea as Ali Hamdan looks on.

enquired after his request for an advance to help repair his father's home. We'd already set up an arrangement for a loan to be repaid through payday deductions. I promised to hurry things along, but frequently these matters took a while to materialise.

Desert goggles, seen here so new they were still adorned with labels, became a status symbol, disallowed when stealth was required, for fear of reflecting sunlight. The leather nose guards between the darkened lenses failed to adequately protect all the nose, the tips of which became badly burnt.

Following each patrol I'd submit a report to Tim and, in his absence, HQ Dhofar, mentioning names and Bedu tribes we'd met, area patrolled and any relevant information, details to be disseminated to the Sultanate Intelligence Officers (SIO). Ours, we had two north of the jebel, based at Midway, Gordon Dawson and Malcolm Hyatt (Queen's Regt).

> *1 Apr – 8620km. YV 5716 – no ramps fm wadi – we need engineers. 8646km at grid YV6902.*
> *1300hrs – sitrep – no ramps. Position YV6607. Two Bedu with excess quantity rice, flour and salt on camel. Suspicious as yesterday we only saw a boy. Father hidden? Brought them plus rations back to Mudhai.*

THREAT TO SALADINS

RTB – 1800

LCpl Abdullah Ali, Ali Hamdan both need new shoes, sizes 10 – request asap. 8698 Mudhai – 78km wadi bashing.

Deep into Wadi Gharah with perpendicular wadi walls rising 45m it'd been another abortive search finding a route onto the jebel.

With provisions exceeding permissible limits we took the two Bedu back to Mudhai for questioning by Said Barakat, the firqat leader. The two were Bayt Kathir, and legitimate. After a couple of days the men were returned to their camel. Left hobbled, Ruqaishi found the camel grazing contentedly, an innocent bystander to war.

My two crew members needed replacement footwear. Aware of our imminent move to Akoot, I radioed requesting new plimsolls. Ridiculous footwear for soldiers on active service, but I never received any complaints. Admittedly, the men claimed the shoes at least enabled a rapid ascent onto a Saladin when the need arose.

2 - 8th April
2nd – EASTER SUNDAY!
Mubarik Musalim – July leave.
Land Rovers x2 – Ali Abdullah, Nasir Hamid, Guide Salim to Midway via Tudho.
Said Mohamed – orderly – has given Ali Abdullah list of kit I need from Midway. My suitcase, with Tim. On convoy – return Mike's rifle & mossie net.

Patrol Report. Done.	*Mission*
End of month servicing – docs.	*Friendly forces*
Punctures – mend today	*Routes found*
	Wells
	Airstrips
	General – caves searched
	Grids – night posns – mileages

1700 – Need another gunner – 12B Mohamed Hamood sick.
JR – lifted AP mine on Salalah plain.

I sent two Land Rovers back to Midway, dropping off Salim, our local FHG guide with his tribe, en route. I was having the balance of my kit sent from Midway and end of month servicing and reports were chores requiring completion. At the 1700 call from Mudhai, I confirmed I needed a replacement gunner for Costello's T12B.

3 Apr – Rifle practice – 303s & Brownings
Six monthly today.
Sgt Fyffe sick, stomach – return Midway with Recce pl.
Hamdan Khalfan managed to drop gearbox dipstick into transmission through filler hole. Wiley Lou Costello, hooked it out using length of wire. Genius. Windy again, cold. Lots of flies.
1300 – Record for a call – under 60 secs. Phew!
Recce pl have pinched 3 of our Land Rover wheels, Lou having just repaired punctures! Ruqaishi will resolve.

4 Apr – Saladins out for a 10 mile run a.m. Akoot preparations with troop.
Plans to dismantle old sangar overlooking camp delayed.
OG firing tmw. Range cards for new sangars.
1300 – valve covers and screws – key for valve covers – delivery by Beaver tmw.

We took the Saladins for a final run, checking roadworthiness and the cars performed well. OG arrived to replace the Squadron at Mudhai as we prepared for Akoot. And as a bonus, our last afternoon was spent on the firing range with .303s and then, more sensibly, Brownings. The boys had earned it.

The Gendarmerie took over the range, zeroing their rifles the following day. My final task was to make range cards for each of the new sangars we'd built, giving OG ranges to registered targets.

5 Apr – 12 extra for nosh – total 17
Askars here demanding more rations.
OG convoy – Tudho – wood and water from here.
Fyffe – to have medical tests. Staff lists by 8th.
Grey – op Jag – 7rds 60mm mors

OG set out for Tudho with water and rations for the firqat. On a more worrying note, Gerry Fyffe was to undergo tests to determine whether he had damaged kidney function. Grey (JR) had a contact on Op Jaguar – 60mm mortars. The adoo were using salvaged British weapons left behind as the British army departed Aden. A mistake armies across the world have frequently been guilty of.

Apart from Olly's absence, my troop were ready to return to Akoot.

THREAT TO SALADINS

Mudhai's Askars (militia), solid fellows to a man, were engagingly contemptuous towards any who'd lived softer lives. Demands for additional rations were agreed quid pro quo against additional guard duties.

17

THEY SAY NEVER VOLUNTEER

Ah! Mud Kars. My troop returns to Akoot and we bid farewell to donkeys. Preparations continue for Op Simba. Rick medevaced to UK. Tom wounded (WIA) and casevaced. First phase (L Day minus 1) – Op Simba. Op Locust – Akoot evacuation. The old army dictum about volunteering. And on becoming an infanter joining 2 Coy Desert Regt.

"The best laid schemes o' mice an' men / Gang aft a-gley." – Burns

BACK TO AKOOT

6 Apr – O Group : Crewing T12 - Hodgson: 80 – LCpl Abdullah Ali, Ali Hamdan
T12A – Oliver: 70 – LCpl Nasir Mohamed, Hamdan Khalfan
T12B – Costello: 72 – LCpl Hilal Ali, Mohamed Hamood
EME – LCpl Ramadhan Chambe
Cpl Mubarik Musalim – 3 Ton – water, petrol, ammo, spare wheels, parts
DR convoy arrives – Alan Howard with ½ 2 Coy
WO1 Bert Kenyon here checking cars – all fit

THEY SAY NEVER VOLUNTEER

AH! MUD KARS

In his photograph, Tim and I pose for our friendly Desert Regiment's Royal Marine, Alan Howard, who'd arrived earlier that afternoon from Akoot, escorting a water and wood convoy.

"Seated right filling his stained briar pipe, a relaxed Tim Cornwell, OC ACS. In bush hat, Paul Hodgson 13th/18th Hussars." – Alan Howard DR.

Shortly before our move back to Akoot and Op Simba, the operation that would eventually lead to winning the war in Dhofar, Alan arrived from Akoot to collect resupplies of water and firewood, required in preparation for flying on to Simba. It was good to meet up again and to hear news of the Akoot crowd, all who were well and sent salaams.

Simba still remained the open secret SAF were mounting an operation to establish a new permanent base west of Akoot. But the location and start date remained tightly controlled. For two weeks, the squadron had been out collecting firewood from the many camel-thorn-lined wadis around Mudhai, ready for DR's convoy, whilst I'd been tasked with searching for routes up onto the jebel.

Alan writes of the time:

"At Akoot Col Nigel and Alex Lamond were planning Op Simba, assisted by DR's three Company Commanders. During the week before Op Simba launch day, I was tasked (as a minor player in the grand scheme of things) to take a convoy of trucks loaded with empty "burmails" and some (empty) water tankers to Mudhai, where there was plentiful water. Off we trundled for the day-long journey over fairly flat terrain. At Mudhai, I was met in the early evening by Paul and his OC, Tim, and I took an iconic photo of them on a Saladin next to the "Ah! Mud Kars" sign – most appropriate for the desert.

The next day was spent filling burmails and tankers, and early on the following day we returned to Akoot, where I had missed a few more days of pre-op feverish activity. Sadly on our return journey one of the trucks hit a TM at Landon's Field. We had a couple of non-fatal casualties, who were casevac'd by Heli. They recovered with no lasting injuries. Whilst waiting for the chopper, mechanics in the breakdown truck stripped the now blasted truck for any useful spare parts, whilst Sgt Major supervised the transfer of undamaged burmails to other trucks. Later Paul's three Armoured Cars followed us back to Akoot, as extra firepower was required to defend the position once the bulk of DR had flown in on Simba/Sarfait."

At significant cost to the unique limestone desert habitat, Akoot's surrounding scrubland had been plundered of vegetation to keep kitchen stoves alight. Now reserves of firewood had to be ferried in from further afield, the culmination of a battalion's 18 months occupation.

> 8 Apr – Oliver fm leave? No, not yet.
> Alan's DR convoy out sparrows – hit L/mine YU 5191. WIAs.
> Bore-sighting – T12 – 2 x HE, 12A – 1 x HE, 12B – 2 x HE
> LCpl Abdullah Ali, Naser Mohd v. good shooting
> Mohd. Hamood is wet.
> Bloody hot – 1300 sitrep on Mike – he seems cleared up – but returning UK for confirmation. Flying back tmw. He'll be gone 4 weeks away?
> New POL point completed.
> Cooked supper over open fire – just like Africa.

Things didn't look good for Mike – now he and Gerry Fyffe were off sick, potentially with kidney problems. Olly still hadn't returned from leave. Alan Howard left early for Akoot, his convoy hitting a mine. We'd been warned to be vigilant. Final adjustments were made to zero the 76mm guns, and we were ready. All I needed was one sergeant back from leave. Our new hand-built POL point (petrol, oil, lubricant) eased the business of refuelling Saladins.

My troop refuelling before our return to Akoot. Out beyond the POL point can be seen what we called 'moon country' leading to the vastness of the Empty Quarter, El Rub Al Khali.

> *9 Apr – 1300 – Lpd – NTR SOAF Venom attack on Dhalkut*
> *White City – mors – no cas*
> *Adoo anti-aircraft guns opened up at jets flying at 8,000ft.*
> *Op Cyclops – contact 1625 – weapons haul – no cas*
> *SMG firing practice*
> *Finish cleaning turrets*
>
> *NFR arrive ½ B Coy – Bob Hudson*
> *1300 – Shopping needs: CO_2 bottle 12A, Rad. cap 12B. Lime juice.*
> *Sgt Oliver. Batteries.*
> *Welfare: OG 9837 Khalfan Nasir Khalfan – no news for 3 months?*
> *Confirm Tango12 move date to Akoot?*
> *Bedu fired at hyena 2330 – caused bit of excitement – all stood-to.*

At 1300, a typical Dhofar sit-rep: Op Leopard with nothing to report, White City mortared, no casualties. Cyclops, a 3 Coy JR op in Wadi Darbat (Dick Fox WFR and his 2ic Jeremy Blatch ex Queen's Regt) discovered an impressive quantity of adoo ordnance, medicines and the body of a civilian, left bound with rope to die a slow death through dehydration. Poor sod.

SOAF jets struck Dhalkut, a coastal village approximately 25km east from the Yemeni border, being used to land munitions shipped from Aden. The adoo replied with anti-aircraft weapons, unsuccessfully this time.

Included in my request for items required for the cars, the elusive Sgt Oliver. Bob Hudson RM arrived with half B Coy NFR en route to Akoot as part of the Simba build up. The remainder of NFR were in Oman, not due in Dhofar until the end of April. And I still awaited orders to move south to Akoot.

> *10 Apr – Completed last checks on cars.*
> *Said bin Salim bin Mikthur walked into my tent demanding FNs for his new firqatmen. With his nerve he must still be a commie.*
> *Nasib back to Midway with donkeys. After many breakdowns, halted 26km away. Dispatched fitter with escort. 1330 – on their way again. Poor b. donkeys!*
>
> *Nusrat tried to resign.*
> *Johnson nearly ate a Bedu boy – boy and father pacified. Dog has 9 lives, now just used one.*
> *B. hot – earache – dust everywhere.*

An eventful day. First a firqat leader demanding upgraded weapons, emphasised in jebali fashion by jabbed finger to chest, guaranteeing to test one's composure. As Thesiger noted 17 years earlier, it was disconcerting to realise the Jebali never doubted our inferiority. We, tolerated as providers of revenue and weapons, they were jebali or Bedu, and Muslim; we weren't. Europeans were Christians, unable to exist in their harsh, unforgiving world without resupply backup. One point above pathetic.

Immediately following my firqat debate, Sgt Nusrat, my Iranian quartermaster, unexpectedly announced he'd resigned and wished to return home. We normally got on well. I politely explained that with two years of his contract still to run there was little likelihood anyone would agree to let him go, so he withdrew. Problem solved.

With a lot going on, Johnson, enforcing his role as tent guardian a little too seriously, nipped a small boy. Fortunately, no more than that and the matter was settled without invoking the customary Bedu law involving blood money. He would have to be watched. Tensions were rising – had the dog sensed that?

FAREWELL TO DONKEYS

With all the preparations going on, Lou and I decided we'd pay a visit to DR's Mortar Platoon donkeys held in a makeshift pound at Mudhai. We'd heard the animals were not in the best shape. The donkeys were used for transporting ordnance on operational patrols inaccessible to vehicles, and after being recently moved to Mudhai they were now unemployed. At some stage these animals had had their voice boxes (larynxes) removed (laryngectomy), denying them the ability to bray, so ensuring they remained quiet on operations. It was reputed to be a simple operation and performed under local anaesthetic. Once cast and held down, an incision removes the vocal cords. Soldiers present at such procedures said it was strange to watch the dazed animals trying to call out afterwards. Hideous treatment for such gentle creatures. The donkeys were also used to carry wounded to safety, but with the advent of helicopters, their transport role had diminished. Now moved to Mudhai, these unfortunate and uncomplaining beasts of burden had seemingly been forgotten.

What we found was shocking. Eight donkeys in a very sorry state, malnourished and looking miserable, ribs showing and two animals with open sores worried by flies. Their pound offered little shade. Heads hung low, repeatedly shaken to free weeping eyes and long ears from the unrelenting swarms of flies, they made a pathetic sight. Then we discovered their diet was limited to dates. Not fresh but putrid, fermenting dates, delivered from Midway by truck, in hard compacted lumps, stored in filthy hessian bags. The feed dates, in a corner of the barusti enclosure, were covered in sand. There was no sign of fresh forage. At least the animals had water, a cut-down drum utilised as a trough. The handlers, asked about the mono diet and filthy conditions, simply shrugged implying 'what d'you expect, Sahb?'.

I ordered the men to clean out the barusti pound, the animals' hooves and bodies of faeces where they'd rubbed against each other in the confined space. The donkey's faces, mouths and eyes were to be cleaned of grime, likewise their filthy hind quarters. And I wanted it done straight away. Lou remained to see that the men complied. I knew he'd muck in, there was no holding him back. I'd inspect once the animals and the pound were presentable. Appalled, I went back to the Mess/ops tent and signalled UAG requesting an immediate supply of green fodder. I added that as the animals were no longer being used, they be taken to a better place before any perished.

That same day, a BATT Vet from Salalah arrived by Beaver with four hessian sacks of green fodder. Inspecting the animals, he confirmed they were severely malnourished and attending to their festering sores agreed it was no place to

keep these animals long term, adding '... not much of a holiday location either!' Mudhai? It was heaven compared to some SAF locations.

Orders arrived to send donkeys and handlers to Midway for flying to Salalah. Duly loaded onto a Bedford truck, the animals were in a considerably better shape having been washed of excrement, sores treated and weeping eyes cleaned using a weak mixture of saline and spring water. It was good to see their faces free of flies at last.

A while later it was discovered what in hindsight should have been obvious. Green fodder was being delivered, but was instead being sold by the handlers to the Camel Firqat and visiting Bedu at hugely inflated prices. Profitable little business until we stepped in.

AKOOT – A RETURN AFTER TWO MONTHS' ABSENCE

11 Apr   Full loads   T12   HE-25, HESH-16, 2 Can = 43
*   T12A   HE-26, HESH-15, 2 Can = 43*
*   T12B   HE-25, HESH-16, 2 Can = 43*

Tim, Sgt Oliver & 2 BATT arrived - Firqat trg.
CO_2 bottle fm Midway tomorrow?
ATU on 80 u/s - swapped with 81. Thimrin
Grey 60 dvr – sunstroke? medevac.
Low-loader arrived 1330 for Akoot convoy

Akoot – incomers 12 rds RCL
Leopard Adonib contact
Plains – airstrikes – W. Jardum,
W/City – drilled 325ft – no water
Cyclops – 82mm attack & s/a – no cas

Finally, an impatient Sgt Oliver was back having been stuck at Midway returning from leave. We restocked on ammo – each car fully loaded following firing practice on our makeshift ranges, a mile out of Mudhai. A day with more than usual traffic into Mudhai, including a Scammell low-loader we'd take to Akoot, to assist evacuating the 5.5in Howitzer.

A soldier was medevaced with suspected sunstroke. Next day another two fell ill with malaria and were flown out by Beaver. Malaria was rare, but we took no chances.

Final battle preparations as my driver, trooper Ali Hamdan cleans the 76mm barrel assisted by a bedu boy, whilst my gunner, LCpl Abdullah Ali strips and cleans the breach-block the day before our return to rejoin Desert Regiment at Akoot. A camp that was still receiving its daily load of incomers.

13 Apr – 2 more cases malaria – worrying as we've no 'anti' medication.
Xtra rations for Johnson tdy.
Q will look out for him.

Recalling my earlier time at Akoot, I toyed with smuggling Johnson in on one of the Bedfords, but thankfully quickly dismissed the idea as perhaps not a place for an independently minded dog. 'Q' promised to look out for him during my 'however long' absence, none quite knowing how long we'd be away.

14 Apr – ETD 0600 Inshallah . . .
Back at Akoot again T12, A, B plus 3-tonners and Bob Hudson's ½ Coy NFR 0900 – 5 breakdowns. Springs on overloaded 3-tonners.
Otherwise plain sailing – arrived late pm. V. Good to see everyone. Mocking comments for having Sundance Kid moustache! All compare idle shaving habits. Camp morale high.

FINAL PREPARATIONS FOR OP SIMBA

Op Simba had been given the green light after months of planning and involvement at the highest levels in Oman, Dhofar and Whitehall. The realisation was clear that once launched, the implications were possibly colossal not only for the progress of the war, but for the future of the Sultanate. This audacious operation had to be the game-changer Oman and Britain needed it to be.

DR-led, Simba would be supported by advance elements of NFR and MR with detachments from Oman Artillery, Firqat and the ACS. Within a couple of months, roulement would happen once again. The two Dhofar regiments, DR and JR, would head back north, and MR with NFR would return to Dhofar following nine months recruiting and training in preparation for another Dhofar tour. There'd been time for relaxation too.

Leading my convoy, we arrived at Akoot to find the place frenetic with activity. I reported to Col Nigel who rapidly outlined my role at the camp. Basically, Graham Sherwell, DR's HQ Coy commander would command the rearguard including my troop whilst the battalion moved out to Simba. Once Simba was established, Akoot would be evacuated, being too large to defend. Instead, a replacement Airhead had been selected, east of Akoot at a place called Janook. My troop would form the bastion of the rearguard. It was good to be back with DR.

15 Apr	HF – 5.5 Rakhyut 0600hrs
Rick medevaced to UK	one 25pdr out of action
Max water economy	
Sit rep: Jaguar contact small	
Cyclops – small contact	
Aden admits 3 killed on mine	contact 1030hrs – 26 bombs. HE,HEAT,Mors.
O Group – 1430	contact 1130hrs – Shpagin - B14
NFR return convoy to Mudhai	

RICK MEDEVACED

Rick Williams, 2 Coy Commander, was casevaced with severe abdominal complications and later flown to the UK after being diagnosed with amoebic dysentery, a result of drinking polluted water. The carcass of a dead cow was subsequently discovered floating in 2 Coy's freshwater supply. Rick was twice decorated, the Sultan's Commendation Medal in 1972 and WKhM for distinguished service in 1973. We'd not meet again until his glamorous wedding the following year. Tom now commanded 2 Coy, with Alan Howard his 2ic.

I was with Alex in the Ops tent when the first mortars whistled in, exploding close by. 'Christ, that's close,' exclaimed Alex as I rushed out from the canvas and stone walled ops room, running bent low towards our cars 250m away. More bombs landed. '*Shiiiit* – they're close to HQ,' I thought, then '*whooooosh – BANG*' to my right I saw through the dust cloud of explosion a running man leap into the air before crashing to the ground. The response is instinctive, I ran towards the fallen man. Calling Sgt Oliver on my Panasonic radio, 'Tango 12A – stand-to – I'll follow!' 'Wilco out,' clicked the instant reply, as Olly and Lou roared off to engage the adoo.

Fully anticipating my next call would be to Babu, I reached the man I'd seen blown up, lying covered in dust and fragments of stone. He was very still. Bending down I made to turn him over when he sat up, wild eyed, disoriented, deafened, with nothing more than cuts and scratches. Unbelievably lucky – a large rock had deflected the blast. Grabbing his shoulder, I pulled him running and stumbling to a manned sangar, before turning towards my car, now approaching fast, my crew having witnessed my detour. Explosions reverberating from bombs dropping out of the sky, 25 pounders responding and Saladins firing, it was as if all hell had been let loose. Adrenaline grinning, I leapt onto the Saladin, hearing Ali's yell from the driver's seat 'Raqm wahid, Sahb!'

Twice that day we were attacked, but without serious injuries. Alex suspected the Salidins' return and increased aircraft activity of late had aroused suspicion of what SAF were up to. Later I blamed Alan: perhaps the adoo had learned it was his birthday? He'd just turned 23. By the end of the day, both his and my plans had been overturned.

SIMBA LAUNCH MINUS ONE (L-1)

Phase 1
16 Apr – O Gp Col Nigel/Alex: 'Probably most important Op carried out by SAF'
Hugh Colley now here
"Securing pty" 1640 fm here – LZ 1700hrs YU239575 – FTZ next pty to YU232578 – (corrected to) YU231575 (1740hrs)
FTZ plans mv. fm. LZ across w. Saiq. picquet 300488 picquet 322482, ambush 3247.
Jets Strike – onto Batendorb area around 1630hrs. Diversionary.
If weather too bad – postpone by 24hrs – POSTHORN.
Saladin (Raysut area) mine TM46, two injured, PN mine one wounded. One SEP, Jaguar.
3 Coy – Bangs 1100hrs (digging funk hole training?)

HF C21 O845	*25 pounder*
B28 0900	*25*
C23 1625	*25*
B40 1940	*25*

Mess full of SOAF pilots
1500hrs contact – Tom injured – casevaced.
Col Nigel / Alex / me – discussion 2 Coy officer strength – Simba goes ahead. Find myself 29A on loan as 2ic 2 Coy DR. Alan now Coy Cmdr. Grab FN – brief boys away few days, LCpl Abdullah Ali commands my car as T12B. Sgt Oliver now T12 loans me spare FN magazine. Met Alan for rushed briefing and grub.
Move out 0600hrs tmw. Hectic, everyone busy – Tom in agony, poor sod. Waved as he's flown out.

All of 7,250km away in an office in Whitehall, a secret operational centre had been prepared with maps outlining the launch of Op Simba, detailing the troops involved, their positions and expected enemy retaliation. And that once committed there was no way out. On duty in that room was a certain Field Marshal's daughter, Alix Baker, a very sweet girl who happened to be romantically involved with Tom, lucky man. Unshielded as others by the cloak of secrecy, Alix was privy to the particular dangers this audacious operation would involve, in taking, holding and establishing a position on the Yemeni border. Additionally, she would have been aware of the expected calculated casualty rate, a given factor woven into all military planning when mounting an offensive. And she just happened to know three of the officers taking part, Tom, Rick and myself. It is sobering to think she could only wait for news.

TOM CASEVACED

Attacked with rockets and mortars, Tom was amongst the early casualties, casevaced by helicopter on L-1, the evening Simba was launching. 2 Coy were now down to one officer, Alan Howard. The battle plan required for three officers to hold Black and White, the two forward positions facing the enemy's front line. Led by two Royal Marines and a Royal Horse Artillery officer commanding battalion mortars, 2 Coy DR were the most experienced unit, critical to the operation's success.

I received a call from the Battalion Ops Room.

OP. LOCUST – AKOOT EVACUATION PLAN

Driving across to the Ops tent I expected a final briefing on Op Locust, Akoot's evacuation and eventual relocation to Janook. My troop with Ruqaishi's recce platoon, supported by a half company of NFR yet to arrive, would hold Akoot as rearguard as DR embarked on Op Simba.

With responsibility for the perimeter defences, I'd be reporting to Graham Sherwell, the large, imposing no-nonsense veteran of bush warfare, who'd learnt his trade with Zambia's Defence Forces. As senior officer he would oversee the evacuation of all military hardware, including the artillery's valuable 5.5in Howitzer. The armoured cars were to remain until all else had been safely evacuated.

THERE'S AN OLD ARMY SAYING – *"NEVER VOLUNTEER"*

Simba, seven months into planning, proposals, meetings, helicopter and foot recces, specialist training and logistical build-up of ordnance, stores and munitions in preparation for this major offensive, had hit a problem. 2 Coy was down two officers, the OC and now his 2ic, who also happened to be the Battalion Mortar Officer. That left just Alan as the new OC.

Walking into a heated conversation, it was obvious what the debate was about. I listened as various options were proposed. To my simple mind, there seemed a possible solution and, waiting my chance, I threw in that I join Alan as temporary 2ic 2 Coy. I had infantry experience, I argued, having once served with the Royal Green Jackets, failing to mention it had been as a potential officer, in the ranks. And anyway, I'd also trained as an infanteer at Mons Officer Cadet School. I'd leave my armoured cars in the capable hands of sergeants Oliver and Costello, with my car commanded by the quietly confident LCpl Abdullah Ali, an NCO who'd later win a SAF commission. Needing a gunner, I'd use the irrepressible LCpl Ramadhan Chambe, our troop fitter, gifted cook and natural mechanical engineer who could also fire the 76mm.

Alex, suntanned face now puce with excitement, tugged unconsciously at his monstrous moustache, an inescapable mannerism when agitated. Time was short. In a little over an hour, Alan was due to fly out with his half company. 'Posthorn', the codeword for postponing the operation was no longer an option, Simba L-1 had begun, helicopters were en route.

From me then back to Col Nigel, Alex spoke with suitable gravity: 'You know it makes sense, Colonel, we can't move companies around now, 2 Company's on Black and White, with mortars. Tom may well return shortly. Meantime Paul can fill in and we'd have Brits commanding both positions,' adding aside to me, 'ahhh, mortars? Shit ... we'll get round that when the time comes – not a problem!'

My proposal had never been an option. As Armoured Car Squadron I was an attached unit, on temporary loan to DR specifically for Op Locust, tasked with the job of covering Op Simba's launch and rearguard at Akoot as the infantry moved out and camp evacuated. The security blackout prohibited radio contact with Tim based at Midway, two days away to the north, preventing a request to 'borrow' me. And it was doubtful Tim would have agreed, I was his only officer and my troop represented half the fighting armour available to SAF at that moment. The remaining three Saladins were at Mudhai, being prepared for deployment to Janook. Mike was still in the UK, sick.

'You're on, Paul,' the CO replied, 'see to your Saladins, I want your troop briefed fully on what I expect in your absence, send me your sergeants... Alex, brief them, this is too bloody big to bugger up now!'

Leaving the Ops tent, I recalled the old soldier's adage "never volunteer". Too soon it'd become clear maybe I'd not fully appreciated the extent of 2 Coy's intended role at Simba. Not surprisingly as I'd not been involved in any pre-Simba briefings.

Eleven days earlier, whilst I was patrolling in Land Rovers with firqat and Ruqaishi's men, a document marked Secret was released; the Op Order for Operation SIMBA. Meticulously prepared, a 34-page briefing document was issued to all participating officers, designed to ensure commanders were fully conversant with every aspect of the operation about to be launched. Op Orders are split into five paragraphs, Situation, Mission, Execution, Administration & Logistics, Command & Signals. It began with an estimation of enemy forces in the area, and ended with codewords for different positions. I never once saw a copy.

I drove back to brief my troop at our night laager, 300m east from DR's Ops and HQ tents.

A CHANGE OF ROLE

Calling my sergeants together I explained the change of plan and warned Olly he would be running radio ops from Alex's vacated ops tent. Costello's reaction was as expected: 'That's ferkin mad, sir, what d'you want to be an infantryman fer?! Won't find me out of me bloody car!' Sgt Oliver was more restrained and with a wry smile remarked: 'Oh well, been nice knowing you, sir – don't fancy it myself, I'll take radio ops any time!'

My immediate problem was whom to leave in command? Knowing both their strengths and weaknesses I was faced with an invidious decision. Once again, I experienced the difficulty of the one being in charge: you can't always be the nice guy.

The two were as chalk and cheese, each had proven skills, were individual and essential operatives within the team. For spontaneity, Costello, who'd act without hesitation, who'd never leave you behind and fight like the devil by your side. Oliver, intelligent and contemplative, preferring to weigh up pros and cons before acting. Then he'd act fast. He was generally correct in his assessments too.

I made my decision. 'When there's an attack on base, Sgt Oliver you're to hand over radio duties to Major Sherwell and take command of the troop. Whilst you both share equal rank, Sgt Oliver will have command in my absence. LCpl Abdullah Ali will command my car with LCpl Ramadhan Chambe gunner, Ali Hamdan, driver.'

Dispatching Sgt Oliver to the Ops tent for briefing by Alex, I drew Sgt Costello to one side and without having to explain my decision, said, 'Lou I'm asking you to take care of Olly, give him the support you give me – he's not me but he'll be OK and will rely on you – as I have always done. He'll be busy on radio duty so look after the boys for me – OK?' before adding 'and thanks'.

With a twinkle in his eye he looked up from the rock he was sitting on and confirmed, 'Don't yer worry, I'll manage him just fine, sir – and don't you worry about us boys here now – you just look after yerself . . . we need you back to take care of us now.'

My gut told me I'd made the correct decision. I also knew that Lou would accept the decision and be fully supportive in my absence. I needn't have worried.

I'd now to brief the boys, which turned out to be a salutary lesson in dealing with the unexpected. I'd not reckoned with their reaction and was taken aback by their apparent shock I was to leave the troop to join the attack. Why? they queried – why leave them at Akoot for Desert Regiment? What was Colonel Sahb thinking? This was not what they'd expected – then as one they began insisting they must be allowed to come with me. 'Where you go, sahb, we go' was their emphatic response.

There'd been talk about anticipated casualties expected in the first few days until Simba had been secured, supporting mortar and artillery dug in, sangars and trenches built and airstrip established. Moved by their concern, I reassured them I would be back shortly, as soon as replacement officers could be flown in to reinforce 2 Coy.

'You don't know these soldiers, Sahb, they're strangers – some have yet to face the bullet . . . and most are Baluchis Sahb, not Omanis, not Arabs like us!'

Again I assured them it'd be just a couple of days. So I hoped.

There followed a sombre shaking of hands. Then Abdullah Ali and Ali Hamdan insisted on coming back to my tent to help me pack my two blankets and rucksack. The request was not expected but I realised it shouldn't be turned down. The process took less than a minute or two and as we emerged from the tent, there, stood in two lines were the whole troop waiting for a final send off: 'Allah kareem, sahb'.

It was a moving moment and as Lou drove me across Akoot ridge to 2 Coy's position I was reminded what a privilege it was to serve with these young Omanis, men who through warfare I had become bonded to – culturally we were so different but as a band, as close as brothers.

We called by the Ops tent where I collected a 7.62mm Belgium FN rifle, ammunition, radio and orders for deployment first light next day. Olly had loaned me a filled FN magazine; I'd no idea how he'd acquired it.

I JOIN 2 COY DESERT REGIMENT

A somewhat relieved looking Alan welcomed me, introducing me to his Arab and Baluchi NCOs. I had wondered how he might view matters, just promoted to acting OC 2 Company and now landed with a cavalry officer as his second-in-command, whom to his knowledge had probably never served as an infantryman before. It was to Alan's lasting credit he kept his thoughts to himself – remaining the true professional, making me feel instantly welcome.

The timing could have been better. It was a hell of a rush – Alan, shortly due out by helicopter with the advance party, the first stick leaving at 1640, needed to brief me. His departure fast approaching, he and I went over 2 Coy's mission for taking and establishing Black and White positions on Mainbrace. His position would be Black, I'd take his earlier designated position, White, which he showed me on his marked up map. Together we hurriedly shared a meal of spiced goat and rice, followed by strong coffee, going over as many possible scenarios that might possibly occur on the morrow. One last look at the maps before wishing each other good luck, and he was off. I was now 2ic 2 Company DR.

The Simba Launch minus one (L-1) Group, the advance party, which included Alan's party comprised the following:

OC L-1 Group – Battalion 2ic: Paul Mangin
OC Red Coy: Ben Hodson with 29 men, OC 2 Coy: Alan Howard with 28 men, FTZ: Mohammed bin Hamed al Ma'sheni with 60 men.
Total payload – 10885kg – 10.9 tonnes to be flown out in 10 Hueys.

At 1640 hrs on 16th April, Op Simba launched with the departure of the L-1 Group, 14 hours ahead of DR's remaining battlegroup, tasked with walking in from the north to secure the main feature of Op Simba, Mainbrace. They lifted off in a series of 205 Huey helicopter flights bang on time. Landing at the designated LZ, grid YU239575, the men spread out, securing the area, awaiting the remainder arriving in a continuous wave of chopper flights. The last stick delivered, the force set off southwards arriving just before daybreak at their objective, the escarpment edge that was Mainbrace. The gruelling 10km night march had been accomplished successfully, in pitch darkness with a new moon. No one got lost or fell into the many steep sided wadis, no one tripped and there were no accidental discharges from jittery trigger fingers. With Simba's LZ secured, the first wave of DR's battlegroup helicopters began flying in as the day dawned, Simba L Day.

Alan recounts briefly on his memories of the events that evening:

> "Many have written about Op Simba, but suffice to say it was thoroughly detailed, with Artillery and Mortars forming a significant part of the Defences, and hence were seen as a key part of the Op. At the last minute, Murphy's Law seemed to kick in, and things looked bleak, when first Rick (Williams, OC 2 Coy) – with chronic Amoebic Dysentery – and then Tom (Bremridge, 2ic 2 Coy) with a back injury – had to pull out hours before the Op. I was then rapidly promoted from bit player to Coy Comd in a very short space of time, as there was no time to find anyone more responsible! The Op was written around key personnel from DR, MR, Firqat, SOAF and others, who each had key roles to play. I thus had to lead the 2 Coy team in to secure the Heli Landing Site, to receive the first waves of choppers at first light. Fortunately yomping and marshalling helis is in every RM's skill set, so on paper the end result was not so catastrophic. I then required a 2ic, pdq. I am not sure how Paul (Hodgson, ACS) was press ganged into it, but he was suddenly "promoted" from Armour to an Infantry Company 2ic, with new call sign 29A – (lost his Tango!) and we were both read into the op in great detail at short notice, and in great haste."

It had begun. DR's advance party were helicoptered to their LZ and night march to secure Mainbrace for heliborne troops arriving next morning. Op Simba had commenced; the largest helicopter operation of the war was underway; the most high-risk of the Dhofar war to date. Simba L Day.

> If it all goes tits up – 'the Battalion, if stranded, can always walk out. . . .'
> Commander Dhofar Area, Col Mike Harvey recalling how he'd done just that in Korea.

Commander in Chief, HM the Sultan, CSAF, his Staff Officers and those in command knew Simba must succeed. The colossal investment in time, men and equipment and over 55% of Dhofar's forces committed, the loss of face at home and abroad plus harm to soldier morale should this British planned and led operation fail, was unthinkable. In Whitehall, Britain's FCO watched and waited.

Admittedly, we could have 'walked out'. It'd have been an almighty slog. A company of the Glosters had done it, famously, in Korea. Yet 130 years earlier

General Elphinstone's huge army had walked out of Kabul, to be massacred by tribesmen.

Eventually I turned in. Above, the bright starlit-filled night persuaded me to remain outside the tent I'd been allocated. My issue blue cotton prayer rug for a mattress would be my bed for the night. All slept fully clothed and booted. I'd been issued a spare FN – that'd not been zeroed, there'd been no time. Loaned webbing, ammo and six magazines produced by Sgt Ali who'd offered to fill my magazines. But I'd declined politely and after we'd chatted for a while, he'd left for a last check on night piquets. As I gathered my thoughts, I loaded my magazines, reckoning it'd been six years since I last held, let alone fired, a SLR, the British version of the FN FAL battle rifle produced by the Belgian armaments manufacturer FN Herstal. That had been as an officer cadet on the Aldershot ranges.

But even as a cadet, my rifle skills had been tempered by the fact that more often than not I was designated Bren gunner, reflecting my experience handling Bren guns as a small arms instructor teaching riflemen recruits light machine gun (LMG) skills at Winchester's RGJ barracks. However, my confidence was boosted by the fact I had recently attained a modicum of rifle skills leading a biathlon ski team, firing bolt action German Mauser rifles.

Rifle oiled and dried, magazines filled, I rechecked my kit before settling down on my mat, with a roll of webbing bunched beneath as a pillow. We had night piquets out, and as many did, given the opportunity, I lay staring at Arabia's clarion night sky, unspoiled by light pollution, never failing to fascinate and draw you in. Welcoming the distraction, I wondered how far the universe went beyond the spaces between stars? Were there indeed parallel universes? Gradually, thoughts returned to the morrow which had already begun. Alan and his men were on the march. Banking on surprise, we hoped they'd reach Mainbrace without interruption. Fortune smiled sweetly, they secured the landing zone, LZ, without contact.

My rifle and kit beside me, I lay wedged against the day's still warm earth and limestone rock of Akoot's ridge. I pulled up my army issue blanket, I had five men close by each also wrapped in blankets against the jebel night's chill. Despite the certainty we faced enemy fire in a few short hours, some were already asleep, snoring gently, making me marvel once more at these soldiers' apparent blind faith in their young commanders, the unquestioning belief that somehow their officers would see them through. And each in command knew that that was a faith which must prevail. Deep in the subconscious is carried the honour of your name, that of your family and ancestors, and for us soldiers, that of your regiment. A subliminal message drummed into you at basic training, and reinforced as an officer cadet being trained to lead, when it is indisputable.

Drifting off I wondered which of the positions on Mainbrace would be the first attacked. It was going to be difficult as I'd heard there was no cover whatsoever on White, my designated position. It was bare arsed, Alex had said, we'd need to dig fast. So how fast was fast? White faced west, nearest to and directly towards adoo-held Yemen. We'd just dig fast. Lying still, watching the skies, I thought this was probably a moment I'd never forget. The men's light snoring amused me, thinking they'd be no good on an ambush. Forcing my eyes shut, I slept.

18

OP SIMBA

L Day – Op Simba launches; the operation that set the seeds for winning the war. No man ducks a bullet. Lightning kills and storms flood. Alan and dynamite. Frankincense. The Sultan's uncle killed. Tom returns.

Callsigns

Desert Regiment

Red Coy	Capt Ben Hodson Sand 19	2ic Capt Ian Thomas Sand 19A
2 Coy	Capt Alan Howard Sand 29	2ic Capt Paul Hodgson Sand 29A
3 Coy	Capt Jonathan Gough-Crispin Sand 39	2ic Capt Dick Morgan-Evans Sand 39A
Artillery	Capt David McFadden Golf 29	2ic Capt Noel McGrath Golf 29A
Armoured Cars	Sgts Alan Oliver Tango 12, Lou Costello Tango 12A, LCpl Abdullah Ali Tango 12B	

Even with the imminency of Simba, Whitehall and diplomats were debating our futures in the war:

SECRET

BRITISH MILITARY INVOLVEMENT IN OMAN   29 March 1972

1. I have seen on my return to Jedda the reference in your telegram No. 89 of 15 March to the forthcoming review of our assistance to Oman.
2. I am aware that there are some powerful – shall we say "Vietnam" – arguments for disengaging ourselves from the Dhofar War if it is our assessment the cause is hopeless or that it can only be won by an unacceptable degree of involvement: but I assume that the review will take full account of the effect of any decision on our relations with the Saudis.

A debate of which fortunately the poor bloody infantry, supporting armoured cars, artillery and other front-line troops were totally unaware.

Patiently we wait airlifting to our positions on Simba. Standing by a Land Rover, David McFadden with his Artillery Recce, waits with time to ponder as we take our turn.

SIMBA L DAY (LAUNCH DAY) – 17 APRIL 1972

17 April – 0630 first lift-off fm Akoot
El Said – deception - firing at Rakhyut first light. Jet strike plus HF
Channel 8 place names – Akoot/Mainbrace
Got 2 Coy up to airfield, after initial muddle. We were 25th Huey out. Dropped onto airfield instead of White. Long, heavy haul to White. Some confusion on 2 Coy positions but soon agreed. Hueys everywhere. Sighted sangars: Two platoons, Mortar section, Pioneer pl, FTZ. Ground v hard – started digging-in immediately and through night. Shallow hole. First contact SA.

Woken at 0500 by last stag on watch. It was still dark. Within 20 minutes we'd snatched a breakfast of chapati and strong, over-sweetened tea before hiking 500m to the airstrip to form up in sticks, lines, to board SAF's Hueys, Agusta Bell AB205 helicopters. We were booked on the 25th out.

The Sultan's naval vessel, El Said, an armoured dhow, had commenced a diversionary bombardment on Rakhyut, a fishing port used by the adoo, approximately 40km east of Yemen's border.

David, an excellent gunner, would go on to win a deserved WB in 1972.

L Day Groups comprised the following:

2ic Red Coy Capt. Ian Thomas (WFR) and 71 men plus 4 mortars, & bombs
2ic 2 Coy: Capt. Paul Hodgson and 47 men plus 2 mortars
OC 3: Capt. Jonathan Gough-Crispin and 59 men
Artillery Recce: Capt. David McFadden and 9 men
Bn HQ 15 men, Defence Stores, Water and Medical Stores.
Total payload 39690kg – 39.7 tonnes: flown in by 35 Huey flights

Twelve fixed wing flights, unable to use the airstrip under construction, delivered equipment by air drop with expected results. Fortunately most of the drops consisted of 78 bedrolls which bounced on landing, but a number of boxes of ammo and spare radio batteries didn't, bursting on impact. Over the next two days another 31 Huey loads were flown in, and 21 fixed wing loads following completion of the airstrip on L+2. Working in relays, pairs of Hueys landed every two minutes, to off-load before heading back to Akoot for a repeat performance. It was an astonishing achievement.

Helicopters are vulnerable to ground-fire. Flying in at 10,000ft to remain out of small arms range, SOAF pilots had mastered the technique of 'spiral descent', dropping within a narrow air column above friendly held ground. An engine failure procedure allows wind to drive the blades like a fan, called auto-rotation when a loss of height might reach 1,700ft a minute. In SOAF, spiral rates of descent were achieved exceeding 7,000ft per minute, 90mph (145kph). Thanks to the extraordinary skill of the pilots that day, none were hit by small arms fire. And just one Huey hit the ground too hard, remodelling a skid.

Someone with greater authority had decided they'd not risk landing Hueys on White, as it was too exposed to enemy fire. Instead, my half company, our gear and mortars, were dumped on an area that later would become the position's earth airstrip. Over 1km away, across a wadi and a steep climb up to my position, was White, where we were tasked with digging in and holding. 'Welcome to the bloody infantry.' I smiled to myself as we began to ferry our gear over three return trips, fetching jerrycans containing 20 litres of drinking water, boxes of ammo, mortar rounds, rations and corrugated iron sheets before we could start digging in. In the event it took over an hour, leaving us as breathless as finishing marathon runners and as drenched in sweat. Two of my men collapsed under the stress of carrying too much. Sitting each facing down the slope we were climbing, I pushed their heads between their knees hoping to get blood back to their heads; it seemed the natural thing to do and worked. I'd not yet learned about blood sugar problems. At one point I too had had to stop with a heart pounding as if to burst;

we've all done it, carrying too much and refusing to give up until the body cries 'enough!'.

I recced the position each climb up to White and returning for the last time, I'd worked out where to site my half company's sangars. It was a bare-arsed feature. What I'd been told was correct: there was absolutely zero cover.

I'd identified my immediate friendly positions, Yardarm and Black, by sight and now assigned section commanders where to position sangars, arcs of fire and lines of communication between sangars. Alan's half-company was just visible on Black to our left and rear, Red Coy could be seen on Yardarm out on a ridge to our north. Once sited, we began digging in. Using picks and shovels against rock and hard baked earth was always going to be an unequal task and we'd only managed shallow scrapes in the ground and begun filling sandbags when the first attack occurred.

'CONTACT – WAIT OUT!'

'A hole in the ground is as important to success or failure in war today as it has been for hundreds of years. Digging is the most hated aspect of a soldier's life in peacetime training, and the most enthusiastic activity when the shooting starts.'

General Sir Richard Barrons KCB, CBE

As one, we flattened ourselves against the earth, dropping picks and shovels, scrambling for rifles. 'Shiiit!' I thought. 'White's first taken out!' Looking around I could see my signaller, flat on the ground, lying prone with hands over ears, presumably hoping he'd become invisible! Comical if it hadn't been so serious. Separated six metres from his radio, the antenna pointing impotently skywards, he wasn't going to be much help.

When an attack comes, you're seldom ready. There's no umpire or referee to start the match. The side fully kitted out attacks whilst the other side are still deciding which boots to wear. There's no whistle to stop play, or cry foul. Yes, you've a plan, but Bang! the first punch breaks your nose, how's the plan now? That initial reaction is vital. Mercenary leader Col. Mike Hoare wrote on being ambushed or attacked, a leader's first reaction must be to shout commands; this tells the men a) you're still alive and b) not lying prone covering your ears with your hands. Good advice.

Reaching for my National radio handset I reported '29A, Contact, wait out!', the obligatory signal on receiving incoming fire. Back came an acknowledgement from an alarmed Battalion HQ ops room, where Alex was sorting maps and papers, in a cave three hundred metres back, tucked into an east facing hillside (the adoo held the country west from White). Of course he asked, but damned if I could make out where they were firing from. What I did know, it was long range, bullets were whistling over, no 'crack!' so had to be 1000 metres at least.

Crawling forward, I dropped into the slight hollow that was to become our sangar, calling up my mortars positioned in dead ground to my rear, for three rounds onto the ridge to our front as our machine guns opened up in response. Suddenly incoming fire ceased, we waited but the action was over. I wrote later in my diary.

> *Long range S/A fire – no casualties and almost as soon as it started, firing stopped. God, I missed my ½ inch armour . . . bullets raked ground around us – hitting kit with dull thuds, other rounds screamed like banshees as ricochets bounced. No crack thump. Astonished no casualties, we're on a bare-arsed feature.*

Digging in on White, just before the first attack – small arms and light machine gun. There was precious little cover except for the shallow holes we'd dug, filling sandbags. Running out of sandbags, a logistical error by a higher authority, we used rocks carried from a wadi behind us, and later those quarried from the earth as we dug.

The adoo held the far ridge across the wadi, a kilometre off. My signaller's radio, my map with stone weight, and three men's kit in the foreground. I wrote "Astonished no casualties" proving yet again life's but a lottery.

Dropping to the ground with the first shots, I'd fleetingly recalled an epigram one Irish Cpl McCarthy, a worthy Green Jacket from 2 RGJ, used to berate us with during basic training. Succinct and to the point, he'd yell 'When some fucker's shooting at you, remember crack/thump, it might just make you a little less fucking useless to the rest of us poor sods!' We were 17-year-olds.

CRACK! THUMP!

> Did you hear that crack Jack?
> 'Twas bullet passed your head.
> Oh! you missed the thump chump
> Well that's because you're dead!

The first indication of an attack might be the audible crack of a supersonic bullet travelling faster than sound, 1235km/h, creating a sonic boom. Unlike a supersonic jet's boom heard over a wide area, the sound of a bullet close by is limited to the immediate area around you, your enemy's personally selected target. The bullet's sharp 'crack' means it's missed you. The subsequent thump is the explosive noise from the rifle's muzzle firing that bullet. Why the time lag? Sound is subsonic.

Detecting the area where the thump is heard allows you to determine where the enemy is firing from and the range may be estimated too, by measuring the delay between the bullet's 'crack' passing overhead and the 'thump' of the rifle's muzzle. Comparing this delay to a table of values, the bullet speed can be calculated and the range to firing weapon ascertained. The theory is similar to estimating the very approximate range of lightning taught to us as children, counting the seconds that separate flash and subsequent thunder.

On hearing the supersonic 'crack' of a bullet, you start counting whilst listening for the muzzle 'thump'. Mentally aligning the crack to thump, directs you to the source of the firing weapon. It's an open ground theory, havoc in echoing wadis.

To estimate the range between you and an enemy, you start counting at a rate of five per second between crack and thump: then multiply the count by 100 to get the distance.

For example, "crack" – *start counting* . . . 1, 2, 3, . . . "thump" = 300 metres, close.

"crack" *count* . . . 1, "thump" = 100 metres . . . too bloody close.

NO MAN DUCKS A BULLET

A bullet fired from a Kalashnikov AK47 zeroed at 100 metres will drop approximately 0.75 centimetres at 300 metres. An average man measures approx. 0.9 metres head to groin. At 300 metres (the argued maximum engagement range) a rifleman aiming at a standing man between head and chest is likely to hit some important part of the body. At 300 metres, the bullet hits the target after just 0.40 seconds. And at 350 metres it might just miss some important part.

To compensate for the drop in trajectory, the rear sights are generally adjusted to battle-sight setting, 300 metres on the rear sight, indicated by the Russian letter "П " standing for – постоянная ('constant'). When zeroed at 100 metres adjustment, the drop in an AK47 round's trajectory over a distance of 350 metres can be shown in the following sketch: time to target is shown too.

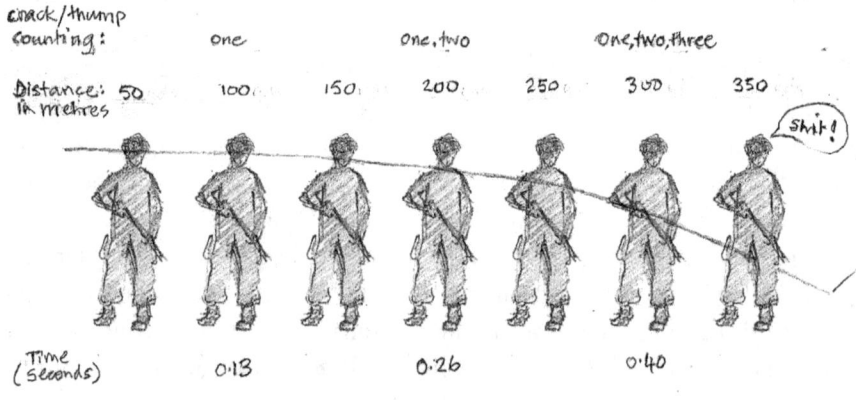

At 100 metres, travelling at 750m/s the 7.62mm bullet's kinetic energy measures 45,000 psi (310,250 kPa). On entry, the projectile will pass straight through soft tissue. Hitting bone will likely cause it to tumble, making it rotate over and over, ripping a larger hole creating a bigger shockwave throughout the body, which requires no further explanation.

* * *

Almost as soon as the attack occurred, it ceased. 'Testing us,' I thought, 'Pop up, blast away, disappear.' It was copybook communist guerrilla tactics – straight from Mao's training manuals.

Throughout history smaller groups of determined fighters have caused mayhem to regular armies. Mao Zedong's writings taught how small irregular groups of combatants, lightly armed, moving swiftly and choosing only to attack when to their advantage, were able to tie down far larger, better equipped but less mobile armies.

The Persian warrior-king Darius I, ruling the world's largest empire and best army in 512 BC, retreated before the nomadic Scythian horsemen's hit-and-run tactics. Two hundred years later and facing guerrilla opposition, Alexander the Great modified his tactics, winning over important tribes to his side, to achieve victory. In the 19th century poorly-equipped Afghans defeated British armies in India and later 90,000 Boers held back the Imperial British Army for two years before succumbing. In the following century using guerrilla tactics, TE Lawrence's force of Arab tribesmen drove the Ottomans from Arabia and in the 1970s Viet Cong guerrillas were driving the world's most powerful and sophisticated army from South East Asia. Other armies since have suffered the same defeats.

Following victory in Cuba, Fidel Castro's plans of exporting Marxist ideology by creating mini Vietnams was already evident on the African continent and South America. And in Dhofar, communist guerrillas, the adoo, sought their place in the history of Marxist revolution, through this proven mode of warfare.

We resumed digging in, our lives depending on building sangars before the adoo brought in mortars and rockets. By the end of the day we'd hit rock beneath a thin layer of baked earth and were still without adequate cover. All we'd achieved were shallow shell holes in the rocky outcrop that was my position, White. Yet with sangars set in depth along the ridge, some forward, some behind facing west to the enemy's front line, I was pleased with the emerging layout of defensive hollows that would become sangars. Alan visited to compliment me, admitting the Cavalry's reputation had risen slightly in his estimation, pretty good from a Royal Marine. He'd given up digging at his position for his was practically all solid rock and had started to build up from the ground rather than continue to attempt digging. He promised to call by the following day with explosives to assist us on White.

By the end of that first day, 17th April, Desert Regiment's objective to take the position around Wadi Sarfait had been achieved with complete surprise. The tight secrecy had held, no one barring senior officers in SAF and those back in Whitehall were aware of the precise date and timings until that day. Simba, 8km from the Yemeni border, now had to be held.

SIMBA L + ONE

Phase 2 until 1200 - Phase 3 fm 1200

18 Apr – Ending day's op orders, Alex wishes us all Happy Easter – 16 days late!

Blasting all day – sangars improving. Hueys impede progress – as we can't dynamite. Half my force taken to work on airfield, not a great help when sangars a top priority. Contact, small arms, est 1400 away. No cas. 29C on White 2 v. slow progress. 29 on Black building sangars up from ground as unable to dig/blast rock for trenches. Khareef down. Second contact pm small arms. Hear 19 and FTZ have also had small arms contacts. Adoo Mors into 29C posn. No cas. Collected more of our ammo this pm – rest tmw. Top cover over White after Skyvan shot up above us. Para dropped supplies, not too successful.

FTZ one WIA. Claim two adoo KIA.

Photograph is representative of what an incomer looks like. This is one of me blasting through rock excavating one of my half company sangars on the bare feature that was White. The adoo held the far hills approximately 1000m distant. Generally photos purporting to show incomers exploding close by are fake, more likely they're of blinds (dud shells) being detonated safely. No one stands snapping photographs of incomers – you've no idea where they might land. Didn't hear the thump chump? That's because you're dead! And you've a job to do.

The day commenced with Alex's ops orders for the day radioed to each of us – which he ended with a loud 'Happy Easter everyone'! Only 16 days too late, but that was Alex at his eccentric best.

On our second day we were resupplied by helicopters bringing water and rations. They also delivered 6ft (1.83m) long rusted angle-iron posts we'd use to build our sangar roofs. As one helicopter approached with its load of posts slung beneath, the straps binding the bundle failed, releasing a shower of these lethal iron spears to fall to the ground. It was like Agincourt from a French perspective. Amazingly with everyone watching, all scattered like scalded cats. Not a man was touched! Five posts embedded in the rock-strewn ground, others flew about bouncing off rocks, stones, stores and kit. The thought of ending up skewered like French soldiers at Agincourt by iron stakes dropping out of the sky held a morbid fascination which appalled. A nightmare incident, never planned for.

The long-range attacks were of little consequence. Without an airstrip the Skyvans continued to drop supplies over Mainbrace, our bedrolls arrived this way, battered but none the worse for wear. One Skyvan was 'shot-up' as it circled over us on White, but suffered no damage. The adoo were close.

SIMBA L + TWO – THE VIOLENCE OF AN ELECTRICAL STORM

19 Apr – Beaver leaflet drop – meant for adoo, blown all over White position. Sangars near completion. Still no big contact. Mors in posn. Registered 81mm mors with help fm Hugh Colley. Mor course lasted 5 minutes. 19B – 3 mors incomers. p.m. – later discovered ex-Brit 3 inch.

First fixed wing onto Mainbrace a.m.
Bloody awful night – huge thunderstorm. Sangars flooded. Bailed water. Whole battalion flooded. In cloud at 3000ft and surrounded by electrical explosions with astonishing lightning flashes, bright as daylight. Lightning killed a corporal in sangar on Black 29's posn – S/Sgt Ali Khamees wounded same strike. Had to force men back to sangars after they'd all come to mine. Explained every sangar was flooded! Ordering them back, it occurred to me adoo could walk straight through this position. Organised some to bail-out, others back on watch. Mess tins make good bailers. Hashish smoked freely . . . Bloody Hell!? Surprised none suffered hypothermia.

Overnight 19th April we experienced a spectacular electrical storm. At first there was no rain, the atmosphere desert dry, making you wonder if the rain was evaporating before it reached us. Clouds filled with lightning and thunder but no rain. The noise deafened, flashing lightning became a constant strobe display.

Growing up in Africa, we'd been directed by concerned parents to straightaway seek shelter in a thunderstorm, and stay inside a car if possible after close family friends had been struck and killed getting out of their car. The theory was the tyres would insulate the charge.* Instructors at the Army Outward Bound School in Snowdonia had emphasised to students what safety actions were necessary if caught in the open during electric storms. And now, sitting crouched in a three-foot deep sangar, rifle and ammo beside me together with some plastic explosive and a box of Mills 36 the other side, snug below a row of steel pickets supporting corrugated steel roofing, albeit covered with a layer of earth and stone, it occurred to me there were possibly better places to be during an electrical storm. We would soon find out to our cost.

It is estimated the Earth's surface is struck by 100 cloud-to-ground lightning strikes every second. Each bolt contains possibly up to three million volts of electricity. What we'd seen was an impressive display of nature's power, presented across a range of mountains bordering Arabia's Empty Quarter.

Then when the rain arrived, our dugout sangars filled within five minutes. The storm's intensity deadened shouted orders and with no radio communication and no idea of the situation in other positions, it occurred to me 'Attacked now and they'll walk straight through White – I'll lose the bloody war!' Fortunately, not even the jebel-hardened adoo were going to risk an attack in such atrocious conditions.

It'd been non-stop now for six days since I'd left Mudhai. And I realised that my men, increasingly dazed through lack of sleep, combined with the physical effort of digging-in, attacks, snacked food and rationed drinking water, were nearing exhaustion. That's when the mind begins to play tricks, for which no amount of training truly prepares you. No matter how hard or arduous the training, reality boots theory into touch.

---

* It's not the tyres which protect you, but the car's metal body acting as a conductive Faraday cage, the current passing around the metal exterior to the ground.

IT'S NOT TOBACCO THEY'RE SMOKING

A face appeared at my sangar entrance pleading assistance. Climbing out, I found men evacuating sangars and running, stumbling in the darkness to mine, not out of concern for my welfare but the misguided belief somehow my sangar might be more waterproof. Like them, I too was drenched. We all looked like drowned rats. Faced with two platoons of soaking individuals complaining bitterly, expecting me to provide some sort of immediate salvation, I raised my hand for silence – lightning constant as daylight ensured they saw me. The storm raged as they crouched waiting; 'What,' I asked pointing skywards, 'do you expect?'

Grabbing the nearest by an arm, I showed him inside my sangar, 1m deep, awash with floating kit and asked if his accommodation was any worse? 'Laa, Sahb' (no sir) and one by one the disbelieving peered into my sangar before being coerced back to theirs. At 0300 it stopped raining. By now bitterly cold, I knew I had to keep the men alert and active. Checking each sangar, I demonstrated bailing out techniques using a mess tin. It worked. We might well have been dinghy sailing in the Solent.

Then I noticed our empty jerrycans were being carefully filled with floodwater for drinking and cooking rice. Good thinking. The work warmed us and soon earlier moans were forgotten. Rotating bailing parties with sentries ensured people kept moving.

Making my rounds, I became aware of a heavy scent drifting from still damp sangars to discover the men were smoking. At least some had somehow managed to keep matches dry to light cigarettes. Except it wasn't tobacco I smelt, but the sweet smell of hashish – available openly in Salalah's market. Too late to stop their medicinal remedy for misery, I prayed we wouldn't be attacked. It was a long night. Next day, as men laid out kit to dry, there wasn't a murmur about the night's storms. It looked like battalion laundry day.

Steaming clothing dried rapidly in the sunshine and I recorded 'amazed no hypothermia'.

MAN DOWN ON BLACK – ALAN SURPRISES WITH DYNAMITE

With no radio communication, I'd sent a runner to Black to report we were secure, to discover two of Alan's soldiers had been struck by lightning. Corporal Said Abdullah had been killed instantly manning a GPMG. On guard and vigilant, he'd had a hand on the GPMG as he watched for movement when three million volts of lightning struck the weapon's barrel protruding out of the sangar's gun slit.

The second man was Staff Sgt Ali Khamees, hit crouching beside his Corporal. Seeing lightning strike the sangar, Alan rushed over to find one soldier dead, the other unconscious. Ali's body had dropped forward into the rapidly filling dugout. He was drowning as Alan pulled his NCO out of the water. There was no response at first as Alan put his weight behind a series of rib breaking compressions, forcing water out of the man's mouth and lungs. Then it was mouth to mouth resuscitation and suddenly Ali coughed water and breathed.

Soaked to the skin at an altitude of 3,000ft and with the sudden drop in night temperature, Alan knew he must increase the man's own body temperature. Dragging his NCO to his own sangar, Alan shoved his patient into his Royal Marines issue sleeping bag. Ali continued shivering uncontrollably when Alan struck on an idea for creating extra warmth.

He'd summoned the company medic to sit beside the incapacitated soldier. There was little a medic could effectively achieve, but he would be able to keep an eye on the patient. Blocking the sangar's firing slits with unused hessian and sandbags, Alan cooly reached into his explosives box and brought out three sticks of dynamite. Unwrapping, he placed the dynamite along a rock ledge inside the sangar and finding a dry box of matches, made to strike one.

Until that moment, none held greater loyalty to the young Captain Sahb. The stand-in OC who'd spent the best part of two days blowing holes in the mountainside enabling us to dig through rock to build life-saving sangars. The Baluchi medic was one of many who revered Alan. But now? In the damp sangar lit by a small torch, crouching beside a barely conscious soldier he watched Captain Sahb unwrap dynamite, push a stick into the sangar wall before taking a box of matches from his Bergen. Unfolding at arm's length in front of him, the man's worst nightmare was about to be realised.

As Alan went to strike a match, the medic let out a primaeval groan, turned and scrambled for the exit, pushing past his patient into the storm, anywhere but remain with demon sahb!

Grabbing the fleeing figure, Alan pulled him back inside the sangar, 'Kull shee zayn, kull shee zayn!' (it's OK!) – before ordering the man to remain with his patient. Turning back to his task, Alan lit the three sticks. 'See – no problem – no explosion!'

Unaware of the chemical and physical properties of Alfred Nobel's magic material, the incredulous medic watched gaping as the dynamite burned, warming the air, safely and without 'infigaar' (explosion). The patient survived to be safely casevaced next morning, making a full recovery. He owed Alan his life. How Alan's star rose as the story spread around Simba the next day gathering embellishment at every sangar.

Walking across to see how Alan was doing, I found him playing with PE again. Cool as mustard, he was preparing to blow another hole in the impenetrable rock. He confessed to having attended an explosives course prior to his language course the previous autumn. One day he'd qualify with a proper job as a Chartered Accountant with one of the UK's top international firms.

Many were photographed posing armed to the teeth with weapons and we'd wondered at their message? 'Better photographed representing day to day realities of a soldier's life,' Alan would say, 'no need for fucking ham.'

Day two and a partially completed sangar. We'd run short on sandbags, and here one of my stoical Baluchi half-sections await delivery of more bags to fill as topping for the walls. I made them bank up the outer walls with earth to replicate the slope found on the front of Saladins, giving the sangars greater protection.

SIMBA L + THREE

20 Apr – 2 L/Rovers arrived a.m.
Boys seem to have fared well after last night's tribulations. Place drying out. More mortar HF. Slight problems with mortar plotting board, but OK. All Simba sangars and helipads now completed. Airstrip too.
Caribous and Skyvans roaring in/out all day.
L/Rovers will help transport stores – save heli hours. Sangars still wet and stink.
29A position now designated White 2 and 3 – might save time getting stores to right place first time! No matches – cold food. All tired. Need to watch that. More storms to north.

Day 3 we were re-supplied with water, rations and rolls of Dannert wire. A welcome sight for I was acutely aware how vulnerable we were to night attack from the dead ground falling steeply to our front. By 2100 we'd hammered stakes and fitted wire, prompting an illogical sense of security now the wire was in place. Ridiculous, given a determined enemy could approach around the outer ends of our new defences. Nevertheless, it felt reassuring we'd done something against a rushed assault. We extended the line as more wire was delivered.

Under cover of the khareef mist, troops lay Dannert wire to the front of White. The work continued into the night. We were all pretty tired by this stage. Modifications were carried out to the wire over the following nights but it was not until after I had left and rejoined my armoured cars, that the area was further secured with mines.

Photographed by Alan, my sangar on White 2, shared with my orderly, Noor Mohammed and here, Abdullah my signaller. Enemy held territory immediately over my left shoulder.

Completed sangars as the khareef closes in. We planted aloe vera on the walls, partly as added camouflage, partly out of contempt towards the adoo.

The airstrip had been completed allowing STOL fixed wing aircraft to land, dropping off supplies, which continued through the hours of daylight.

21 Apr – Mor contact 1.A. chge 6 elev 1218, bearing 4403mils
Msg: 'Capt Bremridge, 11198 Azan Mubarik, 9615 Mohd Mubarik – no flights.'
Yesterday saw sea first time. Dick was right, superb views. The ground below slopes steeply. 8 pl lost yesterday in mist – easily done, I was too for a while. Visibility down to metres. No rain fee layl. Shpagin, and light m.g. firing from east onto airstrip. Deployed 7 pl's GPMG onto strip, 1200.
Shpagin, again pm, deployed 2nd GPMG to strip.
Contacts late into pm. 19 says position nearly assaulted with trip flares set off. May have been jackals?

Indents	
White 2	White 3
water	ditto
4/2 & oil	ditto
rations for tmw	ditto
x 4 corrugated iron, 10 pickets	ditto
matches	ditto
81mm smoke x 20, HE x 100 (white 2 only)	nil
2 inch illum x 18	ditto
Trip flares	ditto

Still no news on Tom's return, nor two men due back from WIA leave. My first daylight visit to Alan's Coy HQ on Black, approximately 850m to my rear and south. The Arabian Sea was clearly visible: Dick Morgan-Evans had been right: the views were stunning. The escarpment dropped 300m vertically to steeply sloping wadis cut into the limestone strata, the slopes all but hidden by verdant scrubland and grass meadows, a result of the annual khareef.

Apart from the promiscuous acacia, vegetation in this area is quite different from Salalah plains. Here aloe vera grows freely, the Arabian Peninsula's evergreen perennial. Alongside, clinging precipitously to limestone ledges grew Boswellia Sacra, the sacred gum-producing frankincense trees with their precious gum that oozed to crystallise on branches, the crystals harvested for uses long immortalised by religious association. These small crimpled leafed trees develop an extended buttress root system adapted for survival against seasonal drought, the shallow roots coping with periods of water stress and nutrient-poor soils. The jebel's northern slopes produced the best frankincense.

With too little time for tourist viewing, I returned to White as the adoo opened up with Shpagin onto the airstrip. Another attack followed as I deployed first one then two GPMG sections to the strip as additional backup. Small arms attacks

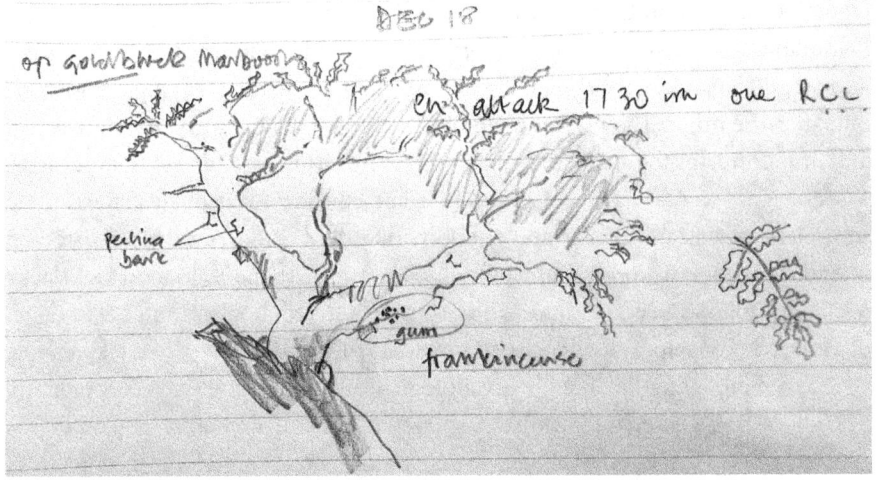

Descending the jebel, numerous varieties of flowering plants, including heavily scented ivory flowers of wild jasmine are found in gorges and the upper reaches of Dhofar's wadis. Myrrh trees (Commiphora myrrha) are also abundant.

continued into the evening, at one stage threatening Red Coy's position as their defensive trip flares were set off. We joked it may have been jackals, but it'd been no joke for the boys on Yardarm, 2,000m away across Wadi Sarfait, isolated from the remainder of the battalion group on Mainbrace. I can still recall the slight level of concern in the radioed messages that night as their flares tripped out.

Hugh Colley commanded Oman's Artillery. On his first visit to Simba and hearing I was on White, he had called to visit, bringing with him a mortar plotting board. Crawling up to my sangar he pushed his gift at me with a triumphant 'Hello, Paul, have a mortar board. Don't lose it, not easy to come by'. Thanking him I replied perhaps he'd better give me a quick tutorial and there followed a crash course on its use directing mortar fire.

Mortar, rockets attack – again my position.

That afternoon, it rained mortars. Undoubtedly amongst the most chilling sounds, the soft 'whoosh - whoosh - whoosh' crescendo building to 'BANG!' as a bomb lands, releasing its murderous circle of death. Shrapnel, jagged shards of metal scream past as you dive for cover behind anything offering protection. Striking limestone, it's not difficult to imagine the effect of a bomb's impact. Amongst steel shards, flying splinters of rock and stone are equally lethal to soft tissue.

Racing to my sangar, I dived behind its wall, scraping hands and shins in an undignified scramble for cover. Limestone takes no prisoners, but offers shelter.

Giving a fire mission to my mortars as shells exploded around us, Baluchi S/Sgt Dad Raman's mortars barked, sending their bombs high into the air towards the adoo positions. Crunch! Crunch! The shells landed with satisfying explosions, one after the other. The playing field had levelled. Unlike direct fire, judgement and time confirms the success of your indirect fire. This time the incomers ceased.

Just eight incomers, a mix of 75mm RCL and 82mm mortar, but fast. Remaining fully alert, you strain to hear and possibly identify the adoo base plate, listening intently for a mortar woosh sound or rocket scream. With the realisation the attack's over, there follows an eerie stillness, quiet but for a stereophonic tinnitus at its dawn of a long relationship. You call up section leaders for casualty rates. We'd taken none.

It is difficult paraphrasing the psychological effects of being shelled. A piercing howl becomes a scream heralding a shell's approach. You shout 'in-comer!' as everyone dives for cover. The ear splitting explosion. Screaming in objection, protesting eardrums numbed and temporally useless exhale in silence's temporary relief before the next crash. There's knowledge each explosion possibly wounds one of your men requiring immediate life-saving aid. Yet duty demands you locate the enemy and return fire to neutralise the attack.

Poseur!! Alan wanting proof of first incomers took this photo as author holds two specimens, tail fins of a 3" mortar and a 75mm RCL. (The 3" mortars were captured British weapons allegedly left behind by a departing army vacating Aden in November 1967.) Newly acquired plotting board, radio, rifle, Panasonic hand radio and combat jackets adorn my sangar wall. Sandbags were filled with earth and rubble excavated during sangar construction. My comfortable sangar Alan would later inherit.

That is what you have been trained to do. A fact of war: the enemy attacks when they have the advantage. It's you who's been caught with your pants down. It has always been so. The response will determine the outcome; that and luck. The saying 'he ducked a bullet' is absurd, no one dodges a bullet but he may with luck dodge a second, unless the weapon's on automatic.

SULTAN'S UNCLE KIA

22 Apr – Requirements:
White 2: FN oil, Mors. // 4 x 2. // 8 corr iron // 10 pickets // 2 x boxes 2 inch illum // Trip flares // Matches.
White 3: oil // 4 x 2 // Trip Flares // 2 x boxes 2 inch illum // Matches

Running short of supplies, my indent included oil and 4x2 flannelette cleaning cloth for weapons, additional 2 inch illuminating mortar rounds plus trip flares, additional corrugated iron sheeting and stakes to strengthen the last sangar roofs. And we needed dry matches. We were eating cold tinned rations.

39 caught at 274486 – Wadi Sarfait – pinned down – 0545 – jets scrambled – 0900 – 4 FTZ KIA, 3 adoo KIA, one FTZ WIA 0600. Jets, good strikes. My sangar and OP completed late PM. Fired White mortars onto camel posn. reported as en. Distressing but saw camels later – pleased they're OK. 39, 39A and FTZ still pinned down east of Mainbrace, pull out tonight once dark. Tom back, I leave tmw. Another FTZ and one DR wounded. Alan's fired 200 rds mortar in support 39 by 1530. 1825 – 19A surrounded. S.A. attack but OK. 29A contact – adoo 222450 firing on 29C – engaged with mortars. Five rounds on White, two onto posn, two short into wire, one over the top, their grid 220461. Brit 3 inch mortars!

HF tonight
1) 1910 chge 6 elev 1135 bearing 3760   3) 1930 6 972 4770
2) 1925 6 1180 4280   4) 1930 4 1127 4460

Still hot at 1630 – khareef clouds drift back 1715 – and getting cold again.

A near disastrous day for SAF. Jonathan (39) and Dick's 3 Coy, guided by the FTZ, walked into a trap, remaining pinned down for most of the day. It was incredible they escaped with so few casualties.

The wounded were brought back but the dead left; something we resolutely tried to avoid. Denying the fallen the dignity of a burial badly affected soldiers' morale. Muslim dead should be buried that day, the body placed in a grave dug parallel towards Mecca, the direction for daily prayers. Leaving a body behind denied closure, adding further to the psychological burden every field commander carried.

With 3 Coy pinned down in Wadi Sarfait, the adoo mounted attacks on a wide front, frustrating completion of our defences. Positioned along Mainbrace's eastern perimeter, least exposed to adoo fire from across the Yemeni border, 3 Coy had completed their sangars ahead of the rest. Patrolling to investigate the steep sided Wadi Sarfait, they had run into a well laid ambush, pinning them down throughout an uncomfortable day.

Calling for support, Alan maintained a steady mortar bombardment, successfully rebalancing 3 Coy's unequal situation. Hugh Colley, who'd remained at Mainbrace, acted as Forward Observation Officer (FOO), relaying targets to Alan. That afternoon I'd noted *'Alan's fired 200 rounds so far: 15.30hrs'*.

Reporting seeing men with camels to my west, I'd been ordered to engage. We landed mortars close to them and they disappeared. Later and to my relief I watched five camels grazing further west and hoped these were the same animals we'd fired at earlier and they'd escaped unhurt. Camels weren't combatants.

Under cover of darkness 3 Coy withdrew, carrying their wounded. At 1825hrs, Red Coy on Yardarm were attacked with small arms, rifle fire, but repelled the adoo without loss. On my position at White, as the sun set, mortars struck around us without causing injuries. Two rounds fell short into the wire, two amongst our sangars and a third 20m back beside my mortar platoon. The adoo had successfully demonstrated they could attack each of our positions on the same day. We'd suffered losses but these could easily have been greater.

We collected tail-fins under cover of darkness later that night as the khareef returned, cloaking us in cloud. Seduced by the temporary cover, the need to remain alert was vital. With positions visible, the adoo knew the ground better than us. And after what had been a good day for them, their tails were up and we could expect further attacks.

A week later, my mortar section received a direct hit when a British 3 inch mortar bomb landed within the circular stone built mortar pit, filled with men and boxes of recently supplied ordnance. On impact the incoming round hit the ground, partially burying itself into the hard earth. The dust settling, the men stared in shocked disbelief at the body and tail fin pointing skywards like a Churchillian 'V' sign. The round was blind. No explosion. A day the gods smiled sweetly.

With Tom's return that afternoon, I'd be returning to Akoot where I was needed. The camp's strength now reduced to my three Saladins, a recce platoon, an artillery detachment and the remnants of DR's HQ Coy, the position was vulnerable. The adoo had sensed Akoot's weakened strength and responding to Simba's advance into their territory, piled on the pressure at DR's old battalion base.

At the foot of the page, my diary entry reads *'Of FTZ KIA – Sultan's uncle. Bodies not brought back.'*

Sheikh Mohammed bin Hamed al Ma'sheni was the Sultan's maternal uncle, a senior member of the Ma'sheni tribe from Taqah, the province of the Sultan's mother. Already proven in battle as a proud and fearless soldier, on seeing 3 Coy and his FTZ firqat were trapped, he led an assault against adoo in caves, sadly to be killed outright at the head of his men. The attempt to silence the enemy machine guns and advance floundered, and SAF's troops remained trapped until finally withdrawing after dark. It had been a gallant attempt to salvage the situation but at great cost. That same day Commander Dhofar Area, Col Mike Harvey, recommended Sheikh Mohammed for the posthumous award of the Sultan's Gallantry Medal, Oman's equivalent of the VC.

My sangar crew, between attacks.

It was amazing how soon they relaxed following an attack, adjusting to being shot at, their faith in my design of sangar protection far outweighing mine. Emerging from the dark, Noor Mohamed, my temporary orderly. The one on the right, my signaller Abdullah leaning against my jacket and shemagh. Also shown, radio, maps, plotting board, list of registered targets, handset, loaned rifle, box of compo rations and mug. In progress on the plotting board, my sketched hand drawn map of DR positions, on the ground one of my three diaries. All sangar roofs were eventually reinforced with sandbags as further protection against falling mortar bombs.

A year later during a particularly fierce contact in Wadi Jarsis above Salalah plain, Abdullah attended to a bullet wound to Alan's arm. I add Alan's comments:

'Abdullah tied my field dressing on my arm after I was shot a year later at the Wadi Jarsis. What a time it was.'

Alan was fast using up his nine lives. It never ceased to surprise the impassive response some of these men and, in particular, Alan, had to wounds – 'it's a bullet wound, treat it'.

Of the constant attacks, one lucky shot amongst many landed alongside a Caribou aircraft, wounding and killing personnel on board. Repairable in ordinary circumstances and given the necessary spares, but here the aircraft became a write-off. Just as at Akoot, shells landing on the runway also spelled the end of STOL fixed wing resupply.

23 Apr – Mortar indent 81mm – 79 boxes HE, 19 boxes smke for 29A = 392 rounds!

Tom's arrived back – half mended. Matches rationing. Soldier's FN flash hider shot off today. Carried on firing! Well, I'm still here – looking fwd to Akoot and wash, but now told stay extended few days. My new c/s 29B, on

Black. Put up more wire in thick mists. View fm Black incredible. When clouds part, through binos you can make out coastal Thalqut, sandy beaches and waves breaking. Astonishingly, we hear children, dogs barking and camels roar. Lined sangar with a used parachute for warmth. Damp, cold night. Rainbows glow around our shadow silhouettes on rising clouds at cliff-face. Tom cooked, just like Kenya safari – 2 tins compo stew! 1st decent meal since arrival. Days of cold sardines, sweet biscuits and compo cheese. Alan taking patrol out tmw. I've 2 Coy mors, Tom 3 Coy's. Both slightly concerned going for a pee in dark and walking over cliff edge, only 3m away. Everything damp – washed feet in canvas bucket – glorious – socks beyond redemption, threw them off cliff at adoo – but updraught blew them back into my face.

My mortar indent reflected the amount fired the day before. Boxes of four mortar bombs had to be fetched from battalion stores approximately 800m away. Sensibly sheltered in a wadi, the ammo dump meant crews had a long haul uphill carrying these boxes back to White's position. There was no other area to store the ammo safely.

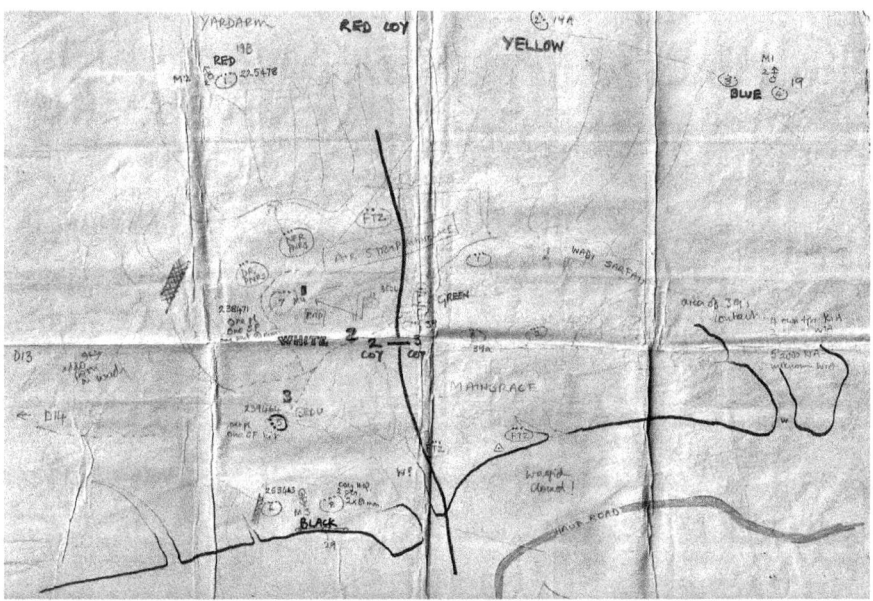

My original sketched map noting SAF positions once established on Simba. Drawn on A4 paper, reinforced with zinc tape, the fall-back treatment for cuts, blisters and generally holding things together. Making the map helped pass the time between attacks and thunderstorms.

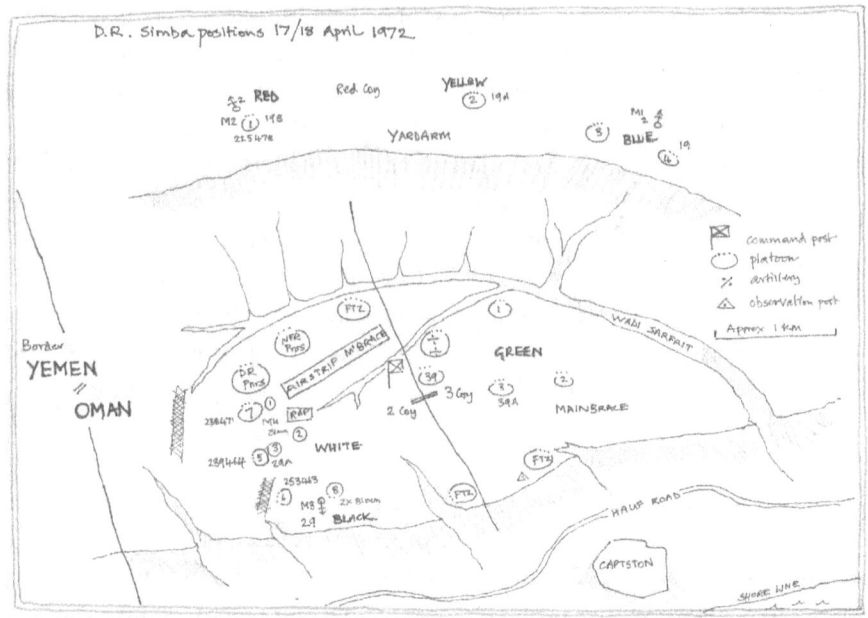

For better clarity, my copy sketch shows Desert Regiment's positions established following Simba Launch Day, 17th April 1972.

The boy soldier, Alan, takes over my position on White.

Tom had returned, on painkillers. Having tasted my efforts on holiday, he insisted on cooking supper. Always an excellent cook, he was worthy of a Michelin Star.

Earlier one of my soldiers had his rifle's flash hider shot away. Unperturbed, he continued firing back at the adoo, not that there was any other option. In addition to my daily indent, one FN rifle.

We were surprised at the ease sounds could be heard from below the cliffs, carried echoing in the wind. Shouting and dogs barking were clearly audible 3,000ft below. Devoid of any polluting background hum, a light updraught and possibly the limestone cliffs themselves contributed to sounds being magnified, like cupping a hand to an ear.

Released from responsibilities on White now under Alan's command, I'd been re-assigned 2 Coy mortars whilst Tom commanded those of 3 Coy. Initially informed I'd remain on Simba for a few more days, no plans remained definite for long and as day dawned on the 24th, I was ordered back to Akoot, increasingly under aggressive short range attacks, a new departure in adoo tactics.

Tom's scribbled message at the foot of a shopping list of gear he required sending up from Akoot was carried up to my sangar by his orderly as I departed. Tom never fully recovered from his back injury and in constant pain he struggled on, seeing out DR's last weeks on Simba. On return to northern Oman he was medevaced back to Britain for a lengthy period of treatment, until eventually informed he was no longer fit for an infanteer's role. We'd not meet again until a year later in the UK, when Rick married Claire, a society wedding at the magnificent home of her godfather, Sir Norman Hartnell, Royal Dressmaker. And I am glad to add that Tom and his dear Alix were married shortly after his return from Oman.

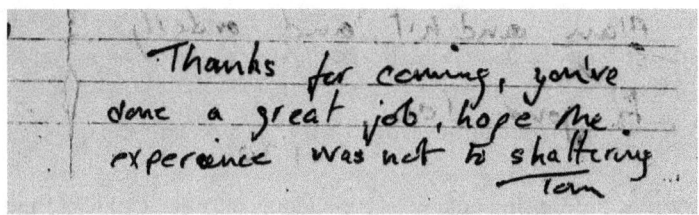

As Simba consolidated and DR handed over to MR on roulement in June, the position became known as Sarfait after the wadi intersecting the battalion position.

19

BATTLE FOR VIMY RIDGE

Return to Akoot under siege. Radio Aden's propaganda. Preparations for Akoot evacuation. Aggressive action – 'show of force'. Ops White Ants 1 & 2. Battles for Vimy Ridge. Jonathan wounded. Casevac using Lou's Saladin, who then resupplies with ammo. Continued attacks leave us surrounded. Olly's extraordinary shooting. SOAF jets arrive and soldiers run out of ammo.

RETURN TO AKOOT

24 Apr – Up before sparrows. Shared flight with Col Nigel in good mood. Akoot – dry and warm.
3 Coy here tomorrow for op. south VIMY – Op White Ants

The Huey's roar prohibiting talk, we sat in silence. Between Col Nigel and me, lay a wretched casevac with uncomprehending staring eyes. His body was strapped tight to a stretcher being accompanied by an attentive medic en route to the surgeons at FST Salalah. It was difficult not to feel the diversion via Akoot must have felt unnecessary to the casualty, having the greater immediacy.

Barely touching down, we alighted beneath the 205's rotating twin blades still thumping the air. 'Home,' I thought, jumping from the shaking helicopter, imagination forcing the involuntarily duck as you lope through a mix of eye lashing dust and burned avgas. Squinting through it all I saw a Land Rover approaching, Lou with some ACS troopers. As we moved away from the Huey's lifting turbine roar, Col Nigel drew me to one side and in a scene more befitting WW1, the English colonel thrust out a hand to shake mine.

Shouting above the din, he yelled, 'Bloody good xxxx' (lost to Huey's turbine) 'xxxx grateful' (again lost) 'xxxx thanks Paul!' Not known for sentiment, praise indeed. Before it became awkward, he'd turned and was striding away to meet Graham, his HQ company commander. Nonetheless, I'd caught the gist. Touched by the unexpected demonstration of gratitude, it was a smiling soldier who greeted Costello with my crew, Ali Hamdan and Abdullah Ali.

Climbing onto the Land Rover: 'Corr! Sir,' remarked Lou, 'no baths on Simba, eh?' Wide grins from the boys as I translated into Arabic. My return was complete as I joined the troop for a homemade brew of roasted coffee and delicious dates they'd ordered from Salalah souq the day before. Sgt Oliver soon joined us from duty in the ops tent – it was good to see him again, red beard fast becoming a tangled bird's nest. The warmth of the troop's welcome was touching. Urgently requesting news of Simba, they would accept nothing less than my relating in full the accounts of the past eight days. Starved of detail due to the continued news blackout, all they'd heard listening on a small transistor radio was limited to Radio Aden's contrived nightly broadcasts claiming successes against those on Simba. My men had yet to hear that the Sultan's uncle had been killed two days earlier. I filled them in on every detail I could recall.

Reaction to DR establishing a battalion position adjacent to the PDRY border had been expected, for SAF had penetrated deep into adoo territory, but unexpected was the direction of retaliation. Sensing an opportunity, the adoo's attention had turned quickly to the now conspicuously weakened position at Akoot. The rules of war are simple: when attacked, retaliate or capitulate. The game was set.

AKOOT UNDER THREAT

The depleted force now holding Akoot had been reduced dramatically to three Saladins, a detachment of artillery, one infantry recce platoon plus the remnants of DR's HQ company en route to join Simba.

Until launching Simba, Akoot had presented a heavily defended forward operating base, fortified and impregnable. On strength there'd been an infantry battalion comprising three rifle companies armed with automatic rifles, two WW2 Vickers machine guns, GPMGs, mortar, recce and pioneer platoons, supported by a three car Saladin troop and an artillery detachment with two 25 pounders and a 5.5in Howitzer. And there was also the balance of FTZ numbering up to 50 irregulars.

Life for those living at Akoot had become increasingly frustrating sitting day after day observing and waiting, sitting targets for repeated attacks by machine gun, mortars and rockets fired by an increasingly proactive adoo. They engaged from a distance, we responded likewise. We suffered casualties, and could only suspect they did, given the occasional Radio Aden reports. Inevitably, morale suffered, and proud soldiers talked amongst themselves but equally to their British junior officers, asking why SAF wasn't taking the battle to the adoo.

Discipline remained paramount, a given, never questioned. Orders were obeyed beyond the 'call of duty'. It was a dangerous place and whilst most reacted to physical danger as drilled into us from the day each had joined up, it became clear younger men, including the officers, often saw a different perspective to that of their seniors. No more apparent was this than when it came to humour, when the 'extraordinarily funny' appealing to younger minds would often be perceived as highly irritating to those almost twice our age, our superiors. Looking back, I am filled with admiration at how the commanding officer put up with the likes of Lamond, Maclaine and Hodgson sharing his Officers' Mess. And Paul Mangin, he of mature years and should have known better, had a wicked sense of humour.

There had been occasions when wrongly I'd failed to see eye to eye with the CO during my months at Akoot. These arose primarily out of heightened tensions we each separately faced, compounded by our Saladins' poor mechanical reliability and ludicrous situation on vehicle spare parts. My troop was also a young unit, where newly qualified soldiers of whom many were unable to read or write, were having to deal with highly technical equipment. Being subjected almost daily to rocket, mortar or heavy machine gun and small arms attacks, it exasperated that by the time we'd reacted, the adoo had disappeared, melting into the surrounding deep wadis, which equally allowed for hidden approach to within small arms range. Thus, in effect, frequently our responses were wasted time and effort. That galled, and then there were always the mines.

Looking back, I regret I failed to fully recognise the pressures Col Nigel faced maintaining his battalion at full battle strength, whilst exhaustively planning in secret for the major push to take and hold a significant position on the Yemeni border. For his part he had an armoured troop attached to his command, yet seriously limited on capability due to the acute lack of spare parts vital to maintain vehicles fit to fight in a desert environment. For my part, frustration born of having to constantly nurse cars that frequently broke down, often with no backup other than a soft skinned Bedford truck and driver ferrying a cheerful, capable

Baluchi mechanic with a few spanners and trusted hammer, the mechanic's tool of last resort.

I am glad to say our mutual friendship and respect, though once tested, remained firm until the old soldier faded peacefully at the great age of 92.

* * *

SIMBA/SARFAIT – KEY TO SUCCESS OR FAILURE?

Much has been written on Simba; much of it by absentees.

Simba would always demand resupply by air. And once adoo artillery successfully registered the airstrip, STOL aircraft could no longer land safely. Every drop of water, rations, munitions and supplies had to be flown in by helicopter; 16,000 lbs (7260 kg) of payloads daily, of which 5,000 lbs (2260 kg) was drinking water. A logistical nightmare, stretching Oman's already war-weakened resources to the limit.

A guaranteed fact of war, plans change with the first rounds fired. Shortly after Launch Day on 17 April, amongst casualties taken was the Sultan's uncle, killed on 22 April; and on 5 May SAF lost their outpost destroyed at Habarut, followed almost immediately by Simba's airhead at Janook on 10 May with SAF forced back, to withdraw north to Manston. And SAF casualties were mounting.

These cumulative effects delayed the assault on Capstan, the feature hoped would give SAF command over adoo supply routes, yet when eventually taken, SAF were again forced to withdraw. And with STOL flights suspended after a Caribou aircraft was hit forcing reliance on helicopter resupply, plans were prepared for Op Trident, the possible evacuation of the Simba position. Jigsaw pieces the critics as hyenas at a kill grab and chew over.

What is easily overlooked is the context. On the ground and to those in command in Dhofar and SAF HQ in Muscat, Simba represented a significant political counterstroke at an opponent commanding 80% of the jebel enclosing Salalah. Not a killer blow but a decisive punch. Strapped by the constraints of finite resources, manpower and limited ordnance, the operation was audacious and brave, launched against a mercurial guerilla force of reportedly 2,000 hard core communists, backed by up to 3,000 irregulars.

Once committed, the Sultanate could not withdraw, the loss of face potentially politically catastrophic to a watching world and significantly, to morale within SAF. Militarily, Simba sent a powerful message to the other side and their allies who could only guess at SAF's overreach to mount the operation. Still of greater importance, it awoke in the Arab world a notice to now respond with support for this newest member state of the Arab League and United Nations, pitted alone against the spread of communism reaching their doorsteps.

As one of the bit players, as Alan would refer to those of us under 25, I never got to ask, but as Sandy later put it to me, it is not inconceivable the concept for Simba may have been based on that of the "Admin Box" in the Burma Campaign in 1944: occupy key ground behind the enemy lines, create a strong defensive position, invest it with considerable firepower, resupply it by air and invite the enemy to expend energy, troops and other resources on attacking it. The risks were considerable, but so were the potential gains.

The perceived danger of revolutionary Marxists overthrowing the Middle East's monarchial countries was now realised. These monarchies reacted quickly to support the young Sultan and his British-led forces, sending supplies of weapons, vehicles and ordnance. Eventually substantial reinforcements in manpower followed plus weaponry gifted or loaned by the kingdoms of Iran, Jordan, Saudi Arabia and the UAE, which combined with the British effort, would lead ultimately to victory over the Marxist threat in the region. Arguably Simba had been the key.

RADIO ADEN: PROPAGANDA BROADCASTS

STATEMENT SAYS THAT TWO HOUR BATTLE TOOK PLACE BETWEEN THE FRONT AND ENEMY FORCES... IN DHOFAR. THE FRONT TOOK THE INFILTRATORS BY SURPRISE, KILLING 20 MERCENARIES AND DESTROYING AN ENEMY MACHINE GUN AND ARTILLERY EMPLACEMENT... THE SAME DAY ANOTHER LIBERATION FRONT GROUP ATTACKED ENEMY CONCENTRATIONS KILLING 15 MERCENARIES AND TWO HIGH-RANKING BRITISH OFFICERS. THE GROUP DESTROYED AN ENEMY WIRELESS SET, AN ENEMY GUN AND ITS CREW.

DHOFAR LIBERATION FORCES CLAIM FIVE BRITISH OFFICERS, 35 + MERCENARIES KILLED AT TAQAH

One of the best channels for ascertaining adoo losses was listening to Radio Aden's nightly radio broadcasts, when mention might be made reporting adoo losses, countered by victories against the Sultan's British imperialist-led mercenary army. Inflated SAF losses against equally understated own casualty rates. A tactic of every war.

It became increasingly common to hear SAF suffering significant loss of life, weapons and armoured cars. At the time, we'd lost one car to rocket fire, one stolen by a defector and a number to anti-tank mines. SEP reports revealed adoo commanders gave priority to knocking out armoured vehicles. With barely six roadworthy at any one time, SAF could ill afford to lose a single Saladin in battle, notwithstanding the effect to soldier morale.

Seen as indestructible to all but rocket attack, the Saladins were known to be capable of withstanding close quarter machine gun fire, even armoured piercing rounds bounced off armoured plate. And mortar shrapnel was of no effect. The loss of a car, as had occurred the previous July, would have represented a considerable blow to SAF, whilst reinforcing the apparent invincibility of a highly motivated communist enemy.

Measured against SAF losing one of their few armoured cars, was the psychological victory to an enemy. And rightly so – man pitched against formidable machine. Little realised was the vulnerability of these machines with their constant oil leaks from engines and gun hydraulics, missing parts and basic equipment, shortages of fuel and ammunition. And in close quarter fighting, crews had to rely on narrow periscopes for vision; a fact discovered to our cost when these glass apertures became prime targets for enemy machine gunners.

Essentially among the primary objectives the adoo craved, were to take out a Saladin or bring down a Strikemaster jet fighter. Either would count as a major propaganda victory, one they were prepared to fight and pay dearly for.

The nine of us crewing my Saladins knew that. Equally so did every pilot.

AKOOT'S EVACUATION

By 24 April and under daily attack, the evacuation of essential equipment and ordnance was stalling. That morning Col Nigel decided to pull me from Simba back to Akoot.

Approximately sixty men, of whom probably fewer than fifty could properly fire a weapon, held Akoot's 1000m diameter natural concave of desolate baked earth, rock and small wadis, dirt tracks and rusting barbed wire. Hemmed in by minefields, both ours and theirs, the SAF rearguard manned a few selected sangars amongst the many empty ones skylining the southern ridge east to west.

Rockets and mortar incomers now reached previously safe areas, including the airstrip north of camp. Akoot base had become a liability. Fixed wing aircraft, required for evacuating our stripped down 5.5in Howitzer, quantities of ammo, ordnance, stores and other equipment deemed too valuable to leave behind, could no longer land safely. Under accurate fire and potholed by incomers, the runway was out of business.

Evacuation at a standstill with the cessation of aircraft landings, Graham's much depleted force continued to hold out against an increasingly confident enemy sensing possible victory, now engaging from ever closer ranges.

SAF had held the jebel stronghold since NFR established the position in 1970, naming it Karlsberg, more in hope than expectation. Situated 5,000m north of the Sheershitti caves complex, the Adoo's stronghold, had allowed for operations south into the adoo-held treeline. Good men had died or been wounded holding the position, or on active patrols from the base. Now we were vacating the place that had been home for many, albeit probably never one close to hearts.

In the lead up to Simba, DR had mined all approach wadis and open ground leading to the camp's flanks and front. Whilst this gave a degree of protection from conventional assault by infantry, it provided none against rocket, mortar and machine gun attack. And in their turn, the adoo had ringed the camp with a necklace of Chinese and Russian mines.

Briefing us that day, Col Nigel decided on aggressive action to push the adoo back in a bid to re-open the runway and 'sew up' Akoot's evacuation. OC DR had a flair for words.

A day later 3 Coy DR flew in from Simba for Operation White Ants, a joint DR/ACS operation over two days, 26/27 April. Dating from WW1, code names were initiated to confuse the enemy. The tradition endures.

OPERATION WHITE ANTS

Callsigns
Major Sherwell – OC Akoot – Sand 9A
Capt Gough-Chrispin OC 3 Coy DR – Sand 39
Capt Morgan-Evans 2ic 3 Coy DR – Sand 39A
Capt McGrath OA – Golf 2
Capt Hodgson – Tango 12
Sgt Oliver – Tango 12A
Sgt Costello – T12B

25 Apr
3 x HE & 2 boxes .30 fired in my absence. Stand-to 1300-1600
1830-1915
3305 stand-to net (channel 6)

Parcel fm Hong Kong – new lighter. Black tape for mug.
3 Coy arrive from Mainbrace. O Group with Jonathan as soon as he arrives. Graham OC. Col's aggressive 'show of force' to open up runway and cover Akoot withdrawal.

Sit-reps
Leopard - 6 SEP. HH Bravo contact - s.a.   Simba - I know.
HF today
1015 - 518632 - 25   1520 - 534639 - 25   See Khalfan ref. Ramp clearing
1115 - 533634 - 25   1610 - 520623 - 5.5
1220 - 542639 - 5.5   1705 - 489611 - 25
1300 - 498626 - 25   1815 - 520631 - 25
1410 - 520618 - 25

It was good meeting Jonathan and Dick again as we made for Graham's O Group. Blunt and to the point, he outlined our mission: 3 Coy with ACS take and hold Vimy Ridge; Pioneers to repair and reopen runway allowing STOL evacuation to continue.

With the airfield no longer viable, Akoot like Simba was now cut off for resupplies of water, rations and munitions. Work dismantling the camp had been suspended. Amongst those of us stranded were a team of British Air Despatch NCOs and FREME (mechanical engineers), up from Salalah to dismantle and airfreight ordnance, the 25 pdrs and 5.5in.

As to Vimy Ridge, we knew the area and knew the form. Moving out before daybreak next day, we'd take adoo-held territory 3.5km south of Akoot, a whaleback ridge spanning 3km east/west, long ago designated Vimy Ridge by Alex Lamond, DR's enigmatic Ops officer. We were to hold the ridge until the airstrip was repaired and airlift completed, allowing for a two-day operation. I planned taking two cars, the third I'd hold at Akoot in depth. We'd ferry GPMG ammo for 3 Coy on our rear decks.

Khalfan's DR recce platoon would mine-clear the south ramp and part of the track leading south from Akoot ridge before first light the next day, remaining on picquet, securing our escape route back.

A fairly sustained HF programme throughout the day was hoped to dissuade the adoo from ranging on the airstrip. It may have worked; there were no incomers that day.

The 'Huey post' delivered a parcel from HK, a much prized Dunhill cigarette lighter and a lens for my camera, ordered on a visit to the UAG Mess, via a catalogue on an earlier R&R. Before online shopping, catalogues proved a reasonably reliable system enabling the purchase of essentials. I also procured some 'gaffa tape' to replace an increasingly pungent frayed section on my tin mug, long past its sensible use-by-date.

26 APRIL – WHITE ANTS DAY 1

Under cover of darkness and with the ramp cleared of mines, we moved out before sunrise. I quote from my diarised notes the ops briefing, 2000hrs, 25th April.

> *Evacuation plan for Day 1: 1 x 25 pdr out? 6 x flights Caribou – inshallah.*
>
> *Op. White Ants 1: T12, 12A with 3 Coy. Aim: Aggressive response: stop adoo fire onto airstrip. 3 Coy move out 0230. Cars 0530 – back, last light. Vimy posns 12 - C14, 12A - B12. 12B cover west 2 Coy's old position. Mors remain Akoot ridge. Jonathan x4 boxes GPMG carried on Saladins.*
>
> *Contact: 1520 Adoo fired fm area of A21 – 2 rounds & 8 fm B14? Hard to tell exactly which wadis they're firing fm. Flies all day. Sun hot, no shirt, having to wear jersey.*
>
> *Contact: 1745 engaged sangar grid 492629 – two adoo ops sighted. SEVEN shots to hit!! My fault, couldn't get range – a <u>lot</u> of dead ground to tgt. Jonathan reckoned range 2500m as well – not the 1700m it turned out to be. Sangar demolished. Dead ground = overshoot!*
>
> *Caribou collected TWO punctures at Mainbrace today, so only one load from Akoot. Same tarteeb tomorrow.*

We joined 3 Company before first light, two Saladins, Olly's T12A and my car, T12. Hull down along Vimy Ridge, we covered 3 Coy building new sangars along the ridge, for none dared use old ones. T12B, Lou, was 3,500 metres to our rear on Akoot ridge.

Both contacts were long range and ineffective, the adoo probably gauging our strength along Vimy. We responded in kind with our 76mm, T12 – 6 x HE/T and 1 x HESH, T12A – 4 x HE/T. Determining correct ranges across desert heat shimmer and the dead ground of wadis between us and the adoo was always difficult. Once a target was bracketed, we almost always succeed with the third round. Firing had to be quick to keep the initiative. The anti-tank HESH round (high explosive squash head), designed to knock out armoured vehicles was, I'd discovered, best for demolishing even the best built sangar at nearly two kilometres. These rounds flattened six inch (15cm) reinforced concrete at that range.

The squadron had been issued with a single rangefinder, a Barr and Stroud 80cm base rangefinder. After his Oman service, Tim Cornwell submitted a paper urging rangefinders be fitted to all armoured vehicles. He questioned 'why have we the British had to rely on the commander's judgement for so long? Anything that gets you to within a thousand metres is useful in Oman . . . although . . . maps should not be forgotten . . . however, we were having to work with old air charts to a scale of 1/250,000 . . . maps which really do not help that much'.

The Squadron's newly acquired rangefinder was fitted to Tim's car. Prerogative? He was the squadron's best technical officer. But by installing the rangefinder on

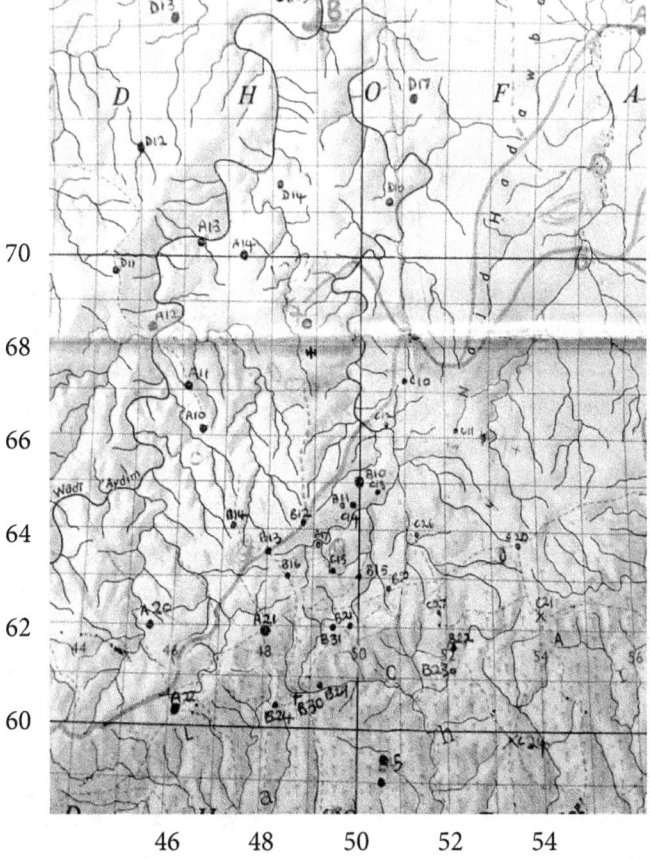

Akoot marked with a cross at grid. 485688; DFs – registered (defensive fire) targets A,B,C,D surround the base and highlighted lines indicate ancient routes through the mountains, still in use at the time. Wadi Aydim, held by the adoo runs north/south to the west of Akoot.

his Saladin for trials, this priceless equipment remained two days' drive away from front line Saladins. So we relied on maps.

The high Qamar jebel, exceptionally hot during the day, grew chilly at night when temperatures dropped dramatically. Still April and at altitude, with no clean shirt I'd resorted to wearing my issue BAOR jersey, warm at night, too hot by day. Three weeks of living rough and any last vestiges at personal hygiene had vanished. Unshaven, water rationed and unwashed as any Jebali, we made for a fragrant bunch.

Working hard, DR's pioneers had soon repaired the airstrip allowing STOL aircraft back, with flights continuing all day.

Jonathan remained with his half company dug in on Vimy when at last light my Saladins covered Dick's men back to reinforce the otherwise unprotected soft target Akoot had become. We took up night positions alongside Dick's men spread thinly along Akoot ridge.

27 APRIL – WHITE ANTS DAY 2

Adoo 496621
LCpl Nasir Hamid 800bzs short on pay – reimburse end month
Out again – in posn C14 – 0540. Best time of day, no flies. Cool breeze, soft light. Eyes sore after yesterday. Good dinner last night – braised steak! Starving after single tin bully beef shared with Ali and Abdullah, plus compo biscuits. Contact 1415 – 5 adoo, engaged – boys saw two adoo fall, I didn't. 1515 heavy contact. Nightmares aren't forgotten, no need for detail. Adoo 40 maybe 100? Own 4 WIA – Adoo 14 KIA, poss 8 WIA? Abdullah caught short, used 76mm shell case, poor bugger. Supper – crashed out, disturbed sleep.
Radio Aden later confirm 19 KIA, up to 20 WIA

Assembling at 0400hrs Nasir Hamid approached on the pressing matter of his pay packet, 800 baizas short (less than a pound). I noted the shortage, promising he'd be reimbursed next payday. Money mattered.

We left camp at 0430hrs reaching Jonathan before first light. Today I had TI2B, Lou, with me, Olly in T12A remained in depth at Akoot. A quiet morning when we'd managed to share a mug of sweet black tea, his signaller brewing on a smokeless fire hidden in his sangar. There was a long-range contact around 1400hrs, from 2km to our south at grid 496621. Nothing else moved. Receiving the all-clear from Graham, Akoot's airlifts now complete, we were ordered to pull back.

BATTLE FOR VIMY RIDGE

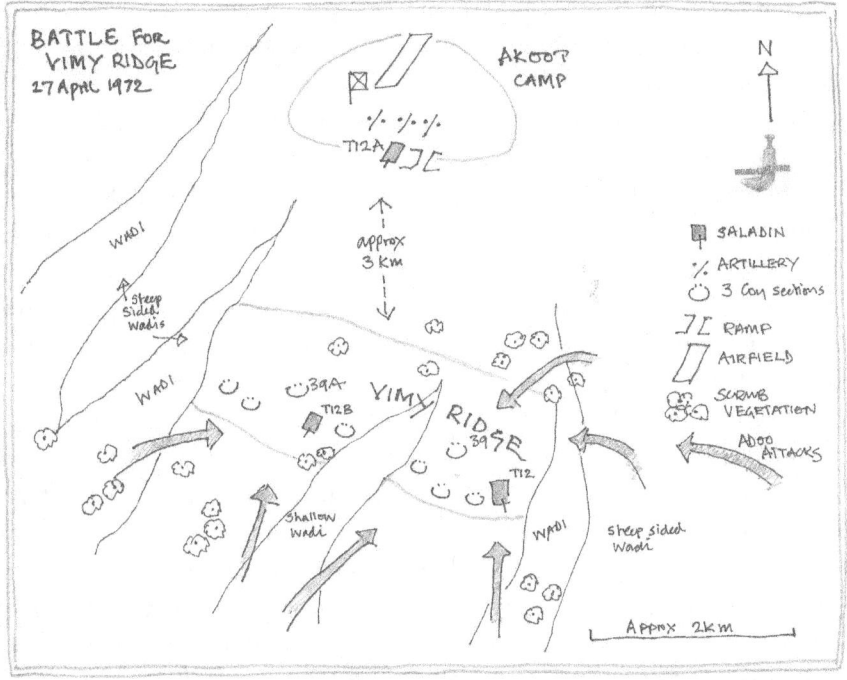

Sketch map showing approximate positions along Vimy Ridge, Saladins and 3 Coy DR

Under a relentless desert sun on an ordinary cloudless Omani afternoon, the ever-present flies buzzed annoyingly as we began to withdraw. It was a little past 1500hrs.

Jonathan withdrew 3 Coy some 150 metres as we waited his signal to fall back past him to cover his next withdrawal, past my two Saladins. We called it leapfrogging. Jonathan radioed 3 Coy were in position covering the vulnerable exit off Vimy. Our turn to pull back.

As we moved, all hell let loose. The first I heard was the sound of bullets smashing into the body of my commander's .30 Browning. 'Crack!' a bullet struck, wedged between canvas ammo belt and the Browning's top cover. 'Bang, Bang, Bang, Bang' another four hit the alloy skinned ammo box, cleanly piercing the thin casing, straight through the belted Browning ammo. I stared incredulously at the holed box above my head. 'No explosions?' The Kalashnikov bullets had missed the belted rounds. 'Yallah!' exclaimed Abdullah Ali, leaning back to stare wide eyed at the damaged gun and holed ammo box, followed immediately by some incomprehensible Arabic shouted to Ali Hamdan in the driver's seat which may have translated to 'Corr f… you should see this!'

I couldn't believe it. Directly above my head, the commander's machine gun was jammed. The adoo were using armoured piercing ammo. Tungsten, I realised, nothing else would be capable of causing such immediate damage to a Browning machine gun casing.

The noise was deafening – as if the turret was being pummelled by hammers. Bullets striking the turret bounced off in every direction, hailstones on a steel roof. Abdullah fired back with his coax Browning. On and on the bullets struck, crash! smash! crash! as I thought 'Shitttt . . . there must be hordes of them to sustain such fire power'.

The attack was perfect in its timing. Furious, your immediate thought's 'how the fuck did they get behind us?'. Managing to move through dead ground they'd now an enfilade advantage direct onto our two isolated cars. Letting the infantry withdraw, they'd timed their attack to hit the Saladins.

Caught trousers down, we'd been ambushed in broad daylight. For two days we'd concentrated on the south, focusing on known enemy-held territory. Overlooked to our east, a hidden wadi system that would have been well known to the adoo. We'd been guilty of making a bloody obvious mistake born from arrogance in our ability to take and hold positions against an assumed lesser foe.

Despite Jonathan's half company remaining on Vimy Ridge through the night, the adoo had stealthily moved into concealed ambush positions to attack as they chose the following day.

Returning that morning with Dick's half company, sweeping the area for mines towards Vimy Ridge, I'd positioned Lou to my right back, facing west as I joined Jonathan on a hillock at C14. Clockwork, all done before stand-to at daybreak. Olly, I'd left positioned 3500 metres back on Akoot ridge guarding our rear. This gave us depth should we be forced to fight a retreat from Vimy. In the event it proved a battle saving decision when we needed our backs covered.

The first day's contacts had been long range. Likewise, this morning's. Overconfident, we'd become blasé. Lulled into a false sense of security and thinking we were good at this stuff, we'd relaxed in the safe knowledge we'd the greater numbers, the superior fire power. After long months taking the shit thrown at us in Akoot, we could take it and survive.

We were wrong. Gifted with two solitary Saladins separated from infantry by 150m, the attack was concentrated and ferocious, the firepower indicating serious numbers. The adoo's plan? Phase 1, remain distant, lob a few mortars and RCL rockets; Phase 2, attack as SAF withdraw. Strike when the other side are most vulnerable. Bag a Saladin. Perfect.

I moved to join Lou who'd called he was surrounded.

BATTLE FOR VIMY RIDGE

EXTRACT FROM TIM CORNWELL'S OFFICIAL CONTACT REPORT:

(The armour/infantry screen was deployed in roughly the same positions as on the previous day with T12 (Capt Hodgson) and Sand 39 (Captain Gough-Crispin) on C14: *(to their rear-right)* T12B (Sgt Costello) and Sand 39A (Capt Morgan-Evans) on B12; and T12A (Sgt Oliver) *(in depth)* on the Akoot Ridge at 488668.

At 1414hrs five men were seen at 497623 and S39A engaged with a very accurate airburst – men were seen to fall.

There appeared to be no more movement and at 1510, ordered to withdraw, S39 moved back to a position at 496648. T12 then pulled back to B10 (496647) and instantly came under heavy small arms fire from the SW. He immediately went forward to join T12B on the B12 position and both cars returned fire onto enemy positions... T12B engaged with HE/T and saw men fall. While this was going on S39 had contact... and T12 telling T12B to remain in position facing SW moved forward to assist Sand 39 who by now was surrounded... During his move back T12 again came under heavy fire causing damage to his Saladin... and saw men on the C14 position which had been vacated by S39 on the initial withdrawal. The air was jammed at this time and assuming these (men) to be enemy opened up with co-ax... ceasing firing when he saw a radio antenna and realised that S39 must have moved forward without his knowledge. T12 drove forward to S39's position and found Capt Gough-Crispin had a bullet leg wound and three soldiers wounded... stone splinters. Parking over the wounded he engaged the advancing enemy. T12 radioed for helicopter casevac and directed the jets which had just arrived, onto enemy positions. The jets could only fire mg as the enemy were too close to use rockets. T12 was anxious to get the wounded out of danger and called up (an infantry) section to evacuate them while he directed mortars onto 505644 and gave covering fire.

During this time the jets were directed at B21 (498620) and T12B with S39A continued to engage the enemy on the SW ridge... T12A meanwhile saw seven men at 505653 which was behind T12 and having confirmed that these were not our own men put down 5 HE/T on target and filled in with one and half belts of .30 co-ax Browning.

T12 was still having a large amount of fire directed at him and the infantry section was having difficulty in making any forward progress to rescue the wounded. He therefore ordered T12A forward to assist him put down covering fire, enabling him to load the wounded onto the rear deck of T12B. Arty fire was brought down onto 496637, 506642, and 500620 and every available weapon put down covering fire while T12B withdrew with the wounded . . . safely back to Akoot.

Once the casualties had been evacuated T12 was able to move further forward . . . engaged a section of three men. Later enemy at 479641, 486635 and 490635 were seen and engaged by T12 and T12A. T12 then engaged a section of six men moving through scrub at 499639 . . . with co-ax and main armament, joined by T12A firing with .30 to confirm the kill.

T12B returned from evacuating the casualties bringing with him Browning for the cars and GPMG ammunition which by this stage was getting very low. Sgt Costello showed great courage by leaving his car and delivering the ammunition to the GPMG section in person, the whole position being under accurate machine gun fire at the time.

T12B moved back to B10 whilst T12 directed jet strikes onto enemy positions at 500620 and 506643. During the jet strike they came under ground fire from positions at 498619 and T12, T12A and S39's GPMG's returned fire. T12A moved back to Akoot ridge to cover the position's back door.

By now the contact had lasted nearly four hours and last light was approaching. The jets had to RTB and under cover of darkness both our own and the enemy forces withdrew. The contact ended at 1950hrs.

5. 4 WIA 3 Coy DR

6. At least 18 enemy were seen to fall.

7. 41 HE/T, 41 HESH, 34 belts .30 Browning

8. The enemy seemed to be either very brave or drugged. They appeared oblivious of any shells that did not land amongst them.

9. T12 had three periscopes smashed during this contact and his commander's machine gun damaged by direct fire. Four rounds penetrated the commander's machine gun feed box, from the front cutting canvas feed belt without striking rounds.

T12 shot out two .30 co-ax barrels, T12B a single co-ax barrel.)

ALL OR NOTHING – THE BATTLE FOR VIMY RIDGE

'Don't bother ducking, the men don't like it and it doesn't do any good'

Lord Longford (prior to leading a cavalry charge over open ground at Gallipoli, 21 Aug 1915. The charge to capture a strategically important hill was accomplished. His body was never recovered.)

As the forwardmost car, mine had offered the best target. Bullets pelted the turret, bouncing away until suddenly smashing my front facing periscopes and vision forwards. Hearing the sights smashed, Abdullah responded, engaging the high ground, firing a burst of coax.

Lou called: he was surrounded. I moved forward to my right to give covering fire. I'd a single spare periscope strapped in its holder. Pulling down on a damaged sight, it wouldn't budge. Stuck fast. I went to another, stuck too. And the third. 'Damm!' I muttered, hitting the last with the palm of my hand which hurt and didn't do any good at all.

Eyes fixed to his gunsight, Abdullah shouted 'adoo!', firing the Browning. The noise added to the furious rattle of rounds hitting the turret. Bang! an incoming mortar landed. Cursing in frustration, sights that removed easily when cleaning wouldn't budge. Then I saw why: striking the exposed alloy framed glass sight, bullets had wedged top sections solid against the steel openings.

'Hammer?' I thought, finding a heavy adjustable spanner. Whacking the most damaged sight smashed the bodywork, splintering glass and alloy fragments into my lap. It worked. Hurriedly fitting the spare top sight, I re-attached the undamaged bottom section. A splinter of glass had cut my eyebrow which bled messily for a while. My one spare sight used, I'd now vision forwards, cracked glass of the other two giving distorted views, but sight anyway.

Peering ahead I could make out a radio antenna close to where we'd just engaged. Then it hit me. I called Jonathan by radio; nothing, airwaves jammed. Communication gone, I grabbed my National handset. Same result, everyone trying to give orders at once jamming the air. I shouted to Ali to take us forward to the hillock above the antenna.

I glimpsed men leaping between boulders towards us. There seemed a lot. Jonathan must have seen them too and rushed to secure the hilltop. Parking past the group I took to be injured, Abdullah let rip with the coax. We had to hold this hill. Who held here won.

Suddenly, firing ceased. I called to Ali to switch off the engine and shouting to the men outside, they called back in confirmation. They were alive! I shouted, 'Get under the car!'. I called for casevac as we restarted engines. Another mortar landed close. Parked over the men, I daren't use main armament I'd loaded with HE/T for fear of deafening them, so Abdullah maintained bursts of fire with the coax, traversing left to right and back again.

Suddenly stillness. Nothing moved. Abdullah looked across at me, shock and dismay written across his face, ashen, sweating profusely. In that split second, we stared at each other, unspoken disbelief amongst the acrid fumes filling the turret. Stunned by realisation at what had happened, I realised it was my responsibility.

A great pit opened in my stomach, threatening to consume me. The car commander takes responsibility.

'Now earn your fucking spurs,' I rebuked myself, reaching across the breech to shake my gunner by the shoulder, shouting, 'Abdullah! It's mine! My responsibility!' repeated again to reassure him. My responsibility, mine. Hearing rounds smashing my sights and Browning, Abdullah had engaged the hill. Of course they were adoo; 3 Coy had withdrawn. He'd done the right thing. Pointing to his gunsight I shouted 'now, look for adoo'!

We had to hold this bluff – losing it and the adoo commanded the eastern ridge. We might survive, most of 3 Coy could be wiped out. And we had wounded beneath the car.

The airwaves cleared and I got through to Graham in the ops tent. He sounded calm, he'd ordered jets. They'd be with us as soon as possible, returning from Simba they'd give us brief top cover. He'd now ordered a casevac helicopter but we needed to get the wounded to Akoot as the adoo 'would drop the Huey'. I knew that. We'd evacuate the men ourselves.

Calling a DR section forward to assist with the wounded, the adoo attacked again, running towards us. I'd no idea they'd worked round behind the hill. Another hail of bullets hit the turret, taking out my one working radio antenna. Now I'd just a handheld National. Despite its limited range I could still speak with Akoot. I also had my Sarbe, the handheld radio designed to assist locating crashed aircraft, issued to Saladin commanders for emergency contact with planes. Operating on the distress frequency 121.5 megahertz, these little radios gave you direct voice contact with men who flew jets. Lifesavers.

The DR section replied they were pinned down. We were still taking a lot of fire as the men sheltered beneath us. Then the jets came in. Announcing their arrival, they screamed in low across our position. No need for smoke grenades; easy to spot, two Saladins on a ridge of barren desert. The air cleared of bullets. Making contact I gave a fire mission, all in front of our two cars held adoo.

Too close for rockets, they dived in from the west, blazing 7.62mm machine guns. This we knew the adoo feared most. Jets' machine guns didn't have to score a bullseye. Able to shelter behind rock from direct rifle fire, it was the madness of jet fired ricochets bouncing off rocks and boulders they most feared. A hailstorm of bullets. Must have been terrifying. The Strikemasters returning from a mission over Simba radioed they could only remain for three more runs. We were promised others would take their place. And they did.

It was imperative I get the wounded out. A long shot, but we might evacuate using the rear decks of a Saladin.

I called T12A forward to join us. Asking jets to 'hold north' until my third Saladin arrived then strafe our front again whilst we evacuated the wounded. Moving Olly to take Lou's position, we'd get the wounded out on Lou's car. Radioing jets to 'take out' each side of the north/south ridge between Akoot and Vimy, I wanted the scrub-filled wadis cleared of any adoo waiting to ambush us carrying the wounded.

With engines screaming at full power, Olly arrived to take Lou's position as he moved across, dropping into the shallow wadi behind me. Through my rear sight I'd seen Lou arrive. Calling Olly to give us covering fire and switching our engine off again, I shouted to those beneath the car not to move. Restarting, we crept forward over the men to the ridgeline's top. Now we were fully exposed but the jets were doing a great job raking the area ahead with their machine guns. Olly moved again to better protect us as the wounded were lifted onto T12B's rear decks. Asking Lou his ammo status, he too was low on Browning. 'Bring us what you can, also Gimpy for 3 Coy.' With a final 'See yer later!', a thumbs up and he'd gone. Olly moved back towards Vimy's western position. Reversing to hull down below the ridgeline, we were ready to recommence battle. With nobody beneath the car we'd use main armament.

Abdullah saw them first and immediately we engaged with HE/T at men advancing across our fronts. Mortar and rocket appeared to be coming from a ridge further back, beyond the advancing adoo and they had our range.

The Saladin's full complement of HE/T, HESH and Canister shells are stored in racks within the turret, the fighting compartment. Projectiles point downwards, 11 between commander and gunner, a further 12 on the left and 11 on the right between commander and driver. The last eight rounds are stored behind the gunner's and commander's seats.

At the centre of each upended shell case is a percussion cap, patiently awaiting attention of the gun's firing pin. It's protected by a high-tensile steel clip clamped to the base, a safety feature against accidental impact. It's a devil to undo hurriedly. Attempts at quick release resulted in cut forefingers. Needing to reload frequently, unclipping singly was taking too long. With each lull in firing, I'd loosen a few, allowing for speedier loading.

Glancing sideways, Abdullah grinned at me, 'sharbash, sahb', before shouting a few unintelligible words to Ali in the driver's seat. With upwards of 40 rounds of TNT explosive inside the turret, it'd take just one unlucky ricochet hitting an unprotected primer – and oblivion.

Reloading, I'd slide the loosened protector clip off the shell case with my left hand, simultaneously gripping the exposed rim with my right and manually lift the vertically stored round into the gun's still smoking open breech. Using a tightly clenched left fist, your arm as a ram, the round is pushed home into the chamber, avoiding trapping fingers or thumb as the breech slams upwards, shut. A satisfyingly heavy metallic clunk signals the round's safely loaded. With a yell 'Mahmal!' (Loaded!), Abdullah'd respond 'Ramee daheen!' (Firing now!) whilst pressing down on the gun's foot-operated trigger.

Each commander was acutely aware of trapping a digit in the breech but none did. It didn't bear thinking about. Best keep thumb and fingers clenched tightly in a fist. Catastrophe awaited the premature firing by your gunner, pushing the gun's trigger whilst the commander/loader still had his fist against the breech. The recoil would pulverise an arm. That's why he waits for your shout of 'loaded!' I hear Gunnery Instructors advise.

The turret's heat increased steadily with each shot fired. Constant reloading was hot work, clothes quickly became soaked with sweat and grime, maintaining a rapid rate of fire.

Still the adoo leapt forward from cover to cover. Reflecting later, I was staggered at their bravery against what must have appeared a formidable objective. Tenacious in battle, they wouldn't give in. Perhaps the prize was worth the sacrifice?

With cut fingers and sweat pouring down aching arms, Abdullah turned to me briefly as I reloaded. We were filling up with empty cases we'd somehow need to throw out of the turret. I received a thumbs up and wide grin back. I would not have had anyone else beside me at that moment, he and Ali, my driver.

THE UNWRITTEN CODE

T12B returned laden with boxes of Browning and Gimpy ammo. Jumping from his car, Lou dropped 7.62 supplies at Dick's position and two boxes .30 in the wadi behind mine. Olly returned to his position on Akoot ridge as Lou resumed his to my right. The DR sergeant nearest me radioed he'd fetch my ammo, heaving the boxes onto the rear decks. We'd collect as soon as we could.

Ensuring safe evacuation of the wounded and for getting the ammo to us, Lou and the Baluchi sergeant had demonstrated conspicuous bravery, each man subsequently mentioned in despatches. Such moments evinces the unwritten code between soldiers, that once down, wounded, in a tight corner (or low on ammo), there'd be someone who'd risk their all to get you out.

During the adoo's first rush we'd fired perhaps 10 rounds in quick succession at close range. The turret, filling with acrid smoke and hot 76mm shell cases, needed emptying to avoid jamming the gun's traverse gearing. Reaching down, I grabbed a spent case and heaved it out through the commander's cupola to receive a burst of automatic fire in response. Back right, Lou'd noticed and opened fire to my immediate front, giving us sufficient respite to clear the turret. 'Thanks, Irish!' I radioed.

Again, I glimpsed movement. Men leaping towards us, effortlessly as wolves, bounding between rocky outcrops and cover, closing in. We opened fire. We were now firing main armament under 150m. Lou's Brownings raked the ground ahead.

The rancid smell of spent explosive can be overpowering. Sweating hands slowed seizing rounds to load quickly. The continuous loading caused arm muscles to protest. Each 76mm projectile weighs 16lb (7.5 kg), an awkward lump to be wielding about in a cramped turret. We'd been in the car since 0430hrs and our drinking water was running low, despite eking out supplies. It was vital we maintained our water consumption, sweating so profusely in the Saladin's confined space.

With another lull we searched the broken ground for movement, detecting none. Reaching to drink from my chargul, I noticed Abdullah's look of discomfort. The man never complained about anything and I realised something was wrong. Sliding off his gunner's seat he'd crouched beside the gun's breechblock. Spent cases still littered the turret floor. He doubled over cursing to himself. At this Ali Hamdan shouted from his driver's seat, only to receive an incomprehensible reply, yet I could detect the dismay in his voice. Without a word, Abdullah whipped down his khaki trousers, grabbed hold of a spent case into which he emptied his bowels, explosively. Having an opening three inches (76mm) wide, a spent case is just nine inches (232mm) high. Remarkably most of what Abdullah intended went into the brass shell case which only shortly before had fired a high explosive round. He'd chosen well – most of the shell cases were burning hot; this was clearly cool enough to handle or indeed shit into. Occasionally extreme danger might speed up the body's normally controlled functions but with Abdullah Ali, it'd been something he'd eaten.

Without time to think how the hell he'd managed it, Abdullah looked round for anything with which to clean himself. I tore pages from my notebook; it didn't work. Passing an old shemagh, I handed him the substitute bog paper. The well worn material tore easily. Nothing needed saying. Wiping himself clean, he dressed and mopped the splattered turret floor. It'd taken seconds.

Lifting the receptacle through the cupola, with a final shove Abdullah heaved it out to land safely away from us with a thud. Without a word, he was back in his seat, hands to gun handles, eye to sights searching for enemy movement. Nothing was moving.

By now eardrums were ringing. Flimsy rubber headsets and no ear defenders left eardrums vulnerable. We relied on shemaghs for helmets – as did every SAF servicemen. Helmets and ear-defenders would have helped.

With the lull, we moved ammo nearer for my loading, traversing the turret left and right, allowing access to the tightly restricted racks around us, selecting our remaining spare ammunition. At the most hectic we'd fired five HESH rounds as fast as I could lift and load them, whilst Abdullah calmly traversed, aimed and fired at the rushing adoo. They'd run towards us despite taking casualties. We'd see them fall, knocked violently backwards or sideways as machine guns fired and 76mm shells burst amongst them.

These men were unbelievably brave. Seemingly oblivious to the fire directed towards them. Just when nothing seemed to stop them, as quickly as a rush had begun, sudden stillness followed. Nothing moved bar dust settling. We'd wait. Then up again another group would put luck to chance and dart forward, rock to rock, shallow hollow to small wadi. 'Adoo yameen!' (Enemy right!) shouted from the driver's seat, Ali searching through his three fixed driver's sights, and rapidly we'd traverse onto target and fire.

Gradually, the lulls became more frequent. Keeping watch through my damaged periscopes, Abdullah lifted the still hot empty shell cases threatening to trap the traversing gear. Jammed, and we'd be finished. Passing me the hot shell cases I'd grab each and, ducking sideways, throw them out, every time drawing a short burst of automatic fire smattering against the turret. They weren't giving up.

GRENADES ARRIVE AND WE LOSE OUR COAX BROWNING

After that last attack Abdullah shouted he'd a problem with his coax Browning. Despite controlled bursts, he'd had to maintain a high rate of fire. When hand grenades landed close, I'd ordered longer bursts to push the adoo back. Stopping only to reload, he was using the coax to its maximum potential.

I should have realised the way he was putting down such a rate of fire, he might shoot out the barrel's rifling. Now telling him to fire a short burst, I saw his tracer rounds spiralling uselessly towards the enemy, still dangerous, but ineffective for the accuracy required.

We'd now no effective coax machine gun. Our left flank was dangerous, we'd seen movement in the wadi's scrub. Radioing Olly to lay down 'covering fire left', we pulled back into the hollow behind us, leaving my DR section on the small bluff we were holding. I'd use the barrel from my damaged Browning. Reaching up, I started to dismantle the damaged machine gun above my head. Immediately automatic fire opened up as I ducked instinctively, whipping head and arms back inside the vehicle's cab. 'Shiiiit, that's close,' I cursed. Needing no translation, Abdullah traversed sharply left ready to fire if we saw anything, I'd already reloaded HE. The adoo had now got to within 100 metres behind us, cutting us off from the balance of 3 Company and Lou's car to my rear right and rear. With me, I'd a three-man section who'd now dropped back beside my car. We had to hold this high ground.

Olly radioed he'd seen the adoo and requested using HE so close to my car – only one answer – and Bang! then again Bang! Olly engaged with five rounds HE from a range of approximately 3,500 metres. He was spot on target. Fearing he might hit us he'd swapped seats with his gunner and using a tactic we'd practised, fired co-ax to range onto target, followed immediately with the 76mm. He then followed with bursts of Browning. It was an incredible display of firing.

'Thanks, Tango 12A – that's very pretty shooting – better watch our backs,' I radioed; 'Wilco, message understood' came the nonchalant reply. 'Thank God for Olly,' I thought, knowing I had to get the spare barrel. Reaching out of the turret again I began furiously unscrewing the Browning's barrel guard and then with a sharp twist, the barrel loosened as I spun it round freeing it from the gun's body. Dropping back into the turret, I cradled the heavy, still warm barrel and again incoming fire cracked overhead, but it was directed at Lou's car who was already firing back in return.

'Tango12 – Tango I2A, adoo to your east – firing now!' Ollie messaged as his 76mm barked twice in rapid succession taking out the adoo group. His shooting was extraordinarily good.

I realised we were low on .30 ammo. Only one thing for it: glancing across I told Abdullah what I had to do and without stopping leapt out of the turret reaching the two boxes the sergeant had thrown onto the rear decks. In one movement I had grabbed the boxes and heaved them through my cupola following them back inside the turret. Olly's covering fire had silenced the adoo behind us.

Meanwhile, Abdullah was having problems unscrewing the coax barrel. After two hours' constant firing, the barrel had expanded in its housing; it was also too hot to touch. Stripping off his shirt to protect his hands from burning, he finally released the swollen barrel, the sweat-dampened shirt's material steaming, adding to the turret's already ripe stench.

As he handed me the useless barrel, I leant across, offering mine to fit into the coax's body. Stashing the still piping hot barrel behind me, I bent down to throw out a number of empty shell cases. The brass empties flying out of the turret still attracted automatic fire. Still small arms fire. And now again hand grenades were thrown landing to our front. What was the DR section doing? The adoo were too bloody close.

My DR soldiers were out of ammo.

THE ADOO RUSH AGAIN

Ali shouted from his cramped driver's seat 'adoo hina – adoo hina, sahb!!' (The adoo are here!) We'd no machine guns. You have to stay cool, I told myself as I reached back for my Sterling, cocking it as I pushed it past my chest out through the hatch and fired a long sweeping burst, spraying the area in front. An unwieldy weapon with two hands, single handed is like trying to control an angry terrier.

Following with shorter bursts, firing wildly, peering through my inadequate periscopes, I soon emptied the magazine's 34 rounds. Pulling back inside, I reloaded. Out again, I now fired short bursts realising I had to conserve this puny gun's ammunition. I called Lou on the Panasonic to hit everything to my front. Typically, he responded as I spoke, Brownings and 76mm blasting the area ahead of us.

I was firing little 9mm bullets against a determined enemy firing Kalashnikovs and throwing F1 hand grenades – small green Russian hand grenades that make a lot of noise. An uneven contest at any time but firing a pop-gun had somehow slowed men leaping towards us. We were nevertheless rapidly losing the initiative. Might have to give up this hill?

I ordered the DR section back – they were useless to me without ammunition.

'We can't lose a Saladin,' I told myself, glancing across at Abdullah on the point of ordering Ali to engage high reverse (armoured corps phrase for 'get the hell out of here') when my cool headed gunner turned, grinned and gave me thumbs up, letting rip with now short bursts of rapid fire, traversing back and forth to our left flank. The moment had passed, and we were back, the playing field levelled.

LCpl Abdullah Ali had moved as lighting, refitting the replacement barrel. Probably took minutes. It'd felt a lifetime. I noticed we both had bloodied knuckles and arm grazes. Adrenalin pumping, you don't feel a thing. We were back in business.

Olly in eliminating the adoo behind our hilltop and Lou clearing our front had given us the space we'd needed. As we went forward again, the jets returned. 'Hello Tangos' crackled the Sarbe handset; Strikemasters. They screamed past low – a roar to make the heart thump, the very best sight imaginable, top cover was back!

I'd had an idea for directing jets to targets. Confirming they were picking out our 76mm tracer trajectory, I asked they follow through with machine guns. Three fire missions hitting target areas after our HE landed, the combination worked seamlessly. We were winning!

It'd grown quieter. Behind us, nothing, the danger neutralised by Olly. Then, 'Sahb' called Abdullah 'barmil maksoor!' (barrel's gone). I'd just seen the last coax burst spiralling into the distance as he fired. With tracers every fifth round, you'd follow the bullets. They were all over the place. I ordered cease fire. No point in advertising we'd shot out our second barrel. We'd no spare. If it came to the worst, with both machine guns 'shot out', we'd be relying on noise and our Sterlings, water pistols against Kalashnikovs. And we were getting low on 76mm.

CANISTER LOADED

I reached down and loaded Canister. This round effectively turns a large-calibre gun into a giant shotgun. Canister was used by American 37mm anti-tank guns in World War II to break up Japanese Banzai charges. During the Korean War, UN tanks facing massed Communist attacks, used canister-type rounds to 'sweep' enemy infantry. Effective. Unfortunately, canister rounds ruin a barrel's lining.

Incoming fire became sporadic small arms. An occasional mortar landed but now these too faded. The ground in front and flanks had become ominously quiet. Jets confirmed they couldn't see any more than we could. Had the adoo withdrawn? A standard tactic. But equally, were they grouping for an assault when we withdrew, as we must at last light? Ahead, bodies lay between rocky outcrops; none moved. Barring the hum of our engines, it was very quiet. Then Dick radioed that his men were dangerously low on ammunition, he'd one GPMG with half a belt left. They were down to rifles and his ammo limited to that in men's magazines. That was alarming, and both Saladins were getting worryingly low on stocks.

Also, he confirmed another fear: the men's charguls were empty, some since midday. The original plan to hold Vimy Ridge for the morning and be back in camp by mid-afternoon, had held until the adoo attacked. Some men had been out on the jebel for two consecutive days.

In the heat of battle even experienced men will forget the fundamental rule of desert survival: conserve water. And on active service, not only water but ammo; 3 Coy were almost out of both.

Jets had had to retire with the fading light and with the battle quietened, it seemed close quarter fighting had stopped. Time to withdraw. It'd soon be dark, but we were favoured by an almost full moon with cloudless skies, ensuring good night vision. Given the sorry state of 3 Coy's men, I agreed to Dick's request they withdraw first with Lou and I remaining to give cover.

Then as they were about to move out, Dick called again requesting we carry his GPMGs on our rear decks. His men were exhausted and the machine guns were dead weight without ammo. 'Make it quick,' I responded as the weapons were brought up to our cars. Scrambling out, Lou and I took their weapons and secured them across our Saladins' rear decks, away from the turrets we didn't need jammed by steel weapons.

LAST OFF VIMY RIDGE

3 Company fell back to take up positions 250m to our rear.

Expecting a counterattack at any minute, we waited, tense, eyes staring through inadequate sights, willing 3 Coy to their positions. Ghostly quiet, except for the purring of our two engines. 'Anything, Bravo?' I asked over the handheld National, to hear his Northern Irish lilt reply, 'No, notting here at all – some ferking bodies I can tell you!' and still transmitting, unforgettably to enquire '... would yer like a Kalashnikov?'

'NO!' I ordered in disbelief, 'Stay in your bloody car!' He was quite mad.

It'd grown deathly quiet. The moon shone over that April afternoon's scenes of havoc; scenes a David Lean movie would have filled with Maurice Jarre's emotive music. Yet as every soldier knows, there's never music, only noise or quiet.

The radio crackled, Dick messaged he was in position.

Moonlight offered sufficient light to motor through the scrub avoiding rocky outcrops. I sent Lou back first, covering his withdrawal. In turn he'd cover us as we withdrew through his position 75m back. We were tight, but in the dark we needed to see the other's silhouette. With no night sights, experience had taught our issue 8x30 Barr and Stroud binoculars were a pretty good alternative. But it meant head and shoulders out of turrets.

Arabia's darkness had dropped like a blanket, exposing the Saladins to a rushed assault. Acutely aware of the danger, six sets of eyes peered out into the darkness. You hardly dared breathe. Both drivers had had to open hatches to better see their route. Yet not a word or question was offered at the decision to cover 3 Company's withdrawal.

Silence was broken by Lou's voice radioing he was in position. Seamlessly we moved back, dropping past to cover him back and Lou moved again. We'd become a single unit, the synthesis complete, commands monosyllabic, reliant and confident in each's abilities and worth. Only death's finality breaks such a team.

Gunfire rang out, a short burst of automatic; totally ineffective. We watched as a stream of tracer floated slowly overhead, orange against silver stars. An adoo's parting shot, a final gesture of defiance, or 'fuck you!' to use a Ray Kane riposte.

Heartbeats thumped in ears lost to tinnitus, we fell back through camel-thorn but also frankincense, crushed beneath our cars, fragile producers of a sap once more valuable than gold.

Finally, Dick radioed he'd reached and was climbing the ramp at Akoot's southern ridge, where T12A had remained our sentinel approximately 30 metres above.

Getting there, Lou dismounted and walked his car up the ramp as I covered him. It was a slow business, the edge was precipitous. Then walking in front of my car, I led

Ali up the ramp using a lit cigarette cupped in my hand as an improvised marker. He stopped twice, losing sight of my hand. Each time I walked back and we'd start again. Progress was painfully slow, the ramp's edge becoming more dangerous the higher we climbed. Reaching the top and safety, we joined the two waiting Saladins and DR soldiers stood-to in sangars along the ridge. As we topped the ridge, Ali reigned back the accelerator and the roar of the Saladin's engine dimmed. Looking round before climbing back on board my car, I could make out the silhouetted lumps of my two other Saladins. With engines now idling, I became aware of cheering coming from the sangars at the top of the ramp. It was a moment not to forget.

Parked back at our sangars I climbed out of my turret thinking, 'We bloody made it. We *bloody* made it!' And the adoo hadn't bagged their Saladin.

The relief was tangible amongst those who'd trudged wearily back to Akoot. I'd seen Dick together with his men as they'd collected their Gimpys from our rear decks. Mentally and physically drained, they were whacked yet exhilarated. The high you reach escaping danger. There was much shaking of hands, slapping of sweaty backs and shoulders.

During the engagement my car had fired 40 rounds of main armament, Lou, 25 and Olly 17 rounds. My car fired 14 boxes of .30 Browning containing 250 canvas belted rounds and burned out two .30 machine gun barrels. 4 commander's turret sights had been hit plus one driver's sight; the commander's .30 Browning top casing damaged, struck by armour piercing rounds, the main radio antenna shot off, and two run-flat tyres punctured by bullets and shrapnel. The turret and forward slopes of the cars bore pop-marks where bullets had struck and bounced off. Lou's car had fired 12 boxes 'shooting out' the coax gunner's barrel and Olly's car, 8 boxes .30 Browning.

Grateful to be alive, exhausted, voices hoarse from inhaling propellant whilst shouting gun commands, hands cut and sore from loading the 76mm, drained of energy, emotion and now cold in damp clothing where earlier we'd been soaked with sweat, we were very thirsty. Olly with his gunner LCpl Nasir Mohamed handed us their charguls – the shared canvas tainted water tasted sweet as nectar.

Tim's contact report ends:

(At last we have proved what we have been trying to preach since we came to Dhofar. Armoured cars and infantry working together on the right sort of ground is a devastating combination.)

20

AKOOT REARGUARD

SAF withdraws from Akoot under constant attacks. The loneliness of the rearguard.

... the ACS ... in that awful Akoot ... fought running battles with the adoo as we were mounting Simba. The latter being no fools twigged what was going on and attacked Akoot, the op. mounting base ... Bloody lucky you were there to support a somewhat alarmed Graham Sherwell (sadly dead) whose pet cat was KIA!

Colonel Nigel Knocker OBE, WO, WKhM

Callsigns
ACS Maj Cornwell – T19
Sgt Fyffe – T1A
Capt Hodgson – T12
Sgt Oliver – T12A
Sgt Costello – T12B
Sgt Begley – T13
Sgt Ali Abdullah – T13A
DR HQ – Maj Sherwell – Sand 9A
NFR Capt Nicholls – Green 19
NFR Recce 2/Lt Ruqaishi – Green 60
JR Recce 2/Lt Nasib – Grey 60
DR Recce 2/Lt Khalfan – Sand 60
Oman Artillery Capt McGrath – Golf 29A

OPERATION LOCUST 29 APRIL – 10 MAY: WITHDRAWAL FROM AKOOT

The Squadron's orders were to establish a base east of Akoot at a place called Janook. It was here, at a long disused airfield, that SAF planned to establish a Forward Airhead to resupply and maintain Op Simba approximately 30km to the west.

Infantry pioneers would rebuild the airfield and in the initial stages the position would be protected by the Squadron in seven Saladins, Tim's as SHQ (Squadron HQ) and two troops, my T12 and Sgt Begley's T13. Joining us, a half company NFR (David Nicholls) and three recce platoons, NFR, DR and JR. Combined, the force would build sangars and fortifications to secure the position. Never intended as a forward operating base, but an operational airhead.

28 Apr – <u>Compass!</u> NFR – arrived Midway.
If Caribou arrives – Tangos deploy airstrip
Signal Tim – Ammo state
Cars sit-rep – Graham / Tim
Graham debrief – me, Lou, Olly, Dick M-E
More ammo on tmw's convoy
Smoking too much
Men seen Vimy – 1815
Congratulations – Tim, Col Nigel and Dfr HQ.
Uneasy about Locust, couldn't give a damn before
Need 3 x Browning barrels, 5 periscopes, antenna
Emptied ammo dump – need resupplies.

Ammo state after reloading

	HE	HESH	.30 boxes	Fired: Main	.30 boxes
T12	10	9	3.5	40 HE/HESH	14
A	3	19	6.5	17 HE/HESH	8
B	8	14	16	<u>25</u> HE/HESH	<u>12</u>
				82 rds	34 bxs

Now all cars – 12 boxes .30

The day was spent cleaning weapons, temporary repairs including punctures, and replenishing weaponry. An urgent ammo indent brought supplies the next day, our ammo dump run low pre-evacuation was now exhausted. A prismatic compass arrived a week later, replacing one destroyed by gunfire with other personal effects stored in an empty Mills 36 timber box, strapped to the outside of my turret.

During the day Graham individually debriefed Dick and I, Olly and Lou. Aircraft continued the airlift as a half coy NFR destined for Akoot arrived at Midway, driving south from Oman.

> *29 Apr – Phase 1 – Op. Locust: 3 Phases – establish Janook – Simba airhead – vacate Akoot*
> *Half A Coy NFR, Mqa FMT tpt and Grey 60 arrive Mudhai*
> *Letter home – Anniversary card M & D*
> *Ramadhan Chambe short RS1,500 on pay*
> *0900 call T19 convoy to M'baosh*
> *Ali Hamdan short 600 bzs*
> *change to channel 6: Question: convoy c/s?*
> *Write Contact Report*
> *Keep 'strip open for Skyvans – two cars on ridge 0900*
> *message Tim on Locust*
> *Skyvan shuttle all day – worked very well*
> *3 Coy back to Simba?*
> *3 mortar bombs, ineffectual, fm West as Skyvan landed*
> *Jim Parsons here, says Jonathan v. happy being sent back to England.*
> *Make new diary*

Akoot, too large and vulnerable for a small force to hold, was to be abandoned for Janook six kilometres east, considered out of adoo artillery range and too far from the treeline for an infantry assault. So it was assumed by those who planned such operational matters.

Domestically, LCpl Ramadhan Chambe and Ali Hamdan's pay packets were short, nothing new but an unnecessary frustration in the field. I'd record shortfalls promising these be recouped. My diaries show numerous such entries.

6th May was my parents' wedding anniversary, marked annually with a card or letter; this year I'd managed a scribbled note, learning later it'd arrived in time. By such simple irrelevances to our daily existence, sanity was maintained.

The withdrawal from Akoot was to be commenced 0600 Saturday 29th April in three phases:

Phase 1 – Assemble force at Mudhai
Phase 2 – Secure Janook, rebuild existing airfield
Phase 3 – Pull out from Akoot

As Dick and 3 Coy returned to Simba, Jonathan was flown back to the UK. Many wounded were treated at tented field hospitals (Sandy, patched up, bandaged and returned to duties on Simba), others sent to the FST, the Field Surgical Team based at UAG where surgeons cleaned, stitched and set bones before returning the white-bandaged to duty (Ben Hodson and then Alan with arm wounds stitched and set in plaster-of-Paris casts before being returned to duty, Tom part-mended and returned to Simba).

Akoot's numbers were now reduced to Graham's HQ Coy, my three Saladins, Khalfan's DR recce platoon and a detachment OA under Noel McGrath. My orders: Rearguard – cover withdrawal of remaining troops, ordnance and munitions. We'd be last to leave.

Akoot ridge and piquet duty. Author enjoys a sandwich and brew, a gift from Graham Sherwell's Mess staff, and kindly delivered by Sgt David Arkless, attached to the SAS and who took the photograph. On a lanyard around my neck is my microphone; binoculars and map in front rest on the turret; and to hand, my treasured wildebeest tail fly-whisk. Behind me a new Panasonic hand radio still to have its aerial bound with a shemagh rag as camouflage and my tin mug displays gaffa tape protection against hot drinks, much needed with a sunburned mouth. At the time we ate in snatches, as and when we could.

OP LOCUST PHASE 1

Tim's forces at Mudhai consisted of four Saladins accompanied by NFR's 2/Lt Ruqaishi and JR's 2/Lt Nasib's recce platoons. To this group were added on a temporary basis, a half company A Coy NFR under command of David Nicholls RM, en route to join us at Akoot. Arriving overland from Oman, NFR moved on to Marboosh with Tim, 25km north of Janook, before motoring on to Akoot.

> *30 Apr*
> *Half NFR Coy & Ruqaishi arrive – David Nicholls. RM, seems OK. Good to see Ruqaishi again. Buy boys cigs.*
> *Water & ammo arrive (60 burmails benz)*
> *Contact reports/map/sitrep to Tim*
> *CFTs 1700*
> *T12 – 1 Browning & 2 browning barrels/5 periscopes/radio antenna & M-switch/Tyres Ammo: 29 HE, 11 HESH – 40 rounds fired – 14 bx m/g*
> *T12A – tyre pump/mic – Ammo: 10 HE, 7 HESH – 17 rounds fired – 8 bx m/g*
> *T12B browning barrel /1 mic//gunner's periscope*
> *Ammo: 13 HE (one misfire), 12 HESH, – 25rounds fired – 12 bx m/g*
> *Rations/Petrol*
> *Caribou shuttle back tdy – inshallah 0915*
> *Flit pumps and flit!*

CFT reports were submitted on each troop's battle fitness, identifying damage and ammo used. Despite the rush, we were still required to submit the data on a regular basis.

David I'd not met before and I found him easy going like all the Royal Marines, and it was very good to meet up with Ruqaishi and his platoon with whom we'd patrolled on numerous occasions before. Graham divided our positions with NFR taking Red and 2 Coy's old positions, my troop with Ruqaishi's men, holding 3 Coy's. A very much depleted force now held a position once defended by a battalion battlegroup. NFR's arrival lifted morale.

DAVID'S WB

Some months later, a patrol led by David was caught moving through a wadi system. They'd walked straight into an ambush. Ordering covering fire, David grabbed a bag of Mills 36 grenades. An experienced climber who'd one day summit Everest, he scaled an almost impossible wadi wall to reach higher ground from where he began lobbing grenades at the hidden adoo. Moving forward as he threw grenades, the firing halted abruptly. The adoo had retreated, leaving behind a dead soldier, escaping with their wounded, evinced by bloodstains on bleached limestone. Examining the dead man revealed he was probably no older than 17 or 18, like many of the Sultan's soldiers. David's example of leading from the front earned him the Sultan's Bravery Medal, one of the best. Equally deservedly, he'd go on to reach the rank of Brigadier in the Royal Marines.

FLIES!

A vital element to our wellbeing and overlooked in the scramble to dismantle the base, was the control of Akoot's fly population. The twice daily task of spraying areas against flies had dropped off HQ Coy's indent. Saladins and tents now crawled with these wretched creatures, partial to any orifice, worrying at our mouths, nostrils and eyes. A pathogenic take-no-prisoners horde. Sitting in a Saladin, they'd settle like a rug across your back. As to their provenance, 100m away, Satan's Pit, the officers' & sergeants' latrine, an unlidded timber box sited over a heaving abyss, now half full after 14 months' usage. Not a place to linger longer than necessary.

Determined to do battle, I'd ordered a spray gun and Flit insecticide, an American pesticide used widely across the globe before the negative environmental impact of this chemical was understood.

Some flies bit, leaving a painful and swollen lump, producing puss which we'd treat with a saline wound-wash provided by Jim Parsons, DR's contract QM. It was a cure-all magic lotion that actually worked!

At the time we'd no idea what Flit did to humans, but it worked wonders against flies. Flit contained DDT and its use was severely restricted, whilst remaining a potent killer of the malaria mosquito.

> 1 May
> Simba – having to recce alternative airstrip
> Bert Kenyon here – dismantling 5.5in.
> 'Bou @ 0930?
> Noel McGrath OA - HF - C70 & B14 - 25pdr - 1615 – one gun only
> NFR had bad night – little nervous. First night – foxes caused stand-to 2330
> Green 60 - 0030 – section leader woke all with plaintive voice on his National – couldn't see other section in the dark . . . Ruqaishi soon sorted that!

News from Simba was they'd have to seek an alternative STOL airfield following repeated shelling onto the site originally chosen.

Bert Kenyon arrived from UAG workshops to oversee the 5.5's dismantling. Recently transferred from NFR to become a gunner with OA, Captain Noel McGrath (ex-RA) was the Artillery's first contract officer. As yet lacking any defined role, Noel had been tasked with dismantling guns, the 5.5in to be taken out by road, the 25 pounders flown out by aircraft.

Twice stood-to, it was a night made memorable by nervous men in sangars shooting at shadows. The experienced suspected foxes. Accumulative sleep deprivation ensured we crashed out instantly, fully clothed and booted, climbing beneath grey wool blankets laid beside Saladins. Blankets ensured easy escape; sleeping bags and you could be trapped. The new arrivals would soon be tested to the full.

ORDERS UNCHANGED – HOLD JANOOK

> 2 May – Skyvan 0915, Bou 0920 – shuttle service.
> 5.5 to be stripped down – now <u>not</u> required at Janook.
> Blow blind HE.
> 1700 call: Radio Aden – Vimy report: 5 en KIA, 19 WIA on 27th south of Akoot. And SAF – CSAF KIA, 2 jets shot down, 3 helicopters casevac numerous Jaysh . . . Armoured Cars not mentioned!
> Graham to speak to Tim on poss. move to Lamdon's Field not Janook. Old hands against Janook favour airhead. Position's absurd.
> 1000 x 5 RCL. 1100 just single RCL. 1430 x 7 RCL all HE incomers to coincide with 'Bou arrivals. Most rounds landed on Red Coy's old area.

'Pops' not audible – bearing 3600 mills? 1600 single RCL east of airstrip.
Msg from HQ – it's still Janook.

Despite reservations by those on the ground with first-hand knowledge of the area, Dhofar Command remained resolute we establish an airhead at Janook. It seemed those sticking pins into Ops Room maps knew best. Lamdon's Field, 1500m north from Janook and the adoo-held treeline would give us better prospects of setting up an airhead we might have a chance of keeping open. Furious at HQ's obduracy, Tim was making himself unpopular. Despite arguments Janook would be a disaster, orders remained: Establish Janook Airhead. Final. Adding to the day's frustrations, none could determine where the adoo were firing from. My diary entry reads *"fed up not locating RCL pops"* (firing sound at base plates).

> *3 May – <u>NO booby traps.</u>*
> *Speak Khalfan/Ruqaishi on decoys*
> *Recce pls to secure Janook & clear for mines? Sand and Green - subsequently cancelled. Pioneers will clear mines fm existing sangars.*
> *Confirmation 5.5 to be dismantled, leaving us one 25 pdr. OK? (no not really!)*
> *0900 one 'Bou expected? Dependent on incomers.*
> *Verify 60 burmails benz remain at Akoot? Affirmative.*
> *Sand 60 to move out 1000 to Janook – escort Guns.*
> *Tim moving fm Mudhai today – now wants our 25pdr in Janook if 5.5 not available.*
> *Ops freqs: T12 - 6, 8 jets*
> *   T12A - 6, 13 HQ Dfr*
> *   T12B – 6, ditto*
> *Sand 60 and Green 60 – build decoys in sangars.*
> *1700 Radio Aden broadcast: Armd Car commander killed and 2 cars destroyed – not jets!! News to me thankfully. Now they're confirming <u>19</u> killed on 27 April – Vimy.*

BOOBY-TRAPS

Tim signalled they'd cleared for booby-traps. The possibility of Janook being mined was high, a previously held SAF position, there was every likelihood old sangars and paths would be mined. But SAF pioneers had swept the camp declaring it safe from this threat. Too soon we'd discover, as JR would nine months later, the area was littered with mines. In addition to adoo mines, SAF had long mined wadi approaches into Akoot, all carefully recorded on maps held at Dhofar HQ for dealing with as time allowed. We hoped they were.

I quote from a SAF Journal at the time, under the heading:

> "Mines and booby-traps. Mines continue to take their toll on both sides in the War ... near Arzat camp a patrol found the remains of bodies of men attempting to lay TM46 anti-tank mines, in conjunction with PMN anti-personnel mines ... a DR soldier and a civilian ... recently killed by PMN mines and in separate incidents four soldiers ... lost limbs ... numbers of vehicles destroyed ... another Saladin badly damaged ... Booby-traps (mines) laid by our forces have successfully taken out an enemy re-supply vehicle ... in another incident Radio Aden confirmed a member of the PFLOAG Economic Committee, a Commissioner and a firqat commander of the Ho Chi Minh unit were killed, nine others wounded."

Mines are and remain a loathsome business.

DECOYS AND VIMY LOSSES CONFIRMED

Receiving orders Janook's mine clearance was now ceded to David's NFR pioneers delighted my recce platoon commanders Khalfan and Ruqaishi. Instead, we were tasked with creating decoy soldiers from sandbags and shemaghs. Despite the seriousness, it was difficult keeping a straight face describing what was required but we successfully fashioned sandbag heads topped with soldiers' spare shemaghs. Over the next two nights, decoy soldiers appeared arranged in sangars to give the impression of greater numbers, sentinels in empty sangars. I've no idea whether our decoys deceived adoo binoculars, but it boosted morale believing perhaps it'd work, and no doubt amused the adoo arriving as we departed.

Conflicting orders for the 5.5in continued; first to dismantle, then reassemble and tow to Janook, before again ordered to disassemble. Noel McGrath was heard muttering he'd never imagined he'd be practising Royal Tournament drills under fire. Worryingly, Tim demanded the last 25pdr sent to Janook where it was needed now the 5.5in would be inoperative. That left Akoot without artillery support.

That evening, Radio Aden announced the demise of the armoured car commander together with the successful destruction of two armoured cars, whilst also confirming the adoo's heavy losses sustained at Vimy.

LOCUST PHASE 2

4 May – Phase 2 Locust – securing Janook
T19 group, Grey 60 moving to Janook. Water convoy.
Sand 60 1400 fm here to Janook.
Orders: Rations. Grease nipple. Large washer.
Simba NTR – Quiet day!
Tim no further than Marboosh – Sgt Begley's car distributor problems. Mr Kenyon – choppered between Akoot – Marboosh. New distributor choppered – Salalah – Midway – Marboosh? Skyvan not enough fuel to fly Mid-Mar-Sal . . .! Pilot wary of his map reading? Tim moving to Janook tmw.
Felt lousy all day – runs. B-hot day. Fly plague, no breeze.

Tim's reinforcements had stalled to an undignified halt at Marboosh, 25km short of Janook, after two armoured cars suffered mechanical problems. This was a setback, with the severe shortage of spares, replacement parts were ordered from Salalah. It is astonishing we managed with such inadequate spares backup. Using up valuable Huey hours, engine parts were choppered some 60km, jeopardising other operations. In an effort to avoid further delays, Bert Kenyon was flown from overseeing the 5.5in being dismantled at Akoot to Marboosh to fix the cars. Whilst Tim fumed, powerless, those at HQ Dhofar seethed at the delays. It was soldiering on a shoe-string.

Meanwhile, three Saladins and David's half company held Akoot with gradually reducing infantry as the evacuation of men and ordnance continued. As the adoo stepped up their shelling and we sought to return in kind, I suffered the effects of a recurring stomach bug and the flies prevailed; it's called soldiering.

LOCUST PHASE 3

5 May – Phase 3 Locust
Grease nipple still needed, washer
Phase 2 Simba – Capstan – postponed (Habarut)
Fished 12 flies from my tea first thing. Expecting a hot day.
5.5 to Janook – in bits.
Akoot incomers, RCL, Mors, MG – keep moving – Bracketed!
Sand 60 – one man on AP mine. 515675. Others wounded.
Habarut taken out – 3 dead and one BATT, others wounded. Relayed all action to UAG through 12, 12A as Habarut radio signal weak. Relay following message:

"DR – TAC warning order – No move phase 2, you can have half coy + mors on standby for heli task fm 0800 6 May. More details later."
1800 – Habarut hit by 60 mors. V. low on ammo – fort in pieces. One more cas. Lunch – single orange shared with Ali and Abdullah – 1/3rd each – but a REAL orange.

As Akoot's strength reduced the remaining DR HQ Coy and both recce platoons departed. Spread across Akoot's 1.5km basin, David and I knew we'd be stretched holding out against a determined attack. With soldiers' humour for tight spots, we'd joked at least we could rely on the decoys standing firm. No one admitted but all wished we'd been with the last trucks departing for Janook that evening.

During their move out, one of Khalfan's men was killed stepping on a mine, with others wounded. The victim had made an elemental error. Running for cover he'd followed a camel track between bushes, treading hard on an AP mine. Nearing the end of his Dhofar tour, he'd made a fatal, avoidable mistake. But who's to lecture? He was under fire at the time. Poor sod.

The extent of our weakened strength would have been obvious to the adoo. For days there'd been a constant movement of men and hardware leaving by vehicle and aircraft. The adoo must have been astonished at SAF's choice of Janook, a position within sight and range, as proved later when they opened fire, on target, without ranging. Now the dice was beginning to roll their way, presenting a chance to balance the books.

Attacked into the evening by small arms, mortar and RCL, we were being tested. They had our range, bracketing the cars, keeping us moving. As day wore into night, we hoped Tim's plan would keep schedule to vacate on the 6th. With tension building, news filtered through SAF's outpost at Habarut had been taken out, SAF, Firqat and SAS killed.

21

HABARUT ATTACKED

International incident. Covert SAS withdrawn after casualties. SAF platoon then pulled out and the position deserted. We lose a fort and the Sultanate responds. Yemen's ensuing anger as they raise questions at the UN Security Council accusing the Anglo-American War Machine. SOAF lose a jet fighter. SAF forced to postpone ops out of Simba. SAF return to a position north of Habarut ordered not to engage unless attacked. Stalemate.

SGT ALAN OLIVER, SULTAN'S COMMENDATION MEDAL, WKHM

On the 5th May 1972 whilst checking frequencies, Olly, ever the diligent radio operative, picked up a faint signal from Oman's Habarut fort, beleaguered and under sustained attack from across the Yemeni border. Their radio antenna shot off, the signal was very weak. Following a number of casualties, they'd been forced to pull back from the fort being demolished by artillery fire. Between attacks on Akoot we relayed messages between the position at Habarut, Dhofar HQ at UAG and DR at Simba until an established radio link had been effected and we stood down.

Significant to SAF and DR's immediate operations, the attack on Habarut became a factor postponing Phase 2 of Operation Simba; taking the Capstan objective.

Akoot Camp. Olly with hair and beard and five of our crew members, returned from a morning's training firing dismounted .30 Brownings. In October 1972 Olly was awarded the Sultan's Commendation Medal for bravery under fire, and subsequently the WKhM for distinguished service during two years in Dhofar.

HABARUT

In a desolate mountainous region 60km northwest from Simba, two major wadis, Difan and Habarut, meet at a confluence named Shafia, becoming Wadi Mudhi and running on northwards to disappear into Arabia's Empty Quarter. The eastern Wadi Difan flows from Oman's Jebel Qamar in Dhofar, and Wadi Habarut in the west flows from the Jebel Mahrat across the border in Yemen; 400m south of this confluence at Shafia where the international border divides Oman from Yemen, there is fresh water at a place named Habarut.

At Habarut are two forts, one either side of the border, both equally jealously guarded and occupied by soldiers of the opposing two countries. A sketched map shows the positions of the Habarut forts in question. There is an ancient camel trail which runs between Mudhai and Habarut, a distance of approximately 64km. As news of the Simba operation reached SAF outposts, unbeknown to those in SAF, members of the firqat FHG (Firqat al-Hudud al-Gharbiyah) attached to the Armoured Car Squadron at Mudhai decided to take unilateral action and launch their own covert operation.

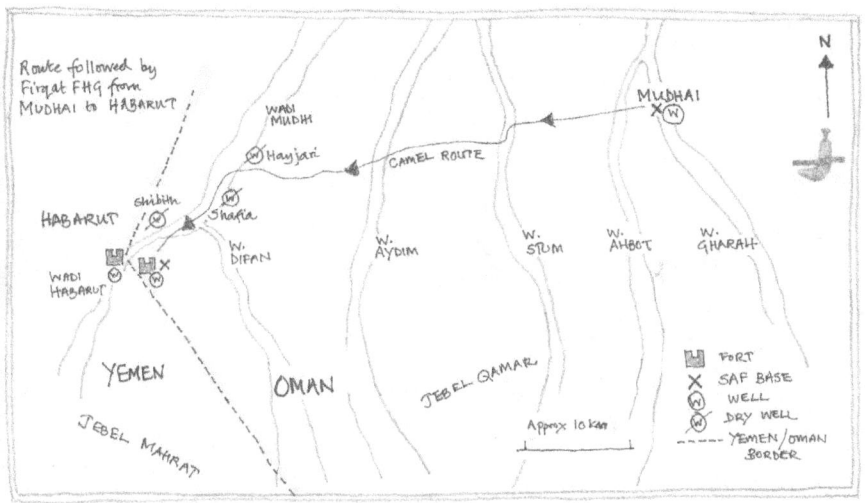

INTERNATIONAL INCIDENT

Despite determined attempts, PFLOAG had yet to make a mark in the newly escalated war. Simba was too established to be pushed back. SAF looked to be staying. Compounding this setback, the recent heavy losses suffered on Vimy Ridge, when at one stage it must have seemed the morale boosting prize of a Saladin Armoured Car was in their grasp. The adoo needed a victory.

Now it appeared SAF had made the error of redeploying to Janook, within reach of adoo artillery and small arms. Of course, in any war there are opposing perspectives. What to SAF was considered a tactical withdrawal, the communists saw as the Sultan's forces driven from their long held strategic base at Akoot and now there was the possibility of Janook too? Suddenly it must have seemed SAF were vulnerable.

And one thing communists like are anniversaries. Approaching PFLOAG's fourth birthday, the adoo had planned and prepared opening up a new front. On 5th May they launched an attack on the Sultanate's lightly defended fort at Habarut, Oman's most westerly position on the border with Yemen. With victory at Akoot, Janook's would follow. Their tails were up.

Author's sketch of Habarut fort before the Yemeni attack, 5th May 1972. Used as a Christmas card that year by friends in SAF intelligence.

PRELUDE TO HABARUT ATTACK

Since March, the Squadron's headquarters were our Mudhai base with its freshwater spring and date palms in Wadi Aybut. Security was shared with the Camel Firqat, Firqat al-Hudud al-Gharbiyah (FHG) who provided picquets guarding hilltops around Mudhai. Brave yet unreliable, it'd become necessary to maintain a watch ensuring they actually bothered to man picquets. This entailed over an hour's solid climbing and scrambling, visiting each of their positions. Keeping us fit and in touch with the firqat, it was hot, thirsty work carrying personal weapons, spare magazines, map, binos and water.

And as with the Firqat Tariq bin Ziyad (FTZ) at Akoot, many was the occasion we'd be stood-to as a nervous Bedu believing he'd sighted movement, shot wildly into the night to find it was just some stray dog or scavenging hyena. More than once a ricocheting round pinged against wadi walls to land with a thud into the sand around our tents, causing consternation but fortunately no casualties.

As Simba kicked off, Tim was fully occupied preparing the Squadron's move to establish the Simba Forward Airhead, which was to become an ACS responsibility. As a former SAF outpost, Janook would first require clearing of mines. Experience had taught us the communists habitually mined ex-SAF positions awaiting the army's return. A lesson learned at cost and repeated each time the four infantry regiments underwent roulement, when freshly trained, keen yet inexperienced troops were first led out onto the jebel. No matter what amount of training, Bang! another explosion told of some hapless soldier fatally following a track, entering an old sangar, or going for a pee under an obvious tree. Theory losing out to practice again. A horrific mistake seldom repeated by witnesses to the event.

Unbeknown to a busy Squadron Leader, eight men from our FHG firqat departed westwards by camel. Following a historic route out of Wadi Aybut, they crossed to Wadi Stumn and over the jebel to Wadi Aydim before cutting to Hayjari's dried well. Travelling south along Wadi Mudhi to Shafla and then Shibith's ancient well sites, they reached the ancestrally disputed freshwater wells at Habarut.

Habarut's wells are found where the international border meets in Wadi Habarut, an area that is intensely hot, arid and forsaken. The only decent drinking water for miles around, the wells sit bang on a purposely angled section of an

Father and son, this FHG firqat member, yet to be issued with a FN rifle, carries a .303 Lee Enfield. After periods of absence, male cousins meeting each other again would rub noses in greeting, all the while exchanging the traditional salaams. The FN (Fabrique Nationale) 7.62mm rifle was used extensively throughout NATO countries, originally being produced in 1953 by the Belgium manufacturer FN Herstal, a former automotive manufacturer.

otherwise almost perfect meridian line dividing Oman from Yemen. Drawn by well-intentioned Europeans, a line that was always likely to harbour tensions, which had in the past and assuredly would again escalate into bloodshed.

The angled section juts into Yemen. Both tribes, the Yemeni Al Mahri and Omani Bayt Kathir, had out of the harsh necessities of desert life, evolved as fiercely proud and independent. Camel raids and blood feuds were perpetuated by mistrust. A way of life from which for centuries we in the Western world have been free.

On my resupply visits to Habarut I'd wonder what it was with politicians and diplomats deciding boundaries with straight lines? They occur across the globe; as evidenced in India, America, Canada, Australia and Africa. The answer naturally is often one of impossibly rugged terrain or other geographical features, as it was here along the Omani/Yemeni border. Yet it is this boundary delimitation, the drawing of boundary lines that is frequently the catalyst for international disputes. And this particular example at the foot of the Arabian Peninsula is one, seemingly drawn with a cartographer's ruler all except for one point, which viewed casually on a map, for all the world has the appearance of an arrow-tip sticking into Yemen.

The two white painted forts at Habarut, one Omani, one Yemeni, stood approximately 250m apart, facing each other malevolently across the wadi bed of alluvium deposits, rounded limestone and sand. Each fort had access to water. An uneasy stalemate endured, both countries reluctant to escalate the situation, wary of causing an international incident. Fighting insurgents within your own territory was acceptable, less so shooting across an international boundary.

Based at Habarut on the Omani side were elements of the squadron's affiliated Omani Mahri firqat, Firqat al Badiyah (FAB) and a platoon of Dhofar Gendarmerie. Also present were a covert BATT troop. With British backing the local FAB commander had sought to establish a union with the Bayt Za'binawt, also Mahri tribesmen but living across the PDRY border. So far so good. Yet to any soldier left to sort out the subsequent mess, the proposal that Yemen's Bayt Za'binawt would come on board surrendering Yemen's fort to the SAF affiliated FAB still seems preposterous. Unsurprisingly, negotiations hit a wall. The Habarut question which had simmered between the two neighbouring countries for 20 years had become a tinderbox.

Whilst noticing an increase in numbers of men wandering around the PDRY fort, suspicion hadn't been unduly raised as groups had previously arrived and departed the vicinity before without incident. As recently as the end of February numbers of men had visited and subsequently moved away. And once again men seemed to be returning. There appeared no undue cause for alarm.

HABARUT ATTACKED

Arriving at Habarut, the Mudhai FHG group had rested a day before deciding they'd walk out to the wells, upholding their ancestral rights. They knew people on the far side of the wadi. There was also mention of some missing camels, but this was never confirmed. Each carried their FN rifle held level over a shoulder in the Bedu's casual version of the 'slope' fashion, a hand resting on the muzzle, rifle butt pointing back. Wearing shemaghs as Dhofaris, wrapped loosely as turbans, they were otherwise clad in the Bedu style of loose shirt and wizar, the latter gathered at the waist by a dagger on a Sam Browne style belt and bandolier filled with 7.62mm rounds. All were barefoot for none owned boots.

Seeing the FHG, a group of Yemeni Al Mahri tribesmen appeared, alerted by the arrogant approach from Oman's side of the wadi. Armed with Kalashnikovs, they were otherwise similarly dressed to the FHG, carrying weapons over shoulders, men who had bought into the communist ideology that promised so much, giving them standing amongst their peers and the prestige of automatic rifles.

A Bedu would choose death before losing face. A single shouted insult was sufficient to provoke a scathing response as the FHG swung weapons off shoulders and as one, opened rapid fire at their would-be abusers. The wild exchange was straight out of a spaghetti western, each side simultaneously reaching for weapons, firing at once. Always a foregone conclusion, Kalashnikov beats FN in such a contest. The FHG fell like ninepins, whilst in return killing and wounding but few of their assailants.

Then mayhem. All hell broke loose, the platoon of Dhofar Gendarmerie and the BATT troop were caught completely off guard as Yemeni mortars rained down onto their positions. The 30 gendarmes in the Omani fort were commanded by 2/Lt Hassan Ehsan Nasib. Camped in a wadi 500m behind the fort, a SAS troop technically 'not in the country' with orders to maintain a low profile. Remaining covert, it was otherwise a safe posting, their job training firqat in fieldcraft; as if these men needed it.

The adoo, members of the Ho Chi Minh Unit, quickly brought into play two Shpagin 12.7mm heavy machine guns. Firing at a rate of 600 rounds per minute, armour piercing rounds hammered the whitewashed stone and concrete walls of Oman's fort. Capable of penetrating 20mm armour at 500m, these machine guns began a steady demolition of the fortress 250m away, mashing concrete walls as easily as if they had been a child's sandcastle. The fort was demolished as 82mm mortars rained bombs around the fort and surrounding encampment, landing amongst DG soldiers, firqat and stores tents, killing many and mortally wounding Tpr. MJ Martin, serving with BATT.

What was essentially a spat between members of Mudhai's Camel Firqat (FHG) attached to the ACS and their Yemeni counterparts, the Al Mahri, now erupted into an international incident. The potential fallout for the young Sultan and Oman was immeasurable. This was a country one year on from a British-led coup that saw the Sultan oust his father. A country still negotiating treaties and seeking allies. The newest independent Middle Eastern state in the Arab League. The Arabian Peninsula is not a part of the world where the other cheek is turned. How to retaliate would be watched and judged closely by neighbours; signs of weakness exploited.

SULTANATE RESPONSE TO THE ATTACK ON HABARUT

Assessing the very real danger of escalation following the cross-border attack, telegrams burned between Oman, the UK and the United Nations Security Council. The concern was immediate, to quote a typical FCO telegram to Commander SAF:

SECRET   *FCO*

...AS ONE OF THE CONSEQUENCES OF THE HABARUT INCIDENT, MINISTERS HAVE DECIDED THAT A (SECRET) DIRECTIVE CLARIFYING THE POSITION ABOUT SECONDED OFFICERS SHOULD BE ISSUED...

...MEMBERS OF THE UK ARMED FORCES...HAVE BEEN MADE AVAILABLE TO OMAN ON THE UNDERSTANDING THAT THE ROLE OF SULTAN'S ARMED FORCES IS THE DEFENCE OF OMAN...ENSURE THAT (NO) BRITISH SECONDED PERSONNEL...ARE EMPLOYED ON OPERATIONS OUTSIDE OMAN, WITHOUT THE PRIOR APPROVAL OF HER MAJESTY'S GOVERNMENT...ALSO AGREED THAT CIRCUMSTANCES COULD ARISE WHERE THE USE OF BRITISH SECONDED PERSONNEL COULD PROVE EMBARRASSING TO EITHER GOVERNMENT, AND THAT, SHOULD SUCH A SITUATION SEEM LIKELY TO ARISE, THERE SHOULD BE CONSULTATION BETWEEN THE TWO GOVERNMENTS BEFORE (further) COMMITMENT OF SECONDED PERSONNEL.

DOUGLAS-HOME   SECRET

Sacrificing the DG platoon and local Firqat for diplomatic expediency, the BATT troop were rapidly helicoptered out, a decision which I'd judge the SAS would have found hard to swallow, leaving their colleagues behind. There'd be no repeat two months later, at a place called Mirbat.

For the next 36 hours, outnumbered six to one, 2/Lt Hasan Ehsan rallied his men against repeated attacks. Only as mortar bombs began landing within the crumbling fort and with ammunition running low, no rations and little water, did the platoon commander lead a fighting withdrawal into the wadi system behind the fort where they held out until relieved. In deserving recognition, he was awarded the Sultan's Gallantry Medal, Oman's highest award for bravery.

Helicoptered from Simba the next day, Desert Regiment's Ben Hodson with two platoons Red Coy arrived to extract the beleaguered Gendarmerie, leaving Habarut abandoned. SOAF followed with a leaflet drop across the border warning against further aggression. The communists fired back. In response the Sultanate bombed the Yemeni fort.

Fearful of the free-for-all becoming a full-blown international incident between two sovereign states, the FCO/HM Government raced to defuse the situation, persuading the Sultan against any further retaliation.

In the temporary stalemate which followed, with British diplomats out of the country, the Sultan sought his Commander's advice on the situation at Habarut. A soldier first and diplomat second, Brigadier John Graham replied as a soldier; he'd retaliate. Within hours, plans for Operation Auqubah (punishment) were being prepared. Oman would strike across the border at Hawf on the coast, an adoo stronghold supplying munitions and weapons to the adoo operating at will in Oman. Reports differ, but I prefer the version where, with a nod to diplomacy, the seconded CSAF's operation order was signed off by his deputy, Col Colin Maxwell, a contract officer. Thus it could be said no serving member of Her Britannic Majesty's forces was involved in what would be a solely contract officer led operation.

Over the 25th and 26th May SOAF jets scrambled from Salalah to strike at Hawf. The attacks had gone well despite a determined return of fire from adoo machine guns when on the final strike, Squadron Leader Peter Hulme's Strikemaster was hit. With amber warning lights flashing and radio dead, the commander of the Sultanate's air force was in trouble. But there were no red lights to indicate fire. Hulme pulled the jet's nose up to gain height. Banking east towards Salalah, he might be able to get the jet home. It was not difficult to decide against bailing out – it'd have been an unfriendly reception party. Ejecting over Simba was no-go, too small an area and anyway with fuel spraying into the cockpit, triggering the ejection seat might have ignited the avtur.

Still climbing, he signalled his wingman, ex-Royal Navy pilot Bob Pointer, he'd try to glide the aircraft home. Switching off nonessential electrics, including the incessant flashing amber, the engine cut. He was now flying a two and a half ton metal glider. SOAF's own Chuck Yeager.

With the cockpit reeking of kerosene, no power and minimum electrics, it took the greatest flying skill to gently nurse the small jet aircraft back to base and to land safely.

His bravery and calmly executed flying skills saved one of the Sultanate's invaluable aircraft. Peter had denied the enemy a significant and dramatic victory. For cool headed tenacity in returning the jet to safety, aware at any moment a catastrophic explosion might occur, Peter was awarded with the Sultan's Gallantry Medal.

YEMEN'S RESPONSE

The attack on Hawf prompted a furious diplomatic row between Yemen and Oman, Yemen issuing the strongest complaint to the Security Council at the United Nations.

IMMEDIATE

RECEIVED IN REGISTRY 17 MAY 1972

FM UKMIS NEW YORK   UNCLASSIFIED

"THE GOVERNMENT OF THE PEOPLE'S DEMOCRATIC REPUBLIC OF YEMEN ... PROTESTS TO THE BRITISH GOVERNMENT ... A DANGEROUS ESCALATION OF AGGRESSION ...

IT IS NOW CLEAR ... BRITISH BASES ... SALALAH, OM-AL-GHWARIF, IN OMAN ARE BEING USED FOR MILITARISTIC ENDS AGAINST THE PEOPLE'S DEMOCRATIC REPUBLIC OF YEMEN ... BRITISH COLONIAL FORCES AND LOCAL REACTIONARY CIRCLES ... PREPARATIONS FOR LARGE-SCALE INVASION OF OUR COUNTRY APPEAR TO BE PROGRESSING.

SINCE ... OUR INDEPENDENCE, IT HAS BEEN EVIDENT ... IMPERIALISM AND ITS LOCAL REACTIONARY POWERS WOULD NOT TOLERATE A PROGRESSIVE REGIME IN THE ARABIAN PENINSULA, WHERE ... VITAL ECONOMIC AND STRATEGIC INTERESTS ARE AT STAKE. THIS LATEST ACT OF

AGGRESSION IS AIMED AT CURTAILING... EVER INCREASING VICTORIES OF THE POPULAR FRONT FOR THE LIBERATION OF THE OCCUPIED ARABIAN GULF AND OMAN... FROM THE REMNANTS OF COLONIALISM.

IT IS NOT ACCIDENTAL... BRITISH COLONIAL FORCES AND THEIR LACKEYS ARE ATTACKING THE PEOPLE'S DEMOCRATIC REPUBLIC OF YEMEN AT A TIME WHEN AMERICAN IMPERIALISM IS... ESCALATING ITS WAR OF AGGRESSION AGAINST THE HEROIC PEOPLE OF VIET-NAM. THE AMERICAN WAR MACHINERY DEPLOYED AGAINST THE DEMOCRATIC REPUBLIC OF VIET-NAM AND THROUGHOUT INDO-CHINA IS BEING RUN BY OIL THAT COMES FROM THE ARABIAN PENINSULA TO THE IMPERIALISTIC ANGLO-AMERICAN WAR MACHINE,

NEVERTHELESS, THE INVINCIBLE REVOLUTIONARY MOVEMENT IN VIETNAM, IN PALESTINE, IN THE ARABIAN GULF AND ALL OVER THE WORLD WILL FIGHT... TO THE END"

ANGLO-AMERICAN WAR MACHINE

Seen from a pro-Marxist perspective the alleged Anglo-American war machine had recently increased the ante with a devastating response in Vietnam. Responding to advances in March by the People's Army of Vietnam, between 1 May and 30 June Nixon's America unleashed 18,000 B-52s fighter-bomber and air gunship sorties against the communists in an effort to slow movement of munitions to the front line.

But in the Arabian Gulf, ostensibly suppliers of oil to the Colonial Anglo-American war machine, efforts were proposed to quieten matters along the Omani/Yemeni border. The Foreign and Commonwealth Office response came from the top, direct to the Sultan hoping to cool temperatures.

> SECRET
>
> YOUR MAJESTY KNOWS THE IMPORTANCE WHICH MY COLLEAGUES AND I ATTACH TO THE ASSISTANCE WHICH WE HAVE BEEN HAPPY TO GIVE TOWARDS THE DEFENCE OF YOUR COUNTRY AND I CAN ASSURE YOU THAT WE SHALL CONTINUE TO DO WHATEVER POSSIBLE TO SUPPORT YOU IN YOUR EFFORTS TO BRING PEACE AND STABILITY THROUGHOUT THE SULTANATE. IT IS BECAUSE OF MY CONCERN FOR OMAN'S INTERESTS THAT I HAVE FELT BOUND TO ASK YOU TO RECONSIDER THE VERY REAL DANGERS WHICH I BELIEVE WOULD ARISE FROM A MOVE WHICH WOULD ENTAIL SERIOUS INTERNATIONAL CONSEQUENCES WITHOUT COMPENSATING MILITARY ADVANTAGE.
>
> WE LOOK FORWARD TO DISCUSSING THE SITUATION IN DHOFAR AND OTHER SUBJECTS WITH YOUR MAJESTY WHEN YOU VISIT LONDON IN AUGUST.
>
> YOUR SINCERELY,
> EDWARD HEATH.

View towards the Yemeni border from SAF's new redoubt at Habarut.

AUGUST? It was still early May! And hot, getting hotter. Seldom was there a better example demonstrating the differing cultures between Western politicians and those who held the torch in the Middle East.

HABARUT ATTACKED

In an effort at de-escalation whilst striving to garner Arab support in his war against Communism, the young Sultan ordered a stand-down. It was imperative the situation be quickly diffused. Yet this was the Middle East when face-saving retaliation was as inevitable as next day's sunrise.

Despite their losses at Hawf, with the attack on Habarut the adoo had successfully forced SAF to postpone Simba's main objective, establishing the Capstan position south of Simba. Planners had long known this objective with direct lines of fire to the coastal road into Oman, the Ho Chi Minh Trail, had to be taken. Looking south the battle group was blind beyond the Capstan feature, allowing unhindered passage along the vital adoo resupply route, the corridor used to supply their forces within Oman. They'd fight tenaciously to thwart SAF gaining this initiative.

Two weeks later, SAF, with orders to maintain a visible presence and not engage unless attacked, returned to take up new positions north of Habarut. And a stalemate was reached at this historically disputed border, where there existed a commodity more precious than gold, frankincense or myrrh: drinking water.

22

LAST OUT OF AKOOT

David's NFR half company departs. We are bracketed by enemy rocket fire. Tim warns of reported possible Yemeni MIG fighters. Lonely wait for orders to withdraw. Treating the wounded, syrettes, death, and a loathing of mines.

As battles raged around Habarut and SOAF attacks went in on Hawf, Desert Regiment's battle group at Simba remained under attack taking casualties. Back at Akoot now under sustained assault, with ever decreasing numbers defending, the position was becoming increasingly vulnerable as the slow process of tactical withdrawal continued.

FOC briefing:

Operations in Dhofar have reached a new and critical stage and it is hard to say which way the chips may fall.

---

6 May – Wedding anniversary

Rearguard: T12 – Graham's reminder! 'last out/switch off lights'   *Janook DFs*

5.5 to Janook	E1 559663
3 Hueys to Mainbrace am Habarut op. Red Coy. 62 mors in.	E2 556664
One Brit officer WIA, x3 jundees	E3 554675
Balance DR – Akoot to Janook	E4 574672
1st convoy out 0630	E5 557652
	E6 552676

LAST OUT OF AKOOT

T12 strike camp 0400 – stand-to 0500. Upset stomach. Slept badly.
No comms with Habarut – no C.W. / voice. silent.
Contact 1230 – 20/25 bombs in RCL, mors – all bloody fast. 10ft from T12B. RCL to me 20ft short. Jockey positions. BRACKETED. They're b. quick to range.
Green 19 – man on AP mine 515675 – KIA. 5 WIA. Assisted David. How I hate mines.
Arrived Janook 1600.

After a sleepless night spent cramped in cars on piquet we were attacked at midday with RCL, 3 inch mortars and 12.7mm Shpagin. It was a busy time as David's NFR withdrew, leaving our three cars the main force covering SAF's exit from Akoot. And it was my parents' wedding anniversary.

I glanced across towards T12B on my right to see him bracketed by RCL in quick succession. Bracketed is when the target (this time one of us) receives an incomer in front and then immediately behind, or vice versa, or either side of their armoured car. The theory being the next rocket lands in the middle, on target. Boom.

In the furious onslaught of incoming fire bursting around us, Lou hadn't noticed a rocket land close behind him. '*Move!!*' my thoughts shouted at what must surely happen next. With a hideous image flashing through my mind, I grabbed the mike at my chest ordering 'Move 12B, move *now*!' In that instant Lou's car shot backwards into a shallow depression, followed by a shaky 'Wilco Out!'. Grinning with relief, I thought 'never seen the old bugger respond so fast ...' The next rocket landed where he'd just vacated.

Then like a bolt it hit home, the realisation that positioned almost 100m east from Costello, we were equally ranged from adoo artillery. A simple traverse right, of course we too were equally 'bracketed'. 'Shiiiit! *SHIT*!' I cursed my stupidity as squeezing the send button on my handset, I ordered 'Ali, *waraa!*' ... ('high reverse!') and Ali slammed into reverse, catching my urgency. Engines screaming, the car leapt backwards down a shallow incline, dead ground away from the enemy's line of sight.

Halting him, I ordered 'move forward right ... halt!' as we climbed to a new firing position below another ridge approximately 75m back from our vacated position, halting hull down, the vehicle's bulk partially hidden behind the rising ground in front. To avoid bunching near Costello, I moved Lou further round to my right. We'd moved less than I'd have liked, but we'd no option on this ridge, and behind and to our left the ground fell sharply into Akoot's basin. We had to make do with what cover we could find.

We'd been extraordinarily lucky. Two rounds landed exploding simultaneously, demolishing the area just vacated. 'F.... you, adoo!' I smiled in grim satisfaction. Concurrent explosions meant two weapons, both registered on our position, 'That's more than luck – they're bloody good ... Where the f... are they?' I thought. Calling the other two, I received negatives.

Coherent as ever Costello radioed back 'F.....g 'ell – you'd have had a f.....g 'eadache if you'd not f.....g shifted then!' Probably another 'f.....g!' was in there somewhere. Under extreme tension, ears ringing, exhaling after close explosions, blood pressure rising to arterial bursting levels, adrenaline induced profanity kicks in, nature's pressure-release valve. Rarely does it ever sound nice, but by hell it works.

'Thanks, Lou, articulate as ever!' I replied, forcing a calm response as adrenaline coursed through swollen arteries and back through veins, heartbeats off-scale, skin tingling, body-hair on end. Catching Abdullah's wild eyed, grinning face across the fighting compartment, we were *so alive!* At that moment, the luckiest in the world.

I quote from Tim's subsequent contact report written in the quiet cold light of day:

> (their bombs landed extremely accurately ... Hodgson's three cars were well bracketed ...)

In glaring sunlight it was near impossible to locate the adoo artillery. I ordered fire on the most likely registered target areas, HE and .30 Browning whilst the last of David's NFR half coy and DR's HQ vehicles departed.

We held the ridge, jockeying constantly between positions now the adoo had us ranged and in their sights, needing to avoid setting patterns the adoo might use calculating our next firing positions. Stationary, we'd become sitting targets. It became a game of chess we couldn't lose.

Explosions followed us like flies. Responding ad hoc at first, gradually we began functioning as a single unit, seamlessly avoiding shell after shell landing between us. No longer chess, it'd become a game of cat and mouse.

Time blurred; it was another hour before the very last troops had withdrawn, leaving Akoot deserted. The adoo rate of fire lessened too, now sporadic bursts of heavy machine guns, automatic rifles and occasional HE rounds. Once in firing positions, we returned fire.

WE AWAIT ORDERS TO WITHDRAW

After days of frenetic activity when men loaded and carted what could be salvaged, the camp was suddenly empty. Before, there'd been organised chaos, now nothing moved except a midday sun's heat shimmer distorting vision. As NFR's last platoon departed, dust clouds obscuring Land Rovers and Bedfords, a glance across the Akoot basin told what I already knew, inducing an involuntary shudder. We were quite alone.

MIG REPORT

Then over the radio Tim called with news adoo forces might be using jets. News like that and instantly the skin crawls, the overriding thought 'jets against Saladins?'. There followed a moment's pause, before Tim added quietly, 'remember – against attacking jets – bursts of 250'. 'Wilco, out,' I replied, before from the wily Costello came the unnecessary clarification: 'That'll be a full belt from yer commander's Browning, press t'ferking trigger and don't let go!' Olly added, 'Fat chance you'd get lucky . . .' With such banter, my troop were prepared.

Three Saladins standing sentinel were all that now held Akoot. Still under sporadic incoming fire, we waited patiently for the signal to withdraw. Gradually the suspense began to rise. We had to remain confident.

In hindsight, against my infantry friends professing dread of ". . . being caught in a tin-can rocket-magnet . . ." much of this confidence stemmed, and perhaps to a reckless degree, from the absolute faith in the up-to-an-inch armour plating directly in front of me. We'd survived direct hits from armour piercing heavy machine guns, albeit at some range, we'd survived Kalashnikov armour piercing rounds at close range, crews had survived mines, we'd avoided rocket, mortar bombs and grenades – I felt in control. We'd been at this game for ten months now. But jets? That was another matter.

Gradually a haunted ambience descended across the camp. With senses on high alert, a dreamlike stillness seemed to descend over Akoot basin. Intermittently HE shells would drop around us, but the adoo had lost their aim, the explosions ineffectual. A greater worry was we'd lost infantry eyes and ears. Now under fire from three sides, we were in danger of being cut off. It'd be difficult if they'd got behind us, but first they'd have had to negotiate the heavily mined wadis laid by 2 Company. I had no option but to rely on that, hoping the mines were still there, live. It was beginning to feel lonely.

Looking about, gone was the smart army camp SAF had held for 14 months against repeated attacks. Dust devils blew on early afternoon winds, spitefully scattering litter and sand as they passed. Discarded rags, cardboard and paper, caught in the winds to be shifted aimlessly until becoming stuck on abandoned barbed wire, too difficult to remove, so left behind. This mix flapped gently in the breeze, calling to mind Himalayan Buddhist prayer flags, blessings for peace in Tibet, here detritus, a reminder of modern man's ability to leave scars on a biblical landscape.

We were nine in three Saladins, but still just nine men, some still teenagers, holding this eerily desolate, now vacated place. Covering each other's backs, the cars never closer than 150m apart, we jockeyed to and fro. We were vulnerable. The adoo knew it would only need a well aimed RPG and bang, result, as they had successfully achieved nine months earlier on Salalah plain.

With the last Bedfords, our fitters too had departed. We now had no mechanical back-up should an engine fail, or electrical circuit cut out, it'd become too dangerous for the vulnerable Bedford truck to remain. We'd have to hold on until help arrived and that'd be Tim's command troop, a minimum 40 minutes away at Janook. With attacks intensifying once more, we pulled back eastwards. We'd become the hunted, I thought to myself, tense and alert, the adoo the roaring lions circling for the kill, sounds of Africa which used to terrify my kid sisters, sending a shiver of excitement through us older boys. I felt no excitement now.

Bang! a shell would burst, flinging up its lethal debris of jagged shrapnel shards, dust and stone. We knew these were not random shots; they had us in their sights. The car nearest the incomer would back away to re-emerge at a different hull down firing position, whilst the other two endeavoured to locate the adoo gun and mortar base plates. Back we'd fall and then advance, constantly forcing the adoo to readjust ranges. Never stationary for long, it was near impossible we'd locate a well concealed enemy. And it was getting hot.

'Hello Tango 12', finally Tim's unhurried radio voice cut in, 'you can move out now – all in position at Janook,' adding, 'thanks for holding out for so long – apologies, lots to do. Good luck!' My reply was brief, 'Tango 12, wilco out'. There was nothing to add.

Ordering Olly and Lou to move first covering them to positions 400m back, they in turn covered me beyond them by another 300m, the classic leapfrog manoeuvre learnt and practised with tanks in BAOR, now used to great effect in the deserts and mountains of Dhofar.

A last look over Akoot basin brought home the fact our withdrawal would be perceived as an adoo victory. The Sultan's Forces finally being driven out from their fortified base, once a constant reminder of the adoo's inability to inflict anything but nuisance attacks, until now. Fourteen months earlier NFR's daring move had established a successful operational base from which to patrol, ambush and frustrate enemy supply lines. In turn Akoot had presented a vast target for adoo gunners bent on killing and maiming soldiers of the Sultan foolish enough to believe they could set up a permanent base deep inside enemy territory and not suffer for it.

Three days later my diary entry for 9th May concludes *'Radio Aden claiming great victory over Jaysh* (Army) *with Akoot . . . now they say they'll push us out of Janook!'*

No matter how SAF might view withdrawal from Akoot (a necessary element of Op Simba), to the opposing side, we were in retreat. We were running, the adoo having ensured Akoot was no longer viable. Making the point, we'd been subjected to a barrage of rocket, mortar and heavy machine gun fire to speed us on our way. Post Simba then Vimy, doubts of inadequacy, or ability to achieve victory over a better armed opponent had now been reversed.

Incoming rounds were again landing at a steady rate. As we fell back, changing firing positions, we'd remain stationary only to lay down bursts of .30 Browning. They had our range denying us any attempt to sit still long enough to locate precise firing positions. They'd moved in from Vimy. I gave orders for three rounds HE each car, along the ridge, followed by machine gun into the treeline to our front.

MINE CASUALTY AND A LOATHING OF MINES

"To die from a bullet seems nothing; parts of our being remain intact. But to be dismembered, torn to pieces, reduced to pulp, this is a fear that the flesh cannot support – and which is fundamentally the greater suffering".
Sergeant Paul Dubrulle, a French soldier, WWI.

Green 19 – AP mine 515675 – one KIA. Others WIA. Assisted David.

Waiting for us, David's half company held scrubland 1.5km east of Akoot. Moving between cover, a soldier trod on an AP mine. Khalfan's DR recce platoon had hit a mine in the same area the day before.

Anti-personnel mines are triggered stepping on them. Their primary purpose, disable rather than kill, thereby increasing the logistical medical/evacuation burden on an opposing force. Horribly efficient, AP mines are not a fragmentation weapon intended to kill, but a blast explosive leaving maimed individuals requiring urgent attention. Momentum is stalled by the compelling need to save life as each man trying to help the injured endeavours not to step or crawl over another hidden mine, frequently laid in groups. An author I've read writes: "There were many scenes of writhing, pleading torsos watched by helpless colleagues who knew that to give help would entail certain suicide." Whilst I have great respect for the author and understand the point he makes, fortunately there were those prepared to take that risk, be it bomb or bullet, for few men can stand aside and watch a fellow soldier die.

The pressure is off-scale, it's every soldier's worst nightmare. In an instant comes the horror of what to expect, followed immediately for the commander, that demanding logistical headache: keep control, save life and keep momentum. A situation made worse by an enemy in pursuit. In this war casualties weren't left to be attended to by the enemy. They didn't keep prisoners and they liked to play with them.

An inevitable secondary result of an exploding mine is the demoralising effect on survivors. Post mine-blast sites are never quite forgotten. With multiple wounded, David radioed calling for additional morphine. Morphine we carried in syrettes, tubes with hypodermics, in appearance similar to tiny toothpaste tubes each fitted with a needle. Pinching a fold of skin between forefinger and thumb, the needle is inserted into the fold, the tube squeezed, a single dose administered. Officers each wore a pair of syrettes taped with gaffer tape to cord looped around necks for ease of carrying, safety and reach.

Ordering Olly and Lou to hold positions facing the adoo to our right flank, I motored over to David where he was attending the wounded. With the two Saladins guarding our rear, I'd reached David as the adoo opened up with automatic gunfire towards us. Treeline, they were firing from the treeline. Abdullah replied with .30 coax as I called the other cars across.

Responding immediately, the two Saladins crashed through the sparse undergrowth, creating clouds of dust, gifting us a temporary dust shield. Taking up new firing positions they too engaged with Brownings. Parked beside David he shouted, 'Could do with top cover' – 'All at Simba,' I replied jumping down beside him, '. . . think they're being taken out too'. Seeing what David was coping with, one grotesquely hurt with leg and groin horribly injured, others lying wounded, groaning and shocked, I cursed in despair, fighting revulsion as already hordes of frenetic flies arrived, frantic at the men's open wounds. Meeting my stare, David cursed, 'God! The bloody flies have followed us from Akoot'.

Stooping down to help, you are met with a questioning face with eyes that stare without comprehension from ghastly wounds then back to you, beseeching you to turn the clock back to when they were whole, before realisation hits home that's never going to happen. That's what gets to you, the unharmed, unhurt, unimpaired, whole and in the wounded's eyes, perfect as he was just seconds ago. Sickened, you wrestle with revulsion, for it's not you but your shattered wounded man you must stay in control for.

'We're going to need more than four.' Handing David the syrettes from my neck, I clambered back into my car for a further supply boxed inside my turret, the troop emergency supply I'd held at Akoot.

Sadly, it was obvious from the start there was nothing we could do for the young soldier who'd triggered the mine. The earliest helicopter was over 30 minutes away, that is if any were available given the emphasis on Simba's needs. He was Baluchi, probably no older than 17 and now lying mortally wounded. As David squeezed a syrette into him, we knew morphine would only alleviate his pain. Through a disfigured and bleeding mouth, he begged we end his life, before sinking into unconsciousness, fading quickly and slipping away. The blast had ripped off his right foot, pieces of which lodged in his throat, severing the right carotid artery. His chest and face had suffered multiple blast injuries, stone fragments blinding his right eye. His groin, non-existent. 'Fucking mines...' David groaned, in anguish. Shocked at the extent of the young man's injuries, we administered morphine to the other casualties whilst a NFR corporal applied field dressings to open wounds. The dead and wounded were loaded onto a Land Rover sent out from Janook by Tim. My two cars were laying down sporadic covering fire, and we'd had no incoming fire towards the wounded. Calling for additional transport, David's men were loaded onto three Bedfords, our soft skinned troop carriers. We'd cover their withdrawal.

Back in my car, I rejoined my two Saladins. We were trained to be ever vigilant to the possibility of mines. Never walk along a track, avoid entering caves or any obvious routes out of wadis, up hillsides or suspicious areas on the flat. Never sit in the soft sand beneath a tree; approach wells only after the site had been cleared and foremost, never enter an old sangar even if under fire.

Regrettably these young soldiers had made the most elementary of errors. In their scramble for cover they'd rushed headlong to the remains of an old sangar, one probably erected during an earlier SAF operation. Abandoned sangars were forbidden territory to everyone, and endless training warned never enter these potential death traps. Told often enough, they should have heeded warnings. Ironically amongst the inexperienced younger soldiers were men with Dhofar tours behind them who knew the drill. Not only were old sangars an obvious mine trap, it was critical that obvious paths be avoided for they'd become notorious first choice with the adoo placing random AP mines. Men going to relieve themselves stepped on mines. Even the cautious were caught, probing the ground in front investigating caves or well sites, or crawling to a firing position only to trigger a mine beneath their bodies. Designed to catch the unwary, the tired and incautious, or in this case the scared desperately seeking cover.

The majority of us had had to push a syrette into a wounded body. There'd been no training. Yes, we'd been shown how to press a field dressing to stem a bleeding wound, but not how to use syrettes. We simply did what we could, acting by instinct. It was expected. No one was exempt. Though clearly upset, David had remained cool, almost detached as together we administered what we could to grateful patients.

> "It was very traumatic to see people, who have served you well and been really good soldiers, die just instantly. One moment they are there full of life and personality, the next instant they are just nothing.
>
> It is very difficult to deal with that."
>
> Col Mike Harvey after The Battle of Imjin River, Korea.

The Bedfords and casevac Land Rover carrying NFR moved rapidly away in clouds of dust towards Janook, about a further 3.5km east as we covered their withdrawal.

There was no longer any firing. It'd become uneasily quiet; calamitous din of explosions, machine gun fire and chaos of earlier, gone. Engines purring on tickover, we sat, searching for movement, shadows or men's dark silhouettes against the pale desert haze. Eyes aching, straining to see into the distance, watching, waiting. Shirts and trousers clung to bodies, chafing, constricting, as our steel cars warmed to roasting beneath an Arabian sun that climbed higher, fading the blue of a desert morning's cloudless sky. And flies massed.

Three Saladins, reeking with pungent empty shell cases tainted by explosive waste gases, nine men's sweat-soaked clothes too long unchanged, slept in and dirt stained. Each car's bouquet enhanced by warm grease seeping from overfilled nipples, spilled petrol fumes and leaking hydraulic oil. Our faithful six wheeled steel chariots on which our lives depended.

Patiently we waited orders to move back.

The initial moments of quiet extended into minutes then stretched out. With each passing minute, the tension rose. I'd moved T12A and B to my flanks, bringing them back from near the treeline as the infantry departed.

We watched for movement or the inescapable silhouette of man in the glaring desert sun. Rarely detected was sunlight reflected off weapon, belt hasp or knife, for these men were masters of stealth, born to hunt, remaining hidden, advancing unseen with a natural ease towards their prey, be it man, desert hare or gazelle. Adept as chameleons at camouflage, they wore buff coloured clothing, with weapons cloth wrapped becoming invisible, until they moved.

We'd discovered that living creatures, particularly man or camel, seen at distance invariably appeared darker, silhouetted against bleached desert. Olly and I had decided the answer was thermal radiation, possibly a body's temperature emitting radiation. It sounded plausible.

Waiting, my mind drifted to events just witnessed, one man dead, five wounded by a mine designed to mutilate. I reflected on a young life lost. He'd have family in Baluchestan who'd mourn their loss, mourn too his soldier's wages on which they'd come to rely, supplementing a non-existent family income that had likely necessitated his joining up in the first place. It's a miserable business.

Death of someone unknown can leave a curious detachment; but we'd spoken and I'd been near him as he died. It'd become personal. How different it is when those killed you've known well, lived, shared food and water with, laughed and fought alongside. I'd come to realise, as often so ably demonstrated by my men when dealing with loss, far better to quote their Arab prayer, 'Allah Kareem' (God is Generous – place your trust in Him).

Many years later I found a passage touching on the intensity of violent death experienced close to hand, fluently put by someone who'd experienced more than most. TE Lawrence had written,

> "Blood was always on our hands, we were licensed to it. Wounding and killing seemed ephemeral pains, so very brief and sore was life . . ."

Time passed before at last the order came to move back.

This was it – time to give the adoo a farewell V sign. Climbing from my turret, I quickly dropped my radio antenna to attach the Sultan's pennant to the top of the thin alloy tube. Olly did the same. Job done, I whipped back inside my turret to shouts of approval from Abdullah and Ali. The pennants flapped defiantly as we drove back across the desert scrubland, out into the more open highlands of the Negd we called moon country, towards the squadron dug in at Janook, and safety.

I quote from Tim's Contact Report:

> (. . . during the initial phases of Op Locust the T12 / Green 19 group (Hodgson/ Nicholls) was deployed forward on the rim of the Akoot bowl to protect the base from enemy attack while the withdrawal (continued). At about 12.30 the enemy opened up with RCL and mortars and it was extremely difficult to locate the firing positions. About 20 bombs landed . . . noticeably accurate . . . cars bracketed. The mortar base plate seemed to be in the area of 462642 and T12 brought down arty airburst on registered targets B13 and B14. The RCL appeared to be firing from further SW and was not located . . .)

23

FIGHT TO SAVE JANOOK AIRHEAD

We rejoin the Squadron with much premature rejoicing. Immediately attacked, men seek shelter beneath my Saladin. Others are caught in the open and forward slopes. Chaos. The charge to save JR recce platoon. Fighting closed down. Snakes. Huw and Twizzle KIA. Under repeated attack, Dhofar HQ finally deem the position untenable. Rearguard again.

JANOOK

6 May – 1600 arrived Janook.
Contact: 1630 – HMG, MG and SA – my position, 24 mors onto us. Very accurate. All caught out of vehs and sangars – made it to my car – alone. Crew later followed. Couldn't move out, Lou and men beneath car. Mors landed 5-10 feet short. Finally had to move – Nasib in trouble. Reversed over our kit. T12A with me, charged down MG posn. Put in air strikes, We have cas. flesh wounds.
2030 Shpagin my posn again. This time we'd reversed into sangar – so able to mount up through driver's hatch. More wounded. Engaged with Brownings, and shelldrake – adoo too close for shelldrake airburst. Adoo mor base plate 533673?
Shpagin impressive at night – silent trace, then crack! crack! crack! followed by boom, boom, boom! No thump! Thank God they use trace.
Twizzle KIA – buried beyond Mess tent.
Snake behind Graham's chair – check where you sit!

FIGHT TO SAVE JANOOK AIRHEAD

Exhaustive reconnaissance by air, vehicle and foot patrols, part of the planning process for Simba, declared Janook a sound location, underwritten by the Firqat, FTZ. We were in for a surprise. Lessons learned defending Salalah's airstrip and Akoot's being eventually rendered inoperable were overlooked.

Handshakes and foolish grins welcomed us, it was good meeting Tim and the Squadron again. Our unshaven stubble, oil and propellant smeared faces unwashed for weeks, quickly earned us unrepeatable pseudonyms. Being no longer in charge felt strange, but learning Mike was again laid up in hospital meant I was once more 2ic.

Janook's strength totalled seven Saladins, three Recce platoons, Noel's 25 pdrs (the 5.5in was in bits) and David's half company NFR. We'd also engineers, Graham's HQ cooks, Mess waiters, clerical staff and pioneers. We were now a reasonable force.

In addition, we still had an Air Dispatch team led by Sgt David Arkless with two others, John and Bert. Attached to BATT at Salalah this three-man unit assisted SAS operations but were temporarily seconded to SAF organising airfreight out of Akoot. Getting the best out of his allocated soldiers, 'Geordie' Arkless somehow overcame the obvious disadvantages of someone not taught Arabic or Urdu, an impressive quality. Vital ordnance was saved; what couldn't be, due to too little time or airfreight space, was burned in great bonfires.

Pioneers had rebuilt Janook's earth airstrip and Skyvans were offloading supplies into purpose built sangars of burmails filled with stone against blast damage, storing munitions, ammo and water in more steel drums.

My troop's new position was on Janook's southwest flank, facing the adoo. To my left, eastwards, Tim's four Saladins with David's NFR and Ruqaishi's recce between us. In depth to the north, Khalfan's DR recce protected Guns, whilst Nasib's JR recce were in sangars southeast and forward, on a spur above a wadi. Tim's men had been busy and the camp was well laid out, with sangars well sited. After allocating my arcs of fire, Tim departed to liaise with David.

Our vehicle sangars were 1m high drystone walls infilled with soil and rubble to approximately 1m width. They offered three-sided protection to tyres against mortar and rocket shrapnel, and bullets from machine gun and rifle fire. Inexplicably, given the freneticism of recent weeks, on arrival I'd not given it a second's thought and we'd driven straight into our sangars, turrets and weapons facing in the direction of the enemy.

We were grateful the wheel-protecting sangars had been built for us ahead of our arrival, but as with specific tasks such as others cleaning your rifle, unless carefully checked afterwards then occasionally the results may not be quite as you might have expected. And you only have yourself to blame.

What hadn't been taken into consideration when building the sangars was that in the event of an attack, the driver couldn't gain access through the vehicle's front as normal without being in full view of attacking forces. The sangars had been built too low. Driving forward instead of reversing into the sangars, I'd let my guard drop. Looking back, I suppose there'd been an expectation we were now safe.

Bedrolls and kit bags had been delivered earlier, including my Bergen and an appropriated 1.5m long ex-SOAF timber rocket box left heaped together beyond our sangars. Collecting their kit, my men ribbed me again about excess baggage.

Being out of the front line, away from danger and back with the Squadron had a tangible effect on the soldiers. Friends came to welcome each other, impulsively yelling greetings, exchanging handshakes and gossip – a special moment, much deserved.

A TIME TO RELAX

At last we'd relax, spirits were high with a promised meal prepared by squadron cooks. God we were hungry. And we were exhausted, I could see it in drawn faces, continuous engagements and meagre rations were beginning to take their toll. Psychologically, being back as a squadron amongst our friends, some not seen for months, and the added promise of full bellies boosted morale to levels not seen for weeks. With the pressure off, we dropped our guard. Janook was safe, we were out of enemy range.

At 1630, the first adoo salvo landed, followed by Sphagin HMG.

Scattering us like startled antelope, spitting machine guns raked the earth, kicking up fistfuls of stone and limestone splinters. Ricochets pinged and whined away. RCL rockets and mortars screamed in, exploding amongst our baggage. Instinctively we'd dived to the ground racing gravity, flattening ourselves as shells crashed in.

Considered relatively secure 6km east and a little over 800m north from the bomb target Akoot had become, my immediate thought was 'Janook's out of enemy range...?' Conspicuously exposed, we'd been caught trousers-down-naked. Caught in the maelstrom of incomers, men crawled towards kit bags to shelter amongst ordnance, including resupplies of 76mm HE rounds and boxes of belted .30 Browning I'd requested delivered to my position. Not the best cover.

Part of Tim's contact report reads:

(... firing from positions at 546676, 541682 and 533673 onto both the main position and forward picquet. T12 (Hodgson) was the only car ... to do anything ... everyone else unpacking kit and the OC (Cornwell) ... caught on forward slope checking sangars ...)

MOUNT UP!

The command to board vehicles, the equestrian call 'Mount Up!' was always given in English. Everybody understood its meaning, once given – all responded.

Spitting dust gulped like everyone else hitting the ground, I bellowed 'MOUNT UP!' hoping to be heard above explosions. Adrenalin surging, heart thumping so much it hurt, I sprinted for my Saladin.

Running unconsciously keeping the car's silhouette between me and the obvious machine guns, I couldn't think about the exploding rockets or mortars. Making it to my car intact, I vaulted onto the Saladin's rear decks avoiding the still-hot exhaust. Scrambling across to the gunner's turret as the nearest opening, I dived headfirst, dropping to crash against the gunner's backrest. It'd been the nearest funk hole. 'Shit, shit, *shit!* that hurt ...' I cursed aloud, rubbing my back. Not the recommended procedure for mounting an armoured vehicle, but it beat the alternative.

Now bursts of small arms struck the otherwise silent turret, making a hell of a din.

Twisting round, I squeezed over to the commander's side, expecting Abdullah's arrival. Apart from superficial scrapes and bruising, I'd cut my head but was otherwise unhurt. Explosions erupting close by and thwack! thwack! thwack! of bullets striking the turret indicated someone had witnessed my ungraceful entry into the Saladin.

No one followed.

Realisation dawned: I was alone. Wrapping my shemagh tight, stemming the sticky flow from my forehead, the last thing needed was blood everywhere; slippery fingers and you can't handle weapons, let alone lift/load a 76mm round. Squeezing back behind the breech-block to the gunner's seat, I fed the coax machine gun Abdullah had only recently made safe and left unloaded after parking up.

Browning loaded!

But the engine was dead. With no access to the driver's compartment and ignition switch, I'd no electrics, no power to traverse the turret. Grabbing the manual traversing handle with both hands, I began winding furiously, forcing the heavy turret to move on its rack and pinion bed. Feigning indifference at my efforts, gradually round it came.

Despite the glaring afternoon sun, tracer was visible. I could make out a machine gun firing at us. The range I judged at approximately 600-700m. All hell was breaking loose, mortars exploding, the machine gun pouring trace towards my Saladin. I'd not yet realised no one else had made it to their cars. Seen, I'd become the adoo's preferred target.

Laying the 76mm onto my assumed Shpagin, I realised 'light machine gun... Shpagin goes through (armour plate) at 600m'.

Firing the 76mm is a two-man operation. A good crew might manage a rate of six rounds per minute. Alone I'd be stretched to manage two. Reaching to my right I wrenched the stubby release handle, dropping the breech open with its reassuringly heavy clunk.

Reaching round beside my seat, I ripped off a safety clip, lifted a HE shell from its stowage rack and steadying it with both hands presented it to the open chamber, ramming it home with my right fist. The breechblock sprang shut with its familiar thump, pushing my fist and arm out of the way.

Loaded! Ready to fire.

I fired a burst of ranging coax .30 Browning. Short. Increasing elevation I fired another short burst, long! Back again, I struck ground around to the adoo's front – position bracketed, on target! The coax rangefinder. Unorthodox, but it worked.

Looking through the sights, I pressed my foot against the mechanical foot-firing pedal. At 640m a 76mm HE round travels 823m per second. At that range the timeframe between trigger and explosion on target is indivisible. It's instantaneous. As I fired, the gun roared beside me, to my front, one huge explosion at the adoo's position. Shrapnel, stone and rock splinters exploded away in an arc at the point of impact. That was what a 76mm gun was designed to do.

The machine gun silenced, I glimpsed more men running to my front right. Achingly slowly, I traversed right. On target! Fire. This time Browning, no time to reload the 76mm. 'How did they get so close?' I hadn't time to wonder.

With no radio response from anyone, I put down a long burst of approximately 40 to 50 rounds of coax followed by a second, raking where the enemy had fired from, hoping to give crews covering fire to mount up, pausing only to reload. Open top cover, pull out spent belt, chuck aside empty ammo tin, lift and position another already opened, feed in new canvas belt of 250 rounds, gun loaded, ready to fire, fire.

It was impossible to locate the adoo base plates; they had extensive cover behind numerous rocks, scrub, hillocks and wadis criss-crossing the terrain to our south and west. 'Bloody hell! This was meant to be a safe position!' I cursed.

I fired the coax again, a wide arc across our front, furiously winding the traverse handle by hand. 'Where is everyone?' I asked myself, sweat pouring from

FIGHT TO SAVE JANOOK AIRHEAD

cramped exertion. I reached down beside my seat for another HE shell, lifted and rammed it into the open breech. Clunk, again it closed reassuringly beside my right shoulder.

More figures emerged further to my front right, crouched and running fast to outflank our exposed westerly position, Olly's empty car. 'On target, Fire!' I fired a second HE round. The adoo were bloody brave, their fieldcraft incredible, we'd the firepower yet still they attacked. But they'd realised only one car out of seven was firing back at them. Their confidence must have soared. A dead Saladin, theirs for the picking.

I called Noel McGrath's guns again, making contact this time to hear his position was being hit by 'overs'. Calling for a fire mission, the 25-pounder dropped three rounds' rapid fire bang on target. Brilliant response. I loaded another 76mm into the smoking breech.

More incomers. Cursing the lack of power, traversing as fast as I could, slowly the heavy turret came round towards another running group. With an 'On target!' more in encouragement than necessity, I was pressing the foot trigger when Abdullah dropped feet first through the gunner's hatch, squashing me hard against the side of the car. Shocked at finding me in his seat, he turned to climb out as I pulled him back. 'Ana bikhayr!' (I'm fine!) I shouted at him, side hurting like blazes where I'd been shoved against the ammo rack. 'Ana bikhayr'.

> (T12 had about half a dozen men under his car at the time but did manage to direct arty fire onto the position at 546676 and fire 2 HE/T and 1½ belts of Browning at it himself.)

Wild eyed Abdullah pointed downwards shouting there were men beneath the car! 'Oh God!' I thought, horrified they'd been concussed by my firing the 76mm. Shouting through the armour-plated floor 'Hal anta bikhayr?' (Are you OK?) I received in broad Irish 'of course we're ferking all right! . . . there's five wit me b'Jesus – one's Said Mohamed.' Said, our 12-year-old Mess waiter had come to greet us on our arrival. 'We're all OK!' adding, 'thought we'd been hit by a ferking incomer!' before incongruously 'would you want me to rescue your camera, sir? – I can see yer kit from here . . .?'!

'NO!' I yelled back. 'Don't BLOODY move! – I'm firing main armament again – OK?'

'That'll be fine, sir . . .' came the reply, 'give'em ferking 'ell from us boys!'

> (Sgt Costello, who was under T12 at the time thought the car had been hit . . . and only realised it was the car firing when the second round went down . . .)

Abdullah had naturally chosen the gunner's hatch. In his haste he dropped like a descending paratrooper crashing feet first into me, propelling my body against the coax and 76mm breechblock. Being of similar build and weight, it hurt. A split second later and I'd have fired. Had that happened, the gun's recoil would have mashed us. That'd probably been it. The gun's recoil system is hydropneumatic, absorbing the explosive energy within the breech on firing, and during run-out the breech is opened by a semi-automatic cam and the empty case ejected, the breech remaining open ready for reloading. You really don't want to be in the way.

Partly winded, my side hurt a lot but on adrenalin highs we scrambled to our respective seats. Squeezing past Abdullah, I noticed he'd too cut his head and was bleeding profusely. Both of us now cut with bloody foreheads.

Climbing across to the commander's seat, I was met by Ali Hamdan. He also jumped feet first, falling through the commander's open hatch thumping me backwards hard against the breechblock. That bloody hurt too. With the direction of adoo fire, sensibly he'd chosen against using the driver's hatch at the vehicle's front – that'd have been suicide.

Seeing Abdullah taking the gunner's hatch, Ali had chosen the commander's. Extricating ourselves, Abdullah laughed, 'you'd not do that with his sister!' inducing a burst of laughter from the bonded unit we three had become. Narrow escapes can induce a flash of delirium. It lasts a split second. Abdullah wrapped his shemagh tight, hiding the scrape to his forehead. We were a match, bloodied faces and spattered shirts. Astonishingly all had escaped serious injury. And Ali reputedly had a very beautiful sister.

In the gunner's seat Abdullah fired a long burst of coax, winning brief respite. With two of us now working the manual traverse handles, we soon pulled the gun turret around, enabling Ali to squeeze through into the confined driver's compartment. The effect was that our turret and weapons were left facing away from a doubtlessly astonished adoo. 'Lou!' I yelled to him beneath the car, 'we're starting up, stay where you are!' 'Wilco!' came the muffled reply as I gave Ali the command to start up. The big V8 roared into life. Now we had power-assisted traverse.

BACK IN CONTROL

With power, we'd regained control. Despite incoming fire concentrated on our car, Costello and five men beneath were safe. Realising Lou couldn't hear me above the engine noise, I needed to warn him we'd be firing the 76mm again. Ali shut down the engine. Above the explosions I yelled I was about to open fire with main armament.

I received his all-clear.

Firing the 76mm must have been deafening beneath the car. Understandably, Lou thought we'd received a direct hit. The closest incoming rocket had landed 3m beyond my car, the blast caught by our baggage and my reclaimed timber rocket box, undoubtedly saving Lou and the others from certain injury, lying bunched beneath the car.

Typically, Lou was concerned about my gear, in particular my camera. The rocket-box had absorbed much of the shrapnel but later we discovered my newly acquired camera had escaped damage, wrapped for safety in a canvas square, against damage in transit . . .

(About 24 mortar rounds had come in . . . extremely hard to move . . . Sphagin raking the whole area. T12A (Sgt Oliver) now managed to reach his car . . .)

For a while it had become clear we'd been the only car returning fire. I assumed we must have taken casualties. Instead, it transpired the rest of the Squadron were sheltering behind and beneath whatever offered any semblance of protection. Then in the short lull after we'd neutralised the closest machine guns, Olly and his crew made it to his car, T12A on my right flank. Climbing into an armoured car under fire is always going to be tricky; they were very brave. Now we'd two cars operational.

Some NFR soldiers had begun returning fire but the situation was still weighted against us. The adoo held the higher ground, RCL and mortars dropped from the sky, rockets with their nerve chilling screams ending in explosions, and the whoosh, whoosh BANG! announcing mortars.

Intermittent on his National, Tim radioed to message he and David were marooned forward, unable to move. Almost in response, Nasib radioed he was being surrounded, requesting immediate support.

(Grey 60 radioed to say . . . enemy very close to his forward position . . .)

Jebel Regiment's recce platoon sited forward of the main camp was now in danger of being overrun; hearing his call, I had to move out. First, warn Lou. Cutting the engine again, I called, 'Any wounded behind us?' A pause, then 'No!' came the reply. Telling him we were moving out and to bunch away from the wheels, a broad Northern Irish accent replied 'We're so f…..g squashed, I might have to get married!!'

'Lucky man!' I yelled back, smiling broadly at the Irish humour. Starting up, we reversed slowly, wheels straight, inching over my prone men lying beneath, before driving over some of our kit behind. There was nothing else for it.

Battle loaded, a Saladin weighs 11.6 tonnes, the clearance a mere 43 centimetres on a level surface. Reversing over my men packed like sardines beneath the car – Lou and his group, one Mess boy and five now very frightened men lay flattened against the earth, not daring to breathe as the Saladin's undercarriage scraped gently against their cramped bodies. Fortunately, the Saladin's armour plated belly has no protrusions that might have snagged clothing. Fortunate too, the ground was mostly flat. In Lou's place I'd not have been happy.

COME ON THE 13TH!

Tim had picked up Nasib's message too. Calling me on the radio, I confirmed both T12A and I now had full crews and we were moving out, giving 'Wilco out!' to his order 'Drive them back, T12!'. 'That's a famous quote!' I radioed back, but didn't hear his reply. Once out of the sangar, my two Saladins moved off gathering speed, swinging south down a slope and out towards Nasib's threatened position. Olly was on my right. With engines roaring, our two cars charged across the open ground. In thanking me later, Nasib told how morale had soared on hearing the screaming engines, the six wheeled cross-country vehicles billowing clouds of fine powder dust, a spectacle always guaranteed to impress. I hoped it did the same for the adoo too.

Machine gun fire now concentrated at our two charging cars. I glanced across at Olly in T12A and realised we still had our Sultanate pennants flying from radio antennas. Smiling grimly to myself, I hoped the sight of his Majesty's fast approaching Saladins flying his flags would be taken as a serious provocation. Afterwards, Nasib confirmed we were right, the rate of fire intensified.

Later over a beer, I congratulated Tim on his 'Wellington order' to charge the adoo positions, receiving a broad grin in response, 'Thought you'd appreciate that!'. Olly wished I'd ordered 'Come on the 13th!' as we'd charged that day, but with adrenalin already coursing fit to burst arteries, there was probably no need for any rallying cry. That, and the fact the armoured car commander racing alongside me was 4 RTR (Royal Tank Regiment) who might not have appreciated the temporary regimental affiliation. How wrong I was, for in an instant with a grin breaking through his magnificent red beard, Olly replied he'd have been proud charging under a cavalry battle cry! (Endorsed when later he served on attachment to the 15th/19th Hussars, who in 1992 merged with the 13th/18th RH to become The Light Dragoons.) Being a proud ex-'B' Squadron troop leader with my regiment, I'd always considered myself a 13th Hussar, 'A' Squadron holding they were the smart lot, as remnants of the 18th! Unforgivable.

Frequently misunderstood by politicians who cut and merge famous regiments, many soldiers seek to join a regiment of their forebears, and whilst every soldier swears allegiance to sovereign and country and will fight accordingly, the greater loyalty is more likely to their regiment and its place in history.

Skidding to a standstill, our pursuing dust cloud formed a screen offering temporary shelter to us and Nasib's men pinned down on the ridge before settling again, drifting lazily in the still air. Too soon it'd disappeared.

(... as the cars moved, the firing almost stopped (at Janook) allowing those exposed to mount up ...)

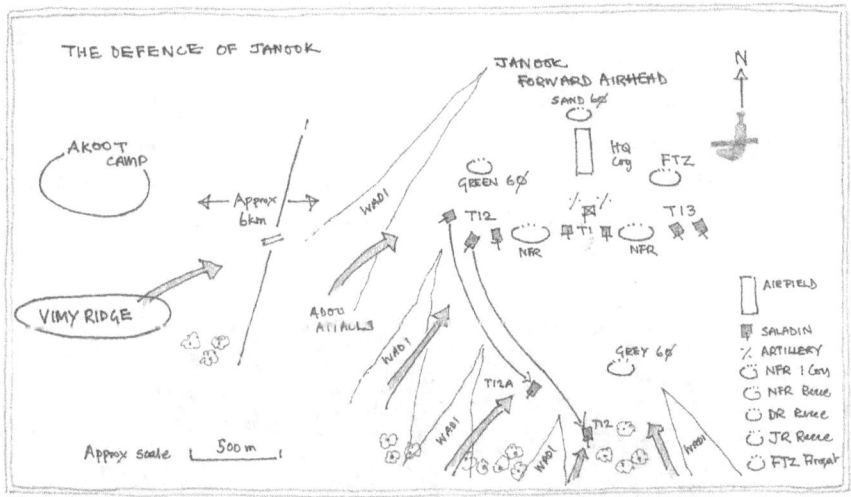

My sketched map shows the direction of adoo attacks against Janook, SAF's Forward Airhead, under continuous attacks between 6 and 10 May. My car and Olly's, T12 and T12A move forward to save Grey 60, Nasib's recce platoon from being overrun.

SOLDIER HUMOUR

Nasib's men had taken casualties, a man I knew shot in the arm, another firing his GPMG had been hit in the hand. Grinning broadly, Nasib held the man's wounded hand high to reveal a missing middle finger, immediately raising soldiers' banter, as again that spontaneous danger-induced flash of delirium had us all laughing, only to be lost to incoming machine gunfire.

Exposed on a forward slope in front of the sangars, we moved out to better hull down firing positions, putting down bursts of Browning.

(T12 had the enemy positions indicated to him by Grey 60, who had absorbed a considerable weight of fire ... T12 redirected the arty onto enemy positions.)

Calling Noel with targets, the 25 pdrs responded accurately despite his position to the rear of Janook still receiving 'overs' from HMG fired at the forward positioned Saladins. We were 500m from Janook, Olly on my right, the adoo around to our front and flanks.

In addition to mortar and rocket fire, we were exposed to armour piercing Shpagin. Squinting directly into the afternoon sun, it was becoming difficult to identify the enemy firing positions. It was Olly who first spotted the HMG firing from 800m. He'd caught sight of tracer against shadows thrown by a wadi wall. Engaging immediately with HE, he scored a direct hit with his second round. His shooting was extraordinarily good.

From the corner of my periscope, I noticed Olly's car suddenly leap forward about 10m. Seen through the restricted 'scope I thought he'd taken a direct hit. Radioing fearing the worst, I received the response 'Tango 12A, we're fine – it's just our kid, Said Mohamed!' Seventeen-year-old Said, so small we'd fixed

The fearless Said Mohamed Harrib, our diminutive driver with his trademark gold lateral incisor.

a bolster cushion to his driver's seat, had seen the second 76mm round hit on target through his driver's periscope. Giving a yelp of delight, he'd thumped his foot against the accelerator pedal, lurching the Saladin forward, before quickly reversing back into a hull down position. The exuberance of youth.

With the adoo's attention drawn to us, Tim, Lou and the remaining Saladin commanders, Sgts Ali Abdullah, Fyffe and Begley, made it to their cars. Tim now assumed command of the battle. SOAF arrived to give top cover, again but briefly on return from missions over Simba also under attack. I directed them onto adoo positions to our immediate south and west towards Vimy, along our old battle ground, giving us good reference points for directing strikes.

(... jets carried out ...strikes at Vimy Ridge and at 533673 ...)

Once again we indicated targets using the 76mm HE, the jets seeing our tracer rounds, followed up immediately. It was seamless. As we'd found on Vimy, the pilots could pick out our HE tracer, enabling them to engage instantly with their much-feared 7.62mm wing mounted machine guns. It was great teamwork.

We'd discovered from captured adoo, jets firing 7.62mm machine guns offered no escape from the hail of bullets raining down, striking rocks, ricocheting, leaving nowhere to hide. Feared for their direct fire engagement, Jets and Saladins had become primary adoo targets, propaganda prizes carrying handsome bounties.

Soon two relief Strikemasters arrived as the first pair left to refuel and rearm. The firefight continued with our two cars directing jets, guns and engaging targets until dusk. With last light the second pair of jets departed with an upbeat farewell 'See you tomorrow, Tangos!'; once again they'd undoubtedly saved us taking more casualties. But for the jets' arrival we might have lost Nasib's position. How we wished they'd had night flying capabilities.

The RCL and Shpagin had ceased firing, gun crews either killed or wounded. An upended Shpagin remained clearly visible, its long barrel pointing skywards at 45 degrees, impotent, Olly's shooting stunningly effective.

In the distance, sporadic bursts of Kalashnikov continued until dark, Ray Kane's adoo 'F ... you!' adieu.

At last light Olly and I covered Nasib's withdrawal before rejoining Lou back on Janook's western flank, facing south and west with Ruqaishi's men. Tim's T19 with Sgt Fyffe in T1A were central with redeployed Nasib, T13 Sgt Begley and T13A Sgt Ali Abdulah covering the eastern flank. David's NFR half-company on Tim's left flank faced east and south. Beside the airstrip, Noel's 25pdr battery with Graham Sherwell's HQ, were dug in approx 1000m north to the rear, protected by Khalfan's DR recce.

(The enemy attack was brilliantly timed... coordinated. The firing of mortars and Sphagin... extremely accurate and one will never understand how we managed to get away with minor casualties. It was rather foolish to have everyone out of their cars at the same time and must not happen again.)

Looking back, we'd all been appalled at the decision made to position the Forward Airhead, essentially a soft target, at Janook. There was high ground south to our front and a string of concealed wadis westwards. Whoever held that ground had a height advantage over the camp whilst also able to approach unseen to within 600 metres through the wadis. The land south offered perfect fields of direct and indirect fire onto the SAF base and any foolish enough to remain there.

An ancient Bedu proverb offers the following doctrine:

"In a place of danger, don't sit waiting praying for a miracle"

POST CONTACT – ORDER RESUMED

There followed the standard post-contact radio check, each position reporting individually as Tim ascertained casualty numbers. We'd none seriously wounded, mainly flesh wounds, one missing finger, cuts and bruises. We'd escaped remarkably luckily. The medics went around bandaging and dressing wounds, two of the wounded being medevaced the following day.

Again I had cut forefingers from hurriedly removing 76mm safety clips designed for peacetime, when I am sure they probably saved many a possible and horrendous turret explosion. In times of acute stress, the clips were a hindrance. As on Vimy Ridge, I was now partly releasing these safety features, yet hands still suffered when working fast, scraping off recently healed scabs. Likewise on knuckles, when rubbed raw ramming rounds into the breechblock. Abdullah's hands were similarly affected.

Tim arrived to thank us, admitting surprise at the adoo's accuracy and how few casualties we'd taken, needlessly reminding us of the need for extra vigilance with night picquets. Lou had paced the distance between the kit drop-off area and my car's sangar. 'You'll be off to the Olympics anytime?' he quipped, reaching for a cigarette. 'With you my trainer, Lou?' I grinned back at him receiving the expected 'Feck no'! Out of training, I wasn't that fit, my dash to the Saladin had been down more to fight or flight's adrenalin rush. The back of a Saladin is just under 1.5m high.

Typically generous by nature, there followed handshakes and muttered 'shadeed, sahb, wagid shadeed' that night as soldiers came round to share their own experiences. One from JR recce displaying a white gauze bandaged hand, fresh stained red, had left the medic's tent insisting he come to thank me. It was humbling to be amongst these most loyal of men.

(At 2000 the adoo attacked again. Sphagin, MMG and SA fire . . . from area of 541603. We had failed to learn any lessons from . . . previous attack and once again T12 (Hodgson) was only Ironside . . . able to do anything about the situation. He called down arty fire and engaged with Browning. T13 (Sgt Begley), T13A (Sgt Abdullah) and T12B (Sgt Costello) all in dead ground to the enemy, and Maj Cornwell once again found himself completely without cover . . . with only consolation he did have Sgts Oliver and Fyffe for company on this occasion!

Reaching his car . . . Maj Cornwell could see trace from . . . Sphagin, but with no illumination for his sight graticule had to fire off the range drum. 2 HESH in target area and ½ belt Browning.

Capt Hodgson had similar problem with lack of sight illumination and decided against using main armament as Grey 60 was to his front. Not being engaged on this contact, Grey 60 was able to pass corrections to arty via T12.

We failed to give the enemy any credit and learnt very little from the earlier contact.

We have been asking for replacement pea bulbs for ages . . . and it seems almost certain

. . . if we had them . . . Capt Hodgson . . . in the gunners seat at the time would have been able to knock out that Sphagin.

2 wounded, Sand 60, Grey 60.)

FIGHTING CLOSED DOWN

"Our drivers and gunners used closed hatches during training, largely to avoid sand and dust getting everywhere. Except for mortar and shell bursts . . . the Commander . . . must not deny himself the use of his ears, nose, corners of his eyes, and that sixth sense he soon develops for danger, by shutting his hatch on the outside world. Those who make people close down on dry training in BAOR are doing more harm than good."

Major AJ Cornwell 2 RTR

T12 – NONE FOUGHT CLOSED DOWN

With temperatures sometimes exceeding 50 degrees Celsius, confinement within a steel armoured car could be overwhelming. My troop operated with open hatches, despite knowing we sat amongst almost a third of a tonne of high explosive packed inside a 200 litre petrol engined vehicle. With hatches closed, heat exhaustion would probably have killed us anyway.

Maintaining a high rate of fire, the Saladin's main armament and coaxial machine gun rapidly built up heat inside the turret; propellant fumes expelled with each 76mm shell case ejected and .30mm machine gun burst, created intolerable conditions with turrets closed. Propellant gases after four rounds fired in quick succession left you choking as coughing, eyes streaming, both commander and gunner failed to function combatively.

I'd taken the calculated decision to operate leaving both turret hatches open, even during contacts. There was no argument for drivers; positioned at the front of the car, it was imperative they mastered driving and operating under closed hatches. Dead driver, dead car. So it was to hell with standard procedures on closed turret hatches. Lessons learned through experience had taught us it was near impossible operating for any extended periods closed down.

I let each car commander decide. Mine followed my example: none fought under closed hatches. Despite the risks, each commander and crew accepted them. Young and confident, we'd had mortars and rockets land within metres causing but superficial damage. We'd also faced hurled grenades on Vimy. After nearly eight months receiving daily incoming mortar and rocket fire, by now we knew the score. The Squadron's most battle-experienced by a considerable margin, we were known for our independent ways. We understood others preferred closed hatches once mortar bombs began falling. Each to their own.

TWIZZLE KIA

Whilst casualties had been light, amongst their number was Twizzle, Graham's adopted small black cat. Included on Desert Regiment's indent had ensured Twizzle soldier status, and us an extra ration of food and water.

The cat was found quite dead, cut almost in two by a rock splinter thrown up by an exploding RCL 75mm round. It upset us all, but particularly Graham, a big bear of a man who'd formed a special attachment to the small cat. Deciding Twizzle deserved a dignified burial, Graham and I decided we'd bury the cat close to our rudimentary Officers' Mess, a cave extended by canvas awning. Here, Graham had confidently predicted, we were safe from incoming fire. A fact unfortunately disproved by Twizzle.

Laying the cat in the roughly excavated hole, it dawned on us perhaps we weren't cut out to be grave-diggers after all, having placed the poor creature with its head facing at an acute angle downhill. Realising we probably shouldn't leave him like that I righted the body so Twizzel's head now rested uphill. Graham said a few words before we covered the small beast's remains. 'That was the proper thing to do,' growled Graham, before adding 'fancy a whisky . . . think I've saved a little somewhere?'

As a postscript – despite loyal and devoted service over a turbulent few months and now KIA, Graham's recommendation Twizzle be awarded a posthumous campaign medal was declined. An unimpressed Staff Officer signalled a reduction in staffing records by one on DR's indent. Graham's subterfuge had been blown.

It wasn't just the front line being taken out by the adoo, those in the rear, HQ and Guns were similarly vulnerable, as evidenced in David Arkless' very readable book, "The Secret War" in which he writes of that night's attacks:

". . . once the firing had died . . . we lay there quietly in the sangar. 'Geordie, Bert?' a voice called out – it was Graham (Sherwell) '. . . everyone OK?'

'I've . . . sausage and beans . . . all over me bleeding trousers . . . yeah, we're OK! Anyone hurt?'

'Finding out!'

'Incoming fire . . . bit heavy? How did they know we were . . . in this sangar?'

'Oh, it wasn't you they're after,' replied Graham looking to the ridge at the Saladins, 'it's just bad luck you were in their line of fire'"

Noel's guns too had received a number of 'overs' aimed at the Saladins, yet resolutely he had his men remain by their guns, responding instantly to our requested fire missions. His fine example of a gunner under fire earned him a WKhM (G), The Sultan's Distinguished Service Medal (Gallantry), Oman's equivalent to the MC.

JANOOK MESS TENT

Next morning, post stand-down, Olly, Lou and I joined DR's second-in-command in the shade of the tarpaulin stretched between rocks that was our Mess, to find Graham relaxed in a camp chair, slumped as only this seasoned major had perfected, chatting to Sgts David Arkless and Dennis Smith, a contract medic. Offered tea, bully-beef and white bread for breakfast, we fell on it gratefully.

Sitting beside Graham, I too sat slumped, weary from endless nights of snatched sleep. Grease, petrol and oil spattered, unshaven and unwashed and reeking of spent gunpowder, I no doubt smelt worse than a dog kennel. Yet no one moved away; we each smelled as bad. None had shaved for over a month, toothpaste was rarer than gold, and our hair wouldn't have looked out of place at Shaftesbury Theatre's current show of that name.

'Busy night?' enquired Graham . . . 'Yup,' I grinned back at the big man, sinking fury teeth into a welcome bully-beef sandwich, compo rations supplied by Graham's Mess staff. The tea was strong and sweet; burmail water, long boiled with black tea leaves added to condensed milk and sugar, the mixture stewed for over an hour; pure nectar to the sleep deprived. The acute tiredness would remain until after R&R and a chance for a good clean up.

Half listening to the chatter about the attacks during the night, my reverie was abruptly interrupted noticing movement behind Graham's shoulder. Asking him to lean forward, a small brightly coloured reptile slithered slowly across the wadi wall just behind him. 'Snake, Graham!' I warned. True to form, the old

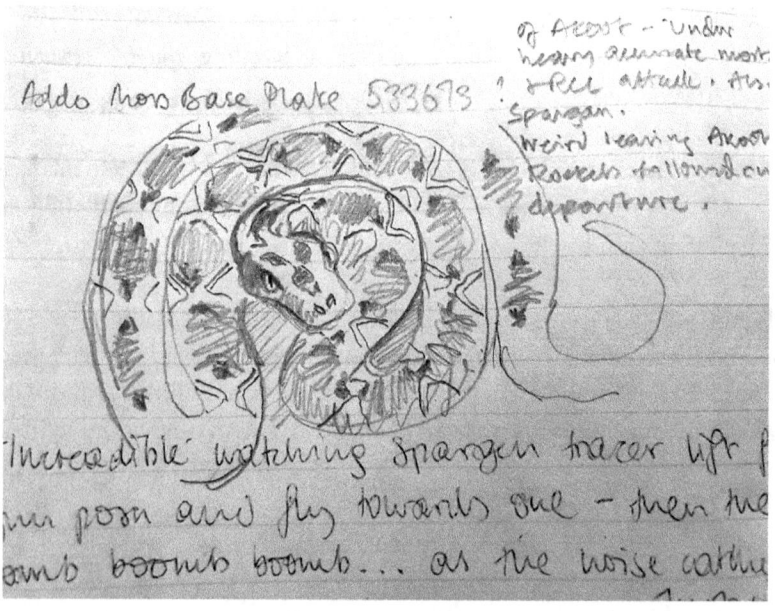

6th May – diarised sketch of the snake, probably Echis Khosatzkii (Painted Saw-Scaled Viper) found in Eastern Yemen and Dhofar. As a species, Vipers have the unenviable reputation for causing the most snakebite associated deaths across the globe. Not one's first choice of breakfast guest. Thankfully we generally encountered very few of these fearsome reptiles.

Africa hand calmly rose from his chair, picked it up and moved to the other side of the cave. The snake, most likely a viper, probably measured 30 centimetres and disappeared almost as soon as seen. Strikingly coloured in shades of burnt sienna and yellow ochre, it looked the business. 'We could be on the set of Walt Disney's Living Desert!' exclaimed Olly, raising a dubious laugh from the rest of us, each now glancing gingerly behind and under seats for any unwelcome guests.

POSITION UNTENABLE

"They put us under a very heavy fire, but luckily for us – and no thanks to any General – a slight rise on our flank ricocheted the balls just over our heads. It was useless, as we could not act."

Captain Jenyns, 13th Hussars, Crimea 1854

Talk continued on the perilous position selected for Simba's airhead, overlooked from the treeline to our south. 'Except that we're presently not totally surrounded, this has the makings of another fuck up,' proposed the optimistic Sgt Arkless, sipping a can of beer. 'Thanks for that, Geordie,' grunted Graham, 'never fear, HQ will come to realise this place is untenable, particularly as an airhead. Now we've filled the place with ordnance, it'll bring adoo in like bloody vultures to a wildebeest carcass! What a cock-up!' Keeping his counsel, Tim told me he'd messaged a disbelieving Dhofar HQ that Janook was clearly a non-starter. Tim's last signal suggested if HQ didn't believe him, perhaps they should visit. Returning to our positions, we wondered how much longer we'd be holding Janook.

As we walked back to our cars, Lou asked in his County Down accent, 'Somebody jes tell me . . . *untenable*, Jasus, what's the ferk's that mean?' 'Fucked,' Olly replied, my intellectual sergeant.

> 7 May – A restless night. Some jundee blasted off at 0430 on automatic – frightened of the dark?? Adoo attacks continued until 2300.
> A.M. – negative reply to Tim's signal that airstrip untenable. Deckchair wallahs in Salalah obviously know better!
> 0530 moved out past Grey 60, not waiting for Green 19 who should have completed his move by first light. Gave them covering fire advancing in the open.
> 1215 – AT LAST! News we're moving back to Manston – Janook untenable as Simba airhead, SOAF declared first plane landing here would be taken

> *out! 1430 Col Mike visited to confirm move out as adoo 83mm fired fm 533673 – confirmed by crater data. Chopper Bravo 1600 – Brit wounded on Red, 'not too serious' (probably was for him?) Troop on stag all day – Rations – 7 biscuits, 3 ounces corned dog, & 2 mugs tea. We've numb bums sitting in cars all day. Sunspots on setting sun. Business getting Green 19 in – no radio contact – radio problems. Huw killed – 3 tonner on TM46 – Taqah road-opening – Wadi Arzat outside Mamurah. F...!! how sad.*

At least we'd slept outside our cars. Interrupted but nevertheless sleep. Stretched flat on the ground on prayer mats, fully clothed and booted, draped loosely with blankets for speedy exit, loaded Sterlings concealed, sleep came quickly. I learned later the rest of the squadron had remained in their cars all night after the last attack. Tim was less than amused T12 had maintained a more relaxed watch with one crewman per car. That, and apparently following the 0430 incident, I'd radioed suggesting some people required weapon training. Of this, I'd no recollection. I was bloody tired. Increasingly at night people were loosing off at shadows, intentionally or accidentally, each occasion causing a full stand-to. I'd total confidence in my troop, highly experienced after months on active service. We were tight. Those on watch would remain vigilant, alert, partly out of loyalty to the troop, partly out of respect for an unpredictable foe.

During the last days at Akoot as it became an ever increasingly remote outpost, we'd survived far worse tension with considerably fewer men than held Janook. Tim and his crews had only just arrived. Reprimanded, I held my tongue, I'd no excuse at all. Tim was right and I apologised. With the pressures he faced, he really didn't need a recalcitrant 24-year-old troop leader just at that moment.

At midday came the best news: we were to vacate Janook for Manston, another place on a map, another arid, desiccated location we had visited on numerous occasions before, escorting Akoot's wood gathering convoys. But it was further away from adoo artillery. Commander Dhofar, flying in by Huey to see Janook for himself, landed as we came under another attack, mortar and small arms. Perfect adoo timing to seal the deal.

My troop moved forward before daylight to take up positions with Nasib's men. Delayed, David's half company joined us later as we covered their advance. Attacks became sporadic with no casualties taken. That night we returned to Janook 1000m behind, to resume night defensive positions.

To our east, Simba was attacked and three soldiers plus Robin Hastie-Smith, a captain with MR, were wounded. Robin was on a brief familiarisation visit to Dhofar before his regiment moved down on roulement. He'd been hit by two 'overs', non-ballistic bullets missing their primary targets only to sail on to strike someone on another position. Medevaced, Robin was heard to comment, 'the adoo got lucky without even knowing it'!

The worst news arrived that evening with news Huw Jones had been killed by a mine on a fairly routine convoy to Taqah, a task we'd frequently undertaken together out of Arzat the previous year. Of equal age, Huw and I had become friends since meeting up after Geoff had been killed. We'd shared the Taqah outpost and a number of convoys and we'd meet occasionally on R&R down from Akoot.

HUW JONES JR

NFR had arrived to take over from JR as Plains Battalion, now looking forward to nine months in the relative safety of Northern Oman. JR's Col Peter Worthy had suggested to recently arrived OC NFR Col Bryan Ray they join a convoy to Taqah as a familiarisation exercise. It was routine stuff. The two colonels would travel in separate Land Rovers with soldier escorts, accompanied by Spike's Z Company Land Rovers. The two Battalion Intelligence Officers (IO), Huw and Dick Simmons (NFR) were travelling in Bedfords with soldiers and provisions.

Following standing orders, once clear of Z Company's daily mine-cleared tracks around Salalah, the extended convoy of vehicles duly followed the truck in front, intent on avoiding mines secreted amongst the numerous existing tracks; hoping also to avoid mortars or rockets taking out more than one vehicle should they bunch together as had occurred on an earlier occasion. As battalion IO, Huw had probably no need to be on the convoy, but he too was showing the ropes to his NFR successor. Commanding the convoy Huw led as point vehicle, a heavily loaded unprotected Bedford truck with stores for Taqah.

Reaching Khor Sawli, one of the frequent wadis traversing Salalah plain and a known ambush point, the front wheel of Huw's vehicle detonated a Russian TM-46 anti-tank mine right beneath his seat. Thrown through the open commander's cupola, Huw fell to the rock-strewn ground badly hurt. Though appearing serious, his wounds were thought survivable. Never issued with helmets, instead, the shemagh, useful as a dust mask offered little or no protection to bullets, shrapnel or violent blows to the head.

Inexplicably Huw's driver had escaped the full energy of the exploding mine. Badly shaken he was otherwise relatively uninjured, the vehicle's transmission between the front seats protecting the driver. Having a steering wheel to hold onto as the front of the truck was blown upwards, the fortunate driver had remained in his seat, unscathed but for minor cuts, deafening and bruising.

The convoy moved on as a helicopter airlifted the casualty to the Field Surgical Team at UAG. Sadly despite the brilliant reputation of these surgeons, they were unable to save Huw. The body of this young contract officer was later flown back to Bayt al Falaj, and buried at the small Christian cemetery outside Muscat.

Gone, that cheerful optimistic individual who'd volunteered to fight a foreign war for political and military masters locally, and those watching remotely from safety overseas. On my last R&R to Salalah, I had joined Huw and Ian Gordon (ex-7 Gurkha Rifles) of MR on a familiarisation visit, and a couple of other off-duty officers taking a Land Rover to the beach, less than half a mile from UAG. We'd swum and relaxed in the warm sea and afterwards sat talking, idly wondering if we might be missed back at camp. Unlikely, as we were off duty. Each was armed so we'd felt safe. An amazing white sandy beach stretched into the distance, the sea's perfect blue reflecting cloudless sky. The talk was of our futures but mostly what we missed most of all, girls, and how we really missed girls. Looking back, I recalled Huw's prophetic words: 'Surely has to be a better way to spend a young life?' . . .

What might we have been doing otherwise with our lives? Little did we realise the true significance of this war against the then omnipresent communists. Indoctrinated with Western propaganda since each had joined up, Marxist Communism was the invisible force intent on consuming democracy. Each had volunteered. Adventurers all, Contract Officers hoping to make a few bucks, seconded on loan from the British Army, hoping to further military careers. And possibly unique at the time, one SSC, a short service commission officer hoping to do enough to gain a regular commission in the army. The last of the honourable professions?

David, Huw's elder brother, a respected major also serving with the Sultan's forces, was transferred to Oman Gendarmerie. After the war, their parents visited Oman, placing an oak cross on Huw's grave. Writing poignantly, they'd taken some small comfort in the legend that frankincense and myrrh gifted at the birth of Jesus originated in Dhofar, where Huw had fought for freedom and died.

How often in discussion we'd recognised parents and grandparents to whom war remained a living memory, and now siblings and girlfriends too, had the worst of it. Whilst we served, we had the support of close friends, and for the most we knew what was going on. At home isolated, fearful, theirs was the ceaseless worry, the dreaded arrival of telegram or unannounced visit. The far heavier burden by a mile.

My diary scribble that day ended once again recalling Housman's lines we'd laughingly misquote over a beer, the last always reaching a crescendo. One day we'd memorise the original prose.

*'Hell man, life's nothing much to lose,
But young men think it is,
and we're too BLOODY YOUNG!'*

LOCUST PHASE 4

*8 May – Phase 4 – Locust:
Janook command passed to me.
Strength:
Elements Oman Arty – 1x 25pdr
Half Coy NFR – another 8 days – David
Green 60 – Ruqaishi
Sand 60 – Khalfan
Elements HQ Coy DR
10 rds. 6:HE 4:HESH
2 x sections MMG fm Z Coy (arrive today)
2 x pls BG (fm 16 May)
Graham away today*

0945 contact – 4 incomers. Time of flight gave us time to finish mugs tea. 1840 contact – s/a and Mors – Adoo seen & engaged – grid 543675 – v. accurate – 3 KIA and poss machine gun seen by Ruqaishi as we scored direct hit, crew attempting to carry MG away to safety. Adoo not wearing headdress – just shirts and wizzars.

(As a result of enemy action . . . (HQ) have decided Janook . . . too difficult to defend to allow fixed wing . . . safe landing

To counter enemy action and to cover move back to Manston . . . armour/infantry screen . . . deployed . . . on forward picquet. Screen consisted . . . all T12 callsigns and Green 19.

(Enemy) attack 1030 . . . RCL . . . T12 (Capt Hodgson) engaged with arty whilst T1 engaged firing 8 HE/T onto 543647.

Rounds landed on forward picquet close to T12B (Sgt Costello) as T12 and T12A (Sgt Oliver) engaged positions at 557652 and 543643 with main armament and arty airburst.)

Tim's troop T1, and T1A (Sgt Fyffe) with T13 and T13A (Sgts Begley and Abdullah) plus Graham's DR HQ Company and Grey 60, Nasib's men, moved out at first light to set up Manston.

Given the rearguard command, my orders were to hold Janook until the last stockpiled ordnance and stores had been evacuated. It would take a while to clear. Tim meanwhile covered the new redeployment and organised repair of Manston's ancient airfield. Leaving two cars and two OG platoons holding Manston, Tim and Sgt Fyffe were kept busy escorting convoys between Janook and Manston.

With David's NFR soldiers we'd also Shelldrake support, Noel's detachment with a single 25 pounder. Making up the balance on strength, Ruqaishi and Khalfan's recce platoons, Mahboob, a Pakistani cook, and one Mess boy. And just arrived, two sections from Spike Powell's Z Company. We made for an eclectic mix.

> (As the last convoy was moving out, the enemy attacked at 1830 . . . firing from 542683 and 543675. The armour/infantry screen was still in position . . . at 550699 1,000 forward south of Janook. G60 was slightly north in an OP at 542702.
>
> T12 (Capt Hodgson) immediately brought down arty fire as he moved his cars to new fire positions some 200M to the W . . . saw 3 men carrying ammunition boxes and opened fire, the men observed by T12A were seen to fall. T12B (Sgt Costello) . . . scored a direct hit . . . with main armament and co-ax.
>
> T1 . . . (back at Janook) . . . after last convoy escort . . . moved forward to assist Green 60 . . . being over-run. They had moved forward onto a crest and were pinned down. T1 was able to follow trace from T12 and opened up with main armament. T12 continued to direct arty fire at enemy positions.
>
> A further 16 mortar bombs fell around cars at 550700. T1 engaged with main armament . . . and . . . T12 engaged with arty . . . same area. Contact ended about 1915 . . . cars pulled back at last light.
>
> Nil casualties taken.)

The morning attack at 0945 was, we considered, inconsequential. The baseplates distant, the bombs had landed short and wide. Time enough we'd reckoned to gulp last mouthfuls of tea before retaliating. We were becoming reckless; a mortar bomb travels over a kilometre a second.

The adoo struck again at 1830. Arriving back from convoy escorts, Tim thankfully joined the battle just as we were getting a little pressed, Ruqaishi's recce platoon being outflanked, with the adoo rushing us. Spotting a crew in action we'd engaged, smack on target, as Tim's rounds followed my trace onto the machine guns, Olly and Ruqaishi observing the direct hits. The contact continued until dark, small arms and mortars we couldn't find.

FIGHT TO SAVE JANOOK AIRHEAD

9 May – 0700 patrolled area of last night's contact, not much found as usual, some blood. All tired. Need to keep moving to stay alert. Better after breakfast. Dug out number of 82mm splinters from my car – horrifyingly small. 2x3mm? We are moving out tomorrow at sparrows – expect a repeat of Akoot withdrawal? Adoo watching every move.
(Radio Aden claim great victory over jaysh with Akoot, now they say they'll push us out of Janook! – Bet they'll claim Manston too?')

Contact 1625. RCL, Mors. RCL at E5 left 200 & Mors at 531673 making earlier calculation from crater pretty accurate! Engaged with 76mm and Shelldrake. About 20 mors and 6 RCL. Saw adoo, engaged 25pdr airburst. Adoo group charged with mgs – wiped out by Lou. God, they're brave. Adoo mors silenced. Estimated adoo losses at 10 KIA. Must be more wounded. Resupply: ammo, petrol, water and akl. Ramadhan is bloody good, he had organised the lot as we came back to our positions.

HE	HESH	.30	6 x Jerrycans petrol
12	22	2	6
12A	11	4	6
12B	5	5	3

(9th May, Janook, Locust Force

The move to Manston was just about complete by mid afternoon . . . and it might have been possible to have withdrawn the remaining Locust Force before last light. But the experience gained on 27 April (Vimy) ruled against this . . .

At 1625 enemy opened up with RCL . . . from 556652 landing on picquet still held by T12/G19. At same time about 10 mortars landed amongst picquet and another 8 landed on main feature (Janook),1200m back.

T12 (Capt Hodgson) engaged with arty, and moved forward to engage with main armament . . . enemy at 533673 and 558652. He spotted an OP at 531673 and asking Green 19 (Capt Nicholls) to continue the shoot, Hodgson engaged the OP with main armament and co-ax. T12A (Sgt Oliver) picked up T12's trace and engaged the target blind.

T1 (leaving convoy organisation duties) moved to Janook's E where he observed mortars firing from 556652 and engaged with 8 HE/T as arty was being used by Green 19.

(As the contact ended) . . . all went back to getting the last vehicles away . . . when at about 1700 . . . men appeared at 548675 . . . engaged T12B

(Sgt Costello) with LMG who replied with HE/T and co-ax. After a pause, mortars again landed on forward picquet and Janook main feature, the (single) gun and T12 cars replied engaging 545660. Contact ended at 1730.)

We moved out on patrol before daylight and later that morning, covered by Olly and Lou, I visited adoo firing positions from the day before. Taking two sections of Khalfan's recce with me we found only bloodstained earth, the adoo long gone taking their dead and wounded.

Six months later and following his departure, I found and read Tim's official contact reports on the Janook actions. I was now Squadron Leader. At the end of his reports, I discovered Tim had generously submitted citations for the three T12 car commanders, the citations falling to deaf ears. Deservedly, Noel had been awarded the Sultan's Distinguished Service Medal (Gallantry) for commanding his gun detachment under fire at Janook. As a gunner, his was through a separate sponsor. Should you ever read this, thanks, Tim, it meant a lot.

(Locust Force pulled back to Manston at first light on 10th May without further contact.
    ... The courage, skill and fortitude displayed by Captain Hodgson and his troop over the period ... has been quite outstanding.)

10 May – Leave application approved. Flights UK & back.
0415 Someone fired belt of 250 rounds .30 into the darkness causing a flap. Asleep, I was dreaming he was testing his weapon! Bloody hell, we now shoot at shadows!!
Withdrew fm Janook 0615. No mishaps. Gut sense of unease returns, last out of Janook. T12 Saladins rearguard, just as Akoot. But adoo remained silent. Know they're watching, they think we're beaten. I'd agreed we fire two short FU! bursts .30 to show we too can be immature in same circumstances ... felt better. But was it dignified?
Manston – a small Akoot. Spirits high. Laager posn. We're held in the rear now, bayts built, Mess too. Wadis have green frankincense trees. Am filthy and stink.

LAST OUT OF JANOOK

Unease returned with each departing truck. Once again, we three cars were alone, on rearguard. Surrounding us, Janook's menacing wadis and gullies so effectively used by an increasingly confident enemy. Chased out from Akoot just days before, we knew we were vulnerable when withdrawing.

Tired as never before, our circadian rhythms non-existent, unwashed and dirty after weeks of fighting, I felt the need to give the adoo a farewell blast. As we moved out, each fired two short bursts of Browning into the watching treeline; pointless, but we felt the better for it. We reached Manston without hiccup. Already an established camp, it was a relief to be free of Janook, a place I'd no wish to see again, twinned with the whole of Akoot.

Again we were leaving a landscape scarred by wheel tracks cut into virgin desert, empty sangars, Dannert wire held firm by iron stakes hammered in for permanence, too deep for easy removal. Abandoned too, litter of a rushed exit, brass empty cases, evidence of contacts littered the place, shiny empty sardine tins and discarded cigarette packets, clothing scraps and random areas of human faeces, nourishment for flies, excrement of a retreating army. All evidence of living vegetation cut down and used for firewood, creating an environmental scarcity where once there'd been chance.

It'd be another eight months before SAF returned to Janook. At the end of their tour, 1 Coy JR mounted an operation south into adoo territory and minefields, paying heavily. If history doesn't repeat, sometimes there's an echo.

My UK leave application had been approved and I'd seen green trees of frankincense in the wadis.

24

GRENADES, HABARUT RETAKEN & MIRBAT

A dropped grenade and time stands still. Brian Jayes joins DR on Simba and is medevaced. Habarut retaken and Saladins break United Nations protocol. Near disaster hunting for meat rations. A lesson learned. Mike unwell again. Battle for Mirbat becomes SAS legend. War decorations and medals.

MANSTON

11 - 12 May – Graham away one week. Continued defence positions. All aircraft using Manston – SOAF now happy.

FAB all present.
Took Khalfan & FAB to search waterhole. x 6 RCL from Janook area.
Today's Orders:

Establish D.F.s		Night attack procedures, armour.
M1	512776	Widen airstrip.
M2	519770	Build S.E.P. compound.
		Nationals – need batteries.
M3	506745	Water – round to all locs.
		Graham – msg – fresh fish on plane!

Hand grenade/Skyvan! Firqatman's clumsy fingers
NB – Contact reports required

Sitrep: water found, drinkable but murky – grid 495798. Water pty: I pl picquet, 1 pl loading, takes 3hrs to fill 6 burmails. We cannot be offensive whilst fetching water.
Also – have upped water ration to 8 pints a man in camp, 16 on Land Rover ops.
Back still painful – will get better.

Tim had done a wonderful job laying out defences, with sangars and trenches requiring finishing. Taking a Land Rover patrol and the Mahri firqat, FAB, as guides, we located drinkable water about 3.5km northwest of Manston, in a Wadi Aydim tributary. Filling burmails was slow work, but a necessity; it was drinking water. SOAF had requested the strip be widened. With MR pioneers on attachment, the existing earth airstrip was broadened using readily available stone to fill holes, as we'd had done at Akoot. There were six RCL incomers, but off the mark. We could relax to getting the Simba airhead established. Of many tasks still outstanding were contact reports covering the last days at Akoot and time at Janook for which I'd now received a reminder or two. Admin / action? Difficult choice.

WHEN TIME STOOD STILL

Boarding a Skyvan to speak with the pilot, I found two FAB firqat whom I'd not met previously, up from Salalah having hitched a lift. They had been sitting perched on the payload, the fuselage being empty of seats. Unloading was in full swing, men offloading boxes of ordnance and munitions, scheduled for onward flights to Simba by Huey.

Offering 'Salaam Alaikum' as I extended a right hand in greeting, they replied 'Wa alaikum assalam'. Rising and, shifting his Kalashnikov to his left hand, one proffered his right in reply, promptly dropping a green Russian F1 hand grenade to the fuselage floor. It bounced twice before rolling to where I stopped its further descent with my desert booted right foot.

Determined to show neither fear nor surprise – we were already dead if the pin was out – I stood foot on grenade, willing raised eyebrows would crease into a frown. Looking back at me, a lightly whiskered expressionless face broke into a gap-toothed smile. Embarrassment or arrogance? Difficult to tell, even after all this time.

Around me, men stopped what they were doing. No one moved. Rooted in suspense they stared, some open mouthed, watching as time stood still. Breaking

Skyvan taking off following resupply at Manston – Arab, Baluchi and FAB Mahri firqat soldiers mill around after unloading stores, and indeed grenades.

the spell, Marhi Firqatman stepped forward and in a single fluid movement retrieved his grenade from beneath my foot. Straightening, he looked at me, impassive, feigning control, yet there it was, fleetingly, the unmistakable flicker of acknowledgement. 'My victory I believe,' I thought to myself.

Turning to collect my gear delivered from Salalah, I overheard the pilot mutter '. . . it's like bloody Russian roulette!'

A fused Soviet F1 hand grenade weighs about 600 grams. The anti-personnel fragmentation weapon, based on the French F1 grenade, has a 60-gram explosive charge (TNT). Earning the nickname limonka for its unforgettable shape and yellow-green colour, these weapons were common to every communist army of the day.

> *13 May – Radio Aden reports 11 KIA since 1st May attacking Janook.*
> *Recce for new route east to Wadi Bal Atawf. Found no water. New route very tight, closed in by wadis.*
> <u>*Need flit*</u> *– fly sprayer*
> *Fridge – Starlight.*

S/Sgt Castle R/R. medic old Hector here, gives us saline solution for hands.
'Bou in 1330, loaded L/R, Doc's fridge, and smoke (25 pdr).
Back 1730 for T12B's crew – special flight for R/R – very good of them. Dick M-Evans on Bou going for R/R – full of life & congrats for us over Vimy and Janook.
Says Simba's going great. Running short on rations.
Sgt Fyffe has decided to stay until end of tour.

The search for better water supplies continued, vital to avoid Manston becoming another Akoot where we'd survived under strict water rationing, supplies either flown in or trucked overland from Mudhai's springs, two days' journey along mined routes, there and back. What had become a critical logistical problem at Akoot and now likely to be repeated at Manston, was fast becoming one on Simba where so far results on finding a water supply hadn't looked promising.

Returning from sick leave, Gerry Fyffe had decided to see out his secondment, easing our crewing problems. That evening Lou's crew caught a Caribou flight to Salalah for R&R, joining Dick Morgan-Evans en route from Simba. Greatly enjoying his temporary role as OC 3 Company, an animated Dick was still full of the Vimy episode, reportedly the largest contact of the war to date he'd heard. As with most records, it'd soon be broken. That July at Mirbat, at a small fishing village in eastern Dhofar, when a furious battle was fought.

BRIAN JAYES – ROYAL HUSSAR (DR)

Fresh and very white faced as we'd all been on arrival, Brian arrived on Simba, DR's latest seconded officer. He and I had met first at our Young Officers course at Bovington Camp five years earlier and then in Münster, Germany when our regiments were part of 4 Guards Brigade. The 10th Royal Hussars dinner nights were always lavish experiences. Learning he'd been posted to Simba, I wondered, needlessly, what Brian would make of Dhofar rations. Our parents were near neighbours in Sussex and I looked forward to seeing him again, not realising it would be sooner than later.

Brian had flown from SAF HQ in Oman directly to Simba via Salalah where he'd hurriedly been issued with kit, a FN rifle, four magazines and ammo before flying on to Simba. As Alan Howard six months earlier, Brian had arrived on Jumea, the Omani weekend. Travelling comfortably in jeans and T-shirt, until issued with kit before joining his regiment, Brian offloaded his bags packed two days earlier at his parents' sprawling home in Sussex, his suitcase and rucksack still bearing smudged chalk markings of a diligent customs official. It was mid-afternoon when Brian stepped off the Huey, and Simba was under attack; his new home.

Sandy, a year earlier, had had the same welcome on arrival when asked to accompany what turned out to be a suicidal mission, when a mortally wounded officer was left behind to die as five men escaped, wounded, an armoured vehicle destroyed and weapons captured.

Given no chance to acclimatise, Brian found himself part of a patrol entering Wadi Sarfait at first light the following day. Descending the precipitous wadi, it was strenuous going. By midday under a burning sun Brian's body gave in to the unaccustomed stress of heat and dehydration. He collapsed in agony with body cramp, unable to move and in extreme pain. His men poured chargul water into his mouth, but he vomited it back straight away, a symptom of dehydration. Dehydration causes muscle cramps. In Brian's case he couldn't move. He'd lost too much liquid and salts and was in very real danger of serious complications leading to renal failure we'd been warned about. DR's doctor Babu ordered Brian be medevaced immediately. Tall yet fortunately of slim build, Brian was gallantly carried back to Mainbrace by his men where Babu administered an emergency intravenous drip, a saline mixture of water and sodium, the body absorbs quicker than water taken through the mouth. Heatstroke kills.

Brian's case had arisen through not being allowed time to acclimatise prior to combat operations. Two days might have sufficed; he'd have at least learned the need to drink more. Suffering from too little water and salt lost through excessive perspiration we all suffered as new arrivals, the arid heat and extreme conditions experienced when under fire, Brian's body mechanisms had closed down. He was lucky. Babu's expertise and rapid medevac to FST Salalah ensured a full recovery. Rehydrated, and suffering no long-term effects, he returned to Simba within a few days.

Meanwhile the position on manning was becoming critical at the Squadron. With Mike away ill with suspected kidney problems and Sgt Fyffe frequently ill with the same complaint, we were short on Saladin commanders. Tim's leave, his first for over a year, was looming, leaving my troop T12 as the only operational unit. Running two locations, Manston and Mudhai, patrols, ambushes and imminently, responsibility for running Habarut convoys, we were busy.

Learning of his escapade at Simba, I urged Tim consider requesting Brian's transfer to the Squadron. Within a week the Royal Hussar arrived to level officer numbers, two cavalrymen to two tankies, once Mike returned from medevac. Brian's health forced him to serve a reduced period on loan service, yet his nine-month tour in Dhofar matched that of his many seconded peers.

> *14 May – 0800 convoy in fm Mudhai*
> *0700 T12 & A with Green 19A – mine patrol. Nil contact. Very dusty, fetched more water fm wells.*
> *Bou in – loaded 5.5 barrel. Took 2 hours.*
> *Stomach bad – can't eat. Water? Registered more DFs.**
> *Water patrol tomorrow.*
> *Last night Radio Aden claimed they'd taken out one Saladin, two Guns, 11 men and 3 x 3-tonners. Admitting to further 3 men KIA at Janook.*
> *T12A R&R tmw – Boys cheered at prospect of Salalah. New moon.*
> *PM gave Tim outline on Akoot/Janook contacts, it took 1¼ hrs but has saved me a lot of paperwork. Soldiers burning frankincense have 'frankincensed' whole valley – but it doesn't matter. Feel like shit.*

*DFs (defensive fire tasks) – pre-registered and numbered targets, used in defensive positions.

The water we'd found to date was drinkable but foul tasting and I'd begun to suffer the effects. Olly, Lou and Gerry were similarly stricken, but not so the soldiers. The incumbent medic prescribed water purification tablets, scrounged from BATT. We couldn't rely on the well water we'd found.

Requiring a Herculean effort we manhandled the unwieldy 5.5in (140mm) barrel, a 4m length of steel onto the Skyvan, a payload approaching the aircraft's maximum at just over 1.6 tonnes. Hot, dusty work, yet undertaken with stoical humour of the Baluchi gunners and Baluch Guard soldiers on loan to us.

All us Brits were suffering stomach cramps, but until fresh water arrived, ferried in by Bedford trucks from Mudhai, we'd had to rely on our well water. With stronger constitutions, the men fared no ill effects and carried on as normal. That evening as meals were prepared over small open fires hidden in wadis, burning branches of dried frankincense wafted scent through the camp, reminiscent of a Catholic Cathedral had the soldiers but known it. Unable to keep my food down, I retired to my bedroll beside my Saladin, feeling too ill to fully appreciate an otherwise ethereal event.

> *15 - 19 May*
> *Mike back Midway? Graham back?*
> *Midway/Mudhai convoy returned – picquetted it in.*
> *Sort positions for BG platoons – water patrol out again, David with 2 platoons.*
> *Fresh water on convoy: 23 burmails. We use 8 per day – less than 3 days ... and only 2 days rations remaining in store. CQMS??*
> *1700 call – Ordered but not on convoy – Artillery 400 HE, 240 cartridges.*

16th: Simba shuttling starts?
2 BG platoons arrive. Green 19 leaves.
MR pioneers build floor for hospital tent
1700hrs – no sandbags on convoy!
Cook KIA – Simba, White.

17th: 'Bou off road . . .
O Gp – BG – Stand-to drill in sangars, radio practice. R&R tmw?

19th: Mike ill again – leaves me OC

Searching unsuccessfully for water, we continued to rely on supplies from Mudhai or flown in from Salalah. Accordingly, water was severely rationed at Manston, limited to two litres a man per day. Saladins being thirsty vehicles we resorted to using Land Rovers and trucks on water patrols.

Ongoing problems with resupply convoys were inexcusable for a position in the field, but the cock-up was further back, not at Mudhai. We faced shortages on

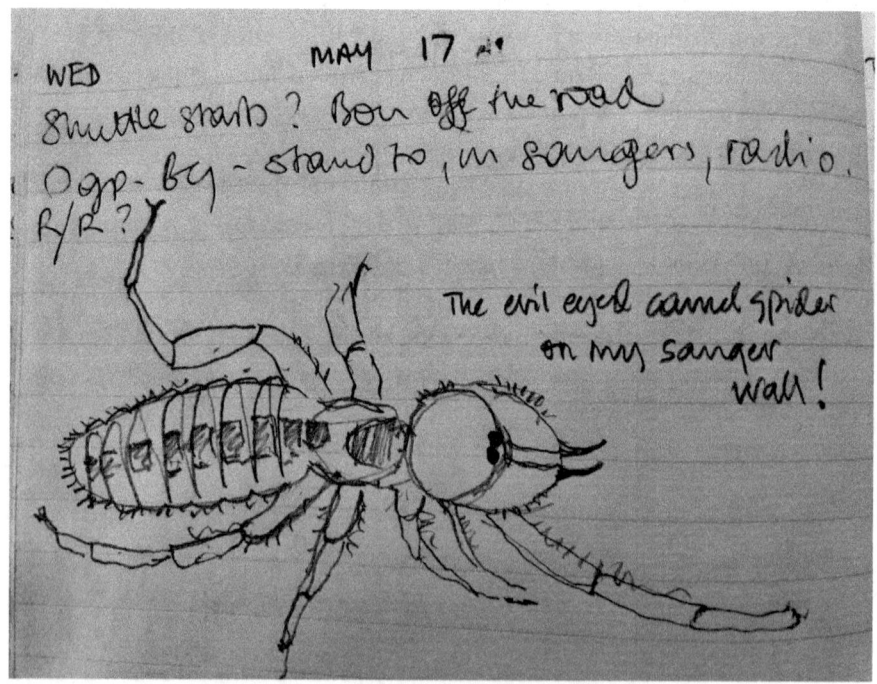

Remains of a Camel Spider dispatched by a concerned Ali Hamdam who'd found this creature in our shared sangar. Expired spider, now minus some legs, was palm sized.

rations, ammo, sandbags for sangar building etc, a constant cause for irritation when there were plenty of other things to be concerned with. Mike, taken ill again as Tim was about to depart on leave, left me in command of the squadron, Mudhai and Manston. And a cook was killed on White, my old position on Simba.

HABARUT RE-TAKEN

20 May - 28 May – Salalah: Habarut convoys O Gp – Op Swing High – RV – C Coy NFR Habarut – 6 cars, 3 reserve / 3 go in.

Tim 4 weeks UK leave.

At the last minute I flew from Manston to Salalah, replacing Mike at an O Group for Op Swing High, the re-establishment of SAF at Habarut. C Coy NFR, Peter Tawell (Queen's Regt) with 2ic Chris Kemball (Royal Green Jackets) would chopper in to secure an area north of Oman's recently demolished castle, to establish a position on the high perpendicular walls of Wadi Habarut overlooking Yemen's fort. The ACS would take in a convoy of munitions and supplies.

It was Tim's plan – I would be taking six Saladins, three I'd keep in reserve 5km north of Habarut in Wadi Mudhi, the other three would continue, taking the convoy to RV with C Coy. I'd been ordered to command from the reserve Saladins. As I protested, Tim told me sharply as acting squadron leader, it was my job to control rather than partake – 'and anyway if it all goes tits up – I can rely on you to get them out. Welcome to command.' With that he left for the airstrip and UK leave, as I caught a helicopter back to Manston.

Op Swing High launched on 22nd May with NFR landing by helicopter north of Habarut to establish their positions. There then followed hectic days escorting back-to-back convoys into Habarut, with our first Saladin escorted convoy arriving on the 24th. The only route available to us ran via Wadi Mudhi south to Habarut, a route that would become known as 'mine alley'. We were taking armed Saladins to the Yemeni border, against internationally agreed protocols we maintain a 10km distance.

Arriving we were mortared but other than the loss of a fine soldier, C Coy's esteemed CSM Abdul Majid, we escaped lightly and the position was secured. SAF was back at Habarut. Within the week we'd taken in a further convoy carrying Oman Gendarmerie who took over the Habarut position, with C Coy moving to our ACS position held at Manston. Following the violent battle 17 days earlier forcing a SAF retreat from Habarut, we'd expected a welcoming reception, but apart from the mortar attack, it'd been clear running. Subsequently, Peter won the Sultan's Commendation Medal and Chris, the Sultan's Distinguished Service Medal (Gallantry).

Handing over command of Manston, we maintained a Saladin troop in support commanded by Brian Jayes with the cheerful Sgts Colin Dick (ex-RTR) and joining him later 'Wimpy' Waite, so named for his insatiable energy, building and reinforcing sangars, runway repairs, clearing paths between positions and erecting wire defences. Wimpy was from Brian's regiment; unstoppable in all matters construction, he should have joined the Royal Engineers, not the Royal Hussars.

29 - 31 May – Brian Jayes ill? Flown to Salalah
Returned to Mudhai fm Habarut – all went well. Buzzed by jets? Adoo? Not ours anyway . . . that's serious . . .
Midway by pm 30 May. End of month servicing, Mess Bills.
Ammo return: HE x 16   HESH x 8 .30 x 8

The introduction of possible Yemeni fighter aircraft haunted us. In this terrain, slow moving convoys would be sitting targets. Fat and juicy at that. It could safely be presumed these aircraft were flown out of Aden where Russian, Chinese and Cuban forces were known to be supporting the communists. However, no doubt it'd been a show of force by the PDRY, baulking against an attack across the border, escalating the fight to war between sovereign states.

The jets returned on a repeat trip as we motored down the beautiful yet confining walls of Wadis Mudhi and Habarut to SAF's new outpost at Habarut. Remembering the Russian MIGs at Aden airport increased tensions, adding to the extant threats of ambush and mines. It was the landmines that would eventually make our Habarut convoys so horrendous, affecting soldier morale and becoming increasingly costly through casualty numbers, losses of vehicles and equipment.

Happily, Brian recovered quickly with treatment on this his second visit to FST in Salalah, returning to Manston on 3 June whilst I, now acting Squadron Leader, was based between Midway and Mudhai camps. In the last mailbag of the month I received a pencilled letter from Tim written in haste from SAF HQ. There was a list of reminders on matters requiring my attention during his absence on leave (naturally), but he'd also penned some kind words on my troop's efforts during the battles at Akoot and Janook, ending with the prophetic words he hoped the actions might have saved the SAF's armoured cars. Time would tell.

What I didn't need was a cock-up.

> Well must get on, but as I will probably not see you before I go on leave, I would just like you to know that I am delighted and extremely proud ——— of the way you and the troop has worked and fought in Akoot/Hanoosh, and I am quite sure this fact has been noted by "them" and —— it may even mean that we might keep the ears in the long run.
>
> Well done
>
> Yours ever
>
> C.

NEAR DISASTER HUNTING FRESH MEAT

1 Jun – Hunting gazelle, meat rations – between Midway and Mudhai ran out of petrol, water. Bloody harebrained.

A day which entered the annals of the Sergeants Mess's "most fabled" war stories – except for the fact most of it was true.

With Tim away, I'd been up at 0500 to finish off his list of jobs I'd been reminded to attend to and having sorted out the priorities, those needing immediate action, I gathered my crew for my return to Mudhai, where I was required for a planned Ferret Scout Car and Land Rover patrol with Gordon Dawson, one of the two Midway-based intelligence officers. Midway to Mudhai was a distance of approximately 80km across desert. I'd a crew of five including my driver. I knew the route well, my crew likewise. Piece of cake.

Crossing Wadi Ghadun's wide expanses 30km short of our destination, we spotted gazelle. 'Sahb, ghizlaan!' (Sahb, gazelle!) came the excited cry from behind me . . . fresh meat, a premium morale booster to men tired of a combat rationed diet consisting generally of tinned sardines in red sauce, served on boiled rice. The paucity of fresh meat in their diet would later become a problem at Mudhai. We stopped the Land Rover as I reached for my Lee Enfield .303, wedged vertically between the front seats beside me, wrapped against dust in a shemagh bound with a used .30 Browning canvas ammo belt. Removing the dust wrapping, I stepped from the doorless vehicle.

A round already in the chamber I released the safety catch taking aim on a sizeable buck about 300m away. I relaxed, breathed out and began to squeeze the trigger. Too late! The animals, possibly spooked by our unannounced appearance in their territory and frozen momentarily with indecision, leapt suddenly into action, disappearing at full gallop, disappearing away up the wide sandy and stone bottomed wadi. 'Damn!' I thought, jumping back into the Land Rover. Setting off in pursuit it was bumpy and all clung on for fear of being thrown out of the vehicle as we careered after our quarry.

The chase in uncharted enemy minelaying territory, in an open Land Rover, six men armed with short range 9mm Sterling submachine guns and a single ancient Lee Enfield, exemplifies the classic head v. heart argument: For – listen to your head (may achieve tangible success) – Against – not follow your heart (increases risk of regret). On this occasion of course I should have listened to my head. We'd travelled possibly 8km before we caught sight of our prey again. This time more careful with my approach, I took aim scoring a clean hit. 'Sharbash!' cried the men, my reputation almost retrieved following my failed first attempt. Driving to the felled animal, a soldier performed the halal prayer, and we loaded the carcass into the back of the Land Rover. It was then we smelt petrol. Looking beneath the vehicle I saw the problem: a damaged fuel pipe dripping fuel. A flying stone or small rock striking the fuel line as we tore across the gravelled plain? This was a Santana Land Rover, Spanish built under licence and widely accepted as not being quite up to British standards.

Crawling beneath the chassis, we fixed the leak with gaffer tape. The fuel gauge showed we were almost empty. A second check revealed fuel still leaking. Fine, use the spare jerrycan to top up. 'I'll radio for a truck and petrol from Mudhai' I said to myself, full of a 24 year old's confidence. Then I noticed no wireless antenna. In our dash across country a soldier had accidently fallen against dislodging the antenna and thinking we'd collect it on our return had said nothing at the time. Kismet. Turning round we began to retrace our steps. Nursing the engine but having to remain in four-wheel drive given the soft sand, we limped westwards towards where I knew we should find the Mudhai track. I reckoned with the heavy going and six men aboard, we'd be getting maybe 16km to the gallon, less with the leaking pipe.

We never found the antenna. Forty tense minutes later we finally broke out of the wadi system onto sandy plain and the multitude of tracks that was the Midway/Mudhai highway. At that point the Land Rover's engine died: we'd run out of fuel. It was midday. Thirty-something km to walk? We might make it at night, not by day. I had one card still to play. A battle aerial.

I'd read a battle aerial could be made from strands of wire, stretched horizontally along the ground. Using morse, a weak signal might get through. It was a chance. But we'd have to wait until sunset when radio waves were stronger. At night a radio signal can travel many times the distance of a signal during daylight hours, all to do with reflection from the ionosphere, a phenomenon known as skywave propagation. Right, now all I needed was some wire. Accompanying me I'd LCpl Rasul Bux, a Baluchi for whom I had enormous respect, a professional soldier, intelligent, smart and loyal.

Explaining I needed wire for an aerial we pulled wires leading to disconnected light fittings. Using my pocket knife stripping casings, we joined single strands to form as long a length as possible. Our battle aerial. Placing a stone on the far end I connected the other to the radio and tried sending a message. A second, then a third, but no response.

'We wait until sunset,' I told the men, 'until then we change picquets every hour, everyone else under cover'. The midday sun was directly overhead and no tree shade for miles this close to the Empty Quarter, but I'd noticed a cave in the wadi wall. Placing two picquets in a hastily built sangar above the cave, I realised our position was easily visible but then so was the Land Rover in this largely flat landscape.

Surprisingly confident in our manufactured aerial, I explained to the men the radio would work at nightfall when I'd radio Mudhai for recovery. They'd looked on with curiosity, seemingly at ease. Touched by their faith in my science, I remained calm; there was no other option. This was no test, it was simple reality. Rationing water, we sat in the shade of the cave, waiting for sunset. It was a stiflingly long, hot afternoon. Towards sunset we were out of water. Taking my driver across to the Land Rover, I drained liquid from the radiator into a plastic army mug, my shemagh as a filter. It was clear of antifreeze. Returning to the soldiers, I offered each dip a corner of his shemagh into the mug and wet their lips. At the end we each sucked our damp shemaghs dry of moisture. It was better than nothing.

As the sun sank in the west, we tried once more; tap, tap, tap, on the Morse key calling Mudhai on the radio, and at the very first attempt back came a response – "WHERE THE HELL ARE YOU?" Never was I more relieved to hear a rollicking in Morse from 'Q' waiting at Mudhai, a man who'd joined the army before I was born, was tough as nails and on whom I relied more than he realised.

With two Land Rovers on their way bringing jerrycans of petrol plus water for the radiator, and charguls of Mudhai's spring water, I turned away from the radio to find a grinning Rasul Bux who had produced an army issue green plastic water-bottle he'd kept hidden in his bedroll. 'Reserve, Sahb, just in case.' The six of us

Arabian gazelle (Gazella arabica)

each took a mouthful of the precious, now hot liquid, none taking more, grateful for the Baluch soldier's sagacity. With men like RB we were going to win the war.

Recovered by an anxious 'Q', watered and refuelled, we returned to Mudhai under a star filled sky. The gazelle, cooked and eaten that evening, was still fresh after a day at 40C. And no, the Sergeants never let me forget the episode.

ROULEMENT JUNE 1972

6 - 10 Jun
Servicing vehicles, my L/R is VOR.
Tmw – Patrol with two FSC + 1 L/R - NW to border. Gordon? 2nd L/R.
10 petrol. 6 water. .30 ammo. charguls, rations.
2 x FSC: Sgt Waite, Jumea, LCpl RB, Mohd' Ali:
L/R me, Gnr. Nasir Ali, Mohd' Ali (Abyad), Said Mohd', Hamdan Khalfan, Aziz Nasir.

(The paler skinned of two sharing the same name, Mohamed Ali without hint of malice or discrimination was known to all as Abyad, Arabic for white).

7 WIA by mors, White, Mainbrace.
MR take over fm DR on Simba. NFR fm JR - plains battalion.
Letters fm home and O – as we left camp – thanks Q!

Unable to join me, Gordon Dawson asked we investigate a Bedu report of activity north west of Fasad. I took Wimpy and ten men, in two Ferrets and my Land Rover. We drew a blank on this occasion. Letters arrived by Skyvan as we departed, 'Q's' parting shot 'somebody still loves you, sir'. Letters from home and my kid sister I'd read later.

Roulement was now in full swing as the four Infantry battalions swapped places, Desert and Jebel Regiments having completed their nine-month Dhofar tours were swapping locations with MR and NFR respectively. As a reception, the adoo hit Simba hard leaving seven men wounded by mortars on my old position, White.

Midway – Shisur – Fasad for night. Incredible hills of sand – they say they don't move. Shisur has good water. Sandstorm fee layl.

Trooper Nasir Hamid mans the Browning, whilst Wimpy who never suffered sunburn has a cigarette beside my .303 rifle. The jerrycans held both drinking water and petrol for the two Ferret Scout Cars and my Land Rover. With no other transport available, carrying petrol was always a risk, one bullet would have been catastrophic, but we'd no option.

Awoke covered in sand – moved off 0700 south to Makinat Shihan. No signs recent activity. Hadn't envisaged getting this close to border. Long drive back, Midway late.

9 Jun – Pay shortages! LCpl Naser Mohd – 43.100 – check – he's grade 2 LCpl.
LCpl Hilal Ali – 45.450 – last pay 49.450 = 4R short.
Letter to Dfr HQ:
Suggesting M.F. takes over admin Midway/Mudhai – leaves me all patrols, Amd Cars, L/Rs, with Green 60 – Op Vulture – Habarut convoys. Much simpler. Requested Midway ACS accmd. moved to priority 1 – we're still in tents.

It was said the well at Shisur was fed by aquifer from another well we used, that at Ma Shadid where we knew water travelled underground from the mountain pools of Ayun. Looking at the map, it made sense, and we relied on both wells for their clean, sweet water.

Monthly pay disputes continued, requiring me to double check with HQ Dhofar and have shortages resolved.

One hundred km apart, my command included Midway and Mudhai, a Saladin troop at Manston, another day's journey away, two firqats, plus at least one infantry recce platoon. We'd responsibilities for Habarut convoy protection, and continuing Op Vulture patrols. Frustrated at the somewhat eclectic structure at Midway and with plenty of time to think as we motored across deserts, I'd written to HQ suggesting a possible restructuring, handing base-camp responsibilities to the company of Baluch Guard under command of the amiable JMF, John Martyn-Fisher (ex Indian Army, and ex Royal Army Ordnance Corps).

It worked, the proposal was accepted without alteration, John assumed command for camp administration, and importantly, guard duties at Midway and Mudhai. Operational duties remained with the Squadron. On 10th June I wrote to Tim on UK leave with the good news.

A LESSON LEARNED, WHEN I SHOULD HAVE KNOWN BETTER

Returning to Mudhai I found preparations in full swing for an early start on the following day's Habarut convoy. All was going smoothly; having completed three convoys to date, all knew their individual tasks. It'd become apparent we'd be running convoys every two to three weeks. I stopped for a word with Lou who

At Mudhai and competing against the distraction of the pin-up above the squadron's op. orders and map board, Lou Costello cleans his AK47 on the table where we'd caught a scorpion at the end of March.

was in the ops tent cleaning his beloved AK47. We were a great team, he, Olly and I, we'd been through a lot recently and it was good to see him so relaxed. We chatted a while before I walked over to my tent hoping for a moment or two's rest.

Entering my tent it was hot; even the sand floor was hot. Removing shirt and boots, I relaxed in a pair of cut down khaki denim shorts, barefoot, pleased to be back at Mudhai, back at base camp, my responsibilities manageable, the Habarut convoy loading under control. Contemplating switching off, I reckoned all I'd still to do was a final check on picquets and night guards.

Just then a shot rang out ending my moment of reverie. Single shot? So not machine gun, so, not an attack. Going to my tent entrance, I could make out an apparent commotion at the head of the wadi where the FHG firqat troops were billeted in caves along the walls, close to the small dam and fresh water. One of my Camel Firqat irregulars, Mohamed Saif, came running across as I emerged from my tent. In the manner characteristic of jebali men, he now commenced to pour scorn on what he thought of my Omanis, emphasising each phrase with an extended forefinger jabbed repeatedly against my bare chest.

This approach always focuses the mind and when first experienced leaves you wondering what might come next. But I'd fought alongside, eaten and shared coffee with Mohamed so stood my ground, and as he paused for breath, interjected quietly that yes, I understood, although hadn't yet quiet grasped what the problem was and yes, I would come with him and yes, I would sort out the soldier who was apparently the idiot at fault.

'Need a hand, sir?' enquired Lou who'd appeared from the ops tent and was silently watching proceedings. 'Nope, I'm fine,' I replied, 'just keep the boys loading up and I'll be back to finish off, I need to brief the men before stand-to.'

Mohamed and I walked over to where the argument had started and been left hanging unresolved. The cause of all the excitement was a certain Mahmood Hassan, an ex-Trucial States soldier, experienced in taking short cuts and living just within the rules of the game. A typical 'barrack-room-lawyer', seen it all, quick to find fault, slow to help, and absent when duty called. What every commander needs.

Mahmood stood a little under my 1.8m, but where I lost any advantage was to his build, broad across chest and shoulders with a good set of forearm muscles, regrettably underused whenever heavy work was required. A good driver, he'd been retained as such.

I approached my driver, the man accused of pushing aside Mohamed Saif's son attempting to water his few goats. Sterling machine gun held nonchalantly in his right hand, Mahmood carried two jerrycans in his left. No small feat, I thought momentarily, wondering how he intended filling the radiator, that'd entail standing on the vehicle's front bumper to reach the filler cap, whilst still holding his weapon.

With my seething firqat now standing alongside me, I realised the atmosphere lacked only a spark to ignite. A primed grenade ready to explode. Insulted Dhofari v Dhofari despiser. Bedu v townie. Stopping in front of Mahmood and exchanging standard salutations – 'Salaam alaikum, Mahmood' he replied 'wa alaikum assalam, Sahb' – I asked what the problem was.

He replied on finding the other vehicle drivers were taking too long, he'd driven across to where the firqat were camped in order to jump the queue. And – Sahb would no doubt agree – given as his business was the more important, he'd pushed through the goats to reach the water to fill his jerrycans. Someone had fired a shot in the air and instantly he'd levelled his machine gun at the young goatherd, shouting at the firqat to stand back. At that, Mohamed had raced across to fetch me.

'Oh Shit,' I thought to myself – well at least it'd stopped there. So far, stalemate. Now how to avoid loss of face by either side, Army or firqat, regular soldier or irregular, many of the latter whom not long before had been in the employ of our enemy, the PDRY regime. And they didn't have any great regard towards their soft North Omani cousins.

Looking at Mahmood directly, I said quietly, 'I want you to put your weapon back across your chest, then I want you to carry those jerrycans and put them in your cab, then you are to climb in, start up and return to our queue across the wadi.'

Mahmood stood his ground, returning my look unflinchingly; 'and where should I join the queue?' he enquired, testing patience to the full. I replied, 'Go to the back and line up as we all do when filling with water, petrol or ammunition or any other load, as you and we have all done on many occasions, Mahmood.'

He didn't move an inch. The firqat irregulars, numbering about 30 men, had now collected around us watching curiously the developing situation. They must have wondered whether the young British officer would stand his ground or would the possibly older and obviously stronger looking Arab make him back down? I say obviously because I'd suddenly realised I was clad solely in a pair of ragged cut down shorts, no shirt, my only other apparel, a pair of camel hide Nizwa sandals. I'd no weapon with me. I'd walked straight into this situation from my tent.

It was as a bad dream. How could I have been so stupid to have put myself in such an avoidable and now dangerous confrontation, relying solely on my perceived authority over hotheaded soldiers and short fuse irregulars under my command.

Standing in front of him it crossed my mind Mahmood must see my heart thumping hard against my chest. Then I noticed a waver in his conceited expression. He'd glanced past me briefly, then after a moment's hesitation slowly he slung his loaded weapon over his head to rest across his back. Picking up his full jerrycans he swung them into the cab, climbed in, started the engine and drove off to the back of the queue of 3-tonners, Ferret Scout Cars and Land Rovers.

I turned to my firqat, Mohamed Saif, who nodded curtly and strode away to join his comrades who dispersed to their quarters along the wadi wall. The young goatherd, victim of Mahmood's intolerance, walked up and extending a thin arm, shook my hand and with a 'mashkoor, Sahb' before turning to gather his flock, returning them to the waterhole.

The moment had passed, it was over.

Wondering how on earth I'd managed to get out of that, I cursed my impulsiveness taking such needless risk with people I knew were by nature volatile, the loss of face paramount. Turning, to my surprise 15 metres away, stood Lou armed with his AK47, Mohamed Said as Siyabi, Ali Hamdan al Regathi, and Mubarik Musalim al Khadim standing in a semicircle, each cradling a loaded weapon. They'd followed; 'T'ought you might be needing a little persuader, sir' as Lou casually put it.

A brew shared with the unflinchingly loyal Mubarik Musalim al Khadim who had watched my back. A Khadim, but now free, Mubarik was born a slave under the previous sultan's reign.

My guardians had appeared from nowhere.

A valuable lesson, I should have worn a shirt before going to deal with the incident, presenting a more authoritative image. In the field none wore badges of rank, but next time, I'd wear a shirt, perhaps carry a weapon.

With the situation diffused, I was only too conscious of the Eddie Vutirakis incident and how that'd ended, and I'd watch Mahmood with particular interest in future. Eventually he 'went AWOL' stealing a SMG.

> 12/14 Jun
> Habarut Convoy. 3 x FSC – Hodgson, Costello, Rasul Bux.
> Backup – 10 mins readiness to move out T12 – S/Sgt Beadle, Sgts Waite, Fyffe
> Trucks:
> 1 x3 ton – 81 x 60mm mor ammo
> 1 x3 ton – POL
> 1 x3 ton – fresh rations
> 1 x3 ton – water
> 1 x3 ton – soldiers – only 14 escort to Habarut?
> 1 x 'Breakdown' 3 Ton

FSC – 2 x 6 men btle rations
Tudho – Qafa – 0400, Habarut 1100 - 1230 – Mudhai 1915 !
Jets again – not ours
Letters – AIWH and Liz

With just 14 Baluch Guard soldiers fit for escort duties, I'd decided to take three Ferret scout cars on this convoy, leaving three Saladins on standby reserve. Operating understrength was a gamble, but Habarut were short on provisions. Leaving Mudhai, we made camp at Qafa, north of Tudho. With so few men, I'd banked on speed. Departing 0400 the following day we made it to Habarut, stopping only to unload, returning exhausted but elated, three scout cars escorting six trucks and not one mined, all back in Mudhai by 1915. It was a record for us. Again, we'd seen unidentified jet aircraft. Again, not ours. We had to remain vigilant.

Letters from home were from my dear grandmother who at 92 had written to soldiers in her family since WW1. Legal guardian to us during early school years in England, my brother and I were blessed with a softly spoken Edwardian Scottish lady whom we adored. Having only met twice during leaves from Africa, she was still a stranger when we arrived from Africa aged 11 for some 'proper' schooling. Our only surviving grandparent, she and an aunt became pivotal to us at a time when we saw our parents once a year for summer holidays. Still unaware we were fighting a communist war, my grandmother was a frequent writer on the peaceful life she led in Iffley, Oxford. The second letter was from Lizzie Furse, a schoolgirl friend of my sister, Odeyne, one of four pretty sisters, family friends back home in Sussex.

15 Jun
Organise Cholera Jabs.
Book smallpox jabs too.
Passport at BAF.

I was beginning to get things sorted for my approaching leave in the UK. Passports, held centrally at SAF HQ who organised international flights, visas and chased us on updating vaccinations.

16 - 20 Jun
Convoy to Manston – water
0900 call: Ramadhan compassionate leave letter and leave dates?
Front diff. Required for L/R
Any news on 78 in Midway?

> *News in fm. FHG patrol in W. Adym – 19 men, women and children fm Hawf with goats.*
> *1300 call: 1) OG Tp roulement 20-23 June – no need to mutiny now!*
> *2) on 3-tonner to Midway – Habarut 10 x SEPs.*
> *3) pax fm Hawf – W.Aydm – Salim Said al Hayfee – son – Suleman bin Salim in FHG.*
> *Apparently quite a few left Hawf after SOAF air strike. SEPS wishing to join Firqats. Only 2 x bolt action rifles amongst the lot.*
> *1700 call: Any news on S/Sgt Ali, LCpl Ramadhan? Confirmed leave for Ramadhan, no news Ali.*

The interesting development were refugees arriving following Hawf's bombing, the Sultanate's 26/27 May retaliation to the Habarut attack on the 5 May. Three families driving goats had trekked across mountains, avoiding both adoo and SAF forces to make it to Wadi Aydm where a FHG patrol out of Mudhai discovered them. Suleman bin Salim, son of one of the refugees, was serving with the FHG, easing the SEP aspects considerably. Gordon Dawson arrived from Midway to question the party whom we ferried to Midway and tented accommodation the next day. The families and goats had trekked a biblical distance of approximately 160km in a little over 20 days in summer temperatures approaching 50C. I never ceased to be amazed at the resilience of the Dhofari. It brought home too, the unnecessary hardship inflicted on innocents in war; these families were simply in the wrong place at the wrong time.

> *18 Jun*
> *Convoy to Manston*
> *Gordon and Nick visit.*

Gordon arrived with Nick Downie whom he was introducing to local firqats he'd be working with. Nick and I had met briefly before. Sharing similar views of the world we currently occupied, we got on immediately.

> *19 Jun*
> *Hand over to Brian – he Mudhai: me to Midway – Cholera jab.*
> *0900 add to Janook write off list : I x shovel, I x crowbar fm Sal 72.*
> *(O.G. losses when panicking as they departed!)*
> *1500 – 20 Hawf Bedu with me in 3-tonner to Midway.*
> *Kalfan – compassionate leave – till 22 June, brother ill. Troop came to wish me good hols!*
> *Inner tubes FSC – sent wrong type! – still x5 punctures!*

As I departed Mudhai my troop came to wish me a good holiday, two asking specifically I buy them hunting knives. It was good of them to see me off. LCpl Rasul Bux who'd always insisted he clean my SMG and Lee Enfield after returning from patrols was one of them. He asked if I might buy him a sleeping bag. I did, but he never received it; killed on the next Habarut convoy five days after I'd departed on leave. He was one of a kind, I'd miss him greatly. Just prior to leaving, I received my annual intravenous cholera booster; probably not best recommended just before a long flight – it aches.

21/22 Jun
Leave Midway – UAG – report Cmdr Dhofar – full sit rep: Done.
Depart Salalah – for Muscat then UK!
Gavin Pike – lunch with PDO

Arriving at Bayt al Falaj I found I had a whole day before my flight back to the UK that evening. Meeting up with fellow cavalryman Gavin Pike (14th/20th Hussars) a staff officer based at SAF HQ, I was invited to lunch with two expat families with PDO (Petroleum Development Oman). It was jolly, but they only wanted to hear war stories from Dhofar, whereas selfishly I'd rather have gone to the beach for the day. Tired but well fed, I finally boarded my flight home.

PDO was a private company, principally owned and operated by Royal Dutch Shell, remaining so until the oil industry was eventually nationalised in 1974; Oman becoming the major shareholder with 60%.

UK LEAVE

Leave blurred into a few short weeks of summer highs. A more complete antithesis to my last 12 months would be hard to imagine. Plunged straight into the Pimm's filled world of Henley Royal Regatta where Father was a Steward, there followed Centre Court seats at Wimbledon, parties, dances, theatres and concerts.

Henley guests of my parents, the Gibbons on noticing my tan enquired whether I was serving in Oman. Vice-Chief of the Defence Staff, Sir John was well positioned to hazard that as a safe bet. The following day he told my parents what was going on in Dhofar. Taking me to one side he said he'd 'checked up' and heard of the recent ACS actions at Vimy and Janook. My cover was blown, so much for the 'secret war'.

I spent many days at the Gatsbyesque mansion that was home to the Furse girls, four beauties, playing squash, tennis and relaxing. Anglo-Americans, they gave a memorable 4th July party with incredible fireworks. Looking up at the explosions of sparkle, I couldn't help thinking there were no tracer rounds in Sussex.

Too soon it was over. Four weeks had slipped away, faster than handheld water. In addition to fun days of tennis and squash there'd been rounds of parties, the last in a small London flat two days before my departure back to Oman. The exquisite Julie Felix was there and sitting on the floor, she'd sung for us as like her, we too sat cross legged as Bedu, entranced, her soft voice in perfect harmony to the gentle plucking of her acoustic guitar.

I'd worked off excess energy scything grass around the village church in Sussex where father was warden. I'd seen the family dentist. I'd purchased hunting knives and a sleeping bag requested of me by soldiers, and two pairs of desert boots for myself. A repeat of a year earlier, when kit packed and ancient car left secure in my grandmother's large empty garage in Oxford, I was ready. This time my family came to Heathrow to see me off. Waving, my mind filled with Julie Felix's earworm of Leonard Cohen's ballad, "Hey, that's no way to say goodbye". Diary entry reads *July 23: flight out – looked back once. Mum and girls in tears, waved.*

19 JULY 1972 – MIRBAT

Four days prior to my return, a SAF outpost in Dhofar held out against overwhelming odds. Defending a fort and 25pdr gun pit were eight SAS, a detachment of OA, a DG platoon and a handful of local militia armed with .303 rifles. The outpost, a coastal village in eastern Dhofar, was Mirbat.

The events that day have been covered extensively in books and journals, widely reported in the media, becoming legend. A battle where eight highly trained men, a platoon of gendarmes, an artillery detachment and a few local militia, supported by jets held off a force two hundred strong.

Attacking at ground level, low flying SOAF jets sustained bullet holes from above. Defending forces lost 20 men killed or wounded. Retrieved adoo dead amounted to 38; the wounded somehow carried away. The 25pdr and fort were saved. The battle would go down in the annals of SAS history.

For several months before, the enemy had planned a major attack against SAF, amassing men from Yemen, the jebel regions in western Dhofar and mountains north of Salalah and Taqah. For some time adoo forces had been disallowed from entering towns, ensuring the plan's secrecy. The attacking force would have included those who'd fought so ferociously at Akoot, Vimy and Janook, claiming victory for driving the Sultan's forces back to Manston. Victories claimed too at Habarut and more recently driving SAF from Capstan leaving Simba effectively at stalemate. So confident were they of success, they now planned to strike deep inside SAF's soft underbelly, nearly 65km east of Salalah.

Using intelligence gathered through their local spy network, they were well informed on the BATT troop movements, but also precise defence positions held by the SAS and Gendarme units. Victory would have seemed assured. Mount a surprise attack and take out the small sleepy coastal village with ancient fort, protected by a handful of sunbathing Brits and a few gendarmes. Piece of cake. Such was the level of adoo confidence, press releases had been prepared ahead for broadcast by Radio Aden.

Approaching silently, the adoo caught the forward picquet asleep. *Asleep!* All had their throats slit. Then at 0530, the first mortars hit Mirbat. The battle raged for over four hours. Peter de la Billière writes "the defenders that day displayed superhuman effort to hold out against a determined and prolonged attack".

In wars brave men fight on each side. Acknowledging the extraordinary courage of Mirbat's defenders, not many would deny the adoo fought just as tenaciously that day. Attacking over open ground, caught scrambling over Dannert wire taking numerous casualties, yet remaining resolute to take fort and gun despite the jets arriving to turn the battle. And there's not much written of those in the Sultan's Forces who gave their lives that day. Militia, old men loyal to the Sultan and their faith, untrained militarily, armed with ancient .303 Lee Enfields, they took on the communists armed with machine guns, nonbelievers who wantonly killed those holding to their faith. Forced to fire from the fort's parapets, they were easy pickings for adoo marksmen. Each time a head appeared, Bang. Like shooting ducks at a funfair.

In addition to the arrival of SOAF jets, another factor in concluding the battle were G Squadron SAS, reinforcements helicoptered in with a platoon of NFR under the command of Capt. Graeme Smith-Piggott. The adoo dead were flown to Salalah where they were publicly displayed as a warning against joining those forces pitted against the young Sultan. Inglorious by Western codes, this was the Middle East where neighbouring countries still carried out mass public executions, severed hands of thieves, stoned the assumed guilty.

Due to the FCO's blanket of secrecy, there was no publicity and no SAS involved received recognition outside their Regiment and SAF, despite consensus some actions warranted the VC. At the time considered politically explosive, capable of endangering all that had been achieved, news about the battle for Mirbat remained silent, covert.

Four years later a number of gallantry awards were finally made:

Captain Mike Kealy: DSO (for gallantry)
Sgt Sekonaia Takavesi: DCM
Sgt Bob Bennett: MM
Sgt Talaiasi Labalaba: BEM, Posthumous Mention in Dispatches (If ever a case deserved greater recognition, it was his)
Tpr Tobin: Posthumous MM

That October 1972, The Sultan's Armed Forces announced awards to their own.

Gnr Walid Khamis: Oman Artillery: Sultan's Gallantry Medal – Oman's equivalent to Britain's VC. Despite being shot through both legs, he never gave in. Dropping to his knees, Khamis continued loading the 25pdr until collapsing from loss of blood. The gun was saved.
Sqn Ldr Bill Stoker: SOAF pilot: WKhM(G) – Oman's MC
Fl Lt David Milne-Smith: SOAF pilot: The Sultan's Commendation Medal for bravery

ON WAR DECORATIONS AND MEDALS

Hansard records:

WAR DECORATIONS AND MEDALS
HC Deb 22 March 1944

"The object of giving medals, stars and ribbons is to give pride and pleasure to those who have deserved them. At the same time a distinction is something which everybody does not possess. If all have it, it is of less value. There must, therefore, be heart-burnings and disappointments on the borderline. A medal glitters, but it also casts a shadow. The task of drawing up regulations for such awards is one which does not admit of a perfect solution. It is not possible to satisfy everybody without running the risk of satisfying nobody. All that is possible is to give the greatest satisfaction to the greatest number and to hurt the feelings of the fewest."
Winston Churchill (Prime Minister) – 22 March 1944

25

ARMOURED BEDFORDS REVISITED?

Return from UK leave to hear Saladins again under threat. Command of SAF upgraded as first Commander Dhofar then CSAF prepared to hand over and depart. Op Shidda when MR are caught in the open and suffer casualties, Lt Saif Hamed killed, Major Malcolm Vining, acting CO and Captain Ian Gordon, acting OC A Coy and others wounded.

RETURN FROM LEAVE – ANOTHER KHAREEF AND CHILLY IN MIDWAY

24 Jul
12.30 Viscount to Salalah with Ali Hamdan, Nasir Mohd – "Mirbat – they died like goats?"
Khareef back again.
16.30 'Bou' to Midway
Learn RB killed after I'd left on leave – Habarut convoy. TM46. How desperately sad.

I found two ACS troopers on the same flight out from Oman's Seeb airport, also returning from leave. Ali and Nasir were full of the horrific end met by DG's Mirbat picquet, 'they died like goats, sahb!' The awful realisation the men died with such ignominy took precedence; to my soldiers the fact there had been a fierce battle was inconsequential.

On arrival and meeting up with an exuberant Dick Morgan-Evans departing on UK leave, we'd shared a drink at the recently opened Falaj Hotel, forerunner to ever more luxurious establishments. Full of the Mirbat story Dick regaled it in detail to a Reuters correspondent we'd met at the bar. Proclaiming proudly Mirbat had been 'even bigger than Vimy, you should write it up,' Reuters man who'd listened quietly, answered ruefully to Dick's hubris, 'agreed, Dhofar's a f.....g big story. But it stops with the 'D' Notice. Period'. And back in Salalah the Khareef had returned.

26 Jul - 17 Aug
Khareef again in Salalah. Midway is cool. Col Mike's farewell visit. Month end indents. Letter fm Louise!
27/30 – 3 day Habarut convoy, NTR thankfully.
FSC driver and Browning training new recruits.
Mike to Manston. Escort Mr Kenyon to Mudhai – Saladin 81 needs new engine, new front wings, new torsion bars – ie VOR . . . for a year?
Stripped 81 of kit – 80 back on road with new exhaust manifold.
Letters out: Furses – big thanks. Charlotte. Louise.
Charlotte: B-Day – Yard-o-led pencil for 2.9.72.

MIKE HARVEY WB, WKHM, OBE, MC

Commander Dhofar, Col Mike Harvey, was departing SAF and called to visit us at Midway as part of his farewell tour of his outlying positions. A quietly spoken soldier, he was hugely respected by us all. And to younger officers, he was instantly recognisable with his smart moustache and thick lensed horn-rimmed glasses. How had he coped as a younger officer commanding a platoon in the rain, we wondered? We needn't have worried. He'd served with NFR before being given Dhofar Command. Twenty years earlier, he had command of D company, the Glosters, part of the British Brigade. Over 24/25 April 1951, the regiment famously held Hill 235 at the Battle of Imjin River, Korea. Outnumbered, the Glosters held off repeated Chinese attacks threatening to overrun their position. Suffering severe losses, B and C Companies were merged to form D company. Attempts to air drop supplies failed. With ammunition low following two days and a night fighting and no longer with artillery support, the position was doomed.

With the rest of the British Brigade withdrawn, the Glosters, surrounded by Chinese, were ordered to fight their way back to British lines. Only 40 men from D Company made it, the remainder of the regiment by then out of ammunition surrendered with 459 men taken prisoner. After three years and at a cost of three million dead, the Korean War ended in stalemate, where it had begun along Latitude 38 North, the pre-war boundary between North and South Korea, known as the 38th parallel, the current border between the two Koreas. Mike Harvey won the MC. In my opinion it warranted the DSO, which he'd achieved fighting the Cold War's secret conflict in Dhofar, the Sultan's Bravery Medal.

18 Aug
Unwell, have a wheezing chest.
Tim being Tim with Bedfords, thinking of mounting .50s on backs surrounded by sandbags for armour protection. First wadi – they'll get stuck – too heavy. Also not armoured cars.

ARMOURED BEDFORDS BACK ON THE AGENDA

Tim had a plan to convert a mine-plated Bedford into an armoured car. Fortunately, it didn't get further than the drawing board.

19 - 22 Aug
Patrol put back one day.
Early start – Land Rovers and trucks to Dauka N/W Midway. Bloody hot. Tim lead veh. Lou and I tail end charlies in choking powder dust. Dauka a great surprise – after 4 hrs of burnt sand and rock, Dauka has green rushes and stinking sulphureous water – but there's a pool away from hot springs – cooler and drinkable. After a brew all had a dip – water leaves skin dry, hair squeaky clean – a first! Firqat hadn't brought rations. Radioed relief truck to deliver tmw fm Midway, with L/R escort.
Sandstorm overnight – everything filled with sand, rifle, kit, mouth, eyes, ears, clothing.
Meerschaum pipe pinched – suspect firqat who'd admired it last night.
Swam again – before winds returned whipping up sands.

22 Aug – 0450 left for Fasad. 0525 sunrise. Beautiful – still cool. By 0800 blistering hot. Fasad 1830, set camp. Dunes majestic as ever, golden sands rise 600ft?

23 Aug – Patrolled west of Fasad. Later met up with Nick and his men in Land Rovers and a Bedford. Stayed for dinner as we discussed handover remainder of FHG – and theft of my pipe! He'd have a word – told him not to worry . . . there are limits.

24 Aug – Father's Birthday.
Left Nick – motored back to Midway. Breakdowns, punctures and veh. rads boiling made for slow, staggered journey back. 2030 Midway. Exhausted, thirsty, hungry, dusty. Showered, beer, dinner, better, bed!

25 Aug
Jumea – an auspicious day! I've a proper room at last. Tiny but air-conditioned!! There's a door that shuts – privacy. Mike next door. Letters from Charlotte, Lizzie, AIWH, M&D, Odeyne. My lucky day.
Prepared New Recruits Dvr training programme.
Pauling's pool open – Brain and I swam after 1300 call. Private rooms, air-conditioned Mess, pool. We're millionaires!

Civil engineers Pauling & Co, a company founded in the 19th century constructing railways in Africa, South America and the Middle East, were constructing Mudhai and Midway Camps. They had invited us to use their newly opened expat swimming pool. Brain and I didn't need to be asked twice.

One free afternoon we witnessed passing swallows sweep into the pool and drink on the wing as lazily as we swam in the warm water, the birds quite unconcerned by our presence. This tiny pool of water created for human use, was to them a sudden lifeline to surviving their incredible journey from breeding grounds in Europe onwards to South Africa's summer. Travelling mainly by daylight, migrating swallows (hirundo rustica) can cover 320km a day at average speeds of 30kph. Silently we watched, privileged at glimpsing another's struggle for existence. Legend tells the swallow's rust red face and breast came about trying to remove thorns from the crown of Jesus. Always raised a smile.

28 Aug - 29 Aug
Dhofar's quiet. Somewhere's going to be hit sooner or later.
Dvr recruits on SMG training. One man without a weapon. There's a shortage – gave him mine. Happy man, may have friend for life. My Colt .45 and .303 will have to do until we get more SMGs.

30 Aug
more SMG firing AM.
New kit arriving fm Persia is mostly U/S. Jeeps are 10 years old, without spares. Guns – same state, with little ammo. Hope their Hueys b. fly!!

Iranians ill-trained. So much for 'war-winning-aid' Have still to see their jeeps driven.

Ordnance received from Persia was basically near useless (U/S). We failed to discover a vehicle that was roadworthy. After hours doctoring and cannibalising parts from the worst, we succeeded in getting a number serviceable. Yet it was still much needed kit, replacing losses to mines, mortars and bullets. We had to be grateful, we weren't in any position to be otherwise.

With hindsight it should have been obvious. Newly seconded to SAF, Iranian troops were likewise unexpectedly ill prepared for guerrilla warfare. Trained to obey orders without question, they were inflexible to the suddenness of guerrilla attack, blindly pushing on. Brave men died needlessly through ground commanders being denied flexibility. Luckily for us, away from BAOR textbook soldiering, we were not so constrained by our chains of command.

31 Aug
Continued SMG practice. It's hot. JMF says he recorded 129F on Tues. Sgt Fyffe back, Sgt Oliver left on lve. And tomorrow is September. I am 25 yrs old! Quarter century!

It was unbelievably hot taking the SMG shoot. Steel became too hot to touch, open Land Rovers became frying pans. The boys never complained, so neither could we. (129F is 54C.) September and we hoped temperatures might cool. And on the morrow I would be another year older.

5 Sep
CSAF here on farewell visit – Squadron formed up on parade – first that I can remember? He gave the troops a resounding speech, not sure what they made of it – 14 months of Dhofar with no prospects of roulement home to Oman. Most would prefer roulement. Sore throat again. Blaming the air-con? We're promised long wk/end ahead Thurs/Fri – The Prophet's Ascension (Al Isra wa Al Mi'raj). MR big punch-up on Simba, out west from White.

BRIGADIER JOHN DAVID CAREW GRAHAM, OBE WO3 (MILITARY)

Following Mike Harvey's visit on 27th July, John Graham arrived to deliver a farewell speech to the troops. We'd miss his natural style of soldiering that had made him a popular Force Commander. Undoubtedly sorry to be leaving, he'd had an exhausting time of it recently, until eventually hospitalised. Listening intently, every soldier stood rigidly to attention. I think they rather enjoyed the parade, a rare event being formed up as a squadron on a hastily prepared parade ground.

In private afterwards with Tim, Mike and I, CSAF acknowledged HQ were aware how hard it was on the squadron being stuck constantly in Dhofar, but with a single unit, there was no alternative. A proposal that additional pay for soldiers might mitigate matters was turned down, with mention the war was already an ever-increasing drain on the Sultanate's budget. It was difficult not to feel that somehow the Squadron fell within that infantry mindset on war budget. Only later would it manifest with tragic consequences. Nonetheless, at the time we each recognised how soldiering with Col Mike, Glorious Gloster and Brig John Graham, A&SH, Para, had been a singular privilege and honour. The two commanders would be missed.

As CSAF was departing, Muscat Regiment took a beating on an op out from Simba.

OPERATION SHIDDA

> 6 Sep
> Op Shidda. MR lose 4 dead, SCO and 10 wounded, 2 Brits, Malcolm Vining in mouth and arm trying to recover SCO and Ian Gordon (ex-Gurkha Rifles) in head. Rumoured he's now talking, one day after! FST must have done a wonderful job. All wounded will live. SAF caught on a forward slope in daylight. Peter Simcock temporary OC MR – Col Bill on leave.

Dhofar HQ's newly arrived Brigade Major, Peter Simcock (Paras), assumed command of Muscat Regiment in the absence of Lt. Col Bill Kerr (Royal Highland Fusiliers) on UK home leave. Of those closely involved was Sandy, promoted major commanding B Company MR making him one of the youngest, if not the youngest serving major in the British Army, commanding a full company on active service. Not many years later Sandy would twice undertake ceremonial guard duties at Balmoral, dining as a guest of Her Majesty, but that's a different story.

On Shidda, I can do no better than use Sandy's account, related to me later:

"Op Shidda – the attempt to search two wadi heads, likely adoo armouries/stores areas west of White at Sarfait.

Malcolm Vining, acting CO, was wounded in the left cheek, mouth and left chest near his collarbone. He was prone, firing his rifle at the adoo. A round ricocheted from the ground in front of him. Entering first his cheek, it passed through his mouth exited below his jaw bone and lodged in his shoulder. Without the loss of energy from the ricochet effect, he probably would have been instantly killed. I suppose it indicates something of the way the Op was going when the Tac HQ group was in direct contact with the enemy.

Ian Gordon, usually 2ic, then acting OC A Company, was wounded in the head. The round grazed his forehead above and between his right eye and that ear. He was operated on first at the FST and, following casevac, in the UK. His peripheral vision is slightly reduced. His local officer, Saif Hamed, had already been killed beside Ian. Saif was shot in the chest and died before the casevac helicopter arrived (another element in the cock up between Bn HQ - HQ Dhofar Brigade - SOAF).

Following Saif's death and Ian's incapacitation, the CSM, Obaid Mubarak, assumed command of A Company. Obaid was a Khadim. Although we never served in the same company, I gained the impression that he was determined to prove his bravery at every opportunity, to demonstrate that he was better than most of those of pure Omani lineage and who may have been relatively better off financially. The tribal/class element to Obaid's situation was clear. He was recklessly brave. That is dangerous. While making a plan for the withdrawal, I had to order him not to lead (for he would have been the first to advance) more soldiers directly against the adoo position opposite his, in order to secure that dominating ground so as to facilitate recovery of the three bodies lying in the intervening wadi. (The first was shot as his platoon/section advanced to secure that sector's dominating ground where the adoo were based. The other two were killed attempting to recover the first body.) I am sure that I did Obaid a long-term favour; without a full company level advance and a dedicated operation in his particular sector to recover the bodies, nothing would have been achieved but increased casualties. Furthermore, such an advance would have created a gap in our line on the east/west feature, thereby near guaranteeing that the westerly company, C Company (Romily David), would be surrounded by adoo. There were no spare troops and the priority was to extricate first C Company from the west, followed by Obaid's, then mine, the most easterly."

SSgt Mubarik Said and CSM Hilal Ali share a tea break with Sandy on Yellow, Sarfait. December 1972.

"The sangar in the photograph of the CSM, a Platoon Commander and me at Yellow was not mine. I then lived at Red at the west end of Sarfait. Red was the adoo's favourite target; 'Al Muaskar al Gharbeea' (The Western Camp) was frequently mentioned on Radio Aden as having been hit by many 75mm and mortar rounds, inflicting many casualties etc. Yellow, the middle position on the Yardarm feature, consisted of two mutually supporting half platoon positions denying adoo access to Yardarm across the watershed between two wadis, one flowing east and subsequently south past Green and the other flowing west, north of Red. The CSM commanded Yellow. The photograph was taken by a soldier using my Kodak Instamatic camera.

In MR's first Dhofar tour, as a Cpl, in 1968 Obaid was awarded the WB. As a SSgt in the next tour, he was awarded a Commendation. He was to be similarly recognised for his action on Op Shidda. Following return to Sarfait, post Op Shidda, I was concerned that the fact that those left behind were Baluch might be held against him. I was wrong; he was held in high regard by all in that mixed

Omani/Baluchi company. I hope that he survived subsequent Dhofar tours and, following retirement from SAF, he flourished, but I never heard.

With hindsight, I consider, given the troops available (three companies, all minus men to ensure continued security of the Sarfait position), the Op was over ambitious. Also, clearly the double checking of details of the plan with HQ Dhofar Brigade and thereby SOAF was not thorough. I remember the COs O Group before the Op; neither HQ Dhofar Brigade nor SOAF were represented."

Op Shidda when SAF attempted to take a position known as Gants Hill, an area from where the adoo were firing into Sarfait, represented a serious failure. Coupled with SAF's various attempts to secure the Capstan feature, the adoo would have taken heart in that they were able to contain SAF expansion out of the Simba position now known as Sarfait. These successes four months after seemingly driving SAF from Akoot and then Janook would have been regarded as victories. There would be more.

Sandy completed his service as the recipient of both the Sultan's Commendation Medal for bravery under fire and the WKhM(G), Oman's equivalent to the MC. Malcolm Vining won the WB for his actions on Shidda and returned to active duty after recovering from his wounds. Ian Gordon's head was repaired and he too returned. Having escaped death by a whisker, Ian renewed his contract to stay on in SAF until 1976. During a period of intense fighting Ian won the WB for operations out of Sarfait.

7/8 Sep
The Prophet's Ascension – Brigade HQ declare a public holiday. Two days off. Brian returns Manston Sat. Delicious meal with the boys. Petrol flap – Midway almost out of juice. What, again?

A recurring problem, Midway was constantly running low on fuel. However, it was never a serious problem until later in the year, when following a catastrophic failure in logistical housekeeping whilst under the command of a temporary OC Midway Garrison, the base famously ran out of fuel.

9 Sep
Brian left. ACS take control of Manston again. Looks like we will be responsible for that area until at least February. One month on one month off?
Parcel – birthday gift a bicycle horn from Odeyne! Have to fit to L/R.

HQ decided to task us with responsibility for Manston and immediate area once again, moving NFR's company to reinforce Sarfait. It was planned the ACS would cover this task on a month-by-month basis. Brian left for Manston, leaving me continuing Op Vulture patrols and convoy duties. And a parcel from my 14-year-old sister contained a bicycle's trumpet horn which I fitted to my Land Rover, following due application of grease and sand to kill reflection. One of many memorable birthday gifts.

> *10 Sep*
> *"Q" on 0900 call – back from leave. Terrific, he can take over the tedious jobs!*
> *Punctures on both course vehicles.*
> *T14, Red 60 escort convoy to Mudhai*
> *Mike back here after Brian's move to Manston*
> *Tim flying Salalah tomorrow for O Group*

SQMS Peter Phereyeshaw John Minvalla, 'Q', joined the army in 1947. Tough, generous in spirit and dependable; Pete, the ex-SAS veteran of many campaigns, who'd fought in Korea, Malaya and the Radfan had won the BEM for gallantry. Retiring from the British Army he joined SAF on contract. Later he was awarded the Sultan's Commendation Medal for Bravery. Pete had married a Kenyan girl and was father to two boys living in Nairobi, one of whom had recently been commissioned into the Kenyan Air Force as a fighter pilot, an achievement of which our SQMS was justifiably proud.

It was good to see Mike again, seemingly fit and relaxed following recuperation in the UK. His home was in Dorset near Bovington Camp where his father Lt. Col Eric Offord was well known and much revered, running the Royal Armoured Corps Tank Museum. A WW2 veteran who still bore the scars of facial wounds received winning a MC.

Mike remarked he'd met an old girlfriend of mine at a dinner party and she'd sent her love. Diana, whom Mike had known for a long time, their fathers serving in the same regiment, had recently married a friend of mine in the 16th/5th Queen's Royal Lancers. Another girlfriend lost. Mike said she was very happy. Somehow I sensed Mike knew I still held a torch for her.

Tim left the next morning for an O group with Dhofar's new commander, Brig. Jack Fletcher and NFR's second-in-command, Major Arthur Brocklehurst (ex-Para). The O group was for a post monsoon operation called Operation Sycamore.

11 Sep
Up early – convoy to Manston. Take Red 60
Brian has two broken down Skyvans at Manston.
Ordered silk shirts from Andrews HK – £4 for two, ordered four.

Another convoy resupplying Manston. Standing forlorn adjacent to Manston's dirt runway were two broken down Skyvans awaiting repairs, their pilots having been safely helicoptered back to their comfortable Officers' Mess at RAF Salalah. How often did we reflect perhaps we'd have been better off as RAF, returning home at the end of each day to a cool gin and tonic served in an air-conditioned Mess against us lot on the jebel, enduring four to five weeks between a one-night R&R. However, all said I'm not sure many would have opted to change places.

"Q" had an address for Hong Kong tailors who for a ridiculously low price would produce handmade shirts. I had followed this through and sent off an airmail letter ordering four rough-silk shirts which arrived safely a month later, by resupply helicopter. The service was an innovation at the time and I wished I'd ordered more. Often admired when worn with a dinner jacket, the shirts lasted a great many years.

26

MIKE, 'UNCLE'

Ops: Sycamore and Hornbeam, and a sense of déjà vu. A bombshell. Revived - 19 century Vedettes, Habarut convoys and funeral.

POST MONSOON OFFENSIVE: OPS SYCAMORE, AND HORNBEAM – 15TH & 22ND SEPT

The three-month long monsoon was drawing to an end. Perpetual mists and incessant drizzle giving way to cloudless blue skies over a lime green, long grassed and tree covered jebel. The verdant grasslands only ever lasted a month before the relentless sun desiccated hilltops, becoming once more a landscape of differing shades of browns and beiges, until the following June when the monsoon's return would kickstart the cycle again.

That September large tracts of the jebel still remained in adoo hands, able to operate on their own terms, commanding the high ground surrounding Salalah plain, free to fire mortars, rockets and machine guns at SAF and RAF Salalah positions. SAF commanders decided to take the initiative mounting two operations, attacking from the south and northern jebel reaches around the area of the closed Midway road. The Armoured Cars would be involved on Op Sycamore from the north.

For those who had been involved in Op Jaguar, the post-khareef push a year before, it was difficult not to reflect that this new initiative had more than a little of déjà vu about it. There was even a diversionary element to the operation as there had been with Jaguar.

MIKE, 'UNCLE'

13 Sep Mike – O Group UAG – Ops Sycamore/Hornbeam

As Mike attended a final briefing at Brigade HQ in Salalah, Tim decided Sgt Colin Dick (ex RTR) who'd recently arrived from the UK on contract, required 'breaking in' and would take my Saladin and crew. Initially included and now told to step aside galled somewhat, I'd been with my two crewmen for the past 14 months.

When Mike returned to brief his troop, I'd noticed a certain air of detachment, but put it down to Tim's imminent departure in two weeks when Mike would assume command of the Squadron. It'd be a tough act following Tim, which, added to Mike's recent sick-leave absences, must have weighed heavily on his mind. And Mike had not been in a contact for the best part of nine months.

With time to spare before becoming embroiled in organising the next Habarut convoy I was leading, I lent a hand with the troop's battle preparations. Banter, typical of soldiers at any time, was sharper prior to an operation, the wise-cracks and quips somehow funnier. They were a great bunch. Bidding my crew well, I'd introduced Sgt Dick asking them to make sure he didn't get himself into any trouble. They'd assured me 'we'll look after him – as we always do for you, Sahb!'

Walking back to Tim's office he asked to have a word. His message was fairly blunt, especially coming from my laidback OC. 'There's a Habarut convoy leaving in five days, there're VOR Bedfords to sort and escorts to organise, the firqat for one – so basically, those are your concerns, not Mike's. Leave him to get to grips with his. Dammit, he commands the Squadron in just under two weeks. Anyway you've had your battles, let someone else have a go!' I held my tongue.

POLITICAL PRESSURE BEHIND OPS SYCAMORE AND HORNBEAM

During winter 1971/72 the FCO had become increasingly concerned at PFLOAG successes in the region. As SAF launched Op Simba to sever enemy supply routes from Yemen, Whitehall had held its breath. And yet despite the initial operational success of Simba, it belied the fact supplies still filtered through to a resurgent adoo.

Facing global pressure, led by a US fearing the unthinkable – a nuclear armed Cold War enemy controlling the Straits of Hormuz and Western oil supplies – Whitehall stepped up their interest in the Dhofar War. The seconded appointments of Commander SAF and Commander Dhofar Area were raised to the ranks of Major General (Tim Creasey, ex-Indian Army/Royal Anglian Regiment) and Brigadier (Jack Fletcher, Queen's Regiment) respectively.

On 22 Sept, Op Hornbeam would be mounted from Adonib in the western reaches of Salalah plains. Eight strongly held NFR outposts would be established, running from Mughsayl on the coast, north some 50km to the ACS patrolled Op Vulture deserts. Known as the Hornbeam Line, it would become an effective border. Further east, SAF and BATT continued to build on the successes of Op Jaguar commenced a year earlier.

As a precursor, this new initiative would kick off with a major diversionary operation, Op Sycamore, an offensive operation with SAF feigning to reopen the Midway road, long held by communist forces. Mounted from Midway, NFR in battalion strength together with the ACS would advance to contact southwards. With NFR's commanding officer, Lt Col Bryan Ray (Queen's Regt) away on leave in the UK, Major Arthur Brocklehurst, his ex-para 2ic handled the operational planning, with both Tim and Mike flying to Salalah to attend O Group briefings.

Closed for 18 months, reopening the heavily mined and partially destroyed arterial dirt road over the jebel linking Midway and Salalah would have represented a major propaganda victory for SAF. The adoo knew they held the upper hand along this easily ambushed route, but uncertainty prevails whenever the other side's plans are unclear.

As part of the build-up to this op, and other smaller probing patrols, the ACS had spent weeks searching tirelessly the jebel's northern approaches from our bases at Midway and Mudhai hoping to establish a route to supply the proposed Hornbeam line positions, saving SAF's reliance on the costly alternative of fixed wing aircraft and helicopter flights. However, locating where a ramp might be built had proved near impossible given the vertical walls of the wadis searched, some extending to over 60m high of limestone rock.

Reopening the obvious route up onto the jebel plateau, the Midway Road, had long been dismissed as suicidal by Dhofar command, due to inadequate strength in numbers available to take and hold the objective. With ordnance in serious short supply, manpower already overstretched and short on time necessary to mount such an operation, that idea was abandoned. A year later it would eventually be accomplished during ten days of fierce fighting in December 1973, involving a huge operation undertaken by SAF with the support of an Imperial Iranian Army Battle Group and supporting allies from specialist Jordanian forces.

OP SYCAMORE AND MIKE, 'UNCLE'

> ... it is all so true and realistic. I had forgotten the ACS being constantly in Dhofar ... with all its implications.
>
> Col Nigel Knocker OBE, WO, WKhM

The day began as any other, 0600 parade, orders for the day, continued preparations for Op Sycamore and my looming convoy along the mine infested wadi Mudhi south to SAF's position at Habarut on the Yemeni border.

THE STERLING L2A3 (MARK 4) SUBMACHINE GUN

As mentioned in various passages, the squadron were issued with Sterlings as personal weapons. Colloquially, they were known by their acronym SMG. An uncomplicated all steel submachine gun capable of firing 550 rounds a minute. Effective killing range, 200 metres. An accurate weapon at short range. Fully loaded, a magazine holds 34 rounds.

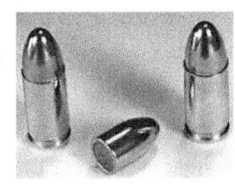

Bullets measure 9mm in diameter and 15.5mm in length with brass case, 29.7mm. Designed by George Luger in 1901, the bullets were named the Parabellum, after the manufacturer's motto "Si vis pacem, para bellum" (If you seek peace, prepare for war).

The Sterling L2A3 (Mark 4) submachine gun had been in use since WW2. Issued to Britain's tank and armoured car regiments throughout the Royal Armoured Corps (RAC) they were a weapon that stowed easily inside armoured vehicles. Omani servicemen, trained on rifles at basic training progressed to the SMG on joining the Armoured Car Squadron, undergoing extensive training, handling and firing the weapon, understanding its capabilities, and shortcomings.

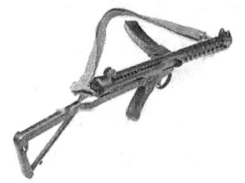

> Sterling L2A3 (Mark 4)
> Weight 2.7kilograms (6.0 lbs)
> Length 686 mm (27.0 ins)
> Folded stock 481mm (18.9ins)
> Barrel length 196mm (7.7 ins)
> Feed system 34 round box magazine
> Sights – Iron

Each day, weapons would be stripped to reveal all working parts, cleaned and very lightly oiled, for too much attracted clogging dust. Barrels would be pulled through, inspected and gun parts reassembled before a last check and the weapon wrapped in an old shemagh, keeping it free from the all-pervading dust.

Magazines would be unloaded, the internal spring checked and cleaned. Each of the 34 rounds would be inspected, wiped free of dust and one by one carefully reloaded to ensure the spring loading mechanism slipped bullets into the gun's breech without jamming. A routine task but one always undertaken methodically for a jammed gun was useless. Thirty-four rounds maximum. No point trying to force in more, it'd only block the works.

Slotting into the gun left of the trigger housing, the curved magazine facilitates a rapid flow of rounds into the gun's breech. A thumb switch on the handle housing alternates between automatic or single shot. As with any weapon, it needs to be cocked before firing. The SMG's firing pin is fixed within the bolt. A sharp pull on the cocking handle moves the bolt back to engage the trigger mechanism where it is held at the rear of the chamber, ready to fire. The spring-loaded bolt is released as the trigger is squeezed, when the bolt flies forward, collecting a round from the magazine, shoving it into the firing chamber.

Ingeniously, the gun's advanced primer ignition means the cartridge is fired while the bolt is still moving forward, a fraction of a second before the round is fully chambered. This propels the bullet down the barrel whilst simultaneously resisting the forward movement of the bolt. The objective? To employ a lighter bolt than if the cartridge was fired after the bolt had already stopped in the chamber. The energy created by the expanding gases on firing then only has to overcome the bolt's static inertia plus spring resistance to push the bolt backwards before sliding forwards to reload again. The lighter bolt ensures a lighter, more controllable gun since there is less mass moving to and fro within it as it fires. However, there's still a fair degree of gun-shake during rapid fire, akin to holding an angry Jack Russell.

Following dinner the evening before Op Sycamore, Mike and I sat chatting in his bayt, his room adjacent to mine, as he cleaned his weapon in preparation for the op next day. It was just he and I this time, as Tim was working late on squadron admin, whereas the three of us had often supported each other this way prior to patrols. We were a close unit. Mike, almost fastidious to the extreme in having a clean weapon, would meticulously ensure every bit of his kit was in best battle order. With his SMG, he had a preference for taping two magazines together, back to back, using black masking tape, giving him double the amount of rounds should he ever need to fight his way out of a tight corner. He'd rebind the magazines each patrol or op, making sure they fitted snugly into the gun's chamber either way. I'd chided him that his remodelled double magazine was too cumbersome inside an armoured car for my liking. It was getting late when I bid him luck with the op, and Mike had replied the same for me on my Habarut convoy departing in two days' time, adding in his patriarchal way, to watch out for 'those bloody mines', spoken as one who was both my senior and in days would become my Squadron Leader.

15TH SEPTEMBER: LAUNCH DAY – OP SYCAMORE

Next morning with kit packed and placed tidily by the locked door to his room, Mike picked up his SMG. Against regulations for we didn't carry loaded weapons on base unless there was an emergency, he loaded his double magazine. Lying back down on his bed, he turned the already primed machine gun to point at his heart, slipped the switch to automatic and fired 16 rounds into his chest.

Lou joined me as we kicked open the locked door and burst into his room, where Mike lay outstretched, fully clothed, booted and ready for battle. Prostrate. Motionless. SMG still pointed at his chest, grasped tight in unyielding hands, guilt ridden corroborators who'd played their part.

Reeling with horror, disbelief at the enormity, the utter stupidity, the ghastly mess, I heard myself shout '. . . *NO!* Mike, *NO!*' as if it'd make any difference, willing the clock to turn back whilst the appalling thought occurred, 'just one would have been enough'.

Instantly, unreasonably, I was very, very angry, with everything, with everybody, with Mike, with Tim, with SAF and the whole bloody business, and with myself. We'd not seen this coming. No warnings, no premonitions, this wasn't the Mike we knew and trusted, the measured, careful, quiet, fastidious, mild-mannered second-in-command. 'Uncle'.

From the word go soldiers are trained to 'get a grip', remain in control whatever situation might present. But nothing prepares you for something like this. The moment when someone is shot, hit by shrapnel or blown up by mine is different, the result of hostile intent, but not bullets self-inflicted. Seeing Mike so utterly still, I stalled as Lou with an oath pushed past me to reach out and gently close Mike's eyes.

In moments of extreme stress a valuable little mechanism engages in the brain, an electrical circuit that's guided us to safety in our evolution. We detach. Momentarily we may view ourselves as if from outside our body. We swear an obscenity out aloud. We forget to breathe. We stare dry mouthed with heart thumping in chest and ears, before realisation reawakens consciousness. Bang. Back with a thud. What levels of desolation takes an outwardly intelligent and meticulously careful individual down that solitary spiral where there is no one to dictate otherwise? Where only eternity awaits? And oblivion.

I remained detached – as a means of staying in control. I offered a short prayer in Arabic, hoping God would grant him peace and a place in heaven. 'Allah kareem' – 'God is generous, peace in death'. I hoped Mike had found his.

Instructing Lou to remain with Mike, and to keep the broken door closed, I left the room to find a group of men now gathering outside. 'Captain Offord has had an accident,' I told them, hoping to sound calm, as if nothing serious had occurred. I added that Tim would brief them later, on any changes to Sycamore and they should continue preparations for leaving in five hours' time. I could tell to a man they knew. Drifting away, there were soft murmurings of concern, more in disbelief. Suicide without cause is prohibited under Islamic teachings.

Walking the 350m to Tim's ancient caravan unit utilised as his office, I approached recognising the unmistakable raised voices of our Squadron Leader and local firqat commander, Said Barakat of the Firqat al Badiyah. I'd interrupted a heated exchange in Arabic with Tim standing his ground against a ferocious firqat leader. Barakat, in his indomitable way, was again demanding better weapons for those FAB men still issued with .303 rifles. Due to an influx of new recruits, there'd been too few FN rifles to issue one to each man. An understandable grievance and one we'd heard on numerous occasions before. We were not alone as a Squadron; other units suffered too, SAF was running just above empty.

Not particularly well known for eloquence, Barakat was employing the accepted method that Bedu/Jebali alpha males employ to add emphasis, jabbing an extended forefinger hard into Tim's chest. Repeatedly he jabbed, with each word requiring attention necessitating a further firm jab to the chest. On a normal day I'd have stood off and watched amused, enjoying the schadenfreude, waiting as my friend and boss would by masterful example demonstrate how to keep one's cool under fierce provocation. He'd learnt to deal with this almost daily occurrence better than most during his two years on secondment. But, as he told me afterwards, seeing my approach he'd realised quickly something was wrong, deftly dismissing our Bedu companion with reassurances 'as soon as weapons became available'. On this occasion Said Barakat departed with grace.

'Hello Paul,' Tim greeted me with his usual wide grin, 'thanks, I really needed rescuing, as you heard, Barakat was not going to take the usual platitudes today...' I raised a hand to interrupt, telling him quietly, 'Tim, I've just come from Mike's bayt, sorry, he's dead. Mike's shot himself'.

Tim hadn't heard the shooting shut in his noisy air-conditioned caravan arguing with Barakat. And the heavy concrete block construction of the new bedrooms 350m away had further deadened the sound of Mike's gun. For a couple of seconds all that could be heard was the communications radio whining in the background against the air conditioner's rattle. As my words sank in, Tim's deeply tanned face paled in disbelief. 'He's . . . *WHAT?*' staring back at me in astonishment, in denial at what I was saying, shocked, refusing to believe yet realising immediately he must. Incredulously he blurted, 'He's done WHAT? . . . He's . . . *No!* . . . what the FUCK??' I went on, 'You'd better come with me, I've left Costello with him.'

We walked back in silence to join Lou standing sentinel outside Mike's room. Entering, the room's silence stifled, threatening to suffocate. For a moment I heard Tim choke, before clearing his throat. Calmly turning to me, drawn features clearly expressing our shared grief, he managed quietly 'Paul – you and Lou tidy up, I will be back shortly. I'll order a casevac.' With that he was gone.

Outside, I heard Tim order Sgts Dick and Begley to keep the soldiers away from Mike's quarters. 'Q' entered the room with a stretcher. Ever the professional, calmly, quietly, he removed the double magazine before taking the still tightly gripped weapon from Mike's hands. We wrapped Mike in his bed sheets and army issue grey blanket, finally wrapping around him his issue bedcover, green with a neat multi-coloured needlework design. SAF's issue bedcover would pass for a shroud. The constantly practicable 'Q' had added two additional blankets folded as wadding to form an absorbent mattress on the canvas stretcher. We lifted Mike gently onto the stretcher before covering both him and his stretcher with another grey issue SAF blanket, finished with its uniform traditional white blanket stitch. A body prone and unmoving beneath a grey blanket evoked memories of Geoff's last journey. That'd been almost a year ago.

I went out of the room to find a growing circle of concerned soldiers had again collected outside. Looking straight at their faces as I spoke, I lied in expressionless monotone. I do not recall exactly what words I used but the gist of my message was there'd been a terrible accident involving Ra'ees Offord when cleaning his weapon. He had suffered mortal wounds and regrettably the Squadron's Second-in-Command was dead.

I was met with a blank silence as the men stared back at me, before gradually soft murmurs became audible 'Allah Kareem, ya sayyidi, Allah Kareem . . .' At that moment Tim returned to add reassuring words helping to defuse the tension born out of disbelief. Mike had been a popular officer.

The inevitable questions followed. 'Not an accident, sahb . . . How could an accident happen?' To a man they each had issue SMGs and the endless teaching and relentless training on safe handling of these unpredictable machine guns and repeated warnings of careless use had successfully ensured none had been accidentally fired. The glaring hole in our story was all knew of Mike's fastidious nature and that one of the gun's magazines had been half emptied. No one looses off a burst of automatic accidentally.

Foremost was the need to quieten everyone down. We were hours away from a battalion operation departing that afternoon into enemy held territory, an op involving us with the NFR, BATT and firqat irregulars. Under Phase One, Mike's task was to lead the battalion battle group into the jebel foothills and secure a position from where the infantry would walk through, having disembarked from Bedford trucks 1km back.

To his enduring credit, Tim remained composed, level-headed and calm. He addressed the men, emphasising that all operational plans remained unchanged and that I would replace Captain Offord, taking command of the Saladins presently being readied. We would leave as planned at 1530, two hours before dark. The men were dismissed, returning to their pre-op tasks.

Tim and I joined 'Q' and Lou and the other NCOs gathered beside the airfield's earth apron to await the casevac aircraft. They'd ferried Mike's body by stretcher secured across the back of the Land Rover I shared with Mike. All were silent. As we'd waited, Tim turned to me, 'You've got Sgts Dick and Begley – I'll accompany Mike's body to ensure a proper funeral. There'll be an official enquiry no doubt. God what a mess! Mike's notes, frequencies and marked maps are in my office – have a good look at them, you move out at 1530.'

I'd time, so we waited. None spoke, or if they did, it was in monosyllabic whisper. Tim seemed miles away, staring at the jebel and sky above, willing perhaps the aircraft to appear. And then came the unmistakable drone of a plane's engine. Squinting in the direction we knew it would appear, we could make out a small spot that grew slowly larger to reveal SAF's Beaver light aircraft. Making a single sweep of the airstrip the plane landed perfectly, taxiing straight up to where we stood.

The de Havilland DHC-2 Beaver was a small reliable aircraft, used extensively by SOAF for reconnaissance, but also emergency resupply of provisions and ammo; occasionally casevacs. We'd used it often, all it needed was a short cleared landing strip. Developed and manufactured in Canada, the plane was a single-engined high-wing propeller-driven STOL aircraft with a wingspan of 50ft (15m). It could cruise at 140mph (225kph).

While the engine was still running, Tim approached and had a quick word with the pilot, rejoining us as gently we lifted Mike's body from his stretcher into the hull of the aircraft, laying him on the floor of the cabin, the seats already removed for casevac. Tim and I spoke briefly before he climbed into the aircraft to sit beside the pilot. He'd escort Mike's body first to the FST hospital at Salalah, before a flight onwards to SAF HQ. Spontaneously we saluted as the small aircraft taxied away.

They buried Mike two days later in Northern Oman, in a small graveyard located by the coast under the dappled shade offered by weeping Casuarina trees at the cemetery called Mina al Fahal. Neat rows of faded Portland stone stand sentinel in the Omani sunshine remembering those who lived and gave, fought and died in the Dhofar war. A foreign field.

A lesson not taught training for war is that you might miss friends' funerals. And that that absence will prolong closure.

With a submachine gun there's no going back. In films it usually involves a pistol to the temple, mouth or from below the chin when the probability of death is 99%. A single bullet through the brain is nearly always fatal. Rarely is the act so violent as a blast of bullets through the heart. He'd have heard the first shots fired. That thought haunted. 'Q' later confirmed there'd been 18 rounds left in Mike's partially emptied magazine, '. . . means he fired 16 rounds, sir'. 'That'd be right,' I replied, 'Mike always filled his magazines to capacity.' I later worked out it'd take less than two seconds to fire a burst of 16 rounds from a SMG.

Over the last few days Tim and Mike had studied and marked up maps, Mike briefing his crews, ensuring everything was ready to move out ahead of and leading, NFR's battalion group. NFR and their OC, Col Bryan Ray, just one day back from leave now began arriving, flown up from Salalah by Skyvan and Caribou aircraft. The battalion battle group's Operation Sycamore had begun. All was set. Except Mike was dead.

I'd first met Col Bryan in April that year, shortly after the Vimy battle at Akoot, then under constant attack. He was visiting David Nichols' half company NFR who'd recently arrived to support SAF's withdrawal from the besieged base. We'd met since on my infrequent R&R visits to Salalah and got on well; he'd a gift for making you feel at ease and welcome. A very popular CO. Intuitively expressing genuine empathy over Mike's death, he recognised the particular loss to the Squadron. Getting on well with Mike, he was appalled by what had occurred. Yet each understood with the op kicking off, when in excess of seven hundred men's lives might depend on Command making the right decision, there was no room for sentiment.

Worryingly, I'd just discovered the full implications of our initial task: we were to depart well ahead of the infantry who'd follow later in Bedford trucks. With two hours' daylight remaining, planners had determined my troop of three Saladins would recce forward and secure a point position, the infantry moving up and through us after dark, much as cavalry's 'vedettes' in 19th century wars.

That was then. This was the 20th century. No recognised teaching, thought or literature on military tactics recommended armour moving at night ahead of infantry into enemy held territory, thick with thorn bush, large anthills and deep wadis that all offered ambush cover. It was asinine planning. At a rapidly reconvened O group, I raised the question on the tactical sense of armour leading infantry into enemy territory at nightfall, to be told flatly there'd be no change to the set plan. It was pointless asking whether anyone had factored in the unplanned delay Mike's death had caused. Outranked, outnumbered and overruled, I left to brief my troop. My six Arab soldiers I knew, being fatalistic, would remain non-committal despite knowing full well how vulnerable armoured cars were after dark. Not so my two experienced British sergeant car commanders. Allowing them some choice words about senior officers, I told them we'd no alternative and with that we moved out.

It was now 1630, an hour behind and 90 minutes before dark. I had Mike's marked-up maps, but you couldn't get lost on this op, it was the Midway Road, possibly the most recognizable feature across the jebel. It was an area Tim and I had recced a year earlier on Op Broadside. I'd checked frequencies and briefed my troop. We would secure and hold a forward position allowing the battalion to motor up, de-bus and walk through our picquet.

It rankled being dismissed out of hand, for having patrolled there on earlier occasions, we were probably at the time the most familiar in SAF with the area we were to penetrate. I should of course have let it go – but it'd been a bloody wretched day. We moved off into the fading light, leapfrogging, first one car forward, mine, then the other two would drive through to take up firing positions three to four hundred metres ahead, shorter distances as it grew dark.

Halting to fix my bearings, I climbed a small rise giving clear views towards the jebel and our intended RV. We remained watchful whilst behind us NFR would soon be leaving Midway in trucks to join us on foot after dark. Not my choice of best tactics for advancing into enemy territory.

MIKE, 'UNCLE'

VEDETTES

Arriving at our grid reference, covered by my two other Saladins, I disembarked with Abdullah Ali, recceing forward to a shallow ridge of limestone offering a view towards the foot of the jebel. We were now vedettes, an expression I'd only seen in history books or depicted in Officers' Mess paintings, dismounted cavalry stealthily approaching to piquet ahead of advancing forces. Only now we'd had to advance with powerful engines killing any hope to stealth, broadcasting our whereabouts, symbolic prizes for the taking. Had to hand it to the ops planners – what half-baked strategy! After about an hour, it was with some relief we heard the first advance sections of NFR approaching. By now it was pitch dark. Dismounting from their Bedford trucks a kilometre back, the lead company began to filter through and past our three Saladins, walking on to take up their night positions.

Vedette – Op Sycamore and I inherit Mike's callsign, Tango 1.

Taking first stag, I forced myself to concentrate on mulling malevolent thoughts on senior officers' planning in preference to the otherwise overwhelming images of that morning. Turning in, I rolled out my prayer mat and blanket, weary and ready for sleep. It'd been a shocking, horrendous day, leaving emotions in turmoil. In a flash – Mike gone; Tim leaving; the Squadron on edge as to their future, possibly now even more precarious than when we'd faced losing Saladins for armoured Bedfords and Land Rovers. Settling down, I saw Ali and Abdullah were already asleep, one snoring lightly. As I dropped off, I caught the end of a conversation between my two sergeants, Colin Dick and Geoff Begley. In a slow cadence, murmuring so I'd not hear, Colin voiced the open question 'What the fuck happens now?' to which Geoff replied quietly, 'S'pose it'll be the boy general?' Sleep overtook and I slept fitfully, till woken at 0300 for my second stag.

I'd choose the 0300 stagg, as habitually I was awake then.

16 Sep
All Coys in posn First light. ACS to 8519 by first light as "Screen Force". Cover Guns and flanks: withdrawal last light.
In posn 0815 – NFR not yet on summit. Around 876176 instead. O.P. sited 0845 – 860135.
Castle feature established: 1100. Flogger visit – contact: flares – Jets fired at grid 895158
'Alpha' feature secured 1410 by A Coy.
Withdrawal 1730 – back to 860316 by last light an hr later. NFR all around – better kip tonight inshallah!

At first light we moved forward to the foot of the jebel joining Battalion HQ. Col Bryan in excellent spirits climbed onto the back of my car for a chat as the battalion fanned out to our front and sides. At around midday the objective was reached and secured without contact. As we watched, a Huey 206 appeared, circling slowly before dropping out of the sky to land on 'Castle', a feature adjacent to a NFR Observation Post (OP). It was Commander Dhofar, aka Flogger. Unannounced he'd decided to pay us a visit. This was to become a familiar tactic of his, never interfering with his commanders on the ground, but being there to give encouragement and advice. His way of being seen to be in touch. Unique and popular with his subordinates, it also kept people on their toes.

The adoo were obviously watching their opponents march laboriously into the hills alongside the Midway road, but for whatever reason decided not to fully play their hand. An exchange of mortar fire and flares were fired from high in the jebel, slightly wounding Noel McGrath, acting as the op's FOO, Forward Observation

Officer. We two had last been together at Akoot and Janook five months earlier. NFR responded with mortars, and an air strike, but that was the limit of the contact.

Following Commander Dhofar's departure, the battalion retraced their tracks to the jebel foothills where we held station. At last light my troop joined NFR's TAC HQ, happy to relax now surrounded by a circle of infantry.

17 Sep
Up before sparrows after good kip – nothing would have woken me! Covered NFR withdrawal after taking transport up to them. Back in time for late b'fast.
Finalise Habarut convoy. Use FHG to supplement convoy escort.
G 60 Sgt Abdullah on comp. leave – return with NFR.
Tim still at BAF
Mike buried today

Up early to collect their transport, we covered the battalion back to Midway, returning in time for a late breakfast at 1100. All had gone smoothly, which from a SAF point of view was encouraging, whatever message the operation had sent the adoo. Noel was soon back in action, his wounds having healed rapidly.

18 Sep
Escort vehs: 4 L/Rs + 2 MessTins + 2 FMT. Parlez with FHG – need 20 men – agreed, eventually. Mudhai for night.
3 x days Battle Rats.

Back at camp – I set to finalising matters for the Habarut convoy, delaying departure by one day. Somehow I'd managed to persuade 20 men from the Firqat al Hudud al Gharbiyah, FHG, to join our escort, but it'd been an uphill task.

19 - 21 Sep
FHG refused to leave Mudhai. Escort now just 11 men. Bloody GREAT! Convoy to Habarut. 0800 first mine XV 9223 – Dvr slightly wounded. No casevac. Second mine 1300 XV 9337 – No WIA – Dvr's name Rasul Bux ... astonishing coincidence, LM was 20 metres fm one which killed our Rasul Bux in June.

A light convoy and we travelled fast. Having been incredibly lucky recently with mines, this time we hit two losing two trucks, but incredibly suffered no casualties.

At the last moment our attached firqat, the FHG, decided against accompanying my convoy, leaving me with just 50% normal infantry support. Taking a risk, I'd pushed ahead, already a day late for our beleaguered Habarut outpost. Foolhardy and probably incautious, but luck favoured us that convoy.

POST FUNERAL

Annual Report for 1972   SECRET

During 1972, 3 of the biggest actions of the war took place on or adjacent to the frontier with PDRY. The incidence of such clashes will probably increase as SAF grow more successful.

    The planned expansion of the armoured car and artillery regiments is, as well as for operational reasons, intended to enable soldiers in those two units to have the same rotational cycle as other units. Presently they serve permanently in Dhofar except when on detached duty in N.Oman for training courses, the supervision of recruit training and other similar occasional employment. Recently this lack of opportunity to escape from the rigours of service in Dhofar has begun to affect morale in these two units.

FOC briefing

Battalions in Dhofar do a ten* month spell and then revert to Northern Oman. Deploy an additional battalion in Dhofar and the relief system would be thrown out of gear, which would in turn threaten the morale of SAF. Close on a year in the active theatre is a long spell by any standards.

FOC briefing note

---

*Author correction – battalions undertook. 9 month (tours)

Tim returned five days later a different man. Gone the cheerful demeanour, the boundless enthusiasm we all admired. We had served together now for the best part of 15 months. In that time the Squadron had been built from scratch. We'd a great team of British, Omani and Baluchi NCOs and loyal troopers sharing bonds born out of shared danger, frustrations and hardships, lengthy periods endured living on cars, under canvas or in hand built sangars. We'd spent long periods on combative and reconnaissance patrols, perpetually escorting convoys, been shot at and mined. We'd survived ambushes. We'd fought and taken casualties but had always come through. With Mike we three had become one, a team built on experiences shared.

The first chance for Tim and I to sit and talk following Mike's funeral was on my return from Habarut. Tired, sweaty and dusty, I called in on him to report how Sycamore and then the convoy had gone. Sharing a cold beer in his caravan, wearily Tim recounted the wretched business of burying Mike. The service had been shockingly perfunctory. Arriving at the military cemetery, saddened by the too few attendees, he was appalled to find he was the only one in full dress, khaki uniform, borrowed Sam Browne and sword. Pausing, he added 'at least they'd organised The Last Post'.

The incident had rightly left him bitter towards the detached comfortable lifestyle HQ staff enjoyed and those who should and could have made greater effort to attend the funeral of a fellow combat officer. Some might say there were mitigating factors, the outgoing Commander SAF's imminent departure, events in Dhofar plus new regimes bedding in at SAF and Dhofar HQs. Yet the apparent indifference engendered disbelief.

Tim opened up: 'This war and the way they're running it killed Uncle. The squadron has always had to exist on a shoestring budget. We constantly chase vital spare parts simply to keep vehicles on the road. Damaged cars are cannibalised, some will probably never run again. We've worked our nuts off here in Dhofar. No break for us every nine months. OK, there's just one Squadron, but if we're lucky we get a day a month R&R in Salalah, and then we're on the scrounge for parts, clothing, shoes or additional rations for the men. With no let up, it's no bloody surprise people crack. Those idiots at Bayt al Falaj denying us kit claiming it's an 'infantry war' – *Bullshit!* When they want Saladins, they shout expecting us to roll up with battle-worthy cars! Well fuck to the lot of them!'

I let him run on. Tim's profanity was pretty rare. It seemed the weight of two years' Herculean effort building the Squadron from nothing, from scratch, constantly striving against a frequently disinterested system had finally become too heavy a burden. I listened into the night as he gave vent to feelings, long held in check by this normally calm, fair and disciplined individual, a man whose greater intellect threatened those in higher authority.

As we shared the sadness of Mike's unnecessary death, I realised what this meant to Tim as Mike's commanding officer. The poor sod had almost reached the end of his two-year secondment, surviving contacts, minefields and ambushes. He'd achieved what had been asked of him, namely the establishment of an armoured car squadron, built for much of the time whilst on active service. He'd reached the stage of quietly handing over command to his number two. Then Mike's death. Not as others killed by an enemy, but from the danger within. The anger and loss at the waste of a thoroughly decent man and fine soldier weighed heavily.

There is bitterness and sadness in equal measure at suicide and the discussion became torrid as the evening drew out, all the obvious angles being brought up and those not quite so but out of respect left aside, such that eventually I made my excuses, needing to retire. I was whacked, as I imagined Tim had to be, both physically and mentally exhausted by the events of the past week. For my part, lack of sleep, confused emotions plus acute weariness that follows operations had become one jumbled mass, blotting out clarity of thought.

Rising I heard Tim's hoarse whisper: 'You know? They can't bloody give us fan belts for cars, but at least they've got three more graves dug, ready for the next unlucky bugger! God, I loathe staff officers! There's a room full of body bags and coffins to fly seconded home. Contract officers have graves already dug, neat rectangular holes, waiting, empty.' After a short pause, he added, 'Funny how at the end of their secondment, staff officers make sure they spend a fortnight somewhere safe in Salalah, becoming eligible for a campaign medal . . .'

I stared back at him, seeing a mental image of what he'd gone through burying Mike. Of course it was only expected someone would have thought ahead to have graves dug. How expedient, how efficient, how sobering. There was probably an army instruction on the topic. Putting down his beer, Tim said quietly, 'We should turn in, you look bloody awful, get some beauty sleep. You'll take the next Habarut convoy too, too much to do here.' Back in my room I collapsed across my bed fully clothed, desperate to escape reality, but sleep eluded, mocking a tired brain. I think I prayed. I am sure I did. Recalling Sassoon's lines, repeating them until becoming an earworm, like some hypnotic sedative seducing the subconscious, sleep eventually came.

> . . . *He put a bullet through his brain.*
> *No one spoke of him again.*

As if singular to war, an unspoken law had been broken, followed by a resounding roar of silence. In place of eulogy, eradication. No mention in the half yearly SAF Journal subscribed to by members past and present, and intended to illuminate an interested readership. No records, papers or articles would make mention of a Captain Mike Offord who'd won the Sultan's Commendation Medal for bravery in action; son of a respected WW2 soldier, a brother, caring friend, admired in the Squadron. Absent now. Gone. 'No one spoke of him again'. Suicide's taboo had pulled up its blanket of silence.

MIKE, 'UNCLE'

> *Crowds... who cheer when soldier lads march by,*
> *Sneak home and pray you'll never know*
> *The hell where youth and laughter go.*
>   *Siegfried Sassoon*

Mike, Uncle, was not yet 40.

27

TIM DEPARTS

The Sultan's brief visit to Midway and overland journey north to Oman. Tim departs a saddened man and command passes to me. Ramadan causes rising tensions. Lou and a desert hare. Major John Martyn-Fisher and another court martial.

THE SULTAN JOURNEYS OVERLAND TO OMAN, AS HIS FATHER BEFORE HIM 17 YEARS EARLIER

21 Sep
Midway
FAB to Fasad, 12 men and a Bedford. + L/R.
Sgt Greeves arrived BAF. ex RTR - WO1
Op Longsafari – HM flew in 1630 to join road convoy leaving tonight for Oman. A trip made by his father in the 1950s? Ian Thomas and Gordon Dawson on Brit escort duty. (Brits awarded R.S.400 each on arrival at Muscat . . . some have all the luck!)

The big news of the day was the arrival by aircraft of our commander in chief, HM Sultan Qaboos to join a vehicle convoy driving across the deserts north to Muscat. Capt. Ian Thomas commanded the half company of Red Company DR soldiers seconded temporarily to royal guard duties. The Sultan rode in one of two new Range Rovers escorted by DR in Land Rovers and Bedfords. Following arrival at Midway, the new vehicles had been thoroughly cleaned, washed and polished fit for a Sultan. We heard later the trip was as uneventful as it was successful, the Sultan's father having made a similar PR drive in 1955, the then first crossing of the Omani desert by vehicle. And of course it didn't matter one jot that those accompanying HM's picnic were awarded thumping bonuses, the equivalent of a month's pay free of tax.

Sgt Peter Grieves, an ex-RTR warrant officer, arrived at Bayt Al Falaj, SAF HQ, en route to join us after briefing and kitting out. On contract, Peter would go on to gain a SAF commission and be awarded a medal for distinguished service, the WKhM, in 1977. More than twice my age, we got on famously once he'd forgiven me for dragging him out on patrol two days after he'd arrived. At the time and experiencing a bloody cold few days, I had no qualms about him suffering heat exhaustion. He'd have been warmer in BAOR.

Responding to a SIO request, we were sending a firqat patrol out to Fasad waterhole more to show a SAF presence, there'd been no intelligence of adoo in that area for a while.

Sharing breakfast on a cold patrol, from left, Mohamed Said, Hamdan Khalfan, Masoud Hamid, Pete Grieves preferring a beret, still yet to master the shemagh and 2/Lt Greadh Jumaah in blanket.

22 Sep
Abdullah Ali on comp. lve – Father dead.
Hamid Hameed NFR recce medevac. CSAF – General Creasey arrived Midway. Long chat Tim and I. We're keeping Saladins! I take over Sqn. Hopefully we're to be rid of Habarut commitment?
SEPs report adoo morale poor.
Dinner with Ruqaishi. We get on well.

An eventful day when I learned officially I'd be taking over from Tim and importantly, that Saladins were safe. The meeting was cordial yet brisk and the topics matter of fact, new Commander SAF, Major-General Tim Creasey was a busy man. Promising to release us from running Habarut convoys, the promise was unfulfilled. If the army teaches you one thing it's as Tennyson penned, "Theirs not to reason why". I dined with Lt Ruqaishi of the NFR that night, planning another patrol with his recce platoon. I did enjoy his company and always felt the better for his conversation.

25 Sep
Convoy to Manston, via Mudhai. Bedford Recovery veh rolled over a wadi edge! Written off – no cas. Lucky.
Sit-rep – Simba and Adonib engaged heavily by mors & RCL.
Manston – boys not happy doing guard duties – Nasir Hamid, Suleyman Said, and LCpl Pir Bux! Need to sort. Convoy returned safely Mudhai.
Habarut – 62 armed men seen in the area.

The escorting Bedford recovery truck, complete with crane and carrying our vehicle spares toppled into a wadi. The overconfident driver, a little short on imagination, had driven too close to a precipitous edge when bingo, over he went. Classic. Sixty metre drop into a wadi. The hapless man, relatively unhurt, had leapt clear and tumbled only 3m or so down the ravine before coming to a stop on a crumbling ledge, one very lucky driver. With time, we salvaged what we could before leaving the wreckage. Back at Midway, cuts and scrapes bandaged, he was brought before the Camp Commandant, John Martyn-Fisher (JMF), charged with reckless driving and fined three weeks' wages. He'd got off lightly given he'd written off a valuable vehicle.

I'd a problem to resolve at Manston, where recalcitrant ACS soldiers considered they shouldn't be included on guard duties. LCpl Pir Bux's involvement surprised me, but following a meeting and reasoned argument, all three resumed guard duties at the base. Sometimes that's all it took, a face-to-face meeting, a chance to air grievances and the matter was settled.

We'd heard adoo morale was low after recent losses. Bombing Simba and Adonib heavily reminded us they could still throw a punch. And there were reports of large numbers of armed men again gathering at Habarut which was giving concern.

TIM DEPARTS

> The Armoured Cars (ACS) were commanded by Major Tim Cornwal 2 RTR... an extremely brave officer.
>
> Lt Col Bryan Ray, MBE WKhM Northern Frontier Regiment

After almost two years' continuous deployment in Dhofar, the culmination of two years' exhaustive slog building the squadron, fighting every inch against the relentless threat of disbandment, Tim was leaving. He had set the foundations for what one day would become the Sultan of Oman's Armour. An armoured force that would be equipped with main battle tanks, light armour and reconnaissance capabilities.

His impassioned struggle for the squadron's survival against a seemingly indifferent hierarchy had left Tim unpopular at HQ. Unjustly this effectively

Tim at Mudhai March 1972, in the lead up to Op Simba.

ruined any chance he might have had of official recognition for his unrelenting efforts. Whilst other commanders departed SAF rightly honoured for their respective services to the Sultan, Tim's efforts went unrecognised – except, that is, by us, his squadron, each to a man holding him in the highest regard. Tim departed as he'd requested with neither fanfare nor parade. It was just another day, 29th September 1972, just another flight out of Midway but this time with his accumulated baggage, his kit and the weight of memories.

In his entertaining book 'Dangerous Frontiers', Bryan Ray writes on the Akoot withdrawal and battles at Janook, commenting that command was with David Nichols and his half company NFR. This is incorrect: NFR had just arrived from northern Oman for another nine-month Dhofar tour. DR's Graham Sherwell commanded the Akoot withdrawal and once out of Akoot, Janook command passed to Tim, with Graham becoming his 2ic. Bryan also credits Patrick Brook with command of the ACS at this stage; this too is incorrect, Patrick would arrive a full year later. That's a long time in a war.

It would be another six months of soldiering in the deserts and jebel of Dhofar before I returned to the UK to rejoin my regiment stationed at Lulworth Gunnery School, in Dorset. Leaving Oman with the rank of acting major, this was reduced to Lieutenant, matching my contemporaries in the UK. That'd been expected. But not so, having been away from tanks for three years, first in BAOR with Ferrets as Recce Troop for a year in Germany, then armoured cars in Oman, I found I'd forgotten most of what I'd once known about Chieftain tanks. Added to which, there was little to be excited about playing soldiers on Salisbury Plain once again. Shortly afterwards, allowed to wear a third pip when granted the unpaid rank of captain, the Regiment already having its full complement of captains, I became 2ic to a good friend, Roddy Cordy-Simpson, commanding the RAC Lulworth Gunnery School Squadron.

I was not alone in losing rank on return to regimental life. I learned later my sergeants, Olly and Gerry, both returned to their regiments demoted to the rank of corporal. Despite ribbons on chests denoting distinguished service in action, their acting ranks in Oman were no longer valid.

Shortly following his service in Oman, Tim took the decision to leave the forces, moving to Australia, where sadly over the years we lost touch, as friends often do.

For a while there was many an evening after dinner when I'd have to leave my cheerful fellow officers in the Lulworth Mess and retire to my room, to go quietly through my collection of 35mm slides. Using a single frame projector, it would throw vivid images onto my room's cream emulsioned wall, and I'd be back in Dhofar. It was during such evenings of memories when gradually it dawned that

TIM DEPARTS

no matter how much you resisted, being present at violent death impinges an unwanted intimacy, leaving a shared secret of secrets, to remain carried at the far reaches of the mind. Memories of the morning Mike died alone in his room, a young life wasted, reoccur every 15th September; they always have, and always will. I'm sure it's the same with Tim.

> *30 Sep Tim left yesterday.*
> *Tpr. Rasul Bux – RS – 10.000 from Sqn. Loan Fund.*
> *Notes for 1st Pde: SitRep – Dhofar*
> *43 bombs onto Simba – no cas/dam*
> *SA onto Simba throughout day – no cas/dam*
> *Habarut – quiet*
> *Plains: B Coy NFR ambushes near Auyn*
> *Adonib/Salalah – quiet*
> *Taqa – firqat contact 12 - 15 adoo. 2 Firqat KIA, 2 WIA. Adoo? One SKS captured. 11 adoo killed in last week above Taqa & NFR 2 KIA, one WIA. Noel now recovered fm wounds.*

My first full day in command. I'd decided I would hold a 1st Parade every morning when I'd outline plans for the day, duties and brief the Squadron on the latest Dhofar news. Apart from proving a success with the men it gave me an easier transition into my new role. That day I heard Noel McGrath, our artillery support at Akoot and Janook, had recovered well from his wounds incurred on Sycamore.

I quickly became accustomed to the many responsibilities of running the squadron, the base at Mudhai, the two firqats, Brian's troop at Manston and escorting Habarut convoys and Op Vulture patrols. I'd excellent support from Brian at Manston, Ruqaishi at Mudhai and my senior NCOs at Midway, together with Midway camp's intelligence duo, SIOs* Gordon Dawson and Malcolm Hyatt. JMF, the consistently cheerful John M-Fisher, became a good ally, in his late fifties and unflappable, he had army life 'sorted'.

*SIO – Sultan's Intelligence Officers

TENSIONS RISE AS RAMADAN STARTS; LOU AND A DESERT HARE

8-10 Oct
Patrol; Me, Lou, G60 – without Ruqaishi, and FAB, departed 0715 – 1¼hrs late – firqat all over the place! B'fast Shisur, where FAB decided on large meal – delayed 1½hrs. Reached Fasad 1630, only 3 breakdowns and one Bedford stuck.
Not pushing on – G60's Bedford VOR. Lou discovered Fitter had been adjusting tappets when it was just a u/s spark plug!! Sorted. Aghhh. Fasad cooler than last time, but winds whip sand stinging face and eyes.
0630 start after a quick water-pump change on a Bedford. Bldy cold last night. Lou snores like a train. Wadi Mitan. Mileage 9956. Met Bedu with FAB – no news. Generously invited for a fuddal of goat, rice and coffee. Bedu tent v. dark. The Rashid, inquisitive for news – blood enemies of the House of Saud. Best to not cross them.
PM, incident with desert hare. Nearly did for us Costello!
Returned Shisur after dark, waking to find we'd slept in a graveyard. Lou very amusing about interrupted sleep!
Finally new moon this pm – Ramadan begins, tmw. Sunburnt.

Leaving the Bedu having eaten well, we'd motored west towards the border, stopping before nightfall. I'd just positioned picquets when there came a short, high pitched scream. Looking in the direction, another scream, this time more insistent and drawn out. I saw Lou rush across to a group of firqat and shove through the throng of men. There followed a shout, an oath and the screaming stopped. Walking over, now more shouting as I noticed agitated men reach for rifles. In that millisecond the promise of some peace at the end of a day's driving evaporated. I refused to run, far better walk, stay calm, whilst my mind raced, thinking 'What the fuck has he done now??!'

The firqat had caught a hare. I'd watched Bedu catch them by hand, the hares sitting tight rather than bolting. Thoughts collided in my brain – 'diffuse this quickly, how the hell d'you do that?'

Acutely aware how quickly matters reached flashpoint, any hint of insult, however perceived or slight, these hotheads were capable of murdering Lou without a second's thought. The instant I reached the men surrounding Lou, I knew what he'd done. Surrounded by men with loaded weapons, there stood my Irish sergeant, shirt stained by oil and sweat, likewise his creased trousers, beret typically pushed to the back of head and face flushed with rage beneath sunburn;

unarmed he was holding a dead hare. My gunner Abdullah Ali had followed me and stood by my side, the rest of my soldiers gathering on the periphery.

The firqat parted upon my approach. This time shirted, I was also armed, albeit with just a WW2 Colt 45 in its leather holster strapped at my waist to my regimental stable belt. As a weapon pretty useless; in terms of confidence, boosting.

Quiet fell as raised voices faltered. Ahead men's eyes fixed on me; behind, I could feel them boring into my back; each man I suspect holding back, curious as to what happened next. I'd no plan. Instinctively, looking directly at Lou I spoke slowly and quietly, 'Lou, just put the bloody animal down, and stand away'. He was about to speak but thankfully caught my glare and responded as I prayed he would. Slowly he placed the dead animal on the ground and moved to one side. He'd wrung the hare's neck as a coup de grâce. Bending to the animal I placed my hand on its chest and called out in Arabic 'mush mayit!' (not dead!). Straightaway an elderly firqat pushed forward, seized the hare from beneath my hand, and in a flash slit the animal's throat. Squeezing the lifeless animal, blood squirted from the wound. Speaking quietly he offered the halal prayer 'Bismillah Allahu Akbar'. Honour was satisfied.

I escorted Lou back to his vehicle meeting an exasperated Sgt Abdullah, NFR Recce Platoon sergeant, commanding recce during Ruqaishi's absence on short leave. A man known for his quick temper. To my surprise he first had a go at me being responsible for Lou, before turning on the humbled Irishman to spell out exactly what he thought of British interference in Arab culture. At least that's what I think he must have said. Ironically, the lesson was completely wasted on Lou who still spoke little or no Arabic.

Once Abdullah had got it off his chest, he relaxed. It had been a tense moment with the firqat and I thanked him for his observations. Turning to Lou I explained in words of one syllable how very close he'd come to sacrificing us all to save a small animal's pain. Given firqat history of the Habarut gunfight, they might have killed us all without questions asked. But Lou wasn't happy. I don't think he ever quite adjusted to Bedu ways.

Reflecting on the halal procedure, it made you wonder how more dignified an end it was for the unfortunate creature about to be consumed, measured against the horrors reported to occur in abattoirs across civilised western countries.

Anyone hearing a hare scream, knows the piercing sound. Lou had reacted out of pity towards an animal he felt was being tortured needlessly. To ensure the hare wouldn't escape, the animal's hind legs had been broken. Disregarding the screams, they'd continued preparing a fire before killing, skinning, cleaning and cooking the animal. Whilst to us inhuman, to them expedient. 'Why catch

Supper is prepared, and the singular Lou Costello comes over for a chat, shortly before the desert hare escapade. He frequently preferred his beret to our conventional shemaghs. 'It gives me dignity', he'd claim.

an animal twice?' Another example of Bedu expediency. When a camel didn't give milk, they'd sew up her anus until she did – apparently worked every time.

Anecdotal evidence abounded; those captured by Mahri tribesmen would have the soles of their feet burned, rendering escape impossible. It was a harsh, brutal environment endured by those hard enough to survive it.

RAMADAN, ITN CREW AND A 13TH HUSSAR VC

11 Oct
Arrived back Midway 1100. Problems – 1) Food/Ramadan – now sorted.
2) Guard duties – resolved with JMF – now a Baluch Guard responsibility.

The Holy Month of Ramadan is the ninth month of the Islamic calendar and begins 10 to 12 days earlier each year due to the Muslim calendar year being shorter than the Gregorian year. Ramadan 1972 began with a disagreement about rations, which proved to be a problem at the Salalah end, where our rations were sourced. A message to Dhofar HQ resolved immediate issues on shortages, and shortly afterwards with Sgt Fyffe seconded as an assistant to the SIO Dhofar based in UAG, we suddenly had a friendly conduit to HQ's quartermaster stores.

> *Dick Morgan-Evans here by Skyvan with ITN Ranulph Fiennes reporter? Apparently he wants 'warry' pictures of Saladins! With majority VOR at present we patrol in Land Rovers. Also JR's Col Roger Jones here, warning not to give 'our reporter' Dhofar War news. Hell, I'm not new, been here nearly 18 months. Met Fiennes, had to decline putting on 'warry' display – too many Saladins VOR. Offered him trip into Empty Quarter by L/R. Accepted, he'll return in few days.*
> *Presumably OC JR delivering HQ edict – guy seems OK to me.*
> *Next convoy to Manston – leaves first light tmw.*
> *Letter to Col John: £5 donation to Malone's VC purchase fund.*

At first I'd taken Ranulph Fiennes and his colleagues to be more visiting BATT, too much hair and dressed in jungle greens. Warned by Col Roger to avoid all comment on operational matters, upon introduction I discovered Fiennes was now part of an ITN recce finalising details before returning to film Saladins. 'We want warry pictures . . .' they said. Having already filmed a mock attack using a group of firqat soldiers running about firing rifles, they needed some action shots of Saladins to complete their war sequence.

Someone might have alerted the ITN film team to a possibly wasted journey. We couldn't even offer Ferrets, the current state of spares being as they were. We'd been reduced to cannibalising parts from cars to keep one Saladin troop active, essentially the last of the Sultan's armoured units, which I wasn't about to jeopardise tearing around kicking up dust for an ITN crew. A tongue in cheek report in the SAF Journal at the time held that the ACS had posed numerous problems for FEME (SAF mechanics) for insisting on operating in the jebel where even donkeys couldn't travel! Being ex-cavalry, but also ex-SAF, Fiennes understood my predicament. By way of consolation, I offered him an escorted trip into the desert to which he quickly agreed. We'd see him again towards the end of the month. We'd made polite, if stilted conversation, my endeavouring not to divulge information Fiennes was quite capable of second-guessing anyway. Having said no to filming, he'd seemed pleased at the offer of a trip into the desert in Land Rovers. I suggested Shisur, promising to send him with Lou and an escort.

And responding to a letter from my parent regiment's commanding officer, John Ansell, I sent off a cheque for the requested £5.00 towards the purchase of L/Sgt Joseph Malone's VC won at Balaklava. With his horse shot dead under him and on foot, the 13th Light Dragoon had remained behind to save the life of a wounded 17th Lancer Officer. The medal, successfully purchased by the Regimental Museum in 1972, was subsequently acquired by the Lord Ashcroft VC Collection in 2017.

The Charge: 25 Oct 1854

"... then somebody said let the light cavalry go on ... and we saw nothing more of them until we saw them coming back by ones and twos, some mounted but mostly dismounted, such a smash never was seen, they were murdered...."

Capt. Michael Stocks, The Royal Dragoons

14 Oct
PDRY celebrations – anniversary Britain's withdrawal fm Aden.
Q – need report on missing SMG.
SITREP:
<u>Simba</u>: alkamayin - walakin mafee adoo - fee yawm MR yashoof sitta adoo min Yardarm wa al gaysh atlaq midfa haawin - hawen, adoo magrueen? la arif.
<u>Habarut, Manston</u>: mafee lil'iiblagh
<u>Mudhai</u>: FGH alkamayin - mafee lil iblagh
<u>Adonib</u>: NFR ambush- walakin mafee adoo
<u>FAN</u>: fawq min wadi Jardum shee contact fee layl - walakin mush mumkin yasoof adoo mayit.
<u>Taqa</u> : NFR shee contact - wahid adoo KIA, mafee jaysh magru
<u>White City</u>: wahid SEP geh

The above is a transcript of Dhofar HQ's daily sitrep for that morning, 14th Oct. Similar to what I'd read out briefing the Squadron each day. It was typical of the messages received 0600 each morning, sent in Morse. I summarise in translation:

<u>Simba</u>: ambush – but no adoo. MR engaged six adoo from Yardarm – result unknown.
<u>Habarut/Manston</u>: nothing to report
<u>Mudhai</u>: FGH ambush – nothing to report
<u>Adonib</u>: NFR ambush – no adoo
<u>FAN</u>: contact wadi Jardum – adoo casualties undetermined
<u>Taqa</u>: NFR contact – one adoo KIA, no SAF casualties
<u>White City</u>: one SEP

TIM DEPARTS

COURT MARTIAL – WHEN COMMON SENSE PREVAILED

Shortly after I'd taken over the squadron, JMF called me to the office we shared, Tim's old one, the antiquated portacabin with noisy air-conditioner. The scruffy exterior belied a now immaculate interior, as only an ex-Indian Army major might achieve. John had a problem. His Baluchi RSM, a mountain of a man, had been caught in flagrante delicto with an Arab boy of 12, one of the Sergeant's Mess boy waiters.

I suspect acts of homosexuality probably occurred discreetly between soldiers. Away from home for long periods of time, some of the Baluchis would spend up to two years between each home leave, in their endeavours to save as much of their pay as possible.

But homosexuality was highly stigmatised and is still forbidden in mainstream Islam. It was also forbidden in Oman, particularly the Sultan's Armed Forces, as it was forbidden throughout Britain's Armed Forces at the time, where, if found guilty, serving personnel would be thrown out of the forces, their reputations shattered. However, the particular objection on this occasion appeared to be one of race, Baluchi and Arab. It seemed it might not have mattered so much had the act occurred between two of the same race.

The Arab soldiers were very angry indeed, demanding retribution. Some had called for castration. Faced with a suddenly ugly and escalating racial incident, John had had to act fast. On arrival, he quickly briefed me. As I took a seat alongside the Camp Commandant who would act as officiating officer, I introduced myself to the third officer, a Baluchi lieutenant sitting at his other shoulder. Thus was the court martial convened. The defendant was marched in and following a remarkably quick hearing, John summed up the case and passing sentence reduced his RSM to the rank of private. For the accused now found guilty, it was a heavy blow, financially but also to his self-esteem, and his standing amongst his kin. However, honour was satisfied, the situation diffused and no blood spilled.

28

THE RAID INTO YEMEN

We take part in a covert raid across the Yemeni border. Nick Downie with Mahri firqat. With me, Malcolm Hyatt, 'Q' Minvalla, Aziz Nasir, Ramadhan Chambe and others. Nick's fort at Sinau & Op Dhib (Wolf). Bounty hunters & prize money. Death of a Sultan.

THE SULTANATE OF AL-MAHRI

Over the border in Yemen lies the Mahri Sultanate of Qishn and Socotra. Established in the 10th century, it became a British Protectorate in 1886, later joined for administrative and military purposes with the Aden Protectorate. Abolished with Britain's withdrawal, the Sultanate was arbitrarily annexed by the Soviet-supported South Yemen in 1967 to become part of The People's Republic of South Yemen; not popular with those whose territories became ruled by Marxist non-believers.

The Mahri hold an unequivocal belief they are descended from Shem, son of Noah. With the expansion of the Persian Empire, the Mahri became a vassal state of Persia and following early conversion to Islam and siding with Medina, the Mahri broke away from their Persian oppressors. Reputed to be the first nation to have domesticated the camel, they dominated the frankincense trade but also local agriculture harnessing wadi floodwaters by constructing dams. Militarily, young men were trained in the art of combat from boyhood and the Mahri enjoyed a ferocious reputation as cavalrymen, playing a significant role in the Islamic conquest of Northern Africa and indeed Spain. Masters in the use of all available weapons, from hand crafted daggers to 19th century Martini-Henrys and latterly .303 rifles, they upheld a reputation amongst Arab nations as "the people who kill without being killed". A fearsome legacy.

Not for them the trappings of capitalism, all the Mahri owned and needed, they carried. Their manner verging on the haughty, they displayed a disdain for what we took as basic necessities. In the early 1970s, Land Rovers, trucks, watches, radios, maps, compasses and binoculars had yet to be considered enviable possessions, remaining the legacy of wealthy European travellers, transients who passed by to disappear back to alien civilizations. However, at the sight of a modern high velocity rifle, their grasp of a weapon's workings was astonishing. Probably the one item coveted most by Mahri tribesmen, it was obvious they had but a singular interest.

In 1970 Britain's Foreign Office initiated early covert measures to encourage the disgruntled Mahri to take up clandestine resistance against the PDRY. Seeking to encourage them, MI6 had been playing on Mahri enmity towards the occupying Yemeni communists. Local intelligence revealed Marxist forces had taken to using ancient Portuguese forts for storing ordnance and provisions, prior to distribution through adoo resupply channels. Despite being few in number, the Mahri armed with British supplied .303s began making occasional raiding sorties against the communists. Whilst a thorn in the foot for the Yemeni-based adoo, these attacks remained little more than nuisance value.

COVERT RAID INTO YEMEN

Two weeks after inheriting command I was still learning the ropes, dealing with the unaccustomed bureaucracy of running the Squadron, my disparate outfit spread over three patrol bases, with an infantry recce platoon, two firqat plus assorted local militia. In addition to Land Rover patrols, setting ambushes, escorting convoys, maintaining and repairing tired armoured cars, submitting indents etc there was the all-important continuation training, upgrading soldiers' trades. The last would ensure men achieved more than a single trade, becoming both gunner and driver, leading hopefully to car commander. And there remained the constant task of keeping peace between recalcitrant firqat tribesmen.

It was at this time I was approached to personally escort a clandestine operation across the border into Yemen. Never codenamed, the op was undertaken without the knowledge of SAF or Dhofar HQs. A secret mission in a secret war.

Involved were the area's SIOs, Midway's local intelligence officers, Gordon Dawson, an Arabist previously of the Aden Protectorate, and Malcolm Hyatt, originally recce platoon leader with MR. Both were impressively fluent in local dialects and equally, as with many of their ilk, adept at playing cards close to their chests. And then also, stationed with me at Midway, a good friend and the op's primary catalyst, Sgt (subsequently promoted captain) Nick Downie, ex-SAS trooper, keen photographer and man with an interesting medical background. Nick also had an enviable knowledge of physics, of which more later. Undoubtedly far better educated than most in Dhofar, as he would frequently remind me, he'd almost qualified as a doctor. Just short of completing his training, he'd dropped out of medical school, to the dismay of his father, a Harley Street consultant. Foregoing a post-nominal MD, Nick departed the world of medicine becoming a 22 SAS trooper. As a medical student he'd joined the territorials, 21 SAS, before winning acceptance to the Regiment on merit, one of the very few to have achieved this feat. Casually he'd mentioned that fewer than five had passed his SAS selection course.

The other members of our party involved a handful of Firqat al Badiyah (FAB), my firqat attached at Midway. I chose two Land Rover crews, ten men and 'Q', my unflappable ex-SAS squadron quartermaster who like Lou was old enough to be my father. He'd become a loyal friend, and one whose judgement I respected.

In 1972 a decision had been taken to increase covert operations across the border in Yemen. The first step: form a Mahri firqat to undertake guerrilla operations within the PDRY. In October a small group from this fledgling firqat, numbering approximately twenty and led by Nick, made a daring raid into Marxist Yemen, once the Sultanate of Al-Mahri.

THE RAID

Reports, books and articles make mention of the raid into Yemen that October, one such as:

> "... a number of ex-SAS personnel led this unit ... and ultimately in one daring raid destroyed the fort at Sinau, 80 miles deep inside PDRY territory."

Ever since, the story has become legend with debate drifting on certain aspects, inevitably generated by people who weren't there. Some reports are in very short compass.

Departing Midway at 2030 on Sunday 15 October, there were four Brits involved: Malcolm, Nick, 'Q' and myself. We'd four 4x4 vehicles, Malcolm and driver in a new Land Rover, Nick (who had no Arabic at the time) and Mahri interpreter in a recently supplied, poorly assembled, Iranian Jeep, and 'Q' and I in our ancient

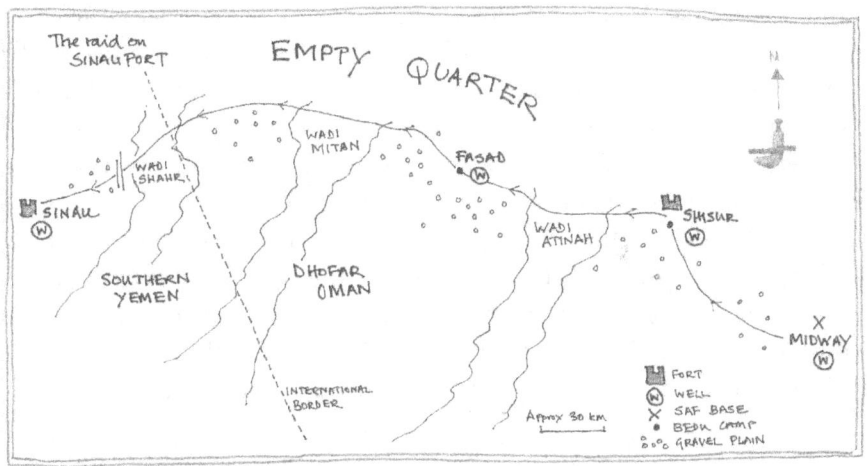

The route across deserts west from Midway to Yemen's border and on to Sinau, in all a distance of over 420km.

Land Rovers with ten ACS troopers. Four Bedford trucks carried firqat from the FAB, munitions, food and water. There was also a quantity of PE4 dynamite.

The Mahri interpreter was small, an uneasy man called Rashid Khalfan. Recently returned after escaping Oman under the previous Sultan's reign to self-exile in Sharjah, he was not firqat, but a civilian returning home. He'd no military training. In Sharjah he'd become a vehicle mechanic. Being small in stature suited his predilection for squeezing beneath a vehicle bonnet, where sitting on his haunches, balanced on a hot engine block he'd stoically sort out most mechanical problems. Possibly not a first-choice acquaintance given his inclination, unlike soldiers, to avoid eye contact when spoken to, his worth was in his mechanical expertise. Recruited by Malcolm, Nick would have to trust him.

> 15 Oct
> With me: Q, LCpl Ramadhan Chambe, Troopers Mubarik Musalim, Suleman Jumea, Suleman Said, Nasir Suleman, Aziz Nasir, Hamid Abdullah, Salim Suleman, Khamis Khalfan, Kamis Ibrahim.
> ETD 2030 – Fasad for the night – inshallah. It's a month since Mike died.
> 0400 still digging out FAB vehicles in Wadi Atinah (wadi half-shaft) Dusty drive. B. annoyed with Nick whose vehs they are – didn't bother to help – but went off to kip!

Our planned morning departure was frustrated by mechanical problems. Despite looking the part, some of Nick's recently delivered grey painted vehicles suffered teething problems. Added to exasperating delays waiting for firqat members to agree who should accompany us, we'd finally left at 2030hrs. Less hot, but not the best time of day to start motoring across desert; however, the night was clear with a half-moon. Progress became painfully slow. Breakdowns and inexperienced drivers getting stuck delayed us, despite that it was marginally easier crossing loose sand at night when it was cooler. Trying to make up for lost time, knowing we had to RV with the Mahri camped across the border, we pushed on, finally stopping at Fasad shortly before daybreak. I'd become short tempered, at one point furious with Nick, finding him asleep in his jeep, when all others were working hard to get his convoy moving! There was very little sleep that night. And the raw memory of Mike's lonely death a month earlier had yet to fade.

16 Oct
0500-0700 interrupted sleep – breakfast before daybreak. 3 Rashid bedouin worked b. hard extracting trucks fm Atinah last night. Departed 0715. Ruddy awful drive to Mitan. Malcolm's Dodge with carb trouble. God, progress slow. V. hot. Met BATT troop – tea and compo biscuits! At RV, dropped off Nick and interpreter with two trucks after fuddal with Mahri. Unpleasant incident with a Jebali. Vimy hangover. Makes you wonder.

After an hour's snatched sleep beside vehicles and about to move out, two trucks refused to start. With patience running on empty, I walked back to the drivers to be informed 'Battery flat, sahb'. There was no use blowing a gasket, and with some effort, I quietly explained to the drivers the basic necessity of switching off the ignition when parking up. I didn't envy Nick with this lot. A tow-start solved the problem and our eclectic convoy was underway by 0715.

We'd been driving for a couple of hours when on a small rise in the arid flatness we came across a BATT outpost surrounded by barren oven-hot desert. The camp consisted of a few tents, various water filled burmails and some Mahri tribesmen the SAS hoped to train as firqat. Expecting us, we shared a brew floating with dead flies, through which we dunked best British compo biscuits as we caught up on the BATT's progress, their thoughts on desert living and the war in general. Exchanging the usual banter between soldiers, Nick, well known to them but now ex-Regiment came in for a jibe or two. We learned they'd not had the best of times with their firqat and with Ramadan essentially curtailing training, I'd the feeling that approaching the end of their four-month tour, they'd had their fill of it. It was out here in the middle of nowhere, I first heard a weary BATT mutter, 'Look at them, sod-it! Far as I'm concerned, who cares *who* fucking wins'. The irony was not lost on us.

Departing, we continued westwards towards the indiscernible Yemeni border. No drawn line in the sand, no fence, not even white painted rocks. The only border, an imprecise line an unknown cartographer had drawn across a map inscribed 'data incomplete'.

We'd crossed over into Yemen without ever knowing the precise time or place, our guides finding the Bedouin tents around midday. Leaving 'Q' with a guard of eight men and the Bedford drivers, we walked over to the reception committee. Nick and I walked together, his interpreter walking ahead shouting greetings to his fellow tribesmen. The responses sounded promising. Malcolm walked chatting with some firqat as we went forward to meet the al-Mahri emerging from their tents.

Following traditional introductions, we were invited inside the largest of three Bedouin tents, a frame of bound acacia poles, over which layers of thickly woven goat and camel-wool rugs had been fixed, shade against the sun's glare. There was no ventilation.

We sat crossed legged in a wide circle, sitting where we'd stood on entry, squeezed against each other as more entered the tent. Hot bodies shuffled for comfort, each cradling a loaded automatic weapon, many with grenade bulging pockets, all with knives protruding from waist belts. The atmosphere was intense and soon the tent's dark interior took on a 'Black Hole of Calcutta' heat. Escaping the sun's brightness, eyes adjusted to the dark as the aroma of unwashed bodies, goat, camelhair, and vintage cooking prevailed. Senses reeled as the assembled men's diet of onions, rice, goat, camel milk, dried fruits and spices was having the expected effect. Too soon it became impossible to distinguish between the competing pungent qualities of unwashed, sweat soaked bodies and the constant release of intestinal sulphur-filled gases.

In the dark, flies seeking shade from the glare outside crawled investigating mouths, eyes, ears and noses, creeping down shirts and up rolled sleeves. Undeterred, the flies didn't bother our hosts one jot and determined to show equal indifference, we sat motionless, hands aching to swipe the itching insects drinking at rivulets of salty sweat running freely down faces, backs and arms. The desert born looked on, amused, waiting for the first to flinch. Malcolm, the urbane SIO, broke first, 'Fuck!' he swore. 'I *hate* flies,' wiping them away from his mouth and face, watched by a row of wide knowing grins.

Coffee was produced, served in shared finjans handcrafted from reclaimed tin. Each took turns sipping the bitter black liquid devoid of additional spices experienced elsewhere. These were people far from markets. There followed a discussion on the mission, Nick's driver translating rapidly between the Mahri's short brusque sentences. The mission: take out an ancient Portuguese fort known to be used by the adoo. Without mortars or heavy machine guns, they needed

Nick to lay sufficient charges to destroy the building. I watched Nick who nodded back at the Mahri, agreeing through his interpreter it could be done. The plan was set, they'd move out under cover of darkness and strike in the early hours the following morning.

We were illegally across Yemen's border. By my reckoning we'd covered between 350 and 375km west from Midway. It was always difficult to be absolutely accurate driving over soft sands. The three of us Brits knew it wasn't possible for my small group to continue any further west. Acting alone with his firqat, a maverick contract officer would attract less media attention should it go tits-up. So it was with heavy heart I bade Nick farewell. Where he was going there'd be no chance of a rescue, helicopter or vehicle. 'You'll be alright, Nick,' I said, hoping the enthusiasm was not too forced. 'Anyway, they look a decent crowd?' 'Yeah ... right,' he replied. 'I'll blame Hyatt,' he said, shooting a glance at the departing figure already walking back to his Land Rover, 'you can blame Dawson too if I don't come back!' We shook hands as he added, 'Now fuck off back across the border before anyone finds out where we are!' With that and a final 'Good luck, chum' I left, accompanied by my two men, Aziz Nasir and Saif Nasir, who'd joined us in the overcrowded Bedouin tent.

I'd taken only a few paces when I found my way barred by a tall jebali, blank face with no distinguishing features but for a three-inch scar running from hairline to right eyebrow. From his left shoulder a Kalashnikov hung loosely by his side. The man had stepped out from a group to stand directly in my path. Of my height, he was typically slim built with wild hair, ubiquitous bullet filled leather bandolier worn loose over a filthy, sweat marked brown shirt, stained through constant wear, a ragged wizar wrapped tight around his waist, from which a belt holding a simple nine-inch jebali dagger was visible. Pretty standard firqat appearance. But why block my way? His was a face I'd not have easily forgotten, yet I didn't know him from Adam.

'Salaam alaikum' came the measured monotone, devoid of any emotion. In that single instant I realised something was wrong. His empty greeting hinted no 'salaam'. He might as well have spat at my feet. The abruptness hit home. What was it about a snake and a Dhofari?

Hairs on neck and arms were rising as his eyes, ebony black, fixed me a narrowed unflinching stare, obvious now. I replied guardedly 'Wa alaikum assalam', responding in the traditional greeting expecting to follow by exchanging a handshake – but there was no proffered hand, no responsive greeting. Instead, left arm now cradled his AK, his right still hung casually by his side. There was none of the desert chivalry expected between meeting strangers, gone any attempt at cordiality, in its stead hostility, radiating in waves. Hatred up close is unnerving.

THE RAID INTO YEMEN

Continuing in monotone, 'Sayarat musfaha' (Armoured Car) was all he said. The tension clear in his voice as I realised, he knows who I am ...

Momentarily, I'd a flash-back to a conversation with Babu, DR's doctor, who'd warned as we sat calmly discussing matters medical, swapping tales over a beer late into a winter's evening, under canvas inside Akoot's Mess marquee. 'Beware the monotonous voice,' he'd said, 'if lacking in emotion ... ask yourself, could it indicate schizophrenia?' Thanks, Babu, I now thought, you never mentioned how to deal with the diagnosis.

It occurred to me how solidly he stood, this firqatman barring my way. Lithe as many of his kind, he looked hard as nails. I realised his right hand had moved to the cradled AK, yet otherwise he stood absolutely still, reptilian and venomous. The impassive face gave nothing away. Deep instinct warns, the lion's steady stare, fixed, merciless, confident at the outcome. Had I eventually met my nemesis?

The time it had taken to reach this point was perhaps no more than three to four seconds, maybe five. As we stood motionless, each holding ground, an audience had gathered in the background. My thoughts raced, how the f... did it get to this? when a second man stepped forward to pull my antagonist away. There was no struggle, no sound made, yet still the man's eyes blazed, locked on me. I didn't move, conscious not to escalate matters, when from behind me the diminutive Aziz Nasir, witness to it all, pulled my arm, quietly repeating 'Alan nadhhab, Sahb' (Now we go, Sahb). I turned to ask Aziz for an explanation to find a determined, steel-eyed look that didn't want discussion.

We moved off as he murmured 'His cousin – killed at Akoot battle'. So that was it, recognition making hackles rise again as I began to rationalise what had just happened. Aziz still gripping my arm led me firmly back towards our Land Rover. I had to warn Nick. Calling across to Saif Nasir, 'Tell Capt Downie' to let him know what had occurred. I knew Nick was clear on this one, he wasn't 'Sayarat musfaha', he'd not been anywhere near Vimy Ridge that day, a fact this Mahri firqat was well aware. Nick was firqat, not Armoured Cars; there was no argument with him.

Reaching our vehicles where I'd left 'Q' and the men on guard, Malcolm called Nick on the handset radio to warn him of what had occurred. But Nick had already heard and replied he'd received assurances he was safe, adding 'tell Cavalry, he should listen to Radio Aden tonight ... they say Commander Armoured Cars had a mention, my congratulations!' There was no comfort in that. I was glad to be leaving.

NICK'S FORT AT SINAU

Many years later over a beer, Nick recounted how after we'd departed he'd taken his bandits further into Yemen, arriving at their objective in the early hours the next day. Seeing the strength of Nick's force and being lightly manned, the fort had surrendered without a fight.

Constructed of stone, Sinau fort was one of many built by occupying Portuguese colonisers in the 17th century. Nick's mission in destroying this adoo storage facility would demonstrate SAF could strike as they pleased, anywhere, at any time.

Nick had two wooden cases of PE4, each holding 40 x 8oz charges. He reckoned by placing his limited explosives carefully, he might cause sufficient blast damage to collapse a few walls, and if lucky the kinetic energy might even bring the roof down. He reckoned the explosive force should have maximum effect on the windowless structure. Get it wrong and it'd make a big noise, get it right, he said as he smiled remembering the moment, he might blow the building apart.

Carefully moulding the malleable material into selected corners of the stone walled construction, he inserted detonators before clamping fuse wires. A last look round the historic building, checking all was ready, Nick knew there'd be no second chance. Satisfied his men were clear, a shouted warning and the fuse was lit.

The explosion was as dramatic as he'd hoped, the ancient roof lifted then collapsed back into the building, the outer walls simultaneously erupting outwards with the shockwave. Two centuries of ancient fort disintegrated. A cheer went up from the motley assembly, as he muttered 'time to leave'. They successfully made it back to the border approximately 125km away. A significant strike had been achieved against the communists deep inside their territory. A solid victory to Nick's bandit firqat. Despite the success of Nick's achievement that day, it was never properly recognised.

Perhaps he shouldn't have named the pet gerbil he kept at Midway after the country's ruler? Research makes me suspect the creature was a Cheesman's gerbil (Gerbilus cheesmani) which would have amused Nick given his fondness for quoting phrases from The Goons Show, generally – well no, always – at inappropriate times. We'd find gerbils were quite easy to catch: all you required was a box, some broken biscuit and a short stick tied to a few metres of fuse wire. With the box propped over the bait, along comes unsuspecting gerbil, wire pulled and hey presto one little pet. Nick decided to keep one in his room at Midway, in a modified, partially sand-filled recycled Mills 36 box, adding to the cigarette smoke and suspect aromas already filling his accommodation. He was a heavy smoker. And when it came time for Nick and I to leave Midway, we set the small creature free amongst the dunes.

The raid, audacious by any standards, carried great risk for Nick and his ragged band of men. Far less courageous actions won recognition, but Nick was never one who cared much for citations and medals. It was merely another episode, part of the enigma that was Nick Downie. Shortly after writing this piece, I learned the sad news Nick had died from Covid. Ironically, in death Nick was honoured with obituaries in the main broadsheet newspapers outshining any citation.

As to the remote place called Sinau, it is mentioned in studies which indicate possibly Yemenite Jews once made a home there having been forced out of Babylon when it fell to the Persians. The Jews created a community, built dams to collect water and remained in Sinau until migrating west to establish themselves in Yemen. The fort, however, was a far more recent addition, built as an outpost by the occupying Portuguese. A sad fact of war: occasionally ancient buildings get destroyed.

OPERATION DHIB

Nick's daring raid was a precursor to Op Dhib (Wolf).

Since before the Sultanate's perceived humiliation with the Habarut attack that May, Sultan Qaboos had urged the British Government raise the bar in the war against communism, by instigating insurrection in Yemen as a form of proxy war. It was muted it might be run covertly out of the UK's Secret Intelligence Service's (SIS) as a substitute against the alternative, overt use of force with all its associated political ramifications. The Mahri tribesmen would be trained by SAS to undertake cross-border raids, an operational escalation the Sultanate hoped would dissuade Aden from further support for the PFLOAG.

On 8th October the Sultan made a direct request for additional SAS troops to those already in Dhofar, specifically to attack the communists in South Yemen. On 18th October Britain's Chief of General Staff, General Sir Michael Carver, visited Oman where he was quoted as being strongly in favour of such a policy if it would shorten the war, admitting to the Sultan there was some fear in the United Kingdom of being drawn into a mini-Vietnam. Soon after his return to the UK, the FCO and MOD agreed, despite the political risks involved, that 22 SAS should train the Mahri firqat, conditional on no serving SAS accompanying any cross-border raids. On 23 November, Britain authorised the secret go-ahead for Operation Dhib, 38 days after we'd first set out on Nick's clandestine mission to blow up the Yemeni Fort at Sinau. Once launched, Op Dhib continued on and off for the next three years.

With the implementation of Dhib, Britain avoided other nations' strategic mistake when fighting a counterinsurgency war, the temptation to employ massive force as might be necessary in fighting a conventional war.

The raid on Sinau had been utterly clandestine. No further such raids followed and Nick was transferred to other firqat duties. Although Dhib never became a priority over SAF operations, there were continuing small successes. An understanding had been realised in London and Muscat, the war against PFLOAG must only be fought and won within the boundaries of Dhofar. And as would be proved, the success in winning an internal war was to win hearts and minds.

A FOC document is silent on the raid, other than that available which reads:

SECRET   *27 NOV 1972*

MILITARY ASSISTANCE TO OMAN   FCO briefing

Following yesterday's DOPC meeting I attach . . . draft telegrams to Oman: the first relates to the Mahra operation . . .

BOUNTY HUNTERS

16 Oct
Made way back, camping two hours west Fasad. Starving all day. Radio Aden have raised price on my head. Boys v. impressed! Crashed out 1930, slept till 0300 stag, then slept again. Discovered Aziz Nasir kept vigil by my side – says I'm too valuable now! A loyal friend. Stopping for 1700 call, heard Lou awarded a MM, Olly, Commendation and me, Bravery Medal for actions in April. B.whacked. Nose, lips badly burnt.

We returned by the route we'd gone in, keeping wide of our original tracks, driving across unmarked ground to avoid any likelihood of hitting mines. Our journey was thankfully uneventful. We set camp for the night back inside Oman, having crossed the unmarked border. Across the flat plains we could make out the huge sand dunes of the Empty Quarter's southern reaches. Where we were was utter emptiness, in all its meanings. The stillness absolute.

At my 1700 call with Midway, I learned of the awards to Sgts Lou, Olly and myself. The WKhM(G) for Lou, Sultan's Commendation for Olly and WB for me. It was later determined the awards were for the battle on Vimy Ridge on 27th April. That we three T12 car commanders had been recognised was gratifying, especially so as the recommendation had come from another unit's commander, Desert Regiment's Col Nigel, submitted five days following the action. Olly was on the radio from Midway and we exchanged congratulations. Sounding elated, he said HQ Dhofar had messaged offering congratulations, and there were similar messages from battalion COs, one from Sandy and one from Graham Sherwell at DR, now back at Bid Bid in Northern Oman, whose typically cryptic message Olly read to me:

General Points:

1. Congratulations on your Bravery Medal. Please pass my congrats to Irish and Olly as well.
2. About Mess Bill. I will agree to your figure 62.755 Riyals, please dispatch ASP.

All the best, Graham.

I didn't really take it in, tired and ready to crash out, we'd slept in snatches since leaving Midway 24 hours earlier. Since then it'd been non-stop motoring through shimmering deserts, mirages, deep sand wadis and flint gravel plains, inevitable breakdowns and punctures. Food, tea and sleep were top priorities.

That night as usual the boys tuned to Radio Aden, catching up and laughing at the preposterous claims allegedly achieved against SAF forces when an excited audience called me over to listen. I missed the actual broadcast, but they assured me 'Sahb, now more for Captain of Armoured Cars!' – I grinned back at them replying 'We are all armoured cars!' adding 'raqm wahd wa shadeed!' (first and brave!) 'raqm wahd!' came the chorus of wide grins in unison as supper was prepared. Apart from 'shadeed' (strong/brave) the highest accolade the troops used was 'raqm wahd' (literal meaning, first class).

Both 'Q' and I had badly sunburned faces, a consequence of endless hours driving in windowless vehicles with sun, wind and sand taking their toll. Even after 18 months in Oman, tanned British white skin burned. Cracked lips splitting, the procheilon (area of top lip) bled with each mouth movement. It hurt, reducing conversation to the necessities. And finger feeding spiced food between sore lips became an unequal contest between nourishment and pain.

Picquets posted, I settled in a hollow scooped out of the sand and gravel, creating a sand mound for a pillow and laid out my cotton prayer mat. Pulling my grey wool blanket over chest and legs, I tried to sleep. But sleep remained absent. Too tired, an exhausted mind refuses to switch off. Looking up, ever incredulous at the display of stars consuming the blackness above us, I was acutely aware of our close proximity to Yemen's border. Then, too, I considered the implications of the armed Mahri we'd collected leaving Nick. There's an arrogance the Bedu have over the more relaxed attitude displayed by my town Arabs and few Baluchi soldiers. The reward offered for the captain of armoured cars was a hefty sum. And here he lay, ready for the taking. Fortune for little risk.

An unease lingered also following the threatening wild staring jebali earlier that day. Blood feuds were the preserve of desert tribesmen. And uncertainty concerning the cumulative effects of Radio Aden's subversive nightly radio broadcasts persisted. On offer as bounty was indeed a king's ransom to these people. More than enough to share. Unknown to us serving at the time, declassified material reveals the FCO were aware the Mahri militia had been infiltrated by PDRY agents feeding reports back to Aden. My fears that night may have been well founded.

Two of my Mahri passengers we'd acquired for questioning back at Midway.

PRIZE MONEY

Throughout history the use of prize money as an incentive has been offered by belligerent nations, tribes and clans. With the abolition of the slave trade in 1807, Royal Navy ships capturing slave carrying vessels were awarded money measured against each slave saved. Monetary rewards were still being paid to British servicemen capturing enemy ships until abolished with the 1948 Prize Act. Prize money and bounties were nothing new.

I must have dozed off; suddenly it was 3am and Aziz Nasir gently shaking my shoulder. Woken from a troubled sleep, I pushed blankets aside to take my stag.

I thanked him and joined the picquet on watch. It didn't occur to me at the time, but Aziz shouldn't have been the one to wake me, it should have been Kamis Ibrahim. Aziz's stag had been earlier. Stag ended, I returned to my scoop in the sand and promptly fell into deep sleep. Half an hour later just before dawn Aziz again woke me, now offering me my tin mug overfilled with sweet tea to its worn gaffa-taped rim. Thanking him, I sat up; shrugging off my blanket I supped the strong brew as slowly I became human again. We were all very tired. Cleaning my rifle, I still failed to connect; the last stag should have woken Aziz as well as me.

Lifting my bedroll mat and blankets bound tight with a canvas Browning belt into my Land Rover, Aziz reached down to where I'd slept and picked up a damaged Shpagin round. I knew it well. Half the copper casing scraped back where the round had struck rock to reveal tungsten, the copper now polished living in a trouser pocket. I looked down at my talisman from that night attack in Akoot a year earlier when the ground had erupted with thundering HMG bullets around my Land Rover. The heavy bullet had fallen from my trouser pocket as I slept. 'Hina, Sahb' (here, sahb) was all he said; there was no awkwardness, many knew I carried it with me, using it as a pipe tamper filling my Kilimanjaro meerschaum pipe. Stupidly, I suppose, I'd allowed this single 12.7mm bullet to assume a far greater importance than its worth, yet another spent round littering Dhofar. It remained with me for 31 years.

Aziz had stayed awake all night seated by my side; 'I don't trust the Mahri,' he'd replied to my question, 'and now you're worth too much'.

Mature beyond his years, 18-year-old Trooper Aziz Nasir, diminutive, loyal and fearless. A man to have at your back.

17 Oct

Temperature, suffering fever. Eyes sore fm wind and sun. Babu warned of sunburned eyes ... 'especially Blue eyes, Paul!' Nick's Dodge still breaking down got stuck again. Responding to radio call, found Malcolm 50yds away sitting in his Land Rover yelling 'FIRE!' Absurd.

This was Malcolm at his most impressive. Not a man to dirty his hands, incapable even of throwing sand onto a fire threatening to engulf Nick's truck. We soon extinguished the smouldering wiring, and with some deft electrics, restarted the jeep. Suffering with a slight temperature from what I suspected to be too much sun, I was not happy with my intelligence officer.

Stopping for breakfast around 1030, it was cooked by LCpl Ramadham Chambe, trusted mechanic, magician with engines, one time Saladin gunner at Akoot and here demonstrating his skill as chapati baker. He claimed it cleaned his hands. A man always in the thick of it, Ramadhan was awarded the Sultan's Commendation Medal for bravery under fire in 1972.

Breakfast typically consisted of sweetened over-brewed tea, chapati and tinned sardines in a curry/tomato sauce.

'Q' with his driver Khamis Khalfan joined me seated by my Land Rover enjoying Ramadhan's cuisine, a meal fit for a Sultan. The old soldier, 'Q' naturally had a supply of aspirins with him and gave me a couple, which helped to alleviate my headache. We sat apart to avoid attracting the persistent flies, found even here in the Empty Quarter, my chapatis balanced on my knee as Aziz took the photograph. Our next stop was Mudhai before motoring back to our base at Midway the next day. Chief Ironside was my new callsign.

MIDWAY AGAIN

18 Oct
Maps for BM – he's leading convoy in Messtin – relief, lets me off!
Feeling under the weather – slept all afternoon. SSM Piórkowski returned from night driving training reporting one FSC on its head !! No cas. Back out to recover car – got back 0300 – bloody tired now.

Popski arrived back from a training run with the news they'd managed to overturn a Ferret Scout Car. Astonishingly no one had been hurt. We returned to the stricken vehicle and with more than a little debate righted it and towed the vehicle back to camp.

19 Oct

BG roulement arrive. Brig Jack Fletcher and Mary here for tea. Peter Simcock here for Habrut convoy tmw. Points for discussion: SQMS, Costello, OC Manston. Sultan's father dies.

Commander Dhofar and his lovely wife Mary arrived with Peter Simcock, released from acting OC MR post Shidda and who'd command the next Habarut convoy in my place. Brigadier Jack and I met as I brought him up to speed on our activities. Together we toured the camp, introducing him to a few startled soldiers unexpectedly meeting Commander Dhofar in person. Never one to stand on ceremony, the brigadier was a man quick to put people at ease, the boys equally quick to reciprocate.

Peter's convoy was taking Baluch Guard soldiers (a recently formed battalion) to relieve the Habarut position when they struck a mine at 1015 the second day out, again close to where Rasul Bux had died. Armoured Cab 905 was written off, one I could ill afford to lose. The blast removed the vehicle's front axle complete with engine. Hurrying to the scene in his command vehicle, my borrowed Messtin, Peter found a solitary individual, Khalifa Mohamed, perched amongst the wreckage, incongruously seated on the passenger side. Khalifa was one of my drivers. Shouting to the temporarily deafened man 'wayn driver?' (Where's the driver?) 'Anna saa'iq!' (I am the driver) came the desolate reply. Peter had excelled in his language exam, yet in times of acute stress it's easy to revert to kitchen Arabic. The tale was related to me by a happy-to-be-alive Khalifa on his return. Slightly deaf, but otherwise unharmed, he told how he'd been blown out of the driver's seat to land on the passenger's. A very lucky man. Following this convoy, I don't recall many staff officers queuing to command Habarut convoys again.

DEATH OF A SULTAN, 19TH OCTOBER 1972

Banished following the British led coup in July 1970, the Sultan's father had withdrawn graciously to the UK, a country he'd long considered his ally. With British support he'd gained the throne in 1932 aged just 21. Created GCIE in 1945 and GCMG in 1965 (respectively, Knight Grand Commander of the Most Eminent Order of the Indian Empire and Knight Grand Cross of the Order of St Michael and St George), the Sultan had been recognised as an important ally in an unpredictable part of the globe. However, like his father before him, he'd failed to move with the times, allowing potential catastrophe through an open door. Five years from receiving his latest honour, he was ousted by his trusted ally.

Departing Oman, his residence became the Dorchester Hotel, W1. London must have seemed like another planet compared to Salalah. On his death he was interred at Brookwood Cemetery, Surrey. Once politically defensible, the Sultan's remains were disinterred and returned with honour to be rightly buried in the Royal Cemetery at Muscat.

29

HABARUT CONVOYS, A FIRQAT AMBUSH, THE EMPTY QUARTER AND JIBJAT ROAD

Habarut convoys and the horror of mine casualties. The support of an exemplary soldier. The farce of a firqat ambush. The beauty and mystique of The Empty Quarter. Wilfred Thesiger. Soldier AWOL with SMG. Pending Tray and paperwork surprises. Blood money. Fiennes escort to Shisur. BATT O Group. Johnny Braddell-Smith & psychology on close quarter fighting. JibJat road recce with BATT and a close shave. Johnny, gallant soldier, KIA.

THE RELENTLESSNESS OF HABARUT CONVOYS AND MINES

One blessing is that we no longer do the Habarut trip all the way, but now use Helicopters for the last 10 miles.

'Q' Pete Minvalla, 8 August 1973, in a letter to me following my departure

Our three weekly resupply convoys ran along a repeat route, Wadi Aydim joining Wadi Mudhi to Habarut. A 12km run along a stone-strewn wadi, in places 300m wide, others less than 125m with limestone walls rising up to 100m. It was mine

HABARUT CONVOYS, A FIRQAT AMBUSH, THE EMPTY QUARTER AND JIBJAT ROAD

Mudhai and a time to relax as our evening meal is prepared, relieved we'd returned safely through the mine alley of Wadi Mudhi. How quickly we learned to relax before taking the next convoy.

'Messtin' puncture repair on a FHG escort vehicle. The great dunes of the Empty Quarter seen behind.

infested. Most trips we hit mines, the Soviet TM46 that would take out a 3-tonner cab, driver and co-driver if there was one. There was no way of clearing 12km of limestone alluvium, rocks and sand. It might be the lead vehicle, or the very last to hit a mine. As expected of any enemy laying mines, the aim was to immobilise a vehicle, kill or wound personnel. So anti-tank mines were laid to catch the truck, and AP mines added to kill or maim the unwary rushing to assist. The wounded slow an enemy's progress, needing to be dealt with, for there are horrific wounds that sicken, hitting morale badly.

It was difficult not to be affected by the constant threat we'd hit a mine each trip. I knew they'd follow my lead, so the remedy was, lead each convoy. Addressing drivers before each convoy I'd reiterate the dangers from mines, stressing the need of remaining in the lead vehicle's tracks that had effectively cleared a route through what was a 12km long minefield.

Occasionally it was the seen-it-all-before cocky driver who'd be the one, who in the fading seconds of life, would strike a mine. More often though, it was the newly arrived from Oman's Motor Transport (MT) School of Driving who'd fall victim. A momentary lapse of concentration, perhaps whilst reaching for a cigarette, or water filled chargul, or glancing nervously up at the enemy held

Looking back northwards from my Messtin, an open partially armoured Bedford truck, I lead a convoy along Wadi Aydim south towards Habarut carrying provisions, food, ammo, wood, water and relief troops. The truck behind has drifted from my tracks.

Two separate mine casualties, the first killed both crew, the second, the passenger. Hitting mines, these unprotected vehicles were death traps.

wadi heights 200m away – and BANG! We'd another stunned, wounded, helpless casualty.

On one occasion an NCO front seat passenger couldn't believe his luck at escaping uninjured after his Land Rover struck a land mine. The rear wheel had hit, being blown to pieces. Those seated in the back were horribly injured. Blown into the sky, a steel 7.62mm ammo box reached its apex of ascent, to fall tumbling back towards earth, landing on the unfortunate NCO's thigh, severing his leg on impact.

Every mine struck halted the convoy. Immediately leaping from trucks we'd deploy against the expected ambush. With the position secured, the pressing need was to extract the hapless victims from the ruined truck. The best approach was to drive an armoured Messtin tight up alongside the stricken vehicle, as protection against any AP mines positioned around the detonated TM46, and deal with the casualties. Astonishingly, not all mined incidents produced serious casualties. You'd deal with the casualties and if required order a casevac Huey. Then, the tense wait for an attack whilst at the same time organising a rapid offload of stores onto other already overloaded vehicles. We got used to it, but it never got easier.

Radioing our friends at Habarut we'd confirm a revised ETA. There was no need for explanation; they'd have heard the explosion echoing up the otherwise quiet wadi. Once the chaos had been cleared, we'd be on our way again. The adoo's objective had been achieved – delay, kill and wound the enemy, destroy equipment. And we knew the Sultan's forces achieved much the same result in return whenever a successful ambush was effected, or our mines activated. It's called war, the brutal cycle of the business of war.

I never ceased to be amazed why the adoo failed to follow up with an ambush from the dominating high ground which offered such potential. The Yemeni border less than a kilometre away presented ample time to attack and withdraw before SOAF jets appeared from Salalah over 150km away. Furthermore, in the event of aerial attack, an abundance of deep caves offered secure safety in the next wadi westwards, Wadi Dhawr, tributary to Wadi Mudhi. The jets would never have found them. Given the adoo's undisputed successes at mine laying, height advantaged and overlooking a stationary, disorientated convoy, there'd have been a massacre. Yet the adoo failed to follow up. They missed a trick there.

And we were unbelievably vulnerable. Regularly, my convoy escorting troops would arrive from Oman, frequently Oman Gendarmerie, young inexperienced soldiers on loan for a week of escort duty, before returning to the relative safety of guarding palaces and fortresses in northern Oman. Not that these young

Another mined Bedford.

The intimidating 150m high walls of the beautiful Wadi Mudhi, the pebble and small boulder-strewn route in which the enemy laid their mines, easily camouflaged, lethal portents of death.

Mined remains of a SAF Land Rover.

men lacked valour, but they were worryingly inexperienced compared with the majority of the squadron, where most had served 15 months on continuous active service, and while temporarily supported by our attached recce platoons and firqat forces, were on every convoy.

SAF's new position at Habarut comprised deeply dug sangars and beyond, in the far distance, almost out of sight, Yemen's Habarut fort.

HABARUT CONVOYS, A FIRQAT AMBUSH, THE EMPTY QUARTER AND JIBJAT ROAD

Of royal blood, the cool headed 2/Lt Yousaf Khalfan bin Zahir al Busaidi, DR Recce Platoon leader attached to the Squadron. As with Ruqaishi, his counterpart in NFR, we became firm friends, sharing patrols and convoys, a friendship heightened through the many horrific experiences dealing with the sad aftermath of mines. An astute leader who held absolute command through a noble bearing, he exemplified all that was good about soldiering. Destined to rise to senior rank in the Sultan's Army, he was awarded the WKhM (DSM) in 1971. He survived the war, rising to the rank of Brigadier, and father to 11 children, many of whom attended universities in the UK.

Sgt. Marahoon DR recce, waits patiently as we await a puncture repair.

An alert picquet – and we're safe as houses?

Moving out of Wadi Mudhi – away from the easily hidden murderous land mines.

HABARUT CONVOYS, A FIRQAT AMBUSH, THE EMPTY QUARTER AND JIBJAT ROAD

George Sommerville comfortably wedges his generous frame into a Messtin. He too was blown up on a TM46, travelling as tail-end Charlie at the rear of the convoy. Retaining his sense of humour, he was lucky to survive with no more than the onset of premature deafness, common to many soldiers.

Four months after I'd left Oman, 'Q' wrote confirming convoys no longer drove all the way to the Habarut outpost, but stopped 16km short, thus avoiding the treacherous mined last leg of the journey, greatly reducing casualties and losses to vehicles. Someone at HQ had finally taken notice.

* * *

CAMEL FIRQAT AMBUSH

My Camel Firqat, Firqat al Hudud al Gharbiyah (FHG) were Bedu. The men, medium height and slightly built, were fiercely proud. Having a culture where death was preferable to loss of face rendered them fearless, accepting death as God's fate, "Allah Kareem".

The FHG, they who had been involved in the Hararut shootout in May, were primarily based at Mudhai with some 40 camels. Known for their resilience in the harshest of climates, a camel can carry 4 hundredweight (200kg) which they kneel to receive. Any greater load and they refuse to rise, resolutely remaining sitting on the ground. Once the load is lightened sufficiently, they will rise with a protesting bellow, to carry their load without much complaint or resistance.

The adoo used camels to great effect moving munitions, food and water through the mountains with minimal evidence they had passed that way. We, on the other hand, clumsy and heavy, scarred the environment wherever we went. Vehicles broke through the desert's skin of sun-baked stone and sand, a surface evolved over centuries of searing heat, undisturbed other than by wind and occasional rain until wheeled vehicles arrived, exposing the powder dust beneath, leaving tracks visible for millennia.

FHG Camels around our camp

Female camel with her young. She's been hot-branded with her owner's mark, two swords above an eyelid. So marked, the theory was they were less likely to be stolen.

HABARUT CONVOYS, A FIRQAT AMBUSH, THE EMPTY QUARTER AND JIBJAT ROAD

Many my age, Firqat irregulars who'd once fought as adoo, now fought for the Sultan.

At times unpredictable, these Dhofaris were undeniably fierce fighters and I was thankful they were on our side. Whilst accompanied by my men, patrolling with firqat added a frisson knowing these irregulars had recently fought for the communists. Many knew their opposite numbers within the adoo forces shooting at us or those we were tracking. There'd be moments after stopping for the night, exhausted and longing for sleep, when unexplained a stone might slide into a wadi, or a different scent waft in on a breeze, sending senses wild, as skin crawled and quietly you reached for your rifle.

Mercurial in any recognised military situation, more often it was their unpredictable, unorthodox approach to what would otherwise be a set piece procedure that threw you. Despite suggesting strict adherence to detailed plans, frequently nothing of the sort would occur. Much more likely the firqat would react in their own fashion that'd be laughable in any other theatre, or indeed result in court martial within the British Army.

One such occasion involved six ACS and myself with Ruqaishi's NFR recce platoon and ten from the FHG. Lying motionless in ambush, bugs biting, sweat and flies ignored, moments pass, anticipation grows and tension builds. Nerves pushed to the edge.

Then, Bang! All hell broke loose as automatic rifle fire and grenades exploded, to be followed as quickly as it had started by absolute quiet, magnified by contemptuous echo. Reaching for my handheld radio, I called the firqat leader for a contact report, expecting to hear he'd had a successful ambush, to be informed they had successfully slaughtered a hyena.

Our position blown, there was no point in remaining. We'd now more likely become the hunted. With no alternative, I gave the order to break and make our way back to our vehicles 600m back in a wadi, protected by a recce platoon section.

Returning to the transport, I was joined by said firqat leader whom I asked for an explanation. Grinning slyly from ear to ear he recounted how the poor wretched animal had been cut in two by the ferocious automatic fire. 'Oh, and musafaha sahb, there are no adoo in this area anyway'. Occasionally as if to make a point, this firqat leader would address me as Musafaha Sahb – Armoured Car Sahb. In this instance it was not meant as an endearment. I refused to be drawn, choosing to ignore the challenge for a point scoring argument. He knew he was in the wrong; equally I knew this ex-adoo was probably far better informed than most on the whereabouts of the enemy. A pity he'd kept his counsel when orders were initially sent up from HQ and we were jointly briefed to lay our ambush in the wadi we'd carefully approached, crept towards and crawled into positions during the black night seven hours earlier.

THE EMPTY QUARTER – BETWEEN DESERT, SKIES AND HEAVEN

> One is struck dumb with astonishment; you are walking in a desert where nothing reminds you of man
>
> Joseph Méry 1853

A three-day patrol had brought us back to the lower reaches of Arabia's Empty Quarter. We were returning in open Land Rovers from Yemen's featureless borderlands, sun and windburnt, thirsty, hungry and tired. Covering approximately 650,000 square km of desolate emptiness, reputedly the world's largest desert, an empty space of sand where but for gun inflicted tinnitus, silence is limitless.

The allure of the magnificent dunes approached from flat, mirage shimmering deserts, draws you in to their special magic, mesmeric for all who make the journey. We were camped for the night on the sandy gravel of Wadi Jadilah west of Wadi Mitan. Here wadis disappear into dunes, golden hills with ridges pencil clear against blue skies, huge mounds of sand created by the twin forces of wind and gravity.

Ramlat Jadilah has been recognised as the world's tallest sand dune, rising 460m above sea level. To us then, it was simply a huge sand dune. Colours ranged between pale camellia pinks, to shades of brick reds, yellows and oranges. The many hues result from the presence of feldspar, a mineral that makes up roughly 60% of the Earth's crust. Devoid of organic matter, the desert sands have the purity of a sea washed beach.

There are watering holes created by man, such as at Shisur, but these are few and far between. A sad fact of war leaves landscapes scarred and misshapen in

HABARUT CONVOYS, A FIRQAT AMBUSH, THE EMPTY QUARTER AND JIBJAT ROAD

Below the Mighty Ramlat Jadilah members of FAB (Firqat al Badiyah) the Mahri firqat, enjoy a meal of hot chilli spiced sardines and boiled rice.

Land Rover patrol with a recently issued shiny Bedford truck, a replacement following mine losses. It had still to be painted with a mix of sand and buff/ochre coloured camouflage paint which dulled reflective surfaces. And Bedu detritus at Shisur's well.

the man versus man contests, with no thought for preserving natural beauty. Landscapes scarred by combatants who fight, wound, kill, die or live until the next time. Fortunately, strong winds may eventually cover tracks through the sands, relieving nature of man's interference.

THE NIGHT SKY AND HEAVEN

Fed, we were relaxing quietly, sipping mugs of strong coffee. Fading embers of a desiccated wood fire gave an additional warmth to the desert's winter evening. Weary limbs stretched under heaven's stars. We smoked cigarettes tipped with smouldering crystals of frankincense, good for the chest I was assured. Tasted foul.

Ruqaishi and I were discussing the constellations above us, exchanging names, Ursa Major was Banaat Nayim in Arabic (Lady asleep; placed in a grave the body is laid in a foetal position, with head facing north). 'Najam Shamal', Arabic for Polaris, the North Star. Likewise Orion's Belt, 'Miayat Zayn' (a good hundred) and our galaxy, The Milky Way, 'Darab Altibana'. We talked of the vastness of space, the Milky Way I'd read was 100 million light years across. The sand still warm, we looked into the skies as mankind has done over millennia, the Empty Quarter absent of light pollution offered stars that seemed within arm's reach. We could only stare in awe at the fantastic free display above, and wonder.

Having scooped away stone and gravel, our cotton prayer mats were laid flat on the cleared surface, makeshift pillows once again formed from sand. We sat as Bedu, crossed legged, army issue grey wool blankets wrapped over shoulders for warmth. It was getting late and we were turning in when I asked what he thought existed in the darkness between the stars? How far did space go? Ruqaishi replied quietly 'Hinaak fee Ganna' with absolute conviction (there lies Heaven). Looking up above at the cosmos filled with its sparkling dots piercing the darkness, I tried to visualise seeing past through to the limitlessness of space, beyond man's vision or indeed imagination, and had to agree. I was aware here was a man with an abiding confidence in his faith, who through his unshakeable beliefs could awaken in another that same conviction.

Thanking him for sharing his wisdom, I pulled my blanket across my body, reassured at his certainty, grateful yet again for these rare insights gifted through another's culture and perspective. For theirs was a culture older than ours. One which Europeans have waged wars against. These soldiers knew their history and would delight in reminding me the reason the squadron's armoured cars were called 'Saladins'. They were equally well versed on the desert victories of WW1, the stories of King Faisal and legendary Bedouin leader, Auda Abu Tayi, and of Lawrence.

Not for the first time was it brought home to me these men were just as informed as we the supposedly educated elite, but within a quite different intellectual framework. Whereas ours was defined by years of established educational systems, theirs relied then on the Quran and survival skills learned in a hostile environment. How often had I been humbled at the generosity of the poorest Bedu, offering to kill a precious goat or camel and share his family's meagre supplies of coffee and water? They had codes by which they lived we could only dream of.

Was this what Europeans had long found so beguiling about the deserts and its peoples? The Burtons, Blunts, Lawrences, Thomases, Philbys, Thesigers? The list, extensive. Was it fascination based on romanticism conjured by thoughts of those surviving under unbelievable conditions, enduring by codes of honour and respect to others, as is written in the Quran? Codes lost to Europeans? Is it a privilege of the rich to be able to revere finding romanticism in poverty, in the safe knowledge of escape back to the comforts of Western civilisation?

When thinking back to my conversation with Ruqaishi that night, I've wondered how it might have drifted, given the evidence now proven through Hubble telescope discoveries. A single grain of sand held at arm's length equals to a measurement of 2.6 arc minutes, concealing beyond a tiny fraction of space. Viewed through that one single random spec in the sky, that negligible hole in the heavens, we are told Hubble Extreme Deep Field explorations revealed a count of more than 5500 galaxies. The most distant galaxies are 13 billion light years away. As if that was not enough, these galaxies are moving away from each other at ever increasing speeds. The speed of light, absolute at 300,000 km per second, means they represent light that has shone from a time when the universe was young, less than 500 million years after the moment of creation, when time began and theorists say there was no light due to the density of dust. Brought up on the Book of Genesis, it is sufficient to make you reflect upon your beliefs, sufficient to raise doubt to doubts. Sufficient to awaken certainly, we are not alone in space.

WILFRED THESIGER

Twenty-six years after Thesiger undertook his remarkable travels in southern Arabia, the Rub al Khali remained still largely unspoiled, a strange hypnotic place enhanced by undisturbed beauty and silence. One of those few wild places on earth where mankind's achievements which have granted him supremacy over all things except nature, are brought into sharp focus and significance lost.

The sands of the Empty Quarter were and remain to this day one of the most remarkable places still left to experience. When introduced to Thesiger as one having soldiered in Oman, he enquired where I'd travelled. More charming than I'd been led to expect, somehow I could tell his enthusiasm was guarded. I replied I'd lived in Dhofar and would often visit Shisur from where he had set out to cross the Empty Quarter, explaining we used the well as a base from where to patrol east to Dawkah, and west past Wadi Mitan to Yemen. Hearing this he sighed, looking past his boxer's long broken nose at me before replying with a hint of censure, 'I see . . . and I suppose we travelled by vehicle?' There really wasn't much answer to that, to someone who'd walked barefoot with camels across Arabia's sands. He spoke with a lilt straight out the 1930s and was equally well-mannered; nevertheless, I recognised an inner sense of superiority, much as that of the Bedu towards those considered would struggle to survive as he and his small band of Rashidi Bedu once had.

Of high ideals, a British aristocrat whom the Arabs referred to as El Mubarak bin Landan (The Blessed one from London), he had lived for long periods with nomadic peoples from the Middle East to Northern Africa. After Eton and Oxford where he gained a boxing blue, he served with the SAS in WW2. A frequent visitor to a farm owned by my father's cousins at Naro Moru at the foot of Mt. Kenya, he was a nostalgist in the purest sense of the expression, highly intelligent, well-read, a man who eschewed the comforts of his birthright, preferring the romantic lifestyle of the nomad.

Despite him complimenting SAF efforts in stemming the tide of communism into Oman and what had been accomplished, it was difficult not to feel, next to his abhorrence of what a Marxist regime might have meant, the image of vehicles in the Rub al Khali probably ranked a close second.

> I grew to feel an increasing resentment towards Western innovations in other lands and a distaste for the dull monotony of our modern world.
>
> Wilfred Thesiger

22-27 Oct
Check Green 60 mine detectors – report results to John MacCallum.
Applicants – post of storeman – 3? We only need one!
'Q' discovered Sterling No. 49 missing: Board of Enquiry – JMF. Result – stolen.
Rain 23 Oct – 1430 – wonders never cease.
Khareef back – same as last year following monsoon. Midway engulfed 0730. Visibility down to 100m. Sun broke through 0845.
Ruqaishi back to command G60 – thank God.
NFR wadi Arzat ambushes – 9 adoo – 2 KIA. Simba – 32 incomers, 23 Oct.
Cleared 'In Tray'! – only to discover a 'Pending Tray' – and some important correspondence – thanks Tim!
Disputed – Khalifa Mohd owes Rashi Mohd RS 9.00? Sorted.
Balaklava Day.

A lost weapon was serious business. It transpired the amiable ex-Trucial Oman Scout, trooper Ali Mubarik was AWOL. In the period immediately following Mike's death, he'd departed on annual leave from Salalah, without handing in his SMG. Despite strict procedures that every man hand in his personal weapon on departing Dhofar, Mubarik had somehow evaded any checks, managing to secrete his weapon amongst his bags and successfully flown north to Muscat and then disappeared. Subsequent searches of his village revealed he'd vanished without trace. Neither Ali Mubarik nor SMG 49 were seen again. The third soldier from the Squadron to abscond with a weapon, the first taking an armoured car with weapons and radios, the other two, machine guns – not an enviable record. As if we hadn't enough to contend with, there followed another Board of Enquiry, another black mark against the Squadron.

The best news of the day was Ruqaishi's return. In his absence, Sgt Abdullah had led NFR Recce for the past two weeks. Whilst a good man, a fighter with ugly bullet wound scars across his belly to prove it, he was no Ruqaishi.

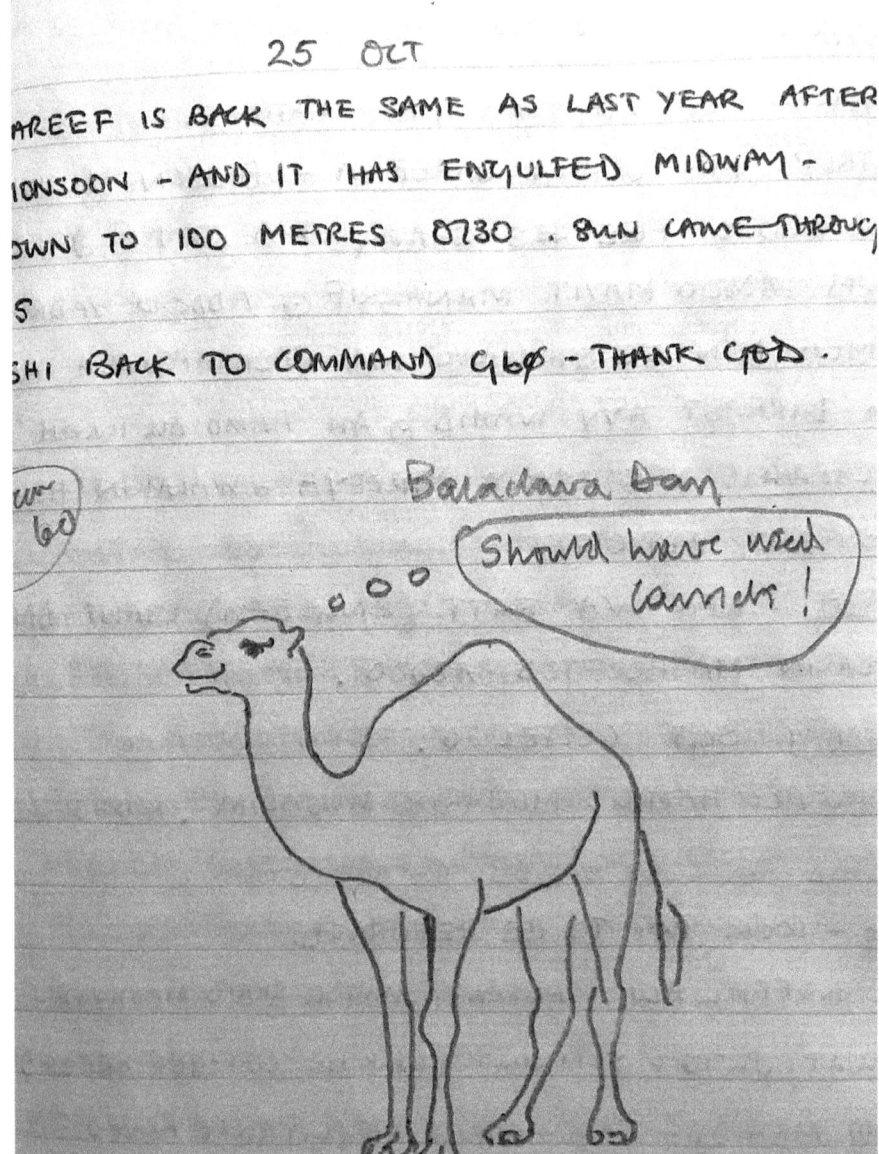

This year was spent enjoying a quiet evening with Ruqaishi, hearing news of his leave, his family and legends of the Green Mountain, Jebel Akhdar in northern Oman, where he told me apricots and lime trees grew.

25th October marked 'Balaklava Day' and a second missed anniversary of my parent Regiment's principal battle honour. In Germany, we'd enjoy a day off from the ordinary, which meant an escape from maintaining tanks, their engines, weapons and radios, and instead there'd be sports fixtures including clay pigeon shooting and, I recall, a lot of beer. It was always memorable for the consumption of alcohol.

PENDING TRAY AND PAPERWORK

Back at Midway and tackling my overladen intray, nestled amongst paperwork I'd set aside to catch up on, I discovered some overlooked letters. These included envelopes addressed: Capt PEB Hodgson 13/18H, HQ Sultan's Armed Forces, Bayt al Falaj, Muscat, PO Box No 602, SULTANATE OF OMAN. Across the envelopes in biro had been added: MIDWAY.

No stamps, so must have come via diplomatic bag? Perhaps news on my application to extend my Short Service to a Regular Commission? 'Never get a job at HQ,' I muttered, realising I should be more proactive with paperwork admin. The first embossed envelope contained a letter from Major General JM Brockbank, CBE, MC – Director Royal Armoured Corps, short and brief as you'd expect from a busy man. There was also a letter on expensive paper from Buck House confirming I may wear the Sultan's Bravery Medal, and a kind letter from Brigadier Jack Fletcher too.

> *28th Oct*
> *No spares B'ford trucks? Manston Convoy – overnight Mudhai. RTB midday. Col David and John MacCallum visit. Fiennes back – sent him with Lou and eight men to Shisur in 2 L/Rs. Our guest now wants to photograph camels. Lou happy as guide. That evening shared a drink, wasn't after war stories at all – just visit to Shisur. They found camels, delighted he'd found newly born black calf with mother. Ginny, his wife, in Muscat researching book. He remembers Desmond at Eton, small world. He recalled fondly his time with MR, 1968/69.*

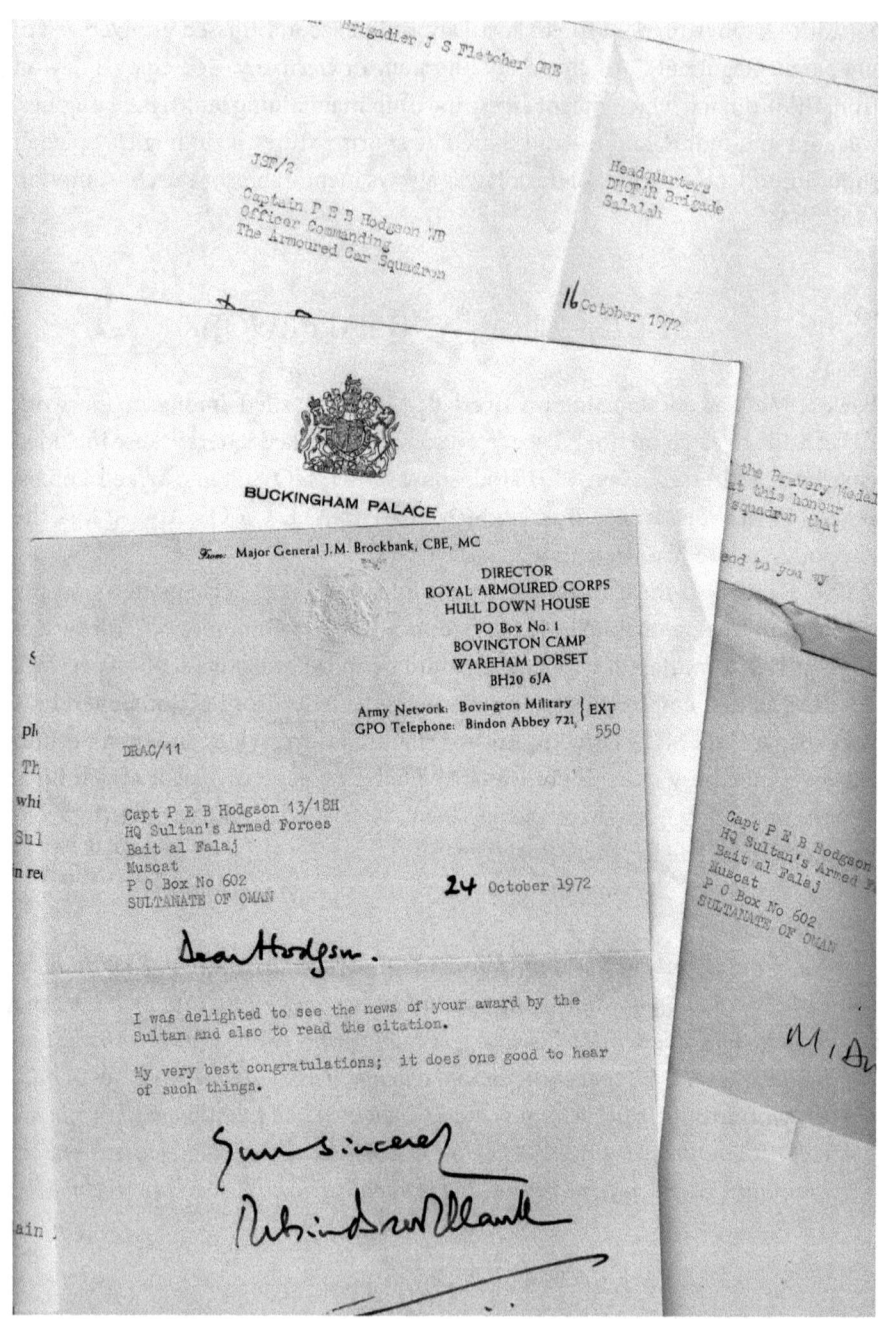

Rising to become Director Royal Armoured Corps, General 'Robin' Brockbank, Eton and Christ Church, Oxford, had been commissioned into the 9th/12th Royal Lancers, winning an immediate MC in North Africa in WW2. In retirement he became a great advocate of conservation.

FIENNES BACK AGAIN, AND I SEND HIM TO SHISUR

One of the first to be published on Dhofar's secret war, Fiennes wrote an absorbing book on his adventures in Oman, titled "Where Soldiers Fear To Tread". Amongst his many exploits, he tells of one in particular, an audacious ambush deep into adoo territory followed by desperate escape under fire, all accomplished without loss. They'd killed two adoo and the contact, a culmination of many 'independent operations' during MR's nine-month Dhofar tour, had earned him the Sultan's Bravery Medal.

Years later and now a record-breaking Polar explorer, Polar explorer, Ranulph Fiennes is quoted as reflecting on his time in Oman as possibly his most fulfilling. Of the many global expeditions accomplished, one sought to discover the fabled Ubar, mentioned in the Quran and referred to as Atlantis of the Sands by TE Lawrence. As he was keen to revisit Shisur, I lent him Lou and an armed escort as promised earlier, to visit our favourite sweet water desert well. We'd discussed the location at some length, for he knew it from his time as MR's recce platoon leader in 1969. As with many aspects of Arabia's long history, there is much that lies buried in the sands, physically and in myths and legends. The subsequent Fiennes expedition 20 years later would revitalise authoritative discussion at many levels concerning the elusive Ubar's 5000 year old existence.

As to local theory, many years later when on a visit to Dhofar, I enquired of my guide, a proud Mahri, veteran firqat and son of an ex-adoo, his opinion on Ubar. His reply, pronounced with typical Jebali assertiveness as to dismiss further discussion, was 'La Ubar, Shisur, bayt al Rashid!' (It's not Ubar, it's Shisur, home to the Rashid tribe). Thus, the irresistible legend lives on.

Desmond Sandford was my twin's socially gifted brother-in-law. Before leaving for Oman, he'd mentioned a certain Ranulph Fiennes as a 'daredevil' friend at school. Charming to the core and certainly no daredevil, Desmond had been expelled for escaping too often to parties in 1960s Bohemian London.

BATT HQ – O GROUP: JIBJAT ROAD RECCE

Ist Nov
O Group – OC BATT caravan. Recce road link Jibjat to Midway. We select route fm 72 to grid area BE 2416. ACS and Green 60. Propose linkup 4 Nov. Overall command BATT, c/s 38 – OK. Their 2 vehs leave JJ 0700 – 4 Nov. RV at 181221 by 1200hrs. Calls: 1230 and 1600. c/s 38. Eventual plan – build road to JJ. Beer with Cols Brian & Bill Kerr before long, deep chat with Johnny B-S in UAG gardens,

Flying to Salalah for an O Group, I reported to BATT HQ's small caravan, meeting the SAS squadron commander, his Ops officer and the Sultanate's resident SIO Dhofar, Major Tony Hazeldine, head of intelligence at Dhofar HQ. Incorrectly assuming I'd been briefed on Jibjat, BATT's eastern jebel position, they were correct. I was the better informed on geography west and north of the Qara jebel.

So soon following the clandestine raid into Yemen, which as yet still no one spoke of, I was becoming wary about what next we might be dropped into. The briefing indicated a relatively simple op. The aim: seek a route between Jibjat and Midway, reportedly viable according to BATT's firqat guides. If successful, the route would be a precursor to building a road onto the eastern jebel allowing access to build civil aid posts, each with a water borehole, concrete wellhead, school, shop and mosque to serve local jebali tribes.

BATT in two jeeps using firqat guides would recce a route down from Jibjat to Wadi Jazal which ran north and down to an area of desert and scrubland I knew but had not fully explored. As a squadron a full year earlier, the Squadron and infantry had had a contact when in Saladins we'd engaged using our 76mm guns. Adoo territory in 1971, patrolling alone in Land Rovers from the north with my small numbers would have been a death trap. With its steep 180m vertical walls the high ground had belonged to the adoo. Now the guides assured their SAS partners the area was free of Marxists, it would be safe to travel in small parties. Meeting the BATT approaching from the jebel with their guides, I was to secure the RV and await their arrival.

I'd lead from 72, Midway's callsign. The BATT callsign was 38. Brian was fully committed at Manston supporting the Simba airhead. I'd take four Land Rovers, 8 ACS soldiers, and 8 from NFR's recce. I had Ruqaishi back from leave. 'No sweat' I thought to myself, thankful it appeared so straightforward. Despite the near useless maps, I was confident we'd find a route into Wadi Jazal through the Qara foothills. I knew the area, BATT had firqat guides – what could go wrong? What transpired was a cock-up with near fatal consequences.

I left to spend the night in a borrowed room at the Officers' Mess, a guest of Bryan Ray's NFR. Lt/Col Bill Kerr, MR was down from Simba on R&R and together they invited me to share a drink before dinner. Bill Kerr I hardly knew apart from introduction, but Bryan I knew well. It was good to see him again. After dinner, I retired to the stillness of the Mess gardens, a calm oasis attributed to an ex-Scots Greys,, JR's Richard John when last stationed at UAG. The air was heavy with the scent of wild jasmine mixed with damp earth, the result of over enthusiastic watering earlier that evening. The waft of cigarette smoke interrupted to drift lazily in the still air, accidental reminder of a passing smoker. It was peaceful, quiet but for the incessant hum envied only by those deprived of air-conditioners.

Following dinner, relaxing beneath drapes of magenta coloured bougainvillea intertwined with free growing wild jasmine, I'd been joined by Johnny Braddell Smith, OC A Coy NFR, six months into their current tour in Dhofar. We were sharing stories as soldiers do, in the knowledge it was better to hear first hand than along the grapevine.

Bougainvillea.

Johnny had had a year's experience ahead of me soldiering in Oman. He'd been at Akoot when Stuart Rae was killed. Greatly respected among officers and men, Johnny had been involved in a number of fierce gunfights on the jebel. With his reputation for cool headed soldiering, there was an empathy with someone who'd fought close contacts. He knew Vimy Ridge and Janook and asked to hear more of our battles. He also wanted to hear about Mike. I gave him a full account of what had occurred, sparing none of the chaotic details. It was strangely cathartic, this conversation with someone who listened attentively without interruption.

When I'd finished, he turned from staring at his feet to look at me. Brushing wisps of receding fair hair from his high forehead, he replied in his quiet Irish lilt, his tone muted, 'That's a problem?' he quizzed. 'Listen, there's not a man out here who's fought close contact can honestly say he's not been involved in something similar. Every patrol we take, we risk soldiers' lives. It's us, we lead them into contacts. You come to a place when suddenly you think *shit! this is bad*, but then it's already too late, bullets are flying. So we send men forward and they're shot or killed. We give orders. We lead men down a route we've selected and someone treads on a mine, it's us, we chose to go there. We bring down jets or mortar or guns too close and men are killed, it's us. Every time we leave our dead or wounded in the field, it's us who decide to do so. It's bloody shit, but that's active service.' In mocking prophecy, how Johnny's words would echo one day.

Pausing before going on, 'So, how d'you cope with that?' he asked rhetorically. 'You know what? It's *how* you cope . . . that's the important bit. Don't move on, you end up dead. Or worse, your soldiers will, whilst you beat yourself up wondering uselessly the what-might-have-beens.'

* * *

JOHNNY BRADDELL SMITH WSH, WB, SULTAN'S COMMENDATION MEDAL

Eighteen months later Johnny was killed attempting to recover a downed soldier. The man on the ground, Johnny had been ordered to push forward against his better judgement by those in command. He and his men were accompanying an Iranian patrol north of Raykhut. Unhappy with his orders, he recognised he'd no alternative but to advance with his irregulars, firqat troops of the FTZ with whom I'd soldiered at Akoot. They ran straight into a fusillade of automatic fire. Pinned down in dense woodland, the adoo held the initiative. His company sergeant-major (CSM) was killed outright, shot at close range. A young firqat attempted to lift the dead man but struggled under the weight. Seeing this, Johnny handed his rifle to one of his men and rushed forward to help. Dragging the body out of the firefight, Johnny was hit and fell, still trying to pull his dead friend to safety.

The automatic fire was close and intense. The adoo dominated. Now the situation was understood by higher command. Deemed too dangerous to retrieve the bodies, Johnny and his CSM were left where they lay, amongst the wild acacia and scented frankincense on the jebel. It was Christmas Day. The men's bodies abandoned where they'd fallen, would be retrieved a year later. Johnny left a widow with small children.

Already the recipient of the Sultan's Bravery Medal, and a Commendation Medal for bravery, Johnny was posthumously awarded the Sultan's Gallantry Medal, Oman's equivalent of the VC, becoming the most highly decorated British serviceman serving alongside HM Forces. Johnny's citation ends with "This action typifies the . . . courage and complete disregard for personal safety shown by Major Braddell Smith during this and earlier actions against the enemy. His gallantry and devotion to duty are beyond praise."

> "Good-morning, good-morning!" the General said
> When we met him last week on our way to the line.
> Now the soldiers he smiled at are most of 'em dead,
> And we're cursing his staff for incompetent swine.
> "He's a cheery old card," grunted Harry to Jack
> As they slogged up to Arras with rifle and pack.
>
> But he did for them both by his plan of attack.
>
> Siegfried Sassoon

2 Nov
Caught Skyvan, Mike Butler on board. Met Landon, knew of the Sinau raid. Back via Manston to see Brian's crowd, Wimpy and Colin Dick, all growing beards and well tanned! Al Mutasim Hamood, Red 60 has joined us – posted following incident at Simba. Very affable, speaks excellent English – Busaidi – royal family.

The following morning as I made to board a skyvan carrying ordnance and provisions north to Midway I saw there was one other passenger, Mike Butler, an ex-13th/18th Royal Hussar. He had served with MR as recce platoon leader prior to Rannulph Fiennes and having since left the British army, was now a civilian working for the Sultanate as an agricultural advisor. We'd met once before but not so his companion, Tim Landon, another cavalryman, ex-10th Hussars and about whom a lot has been written elsewhere. As a SAF Intelligence Officer he had played a pivotal role in the Sultan's successful accession to the throne following the coup, and since remained a close associate to the Sultan. On introduction, Landon shook my hand and after a moment remarked casually how well the raid into Yemen had gone. With that he turned and bidding farewell to Mike, strode off to his waiting Land Rover. It was the first and last official acknowledgement I heard of the operation having occurred. We flew back to Midway via Manston where I

The Manston contingent, Brian with Sgts Colin Dick and Wimpy Waite, showing signs of having gone native.

met with Brian and his crews. Also present was a young lieutenant, Al Mu'tasim bin Hamood bin Nasr Al Busaidi of Muscat Regiment. He'd just been posted to the squadron, following a serious incident at Simba. Affable and outwardly confident, he spoke perfect English.

'DIYA' – BLOOD MONEY AND AL MU'TASIM HAMOOD

Under difficult circumstances, Sandy had been promoted in the field to replace the existing officer commanding B Coy MR on Sarfait, when he was sent out to investigate the sad shooting of a little girl. He later related the following account:

> I took over as OC B Company from Willie Harris. Willie was removed from post by Bill Kerr. I was Adjutant and summoned to Sarfait from UAG; my handover was to get off the Skyvan and ensure Willie get on it. Al Mutasim was the Company 2ic. He did not inform me that he was taking out a patrol that evening, and I failed to ask about such things. Having walked around the Company position, on Green, and noted various tasks requiring to be done, at his invitation I had my evening meal with John Dean whose guns, as you will remember, were positioned near Green. While we were sharing our rations, small arms firing started. It was dark. Following the usual confusion, we realised that the "contact" was Al Mutasim and his patrol in the wadi north of Green. The wadi was aligned west-east, becoming gradually shallower at its western end towards the Battalion's Tac HQ area; you may remember it.
>
> It took some time for me to arrive on scene with a couple of Jundees and a signaller. When I arrived with Al Mutasim, on the south slope of the wadi, he told me that there was an adoo party in the cave opposite. That was the target. I thought this was nonsense because there was no return of fire. I ordered stop firing. It was then clear the adoo small arms fire was a flickering cooking fire in a cave.
>
> Leaving Al Mutasim to secure the south side, eventually, by crossing the wadi near the Tac HQ position we approached the cave from the north side of the wadi. There we found a Jebali family frightened and distraught. One of the daughters, perhaps aged about eight, was seriously wounded, I recall in the body, and unconscious. The remainder of the family were unhurt. Having applied a FFD, we carried the girl to the top of the north side of the wadi where someone had sensibly pre-positioned a Land Rover. We used that to transport her and her family to the Tac HQ area where the RMO, Jaya Mohan, tried in vain to save

her. I remember afterwards Jaya invited her parents to see the body, her parents standing in misery outside the Medical tent. I do not know who looked after them, but understandably they left the area the following day.

The concern was of a likely blood feud developing from the family against Al Mutusim. Accordingly, about two weeks later Al Mutasim left Sarfait for Salalah. I think at least temporarily he was employed in the Royal Palace. If so, the logic perhaps was to allow time in which to settle any blood feud compensation and to protect him while that happened. As you know, subsequently Al Mutasim was OC Recce Platoon MR at Midway with you.

The friendly, easy going Lt Al Mutasim Hamood serving with Muscat Regiment as 2ic B Coy, was another member of Oman's royal tribe. Being of royal blood, and facing potential demands for 'Diya' (blood money) Al Mutasim had to be removed from the scene. Eventually he ended up with us at Manston then Midway until negotiations had been finalised. In Islamic law Diya is the financial compensation paid for causing death, injury or damage to another. It will only apply where the victim's family agrees to the compromise, against the alternative punishment, 'Qisas' (equal retribution). The wadi Sandy refers to was a tributary of Wadi Sarfait.

OP – JIBJAT ROAD RECCE

3 Nov
1300 departed Midway for Wadi Jazal. Thought I knew this area but map reading all over the place. Finally found right camel track, inshallah. Looks like poss. thunderstorm over the jebel, not perfect. Night position secured and men fed by last light. I take 3am stag.

4 Nov
Radio contact – 38 – confirmed on the move. We entered Wadi Jazal. Made stop for quick breakfast. Wadi J. full of trees, really very attractive. For the most part, going good. Saw gazelle but no other signs of life. Reached RV at 1130. Wadi walls 600ft high? Picquets set both sides. Overlooked, classic "place of danger". Made radio contact. BATT arrived 1215 chasing gazelle galloping through our position – bloody firing automatics! Diving for cover, bullets flew striking trees we were sheltering under. Yelling 'HOLD YOUR FIRE!' to my lot, called 38 'Cease firing, you idiots!' Firing stopped. Vehs. stopped. Ruqaishi and I went forward to remonstrate. Three large BATT and

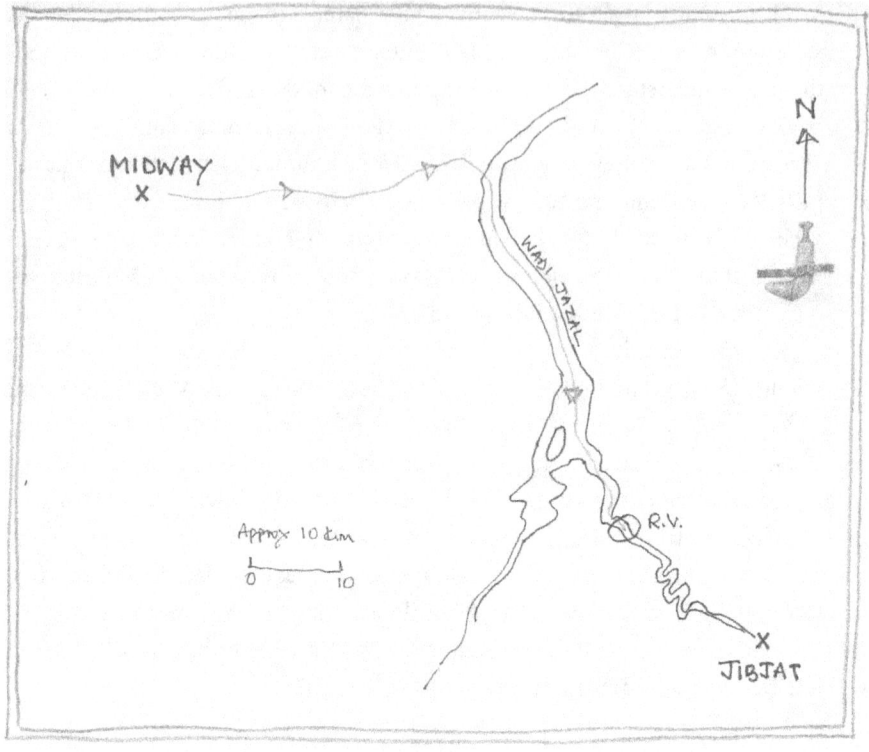

The route to our RV with BATT along Wadi Jazal.

> *six or eight firqat. Livid – I pointed out my positions. Told them we'd have slaughtered them had we fired back. Impassive response. An angry Ruqaishi beside me, I told them to bloody follow our tracks and make their own way to Midway. Utterly unprofessional but I had enraged soldiers to placate. Picquets down, drove out of w. Jazal, stopping for brew and majlis in wadi. All resolved, I hope. BATT gone by time we returned nightfall.*
> *Shot 2 gazelle on way back. Eid grub.*

There is little to add to the above diarised events, it was sheer bloody lunacy. Out in the open at 100m the two jeeps were easy targets. We wouldn't and didn't, but had we fired back, that'd have been it, *khalaas!* finished! as the Arabs say, illustrating the point with a swift swipe of one palm across the other.

Walking towards the jeeps accompanied by a furious Ruqaishi, I heard him mutter through gritted teeth he thought Brits were meant to be helping win the war. After a few unsatisfactory words, I told those in the jeeps they'd better make their own way, we'd no need for each other and that they and we were probably safer having never met. With that the BATT jeeps disappeared in clouds of dust as Ruqaishi and I brought our men back down from their high picquets. It occurred to me I was probably being unprofessional, but just then I couldn't give a monkey's. Still livid, we drove out from the high walled wadi towards the plains. Stopping beneath the shade of some acacias I ordered a brew, realising I must debrief my men on what had occurred. We didn't need to carry this incident back to base where there was every chance they'd meet up with the firqat or those BATT involved.

Sitting crossed legged with my soldiers around me, we held what might be called a 'maglis' in Arabic, a council where I invited each of those who wished to express their views to have their say before I concluded the debate saying at least none had been injured and weren't we lucky their shooting had been so wildly off target! After a while, they'd calmed down and were soon joking at the poor marksmanship they'd witnessed, 'Al Hamdallah!'.

As we prepared to leave, my picquets gestured they'd seen gazelle. Ruqaishi called across with the obvious question. It was 4th Nov and the closing stages of Ramadan. Fresh meat was up there together with the only other thing on every man's wish list. Carrying our rifles, Ruqaishi and I stalked to the rim of the wadi 50 metres away. Three hundred metres off, stood a herd of gazelle, one or two keeping vigil, heads raised whilst others grazed. Quietly lining up on two males, we were ready. On my whispered command of three, we fired. Ruqaishi's FN, my ancient 303. A single shot each. 'On target!' – twice. Running forward, two men performed the halal prayer 'Bismillah Allahu Akbar'. Meat ration prayers had been answered. The day had ended well after all.

Returning to Midway, the carcasses were dressed before being stored in the cookhouse's newly arrived freezers, ready for Eid al Fitr in four days, the 8th Nov. The BATT had disappeared, helicoptered back to their base at Salalah. Their firqat too, had melted away.

30

MEDEVAC AND THE SULTAN'S PALACE

Eid al Fitr. Medevac to Cyprus, finding on return nothing had changed. Another roulement, another Dhofar Christmas and firqat problems. Salalah Palace to meet the Sultan. An aborted take-off and another Habarut convoy. Old Kenya hand Geoff Harcourt. 1973! Patrolling with Ruqaishi's NFR. A geology talk, map reading, half-shafts and a reminder of one's ethnicity.

7 Nov
Simba mortar incomer landed inside MR mortar sangar but was blind – No cas. UNBELIEVABLE.
Hilal sighted 1807! Gazelle fuddal with the boys in celebration. Delicious. Later – Drinks in Mess – JMF's birthday.

EID AL FITR

8 Nov
Delicious nosh last night. Eid al Fitr breakfast this AM. Didn't eat much, but very good. The boys to eat the rest this pm.
I organised target shooting 10am after breakfast – everyone happy.
Tpr. Said Mohd Harrib – medevac.
Letters away – home and Charlotte.

10 Nov
Eid Al Fitr breakfast with Wali – Burayk bin Hamud al-Ghafiri. Quite a surprise meal: cornflakes and camel milk, goat and rice – tea and Halwa.

As the two senior officers on base, JMF and I were invited to breakfast with the Wali, Governor of Dhofar, in his encampment beside our base at Midway. We arrived and were welcomed into his copious tented home. Following introductions, seated on the carpeted ground we were offered what might best be described as a British/Arab take on breakfast with Middle Eastern trimmings. Served on enamelled tin soup plates we enjoyed cornflakes in warm camel milk. There followed roast goat and rice, not on the expected communal dish but again on individual enamel plates, mugs of tea, coffee and finally Halwa, a flour paste (semolina) fried in oil and sugary syrup. Wali Burayk bin Hamud al-Ghafiri, a strong supporter of the Sultan in the overthrow of his father, now held significant sway governing Dhofar Province. He was an important ally and one I did my utmost to keep on side, as proved necessary following a diplomatic faux pas early the next year.

11 Nov
Midway – Driver trg. End of course.
Feeling feverish – but put it down to food. Left for Mudhai with Said Suleman. Met SSM Ali Abdullah patrol at Wadi Ghadun – fixed his radio. Running a temperature. We drove on to Mudhai. Two punctures! Evening meal with Ruqaishi. Gave orders to FHG who only have a Cpl i/c at present. Mohamed Mahadi is in Salalah, everyone else has disappeared!! Informed Ruqaishi of future plans, grids to ambush and patrol and impending visit by Col Bryan. Ruqaishi gave me two replacement tyres, he'll have punctures mended. Motored back to Ali's position. Very cold night yet sweating wrapped in blanket. Made cock-up of midnight call. Feverish. Remembrance Day.

12 Nov
Returned Midway to find Messtins VOR. Only one fit for convoy. Saw Midway medic, retired bed with aspirins.

13 Nov
Feeling slightly better. Rose late at 8. Popski took parade. Caught up in office – work just grows! Retired 1600 after hot toddy. Wheezing and coughing.

14 Nov
Op Vulture planned ambush south Tudho – G60.

Cancelled ambush discovering Gordon's made horlicks of briefing guide where to take Ruqaishi. . . . 28 miles from my grid reference?? . . . We must win one day.
Made arrangements for flight to Muscat for investiture, but not sure I'll make it. JMF kind loan of his uniform.

MEDEVAC

15 Nov
Capt GHD Sommerville arrives Oman.
<u>*Capt H medevac.*</u>
Op. Condor – ambush sprung. Own cas. 4 KIA, 1 WIA. En cas: 1 KIA, 3 reported KIA, 2 reported WIA. En KIA – Mohamed Ali Salim Abu Jabal Kashawb – platoon cmdr. Central Area.
FHG ptl RTB fm SW Mudhai. NTR.

The above entries were written by 'Q', who with SSM Piorkowski had taken over command of the squadron at Midway. Radioing Brian at Manston, Brian had suggested he remain at Manston with responsibility for Midway left to SSM Piorkowski and until further notice they should await orders from Dhofar HQ.

During my stay in hospital I endeavoured to keep notes, written up on my return to Midway.

Collapsed with high temperature/difficulty breathing, medevaced on Viscount. Martin got me to FST. Romily to take convoy in my place. Penicillin injections – Pneumonia. Bloody hell!

I'd been looking forward to seeing Romily David again. We knew each other when stationed at Münster as part of 4 Guards Brigade. A Welsh Guardsman, he'd recently joined MR and flying in from Simba, he commanded the next Habarut convoy leaving on the 18th. Romily later won the WKhM(G), Oman's equivalent to the MC.

16 Nov
Investiture Day – Muscat.

Brigadier Jack visited hospital to be briefed on Vulture and ACS locations. He never stops, extraordinary. Suggested Brian to Midway and on arrival,

MEDEVAC AND THE SULTAN'S PALACE

George to Manston.
Abdul Wathik visited asking to re-join – with commission! Cheeky sod.
Reckon injections every 3 hours are keeping my temperature up.
1 x WIA arrives from Simba; slight shrapnel to shoulder.

17 Nov
1 x WIA arrived pm, shot in bum, sciatic nerve OK.

Returning to Midway as I was organising another Habarut convoy, I'd collapsed. Helped to my room and put to bed by my men, they alerted the base medic, Elsa Williams, wife of the contractors building Midway Base. A trained nurse, Elsa took one look at my condition and put me on an awaiting aircraft, a Vickers Viscount. The Sultanate had two of these British medium-range turboprop aircraft and one had arrived at Midway with soldiers returning from leave. Fortunately for me, Martin Robb of MR was also on board, en route to Salalah, and kindly delivered me to the Field Surgical Team army doctors. The hospital, a single storey concrete block was home to some of the most highly talented surgeons, more used to mending and sewing up bodies.

I lost consciousness shortly after being admitted. The next two days became a blur of waking to penicillin injections every few hours, my backside initially, then into my thighs. This hurt, and once my thighs became too bruised the single minded medics returned to my blackened, less bruised backside.

'Oh you're awake,' enquired a man dressed in green overalls, 'you gave us quite a headache, but we think we've discovered the problem, pneumonia. Both lungs were dangerously full when you arrived,' adding, 'you don't smoke, do you?' – 'No,' I lied in a whisper, 'I'm a langlaufer'. This provoked a roar of delight and I realised there were three medics. 'Well that's a first,' said Dr Friendly Face. 'Gentlemen, it would appear what we have is a cross-country skier obviously suffering some degree of disorientation becoming lost somewhere on the edge of Arabia's Empty Quarter where naturally he succumbs to double pneumonia.' I failed to see the funny side as an orderly arrived with another stainless steel kidney dish with two hypodermics swimming in methylated spirit.

My ex-squadron NCO, the recalcitrant LCpl Abdul Wathik, had heard I was laid up at the FST. News travels fast and calling on spec requested an urgent meeting with me. The British Army medic asked if I wished to see him and of course I agreed, though feeling wretched. What did Wathik want that had become so urgent after all this time? I soon found out. Getting nowhere at DG he wanted me to arrange his immediate transfer back to the Squadron, naturally as an officer. I managed a whispered reply promising I'd look into his request, but as to a commission, he'd have to follow the correct selection process. It was then time for more injections and Wathik was asked to leave. Subsequently offered a transfer, he never followed it up.

Later the same evening I was visited by OC Dhofar, which took me by surprise. But he explained he needed a debrief on our operations north of the jebel. Pneumonia takes your breath away, leaving you forced to speak in short gasps, rendering you practically incapable of sustained speech. He crouched beside my bed, so as the better to hear me, and I responded to Brigadier Jack's questions confirming what was happening on Op Vulture. He was up to speed with the raid to destroy the castle, "Downie's Folly", and one version of the joint op with the Jibjat BATT. There was no point now in presenting the alternative of what had occurred. I reported on the positions at Mudhai, Manston and Midway camps, Tudho in Wadi Aydim and Habarut re-supply convoys, ambushes and patrols into the Empty Quarter past Shisur out to Fasad, and Ma Shadid to the west with the two firqats, FHG and FAB.

Following arrival as Commander Dhofar a couple of months before, apart from a brief visit to Midway, we'd barely touched base. He was an extremely busy commander, with operations out of Simba, Sycamore, Hornbeam, Vulture, Hawk and Wolf – all post Jaguar. Graciously his opening remark was an apology. I replied all knew how busy he'd been, thinking to myself 'we're doing fine left alone'. His eyes widened visibly as I outlined the responsibilities and areas involved. There was no bullshit – like everyone else in Dhofar, we were all managing with what we had, the best we could.

Agreeing to my suggested command restructuring, Brian took over in my absence, moving to Midway from Manston; George Sommerville, poor chap, would go straight to Manston on arrival. There'd be no acclimatisation for George. Thus the command structure altered within the squadron and would remain so until my return. It was very good of Brigadier Jack to spare me the time in his busy schedule and I was bolstered by the visit.

Wounded continued to arrive at the FST, keeping the medics busy – and on the 18th November I received confirmation I was to be medevaced to Cyprus for specialist treatment. The same day I received a visit from the Squadron's newest recruit, Captain George Sommerville, ex 3rd Carabineers.

> Met George – gave him briefing which left me panting like a dog. GS – not the lean mean killer type; happy and easy-going. Hope he knows what's let himself in for. Claims he'd been briefed by MI6 before departure.
> News arrives, Habarut convoy went OK.

21 Nov
'So, langlaufer, now we've stabilised your condition, we're flying you to Cyprus for treatment – they'll clear your lungs and get you sorted out – you may even get back home for Christmas lucky lad!'

Stretchered on board Herc and loaded amongst kit and supplies. Amongst end-of-tour RAF, I have an orderly i/c some sort of drip into my arm. Couldn't move being strapped in stretcher. B awful flight.
Ward 5 – Akrotiri hospital comfortable, smells of hospital.

27 Nov
More X-rays and continued injections. Can you overdose on penicillin? Box of fruit delivered by pretty Red Cross lady in uniform! Gift from Father (fruit!) Army had alerted home. I'm impressed.
Stuck here for another week, minimum. God there's going to be chaos by time I get back . . . January leaves and courses to organise. Signalled SAF.

There is really nothing to add to my diarised notes above. Lying strapped tightly on a stretcher unable to move for the entire flight in a noisy Hercules C-130 aircraft, I was surrounded by end-of-tour RAF personnel jubilant at leaving Dhofar and returning to their families, wives and girlfriends in the UK. It was hard not to feel a little envious. The nurses and medics at Akrotiri worked wonders and I was soon able to walk about the hospital grounds regaining my strength. And no doubt my recovery was speeded by the box of fruit delivered by a pretty lady in Red Cross uniform.

RETURN TO DHOFAR

29/30 Nov
Bags of letters arrived – Home, William, Ann, Odeyne, AIWH. Weather improving – could be summer.
Khadim route recce postponed. Concerned about Squadron.

8 Dec Signal arrives ordering return Dhofar.

I managed to signal Dhofar Brigade HQ about my predicament. This caused a flurry of signals between Dhofar and Akrotiri, the former demanding my return, the latter refusing my release. There was talk I should be repatriated to the UK for further specialised treatment. Impasse ensued until eventually on 8th Dec, a single line signal arrived:

"Urgent: Return Hodgson soonest – repeat urgent."

'You must be bloody important,' remarked OC RAF Akrotiri Hospital – 'I'd planned to send you back to the UK for further tests, something's not right with your chest – but you seem to have recovered sufficiently so it would appear you are to return to active duty. I'd add a word of advice, forget smoking and keep away from dust – appreciate the irony but best keep clear of dust entering your lungs again.' Apart from my growing concerns about the Squadron, I'd have enjoyed a Christmas at home, it'd have been my first since being commissioned, five years earlier.

I'd joined a resupply Hercules C130 flying to Salalah in the company of a bunch of nervous RAF personnel, virgin soldiers en route for a nine-month tour at the RAF base. Later that day I cadged a lift in a Beaver aircraft to Midway to rejoin my squadron. It was 10th December; I had been away three weeks.

Arriving back I was loath to return to my bayt, my room adjacent to Mike's, a still locked and vacant space. The few weeks away though pretty wretched and painful at times had been an escape from all that had happened that day in September. But there was no alternative, there weren't any other spare rooms. It was miserable to be back.

I was still coughing and my chest still hurt. It was Brian who pulled me up, Brian who had stoically held the fort in my absence now telling me sharply I needed to get fit again, both mentally and physically. Dragging me out each evening before stand-to, he dug me out from my navel-gazing with painful runs when I coughed for Britain, as he kindly put it. But running worked and the coughing decreased.

Separately, despite the hoped-for success of the eastern route onto the jebel, the Jibjat route, the constant search for vehicle access onto the western jebel remained a priority. A recce of the Khadim route, reputedly an ancient slavers' route northwest of Ma Shadid had been postponed until after my return. Despite firqat guides' sworn knowledge the route existed, we never found the mountain pass, pitifully named and we imagined filled with ghosts of betrayal and despair.

NOTHING HAD CHANGED

11 Dec
Bde HQ – Orders Group: 1400.
JMF away on leave – Charles Butt here instead. Oddball. Might improve? Inshallah.
O Group – future operations up until next monsoon. Op Vulture and Habarut convoys to continue.
Met Col Bryan – said I looked ill. Still coughing.

> *Simba – 9 incomers – one slight WIA.*
> *Adonib – 3 adoo – Wadi Ashawq – mortared.*
> *Plains – 4 incomers – near HH Echo.*
> *W. Arzat – now confirmed adoo losses 11 KIA, 6 WIA in contact/ambush of 9 Dec by NFR/BATT – good show. Johnson lame, kidnapped by resupply convoy yet escaped, returned limping. God knows how far he'd trekked.*

After a week in the FST and two in Cyprus, the feeling of detachment was hard to shrug off. Nothing had changed, yet it felt I'd been away months. The war continued unabated. NFR were achieving successes and MR's Sarfait, hit on a daily basis, absorbed mortar and rocket fire that otherwise would have been directed at Salalah. Attritional, like Akoot, but Sarfait were well dug in and the position secure. And yet the question remained, how long could SAF maintain their presence on the jebel when every bullet, mortar bomb, artillery shell, rations and water had to be flown in by helicopter, fixed wing capability having been lost to the adoo. At the O group and welcoming me back, Commander Dhofar reiterated the importance of continuing Op Vulture. Whilst admitting to the parlous state of our armoured cars, he added 'I'm really sorry, you must do what you can.' The situation on vehicle spares and ordnance had become critical, but the infantry were suffering likewise.

On my return to Midway, I discovered a changed dog in Johnson. In my absence, he'd disappeared and it was assumed he had been stolen by civilian convoy drivers from northern Oman delivering resupplies. Escaping his captors, he must have retraced the journey back to Midway, skirting the Empty Quarter's southern deserts, returning with two bleeding front paws, skinny and extremely thirsty. Thankfully he was now on the mend. Ridiculously overjoyed to see me – as I was to see him – he leapt up, placing great big paws against my chest – when it was always 'Ugh! Johnson! What have you been eating?!' I'd scold, his breath ever in need of a visit to a dental vet.

And I found JMF in high spirits, nothing to do with my return but rather his imminent departure to the UK on Christmas leave.

> *12 Dec*
> *Live firing – end of course: 16th - 20th Dec.*
> *LCpl Said Mohd Harib's father killed in accident on 10 Nov! Sending him home 10 days compassionate leave. No flights until 17 Dec. Cpl Nasir Mohd will take his place at Manston.*

News travelled slowly and there followed a five day wait for an available flight home for Said Mohamed whose father had been killed a month earlier.

A promising young NCO, LCpl Said returned promptly from compassionate leave, to rejoin the Manston troop.

> 16 Dec
> Salalah – see Col Jones J.R. re Manston convoys.
> Cpls Nasir Mohd (for Manston) and Musalim Dhait to police station for dvr. licence.
> Found mad rush on. All 4 battalion COs here. Saw Cols Nigel, Bryan briefly. Busy!
> No chance of flight back – but managed to get Cpl Nasir Mohd booked on flight tmw. 1300. Bought food for the boys at Manston which Nasir will take tmw.
> Met Said Mohd Khamis – bride found for him by his father – now Dad wants marriage to take place! Said is still broke after 6 weeks away, going to wait for two/three months. Can't be older than 15? Grabbed 206 flight back, via White City. Shot at crossing jebel – spiral in and out. Nightmare thoughts – being shot at from underneath!

ROULEMENT – DECEMBER 1972

The hubbub at Brigade HQ was due to the imminent four battalion roulement, NFR and MR about to depart for Oman, DR and JR about to return for another Dhofar tour. It was good to see Col Nigel once again; we'd last met as I'd left Simba to rejoin my troop at Akoot in April. His battalion would be based at UAG, Plains Battalion this next tour, with JR on Simba.

The boy betrothed, Said Mohd, was based at Salalah with Gerry Fyffe still on loan to HQ Ops Room. Said sought me out almost beside himself with excitement. His father had found him a bride. As he'd only recently returned from short leave following a radio course in Oman, added to the fact he was presently flat broke, he accepted perhaps a wait to recuperate funds might be a good idea. He was probably no older than 15.

I hitched a lift with ex-Army Air Corps Nick Holdbrook flying an Agusta Bell AB206 JetRanger, an Italian built two-man helicopter. For all that, an excellent aircraft. We detoured via a BATT outpost making a spiral descent akin to being sucked into a whirlpool, dropping us 7,000ft per minute to a jebel LZ (landing zone) indicated by smoke grenade. Ten minutes later our spiralling ascent lifted us out when Nick remarked calmly over the headsets, 'Hang on, we're being fired at.' On we climbed, the 206 engine screaming, round and round circling upwards. Peering out of the clear glass, I thought I caught sight of tracer arcing towards us, but wasn't certain.

The sudden apprehension of receiving burning tracer up the rear-end causes an involuntary tightening of the sphincter muscles at the floor of your pelvis, surpassing even St Moritz's Cresta Run as the ultimate laxative controller. Nick, a gallant pilot and friend was awarded the Sultan's Bravery Medal in 1973, adding to his Sultan's Commendation Medal in '72.

17 - 19 Dec
Visited Manston staying overnight. George, Sgts Dick and Wimpy on good form.

20 Dec
Roulement convoy to Manston.
Report: A Coy NFR – big contact – 25 adoo ambushed by jaysh. Ambush caught 4 KIA, I WIA. 8 took cover in two caves which SOAF filled with a rocket in one, two the other. I KIA. NFR 1 KIA.

Our convoy to Manston carried roulement troops and provisions. We returned on 22 December without incident.

Following a night contact on 17th Dec, Simon Hill (Parachute Regiment) took A Coy NFR from Adonib and set a daylight ambush catching a camel train, killing four adoo and capturing one seriously wounded. NFR lost a soldier killed. Adoo seen taking cover in caves were taken out by SOAF jets. Following up, NFR discovered a body, recovering an extensive haul of provisions, small-arms ammunition and importantly, a RCL sight. Simon's company, constantly in the thick of it patrolling and ambushing out of their Adonib base in the western reaches of Salalah plains, gained many successes against the adoo. He was awarded the Sultan's Bravery Medal that winter.

22 Dec
FAN patrol & NFR discovered stores dropped by the ambushed adoo convoy. 67 bags of rice, an unknown quantity of sugar, 9 boxes of 7.62 ammo, 20 HE 81mm mor. rds, one sack tobacco, and documents. Close by discovered further 7 sacks rice, 6 packs sugar, 2nd RCL/Mor sight to one found earlier. All food burnt, other stores, docs recovered. Terrific result.
Also Boom had a successful contact at Thalfutt – attacking another convoy on beach, aided by jets firing rockets. Jaysh contacts becoming more successful. Heard Sandy wounded – shrapnel. He's OK – treated at Mainbrace tented hospital. Kept in bed with other wounded until after HM had flown to Sarfait and visited the wounded! Sandy'll never live that one down!

The Boom, an Arabian dhow, represented the extent of the Sultan's navy on active service. Sailing off the coast keeping out of range of small arms fire, they sighted a camel train making its way along the beach at Thalfutt, SW of Sarfait. Standing off, they directed jets onto the enemy convoy. Militarily a successful strike, yet none were ever happy taking out camel trains, killing innocent beasts of burden.

I learned Sandy had been wounded at Sarfait and was treated at the Simba tented hospital. Coincidentally HM happened to be visiting to see the place that day and Sandy was kept in hospital until after the visit, greatly to his embarrassment. He'll say the wounds certainly didn't warrant a stay in bed, whilst we say it was one way to seek an audience with HM.

24 Dec
LCpl Ali Hamdan on lve.
LCpls Abdullah Ali, Nasir Hamid and Suleyam Said back fm lve.
One L/R and 3 tonner to Mudhai for water then Manston. LCpl Abdullah Ali & Said Saif for Manston.

CHRISTMAS DAY 1972

25 Dec
Christmas Day – a working day
5 x FHG refusing to patrol
Dissidents:
8511 - Pte Al Haraisi Musalim
8533 - Sgt Said Achmed Rubaat
8525 - Sgt Salim Musalim
8506 - Pte Musalim Mohd
8507 - Pte Said Mabkhout Salim
Still away on Haj
8509 - Sgt Aboub al Obaida
8515 - Pte Ali Said
8516 - Pte Mubarik Ali
Discharged:
8530 - Pte Ali Achmed bin Ali

Christmas morning and formed up outside my office were elements of one of my two firqats, the FHG. Following the customary exchange of greetings, everyone spoke at once. Calling for quiet, it transpired five men were unhappy with their rations and guard duties, the latter a direct consequence of three FHG being still away on Hajj. One firqat no longer wished to fight for the Sultan. It was a lengthy meeting, for it seemed they had all the time in the world, but finally the duty roster on guard duties was resolved, the men returning from Hajj would indeed undertake extra duties on their return and Pte Ali Achmed bin Ali handed back rifle and ammunition and was officially discharged. A normal firqat admin morning really.

26 Dec
Habarut convoy: 28 Dec – preparations in hand: I'll take LCpls Abdullah Ali, Hilal Ali, Jumma Musalim, and Tprs: Mohd Ali Hamid, Mohd Hamood, Said Suleman, Khamis Hamid, Mohd Ali Salim.
Geoff Harcourt OG will be accompanying us with half coy OG. One troop OG for roulement Habarut.
Investiture: 1200, 27 Dec.

THE SULTAN'S PALACE, SALALAH

27 Dec
Flew down by Beaver yesterday pm. Bit of a party in Mess last night. Four of us attending investiture. Others all OA – Gunners John Dean, Mike Hardy both WB – Noel McGrath WKhM(G).

Third to be called, I marched in, smart as a Guardsman in JMF's borrowed jacket, halted & saluted as directed, one pace in front of HM, he immaculate in uniform, surrounded by six officers, two Omani and four HQ SAF, including Flogger. David Glazebrook read out citation. A surprise – it was for Vimy – not Janook? HM stepped forward to pin medal, congratulating me. Softly spoken, a voice that demands attention. I replied 'Thank you, your Majesty', he stepped back, I about-turned and had taken a step when from behind caught hissed stage-whisper, 'Salute!'

'OH Shiiiiit!!' I thought in disbelief. Halting, I about-turned to find everyone saluting. Wishing the floor would open up, I returned my smartest parade-ground salute, about-turned once more and marched out. What an idiot! Would never have made the Brigade of Guards.

Invited for refreshments in airy first floor loggia, sat on soft cushions after the Sultan joined us for black coffee and exquisite fresh dates. HM asked where each was based with questions on our activities. Engaging to talk with. Looks young for his age and undoubted worries of state. I replied I was leaving for Habarut next day. Incredibly well informed, he believed we did so every three weeks? Talk moved to Midway's climate we locals called "millionaire's weather" once the winds ceased. I'd liked to have mentioned the fort at Sinau – but thought better of it. Sensibly.

'Ah Midway,' he replied smiling broadly to my suggestion it was a place to build a palace, 'the Shimaal blows from the North . . . better you than me.'

All too soon time to leave. Gracious and elegant, our C-in-C looks you straight in the eye, devoid of hauteur, making you feel at ease. This is who we are fighting for. Reckon he's only a few years older than me. Remarkable man.

A synopsis of the Investiture and citations reads:

Investiture by The Sultan, 27 December 1972, Salalah

The Sultan's Bravery Medal – WB

1. Major MH Hardy 1st Regt Oman Artillery
   For actions during preceding year . . . particularly Op Jaguar . . . when his skill and bravery as an FOO earned . . . admiration and respect of the units he served.

2. Capt JGW Dean 1st Regt Oman Artillery
   For bravery on operations from Akoot 1971 monsoon and later Op Jaguar . . . three helicopter borne assaults . . . during one continued to engage enemy over open sights . . . as mortar bombs landed on his position.

3. Capt PEB Hodgson Armoured Car Squadron
   For bravery 27 April 1972 . . . in support Desert Regt . . . despite damage to armoured car . . . evacuated wounded . . . took command half company . . . covered withdrawal remaining until last to ensure all safely back in Akoot . . . Hodgson's armoured car . . . down to last four rounds of machine gun ammunition and two rounds HE from a full load by end of the engagement.

The Sultan's Distinguished Service Medal (Gallantry) – WKhM (G)

4. Capt NH McGrath 1st Regt Oman Artillery
   For actions at Janook and Manston May 1972 . . . commanded 25 pounder detachment . . . provided accurate supporting fire despite enemy fire striking his position . . . an inspiration to his gun detachments.

The Sultan was 31 on 16th December. Leading his country out of the Middle Ages while at war with an ideological enemy still very much in command of the high ground, this was a man under unbelievable pressure. Yet he seemed to carry his responsibilities with a grace and natural ease. Blessed with that rare ability when speaking with you of treating you as an equal, there was no awkwardness, no hint of imperiousness as we sat on cushions in conversation with the county's ruler, our Commander-in-Chief.

I caught a Skyvan to Midway that afternoon, calling en route at White City, a jebel outpost. The Baluchi loadmaster gestured me to the co-pilot's seat, next to the indomitable ex-Strikemaster pilot, Barrie Williams. The flight carried stores and equipment.

Barrie was now flying Skyvans, having recently recovered after serious injury caused ejecting from a low flying jet hit by small arms fire in September 1972. Delighted at having a front seat, I'd a bird's eye view as we nearly crashed. Speeding to take-off along the jebel dirt strip our load shifted. Aborting take-off, Barrie reversed thrust whilst also jamming on the brakes; running out of runway, we careered directly for the rocks. Simulating a slalom run, he weaved and bumped the aircraft around boulders until bringing it to a shuddering standstill. 'Allah Kareem,' I heard over the headset as the loadmaster picked his way forward past the now mix of loose containers and jute bags of food. Due entirely to Barrie's driving skills in avoiding rocks, we'd escaped any visible damage. Together with a group of excited firqatmen and BATT who'd witnessed the near-disaster, boulders were cleared by hand enabling the aircraft to reverse under its own steam, taxi back and this time successfully take off for Midway. 'Enjoy that?' enquired Mr Cool. 'Not bad,' I'd replied, not to be outdone. Definitely my choice of pilot. The fault had not been the loadmaster's, but a worn cargo net which had split on take-off.

HABARUT WITH OG

28-30 Dec
Habarut convoy – OG troops roulement. Night at Tudho. Abdullah wanted to camp in usual position. Bloody hell, the area he preferred there was greater likelihood of AP mines, near where 3-tonner struck last convoy. We camped as I directed. Abdullah needs watching.

Good to have Geoff along, old Africa hand. Learned he'd been Jomo Kenyatta's bodyguard. Not a recommended occupation. Took Geoff to visit each picquet, complained he was unfit! After coffees, talked into the night of Kenya.

Picquets climb towards the skyline above our night stop position. Each to be visited, checking sangars, arcs of fire, stags. Geoff's past had included heading up the bodyguard for Kenya's first president, the ex-Mau Mau leader Jomo Kenyata. Interesting times, he called it.

Geoff strenuously supervises repairs to the broken spring . . .

MEDEVAC AND THE SULTAN'S PALACE

The colour of our fresh water drawn from a well amuses Geoff. 'No need to add tea leaves,' he'd claimed. On leaving OG, Geoff was promoted to Colonel commanding the Sultan's Royal Guard, a position he held until retirement. Sadly, Geoff died in France soon after retiring from what had been a full and interesting life.

The next day and another Habarut convoy, one when I was accompanied by Geoff Harcourt of the Oman Gendarmerie.

> *Habarut v. hot. Arrived 1230. Departed 1400 – worst timings yet. Pitched camp 1½ hrs south Tudho – mine country. Cold night again.*
>
> *RTB –1530 – back late after breakdowns. OG and Geoff missed today's plane. Combination of wind and sun. Both badly sunburnt.*
>
> *31 Dec*
> *Book flight – Said Mohd Khamis for Weds. Wedding leave brought fwd – compassionate grounds. Brian away to buy food for Mess.*

The 15-year-old Said's promised wedding leave was brought forward, his father having died. I organised his return for funeral and marriage.

1973

1 Jan
Warning Order – Op. 4 Jan. Recce south from Mudhai teaming up with 3 Coy NFR, Nomads and Tigers. We leave tmw. Not feeling too good. Couldn't face dinner – early bed. Slept badly.

Nomads and Tigers were code names for Firqat and BATT who'd be joining us, together with 3 Company NFR.

2 Jan
Feeling better. Took Saladins out this A.M. Brush-up. Went well. Taking T1A Sgt Greaves, Lou T1B, Ruqaishi Green 60: O Group 1230 – meal 1500: leave 1600 to RV tmw AM.
Left 1650 – at last moment two radios on blink. Motored out west – took up night positions. First stag. Looks like a cold night. Strong winds. Put up covey of sandgrouse, beautiful creatures.

Ruqaishi, after we'd halted for lunch at around 1500. That morning we'd put up a covey of chestnut-bellied sandgrouse (Pterocles exustus), the same species found across East Africa. Pretty birds.

The Squadron was particularly fortunate having Recce Platoons attached from regiments stationed on the jebel, Akoot, Manston and Sarfait. These soldiers were exceptional, their commanders leading from the front. I can attest to the special bond with each Recce Platoon commander I was fortunate to have attached to me, sharing a special camaraderie as for a short while they became integral to the Squadron.

I'd found a good friend in Ruqaishi, with whom many a night the world was put to rights. To give him his full name, rank and post-nominal – 2/Lt Mohammed bin Said bin Zahran al Ruqaishi WB. Decorated for bravery, he'd won the Sultan's Bravery Medal as NFR's Recce platoon sergeant in 1968. I discovered he was the sole member of his tribe serving in SAF. During the Jebel Akhbar rebellion in 1957-59 a number of the Ruqaishi tribesmen sided against the Sultan, choosing to support the Imam. Losing the battle none since had volunteered to join SAF, until young Mohammed joined up some ten years later. An outstanding soldier, he would one day command NFR and eventually retire a Brigadier.

A GEOLOGY TALK

Towards evening and halted, we'd built sangars as cooks prepared a meal served with chapatis prepared earlier in the day, stored rolled in a cloth. We'd used desiccated acacia sticks and would be fed ready to stand-to before dark, all vestiges of smokeless fire extinguished.

Collecting rocks for sangar walls, I'd noticed a stone with what appeared to be an imprint. Limestone rocks came in funny shapes, and there were plenty of fossilised seashells, but on second glance this was different. I shoved it into a jacket pocket before carrying rocks back to the sangar. Perhaps an ungulate, an even toed mammal's footprint. Antelope? I showed it to Ruqaishi. Staring at it he confirmed it was definitely antelope, but how, he wondered, was it set in stone? We'd no time to discuss the matter further but hurried to complete our fortifications, sort stag watches, eat and settle down.

Our position secured, sangars built and all fed, we relaxed sipping coffee. Tonight we'd dined well on fried corned beef, onions and rice and it was then there followed a deep conversation I'd not seen coming.

'Explain stone footprints,' the men asked. Where to start? I thought, and pointing to the surrounding limestone around us, explained it'd once been soft mud which over millions of years had been compressed and hardened, forming rock. Expecting disbelief, they urged I go on. Drawing on 'A' level geology memories, I was now being taxed to the full. Explaining animal and plant remains left in the

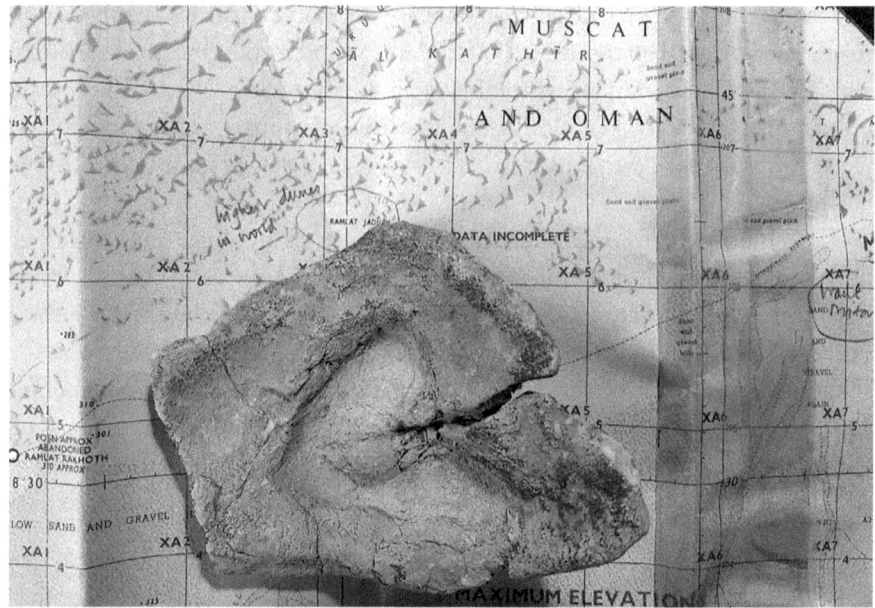

Fossilised imprint measuring approximately 80 x 120mm in limestone. I felt somehow this stone eclipsed that of finding a fossil. Whereas a dead creature's fossilised remains represented the physical, an imprint was ephemeral, evidence of some living creature's fleeting passage leaving a geological shadow of where it had once trod, a mark to last for millions of years, innocent, unlike those of our tyres. I was thrilled.

mud were also turned into rocks, very rarely the imprint of an animal's foot might remain and too be turned into stone. Amazingly I still held a captive audience. I recounted how up to 65 million years ago, reptiles, the same scaly spiked lizards we found under rocks, had ruled the world for about 160 million years, some being large as Saladins. These creatures had died out and nobody knew why. Looking again at the stone being passed round, I told how smaller animals later inhabited the earth, with many species also becoming extinct. Then birds and mammals arrived. I looked at them; all had listened with remarkable intensity, or was it just good manners? I believe it was the former, for there followed an avalanche of questions – leading me to confess sadly I'd just exhausted what little knowledge I had of palaeontology.

There followed a brief silence before the obvious question, would we too become extinct? Realising we were now touching on a possible minefield of religious beliefs, that void which exists between absolute faith and the doubts suggested by science, I paused. These were deeply religious men, many would pray their designated five times a day, stopping to pray each time we halted to change a tyre, half-shaft or attend to a mechanical breakdown. Even as we halted to clear for suspected mines, one or two would stop, kneel towards Mecca and begin to pray, not out of fear, but religious obligation.

Very carefully I replied, hoping to put an answer into context. I explained we were fighting an adoo who were humans too but with different beliefs. They followed communism which recognised no God. And that humans with their differing beliefs, who'd evolved from small groups hunting with sharp stones, the same we sometimes found lying in caves and open wadis, could indeed end up destroying mankind with their bombs.

It was a reflective group who turned in that night to sleep beneath the stars. Generally, on nights like these, men spoke of the endless nightly display above our heads. These and our shared discussion that night on fossils are ones which return to me to this day.

> 4 Jan
>
> *Cold again. Coldest night yet in Dhofar? Difficult map reading – featureless gravel plains, but reached RV OK – think I must have resigned 4 times during day! A day of broken half-shafts... Around midnight khareef had blown away giving us sunshine all day. Perishingly cold winds, any sleep, I stole from the cold. Joint recce successful. G39 – Chris Kemball also has bad cough, and suffering from mist and wind. We're low on petrol. The claimed Saladin's 140 miles range was never measured in desert conditions. Returned same route arriving back, frozen at 1330, tired. Showered and refreshed, remained in Mess until 11ish. Tomorrow lie-in.*

A particularly cold patrol in Saladins to RV with NFR's Chris Kemball (RGJ) went without incident, apart from broken half-shafts and testing my map reading skills to the limit. After an action the following year Chris was awarded the WKhM(G).

MAP READING AND HALF-SHAFTS

Accurate map reading presented a constant difficulty. We relied solely on issue maps scaled 1:250,000 overprinted with the confidence inspiring phrase – "RELIEF DATA INCOMPLETE" – every 5 grid squares. Rarely did we have guides who in truth were only of use in determining named wells and wadis. And tribes. Understandably they'd no concept of how to associate physical landscape to chart.

Tango 1B brings up the rear with POL Bedford (fuel truck). One of Ruqaishi's Land Rovers' tailends. Not ideal map reading country.

Wadi Mitan – I cover Green 60 moving through.

Given the vast areas we travelled, stuck at the back of my mind I carried the reality we operated at the limits of helicopter response for casevac or reinforcements. The Hueys and STOL aircraft constantly serving operations on the jebel were fully stretched. Despite often agonising delays, SOAF pilots who picked up our dead and wounded, delivered men or supplies, never let us down, whatever the conditions.

Whilst these difficulties were testing for us given the distances we operated over, they were equally challenging to SAF infantrymen.

Wadi Mitan runs diagonally southwest from the fringes of the Empty Quarter to the higher ground in Yemen. Frequently there'd be no traces of camels or vehicles. Often, we'd find wells dried out and we'd be forced to turn back low on supplies, petrol and increasingly, Land Rover half-shafts. Overladen Land Rovers struggled through a combination of factors, an over-optimistic driver, the wrong gear meeting soft sand and hey Bingo! bang went another half-shaft.

Without the horror of a mine, the effect was as disruptive, we'd halt, dismount and set picquets as fitters and excited driver attempted to beat the record for replacing a half-shaft under the target time, nine minutes.

> *5 Jan*
> *Jumea – Midway. Up at 0715 to talk to 58A – They wanted to know what the weather was like! Still cold but wind's dropped. 39F – colder than a German autumn! Wrote letters home.*

So much for a weekend lie-in – Salalah called me up on the radio asking for a forecast. I'd replied it might be warmer in BAOR.

> *6 Jan*
> *A cook required Mudhai, plus kit.*
> *Manston visit in Iranian Huey. Departing ½ hour early, they'd left Sgt Fyffe behind so made them fly via Salalah then on to Manston. George and team well. Letters fm home, Regt. and Tim. Good news on prospects of regular commission – signalled for paperwork. Confirmed: Col Nigel instrumental in my getting WB. Not Tim nor Janook. Tim's letter, he leaves UK for Münster today. Must try to visit whilst on leave.*

The arrival of Iranian helicopters, men and ordnance was beginning to pay welcome dividends. There were the occasional hiccups, mostly lost in translation.

I needed to complete paperwork transferring my three-year extended short service commission to a regular commission. The Regiment was very supportive, but I would only receive an answer on my return. And I'd heard from Tim, he was being posted to Münster, my old stamping ground and I hoped to see him on my eventual return.

> *7 Jan*
> *Unexpectedly – to Mudhai – 1600 fm Midway. With FHG - patrol tomorrow, Salim Hamees and Nashran Mohamed. Reports of mortar explosions southwest Mudhai. Patrol to investigate. Have had to borrow Walnut vehs to supplement ours. VOR for one reason or another – one, a fitter attempting to fit fire-extinguisher had drilled holes piercing the petrol tank!!*

We departed in three Land Rovers and a Bedford for Mudhai at 1600hrs, a little late but I wanted to be there for an early start the next day. I'd be taking Ruqaishi and his NFR recce platoon with me. 'Walnut', Gordon Dawson's codename, the local SIO had kindly loaned me two new Land Rovers to replace my two in workshops, one Land Rover having had its petrol tank holed by a hapless but enthusiastic driver attempting to fit a fire extinguisher.

AFTER 18 MONTHS, A REMINDER OF HAVING WHITE SKIN

> *7/9 Jan*
> *B. cold still. Patrolled long way down W. Stum then east to YV4600 W. Aseebu, trib. fm W. Stum. Met jebali family – shared camel milk. Reported no signs adoo, explosions, mines. Donated salt, sugar, rice, small bag of onions plus raisins we'd not used, and some coffee beans. All gifts graciously received, each treated as important as the other. Ancient shaibah pinched skin on my arm, muttering 'abyad giddaan' to much laughter fm Ruqaishi and others. Says a lot for my suntan! Difficult driving, took much longer than expected. Back late, Mudhai. Fed and shared beer with Ruqaishi into night discussing different cultures. With borrowed extra blanket, slept much warmer.*
> *RTB 1100 – v. hungry. Discovered "all the hard work" BJ had talked about over the radio was b-shit! He's demob happy. Bed early.*

We patrolled deep into the mountains from Wadi Stum then up Wadi Assebu ending finally in a precipitously walled limestone wadi and jebali camp, known to Salim and Nashraan. I still placed picquets who set off uncomplainingly to the high wadi ridges. Glancing at their progress, I did not envy their 180m climbs. These were good men.

Greeted with the unique cordiality of desert peoples, we were entreated to share their camel milk, and responding with a gift of provisions, our hosts insisted we stay for coffee. It is surely one of life's noblest gestures, this unconditional giving by people whose lives are lived on the edge, who having little are yet insistent on sharing what meagre supplies they have without a thought as to how little they can spare.

The observation *'abyad giddaan'*(very white) was a reminder that even after 18 months in the desert, a European skin remains white measured against the sunburned browns of the Middle East. A constant to be aware of and how easy it was to pick out a Brit from a distance.

Arriving back late to Mudhai, Ruqaishi and I shared a warm beer outside the Mess tent, sitting beside a dying fire used to heat our hastily prepared supper of sardines in tomato sauce, the easiest go-to meal when satisfying hunger was uppermost amongst our needs. During our conversation we were idly discussing regional differences in dialects, and variations in Arabic vocabulary between tribes, when I asked a question I'd often pondered during my almost two years in the country. Whereas Arabic was written from right to left, when it came to numbers, these were written left to right. Why the anomaly? Ruqaishi had no answer, but that was as it had always been, he replied smiling.

Looking up at the sky and noticing the waxing moon was a few days short of full, we speculated perhaps the origins of Arabic being written right to left had something to do with the moon phases? Could it be in ancient times it had been decided thus, to reflect the moon waxing from the right (north of the equator). That theory he'd not heard before, but it made us think and talk continued into the night, touching on the minutiae and subtle differences between cultures, marvelling once again how little there was to distinguish between men who trained as soldiers. It was cold away from the fire and turning in, Ruqaishi loaned me a spare blanket against the chill.

Leaving at daybreak after a welcome mug of sweet tea and a cold chapati, the extent of an early breakfast, we made good progress returning to Midway. Brian's apparent lack of effort to make inroads into my bulging in-tray was easily explained, my outburst at him unjustified. He'd been working nonstop on our Land Rovers and decided correctly that was the priority. It was for me to apologise.

31

THE LAST OF THE BEDU?

Tragedy strikes a friend. Patrolling with Ruqaishi and an invitation to become bedu. The Ambassador's visit and diplomacy. Brian departs. Roulement February 1973. Building JibJat Road. Charles Butt arrives as OC Midway Garrison & runs out of petrol. JMF returns, and sanity regained. End of Saladins again? Promotion. Malcolm leaves. Op Dragon and the death of a tiger. JibJat road completed and final Vulture patrol. Smallpox scare. I ponder on the last of the Bedu?

TRAGEDY STRIKES

10 Jan
Dreadful news – Stepping off plane fm UK, JMF told signal received – his wife killed, son injured – car accident after dropping him off at Heathrow. Put straight back on plane to UK. Poor bloody sod.

A thoroughly decent individual, genuine, easy going, unflappable, always fair and reasoned, popular with his Baluchi and Pakistani soldiers. No one deserved the knock he'd received. Remaining on compassionate leave for just two weeks, he rejoined us at Midway in the run up to my departure, putting on a brave face for what were unimaginable personal circumstances, saying it was easier to be back at work than feeling sorry for himself in the UK. His son had returned to boarding school. After Oman, we remained in contact and I was delighted when a while later he wrote with the news he'd married again.

THE LAST OF THE BEDU?

12 Jan
0500 – 2 LRs and Bedford patrol north Shisur, more a flag waving exercise. Amazing desert colours this AM – browns, yellows, purples, maroons, blacks, greens. Laa adoo, laa ghazal – presumably all shot? Reached Shisur just under two hours, good going in cooler sand. Faddal with Bedu west of Shisur – dates, coffee and scented tea. NTR. Exchanged salt, onions, raisins and bag of rice, insignificant to us, precious to a nomad. The Rashid, a proud people. Banaat giggling behind screened-off tent area – we were being spied on, evinced by occasional movement of tent flap. Ruqaishi tells me they like the yellow haired soldier – did I want to stay?!

'Laa adoo' means no adoo and as mentioned before, colloquially 'Tafaddal' implores acceptance, an invitation to join for refreshment or meal. Colloquially I'd abbreviated 'faddal' as a noun. The code of nomadic generosity, almost impossible to decline without causing loss of face.

Nothing to report – NTR – with no reports of any cross-border activity we returned to base that evening.

Rashid encampment west from Shisur. North from here lies the Empty Quarter. The burmails held water from Shisur's wells carried on camels in goatskin sacs. It transpired the giggling heard behind the tent flaps was from young Bedu girls. My fair hair apparently amused them and despite Ruqaishi's encouragement, I turned down the offer to turn Bedu.

13 Jan
Barut Mubarik, Yaqub Abdullah, Khamis Khalif away on Eid Leave. .50 trg, firing, FN trg. Letters to Charlotte, Sandy, M&D.
Viscount arrived with <u>mail</u> – 9 letters – Home, AIWH, Louise too!

14 Jan
John MacCullum and Eric Butler arrived – Roulement conference. Convoys to stay over at Midway.
Jets using ranges North Midway next wk.

SOAF confirmed they would be using an area of 'our desert' for target practice. Pilot training continued even in a war zone.

15-18 Jan
BH away Thank God! (BH entry to diary!) – Has decided to stay until 20th Jan – No comment. (PH entry)

Convoy – 16th – Mid – Mud – Man – Mud – Mid. 1700hrs 18th: all in safe. Brig visit to Mudhai. Mist – khareef all day. Sandstorm warning – never arrived.

Brigadier Jack paid us an unscheduled visit by Huey 206 catching the convoy leaving for Manston. Unannounced as ever, it was his way of keeping in touch. Always friendly, positive, upbeat, his visits boosted morale. Like John Graham before him, Jack Fletcher had the natural ability to inspire. The Manston convoy was accomplished without incident.

THE AMBASSADOR'S VISIT

19 Jan
Received msg. Ambassador arrived Dhofar, wants to visit Midway with wife and meet Wali.
Descending gangway, asked me 'Who's in charge here?' Replying I was, prompted a 'Huh'. Admittedly I was in Dhofar uniform – my shirt, no badges of rank, slacks, shemagh and worn out desert boots seemed to wrong-foot HE. Behind, David Glazebrook caught my eye with raised eyebrows. Good seeing David again. Took party out to Wali's camp 500m east of Midway. Following introductions offered coffee and dates. Meeting cordial, but lengthy with

incidental chat. Amused at HE's growing discomfort seated crossed legged on tent's carpet, stretching first one leg then the other. Looked uncomfortable. David too. Here we sit on the ground crossed legged every day, admittedly we've young joints! Ambassador's wife caused bit of a mushkilla, apparently she offered to buy jewellery off Bedu ladies' ears, necks and arms. Wali b. furious. Summoned after everyone had departed, I caught it in the neck. So much for British diplomacy.
Letter to Louise, and HQ.

My diarised notes tell it all, not the most satisfactory of PR visits. Following the ambassador's visit, I was recalled to the Wali's tent, where I was subjected to some harsh words. It was some time before this important local dignitary, the Sultan's Governor of Dhofar, had quietened down. We eventually departed amicably, my profuse apologies accepted for actions of those with higher authority than me. I had been fortunate having Ruqaishi to assist me in smoothing matters with a man I needed to keep on good terms.

20 Jan
BH departs & Sgt Greaves on lve. SSM Ali, Suleman Jumea, Ali Nasir, RTB after Eid lve. Convoy Mudhai-Man-Mudhai. BG platoon to Salalah on Viscount. JMF back?
Sad to see Brian go – will miss the 10th Hussar. He's so bloody happy. Promised invite to wedding after my return 'so stay alive!' Ali – back to Oman – 7 days comp. leave – house washed away in rains.

Receiving news his father's house had been washed away in floods, SSM Ali was allowed the requisite seven days compassionate leave to sort things out before returning to Dhofar, where he was also needed. Being the professional soldier he was, he duly returned, his father's house repairs resolved.

And Brian, packed and raring to go home, had reached the end of his truncated secondment. Serving nine months in Dhofar, he'd matched the typical tour of a seconded battalion officer. Climbing into the aircraft he turned shouting 'Bloody made it! Can't tell you how good it feels! Just fucking stay alive, Hodgson – not getting married till you're home too!' He'd gone as I shouted back 'I'll be there!'

ROULEMENT FEBRUARY 1973

> *21 Jan*   *LCpl Nasir – Guard duty*
> *Convoy RTB Midway – no problems.*
> *Gray Mackenzie rep in Salalah.*
> *1500 – Sand 60 arrived overland fm Bid Bid – brand new L/Rs!!*
> *Great to see Kalfan again.*
> *Cpl Salim here with first half of Green 60 – Ruqaishi arrives tomorrow.*
> *3 Coy JR to Manston – Simba?*
> *Odeyne now 15!*

With roulement underway, Khalfan, now a full lieutenant, arrived overland leading DR's recce platoon, as Ruqaishi with his NFR recce platoon prepared for their move back to Oman. It was good to see Khalfan again. Gray Mackenzie, civil engineers, had opened offices in Salalah. Although incidental news to us in Midway, it demonstrated confidence in the country.

> *22/23 Jan*   *Sand 60 – Guard duty*
> *Ruqaishi here with the rest of Green 60 – all happy going home!*
> '*BASE CAMP FR FUTURE TROOP SET UP MUDHAI. DR RECCE UNABLE TO FAMILIARISE AREA DUE TO LACK OF MOGAS. HOPE YR DECODE BETTER THAN MINE //*'
> *Col Bryan, Medi, John White & two others here for night - leave with G60 early tmw. Last here 4 months ago?*
> *BAD DAY . . . big flap – Midway garrison out of petrol – managed to scrounge some fm ACS POL for Ruqaishi tmw. Sorry to see a good friend go. He's been great company.*

As to the message from DR's Khalfan now at Mudhai - Mogas? I hadn't a clue what the word meant, but it materialised that they'd arrived without Dhofar maps.

    Colonel Bryan accompanied by Captain John White (Sultan's Commendation) and a platoon of NFR soldiers had flown up from Salalah to join Ruqaishi's returning convoy and were in an ebullient mood. We'd last been together as a battalion group for Op Sycamore the previous September. That seemed an age ago, yet it was just four months. It was with not a little envy we saw them off across the deserts up to Oman. Roulement was as usual chaotic as people arrived unannounced expecting to stay, demanding preferential treatment, theirs the more important task. Just like firqat really. Midway, short on petrol, delayed Col Bryan's departure.

THE LAST OF THE BEDU?

BUILDING JIBJAT ROAD

25 Jan
Patrol – 30th Jan – 20km to Wadi Jazal with Holdfast – site of Jibjat rd. route.
No news yet JR's move to Manston. Don't think they've planned further than Salalah? My new room finally ready – moved across after prayers.

Still at Manston we awaited JR's arrival to take over command where I had George holding the fort with three Saladins and a NFR half company, awaiting their chance to relocate back to the north.

Following the successful recce with BATT's firqat to navigate a route from the northern desert plains to Jibjat, a 'road-gang' was created incorporating a civilian workforce, heavy earth moving equipment and SAF protection. We provided a three Saladin troop during the construction stages, initially commanded by my sergeants, Lou, then Wimpy. Towards the end of February, command moved to Captain Robin Amoore (17th/21st Lancers), recently arrived on secondment. Robin went on to become Squadron 2ic, serving with distinction winning the WKhM(G), equivalent to the MC. The road we'd recced and helped to build, from the plains up to Jibjat was little more than an earth track, yet it remains in existence to this day.

27 Jan
JMF back from comp. leave. Quietly and thoroughly professional, he's straight back into role. Replaced CB whose stay as OC Midway garrison has not been without incident. V. good to see JMF again.
Col David on visit. Now HQ talk of creating a Recce Sqn?
Promoted Major.
Barut Mubarik RTB? – extension 4 days.
Msg. JR convoy complete this loc. JR vehs stop this loc tdy.
Tangos end of month servicing.

John's return was more than welcome. I met him off the aircraft and over strong coffee served in his semi-air-conditioned office, I brought him up to speed on the situation at Midway. JMF, to his great credit, took it all in and replied his main objective now was to get back into role as seamlessly as possible and keep focussed on his responsibilities. Adding, 'Fortunately I also love my job.' John would go on to serve out an extended contract before finally returning to a well-earned retirement in the UK.

To cover for John's absence on compassionate leave, Major Charles Butt (CB) had arrived on temporary loan from Oman Gendarme, where he was HQ Coy commander. Regrettably, he and I had failed to establish the rapport I enjoyed with John. Never would the garrison have run out of fuel under John's command. Of the many CB anecdotes, perhaps his best was whilst seriously intoxicated and attempting to reopen the enemy-held Midway Road. Setting out alone in his Land Rover, dressed in parade uniform, he managed to negotiate the camp entrance's two burmails and barbed wire, before tearing off towards the jebel road to Salalah. Up went the alarm and only the quick thinking of newly commissioned 2/Lt Greadh Jummaah averted what would undoubtedly have involved a messy ending. Leaping into another Land Rover, Greadh roared out in hot pursuit, rapidly overhauling the wild Major Butt, who by now had drawn his sword in his erratic charge towards the jebel. Driving alongside, Greadh drove into the side of the now stalling OC Midway's Land Rover, forcing it to a halt. Major Butt's last charge. You couldn't make it up.

THE SUBJECT OF SALADINS AGAIN AND PROMOTION

David Glazebrook DAA & QMG (Deputy Assistant Adjutant & Quarter Master General) arrived on a flying visit. Amongst other topics, he wished to discuss the perennial topic of possibly reorganising the Squadron into a reconnaissance outfit, using lighter vehicles. He sought out my views but I replied I couldn't agree. Borrowing Tim's well-versed arguments I reminded David of what had been achieved when the Saladins had fought, that but for the situation on spares, we had the technical abilities to operate as a viable force. And that without Saladins, the battle at Vimy, followed by the lengthy withdrawals from Akoot, then Janook when so much vital equipment was saved, would have been different stories but for the Saladin. Feeling I now had nothing to lose this near to the end of my secondment, I reminded David that the subsequent chaos that was Janook was due solely to bad planning by an indifferent HQ, and that had it not been for the Saladins, then on that occasion too, there'd have been bloodshed. SAF needed armour.

Maybe it was the passion of the argument, Tim's argument, that took David by surprise and after reassuring me the subject was still theoretical it was dropped and we moved on to other matters. As the meeting ended and David rose to leave, he happened to notice my spare shirt hanging off a peg in my office displaying a captain's rank. At this David remarked he was astonished I'd not been promoted.

Given my role as Squadron OC and the various firqat and SAF outposts we operated, on a simple handshake I became acting major. Adding further to my surprise and delight, I later discovered he had arranged back-pay to when I'd taken on the squadron four months earlier. With friends like David . . .

Fortunately, the conversation regarding trucks with canons remained inconclusive, and was to remain so, presumably destined to be only ever an idea for senior officers' after-dinner discussion. Sadly, the point highlighted of Saladin and infantry working together as we'd done months earlier would be proven as soon as the following month when JR fought alone in a fierce action south of our old doomed position Janook.

28 Jan
Sgt Waite moved out 1030 – fuses! Inevitably something goes wrong when we want an early start – invariably it's radios.
Grey convoy to Mudhai – 32 vehicles!
Three Somali nationals rounded up by Sand 60 near Mudhai. Two had passports – last stamped in Aden. Found hiding under a bush . . .

Plagued with unreliable radios, we'd become adept at swapping them between vehicles. Blown fuses were replaced but given shortages on spares and equipment, running the cars remained a constant battle against the odds. Wimpy Waite now joined the road gang, Lou and his crew returning for some well-earned rest. And DR's Khalfan had his first success at Mudhai. We handed the Somalis over to Gordan, who sent them on to Salalah as 1 Coy JR finally departed for Mudhai then Manston.

MALCOLM DECIDES AGAINST RETURNING TO OMAN

My soldier friend turned intelligence officer had failed to return from UK leave. Making contact with Gordon, he'd learned of a potential stink concerning alleged covert efforts to supply arms across the border in Yemen. There was also the question concerning who had ordered the operation to demolish a certain fort in Yemen. In answer to Gordon's warning, came the reply 'Oops, has Malkie-baby made a booboo?' which we took to be spook rhetoric for 'Oh Shit'; he sensibly stayed away. An enigma, who had once been presented at the Court of Emperor Haile Selassie. Malcolm's air-conditioned caravan was adorned with photographs to show for it, seeming to grant him a gravitas mere soldiers could only dream of.

I met Gordon shortly afterwards who elaborated on a covert plan straight out of a Fleming novel concerning the secret supply of weapons across the border. Somehow covert became overt, triggering a monumental ruckus locally and with the two HQs, Dhofar and SAF. Doubtlessly causing a stir also at what London cabbies called "City's worst-kept secret address known to every cabbie, tourist guide and KGB agent", 100 Westminster Bridge Road, SE1 7XA, home to MI6.

Some deft diplomacy was required to calm highly charged expectations centred on the supply of rifles and the demolition of Yemeni forts. It also brought to an abrupt cessation further involvement of someone whose role had been to gather intelligence – not arm private armies. We would miss his intellect and wit.

> *30 Jan – Message: SUNRAY HOLDFAST THIS LOC TO YOU TDY. KEEN TO DRIVE MIDWAY/JIBJAT RD. PSE ACK ESCORT CAN BE PROVIDED THROUGH SYCAMORE AREA.*

We'd received a message that OC SAF engineers (codenamed Holdfast) wished to visit the 'road gang' and requesting I provide an escort. With most of my next Habarut convoy organised, and with plenty of notice this time, we safely escorted the engineers to the roadworks site and back the same day.

> *2 Feb – Have had to postpone Habarut convoy ETD until 0800 4 Feb as No escort.*
> *Grey 60 arrived 1430 – towing 2 LRs, one misfiring.*

As part of Jebel Regiment's continuing roulement, our old friends Grey 60, their recce platoon, arrived down from northern Oman limping in with two Land Rovers under tow and a third faulty. Nothing really surprised me anymore, but on discovering my promised convoy escort troops had still to arrive, I had had no option but to postpone the scheduled Habarut convoy by two days. And Grey 60 now had a new commander, the instantly likeable 2/Lt Rashid.

> *Rashid of Grey 60 seems a good man. Worked on paperwork all day – cleared a lot – only 2 interruptions. Too busy to write home.*

> *3 Feb – Muslim New Year – half day for the boys.*
> *OG unit arrive by Viscount – Habarut convoy support.*

> *4 - 6 Feb Habarut resup. convoy. All went well. OG boys keen as mustard. Roulement platoon leaving Habarut delirious to be returning home.*

This was to be my final Habarut convoy and fortunately passed without incident. The next, in three weeks would be commanded by George Somerville who, poor chap, drove smack over an anti-tank mine leaving him prematurely deafened, his indomitable cheerfulness undented. On leaving Oman, George re-trained to become a respected schoolteacher in the highlands of Scotland.

> 6th Feb.
> Met up with Gordon and FHG at Qafa on return. No activity to report.
> Op Dragon: 1 Coy JR caught south Janook! Tiger Wright KIA with others, many WIA. How bloody sad. He'd reached the end of his secondment.

OP DRAGON – 6TH FEB 1973

The powerfully built Paul Wright I'd known since my early days in Dhofar when attached to 1 Coy JR at Razut in September 1971 for joint operations on Salalah plains. Paul had gained the pseudonym Tiger. Only later I learned this was due to none other than Nick Downie, attending the same SAS selection course as Paul and naming him Tiger, as in his own words, 'to take the piss'. It remained Tiger Wright from that day.

We'd recently met at Salalah and I'd not seen him since JR's last Dhofar tour when he won the WB. Now nearing the end of his SAF secondment, he still had Mike Austin as his 2ic and Bob Aplin as 2nd captain. Again we'd not met since they'd departed Dhofar nine months earlier.

Tiger was interested in learning more of what had happened on Op Locust when SAF was pushed out of Janook, taking a beating, wrongly positioned by those who planned matters elsewhere. As described earlier, withdrawing under fire from Akoot we'd hit mines taking casualties. Managing casevacs we'd made it successfully to Janook where we were to establish the Simba airhead. Driving into camp to join the squadron who'd arrived days before, we were climbing out of vehicles, greeting friends not seen for months when all hell let loose. To the watching adoo we must have looked like a bunch of end-of-term school kids. The position was dominated by high ground occupied by the adoo on three sides. At least we had a back door to the north.

Holding the position for three days, a disbelieving Commander Dhofar had visited as on cue the adoo attacked again hitting the airfield. Tim's message 'the position's untenable as a Forward Airhead' was finally accepted, revised orders issued and we withdrew to Manston following five hectic days fighting. Little was broadcast about this particular episode for obvious reasons and I doubt will appear in many books about the Dhofar War.

Tiger, however, wanted to know all about it, asking where the enemy had attacked from, in what numbers, with what weapons and layout of the ground. I told him in as much detail as I recalled, mentioning also he should verify details with David Nichols in NFR, whose half company was attached to the squadron at the time. He said he'd like to have a go at the adoo south of Janook.

Within days of completing his secondment and rejoining his regiment, the Royal Engineers, Paul Wright led his company out on Op Dragon. The aim, to draw the adoo into positions where the better equipped SAF might engage with artillery and jet aircraft.

On 6th February, 1 Coy moved through Janook, dominated by adoo vantage points, close to the treeline and wadis offering unseen approach. An untenable long stay proposition, as proven a year earlier. As with Akoot, the area was littered with mines which we'd found to our cost.

At 0615 a soldier triggered an AP mine, and in that single moment broadcast 1 Coy's whereabouts. It is probable the adoo were already awake to SAF's presence, for no matter how lightly the army tried, to a jebali's acute ear we trod as elephants.

Within a short time, the adoo had assembled a significant force, seamlessly moving men into attacking positions, strategically deploying with automatic rifles, heavy machine guns, mortar and RCL. The attack came around 0730 with such force that for a while it seemed the defenders must be wiped out. For the next six hours 1 Coy gradually fell back, holding off their pursuers, carrying their wounded, fighting a textbook withdrawal. Tiger Wright, standing head and shoulders above his men moved nimbly for a big man, rushing between positions, giving orders, encouraging and inspiring his men to hold their ground against repeated attacks thrown at them.

At 1545 Tiger was hit by an artillery airburst. Shrapnel takes no prisoners and he was killed outright. He'd been pulling wounded back to the safety of sangars, helping distribute ammo to his sections, all the while directing airstrikes onto adoo positions.

Mike now took command. He'd called for helicopters to evacuate the wounded and killed. Speaking with him afterwards, he related how whilst directing jets to targets, an airburst exploded overhead taking out the two men either side of him. Ordering his reserve platoon forward to give covering fire, Mike attended to the increasing problem of the wounded. Staff-Sergeant Salim Khalfan Hamad al-Siyabi pushed forward leading his platoon to draw adoo fire. For over two hours Salim steadfastly held his exposed position. Wounded and at one point outflanked on two sides, Salim remained calm, inspiring his men, driving off repeated attacks. A quite outstanding display of soldiership.

The jets once again were the saviours, screaming in low with murderous machine guns blazing, forcing the adoo advance to a standstill, allowing JR to gradually fall back to an area where a total of 11 wounded and dead could be airlifted out by Hueys.

In his typical self-deprecating fashion, Mike related to me how loading the wounded onto the aircraft, he was forced repeatedly to drag self-appointed 'medics' from remaining on the rapidly filling helicopters. He needed every man who could fire a rifle. 2 Coy JR under Nick Ofield, his commander Mike Ball being on leave, were flown in from Manston to assist 1 Coy's beleaguered men. Finally, after nearly eight hours fighting, the adoo called off their attacks as JR were pulled out by helicopters to the safety of their base at Manston.

JR's ops officer Simon Steward had volunteered sending in Nick Downie by helicopter, but misunderstanding the message Mike had declined the offer to his lasting regret for they were good friends. And Mike could have well done with Nick's assistance, an ex-SAS medic. In the rush to vacate the position, a large quantity of 81mm mortar bombs were left behind. It was Nick to whom JR turned knowing his expertise with explosives and the dumped ammo was dutifully blown up in a daring covert mission later that night.

1 Coy losses were 2 KIA, 1 missing in action and 10 WIA; the adoo, 9 dead. This was not a war of vast numbers, contacts lasting all day rarely exceeded this casualty rate. It was more an individual conflict pitching one against the other as opposed to the mass scales of World Wars. For all that, every individual would attest that it only takes one bullet, one shrapnel shard or single mine to maim or end life.

That day JR's medal tally was increased significantly: Tiger Wright and S/Sgt Salim were each awarded the Wisam Shuja'at (Wsh), the Sultan's Gallantry Medal, equivalent to the British VC, the very rare level 1 Gallantry medal. Mike Austin and three soldiers the WB, the Sultan's Bravery Medal, British equivalent DSO/DSM for Gallantry and three men the WKhM(G), British equivalent MC/MM.

Tiger's death shocked us all. A man who led from the front and had survived many a close contact. He became the most highly decorated British seconded soldier to have served in SAF, having gained the two highest awards for Gallantry under fire: the WSh and WB.

All felt for JR who'd lost a fine soldier, killed as he completed two years' loan service. Almost there, someone who had all but made it. A soldier who'd been awarded

The Sultan's Gallantry Medal – Wisam Shuja'at. (WSh.)

medals that would never be worn, more likely destined to end up in a regimental museum, or someone's collection. Had this been a Hollywood movie they'd have had Tiger walking away silhouetted against an angry red and yellow artificial mushroom cloud, always a poor substitute for high explosive – but in reality fate plays a hand, and a chance splinter of exploding rocket records a different ending.

Two weeks later down from Mudhai I met up with Mike at UAG. He too was there for a night's R&R and we'd both been put up in rooms borrowed from occupants out on operations. Accommodation was always tight at the Mess. Sitting with him outside his bayt as we shared a cool beer, catching up on what we'd been doing since we'd last met nine months earlier, I found a relaxed soldier. We sat into the fading light, seated on camp chairs. Mike had reached the end of his three-year contract and I had just a few weeks to go before the end of my secondment. We'd gone over the still vivid details of Op Dragon and the contact south of Janook, recognising we both knew the territory well. Apart from being there during SAF's beating at Janook in May the previous year, I'd frequently escorted convoys into the tree line collecting firewood for DR's Akoot cookhouses. We'd always patrolled in force, a half company of DR escorted by three Saladins. And we'd experienced mines too; the place was riddled with them.

Whilst I was readying to leave at the end of my time in Dhofar, I regretted not having had the chance to explore Northern Oman with its many varied treasures, historical and geographical. Mike enthused about an Oman I should visit – urging I consider returning on contract. I replied I'd had enough, too much Dhofar I reckoned, but the option was there; after all, I only had five months left of my extended short service commission back home in the UK. Mike was staying on, and learning he'd recently renewed his contract for another three years, I remember my reply: 'You'll have saved enough to buy a farm by then!' Mike served out his second contract and we met again ten years later on a SAF visit to Oman as guests of the Sultan in 1983. Mike was fit and healthy. He'd not changed one bit.

JIBJAT ROAD COMPLETED

16 Feb
J/J road will progress 3km tmw. Sand 60 moving to Rd Camp tmw.
Op Vulture – Recover abandoned oil rigs and equipment – Wadi Mitan area. I'll take Q, Khalfan with a section from Sand 60 and ACS x 6 – three Land Rovers, three Bedfords and Breakdown.
Sand 60 need new medic – check.
Saif Nasir – AWOL – 37 days lve? Chase.

The road gang were making astonishing progress – and on 17 Feb, I messaged Dhofar HQ/BATT

'J/J rd now reached BE Northing 24. Will reach point alpha tmw. When earliest can expect escort fm South, ques.'

We met the escort driving from Jibjat on 22 Feb, the connection from the golden sands and gravel plains north of the Negd and the high jebel plateau, had been achieved.

FINAL OP VULTURE PATROLS

My last but one op under the wide-ranging remit of Vulture was to recover derelict oil rig equipment, abandoned in the desert bordering the great sand dunes of the Empty Quarter. This equipment had been left behind following an attack by Yemeni forces killing Mecom Oil Company's prospectors six years earlier. Houston-based American John Mecom had once ranked alongside J. Paul Getty as one of the few individuals running large-scale oil operations.

On this rare occasion I took a couple of the Al Mahri firqat as guides, Hathi al Kamam and Hamid, his younger brother, just a boy yet already proud owner of

a .303 rifle. Hathi with his rifle muzzle sealed with material against wind-blown sand stands beside Hamid, barely taller than his rifle length.

Leaving Midway on 17 February, we struggled to make progress, being forced to stop west of Shisur for the night. The going was slow. Apart from the usual soft sand alternating with gravel plains, we'd not travelled 16km before running into a shimaal, a dust storm which even with goggles made driving in open vehicles difficult. Blown sand penetrated everything no matter how well wrapped, clogging weapons, clothing and vehicles. Men became caked in the stuff, causing skin irritation wherever clothing chafed or soft skin rubbed, lending conviction to the reason for circumcision in Middle Eastern countries. And eyes filled with grit, defeating our issue WW2 leather rimmed 'Rommel' goggles.

Decreasing at night we welcomed the brief respite, but I feared we were in for another dust storm the following day. Rising before sunrise, we crossed the wastes of Wadi Ghadun named wadi half-shaft for self-explanatory reasons. The secret was to cross this wadi at first light with the sand still relatively cooler and thus marginally firmer. We crossed this time with no half-shafts stripped, a record. The drivers were getting better.

Winter shimaals are caused by strengthening high pressure abutting a deep trough of low pressure and can blow constantly for up to five days. On this occasion we were fortunate that by the time we arrived at the northerly reaches of Wadi Sahhr on the Yemeni border, the wind had blown itself out and a period of quiet descended as we made camp that night. We'd travelled 240km across desert in atrocious conditions and were relieved to be free of wind-blown sand. The men were soon cooking our meal over an open fire, joking at endured hardships, whilst we brushed down equipment and cleaned weapons. That night we dined on tinned meat added to braised onions and sultanas generously spiced with red and green chillies, cooked in a vast 30 inch (76cm) diameter battered aluminium pot that accompanied us on longer patrols, the meal shared, served on a large communal tin plate of steaming rice, just reward for effort. As usual once we'd eaten, cooking pots and serving dishes were scrubbed clean using the desert's still warm sand, as free of bacteria as any hot tap water. Another cold night, but all slept well after two days battling sandstorms, each taking turns on stag for it remained no man's land.

19 Feb
Found old camp site – littered with abandoned, rusting oil rig equipment. Beggars question – worth recovering? Orders we do. Mine clearing took long time. No booby traps. Loaded equipment using winches on Bedfords. Back to Shisur for night – much in need water. Desert is turning green, when looked at from ground level.

On patrol and an evening meal prepared.

Early next day we found the oil rig. Our first job was to ensure the area was free of mines which we accomplished using Sand 60's detectors, our bayonets and knives. It was delicate work. Eventually having cleared the site we inspected the presumably once painted steel of plant and equipment that had suffered too much sun and shimaal winds. No single piece of equipment had escaped oxidation, begging the question whether they were worth recovering. Then began the task of lifting and manhandling the heavy sections of rig onto Bedfords, winching on board the heaviest pieces. This took us until mid-afternoon and despite the continuous effort put in, I decided we'd try to make Shisur and its fresh water that night.

Slowly the loaded convoy formed up behind my Land Rover and with Khalfan's Sand 60 bringing up the rear, we began the long haul away from the abandoned drilling site. Looking back, waiting for the crawling Bedfords to catch up, my binoculars picked out the scars of man's interference on this magnificent landscape; blackened drill heads, burmails and rusting poles defiantly pointing skywards, abandoned litter we'd no room for.

Motoring across the flat expanse of flint and gravel plains, I called a halt noticing the desert was turning green. There must have been rain, when, I had no idea and now as far as the eyes would focus stretching into the distance the desert was suddenly green. Yet when looked at from above, the tiny shoots spread metres apart disappeared. It was hard to conceive how life existed in such an arid place. Subconsciously alert to any irregularities, I'd also seen a round stone, pretty obvious against the desert's flatness. Picking it up from beside my Land Rover tyre, the fist sized ochre tinged object was a geode. How on earth it had been deposited out here, so far from any noticeable wadis escaped me. Today, it sits beside me on a window sill.

We made Shisur in the dark. The local Al Rashid came asking for rice and rations, which we were able to give them. Drawing fresh water from the well under the cave we ate lightly, a quick meal of chapatis and tinned sardines before crashing out.

SMALLPOX SCARE

20 Feb
Awake before light as Bedu had come into our position asking for me clearly distressed. Sick? Yes – But I don't need a pointed finger prodded into my chest by a Bedu demanding 'ureed dawa'. All we had were our first-aid boxes on Land Rovers. Sand 60 has no medic as yet. Inspected the patients

Stoically queuing for smallpox inoculations, before we were allowed through the gates.

– blisters and sores evident. Interesting. Handed out aspirins – broken in half, one to each man and one for each spouse. Two men had two wives. Quartered tablets for affected children. Chicken pox? Radioed Midway with report. Broke camp and motored 5km south before halt for an uninterrupted breakfast.
Arrived back at Midway to be halted outside camp – HQ Dhofar fearful it's smallpox! All to have jabs immediately – Beaver on its way with vaccines. Shit! Smallpox?

Next day, I returned with two Land Rovers and a medic flown in from Salalah to treat the Shisur Bedu. Arriving, we received a radio message it was chickenpox, not smallpox. We'd been inoculated out of expediency leaving sore arms and a few who feigned sickness. Still, it beat the alternative. In 1973 it was still considered imperative people exposed to the virus receive a booster without delay. Whilst we Brits underwent regular inoculations against smallpox during army service, it seemed we still required a booster on exposure to smallpox. My men had not received vaccinations before and some suffered slight side effects, fever and headaches for a few days. It was not until 1980, seven years later, that the World Health Organization declared smallpox eliminated.

It's a highly contagious and deadly disease, caused by the variola virus transmitted directly person to person. In 1796 Edward Jenner successfully inoculated a child with vaccinia virus (cowpox) demonstrating immunity to smallpox. Within two years the first smallpox vaccine was developed. Estimates of up to 300 million people across the globe became infected in the 20th Century before the disease was finally eradicated – the only human infectious disease ever to be completely eliminated.

Thought to have originated in India or Egypt at least 3,000 years ago, there is evidence the young Pharaoh, Ramses V who died in 1157 BC had suffered from smallpox, his mummified remains showing telltale pockmarks/small lesions on his skin. Other members of the Royal household received substandard mummification, presumably the result of a hurried burial in an apparent epidemic.

THE LAST OF THE BEDU?

"I pondered on this desert hospitality and compared it with our own. I remembered other encampments where I had slept, small tents on which I had happened in the desert and where I had spent the night. Gaunt men in rags and hungry-looking children had greeted me, and bade me welcome with the sonorous phrases of the desert. Later they had set a great dish before me, rice heaped round a sheep which they had slaughtered, over which my host poured liquid golden butter until it flowed down on to the sand; and when I protested, saying 'Enough! Enough!', had answered that I was a hundred times welcome. Their lavish hospitality had always made me uncomfortable, for I had known that as a result of it they would go hungry for days. Yet when I left them they had almost convinced me that I had done them a kindness by staying with them"

Wilfred Thesiger – Arabian Sands

The word Bedu comes from the Arabic word, badawi, desert dweller. Some will say the plural is Bedouin, but the Bedu will say it is Bedu.

Despite the exhausted state of our armoured vehicles, my orders remained we maintain blocking operations towards the Yemeni border. As such we had continued long range Land Rover patrols up beyond Shisur, generally taking three Land Rovers and a Bedford pick-up truck with a fitter/mechanic, water, fuel, rice,

The author about to explore the depths of the well at Shisur. The place was a haven for bats, spiders and scorpions. Where I stand at the mouth to the cave, the sand is littered with camel and goat faeces.

tinned food and spares. It had become habit to take extra rations to distribute to Bedu families we encountered, for they would always insist on feeding us, producing coffee or just camel milk for us.

A remote place yet to find fame through Fiennes' expedition seeking the fabled Ubar, Lost City of Atlantis, Shisur was our popular stopping-off point, the water sweet and plentiful. Found below an ancient stone-built fort and hidden deep within the far reaches of a limestone cave, there's a pool of cool fresh water. The back of the cave is shaded to an almost impenetrable darkness where, combined with the chill of cold water, the air temperature is noticeably lower in stark contrast to the desert's heat and blinding sunshine outside. We'd refill our canvas charguls here, the water untainted by camel urine found at other desert wells.

Although warned by the Bedu against snakes, we never saw any. What we found instead were bats, but also camel spiders lodged in the craggy cavernous roof, and the occasional black scorpion, always large specimens which scuttled across the sandy floor. Inside the cave these creatures would watch menacingly, waiting their turn, invoking the spirit of Cerberus, guardian at the entrance to Hades . . . a presence sufficient to induce an involuntary shiver, or was it just the chill?

From Shisur, we patrolled west then north to Fasad and the Makinat al Haiz waterhole. Stretching to our area limits, we'd journey further into the Empty Quarter on to Fasad North's sulphur-tainted waterhole before striking west past Wadi Mitan to where Wadi Jadilah disappeared, swallowed by 180m high dunes. Colossal tsunami waves of rolling golden sands, colours fading through the day as the desert sun's white light robbed the spectrum of colour. Windswept by shimaals, these huge silent mounds of sand inspired awe in a stillness unchanged for millennia. So utterly remote and so uniquely beautiful were my surroundings, it was growing difficult not to fall under its spell, stirring a temptation to remain, as Mike (Austin) had chosen to do.

This was the province of the Bedouin peoples who ranged Arabia's deserts. In my short time amongst them, I had noticed how the desert Bedu walked with an effortless cameline stride. This in contrast to those peoples who lived on the jebel, where the jebali walked with an almost bandy legged gait, accustomed as they were to navigating routes around or over boulders, along stoney wadis, dry river beds and steep wadi passes.

In a caravan, women bring up the rear, camels laden with baggage, tents and provisions en route to a waterhole secured by their menfolk travelling ahead. A way of life about to be eclipsed forever through the advent of motorised transport. Gladly exchanged, ancient, unhampered ways lost to consumeristic, packaged livelihoods intent in the pursuit of materialistic trappings.

Men of the Al-Rashid at Fasad. They'd arrived from the west with a caravan of camels, along an ancient trading route running south of Ramlat Mitan's dunes. Bedu warriors, tribesmen greatly admired by the British explorer Wilfred Thesiger. It was at Shisur's well in 1946 where he arranged to secretly meet guides of the Al Rashid before setting off to traverse the Empty Quarter by camel, becoming the first Western explorer to cross this desolate, beautiful place, then a region forbidden to Christians under the threat of death. He did it barefoot so as not to arouse suspicion in leaving boot imprints. A quite extraordinary man.

A Rashid camel caravan approaches, stretching back over 150 metres.

THE LAST OF THE BEDU?

The desert shown here is typical of the sand and gravel plains of the Negd and in the far distance, shimmering through the heat of the day are the golden sands of Al Rub Al Khali, The Empty Quarter. An unbroken landscape, devoid of movement, utterly barren, very hot, very dry, it held an absolute stillness, a quiet that brought an exquisite beauty to it all.

Here lived people devoid of excesses, who followed a noble course, structured by established rules of desert survival, bound by chivalry and honour long since vanished from our Western World with its 21st century successes. Yet for all our achievements, our industrialised, meteoritic progress, our sophistication, there has long been a fascination with the simple values displayed by peoples with apparently so little in terms of material wealth. Aloof, uncomplaining, sometimes distant and often contemptuous towards the choices we have made, it is difficult not to wonder who had chosen wisest?

Co-existing in this harsh biblical environment amongst and alongside family units living, not simply existing, were we, trespassers in a paradise, perhaps witnesses to the last of the Bedu?

> "On the face of it, we should find that the Bedu, the nomadic peoples of Arabia, have many of the trappings as we, most of our virtues and perhaps fewer vices. The principal difference is that in their case, nature wants tending, whereas in ours, nature wants *for* tending. For we have ridden roughshod to spoil its beauty, through an insatiable consumption. So, is this sophistication?"
>
> anon

32

HANDOVER AND FAREWELLS

My successor, Patrick Brook, arrives on a recce. Meetings with CSAF and I witness the winds of change at SAF HQ. Rick is wounded and separately Alan too winning a good WB. Final duties, Johnson and farewells before a last parade and return to the UK.

Patrick Brook arrived at Midway late afternoon, 22 February; he'd flown from Muscat and prior to that from Trucial Oman (UAE) where he was currently serving on secondment. A day later, I'd returned from my final Op Vulture patrol. Other than visiting some bedu camps and punctures there'd been nothing in particular to report. And it was hard to suppress the growing sense of melancholy that had been growing within driving back across the gravel plains and sandy wadis towards Midway Garrison. Parking my Land Rover, I realised that was it – my final patrol. I would be handing over to George, and Robin recently arrived at the start of his two year secondment. And there was Johnson happily wagging his tail in greeting.

As I called to dump maps and cast an eye over any urgent messages, I found Patrick sitting reading documents in my office. We'd not met before, and being sweat stained and dusty, in bad need of shower and clean clothes, I was a little taken aback to find seated before me an impeccably turned-out officer sitting behind my desk. So smart an officer was a rare sight in Dhofar – but it transpired he'd flown direct from SAF HQ in the north. Rising to greet me, he introduced himself before going on without pause to explain he'd be taking over after I'd left.

That came as news to me but by then I was long past being ambushed by surprises. At that instant I realised with huge relief it meant I could now leave for home at the end of my secondment in nine days' time. A fellow cavalryman, Patrick's parent regiment was the Blues and Royals.

I was all in, but Patrick, fired up with the newly-arrived's enthusiasm, wanted to chat. So I sat down and began an outline briefing on our current battle strength, planned operations, training, vehicles, the last being in a sorry state following 24 months' active service, lack of spares, wear and tear and mines. The meeting went on until I had to insist on a shower and change of clothes. We agreed to meet for dinner in the Mess. He'd already met everyone on base so needed no introductions.

At dinner and sitting apart from the others, the debriefing continued. Wishing to learn about the Squadron's personalities, Patrick asked we continue in my newly acquired accommodation, the same he'd inherit arriving in May. Recently decorated rooms still smelled of emulsion, a rare scent in the desert. The accommodation, a two-roomed suite, fitting for a future Colonel commanding the Sultan's Armour. There was even an ensuite shower and its own loo. Up until then, as with many SAF commanders, all kept open house, be it sangar, tent or armoured vehicle. Until now, there had been little or no privacy, no retreat from those wanting, often demanding, answers to a whole myriad of questions and problems requiring immediate resolution. Now we enjoyed running water and a reliable electricity supply. I'd also just received a music centre imported from Hong Kong, astonishingly delivered unbroken to Midway. I'd mentioned my room had become the best place to escape to find solace, of the kind all in command need on occasions. The walls were painted a frankincense green, rare on the fringes of Arabia's Empty Quarter.

Author, badly sunburned, a little wild and in need of a wash. (Tom Brembridge's photograph)

'Good, we can listen to your Rachmaninov...' Patrick had volunteered. Weary from lack of sleep and four days on the road, face, ears and arms badly sunburned, all I really wanted was my bed. But Patrick had booked us flights to Bayt al Falaj the next day, so needed all the information he could gather prior to our meeting CSAF. I recognised a debrief was probably of more use than what he might have gleaned from scouring the Squadron's confidential papers over the last two days and so agreed we continue, away from the Mess in the comfort of my new bayt. Rachmaninov I had on cassette tape. I would rather have listened to my Leonard Cohen or Neil Diamond's haunting 'African Trilogy'. Sadly my Carol King Tapestry tape was long broken.

We talked into the night. Much of what I had to tell him he'd already heard about albeit in scant detail as he passed through Bayt al Falaj. Naturally he was interested primarily in our vehicle strength and personnel, those I felt to be outstanding individuals, details of soldiers' gunnery/radio/driving and maintenance skills and levels of continuation training. To this I added what I'd always considered of paramount importance, squadron and individual soldier morale. It was always going to be a long session.

He told me learning of the approaching vacancy (my departure) he'd applied for transfer to SAF to command the Squadron. He was the ideal candidate, having served in SAF three years earlier with MR, the regiment's second cavalryman to Ranulph Fiennes. I learned he'd been wounded, a bullet catching Patrick under an arm to leave a neat set of entry and exit holes. Proving the point, he proudly showed me his scars – mine would come later and remain hidden to all but the medics and my wife. One glance told me another fraction of an inch, or a high velocity ricochet from any other direction, it'd have been a smashed humerus and arterial wound. Instead, he'd a soft tissue souvenir. Lucky.

Of war stories exchanged that evening, one he failed to relate involved his near demise. During an otherwise undramatic convoy between Oman down to Midway accompanying Fiennes, Patrick had very nearly come to grief. As retold first hand in Fiennes' books, Patrick had apparently fallen asleep whilst travelling at night in a stripped-down Land Rover without doors. He'd somehow rolled gently out of the vehicle, unseen. I'd like to think this would never have happened with one of our more alert drivers. Patrick's vehicle was the tail end of the convoy. Unlike BAOR convoys in Northern Germany travelling in file along tarmac roads, any large convoys motoring across desert always spread out wide to avoid trailing behind others' choking dust.

Rudely woken from his slumber as he rolled in the soft 15cm deep powder dust, he came to a halt, spitting the stuff out of his mouth, rubbing it out of his eyes, only to watch in dismay the convoy slowly disappearing behind its mushrooming dust cloud. Astonishingly, the dozy driver hadn't noticed the undignified exit, whilst any paratrooper observing Patrick's forward roll would have applauded his effort at dismounting from a moving vehicle.

Battered but otherwise unhurt, he realised whilst lucky there'd been no other vehicles following to run him over in the dark, he was now quite alone, without weapon, map or water on the edge of Arabia's Empty Quarter. With no alternative but to start walking, he set off after the still billowing dust cloud, final evidence of a disappearing convoy.

Eventually, the convoy halted when a vehicle broke down. It was then Patrick was discovered missing. Tearing a strip off the hapless driver, Fiennes turned the convoy round and with great presence of mind formed the vehicles line abreast, stretching hundreds of metres either side of the main tracks, to give them as great a spread as possible in their search for their missing passenger. They then set off retracing their tracks in the search for Patrick who was discovered walking westwards, tramping stoically through ankle deep powder dust, very dirty, extremely thirsty but doggedly striding along following the mix of vehicle tracks. With day temperatures reaching high 40 degrees Centigrade, Patrick had cheated almost certain death, one which would have been very lonely.

At a point I could no longer keep my eyes open, Patrick kindly excused himself and retired to his bayt next door. I wrote in my diary – *seems a good man, bloody keen – just what Squadron needs*. He'd later win a bar to his WKhM.

25 Feb
Seeb Airport amazing. Tarmacked roads, what an improvement. New bayts in BAF wadi. Takes Oman 100 years ahead of Salalah, 200 ahead of Bayt al Falaj in July '71. Rick blown up on Taqah convoy, injured.

We'd flown first to Salalah then on to Seeb, Oman's recently opened airport. It was my first visit and I'd not expected so rapid a transformation, barren desert to airport. Commenced in 1971, the airport was officially opened in December 1973. That February, work was still in progress but the main runway had been laid and most airport buildings opened. Originally named Seeb, it would be renamed Muscat International Airport in 2008.

Our first meeting was with Commander SAF, Major General Tim Creasey, in his airy office at Bayt al Falaj. We'd met only once after Mike's death when he confirmed I would take on the Squadron. He'd also promised we'd keep the Saladins (promise kept) and furthermore we'd be relieved from organising and escorting Habarut convoys (promise broken). A big man with huge handshake, direct stare and imposing appearance, he wore an immaculate SAF Staff Officer's uniform and one enormous gold Rolex decorated with the Sultanate emblem. Patrick, equally smart as a Trucial Oman Scout, reinforced the fact smart uniforms were rare in Dhofar, clearly very different armies in the north. As any on day-release from Dhofar, I was feeling decidedly the poor relative in a freshly pressed borrowed shirt, my one-size-too-large borrowed trousers held up by a regimental stable belt that had seen better days, and a pair of oil stained desert boots. Recently supplied major's crowns dragged heavily on cotton epaulettes. Introductions over, we each took our seats. Coffee was served, it was all very cordial.

THE WINDS OF CHANGE

We got straight down to business, CSAF was a man in a hurry, indifferent to the past, planning the future. Giving him a report on the parlous state of my Saladins, he gave his word to Patrick that things would change. It was almost 'Give me your shopping list, I'll supply'. Saladins were indeed safe. Too late for Tim, but music to worn ears. The Squadron's future was secured in that sentence.

I learned later this positive change in our fortunes was closely linked to the arrival of Iranian and Jordanian troops on the ground, with UAE and Saudi as supporting allies. The Middle East's monarchies, facing the same ideological threat seen spreading from the revolutionary People's Republic in Yemen, now gave their support in arms, men and machinery greatly boosting the Sultan's war effort, accepting that only by facing communism together, they would prevail.

Leaving elated, I couldn't believe all that wasted time and effort trying to maintain vehicles with little to no spares, was over. No more we'd patrol with Saladins and Ferrets constantly vulnerable to breakdowns, relying on cannibalising VOR cars to use worn and repaired parts. The rules of the game had been altered at last, the Squadron could move ahead. The effort needed was still huge but Patrick was up to the job, and with the promised support from CSAF, the future for the Sultan's armour looked certain.

The Rolex was a gift to CSAF, or as overheard in the irreverence of Salalah Mess, 'goes with the fucking uniform man!' A typical Rhodesian riposte.

News arrived Rick had been blown up taking a convoy into Taqah and been wounded. At the time it didn't sound too serious, but it turned out the injuries would be long lasting. Like me he too was within days of completing his secondment.

There was another anomaly between contract and seconded personnel; of those wounded and debilitated in action, seconded servicemen would be eligible to receive financial compensation from the MOD, but not so those on contracts, albeit the Sultan was known to look after the more seriously wounded.

LAST DUTY

I had one last duty to perform before departure. Quite suddenly I'd had enough of the merry-go-round of briefings, introductions and repeated questioning. Not all, but many I'd begun to realise displayed a myopic, almost detached view to operations being undertaken beyond Jebel al Qara, north of Salalah. How long had this been the case, I wondered? Could it have been the best part of a year, since the time we'd been forced to retreat from the ludicrous Janook?

No wonder Tim had left so dejected. What effect had it had on Mike taking over the Squadron? Suddenly I didn't care; Patrick, my senior both in rank and years, was as a loaded spring, bursting-full of energy, passion and ideas. Here was the fresh new broom so urgently needed to revitalise the Squadron, unaffected as he was by relentless days, weeks, months into years of improvising and cannibalising damaged vehicles. Little wonder we called it shoestring-soldiering. All accept soldiers have to improvise, but it was bloody hard keeping a squadron of armoured vehicles running and battle ready/effective without essential spares.

The continuous Dhofar posting took a toll on our soldiers' morale – not for them the regular roulement enjoyed by others. We'd spent our time either on patrol, escorting relief convoys, on operations with infantry and firqat whilst fitting in essential training, all with little logistical support. We'd remained on continuous active service across Dhofar, operating out to the far borders of Yemen. And once beyond.

Like many, I had lost good friends from almost the beginning of my secondment 20 months earlier. Both physically and emotionally I was wearing out. Mind and body had had enough. The majority of us had started as subalterns promoted to acting captains, still in our early twenties. Increasingly Huw's words recurred 'what a bloody daft way to spend a young life . . .'

With Patrick still networking, I excused myself and found an off-duty Jack Sullivan, a contract officer in his 50s relaxing in the Mess with an overseas copy of The Daily Telegraph, catching up on UK news. We chatted for a while before I asked if he would take me to the expat war cemetery. 'Of course,' he'd replied graciously, adding, 'it's called Mina al Fahal, you'll not have had the chance before, it's a place everyone should visit.' I was glad of Jack as guide. An old friend to us, he'd visited the Squadron on a number of occasions, arriving often with a box of vital Saladin and Ferret spares he'd somehow managed to procure. Always good company, jovial and unfussed by the minutiae of army life, he'd become a valued friend to have at HQ.

Arriving at the cemetery, I walked over to the graves. It was a desolate looking place, dusty and unkempt. There stood the simple headstones beneath which lay people the army had buried. These were contract officers and NCOs who had died in war. Not for them or their families the comfort of loved one's bodies returned as was the case with us seconded. For them, the corner of some foreign field. Geoff – lean, tall and fit, a man killed just as he'd begun to feel fulfilled by his efforts to pass on soldiering skills; Huw with his too-young-to-grow whispery moustache, slightly on the plump side of svelte, carefree happy-go-lucky younger brother to David, a major now serving with OG. And then Mike, 'Uncle', who'd taken his lonely escape from unwanted responsibility, shocking us all deeply, leaving entrenched bitterness. Each fine soldiers in their singular ways, each I had been lucky to know well. This was the Christian expat war graves cemetery; one day it would be tidied up and Casuarina trees planted offering shade from the relentless radiated heat of an Omani sun. There were other graves, but none I'd known personally. And there were holes dug that'd be filled.

Unexpectedly, I was unsure what to say or do. Now I'd seen where they were buried, I'd begun to feel awkward. Looking up, I saw Jack watching. He simply nodded and turned to walk to the Land Rover as once more I looked back at the graves. We'd all volunteered. All that optimism, that 'can do energy'? Thoughts unscrambled as memories flooded back and I caught myself saying '. . . remember the laughs we had? You never came out here to die . . . that happens to others.' And I too turned, following Jack. 'It's a sombre place,' he said quietly as we drove away. My soldiers would have added in finality 'Allah Kareem' and moved on, leaving emotion behind. We returned in silence.

Back in Salalah I'd met Said Suleman returning from home leave, and borrowing a Land Rover we drove to the Muslim Cemetery outside town, a dusty solitary place with lumps of rock for headstones, some still painted with white Islamic script. Acting as my scout, Said searched through the rows of stones, but try as we might, we failed to find the grave I sought, LCpl Rasul Bux. Already fading inscriptions distressed by blown sand and sun would all too soon disappear until nothing but lines of stones remained, marking soldiers' graves in a foreign land many miles from home and their people.

Turning to leave, and free of inhibition, I placed my issue green plastic water bottle in its canvas webbing beside an unmarked grave, so bidding farewell, wishing I had had a chance to say so directly to RB when he'd been alive. A final gesture to a friend who'd once produced a similar bottle he'd hidden behind my Land Rover seat, on a desolate day when we'd much need for water, a long time ago at the edge of the Empty Quarter. I knew the bottle would disappear, not stolen but recycled by someone needing it more.

Recognised by those with so little, the Bedu use a single word, 'Maktub' – it is written.

JOHNSON – OLD FRIEND

And then there was Johnson, the dog I'd shared with Brian, who was left at Midway under the loose guardianship of the Sgts Mess with whom he was popular, if admittedly on a more 'tolerated responsibility' basis. Like any dog he'd been fond of being tickled behind ears, his head stroked and back rubbed.

Parting, he'd glanced up as if to say 'What the hell are we waiting for? Time for hunting!' My fondness for this dog went back to our days at Mudhai, when he'd run for miles beside my Land Rover, just out of dust range, long pink tongue flapping from the side of his mouth, glancing nonchalantly across at the slow moving vehicle, then ahead again in the direction we travelled. And all those times he'd kept vigil outside my tent, allowing only my soldiers to enter, growling at firqat whom no doubt he still regarded as adoo.

We'd shared water and food, spicy Arab dishes and chapati which seemed to do him no harm. I had often wondered what sort of diet he'd existed on before arriving at my tent door that morning just before eight, when as the Bedu would tell us, the sun becomes especially hot. Staring fixedly at me, he stood as if moulded to the sandy floor of the tent, his eyes daring me to shoo him away, before turning round a couple of times, scratching a hollow and settling down as if he'd always belonged there. This was his territory, I'd been adopted. Or more probably, 'Suit yourself, you can stay if you like'.

Gradually the realisation dawned I could no longer deny the day would arrive when I'd have to leave him behind. My consolation was he knew nothing of my imminent departure, it was just another patrol and I'd be back. Such is it with man's best friend, faithful, offering uncomplicated company. I hoped the best for him.

Possibly missing the three-way interaction he'd enjoyed between Brian, me and dog, Johnson began to roam from camp. Not long afterwards I learned he'd escaped one evening to wander across to the local Bedu encampment where, giving in to temptation, he'd allegedly helped himself to a prize, a goat kid. Momentarily forgetful of his whereabouts or perhaps grown carless through overconfidence, clearly he'd not realised he'd been seen. With no warning a single shot rang out, the high velocity bullet knocking Johnson over and over. As he tried to stagger up again, a second shot struck, killing him instantly. Rarely do Bedouin miss a target. Every bullet, either bought, gifted or stolen, has been treasured and carried, kept clean, oiled and ready for use. And always, always made to count.

Alone on the desert floor his body would have been left for carrion scavengers; Bedu don't bury dogs. 'Allah Kareem', Johnson – one hell-of-a-dog with that special dog's gift, unconditional trust.

FINAL DAYS

I'd returned to Midway via Salalah by Viscount first, then Skyvan for the last stretch back to base. I had bid Patrick farewell and good luck at the airport, he travelling back to organise relinquishing his post in the Trucial Oman Scouts, whilst I was bound for Midway and temporary handover to George Sommerville and Robin Amore, who'd hold the reins until Patrick's arrival in May.

Briefly I'd met up with the DR boys down from the north; it was good to see them again. Jonathan, back as a company commander, fit and recovered, told me over a beer in the Mess gardens, he had volunteered to take on responsibility for them in his spare time. It was a special place to us all. On my return I sent out some packets of seeds from the UK, annuals mainly, hoping they might germinate. Col. Nigel, Graham and Alan were there too, but not so Tom and Rick, absent recovering from wounds. And of course there were also a few new faces. Shortly afterwards Alan was involved in a fierce battle on the Qara jebel north of Salalah.

ALAN HOWARD WB

Alan had remained a close friend from our days at Akoot, but particularly since as acting 2 Coy commanders we'd dug in and suffered the first attacks on Simba's Black and White positions. On returning to the UK, Alan left the Royal Marines in 1974, to train and qualify as a Chartered Accountant with Deloittes in Rhodesia. There he volunteered for service with the Rhodesian Army Reservists alongside another Dhofar veteran, Spike Powell, who'd left SAF for the counterinsurgency against Mugabe's forces. Spike and his companions were aboard a civilian Rhodesian Airways Viscount, when their aircraft was shot down leaving Kariba National Park where they'd been holidaying. The terrorists used a SAM7 missile. It's a war crime to attack civilian aircraft.

As I was leaving Oman, Alan, now commanding 2 Coy DR, deservedly won the WB in a ferocious close contact at Wadi Jarsis, a wadi adjacent to where Mike Campbell had been killed two years earlier. Alan kindly let me have a copy of the contact report, it was almost to the day one year on from the Vimy Ridge battle. We've remained good friends since.

CONTACT REPORT: WADI JARSIS 24 APRIL 1973

In early March 1973, DR deployed 3 Coy to jebel positions known as the Dianas (1 & 2) against rocket and heavy machine gun attacks on Salalah.

On 24 April 1973 2 Coy relieved 3 Coy, who'd been relatively static during their deployment. The objective: take the offensive to the enemy. Attached was a subunit of BATT with an 81mm mortar in addition to 2 Coy's 4 x 81mm mortars.

Under daily 82mm mortar, and small arms attack, OC 2 Coy identified the enemy's OP 2km away on a wooded hill feature. The attacks fitted a pattern, which OC 2 Coy did not disturb, but encouraged.

On the night of 28/29 April, under cover of darkness, OC 2 Coy led 12 men onto the hill overlooking Wadi Jarsis, where they laid in cover until dawn, awaiting the adoo OP group, assumed to be max 3-4 men. At dawn 29 April, 12 enemy personnel approached the hill – a considerably larger group than expected, but 2 Coy's party retained the element of surprise. As the group approached DR opened fire at a range of 50m, killing or wounding all 12 men. As intelligence later confirmed, the party consisted of an Area Commander, a Sector Commander, the Area's Political Commissar, and other high ranking subunit commanders; their purpose, to recce 2 Coy's position on Diana 1, with a view to mounting a full scale assault. The significance of this was the party was not alone, but supported by over 100 adoo who immediately mounted a full scale assault on 2 Coy's position.

A pitched battle took place in the scrub at distances as close as 10m over several minutes, following which OC 2 Coy conducted a rapid withdrawal under cover of 2 Coy's mortars, which Major Howard had called down on his own position. As the group withdrew from the crown of the hill, the mortars were joined by artillery and jet strikes called down by Capt Rycroft RE, 2ic 2 Coy, based on the main position on Diana 1.

During the close quarter battle, a firqat soldier attached to 2 Coy, was shot in the face and arm beside Major Howard who was also shot in the arm. The withdrawal took over an hour to cover 2km, but all 2 Coy's personnel were successfully withdrawn, despite enemy attempts to cut them off.

Both casualties were casevaced, along with a prisoner whom 2 Coy had captured during the fighting.

Enemy casualties were in excess of 12 dead and 20 wounded, among them key enemy personnel mentioned above. Intelligence later confirmed this action and a patrol carried out by 3 Coy the following night near the same position, encountering another enemy recce party, deterred further large scale operations around Salalah.

SOLDIERS OF THE SULTAN

* * *

There were many people I wished to see before I left. Now began the rush to tidy up a multitude of paperwork for my incoming successor, aspects of our operations but additionally the minutiae of running a squadron and two recce platoons plus elements of two firqats spread between Jibjat road, Mudhai, Manston and Midway and out to Tudho. My days became filled with farewells, all taking longer than planned, for each knew we would not meet again. No longer the shared sangar, Saladin or Land Rover, patrol, ambush, or dusty convoy. The laughs and meals around a fading fire built between lumps of limestone, smoking frankincense attached to a cigarette tip meant to clear the chest, sharing water from charguls, fight or flight danger and quiet periods of reflection, these and the many frustrations stoically borne, would soon be endured and shared with someone else.

I had arranged for an 'indulgence flight' on a RAF C-130 Hercules, to carry my assorted kit assembled over two years. I still had my shrapnel-pitted timber rocket box requisitioned from SOAF, used for safe storage of morphine syrettes, grenades and personal kit. Repaired after Janook, although still visible, were splintered holes containing tiny steel fragments embedded in the timber. Now packed, it held my collection of geodes, flints, fossils and the Mesozoic Era limestone imprint, over which I'd shared stories with Ruqaishi's men. Amongst other essentials, a number of rocket and mortar fins, spent Shpagin and AK rounds, shrapnel mementos and four smashed Saladin sights. And finally, two spent 76mm brass shell cases cut down and remodelled as ashtrays. Souvenirs all too recent to be abandoned. My maps and diaries would go in there too.

In addition, I'd an Iranian rug and my well used woven blue cotton prayer mat, my mattress at night on patrols. There was no way the box, rugs, a rucksack and my Globetrotter suitcase would fall within the recognised weight limit permitted for a scheduled civilian aircraft. I faced an uncomfortable flight, yet the cost to my pocket for flying home by C-130 was just £3.00.

One of the many farewells was to Aziz Nasir, who after we'd dropped Nick across the Yemeni border had maintained guard whilst I slept, considering I was possibly exposed to bounty hunters. I was packing and on the point of closing the lid to the rocket box when he called by. This was one man to whom I owed a particular gratitude and dismantling my web belt I said 'Hadha lak' (this is for you) handing him my Bowie hunting knife.

At first, as tradition demanded, he firmly refused to accept the gift, handing the knife back to me saying he must decline, but I insisted he take it, and handed it back to him, handle first. A serious young man, I watched Aziz as a normally passive face broke slowly into his wide lopsided grin. Again attempting to refuse, he acknowledged I meant him to have the hunting knife as a parting gift. Had I produced Excalibur itself it could not have generated a greater glow of pride than Aziz expressed at that moment. Drawing the blade out of the sheath, he raised his hand, letting the sunlight catch the spotless Sheffield steel before slowly bringing the knife back down to catch his reflection in the mirror finish blade, as he had done on many occasions when cleaning this knife for me, on return from patrol or operations. How often they'd squabbled over who'd clean my rifle or submachine gun and occasionally my hunting knife on returning from patrols, ambushes and convoys! 'That's a number one knife, sahb, thank you. I will carry it with honour always.'

LAST PARADE

Farewell Parade – Midway Airfield, waiting for my aircraft to arrive.

I had seen and spoken with each of my Squadron individually, thanking and wishing them every good fortune ahead. It had been an emotional time. Finally, I'd retired to my bayt intending to finish packing only to find it'd all been done.

A last look around my rooms confirmed everything had been cleared away and faithfully packed by my orderly, Said Mohamed. My army issue prayer mat holed by shrapnel at Janook with the canvas tent door from Mudhai similarly holed, and which I'd used as an added ground sheet when sleeping in the desert, plus my Baluchi rug, a gift from Rasul Bux, all three had been wrapped into a neat roll and securely tied using a spent canvas .30 Browning ammo belt. I had to leave, the Skyvan was due shortly on the earth airstrip.

Washed, brushed and dressed in my cleanest uniform to impress my RAF hosts, I was ready to fly to Salalah where later that day I would be the sole guest passenger aboard a returning RAF C-130 bound for the UK.

Together with Said, I loaded my kit onto my Land Rover and drove off to wait for the Skyvan's arrival. I did wonder where everyone was, half expecting a few to come to my bayt for a final farewell, but no, there was no one. That's fine, I thought, all to say's been said.

When we drove out through the garrison gates I found to my astonishment, the Squadron, that is those still stationed at Midway, formed up on parade on the earth apron. 2/Lt Greadh Jummah brought them smartly to attention as we drew up. Greadh, our first commissioned Arab officer, was Khadim, ex-slave by birth. Selected on merit for officer training, he'd been commissioned into the ACS and was subsequently the first Omani officer to attend further training courses in

Jordan. Back at the Squadron he held his authority with a natural ease, devoid of hang-ups a few of his tribe expressed or suffered from.

As I climbed out of my Land Rover for the last time, I found myself in the invidious position, that of not being a natural speech maker and suddenly having to make one unprepared, to people whom I shared and owed a strong bond. I'd not realised parting would be so difficult. One last challenge. 'Dammit!' I swore gently under my breath, 'bloody ambushed!'

Swallowing hard against the restricting lump that'd now appeared in my throat threatening breathing, I blinked back firmly at wetting eyes hidden behind dark glasses.

Standing in front of the Squadron I realised not only was this the first full Squadron parade I'd taken, for most it was also the first time the whole squadron had been formed up for a parade. I solemnly returned their salute. I stood them at ease, hoping to relax the increasingly charged atmosphere. Pausing to collect myself, I cleared my throat and then made what I hoped sounded like a speech from the heart, praising and thanking them for all they'd, we'd, achieved together over the past two years. Unprepared, it was an unexpectedly difficult speech to make and I was thankful for my dark glasses, for the tears they hid. Seeing men's tears before me only compounded matters. There was a lot to remember, there'd been a lot we'd done. Two years ago, some had been just boy soldiers, joining up with the irrepressible enthusiasm and confidence of the very young, now hardened men.

As my speech ended, Greadh brought them up to attention and there rose a shout, 'Allah Ma'ak, Sahb!' (God be with you, Sahb!). In Arabia, etiquette demands you shake hands when you meet and likewise on departing. I now walked around to have a final word with each individual and shake each by the hand. That was especially emotional.

HANDOVER AND FAREWELLS

2/Lt Greadh Jumaah escorts me around as I say my farewells, shaking hands with Tpr Said bin Mohamed bin Harrib al Muqbali, once so small we'd used a folded blanket to raise him sufficiently to see through the driver's shut-down periscope. And informally, I bid farewell to LCpl Nasir bin Mohamed al-Salmi (Sultan's Commendation Medal), a man I'd trust with my life. To his right Ali bin Hamdan al Regathi (Sultan's Commendation Medal), who'd tried to beat the coconut-juice-drinking-record with dire effects, a guaranteed safe driver in many contacts. Then LCpl Hilal bin Ali as-Shezawi, who on patrol had knocked me unconscious, gashing my eyebrow against an unforgiving steel turret, as he dropped our Ferret into a Salalah Plains wadi having accidentally selected neutral gear. He'd called me father of the squadron and begged me not leave. And at his shoulder the incomparably courageous LCpl Abdullah bin Ali al Shibili, probably the best gunner in the Squadron at the time, later commissioned but sadly later killed in a Land Rover. Selfless, brave and honest to a man, it would be hard to meet the likes of them again.

RETURN TO UK

As I landed back in the UK, I learned the sad news my dear grandmother had died. I had missed her by two days. A focal point in my life, my one-time guardian. She who'd nursed my 10-year-old twin and I through childhood measles and bouts of homesickness for parents and home in Africa, had written faithfully each month. Someone who'd lost a brother and cousins during WW1, shortly afterwards a son and then acquaintances in WW2, knew the importance of letters. Hearing I'd won a medal, she wrote to confess how in great age the difference between life and death becomes paper thin and nothing would cause her greater pain than the thought of losing another to war. Unaware till then I had been on active service, despite staying with her during my one UK leave, her letter ended imploring I stay safe. My last letter back was unread. A quiet and much loved gentle Scottish lady who had made Oxford her home. Her funeral filled Iffley Church.

Not long after my return I received a letter from a girlfriend's father, John Cordle, writing on Houses of Parliament embossed headed paper. He was a senior politician and I'd been close to his daughter Roseanne (Moo) in Germany, when tragically she'd died shortly before I left for Oman. He wrote saying he'd heard I had returned to the UK 'covered in medals' and invited me for a celebratory welcome-back lunch, after which he'd be delighted to follow up with a tour of the Palace of Westminster. A most kind and generous invitation. However, rather selfishly, all I wished for was a little time and space to get my thoughts into some kind of perspective. It was an invitation I regret I was in no mood to take up and I declined.

To most level-headed people I suspect it's blindingly obvious, but still it hits like a thunderbolt, the sudden realisation you're not at war any more. Abruptly, no more casualties, it's safe to walk along footpaths, run through woods, cross or walk along ridgelines, use a torch after dark. Gone, the need to always carry a loaded weapon. Free from all that. Yet still to sink into my 25-year-old brain, the dark realisation of having survived, like others before me and many subsequently, ours was the burden of having achieved just that.

I had to move on.

33

VALETE

I rejoin my regiment in the UK. The episode at dinner when I realise my future lies elsewhere to soldiering. Denouement and the end of the Dhofar War. Sultan Said bin Taimur's response to 'The reason I like the British?' Reflections and That Question.

RUN-OFF

In June that year following a generous post-secondment leave, I rejoined my Regiment at Lulworth Gunnery School in Dorset. One evening, dining quietly in the Mess with Roddy Cordy-Simpson, my squadron leader, our attention was drawn to a conversation between a group of young officers at the mention of Oman.

Young officers are always loud. One remarked 'wasn't that the place where Offord was killed?' . . . 'Oh yes,' came the confident reply, 'bloody unlucky, stung by a scorpion'.

Sitting to my right, Roddy glanced at me then towards the group. 'Perhaps you should get the story straight if you're going to talk about Mike Offord, Paul was there.'

I looked at the finished products of Sandhurst, each exuding an arrogance and self-confidence born out of a testing two years of parade ground, classroom, gym and fieldcraft training. 'Shit,' I thought, 'they'd have been joining Sandhurst as we arrived in Oman.' Newly commissioned, still groomed by youth's impetuosity, they represented the promise for the future of the Royal Armoured Corps.

That afternoon these young officers had toured the Tank Museum at Bovington, an iconic institution run by a retired officer, Lt Col Eric Offord MC, Mike's father, badly burned in WW2. The Colonel, an institution himself, was greatly respected within the RAC.

As once Roddy, and as then I had been, this group were now attending their continuation training in tank warfare at the RAC Gunnery School; brand new Second Lieutenants in their early twenties. At 25, I was older by a year or two, but with the rank of acting captain (at the time unpaid, my return to regimental strength having left the Regiment's captain quota exceeded).

Surprised and a little taken aback at Roddy's sudden interjection, they now turned to me, raised eyebrows feigning interest, careful not to answer back given Roddy's rank. I shook my head; so this was the latest idle talk about Mike, an active service soldier pushed beyond limits, his death reduced to casual dinner table gossip. I hadn't realised there still remained a pulse to the anger felt that day last September. A scorpion sting? Fuck – he'd have survived that.

The small audience of fresh-faced individuals waited expectantly as I began to correct them on events. I told them the truth. And that no, Mike had not died from a scorpion sting. The large dining hall fell silent, as others at near tables listened in. Flooding back with a disturbing rawness, that moment of realisation and disbelief as I burst into Mike's room. I pushed my hands under the table, hoping to hide uncontrolled shaking and my voice strained the more I went on.

'What *is* wrong with me?' I wondered, realising I had meant to shock, to tell them as it was. Selfishly, I'd thought why should they get away with spreading fallacious stories? I doubted they understood the impact unexpected death had on the morale of battle-hardened men, those whose respect and admiration had been deservedly earned. And suicide against their religious beliefs.

Then I realised it had been the first time I'd spoken to anyone outside Oman about that day, other than to make mention briefly and without detail to Roddy, a close friend with whom I shared an office at the camp and was later best man at my wedding. A soldier who'd one day rise to high command as a Lieutenant General.

It only takes a chance remark, scent or taste or date and there in vivid recall, images flash. Today it was Mike very still, clutching his machine gun, remembered so strongly as if within touch. The past would never be less than it had been. Fearful of losing control, I realised it'd become difficult to breathe. The pressure in my chest felt it would burst through my ribcage, the antithesis to those same high velocity bullets and I knew then I would not continue soldiering.

Despite generous and kind efforts to persuade me to remain, I resigned my commission. Not long afterwards and like many after a short period as a civilian, I attempted to rejoin. With the support of a family friend, General Sir John Gibbon, it seemed a formality. But no, I hit a solid wall learning I was now considered medically downgraded, unable to rejoin a line regiment. The options offered were not that attractive and I returned to seeking a career elsewhere.

On leaving the army patched up by military doctors I'd no knowledge of any possible financial support or compensation that might have been available. And in a way I was fortunate, for had I been offered such support I wonder how it might have softened the willpower needed to study for endless professional qualifications and climb the greasy ladder of corporate life. Having nothing to fall back on can be the greatest incentive.

As many find, it's a curious business leaving the forces, you feel cut off, even unwanted, quite alone, needing to adjust to an entirely new environment. New rules, new standards. Many experience far greater traumatic events than I ever did and escape unmarked. More will inevitably experience worse in the future. Best not to become engrossed by it. You have to move forward.

Of SAF friends who stayed on in the forces, many retired early. In moments of reflection, I'd wonder if they and others with whom I'd served felt as I did. Did we ever really find fulfilment afterwards, to match that which we shared serving in a foreign army fighting a foreign war the consequences of which Western Democracies knew defeat was inconceivable? I realised I was undoubtedly exchanging a life of the remarkable for the everyday, the wild for the tame, but it was a challenge I was forced to take, that and to keep memories locked away.

DENOUEMENT – THE END OF THE WAR

With the arrival of Jordanian and Iranian troops together with vast quantities of serviceable ordnance, the 'unwinnable war' in Dhofar was eventually won. In December 1975 the Sultan declared the region safe for civil development. The Marxist communists' hold on Dhofar had been broken. The British would stay on to train Oman's armed forces which rapidly progressed to become fully Arab led, the country remaining to this day as one of Britain's staunchest allies in the Arabian Peninsula. A country that five years earlier seemed destined to a catastrophic future under communist rule, was free to emerge from its Middle Ages time warp, becoming the extraordinarily successful, open, peaceful and fair country it is today. In 2023 GDP was estimated at just over $122 billion, with state education and healthcare free across the country. A member of the United Nations (UN) and Arab League, Oman is a founder-member of the Gulf Cooperation Council, and a firm ally to the West.

So, what might have happened had Oman lost the war, at a time which saw a resurgence of Cold War tensions rising to levels not seen since the 1962 Cuban

Missile Crisis? The Russians or Chinese would have secured a warm water port commanding the choke point at the Straits of Hormuz. What could then have followed would have determined a radically different path to that achieved by Oman's victory.

Here there are messages for 21st century strategists. As of 24 February 2022 with the invasion of Ukraine, the free world faces a new Cold War that echoes the old, where proxy allies are armed and trained to attack Western allies and interests. The West's performance in responding to Iraq, and later the 'War on Terror' and Afghanistan, demonstrates the unique problems staid strategists face.

The respected Dr Simon Anglim, Teaching Fellow at the Department of War Studies at King's College London has written:

> "... the 'War on Terror' is not over and Allied performance in Afghanistan in particular indicates some considerable room for improvement in fighting it. So, careful study of possibly the most successful counterinsurgency in history might hint at good counterinsurgent practice, capacity building and repelling covert attack and the vital role of political leadership in hindering or enabling these." ... "Perhaps the main message of (Sultan) Qaboos's victory is that clear-minded leadership, based in moral and physical courage, is a prerequisite for any successful strategy".

* * *

And back in the summer of 1973 a young soldier destined for greatness joined the Armoured Car Squadron. With the promise of new equipment and given the choice of any army recruit under training, Patrick Brook selected a young Ahmed bin Harith bin Nasser al Nabhani for training as an armoured car driver. Rising through the ranks Ahmed Harith would one day become Chief of General Staff, Sultan's Armed Forces reporting direct to his Supreme Commander, Sultan Qaboos bin Said Al Said.

* * *

VALETE

'THE REASON I LIKE THE BRITISH?'

Almost fifty years on, the Head of the British Army is reputed to have said on lessons learned in Afghanistan,

> "... we came to realise that the main priority was to build up the Afghan Security Forces so they could independently manage their own. These lessons were learned in the East India Company and more recently in the Sultan's Armed Forces when keen young British officers led Oman's troops.

As Sultan Said bin Taimur had once remarked, "The reason I like the British? They lead from the front."

* * *

REFLECTIONS

"No one can live this life and emerge unchanged"

Wilfred Thesiger

Of those who served, very few threw in the towel. Amongst our number, some sought reduced secondments and a few on contract simply didn't return from leave; likewise, a number of soldiers absented themselves. There'd been those who deserted straight to the adoo, one after murdering his officer. All took weapons and in some cases vehicles with them. Most of these soldiers received recognition and were accepted into adoo ranks. Others faced summary execution. There were those who claimed the war wasn't worth fighting for. In doing so the deserters left behind those who, despite the high casualty rate and possible occasional doubts about decisions made by those in authority, remained committed and stayed on. Yet people did leave, to deal individually with their decisions and for some no doubt, nightmares.

So, what was it that made people stay? Adventure, courage, or perhaps fear of letting down those whom you'd got to know in Dhofar and in cases known through Sandhurst or Mons as fellow cadets? For the seconded British, was it fear of tarnishing a promising military career? After all, there was no other conflict other than Northern Ireland for a soldier to demonstrate potential. However, this of course did not apply to those on contract who'd already resigned British army commissions. Maybe it was a combination of the above, that and money, the wager of soldiering abroad for a lucrative return.

And what makes young men volunteer for war? Jingoism? Land of Hope and Glory, Rule Britannia? Or is it patriotism, mirroring the romantic notion of the schoolboys who fought in the world wars, joining with those seeking camaraderie amongst the trenches. A belief they can do something against wrong for good, rekindling the romance of a bygone age when young men trod on the edge of eternity. Political failure sets the traps, which, when sprung, it's the young who are sent to war and in the aftermath must deal with the consequences, each in their own way.

And eventually after it is all over, comes the sad discovery that different choices, occupations and chance combine to reduce contact with those whom once you knew as closely as any next of kin. Gradually the impossible becomes reality, the realisation somehow there's little left in common with past brothers in arms, other than the 'when we . . .' and 'do you remember . . .' conversations. Sworn friendships slowly fade, revived briefly in stilted conversations during the occasional reunion dinner. Christmas cards slip. The silences between become more difficult to deal with, until in time friends become no more than numbers in an old address book, or occasional email.

THAT QUESTION

The after-dinner speeches drone on. I am employed. I am earning again, albeit a pittance measured against previous salaries. I can manage, it's a start. No longer dependent upon medical diagnoses, I have my self-esteem returned. My torso, front and back ache, still stiff, sore and lined with neatly stitched long purple scars, evidence of recent operations. The surgeon's stitching is immaculate, he could have made it big on Savile Row.

I am attending an institutional dinner in Glasgow where every insurance company and affiliated organisation is represented, seated at long trestle tables, row upon row upon row. There are probably near to 600 seated in the hall. To my left, newly met work colleagues and future friends, to my right a few small-minded strangers. And it's that question again, reaching through the smoke haze, exhaust fumes expelled from mouths of braggarts chewing on pretentious cigars, others exhaling fumes from filter tipped cigarettes. Everyone seemed to be smoking. Was it to calm nerves? What was it they feared? My dinner jacket would stink tomorrow.

Considered too newly joined to warrant a hotel room, I am stone cold sober as I have to drive back to my Edinburgh flat that night. Pleasantries have been exchanged with those on my right, but little more and I've watched, observing the throng, not yet recognising their ilk. I half listen to the corporate speak, a new language to be learned. After five months handicapped by debilitating kidney damage, I have begun the fight back from isolation faced by many an army leaver finding work in an employment wasteland where soldiering standards don't always fit.

On paper, unqualified means a mountain of professional exams ahead, starting again on the lowest rung of a new career's ladder. A veteran at just 26. Once again new recruit. Watchful, on guard.

The question this time had been delivered from a diner in the adjacent party across the table. An individual grown weary of his colleagues and who had eavesdropped on Ross's earlier question. Presumably hoping to impress, make a point, he leant forward unexpectedly, as if unable to contain himself any longer, inquisitiveness winning, self-control exhausted. I watched his corporate-lunch-bulk spread onto the table to spill across his side plate, button-bursting stretched white shirt and hired dinner jacket neatly squashing half-finished ripe blue cheese and biscuits. Gesturing with fat fingered cigar, a face flushed and brain fogged by wine, there came an utterance. Slurred speech, offensive in its demanding inflection, scoffed, adding nuance to the earlier question,

> '. . . So, you say you were in the Army, eh? . . . Yer, reckon could've hacked that . . . last of the honourable professions they say . . . Trained to kill eh?
>
> Well my man . . . emm, tell me . . . did you ever . . . emm, actually ever *kill* anyone . . . ?'

Why the challenge? Hell, I didn't know this man from Adam. Yet the sarcasm? Obvious with the 'honourable professions' gibe. Fleetingly I wondered whether my firm worked for his? Did he pay our fees? Best not rock the boat. The clipped Glaswegian intonation only added greater emphasis to "Army" and the overstress on "kill". What an idiot.

I met his gaze and stared back in silence, as drifting back came that mad Irishman Ray Kane's brush-off riposte. I couldn't help my smile. 'F... you' I thought, at the same time conceding I'd better do something about my f...... language.

My inquisitor's words hung suspended in the air, unanswered. All that stuff was locked away in a rocket box; I had a life to get on with.

The Dhofar Campaign Medal

And the night shall be filled with music,
And the cares that infest the day,
Shall fold their tents, like the Arabs,
And as silently steal away.
              Henry Wadsworth Longfellow.

POSTSCRIPT

On Tuesday 24th October 2023 a short ceremony and service of dedication was held at the Royal Memorial Chapel, the Royal Military Academy Sandhurst, when the Sultan's Armed Forces' Roll of Honour was re-dedicated. Fresh amendments corrected dates when men had died and righting a wrong, added missing names to those we should not forget. Included in their number, Captain Geoff Mawle late of the Duke of Edinburgh's Royal Regiment and Dhofar Gendarmerie, and Captain Mike Offord, Sultan's Commendation Medal, late of the 1st Royal Tank Regiment and Armoured Car Squadron, The Sultan's Armed Forces, together with others killed whilst on duty in Oman.

    Forever young, remembered, not forgotten.

Appendices
THE SALADIN ARMOURED CAR

Alvis Car and Engineering Company Ltd produced the Saladin, a six wheeled light armoured car with a big gun identified by its official ordnance title as: (FV601B) Fighting Vehicle: Armoured Car Heavy 76mm Gun.

The second of two prototypes, FV601B was designed as a mobile platform for a 76mm main armament plus two .30mm Browning belt fed machine guns. These punchy vehicles were a huge and tactically vast improvement on the bouncy little Ferret Scout Cars. In homage to British Fighting Vehicles, I offer a brief résumé of armoured vehicle history.

The use of fighting vehicles probably dates back 4,000 years when horse-drawn war chariots were used by Egyptian and Chinese empires. Soldiers had long used shields for protection, and ideas for protected battle carts led to designs by many including Leonardo da Vinci. But it was the 20th Century wars that spearheaded development of the self-propelled fighting vehicle.

In February 1915 with stalemate on the Western Front, First Lord of the Admiralty Winston Churchill created the Landship Committee to design and develop armoured fighting vehicles capable of breaking through German barbed wire whilst remaining impervious to machine gun fire. The committee started with just three members:

1. Chairman: Sir Eustace d'Eyncourt: Director of Naval Construction, a Royal Navy architect and engineer.
2. Flight Commander Thomas Hetherington: Commissioned into the 18th Hussars, he'd been an exceptional horseman. A riding accident leaving him unable to ride, he gained his flying certificate and transferred to the Royal

Naval Air Service (RNAS). In November 1914 the RNAS built 15 Wolseley armoured cars. These were split into troops of five cars, to form The Armoured Car Squadron. Their primary task was to rescue airmen forced to land behind enemy lines. Prominent amongst the first section commanders were Hetherington and the Duke of Westminster. Together they set about aggressively harassing the German advance into Belgium until with the advent of trench warfare, armoured cars became no longer viable. In February 1915 the two placed a proposal for an armoured landship to Winston Churchill.
3. Colonel Wilfred Dumble: A former Royal Engineer now serving with the Naval Brigade. Before the war he had managed the London Omnibus Company. In 1915 as part of a team looking to develop cross-country vehicles for the Army, he was asked to join the Landship Committee which gave us the first tank.

With the advent of WW2, the various military design establishments were consolidated, first into the Department of Tank Design (DTD) in 1940 which spawned the Fighting Vehicles Proving Establishment (FVPE) based at Chertsey and the tank testing area at Chobham Heath. The Wheeled Vehicles Experimental Establishment (WVEE) followed, merging with the DTD to form the Fighting Vehicle Design Department (FVDE) in 1948. The Government's love of acronyms lives on today, as in any large organisation, seemingly matched only by small empires.

* * *

Designs for the Saladin date from the end of hostilities in 1945, when the concept was for a four-man vehicle with a 2 pdr gun, the already proven 40mm cannon, designed in the 1930s by the Swedish arms manufacturer AB Bofors, the Bofors gun. A contract was awarded to Alvis in 1947 and a mock-up completed in 1948. There followed a delay in production when it was decided to upgrade the armament to the 76mm gun then under development. The L5A1 76mm gun was designed to be fired mechanically using a foot-firing pedal. The recoil system is hydro-pneumatic. To initiate firing, the breech is opened pulling back on a mechanical lever beside the breechblock and a round loaded by the vehicle's commander. During run-out the breech is reopened by a semi-automatic cam and the brass empty case forcibly ejected; the breech then remains open ready for reloading.

Finally in 1953 the first of two prototypes was produced, designated Fighting Vehicle 60-FV601A.

However, faced with the increasing demands of the Malayan Emergency (1948-1960), the call for Armoured Personnel Carriers in place of Saladins forced Alvis to concentrate production to the Saracen. With Alvis now fully committed, pre-production work on Saladins was transferred to the military wing of motor and aircraft manufacturer, Crossley Motors of Manchester (pioneers in the development and production of the iconic double decker bus). Crossleys had sold their aviation business to Fairey Aviation, but motor manufacturing continued with development of military vehicles including the FV601. In 1958, production of the Saladin returned to Coventry, where between then and 1970 Alvis built just under 1200 Saladins, selling to the British and various armies across the globe.

A summary of the Alvis Saladin's technical details is shown as follows:

weight	11.6 tonnes
length	4.93 metres
width	2.54 metres
height	2.39 metres
crew	3 (driver, gunner, commander)
armour	8mm to 32mm
primary armament	L5A1 76mm rifled gun
	Ranges: 2,000m direct / 7,000m indirect
ammunition:	full load
primary armament:	43 x HE/T, HESH, and 3 Canister rounds
secondary armament:	two .30 mm Browning machine guns, Range: 2,000m direct
	one coaxial to the primary armament:
	second fitted in front of commander's turret:
	each – 2750 canvas belted rounds
	12 x forward facing phosphorus grenade launchers
periscopes	4 x forward periscopes: commander
	2 x rear facing periscopes: commander
	1 x forward periscope sight: gunner
	1 x forward periscope: driver
engine	Rolls-Royce B80 Mk 6A. 5.67 litres, V8, 170 hp
	suspension 6 x 6 drive wheels
tyres	rubberised run-flats
range	400km
speed	72km/h (tarmacadam roads)

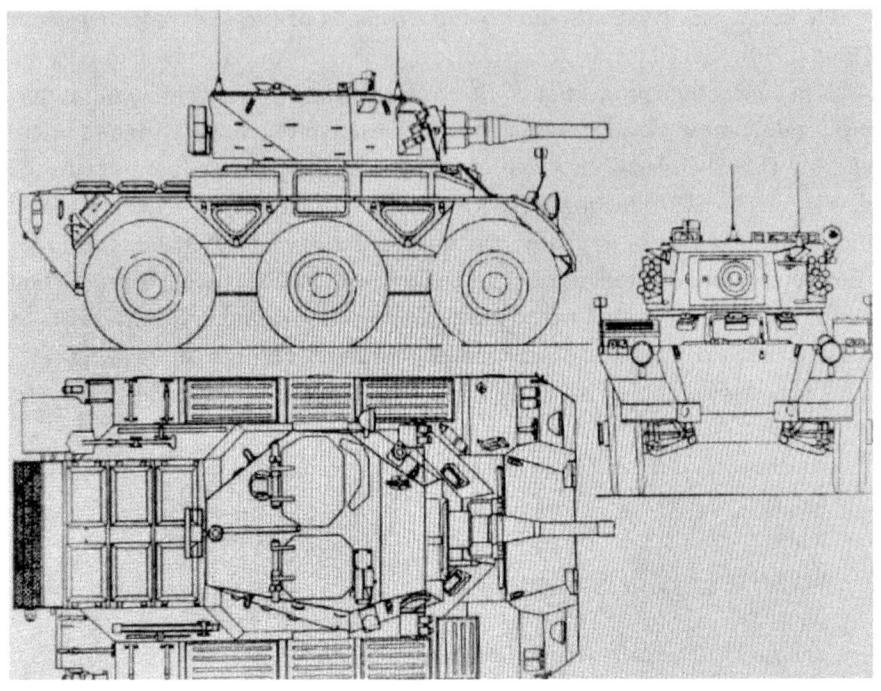

The FV601 Alvis Saladin Armoured Car (Soviet technical drawing).

Glossary

MILITARY CALLSIGNS

9 – Officer commanding (Sunray)
9a – Second-in-command (Sunray minor)
60 – Reconnaissance Platoon/Troop
Roger – (message/order) understood
Wilco – (message/command) will obey
Acorn – Intelligence Officer
Foxhound – Infantry
Golf – Artillery
Holdfast – Engineers
Tango – Armour
Rickshaw – Ordnance Officer
Shelldrake – Artillery
Starlight – Medical Officer
Red – Muscat Regt
Grey – Jebel Regt
Green – Northern Frontier Regt
Sand – Desert Regt
Ironside – OC Armoured Cars

MAPS

Oman	page 5
Op Vulture area & route to Habarut	page 304
Simba positions 17 April 1972	page 376

Akoot and DFs	page 387
Battle for Vimy Ridge	page 389
Firqat FHG attack at Habarut	page 417
Attacks on Janook	page 447
The raid into Yemen	page 533
Jibjat road recce	page 576
Example of 1:250,000 scaled map	page 596

ACS	The Armoured Car Squadron – Al Musaffahaat
Adoo	Enemy
Al-Gamal	Dhofari for camel
Al-Haar	Heat
Al-Khareef	The monsoon mists arrive each June, lasting until September
Al-Qamr	Moon
Al-Hilaal	Crescent moon
Al-Badr	Full moon
Al-Matar	Rain
An-Nagma	Star
Ash-Shams	Sun
AK 47	Russian automatic assault rifle designed 1947. Chinese copy – AK56
Ayn	Beautiful (place)
BAF	Bayt Al Falaj – Headquarters, Sultan's Armed Forces
BAOR	British Army of the Rhine, deployed in Western Germany
BATT	British Army Training Team. The name under which the SAS and their attached personnel operated
Barusti	Shelter constructed from palm fronds over timber frame
Bayt	Room, house
Blind	Unexploded bomb, or shell
Burmail	45 gallon drum. Apart from its normal fuel or water carrying role, also used to build defences and blast protection walls
CAD	Civil Aid Department
Contact	Enemy engagement
CENTO	Central Treaty Organisation
DG	Dhofar Gendarmerie – Gundaarnat Dhuffaar
DR	Desert Regiment – Firqat As-Sahraa
Falaj	Water channel
Fee layl	That night
Fee yawm	That day

GLOSSARY

Firqat	Group of irregulars working with SAF, normally Coy strength Many were ex-adoo, now fighting for the Sultan. The enemy also called their sub-units Firqats
FAB	Firqat al Badiyah
FAN	Firqat al Nasr
FHG	Firqat al Hudud al Gharbiyah
FTZ	Firqat Tariq bin Ziyad
FOO	Forward Observation Officer. An artillery officer attached to an infantry regiment to direct artillery fire
Ghazal	Gazelle, buck
Hedgehog	Salalah Plains defensive location, built using burmails filled with sand, roofs reinforced with iron pickets topped with sandbags, the whole usually consisting of a series of OP towers and sangars protected by Dannert wire fencing
IAMC	Indian Army Medical Corps
JR	Jebel Regiment – Firqat Al-Gibaal
Jaysh	Army
Jebali	Mountain people
Jundee	Soldier
Khareef	Dhofar monsoon
Khadim	Slave
Khunjar	Omani curved dagger
Khor	Wadi estuary into open sea
KIA	Killed in Action
Loomi	Fresh lime drink
LRDG	Long Range Desert Group (WW2 British reconnaissance and raiding unit)
Majlis	Meeting, conference
MR	Muscat Regiment – Firqat Masqat
No Duff	Clarification - not a drill
NFR	Northern Frontier Regiment – Firqat Al-Hudood Ash-Shimaliyya
OA	Oman Artillery – Midfaeeyat Oman
OG	Oman Gendarmerie – Gundaarat Oman
OP	Observation Post – a position from which to observe enemy movement, or to direct artillery fire
PDRY	People's Democratic Republic of Yemen
PFLOAG	Popular Front for the Liberation of the Occupied Arabian Gulf
PFLO	Popular Front for the Liberation of Oman
PMN - 1	Soviet anti-personnel mine

Qaa'id	Leader
RAC	Royal Armoured Corps
Roulement	Rotation – of battalions / SAS BATT teams
Rub Al Khali	The Empty Quarter
SAF	Sultan's Armed Forces
Sahb	Sir
Sangar	Rock and random stone built buttress, some tin roofed over iron stakes, supporting layers of rock and earth against mortars
SEP	Surrendered Enemy Personnel
Shemagh	Arabian headgear
Shimaal	Sandstorm winds from the north
Shpagin	12.7mm Heavy Machine Gun – Russian and copied by Chinese
SHQ	Squadron Headquarters
SIO	Sultanate Intelligence Officer
SKS	Russian semi-automatic rifle in use since 1943. Copied by Chinese
Souk	Marketplace
Tafaddal	Entreatment to join – generally for a meal, coffee or conversation
Tango	Generic military callsign for Armour – Armoured Cars
TM46	Soviet anti-tank mine
Topkhana	The Oman Artillery (OA)
VOR	Vehicle Off Road
Wali	Local Regional Governor
Wizar	Sarong like garment (Kanga in Swahili)
WIA	Wounded in Action

SOURCES

RAC Centre Bulletins
SAF Journals – 1971-73
13th/18th Royal Hussars QMO 1947-1992 (The Light Dragoons Charitable Trust 1996) – Eric Hunt
The Secret War – David Arkless
Where Soldiers Fear To Tread – Ranulph Fiennes
Atlantis of the Sands – Ranulph Fiennes
Coup D'état Oman – Ray Kane
Storm Front – Rowland White
Looking For Trouble – Peter de la Billière
Sultan in Oman – Jan Morris

GLOSSARY

Seven Pillars of Wisdom – T.E. Lawrence
Arabia Through The Looking Glass – Jonathan Raban
The Consolations of Physics – Tim Radford
SAS Secret War – Tony Jeapes
In The Service Of The Sultan – Ian Gardiner
Oman's Insurgencies – JE Peterson
Dr Simon Anglim – Department of War Studies, King's College London
FCO Archives

Acknowledgements

Louise Hodgson, Toby Hodgson ABH, APHH, AIWH, Sandy Blackett, Alan Howard, Tom Bremridge, Rick Williams, Tim Cornwell, Alan Oliver, George (Wimpy) Waite, Colin Dick, Pete Greaves, Geoff Begley, Nigel Knocker, Bryan Ray, Fergus Mackain-Bremner, Ben Hodson, Ray Kane, Jonathan Gough-Crispin, William Hodgson, Ann Gude, Odeyne Griffiths, Catherine Maddocks, Euan & Bethia Colam, Clare Jayes, Ranulph Fiennes, Patrick Brook, David McFadden, Chris Long Price, Charlotte McKim-Furse, Lizie Furse, Roddy Cordy-Simpson, Robert ffrench-Blake, Adrian Wright, Dick Rowe, Gerry Loughney, Beryl Lilley, Douglas Simpson, Jonathan Clark, David Martin, Paul French, John Shaw, Robert Morris, Jon Ballantyne, David Arkless, Sally McBean, John Balding, Stephen Hayes, Gordon Allen.

The men of The Armoured Car Squadron and those of NFR, DR, MR and JR recce platoons with whom we served.

And Ruth Lunn , Judith Barker and Jay Thompson of UK Book Publishing for their help and support.

REMEMBERED

Lou Costello, Mike Campbell, Tim Taylor, Geoff Mawle, Mike Offord, Huw Jones, Rasul Bux, Donald Rankin, Paul Wright, Johnny Braddell Smith, Abdullah Ali, Nasir Mohamed, Aziz Nasir, Mubarik Musalim, Jan Mohammed, Geoff Harcourt, Alex Lamond, Robert Tomlinson, John Martyn-Fisher, Graham Sherwell, Paul Mangin, Babu Chacko, Gerry Fyffe, Brian Jayes, Spike Powell, David Nicholls, Harry Wooley, Nick Downie, Martin Ward-Harrison, Fiona Warton, Dick Morgan-Evans, Noel McGrath, Mike Ryan, Stan Piórkowski, Pete Minvalla, Johnson.

Index

Abdul Wathik, *LCpl* 43, 45, 56, 97, 98, 112, 113, 122, 127, 133, 134, 135 - 137, 140 - 142, 581, 582

Abdul, *CSM Majiid* 471

Abdul, *L/Cpl, Raja bin Faraz* 43, 82, 97, 122, 134, 136, 142

Abdullah *Sgt, bin Hamed* 327, 513, 525, 566, 591

Abdullah, *Sgt, bin Ali* 315, 319 , 404, 449

Abdullah, *Tpr, LCpl, bin Ali al-Shibili* 43, 45, 46, 56, 111, 115, 121, 134, 136, 149, 150, 153, 187, 197, 300, 328, 329, 332, 334, 339, 342, 344, 346, 351, 379, 389, 397, 400, 520, 525, 588, 589, 637, 656

Aberdares 279

Aboub, *Sgt, al-Obaida* 588

Abu Dhabi 4

Acacia *(Vachellia tortilis)* 104 - 595

Acland, *Sir Arthur (AA)* 77

Adam 118

Addis Ababa 265

Aden Protectorate 530, 531

Adonib 20, 98, 112, 121, 122, 136, 137, 152, 169, 176, 184, 262, 338, 502, 520 - 523, 528, 585, 587

Afghanistan 642, 643

Aflaj 71

African grass rat *(Arvicanthis niloticus)* 171

Ahmed, *Lt Gen, bin Harith bin Nasser al-Nabhani* 642

Ahmed, *Pte bin Salim* 326

AIHW 321, 483, 492, 583, 604, 656

Air Dispatch 439

Airey and Wheeler 31

Airworks 71

Akoot v, vi, 14, *et passim*

Akrotiri Hospital, *RAF* 263, 583, 584

Al Haraisi, *Pte, bin Musalim* 588

Al Khalas, *dates* 46

Al Negd 304

Al-Mu'tasim, *Lt, bin Hamood* 573 - 575

Al-Ruqaishi, *2/Lt, Mohammad bin Said bin Zahran* 327, 329, 330, 404, 408, 410 - 412, 459, 460, 520, 523, 524, 555, 562 - 566, 570, 575, 576 - 580, 594, 595, 600 - 606

Ali, *Pte Mubarik bin* 588

Ali, *Pte, Achmed bin* 588, 589

Ali, *S/Sgt, bin Khamees* 361, 363

Ali, *Tpr bin Mubarik* 565

Ali, *Tpr, bin Hamdan al-Regathi* 43, 45, 107, 136, 138, 153, 173, 187, 221, 251, 300, 327, 328, 329, 332, 339, 346, 379, 389, 397, 406, 444, 481, 489, 588, 637

All-African (1st) Trade Fair 266

Aloe Vera 367, 368
Amilhayt, *waterhole* 311
Amoore, *Capt Robin* 607
Anderson, *Maj RGH, (The Drum) Garrison Commander BAF* 176, 177
Anglim, *Dr Simon* 642, 655
Anglo-American War Machine 415, 425
Anopheles Mosquito 80
Ansell, *Lt Col John* 527
Aplin, *Capt Bob* 121, 137, 611
Aqabat Thifah 149, 150
Arab League 4, 382, 422, 641
Arabian Gazelle, *(Gazella arabica)* 153, 287, 436, 473, 476, 575 - 578, 653
Arabian Pipistrelle Bat 308
Arabian Sea 36, 71, 78, 136, 222, 368
Arkless, *Sgt David (Geordie)* 407, 439, 453, 455, 634, 656
Arusha 269, 272, 277, 278, 280, 282,
Arusha Chini 278
Arzat 15, *et passim*
Ash Shimaal 302, 590, 616, 617, 654
Ashcroft, *Lord Michael* 528
Austin, *Capt Mike* 121, 137, 611, 613, 621
Azan, *Pte, bin Mubarik* 368
Aziz, *Tpr, bin Nasir* 476, 530, 533, 536, 537, 540, 542, 543, 545, 634, 635, 656
Baba the Elephant 286
Baez, *Joan* 162
Baiza 37, 248, 388
Baker, *Alix* 343
Balaklava 172, 527, 565, 567
Ball, *Maj Mike* 613
Balmoral 494
Balochistan 115, 177
Baluch Guard 469, 478, 483, 526, 546
Banagi 287, 288
Barker-Schofield, *Maj Ray* 170

Barr and Stroud 127, 387, 402
Barracuda 130, 131, 132
Barrons, *Gen Sir Richard* 355
Barut, *Pte, bin Mubarik* 604, 607
Battle of Imjin River 27, 436, 490
Bayt al Falaj 26, 32 - 34, 70, 81, 82, 87, 113, 117, 176, 177, 243, 298, 458, 485, 515, 519, 567, 626, 627, 652
Bayt Kathir, *tribe* xviii, 139, 305, 310, 320, 325, 326, 329, 420
Bayt Qatan 135
Bayt Za'binawt, *tribe* 420
Beaconsfield 26, 27, 47, 206
Beadle, *S/Sgt Geoff* 26, 482
Beau Geste 69, 78
Beaver, *de Havilland DHC-2* 316, 323, 330, 337, 339, 361, 508, 584, 589, 619
Begley, *Sgt Geoff* 26, 48, 49, 404, 449, 451, 459, 507, 508, 512, 656
Beirut 296
Bennett, *Sgt Bob* 488
Bethlehem 264
Beverly & Joan 272, 273, 275, 277
Bid Bid 41, 59, 65, 69, 70, 73, 81, 91, 118, 188, 541, 606
Bidmead, *Capt Steve* 64
Bingol 108
Bismarck Hut 269, 271, 273
Black, *OP Simba position* 343, 344, 347, 355, 360, 361, 363, 368, 375
Blackett, *Capt Sandy* 27, 31, 40, 46, 75, 85, 87, 92, 111, 113, 150, 201, 206, 250, 256, 321, 322, 382, 407, 468, 494, 496, 497, 541, 574, 575, 587, 588, 604, 656
Blatch, *Capt Jeremy* 335
Blood money *(Deya)* 336, 548, 574, 575
Blunt, *Anne, Baroness Wentworth* 563
Body armour 130, 146, 147

INDEX

Boers 359
Bofors, *40mm gun* 15, 648
Booby trap 104, 226, 326
Boom, *Arabian dhow* 174, 587, 588
Bougainvillea, (*Bougainvillea glabra*) 82, 571
Bounty Hunters 530, 540, 634
Bovington, *Camp* 467, 498, 639
Boy's Brigade 261
Bracketed 207, 214, 387, 413, 428, 429, 430, 437, 442
Braddell Smith, *Maj Johnny* 548, 571, 572, 656
Bramwell, *Peter* 287, 288
Bremridge, *Capt Tom* 27, 31, 32, 35, 41, 46, 58, 66, 70, 150, 180, 181, 197, 199, 202, 205, 207, 208, 216 - 218, 233, 246, 250, 252, 256, 262, 266, 267, 269, 270 - 275, 279, 280, 282 - 284, 286, 288 - 290, 293 - 297, 299, 332, 341 - 344, 348, 351, 368, 371, 375, 377, 407, 625, 632, 656
Brice-Bennet, *Peggy* 269
British East India Company 121
British Protectorate 3, 275, 530
British Red Cross 108, 295
Broadside, *Op* 166, 188, 510
Brockbank, *Maj Gen John* 567, 568
Brocklehurst, *Maj Arthur* 498, 502
Brook, *Maj Patrick* 522, 624 - 629, 632, 642, 656
Brookwood Cemetery 547
Buckingham Palace 190
Bullah, *LCpl Habeeb* 192
Buraimi, *Al Buraimi Oasis* 4
Burayk, *Wali, bin Hamud Al-Ghafiri* 579
Burton, *Richard Francis* 563
Bustani 224
Butler, *Eric* 604

Butler, *Mike* 573
Butt, *Maj Charles* 584, 602, 608
Bux, *LCpl Pir* 520
Bux, *LCpl Rasul* 120, 121,198, 475, 482 , 485, 513, 546, 630, 635, 656.
Bux, *Tpr Rasul* 198, 513, 523,
Calcutta, *Black Hole* 535
Camel milk 142, 320, 326, 535, 579, 600, 601, 621
Camel Spider, (*Solifugae*) 69, 70, 80, 470
Campbell, *Capt Mike* 24, 47, 48, 85, 91, 314, 632, 656
Canadians 277
Cape Buffalo, (*Syncerus caffer caffer*) 280, 290
Capstan 381, 413, 415, 427, 487, 497
Caribou, *de Havilland DHC-4* 15, 70, 73, 117, 203, 250, 374, 381, 386, 405, 408, 467, 509
Carter, *Lt Anthony* 24, 25
Carver, *Field Marshal Lord Michael* vii, 539
Casevac 15, 26, 198, 257, 378, 391, 393, 394, 410, 436, 495, 507, 508, 513, 551, 599
Castro, *Fidel* 359
Casuarina trees 508, 630
Caucasian condition 255
Cerberus 621
Chacko, *Capt Babu* 41, 61, 62, 180, 181, 194, 237, 242, 243, 255, 341, 468, 537, 544, 656
Chagga, *tribe* 269, 271, 272
Chagul 6, 51, 52, 63, 173, 232, 397, 401, 402, 468, 475, 476, 550, 621, 634
Chameleon, *Sibelius* 104 - 106, 111, 112, 116, 157, 166, 172 - 174, 313
Charles Kendall *and Partners* 16
Che Guevara Unit 19

Cheesman's Gerbil, *(Gerbillus cheesmani)* 538
Chieftan tanks 522
China 3, 6, 8, 18 - 20, 281, 282, 425
Cholera 58, 61, 62, 64, 483 - 485
Christmas *1971, 1972* 246, 251, 418, 572, 578, 583 - 585, 588, 644
Churchill, *Sir Winston* 85, 488, 647, 648
Ciguatera, *food poisoning* 132
Civil Aid Centre 309, 310, 314, 652
Claire 377
Cleghorn, *LCpl, A&SH* 322
Cockroaches 172, 209, 237, 266, 327
Coconut, *(Cocos nucifera)* 73, 110, 153, 173, 327, 637
Cohen, *Leonard* 626
Cold War 7, 8, 249, 501, 641, 642
Colley, *Maj Hugh* 342, 361, 369, 372
Colobus Monkey, *(Colobus guerezais)* 280
Confidential Reports 324, 325, 626
Cordle, *John* 638
Cordle, *Roseanne* 638
Cordy-Simpson, *Lt Col John* 18
Cordy-Simpson, *Maj Roddy* 552, 639, 640, 656
Cornwell, *Maj Tim* vi, 23, 26, 42, 44, 48 - 50, 59, 61, 62, 82, 86, 116, 118, 119, 142, 166, 167, 176, 178, 179, 184, 193 - 195, 197, 214, 217, 221, 222, 224, 257, 299, 300, 302, 306 - 308, 316, 317, 319 - 321, 323 - 326, 328, 329, 333, 334, 387, 391, 404 - 406, 408, 410 - 413, 418, 428, 431, 435, 439, 441, 445, 446, 449, 450, 451, 456, 460, 462, 465, 468, 469, 471 - 473, 478, 491, 494, 498, 501, 502, 504 - 510, 512 - 516, 518, 520 - 523, 565, 599, 600, 628, 629, 656

Costello, *Sgt Lou (Irish)* v, xiv, 26, 42 - 46, 48, 49, 52, 56, 57, 64, 65,72, 74, 79, 82, 97, 98, 107, 109, 112 - 115, 118 - 120, 122, 124, 126 - 128, 133, 136, 149, 150, 158, 161,163, 166, 169, 171 - 173, 179, 185, 187, 188, 193, 194, 197, 223, 243, 247, 303, 307, 308, 313 - 315, 319, 323 - 325, 327, 330, 332, 344 - 337, 341, 346, 351, 379, 384, 386, 388, 390, 391 - 393, 395 - 397, 400 - 406, 429 - 432, 434, 438, 443 - 446, 449, 450, 453, 455, 459, 460 - 462, 469, 478 - 482, 491, 505 - 508, 518, 524 - 527, 532, 540, 541, 546, 567, 569, 594, 607, 609, 656
Counterinsurgency 3, 540, 632, 642
Court Martial 83, 140, 166, 176 - 178, 211, 518, 529, 559
Cowie, *Capt Nigel* 266
Cowie, *Mervyn* 266
CSAF, *Creasey, Major General Tim* 501, 520, 624, 626, 627, 628,
CSAF, *Graham, Brig John* 21, 71, 72, 96, 100 - 102, 109, 143, 152, 178, 256, 348, 410, 423, 489, 493, 494
Cuba 20, 359
Cuban Missile Crisis 641
Cultural Revolution 79
Cyclops, *Op* 335, 338, 341
Cyprus 256, 262, 263, 578, 582, 583, 585
D-Notice 3, 22, 183
Dad, *S/Sgt, Raman* 370
Dannert wire 111, 263, 366, 463, 487, 683
Dar-es-Salaam 32, 50, 55, 63, 85, 130, 131, 278
Darius I 359
Darwin, *Charles* 99
David, *Captain Romily* 495, 580,

INDEX

Dawson, *Capt Gordon* 320, 321, 328, 473, 476, 477, 484, 518, 523, 531, 536, 600, 609, 610, 611
de la Billière, *Lt Col Peter* 164, 487, 654
Dead Sea 264
Dean, *Captain John* 574, 589, 590
Deathstalker Scorpion, (*Leiurus quinquestriatus*) 70, 190, 298, 324, 325, 479, 621, 639, 640
Deloitte's 632
Desert Black snake, (*Walterinnesia aegyptia*) 55
Devil's Delight, *Op* 211
Dhalkut 335, 336
Dhib, *Op* 530, 539, 540
Dhofar Campaign Medal 50, 453, 516, 646
Dhofar Gendarmerie, *DG* 15, 43, 45, 69, 74, 79, 80 - 81, 96, 97, 99, 103, 104, 107, 110, 113 - 115, 123 - 125, 141, 142, 144, 151, 157, 160 - 162, 167, 169, 170, 172, 178, 185, 420, 421, 423, 486, 581, 646, 652
Diamond, *Neil* 626
Diana 498
Diana 1, *position* 633
Dick, *Sgt Colin* 472, 501, 507, 508, 512, 573, 587, 656
Dien Bien Phu 21, 77
Distinguished Service Medal *(Gallantry) WKhM (G)* 233, 453, 462, 472, 590
Distinguished Service Medal *(WKhM)* 81, 177, 189, 341, 416, 519, 522
Diya 574, 575
Dodoma 282
Donkeys 192, 197, 322, 332, 336 - 338, 527
Dorchester Hotel 547

Douglas-Hamilton, *Oria, Ian, Saba, Dudu* 284, 285, 286
Douglas-Home, *Sir Alec* 422
Downie, *Capt Nick* 484, 530, 532, 537, 539, 611, 613, 656
Dragon, *Op* 602, 611, 612, 614
Du Pre 26
Dubrulle, *Sgt Paul* 433
Dülfer, *Hans* 201
Dülfersitz 201
Dumble, *Col Wilfred* 648
East African Airways 293, 295
East Germany 20
Easter Sunday 329, 360, 361
Egyptian vulture, (*Neophron percnopterus*) 223
Eid al-Adha 257, 258
Eid al-Fitr 186, 199, 202 - 204, 577, 578, 579
El Said 353
Eldoret 40, 279
Elephant, (*African Bush, Loxodonta africana*) 266 - 268, 280, 282, 283 - 287, 612
Elephant, (*Forest, Loxodonta cyclotis*) 280
Elliott, *Sir Hugh* 285
Elphinstone, *Gen William* 349
Empty Quarter vi, xix, 3, *et passim*
Equator 32, 275, 279, 601
Everest 281, 409
FAB, *Firqat al Badiyah* 167, 217, 305, 306, 420, 464 - 466, 506, 518, 524, 532, 533, 561, 582, 653
Fairey Aviation 649
FAN, *Firqat al Nasser* 112, 128, 139, 144, 528, 587, 653
Fanbelt, *Op* 213, 215
Fanja, *castle, Wadi Fanja* 41, 58, 59, 61
Faraday cage 362

FAS, *Firqat al Salahadin* 128
Feldman, *Marty* 105
Felix, *Julie* 486
Ferrán, *Jaime* 62
ffrench-Blake, *Capt Robert* 182, 656
FHG, *Firqat al Hudud al Gharbiyah, Camel Firqat* 305, 310, 320, 321, 338, 329, 416, 418, 419, 421, 479, 484, 492, 513, 514, 549, 557 - 559, 579, 580, 582, 588, 600, 611, 652, 653
Field Surgical Team *(FST)* 64, 142, 161, 181, 319, 324, 378, 407, 458, 468, 472, 494, 495, 508, 580, 581, 582, 585
Fiennes, *Ginny* 567
Fiennes, *Ranulph* 182, 308, 527, 548, 567, 569, 573,621, 626, 627, 654, 656
Finjan 60
Firefly, *Op* 219
FKW, *Firqat Kalid bin Waalid* 128
Flamingo, *Greater, (Phoenicopterus roseus)* 168
Fletcher, *Brig Jack (Flogger)* 498, 501, 512, 546, 567, 589, 604
Forward Airhead 405, 418, 448, 450, 611
Fox, *Maj Dick* 335
Fragging 35
Francois 38, 40
Frankincense, *(Boswellia sacra)* 51, 151, 220, 240, 258, 298, 368, 402, 458, 462, 463, 469, 530, 562, 572, 625, 634
Freeman, *Ellen* 278 - 282
Freke-Evans, *Maj Patrick* 87, 170
French Foreign Legion 1, 77
French Indochina 21
French Resistance *(Popski)* 188
FTZ, *Firqat Tariq bin Ziyad* 186, 191, 197, 199, 215, 217, 218, 223, 236, 253, 254, 257, 342, 347, 353, 360, 371, 373, 380, 418, 439, 572, 653

Furtwangler, Walter 276
Fyfe, *Sgt Gerry* 26, 27, 166, 174, 189, 190, 194, 204, 221, 260, 319, 330, 334, 467, 469, 522, 586, 656
Gants Hill 497
Garden of Eden 127, 280
Gardens of Gethsemane 264
Geneva Convention 67, 90
Geode 298, 311, 320, 618, 634
Getty, *John Paul* 615
Ghost Crabs of Oman, *(Ocypodidae Saratan)* 130, 132, 144, 145
Ghutra 146
Gibbon, *Gen Sir John* 485, 640
Gibson 273 - 277
Gilman's Point 275
Giraffe, *Maasai, (Giraffa tippelskirchi)* 266, 267, 281, 287
Glazebrook, *Maj David* 298, 589, 604, 605, 607 - 609
Glenfiddich 296
Gold Block, *Op* 213, 227
Gordon, *Capt Ian* 458, 489, 494, 495
Gough-Crispin, *Capt Jonathan* 218, 351, 354, 391, 393, 406, 407, 632, 656
Gray Makenzie 606
Greadh, *2/Lt, bin Jumaah* 141, 519, 608, 635, 636, 637
Great Game, *19th Century* 3
Green, *Op Simba position* 496, 574,
Grieves, *Sgt Pete* 519, 656
Guards Brigade, *(4)* 24, 467, 580
Gulf Air 32
Gulf Cooperation Council 641
Habarut 152, 217, 304 - 306, 317, 381, 416, 484, 487, 521, 523, 525, 528, 651, 652
Habarut, *attacked, International Incident* vi, 413 - 423, 426, 427, 428, 429, 464, 471, 472, 539

Habarut, *convoys* vi, 257, 468, 471, 472, 478, 479, 482, 483, 485, 489, 490, 500, 501, 503, 504, 513 - 516, 520, 523, 546, 548, 550, 552, 554, 557, 578, 580 - 582, 584, 589 - 591, 593, 610, 611, 627
Habkah 307, 308
Hadramawt 321
Hajar, *Jebel* 41
Hajj 589
Halal 474, 525, 577
Halwa 58, 60, 579
Hamdan, *Tpr, bin Khalfan* 185 - 187, 233, 330, 332, 476, 519
Hamed, *Lt Saif bin* 489, 495
Hamid, *bin Rashid* 306
Hamid, *Pte, al Kamam* 615, 616
Hamid, *Pte, bin Hameed* 520
Hamid, *Tpr, bin Abdullah* 533
Hansard 488
Hansen's disease 64
Harcourt, *Capt Geoff* 578, 589, 593, 656
Hardy, *Maj Mike* 589, 590
Harris, *Maj Willy* 87 - 89, 91, 92, 313, 314, 574
Hartnell, *Sir Norman* 377
Harvey, *Col Mike* 100, 178, 218, 219, 348, 373, 436, 490, 491
Hashish 361, 363
Hassan, *2/Lt Ehsan bin Nasib al Naseeb* 421
Hastie-Smith, *Capt Robin* 456
Hathi, *Pte, al Kamam* 615
Hawf 248, 423, 424, 427, 428, 484
Hawk, *Op* 582
Hawker Hunter 67
Hayma 118
Hazeldine, *Maj Tony* 570

Headley Court 129
Heath, *Edward, PM* 10
Hedgehog(s) 64, 75, 93, 103, 113, 122, 126, 135, 137, 149, 176, 653
Henley Royal Regatta 28, 485
Her Majesty The Queen 94, 494,
Hess, Rudolf 27
Hetherington, *Flt Cmdr Thomas* 23, 647, 648
Hilal, *CSM, bin Ali* 496,
Hilal, *Tpr, LCpl, bin Ali* 43, 45, 98, 110, 111, 134, 136, 478,
Hill, *Maj Simon* 587
Himalayan Buddhist prayer flags 432
Hitler, *Adolf* 272
HM Mazoon bint Ahmed Ali Al-Ma'sheni, Sultanah 97, 148
HM Qaboos bin Said Al Said, Sultan of Oman 3, 4, 10 - 12, 59, 102, 141, 162, 518, 539, 642
HM Said bin Taimur, Sultan 4, 10, 11, 36, 43, 50, 94, 102, 141, 162, 643
Ho Chi Minh Unit, *Trail* 20, 412, 421, 427
Hoare, *Col Mike* 94, 355
Hodgson, *Ann* 30, 85, 246, 262, 583, 656
Hodgson, *Capt Paul* xiv,xv, 25 - 27, 32, 35, 65, 74, 87, 101, 166, 169, 185, 332, 333, 348, 351, 354, 380, 384, 391, 404, 437, 441, 451, 459 - 462, 482, 567, 584, 590, 605, 656
Hodgson, *Odeyne* 30, 107, 108, 246, 269, 483, 492, 497, 583, 606, 656
Hodgson, *William* 30, 131, 246, 583, 656
Hodson, *Capt Ben* 217, 227, 228 - 233, 347, 351, 407, 423, 656
Holdbrook, *Flt Lt Nick* 586
Honeymoon Island 131

Hong Kong 1, 303, 385, 499, 625
Hornbeam, *Op* 500, 501, 502, 582
Horombo Hut 272
Housman, *AE* 183, 458
Howard, *Brig CS* 200
Howard, *Capt Alan* 25, 178, 181, 213, 217, 246, 253, 332 - 334, 341 - 344, 347 - 349, 351, 359, 363 - 367, 370, 372, 374 - 376, 382, 407, 467, 624, 632, 633, 656
Howard, *Lt Col John* 25,
Hubble *Extreme Deep Field* 563, 564
Hudson, *Capt Bob* 335, 336
Hulme, *Sqn Ldr Peter* 423, 424,
Hunters Lodge 266
Hyatt, *Capt Malcolm* 328, 523, 530 - 533, 535 - 537, 544, 602, 609
Ibadi Islam 4
Iffley Church 638
Imperial British Army 359
Imperial Iranian Army 502
India, *Indians* 29, 94, 359, 420, 619,
Iqal 146
Iran 2, 5, 249, 382
Iranian forces 2, 6, 336, 493, 502, 532, 572, 599, 628, 634, 641
Iraq 2, 18, 249, 642
Iski 118
Islam 4, 59, 154, 529, 530,
Israel 262 - 264
Jack Russell 323, 504
Jadilah, *Ramlat, Wadi* 560, 561, 621
Jaguar Cars 43
Jaguar, *Op* 148, 151 - 155, 170, 172, 214, 304, 326, 330, 341, 342, 500, 502, 582, 590
Jan, *Sgt bin Mohamed* 185, 208, 221, 248, 250, 251, 261

Janook vi, 260, 340, 343, 344, 381, 405, 406, 408, 410 - 414, 417, 418, 428, 429, 432, 433, 435 - 440, 447, 448, 450, 453, 455 - 467, 469, 472, 484, 485, 486, 497, 513, 522, 523, 571, 589, 591, 599, 608, 609, 611, 612, 614, 629, 635, 652
Jasmine, *Royal (Alyasimayn almalakiu)* 82, 107, 110, 224, 369, 570, 571
Jayes, *Capt Brian* 312, 323, 464, 467, 468, 472, 484, 497, 498, 499, 523, 570, 573, 574, 580, 582, 584, 593, 602, 605, 631, 656,
Jeapes, *Maj Gen Tony* 126, 154, 655
Jebel Akhdar 41, 322, 566
Jebel al Qara 71, 96, 122, 123, 152, 175, 304, 308, 570, 629, 632
Jebel ash Shams 41
Jebel Mahrat 416
Jenner, *Edward* 619
Jenyns, *Capt* 455
Jericho 264
Jerusalem 263, 264
Jibjat vi, 548, 569, 570, 575, 582, 584, 602, 607, 610, 614, 615, 634, 652
Jibjat road vi, 548, 569, 575, 602, 607, 614, 634, 652
Job's tomb 148, 154
John, *Maj Richard* 570
Johnson 298, 309, 312, 313, 336, 340, 385, 624, 631, 656
Jones, *Capt Huw* 167, 168, 171, 183, 243, 438, 456 - 458, 630, 656
Jones, *Capt Ian* 136, 137
Jones, *Lt Col Roger* 527, 586
Jones, *Maj David* 458, 630
Jordan 141, 382, 636
Jordanian, *Special forces, army* 2, 6, 298, 313, 314, 502, 628, 641

INDEX

Joshua 277
Jumea, *Tpr bin Musalim* 185
Jumea, *Tpr, bin Suleman* 476, 533, 605
Kalashnikov xv, 7, 79, 89, 107, 114, 115, 118, 126, 138, 139, 143, 144, 232, 246, 326, 327, 358, 389, 402, 421, 431, 449, 465, 536
Kalashnikov, *Mikhail* 326
Kamis, *Tpr, bin Ibrahim* 533, 543
Kane, *Maj Ray* 81, 162, 163, 165, 177, 210, 211, 217, 223, 224, 232, 233, 246, 402, 449, 645, 654, 656
Kaptagat 279
Karachi 293, 296, 297
Kariba National Park 632,
Karlsberg *Airport* 236, 384
Katangese Gendarmes 95
Katyusha, *rocket* 257
Kealy, *Capt Mike* 488
Keekorok Lodge 290
Kemball, *Capt Chris* 471, 597
Kenya 1, 39, 94, 263, 265, 266, 268, 277, 278, 279, 285, 290 - 293, 296, 375, 564, 578, 592
Kenyata, *Jomo* 592
Kenyon, *WO1, Bert* 83, 110, 199, 332, 410, 413, 490
Kerr, *Lt Col Bill* 494, 569, 570, 574
Khadim, *tribe* 42, 43, 69, 81, 96, 114, 115, 135, 141, 142, 481, 482, 495, 635, 653
Khadim, *well, route* 306, 583, 584
Khalfan, *Pte, bin Nasir bin Khalfan* 335
Khalifa, *Tpr, bin Mohamed* 246, 546, 565
Khamis, *Pte, bin Khalif* 604
Khamis, *Tpr, bin Hamid* 589
Khamis, *Tpr, bin Khalfan* 533, 545
Khareef 69, *et passim*
Khawr ad Dahariz 77, 99, 144
Khawr Qanat 167

Khawr Sawli 119, 123, 151, 159, 167, 168, 178
Khunjar 94, 138, 653
Kibo 267, 272, 273, 277, 280, 281
King Faisal 563
King, *Carol* 626
King's College, *Dept of War Studies* 642, 655
Kipling 200
Knocker, *Lt Col Nigel* 110, 188, 189, 191, 205, 208, 210, 211, 214, 215, 227, 233, 237, 251, 256, 333, 340, 342, 344, 378, 379, 380, 383, 384, 404, 405, 502, 541, 586, 599, 632, 656
Kodak *Instamatic* 265, 496
Konig, *Walter Siegfried* 276
Korean War 401, 491
Kyrenia 263
L Day 332, 348, 351, 353, 354
Labalaba, *Sgt Talaiasi* 488
Lake Victoria 32, 39, 278
Lamdon's Field 410, 411
Lamond, *Capt Alex* 46, 47, 189, 190 - 192, 197, 210, 216, 227, 237, 241, 250, 254, 256, 333, 341, 342, 344 - 346, 350, 356, 360, 361, 385, 656
Landon, *Tim* 573
Larnaca 263
Last Parade 624, 635
Latitude 38 North 491
Lawrence, *TE* 44, 47, 437, 563, 569, 655
Le Marchand, *Capt Peter* 169
Lean, *David* 402
Lenin Unit 19
Leny, *Erika* 269
Leopard, (*African, Panthera pardus pardus*) 39, 158, 271, 279, 283, 284, 287 - 290, 292,
Leopard, *Op* 152, 326, 335, 338, 385

Leper *(Hansen's Disease)* 58, 63, 64
Lewis, *Jock* 132
Lightning *(atmospheric electricity)* 351, 357, 361, 362, 363
Limonka 466
Lion, *(African, Panthera leo)* 139, 158, 266, 268, 280, 288, 290, 291, 292
Lizzie 483, 492
Locust, *Op* 332, 343, 344, 405, 406, 408, 413, 437, 459, 461, 462, 611
Logie, *Ross* xi, xii
Lone Tree 153, 216
Long Range Desert Group, *(LRDG)* 255, 301, 653
Longfellow, *Henry* 646
Longknives, *Op* 186, 197, 199
Longsafari, *Op* 518
Looting 107, 119
Louise 490, 604, 605, 656
Luger, *George* 503
Lulworth Gunnery School 522, 639
Lüneburg Heath 24, 57, 87, 200
Ma Shadid 306, 307, 308, 315, 316, 478, 582, 584
Ma'sheni, *tribe* 373
Maasai 281, 287, 290, 291, 292
Maasai Mara 290
Macbeth, *Op* 151
MacCallum, *Maj John* 565, 567
Mackain-Bremner, *Lt Col Fergus* 48, 85, 87, 90, 112, 119, 656
Maclaine, *Capt Douglas* 207, 208, 221, 237, 241, 250, 251, 380
Maddocks, *Catherine* 30, 656
Maglis 577
Mahmood, *Tpr, bin Hassan* 480
Mahri Sultanate of Qishn and Socotra, 530, *et passim*
Mahri, *tribe, Firqat* xviii, 110, 305, 420, 421, 465, 466, 526, 530 - 537, 539, 542, 543, 561, 569, 615
Mainbrace 218, 347, 348 - 350, 353, 361, 369, 371, 372, 385, 386, 428, 468, 477, 587
Makinat al Haiz 621
Makinat Shihan 478
Malaria 339, 340, 410
Malaya 201, 498
Malone, *L/Sgt Joseph* 527
Mamurah, Royal Gardens 140, 173
Mandara Hut 271
Mangin, *Maj Paul* 59, 61, 218, 219, 222, 223, 236, 237, 244, 245, 259, 347, 380, 656
Manston 196, 197, 213, 215, 243, 381, 455, 456, 459 - 468, 470, 471, 472, 478, 483, 484, 487, 490, 497 - 499, 520, 523, 527, 528, 546, 567, 570, 573, 575, 580, 581, 582, 585 - 588, 591, 595, 599, 604, 606, 607, 609, 611, 613, 634
Manyara, *Game Reserve* 282, 283, 286
Map reading 201, 240, 316, 413, 575, 578, 597, 598
Marahoon, *Sgt* 555
Marangu 268, 269, 277
Marboosh 227, 259, 408, 413
Marie-France 322
Marina, *Sister* 108
Martin, *Tpr MJ* 421
Martini-Henry, *rifle* 174
Martyn-Fisher, *Maj John* 478, 518, 520, 656
Marxist ideology ix, 4, 7, 10, 35, 294, 359
Masirah, *Island* 13, 77, 249, 262, 263, 300,
Masoud, *Tpr, bin Hamid* 519
Mau Mau 94, 279, 592

INDEX

Mawenzi 268, 272, 274, 275
Mawle, *Bill, Robert* 164, 178
Mawle, *Capt Geoff* v, 69, 74 - 76, 78, 79, 81, 82, 84, 97, 98, 105 - 107, 111, 113 - 116, 122, 123, 125, 128, 135, 148, 155, 157 - 164, 167, 168, 457, 630, 646, 656
Maxwell, *Col Colin* 423
Mayne, *Lt Col Blair 'Paddy'* 223
McCarthy, *Cpl* 357
McFadden, *Capt David* 351, 352, 354, 656
McGrath, *Capt Noel* 351, 384, 404, 407, 410, 412, 443, 448, 462, 512, 513, 523, 589, 591, 656
McKim-Furse, *Charlotte* 490, 492, 578, 604, 656
Mecca 372, 597
Mecom Oil 615
Medevac vi, 338, 468, 520, 578, 580
Medina 530
Mercenary 1, 2, 12, 47, 67, 94, 170, 228, 295, 355, 382, 383
Méry, *Joseph* 560
Mesozoic 634
Meyar, *Hans* 273, 275
Meyer, *Professor Hans Furtwangler* 275, 277
Midway *(Thumrait)* xviii, 19, *et passim*
Midway road 19, 20, 500, 502, 510, 512, 608
Milky Way, *Darab Altibana* 562, 563
Millbank Military Hospital xi
Milne-Smith, *Flt Lt David* 488
Mina al Fahal 509, 629
Minvalla, *SQMS Pete, 'Q'* 26, 48, 306, 340, 475, 498, 507 - 509, 530, 532, 535, 537, 541, 545, 548, 557, 565, 580, 614 656

Mirbat vi, 15, 20, 137, 152, 423, 464, 467, 486, 487, 489, 490
Mitchell, *Joni* 238
Mohamed *Pte, bin Mahadi* 579
Mohamed, *Pte, bin Saif* 479, 480, 481
Mohamed, *Tpr Ali bin Salim* 580
Mohamed, *Tpr bin Said* 221
Mohamed, *Tpr, bin Ali (Abyad)* 476
Mohamed, *Tpr, bin Hamid* 519
Mohan, *Capt Jaya* 574
Moïse, *Tshombe* 94
Mons Officer Cadet School 200, 344, 643
Moore, *Flt Lt Del* 71
Moore, *Tom* 288, 290
Morfa Camp 182
Morgan-Evans, *Capt Dick* 196, 202, 211, 218, 222, 368, 384, 391, 401 - 403, 405 - 407, 467, 490, 527, 656
Morrison, *Sgt* 169, 185
Morse Code 28, 199, 207
Moshi 32, 268, 269, 272, 278, 279, 282
Mountbatten, *Earl* 94
Mt. Kenya 564
Mt. Kilimanjaro 32, 206, 250, 266, 268, 269, 271, 272, 277, 279, 280, 543
Mubarik, *Tpr, bin Ali* 185 - 187, 193, 209, 246, 565

Mubarik, *Tpr, bin Musalim al-Khadim* 329, 481, 482, 533, 656
Mubarik, *Tpr, bin Salim* 309
Mudhai 71, 152, *et passim*
Mugabe 632
Mugshail 224, 225
Mugshin 118
Munster 24, 43, 467, 580, 599, 600
Musalim, *Pte, bin Mohamad* 588
Musalim, *Tpr, bin Dhait* 586
Muscat 3, *et passim*

Muscat International Airport 627
Musoma 285, 286
Mutiny 65, 107, 113 - 115, 178, 484
Myrrh, *(Commiphora myrrha)* 51, 220, 369, 427, 458
Mzima Springs 267
Nairobi 256, 263 - 266, 279, 280, 292, 293, 299, 314, 498
Nairobi National Park 266
Naro Moru 364
Nashran, *Pte, bin Mohamed* 600
Nasib, *2/Lt, bin Hamed al-Ruwehi* 307, 308, 315, 316, 323, 336, 404, 421, 438, 445, 446, 447, 449
Nasir, *LCpl, bin Mohamed bin Mahoon* 185 - 187, 204, 208, 233, 234, 248, 332, 403, 656
Nasir, *Tpr, bin Hamed* 43, 45, 63, 109, 110, 136, 149, 150, 153, 185, 198, 204, 221, 329, 388, 477, 520, 588
Nasir, *Tpr, bin Hamid* 43, 45, 63, 82, 109, 110, 136, 149, 150,153, 157, 185, 198, 204, 221, 329, 388, 477, 520, 533, 588
Nasir, *Tpr, bin Suleman* 630
Nazi 27, 188
Negd, *Al, (The Highlands)* 304 , 437 , 615, 623
Neville, *Maj John* 218
Ngorongoro 285, 287
Ngurdoto 280, 282
Nicholls, *Capt David* 404, 405, 408, 414, 429, 433 - 437, 439, 445, 459, 461, 469, 509, 522, 612, 656
Nicosia 263
Nile rat, *(Arvicanthus niloticus)* 171
Niven, *David* 170
Nobel, *Alfred* 364
Noor, *Pte, bin Mohamed* 367
North Korea 19, 20

North Star, *Namjam Shamal* 562,
Northern Ireland 3, 8, 164, 643
Nusrat, *Sgt* 336
Nyabogati river 288, 290
Nyerere, *Julius* 282
Oath of Allegiance 11
Obaid, CSM Obaid bin Mubarik 495, 496
Offord, *Capt Mike (Uncle)* vi, 26, 42, 48 - 50, 65, 81, 113, 166, 167, 172, 174 - 176, 184, 185, 224, 298, 303, 305, 306, 309, 310, 314, 317 - 319, 323, 324, 334, 348, 439, 464, 468 - 471, 490, 492, 494, 498, 500 - 502, 504 - 509, 512, 513, 515 - 517, 523, 533, 571, 629, 630, 639, 640, 646, 656
Offord, *Lt Col Eric* 498, 639
Ofield, *Capt Nick* 613
Oliver, *Sgt Alan (Olly)* 26, 27, 166, 174, 185, 189, 190, 197, 198, 204, 208, 209, 237, 239, 243, 256, 258, 261, 303, 307, 308, 323, 332, 334 - 336, 338, 339, 341, 342, 344 - 347, 351, 379, 384, 388, 390, 391, 395, 396, 398, 399, 400, 403 - 406, 415, 416, 431 - 434, 445, 436, 437, 445, 446, 448, 449, 451, 453, 455, 459 - 462, 469, 479, 493, 522, 540, 541, 656
Oman Gendamerie, *(OG)* 15, 321, 322, 330, 335, 458, 460, 471, 484, 552, 589, 591, 593, 610, 630, 653
Oman National Day (1st) , *23 July 1971* v, 58, 63, 64,
Organisation of African Unity 266
Orinka 291
Orion's Belt, *Miayat Zayn* 562,
Overs 239, 244, 245, 443, 448, 453, 456
P-bulbs 208, 210, 255
Painted saw-scaled viper, *(Echis khosatzkii)* 454

Panasonic 186, 205, 341, 370, 400, 407
Pandora's Box, *Op* 213, 217
Paphos 263
Parabellum 503
Parkistan, *Pakistanis* 29, 249
Parsons, *Capt Jim* 217, 406, 409
Pauling and Co 492
People's Republic of South Yemen / Mahri Sultanate of Qishn and Socotra 530 *et passim*
Persian army 41
Persian Empire 530
Persian Gulf 6, 7
Peters, *Dr Karl, Hut* 272, 273, 277
Philby, *John* 563
Phillips, *Maj Chris* v, 69, 70, 79, 80, 81, 107, 111, 113 - 116, 121, 125, 130, 135, 142, 156, 160, 163, 169, 170, 178
Pike, *Capt Gavin* 485
Pink eye (conjunctivitis) 213, 235
Piórkowski, *SSM Stan* 26, 166, 174, 176, 178, 179, 188, 189, 256, 545, 580, 656
Piquet 114, 163, 193, 248, 250, 251, 260, 324, 349, 407, 429, 511
Pitman, *Capt Charles* 290
Plains, *Light, Sabre, Recce Troop* 14, 26, 42, 48, 119, 210, 136, 166, 171, 176, 199, 299
Plessings 280
Pointer, *Flt Lt Bob* 424
Poland 188
Popski 189, 251, 545, 579
Porcupine, *(African brush-tailed, Atherurus africanus)* 282, 283,
Portuguese 159, 531, 535, 538, 539
Posthorn 342, 344
Powell, *Maj Neville (Spike)* 85, 91, 93 - 95, 104, 151, 153, 224 - 226, 460, 632, 656

Prize money, *(1948 Prize Act)* 530, 542
Promotion 602, 608
Propaganda 4, 59, 205, 295, 378, 382, 383, 449, 458, 502
Qafa 483, 611
Qara *Jebel* 152, 175, 304, 308, 570, 632
Qatan, *tribe* 135
Quetta 177, 243
Quran, *Koran / Qur'an* 28, 563, 569
Rabies II, Op 170
Racal TRA 906, *Squadcal* 108
Rachmaninov 626
Radfan 67, 498
Radio Aden 59 - 541
Rae, *Capt Stuart* 27, 28, 48, 571
RAF Aden 67
Rakhyut 257, 341, 353
Ramadan 152, 154, 170, 186, 198, 199, 203, 518, 524, 526, 534, 577
Ramadhan Chambe, *LCpl* 332, 344, 346, 406, 461, 483, 484, 530, 533, 544
Ramlat Fasad 311
Ramlat Mitan 622
Ramlat Umm Hayat 311
Rankin, *Capt Donald* 292, 293, 656
Rashid Khalfan, *mechanic* 533
Rashid, *orderley* 259, 261
Rashid, *Pte, bin Khalfan* 533
Rashid, *tribe* 524, 534, 569, 603, 618, 622
Ray, *Lt Col Bryan* 457, 502, 509, 512, 521, 522, 570, 579, 584, 586, 606, 656
Raysut 49, 98, 111, 113, 115, 118, 136, 178, 342
Razfa Ardah, *sword dance* 59
Red 60 498, 499, 573
Red Coy 369, 372, 408, 410, 423, 428, 456, 496, 518
Red Cross, *British* 583
Remembrance Sunday 166, 179, 183

Reuters 490
Rhino, Black *(Diceros bicornis)* 266, 283, 284, 285, 287
Rhino, Northern White *(Ceratotherium simum)* 284
Rhodesia 1, 632
Rial, *Omani* 248
Rift Valley 39, 279
Rinderpest 287
Riyal, *Saudi* 63, 104, 191, 219, 223, 541
Robb, *Capt Martin* 31, 87, 581
Robinson, *Heath* 75, 300
Rolex v, 107, 125, 170, 628
Rosencrantz, *Capt Andrew* 35, 217
Roulement 2, 14, 64, 121, 143, 148, 150 - 152, 174, 189, 218, 340, 477, 419, 456, 476, 477, 484
Royal Oman Police 61
Royal Stables, Happy Warrior 30, 38, 125
Rub Al Khali, *The Empty Quarter* 3, 304, 335, 564, 565, 623, 654
Ryan, *Maj Mike* 66, 67, 656
Said Barakat 320, 329, 506
Said bin Ghia 135
Said *Sgt, Achmed Rubaat* 588
Said, *bin Mohamed bin Khamis* 586, 593
Said, *bin Mohamed, orderly* 239, 443
Said, *bin Salim bin Mikthur* 336
Said, *Cpl, bin Abdullah* 363
Said, *LCpl, bin Mohamed bin Harrib* 185, 208, 214, 448, 585
Said, *Pte, Mabkhout bin Salim* 588
Said, *Sgt bin Mubarik* 321
Said, *Tpr, Abdullah* 149
Said, *Tpr, bin Suleman* 579, 589, 630
Said, *Tpr, L/Cpl, Mohamed bin Harib* 185, 208, 214, 448, 578, 585, 637
Saif, *Tpr bin Nasir* 536, 537, 588, 614
Salalah, *Convoys* 96
Salalah, *Enemy presence* 19, 20
Salalah, *Hedgehogs, Airfield defences* 64, 75
Salalah, *mine threat* 75, 78
Salalah, *monsoon isolation* 72, 73
Salalah, *Post monsson SAF Initiatives* 152
Salalah, *RAF presence* 13
Salalah, *SAF armour presence* 47, 48
Salalah, *SAF presence* 14, 69
Salalah, *Salalah Plain / FCO Concerns* 9, 21, 22, 77
Salalah, *Tribal tensions* 113, 114, 115
Salim, *bin Said al-Hayfee* 484
Salim, *Pte, bin Hamees* 600
Salim, *S/Sgt, bin Khalfan bin Hamad al-Siyabi* 612
Salim, *Sgt, bin Musalim* 588
Salim, *Tpr, bin Suleman* 533
Salisbury Plain 522
Sandbeach, *Op* 213, 218
Sandcastle, *Op* 259
Sandcloud, *Op* 259
Sandfly, *Op* 243
Sandmartin, *Op* 213, 218
Sarbe radio 394, 400
Sassoon, *Siegfried* 517, 572
Saudi Arabia 3, 4, 6, 304, 382
Savile Row 31, 644
Screen Force 512
Scythian, *nomadic horsemen* 359
Seeb Airport 489, 627
Seely, *Capt Victor* 34, 38, 40, 125
Seifert 66
Selassie I, *Emperor Haile* 609
Semaphore 69, 83, 111
Semple, *Brig R Ferguson* 34
Serengeti 32, 220, 285, 287, 290
Seronera Research Institute 287, 288, 289, 292

INDEX

Shafia 416
Sharjah 169, 185, 533
Shayla 63
Sheershitti caves & *Chillisherryshitti* 192, 215, 219, 238, 241 - 243, 248, 257, 287, 384
Sheikh Issa *al Ma'sheni* 133
Sheikh Mohammed *bin Hamed al-Ma'sheni* 347, 373
Shem, *son of Noah* 530
Sherwell, *Maj Graham* 92, 183, 236, 237, 313, 340, 343, 385, 379, 384, 388, 394, 404 - 408, 410, 449, 452 - 455, 459, 464, 469, 522, 541, 632, 656
Shidda, *Op* 489, 494 - 497, 546
Shira 268, 281
Shisur *(Ubar)* xvii, 477, 478, 524, 527, 548, 560, 564, 567, 569, 582, 603, 616 - 621
Shpagin round, *talisman* 202, 212, 423
Simba, *Op, L Day* 351, 352, 353, 359
Simba, *Op, L Day + 1* 360
Simba, *Op, L Day + 2* 361, 363 - 365
Simba, *Op, L Day + 3* 366, 367, 369, 375 - 377
Simba, *Op, launches* 342 - 348
Simba, *Op, Spring Offensive* vi, 143, 152, 213, 215, 217, 218, 222, 248, 256, 288, 297 - 299, 305, 332 - 334, 336, 340
Simba, *Op, Success or Failure?* 381, 382
Simcock, *Maj Peter* 494, 546
Simmons, *Capt Dick* 457
Simon and Garfunkel 241
Simonov, *Sergi Gavrilovich* 89, 326
Simpson, *Douglas* xii, 656
Sinau 530, 532, 533, 538, 539, 540, 573, 590
Sind Bats 308
Slaves 15, 35, 42, 43, 69, 141

Sleeping sickness *(African trypanosomiasis)* 285
Smallpox 483, 602, 618, 619
Smith-Piggott, *Capt Graeme* 487
Snowdonia 200, 362
Sommerfield, *Capt George* 1447,
Soviet Russia ix, 3, 8, 19, 20, 31, 77, 103, 137, 249, 262, 466, 530, 550, 650, 653, 654
Sparrows, *(Passer domesticus)* 34
Speakes, *Capt John* 111
Spent-Case-Cartridge-Bag 157, 158, 172
Spiders Web, *Op* 213, 216
Spitting cobra, *(Naja nigricollis)* 289
Stanleyville, *Congo* 94
Steward, *Capt Simon* 613
Stirling, *Col David* 132
Stocks, *Captain Michael* 528
Stoker, *Sqn Ldr Bill* 488
Straits of Hormuz 5 - 8, 12, 102, 501, 642
Strike Force 90, 93, 148, 151 - 154, 171, 172, 176, 178, 317
Strikemaster, *BAC 167 jet fighter* 15, 90, 126, 128, 383, 423, 591
Sudh 15, 20, 113, 152
Suleman, *Pte, bin Salim* 484
Suleyman, *Tpr, bin Said* 520
Sullivan, *Capt Jack* 629, 630
Sultan's Armour 625, 628
Sultan's Bravery Medal *(WB)* 67, 93, 94, 163, 255, 327, 409, 491, 540, 541, 567, 569, 572, 587, 590, 595, 613
Sultan's Commendation Medal *(Commd)* 50, 87, 179, 182, 233, 234, 341, 415, 416, 472, 497, 498, 516, 540, 544, 572, 587, 606, 637, 646
Sultan's Gallantry Medal *(Wsh)* 373, 423, 424, 488, 572, 613
Sultanate of Oman 7, 22, 33, 567

Sumail 118
Summiteer's Garland, *(Helichrysum Kilimanjari)* 277
Sunburn 46, 122, 201, 204, 298, 321, 323, 407, 477, 524, 541, 544, 601, 625, 626
Swahili 29, 45, 50, 51, 65, 131, 270, 272, 284 - 287, 654
Swallows, *(Hirundo rustica)* 492
Sweat 33, *et passim*
Swing High, *Op* 471
Sycamore, *Op* 498, 500 - 506, 509, 511, 515, 523, 582, 606, 610
Syrettes, *morphine* 92, 191, 428, 434, 435, 436, 634
Takavesi, *Sgt Sekonaia* 488
Tanganyika 39, 85, 139, 271, 278, 279, 326
Tanganyika Planting Company 278
Tanzania 263, 266, 268, 278, 292
Taqah 15, 20, 83, 96, 97, 103, 107 - 109, 111, 113, 114, 119, 122 - 124, 126, 128, 133, 135, 137, 144, 145, 148, 151, 152, 155 - 162, 167, 171, 178, 193, 194, 256, 306, 326, 373, 382, 456, 457, 486, 627, 628
Tawell, *Maj Peter* 471, 472
Tawi Ateer 137
Tayi, *Auda Abu* 563
Taylor Woodrow 112
Taylor, *Col, Military Attaché, Nairobi* 266, 392
Taylor, *Maj Tim* 166, 179, 180, 181, 182, 183, 656
Thalfutt 587, 588
Thames Television 170
The Daily Telegraph 16, 17, 629
The Empty Quarter vi, 44, 153, 212, 303, 304, 306, 308, 310, 311, 317, 335, 475, 545, 548, 549, 560, 563, 564, 582, 599, 603, 615, 621, 622, 623, 630, 654

The Milky Way, *Darab Altibana* 562, 563
The Prophet's Ascension 493, 497
Thesiger, *Wilfred* ix, 281, 308, 336, 548, 564, 565, 620, 622, 643
Thomas, *Capt Ian* 351, 354, 518
Thomson's Gazelle, *(Eudorcas thomsonii)* 153
Thumrait xvii
Timboroa 279
Tobin, *Tpr Tommy* 488
Tomlinson, *Maj Bob (Poppo)* 85, 87, 88, 90, 656
Trident, *Op* 381
Trinity College Cambridge 132
Trucial Oman Scouts 26, 632
Trumpers, *Mr Bird* 28, 149, 228
Tsavo West *Reserve* 267
Tsetse Fly, *(Glossina species)* 285, 288
Tudho 217, 320, 321, 329, 330, 483, 579, 582, 591, 593, 634
Turandot, Nessun Dorma 254
Turkey 107, 108, 249
Turkish Red Crescent 108
Turnbull, *Richard* 85
Tusker *beer* 278
Twizzle 313, 438, 452, 453
UAE 382, 624, 628
Uganda 278, 279, 290
Uhuru Peak 268, 272, 275
Ukraine 642
Umm Al Ghawarif *(UAG)* 14, 15, 49, 50, 69, 78, 82, 83, 93, 95, 97, 111, 126, 136, 139, 160, 170, 172, 176, 183 - 185, 196, 197, 223, 224, 238, 239, 250, 299, 337, 386, 407, 410, 413, 415, 458, 485, 501, 527, 569, 570, 574, 586, 614
UN, *Protocol, Security Council* 95, 401, 415, 422, 464, 641
United Nations 382, 422, 424, 464, 641

Ursa Major, *Banaat Nayim* 562
Valerie 321, 322
VC 93, 121, 373, 487, 488, 526, 527, 528, 572, 613
Vedettes 500, 509, 511
Venn, *Capt David* 111
Venom 241, 242, 243, 335
Viet Cong 313, 359
Vietnam 3, 7, 8, 9, 19, 21, 22, 46, 64, 70, 76, 77, 86, 322, 352, 425, 539
Vimy Ridge, *South of Akoot* vi, 197, 215, 378, 385, 386, 387, 389, 390 - 393, 395, 397, 399, 401 - 403, 417, 449, 450, 537, 541, 571, 632, 652
Vining, *Maj Malcolm* 489, 494, 495, 497
Viscount, *Vickers-Armstrong* 489, 580, 581, 604, 605, 610, 632
Voi 279
Vulture, *Op* 152, 217, 298, 304 - 306, 317, 326, 478, 498, 502, 523, 579, 580, 582, 584, 585, 602, 614, 615, 624, 651
Vutirakis, *Capt Eddie* 35, 482
Wadi Ahboot 310, 311
Wadi Arzat 109, 128, 456, 565
Wadi Assebu 600
Wadi Atinah 533
Wadi Aybut 418, 419
Wadi Aydim 215, 217, 320, 387, 419, 465, 548, 550, 582
Wadi Ayun 308, 316
Wadi Bal Atawf 466
Wadi Banut 309
Wadi Darbat 256, 306, 335
Wadi Dhawr 552
Wadi Difan 416
Wadi Ghadun 306 - 308, 316, 318, 319, 579, 616
Wadi Gharah 193, 311, 323, 329

Wadi Jardum, *Ayn* v, 48, 85, 87, 88, 117, 121, 122, 124, 148, 149, 153, 154, 171, 338, 528
Wadi Jarsis, *Ayn* 124, 135, 374, 632, 633
Wadi Jazal 570, 575, 576, 607
Wadi Madi 217
Wadi Mitan 212, 524, 534, 560, 564, 598, 599, 614, 621
Wadi Mudhi 416, 419, 471, 503, 548, 549, 552, 553, 556
Wadi Nahiz 169
Wadi Sahalnawt 77, 123, 169
Wadi Sahhr 616
Wadi Sarfait 359, 369, 371, 372, 468, 575
Wadi Stum 600
Wadi Thimrin 154
Wadi Thuayt 309
Wadi Umran 122, 126, 127
Waite, *Sgt 'Wimpy'* 472, 476, 477, 482, 573, 587, 607, 609, 656
Walid, *Gnr, bin Khamis* 488
Walnut, *Gordon Dawson* 600
War on Terror 642
Warsaw Pact 8, 167
Warton, *Fiona* 67, 656
Watts, *Maj Johnnie* 154
Wehrpass 183
Western Approach Bn, *Western Reaches Bn* 14, 19, 137, 152, 215
Western Military Unit 19
Westminster, *Duke* 23, 648
White Ants, *Op* 378, 384, 386, 388
White City 335, 528, 586, 591, 632
White Nile 290
White, *Capt John* 606
White, *Op Simba position* 343, 344, 347, 350, 353 - 356, 359 - 362, 366 - 369, 371, 372, 376, 377, 470, 471, 477, 493, 495

White, *Rowland* 654
Wilayat 59
Wilhelm II, *Kaiser* 272, 275
Willaims, *Elsa* 581
Williams, *Capt Rick* 27, 31, 32, 33, 41, 46, 70, 150, 177, 178, 180, 181, 202, 205 - 208, 215 - 217, 246, 250, 252, 256, 332, 341, 343, 348, 377, 624, 627, 628, 632, 656
Williams, *Flt Lt Barrie* 129, 591
Williams, *Lt Col John* 27
Wilton Park 26
Wolf, *Op (Dhib)* 530, 539, 582
Wolseley *Armoured Cars* 23, 648
Wooley, *Maj Harry (Uncle)* 69, 79 - 81, 83, 84, 111, 115, 116, 125, 130, 132, 135, 163, 170, 172, 173, 656
Worked flints 311
World Health Organisation 619
Worthy, *Lt Col Peter* 457
Wright, *Maj Paul (Tiger)* 121, 137, 611, 612, 613, 614, 656
Wright, *Sgt Tony* 26
Yaqub, *Tpr, bin Abdullah* 604
Yardarm 218, 355, 369, 372, 496, 528
Yeager, *Chuck* 424
Yellow, *Op Simba position* 496
Yemen, *Soviet and Chinese led threat* vi, 2, *et passim*
Yemenite Jews 539
Yousaf 2/Lt, Khalfan bin Zahir al-Busaidi 385, 404, 407, 411 - 414, 433, 439, 449, 459, 460, 462, 464
Zanzibar 65, 159, 212
Zanzibaris 29
Zedong, *Chairman Mao* 78, 282, 293, 359
Zulu Company 90, 226 530, 531

Regiments

REGIMENTS, BRITISH:

Infantry:
Argyll & Sutherland Highlanders, 91st/93rd of Foot   27, 101, 322
Duke of Edinburgh's Royal   81, 123, 646
Cameroon Highlanders   10
Coldstream Guards   24, 48,
Glosters   27, 348, 490, 494
Green Howards   176
Gurkha, Royal Gurkha Rifles   31, 79, 458, 494
Irish Guards   169, 185
London Irish Regiment   94
KRRC – Kings Royal Rifle Corps   182, 357
Northamptonshire   236
Queen's   328, 335, 471, 501, 502
Queen's Lancashire   218
Royal Anglian   85, 137, 501
Royal Green Jackets   64, 182, 183, 344, 471
Royal Marines   xi, 25, 27, 28, 32, 64, 181, 206, 217, 333, 343, 359, 364, 408, 409, 632
Royal Highland Fusiliers   494
Royal Irish Rangers   218
Royal Sussex   35
Royal Welch Fusiliers   167
Scots Guards   169
Welsh Guards   580

Armour:
Blues and Royals   625
Royal Scots Greys   570
Queen's Royal Irish Hussars   26, 74
3rd Carabineers   80, 116, 147, 181, 582
5th Inniskilling Dragoon Guards   26, 30
9th/12th Royal Lancers   568
10th Royal Hussars   467, 573, 605
11th Hussars   26, 34, 189
13th/18th Royal Hussars   40, 169, 172, 182, 333, 446, 573, 654
14th/20th Kings Hussars   266, 485
16th/5th Queen's Royal Lancers   293, 498
17th/21st. Lancers   26, 607
1st Royal Tank Regiment   1, 26, 646
2nd Royal Tank Regiment   26, 87, 251, 451, 521
4th Royal Tank Regiment   26, 446

Artillery:
3rd Royal Horse Artillery   27, 206, 343
45 Commando   189

Engineers:
Royal Engineers   35, 217, 472, 612

REGIMENTS, EMPIRE:

King's African Rifles 85, 94, 279
Rhodesian Light Infantry 94
Rajputana Rifles 176
Duke of Connaught's Own Baluchis 121

Addendum

On 11th August 2024, I stood before 300 diners seated at tables in a large marquee. It was the culmination of the town's annual agricultural show and hungry people were waiting for their more than generous portions of roast beef, turkey and all the trimmings; for many, the highlight of a long weekend.

Asked to say a few words, I wondered whether I'd be heard above the constant murmur of the now hungry and already partially inebriated assembly, (the bar had been open two hours). I called for quiet, and to my astonishment the marquee rapidly fell silent as I told a story leading to a Grace, neither of which I had related before.

* * *

"….. and here today, in this beautifully decorated tent, surrounded by our community, we are in for a feast – and, such a feast! I've had a sneak preview of what's on offer, and can promise you, no jelly … but a meal fit for a Sultan. Please join me in applauding the efforts of our Montgomery Show organisers and friends.

* * *

A great many years ago, I soldiered for a Desert Sultan. It was his desert. The largest beach in the world. At 24, I'd been there two years and thought I knew it all; fluent in Arabic, a bit player on secret loan to an Arabian army.

I was patrolling the Yemeni border with 8 of my Arab soldiers and my 40-ish Irish sergeant, Lou Costello. Back then, my golly how old 40 seemed to be…! Now Costello – that's a name to conjure with. But for Lou Costello, I'd not be here, … and he too, because of me. Which sort of made us quits, in a way.

Transport comprised two stripped down Land Rovers, no roofs, doors or screens, to which we'd welded Brownings and each carried sub-machine guns, pistols, grenades; the usual stuff… We were dressed as Arabs, and as Costello was wont to claim, (expletives deleted), *'we're armed to the teeth - and not very nice to meet.'* Probably more in reference to our rationed, once-a-month, shave and shower.

Ever disdainful of our habits, the Bedu claimed they could smell soap a mile away.

Costello spoke no Arabic, often unintelligible English, and had little regard for senior officers, or their occasional daft orders. To get by, he'd grunt or shout, wave his arms and say *'By Jesus!'* a lot, whilst overusing his adjectives; the type that rarely translate terribly well. I never regretted having selected him.

On this patrol we'd happened upon a desert encampment, a brown coloured Bedu tent of goat and camel hair, the fabric that ensured it was dark and supposedly cooler inside. Whilst a very welcome escape from the blinding desert sun, the interiors were always stiflingly hot, rank, and airless. And in Arabia's Empty Quarter, summers were hot. Very hot.

As we approached and dismounted from our vehicles, two young boys appeared from behind rocks, pointing rifles larger than themselves, levelled chest height towards us. Back then, every male over 10 carried a rifle, and could shoot like a Bisley champion. Rifles it seemed, were part of their DNA.

A figure emerged from the tent; authoritative, tall and regal, looking arrogantly at us along his hooked nose. He was of the Mahri tribe, this was his well, his tribal land.

"You've met my bodyguards" he growled as a welcome, before commanding we stay for a meal. This was Bedu custom, and to decline would cause offence, Yet, you knew by joining them, even having gifted some of our meagre rations, you'd leave them hungry later.

There was rice flowing with melted butter, fresh goat in a hot chilli-pepper sauce, that stung like fury in contact with cracked sunburned lips, and there was warm frothy camel milk to drink. Seated crosslegged, next to the old bedouin, he placed a goat's eye in front of me. It was a test, only the naïve would eat it and I thanked him but declined, whereupon he smiled knowingly, for he had tried that 18 months earlier for the same result. He removed the eye and murmured, *'Welcome my friend'* then quietly he blessed the meal with a Grace.

* * *

I am privileged to have been asked to say Grace today. It won't be in Arabic. Someone suggested it should be in Latin, but no, fortunately for you - that was said at the President's Evening a week ago, and no one understood it then either!

ADDENDUM

The wise words used by that old bedouin, translate roughly as follows:
  'Where many live with hunger and thirst,
  Be thankful, for food and water. Welcome, I entreat you,
  Come, eat and drink,
  And live in peace, thereafter'

Amen